Trading Blocs

Alternative Approaches to
Analyzing Preferential Trade
Agreements

Edited by Jagdish Bhagwati,
Pravin Krishna, and Arvind
Panagariya

The MIT Press
Cambridge, Massachusetts
London, England

This book was set in Palatino on the Monotype "Prism Plus" PostScript Imagesetter by Asco Trade Typesetting Ltd., Hong Kong.
Printed and bound in the United States of America.

Library of Congress Cataloging-in-Publication Data

Trading blocs : alternative approaches to analyzing preferential trade
  agreements / edited by Jagdish Bhagwati, Pravin Krishna, and Arvind
Panagariya.
    p.   cm.
Includes bibliographical references and index.
ISBN 0-262-02450-0 (alk. paper)
  1. Trade blocs. 2. Commercial policy. I. Bhagwati, Jagdish N.,
1934–   . II. Krishna, Pravin. III. Panagariya, Arvind.
HF1418.7.T73   1999
382'.91—dc21   98-30485
                                                          CIP

Contents

Contributors

Kyle Bagwell

Richard E. Baldwin

Richard A. Brecher

Jagdish Bhagwati

C. A. Cooper

W. Max Corden

Alan Deardorff

Ronald Findlay

Earl L. Grinols

Gene M. Grossman

Elhanan Helpman

Harry G. Johnson

Murray C. Kemp

Kala Krishna

Pravin Krishna

Anne O. Krueger

Paul Krugman

Philip I. Levy

Richard G. Lipsey

B. F. Massell

Robert Mundell

Arvind Panagariya

Martin Richardson

T. N. Srinivasan

Robert W. Staiger

Robert Stern

Lawrence H. Summers

Jacob Viner

Henry Y. Wan Jr.

Preface

This collection has grown out of our conviction that the recent proliferation of preferential trade agreements (PTAs) poses a considerable problem for public policy and a compelling agenda for theoretical research by international economists. It has already prompted a massive, but disjointed, outpouring of analysis by trade theorists. The field cries out therefore for a creative synthesis and sorting out of the different analytical approaches to the understanding of the implications of PTAs.

This volume addresses precisely this need. It puts together many of the major analytical contributions that have appeared over nearly half a century since Viner's pionering analysis of PTAs in 1950, including recent policy papers and overviews that have played a role in the ongoing debate and research. An in-depth introduction ties together the articles reprinted in the volume.

Our thanks go to Kyle Bagwell, Don Davis, Vivek Dehejia, Elias Dinopoulos, Gene Grossman, Robert Staiger, T. N. Srinivasan, Alan Winters, and many others, including three anonymous referees, for valuable suggestions in arriving at our final selection. Finally, Michael Robbins, a graduate student in the doctoral program at Brown University, deserves special mention for his excellent proofreading. A larger volume would have permitted us to include the important writings of yet other economists, among them Eric Bond, Wilfred Ethier, Jeffrey Frenkel, Raymond Riezman, Sang-Seung Yi, C. Kowalczyk, Elias Dinopoulos, and Costas Syropoulos, in this selection. But, alas, an economist must admit that constraints are a fact of life.

Jagdish Bhagwati, Pravin Krishna, and Arvind Panagariya

Introduction

The recent proliferation of free trade areas (FTAs) and customs unions (CUs) in the world trading system has led to a revival of interest in the economic analysis of such preferential trading arrangements (PTAs).

The first burst of such interest came in the 1950s when Jacob Viner (1950) began his seminal examination of PTAs (which he described generically and confusingly as "customs unions") for the Carnegie Endowment as part of a study of the optimal trade arrangements in the postwar period. The prospective signing of the Treaty of Rome in 1957 also gave the spur to further examination of the issue of PTAs by several economists at the time, including James Meade (1955), Richard Lipsey (chapter 4), and many others such as Harry Johnson, Max Corden, and Kelvin Lancaster. The principal issue that these authors focused on was the welfare effect of such a PTA and, in particular, whether the presumption that a discriminatory cutting of tariffs was necessarily welfare improving, simply because tariffs were being reduced, was valid. In distinguishing between trade diversion and trade creation, Viner undermined this presumption and set off a massive theoretical literature on the "static" welfare effects of PTAs.[1]

While there were other non-Vinerian approaches to the static analysis to follow,[2] and most of them in turn reflected some policy concerns, the second major burst of interest in the theory of PTAs came when the United States turned in early 1980s to embracing PTAs (under GATT Article XXIV) as a method of reducing trade barriers when multilateral trade negotiations (MTNs) on an MFN basis under General Agreementon Tariffs and Trade (GATT) auspices seemed to have been foreclosed by the rejection by the European Union (EU) and by developing countries of the U.S. demand at the November 1981 GATT ministerial meeting to launch a new MTN Round.[3] The principal question addressed by the theoretical literature that developed during the late 1980s and the 1990s has therefore dealt with what Bhagwati (chapter 1) has called the "dynamic" time-path issue. In broad terms, do PTAs provide an impetus to, or do they detract from, the worldwide nondiscriminatory freeing of trade? In other words, in the phrasing of Bhagwati (1991), are PTAs "stumbling blocks" or "building blocks" in the freeing of trade multilaterally?

In the twenty-six essays collected here, we have brought together many of the principal contributions to the several analytical approaches that have developed in examining these two, the "static" and the "dynamic" time-path, issues.[4] Part I begins with two substantial overviews of the entire set of issues raised since Viner. Part II addresses the Vinerian and non-Vinerian approaches to the static analysis of PTAs. Part III contains major contributions to alternative ways of analyzing the dynamic time-path question. Part IV concludes with chapters that provide policy perspectives more directly.

While the overviews in Part I offer a detailed synthesis and extension of the issues raised over the years by the growth of PTAs, we provide the readers here with a complementary roadmap to the different analytical approaches that have developed in the literature on PTAs, and that are distinguished and represented in this volume. This should enable graduate students and research scholars to see more clearly the rich texture of the theory of PTAs as it currently exists and to grasp firmly the relationships among what appear to be wholly disparate contributions to that theory.

Part I: Overview

We begin with two complementary overviews of the theory and policy of PTAs that have received some attention in both scholarly circles and in the economic media (such as *The Financial Times* and *The Economist*).

Chapter 1 was written by Bhagwati for a World Bank Conference on Regionalism in 1992 and introduced into the literature the major themes that have now emerged in the theory of PTAs. In particular, the paper developed the distinction between the First and Second Regionalism, the First corresponding to the 1950s and early 1960s while the Second corresponded to the 1980s and thereafter. It analyzed the differential policy issues within each period and the reasons for the different "success" of regionalism between them: the former resulting in abandonment, the latter in proliferation, of PTAs. The paper is also notable for introducing the key analytical distinction between "static" and "dynamic" time-path analyses, the former being the central preoccupation during the First

Regionalism, the latter being the main focus of theoretical analysis in the Second Regionalism.

Regarding "static" analysis, chapter 1 makes a contribution principally by probing further the question of trade diversion and synthesizing different contributions aimed at devising different ways, including the reform of GATT Article XXIV that sanctions PTAs in shape of FTAs and CUs, to deal with it. In regard to the "dynamic" time-path issue, the chapter raises and discusses many questions regarding the then-prevalent view in policy circles that PTAs, or "regionalism" as they are often described misleadingly,[5] were to be embraced as a desirable trade-policy option that was even superior, on some important dimensions, to multilateral MFN-based trade negotiations and liberalization. These assertions by the PTA proponents state that regionalism is quicker, more efficient, and more certain.

Chapter 2 is a more ambitious overview, offering both syntheses of existing theoretical literature and extensions thereto, which is also complementary to the overview in chapter 1.[6] The Bhagwati-Panagariya essay is notable in its critical examination and rejection of the popular hypothesis that trade diversion would be minimized if PTAs were established among "natural trading partners," namely, countries in geographical proximity and/or with large initial volumes of trade with one another.[7] The authors also extend their theoretical analysis to the question of the effects of the endogeneity of tariffs, showing how trade creation can be converted into trade diversion if it is accommodated by raising trade barriers endogenously against nonmembers, as indeed seems to have happened after the peso crisis in Mexico when NAFTA trade was exempted from the tariff increases that were confined mostly to non-NAFTA items.[8]

In regard to the "dynamic" time-path analysis, the authors contribute an analytically sharp formulation of the issue whether the incentive effect of PTA formation is toward continued expansion eventually leading to worldwide free trade or whether the incentives are in the opposite direction. Alternative approaches to the precisely formulated analytical questions are distinguished and the new literature growing up around them (much of it reprinted in part III of this volume) is systematized and reviewed.

The two overviews, chapters 1 and 2, therefore provide between them a necessary introduction to how, and in what forms, the theory of PTAs has evolved. The only serious omission is the non-Vinerian approaches in "static" analysis (which are the subject of the last four sections of part II in this volume), an omission that we repair below in this introduction.

Part II: "Static" Analysis

We distinguish among five different analytical approaches to the static analysis of PTAs in the theoretical literature, of which Viner's (1950) is evidently the pioneering one, and with the most profound impact. We begin with the Vinerian approach, which includes excepts from Viner's own seminal work and a set of the more notable contributions that followed at the time.

Trade Creation and Trade Diversion: Vinerian Analysis

Casting the problem in a three-country framework, Viner introduced the key concepts of trade creation and trade diversion, ideas that have remained central to the literature on static welfare analysis of preferential trading that has emerged in the past forty-five years. The excerpts chosen in chapter 3 from his classic 1950 book highlight the way in which Viner developed his central insights.

It is interesting that Viner presented his analysis verbally, as was often the case with his contemporaries, and did not employ formal models. As is well known, however, from several textbook treatments of Viner's analysis, he implicitly deployed constant-cost assumptions and focused on shifts in given volume of trade, and hence production, among alternative locations of production within and outside the PTA in question. Trade creation, argued to be welfare improving, implied a shift from a higher-cost member country to a lower-cost member country; trade diversion, considered welfare reducing, implied a shift of production from a lower-cost nonmember source to a higher-cost member source.

The precise way in which Viner introduced this key distinction and then worked with it, and also the way in which he related his analysis to earlier writings on the subject by eminent economists such as Haberler, Hawtrey, and Robbins, is reprinted in chapter 3 here and should prove to be of great interest.

Inevitably, Viner's work led his contemporary theorists, such as James Meade, Harry Johnson, Max Corden, Richard Lipsey, and Kelvin Lancaster, to turn to a formal analysis of the issues that had been dramatically opened up. Thus, Meade's (1955) slender book, based on the de Vries Lectures, provided an influential full-scale general-equilibrium analysis of the PTA problem, with Meade focusing, typically as in all his work, on the effect on world welfare, as noted by Panagariya (chapter 7) in his analysis of the Meade model of preferential trading.[9] Meade's analysis showed precisely how the welfare effects of trade diversion and trade creation, when jointly present, could lead to world welfare improvement or reduction, depending on parameters such as the initial levels of tariffs on the goods subject to trade diversion and creation respectively.

In a classic article reprinted as chapter 4, Lipsey focused exclusively instead on the fact that Viner's conclusion that a wholly trade diverting union is harmful to its members is based on his implicit exclusion of consumption effects.[10] Using a three-country, two-good general-equilibrium model, Lipsey demonstrated that, after the union is formed, the gain in consumption due to a reduction in the price of the imported good by a union member could more than outweigh the loss from switching imports from the low-cost outside country to the high-cost union partner.

Johnson (chapter 5) instead argued that it was natural to incorporate *both* production and consumption effects into the definition of trade creation and trade diversion, instead of restricting the definitions à la Viner to production effects. According to him, "Trade creation entails an economic gain of two sorts; the saving on the real cost of goods previously produced domestically and now imported from the partner country; and the gain in consumers' surplus from the substitution of lower-cost for higher-cost means of satisfying wants." Thus, in Lipsey's article (chapter 4), the consumption effect, which produced welfare gain and created added trade, was to be classified as "trade creation" as well. In redefining trade creation this way, Johnson drew a more direct and natural link between the definitions and the welfare effects of the PTA than was done by Viner and Lipsey.

In addition to trade creation and trade diversion, the welfare effects of a PTA also depend on the changes in the terms of trade between union members and between the union as a whole and the rest of the world. Thus, though the terms of trade effects were present in Johnson's partial-equilibrium analysis (chapter 5), it was Mundell (chapter 6) who provided their first systematic analysis. Mundell employed a neat geometric technique to study the terms of trade effects of a small tariff preference granted by a country within the three-good Meade model. In this model, each country produces and exports one good and imports the remaining two. Assuming substitutability in consumption, he demonstrated that a discriminatory tariff reduction by a member country improves the terms of trade of the partner country with respect to both the tariff-reducing country and the rest of the world. However, the effect on the terms of trade of the tariff-reducing country with respect to the rest of the world is ambiguous in general. Mundell also derived the important conclusion that the gain to a free trade area (FTA) member is larger, the higher are the initial tariffs of the partner country. A key implication of this conclusion is that in an FTA involving the United States (EU), which has low external tariffs, and Mexico (Poland), which has high external tariffs, the former is likely to benefit while the latter may lose.

A recurrent theme in the policy literature has been that PTAs may be welfare improving in the presence of scale economies. In Corden's analysis of this issue (chapter 8), because of trade diversion, economies of scale do not establish a stronger presumption in favor of PTAs being welfare improving than was the case under constant or increasing costs. It also remains true in Corden's model that the union members could do better by liberalizing unilaterally on a nondiscriminatory basis than by going the PTA route.

Making a Necessarily Welfare-Improving Customs Union

While the Vinerian approach and distinction between trade creation and trade diversion proved to be potent in trade theory and policy, it violated the pre-Vinerian commonsense intuition that *any* form of trade liberalization should be good—that a movement *toward* free trade (even when preferential or discriminatory) was desirable just as the movement *to* free trade was.

The beauty of the influential paper by Kemp and Wan (chapter 9) is that, in little more than a few pages, these authors restored a sophisticated form of the pre-Vinerian intuition. They did not show that *any* PTA among an arbitrary subset of countries in the world economy would be welfare enhancing for the members and for the world, for that simply cannot be done and would violate Viner's important insight. What they showed instead was that a customs union could *always* be devised, among an arbitrarily specified subset of countries, which would have the property that it would leave the nonmember welfare unchanged while increasing the welfare of at least one member without harming any other member. It would thus be a Pareto-better move compared to the initial uniform-tariff situation of each member country. Kemp and Wan did this by essentially turning the external tariff of the CU into an endogenous policy instrument where as Viner was taking it as given at the initial level.[11] While Kemp and Wan had the proof of this remarkable proposition essentially laid out in their first contribution, they later provided a more satisfactory proof (chapter 10).

The Kemp-Wan demonstration, however, constitutes just a "possibility theorem." Its implementation faces at least two operational problems: one has to devise the common external tariff and one also has to figure out the lump-sum compensation among members, both associated with the Kemp-Wan CU. Grinols (chapter 11) attacks the latter problem, by devising a particular Pareto-compensation scheme that is always feasible and where the compensation to each member country is simply determined by its preunion trade vector so that implementation is easy. Srinivasan (chapter 12) examines the former question instead and proceeds to compare the Kemp-Wan external tariff to the different Article XXIV requirement that the common external tariff should, on average, be left unchanged.[12]

Welfare-Improving Customs Unions Among Developing Countries Seeking Industrialization

After the Treaty of Rome, many developing countries sought unsuccessfully to form similar FTAs or CU's on the ground that, given the protection against the industrialized North in order to achieve a certain targeted level of industrialization, they could liberalize trade among themselves and reduce the cost of their industrialization, and idea that was developed independently in Cooper and Massell (chapter 13), Johnson (1965), and Bhagwati (1968).

The precise mechanism by which this intuition was arrived at relied on scale economies: that small, developing countries would open specialization in different industries, with greater scale economies being exploited, and thus the total value of industrialization desired by each country could be achieved but its cost reduced by specialization among the members on different industries.

As it happens, only recently was a proper proof of general proposition provided by Krishna and Bhagwati (chapter 14), who saw that the argument could simply be proved, as a version of the Kemp-Wan theorem with an added policy instrument thrown in to achieve the targeted degree of member-country industrialization, by combining the Kemp-Wan logic with the Bhagwati and Srinivasan (1969) analysis of noneconomic objectives. This also meant that the essential rationale for such a CU among developing countries is really independent of scale economies: it comes through with constant costs, and is really a variant of the Kemp-Wan argument.

Impact on Members of Policy and Parametric Variations in a Common Market

Consider, however, a different set of questions that relate to a functioning common market such as the European Union, where the CU is characterized additionally by full factor mobility across member countries. In this case, questions such as the effect of policy and parametric changes (e.g., change in the common external tariff or admission of new members or growth in one member country) on the welfare of specific member nations can be answered just the way income-distributional questions (defined on a set of factors, e.g., gender or race) can be analyzed within a nation state.

Brecher and Bhagwati (chapter 15) recognized this essential analogy, proceeding from the earlier analysis by Bhagwati and Tironi (1980) of the effect of such changes on domestic, as distinct from national, welfare when there were foreign-owned factors of production in a country. Their analysis therefore provides the techniques to address these common market problems. More recently, Alessandra Casella (1996) has analyzed a similar problem, differentiating the effect of a new entry on member countries of different size, in the framework of the theory of imperfect competition with scale economies.

Political-Economy-Theoretic Analysis of the Formation of PTAs and Their External Tariffs

Finally, the cutting edge theory of PTAs has moved into modeling the incentives to form PTAs, as in Grossman and Helpman (chapter 16). Their analysis uses a detailed and rigorous specification of the political economy process where special interest groups make donations to policymakers (whose objective function depends upon both contributions and the aggregate welfare level) to influence policy stances in their direction. They show that FTAs would be politically most viable exactly when they would divert trade and result in increased protection to domestic producers.[13]

In addition, the political economy analysis of PTAs has been extended, by Panagariya and Findlay (chapter 17) and earlier by Martin Richardson (chapter 18), to considering the question as to what is likely to happen, incentivewise, to the external tariff against nonmembers, within CUs and FTAs alternatively. Thus Panagariya and Findlay (chapter 17) showed, using a three-country, three-good Meade model, that the formation of a PTA would likely result in an increase in trade barriers against other countries. In particular, these authors show that the formation of a PTA could result in an increase in the trade barriers against nonmembers; and that, with external tariffs being endogenously determined in their models, CUs and FTAs cannot generally be rank-ordered with respect to their welfare impacts.

Part III: "Dynamic" Time-Path Analysis

As indicated at the outset, in contrast to the question of whether the immediate "static" effect of a given PTA is good, one may ask whether the "dynamic" time-path effect of the PTA is to create incentives that lead to addition of more members so as to continue moving toward worldwide free trade or opposite incentives to freeze membership. That is, we now have, in the "dynamic" time-path case, the key concepts introduced by Bhagwati of PTAs acting as "stumbling blocks" or "building blocks" toward worldwide nondiscriminatory trade liberalization, just as Viner introduced the key concepts of trade diversion and trade creation for the "static" analysis. That the two questions, static and dynamic time-path, can point policy in different directions is evident from a simple example. If, say, Chile were added to the North American Free Trade Agreement (NAFTA), this may be undesirable on "static" grounds if it leads to net trade diversion. But it could be considered desirable on "dynamic" time-path grounds because it signifies expanding membership and hence progress toward the goal of achieving multilateral free trade.

A full analysis of the time-path questions is included in the survey in chapter 2, so that we can refer the reader to it. It should suffice to say here simply that there are two fundamentally different approaches to the question in the theoretical literature. One consists of simply assuming that PTAs expand in membership and examining their impact on welfare. This literature is aptly described as one where the PTA expansion is *exogenously* determined. The other, which is based on political-economy-theoretic modeling of incentive structures to expand or deter new membership, is the relevant and important literature where the PTA expansion is said to be *endogenously* determined. Part III distinguishes and deals successively with both approaches.

The chief contribution to the exogenously determined PTA expansion literature is by Krugman (chapter 19). Krugman models a world where there are many distinct geographical units ("nations"), each specialized in the production of a different good that is demanded symmetrically by all countries. The world is then assumed, in this exercise, to be organized into n blocs of equal trading size, with free trade within each bloc and a noncooperative, optimal tariff set by each bloc on its imports. A reduction in n then means more such uniform blocs. Krugman then simulates this model over a large range of parameters, arguing that the best outcome for world welfare is when there are few or many such blocs, the worst being the case where the blocs number three!

This exercise, which does not bear directly on the incentive issues related to whether PTAs will expand membership or not, has drawn attention and response from some trade theorists. In particular, Srinivasan (1993) and Deardorff and Stern (chapter 20) have shown, not too surprisingly, that the Krugman conclusions are not robust to changes in key assumptions. For instance, in the ingenious Deardorff-Stern analysis that allows for Heckscher-Ohlin trade, world welfare rises monotonically with the size of the blocs.

The important, and to us interesting, contributions to the time-path analysis relate, however, to the work of authors who have examined the incentive structures in a political-economy-theoretic framework. Chapters 21 and 22 offer the recent analyses of Levy and Pravin Krishna, respectively, that formalize the proposition that PTAs will undermine the multilateral freeing of trade by reducing the incentives of member countries to seek multilateral free trade. Chapter 23, on the other hand, presents Richard Baldwin's analysis that goes the other way, formalizing the notion that the *nonmembers* left outside the PTA will have an incentive to join the PTA.

This latter area of analysis is clearly going to be the most popular one among trade theorists, reflecting both the policy concerns and issues of the Second Regionalism as well as the hugely expanding interest in the theory of political economy in the economics profession today. The Levy, Krishna, and Baldwin papers are only a sample of the theoretical contributions that we can confidently expect in the coming decade.

Part IV: Theoretical Analyses

The volume contains three more theoretical chapters that are best seen as analyzing the implications of certain well-known "institutional" features of trade institutions and treaties for the analysis of PTAs. The Bagwell-Staiger analysis (chapter 24) examines how the institutional features of the GATT, especially its reciprocity provisions, bear on the issue of whether PTAs will undermine multilateralism. The Levy-Srinivasan article (chapter 25) shows, on the other hand, how the interaction of domestic lobbying

Bhagwati, Jagdish, Greenaway, David, and Panagariya, Arvind. 1998. "Trading Preferentially: Theory and Policy." *Economic Journal* 109 (May).

Bhagwati, Jagdish, and Arvind Panagariya. 1996. "The Theory of Preferential Trade Agreements: Historical Evolution and Current Trends." *American Economic Review* 86: 82–87.

Bhagwati, Jagdish, and T. N. Srinivasan. 1959. "Optimal Intervention to Achieve Noneconomic Objectives." *Review of Economic Studies* 36(1): 27–38.

Bhagwati, Jagdish, and Ernesto Tironi. 1980. "Tariff Change, Foreign Capital, and Immiserization: A Theoretical Analysis." *Journal of Development Economics* (February): 103–115.

Casella, Alessandra. 1996. "Large Countries, Small Countries and the Enlargement of Trade Blocs." *European Economic Review* (June): 391–405.

Gehrels, F. 1956–57. "Customer Unions from a Single-Country Viewpoint." *Review of Economic Studies* 24.

Johnson, Harry. 1965. "An Economic Theory of Protectionism, Tariff Bargaining, and the Formation of Customs Unions." *Journal of Political Economy* 73 (June): 256–283.

Krugman, Paul. 1991. "The Move to Free Trade Zones." In *Policy Implications of Trade and Currency Zones*, 7–41. Kansas City: Federal Reserve Bank.

Michaely, M. 1976. "The Assumptions of Jacob Viner's Theory of Customs Unions." *Journal of International Economics* 6(1): 75–93.

Meade, James. 1955. *The Theory of Customs Unions*. Amsterdam: North Holland Co.

Serra, Jaime Puche, et al. 1996. *Regional Trade Agreements*. Report issued by the Carnegie Endowment for International Peace. Washington. DC.

Srinivasan, T. N. 1993. "Discussion." In *New Dimensions in Regional Integration*, ed. J. de Melo and A. Panagariya. Cambridge: Cambridge University Press.

Viner, Jacob. 1950. *The Customs Union Issue*. New York: Carnegie Endowment for International Peace.

I   Overview

1

Regionalism and Multilateralism: An Overview

Jagdish Bhagwati

The question of "regionalism," defined broadly as preferential trade agreements among a subset of nations, is a longstanding one. As with all great issues, economists have long been divided on the wisdom of such arrangements. So have policymakers.

While this may not be evident to the many economists who are not inhibited by lack of comparative advantage from pronouncing on these matters, and whose pronouncements are a testimony to the enduring value of the theory of comparative advantage, preferential trade arrangements were debated by economists, as such, during the very formation of the General Agreement on Tariffs and Trade (GATT). The context, of course, was the difference between the British, led by Keynes, who were devoted to the continuation of the discrimination in Britain's favour through Imperial Preference, and the Americans, with Cordell Hull to the fore, who were strongly opposed, and embraced multilateralism and most favoured nation status (MFN) instead. Keynes, quite characteristically, at first denounced the American attachment to non-discrimination in trade and then later, when the British had virtually capitulated, celebrated its virtues with equal passion. I will juxtapose the two positions in Keynes' inimitable words, quoted in Bhagwati (1991a):

My strong reaction against the word "discrimination" is the result of feeling so passionately that our hands must be free... [T]he word calls up and must call up ... all the old lumber, most-favored-nation clause and all the rest which was a notorious failure and made such a hash of the old world. We know also that it won't work. It is the clutch of the dead, or at least the moribund, hand.

[The proposed policies] aim, above all, at the restoration of multilateral trade ... the bias of the policies before you is against bilateral barter and every kind of

Originally published in *New Dimensions in Regional Integration*, ed. Jaime de Melo and Arvind Panagariya (Cambridge, UK: World Bank and Cambridge University Press, 1993), 22–51. Reprinted with permission.

discriminatory practice. The separate blocs and all the friction and loss of friend-
ship they must bring with them are expedients to which one may be driven in a
hostile world where trade has ceased over wide areas to be cooperative and
peaceful and where are forgotten the healthy rules of mutual advantage and equal
treatment. But it is surely crazy to prefer that.

Closer to our times, the question of customs unions (CUs) and free-
trade areas (FTAs), both permitted under GATT Article XXIV, became a
major topic of theoretical research. The focus, however, since Jacob Viner's
(1950) classic treatment, distinguishing between trade diversion and trade
creation, was on showing that CUs and FTAs were not necessarily welfare-
improving, either for member countries or for world welfare: in other
words, the case for preferential trade arrangements was different from the
case for free trade for all. The latter, enshrined in Adam Smith and
Ricardo, and rigorously proved later by Samuelson (1939), Kemp (1972),
and Grandmont and McFadden (1972), is a first-best case. The former, by
contrast, reflects second-best considerations and was argued by Lipsey
and Lancaster (1956–7), Lipsey (1957), Meade (1956), Johnson (1958a,
1958b) and others.[1]

But if the main focus of these analyses was on disabusing the faith in
regionalism as being desirable (on static immediate-impact grounds) by
analogy with the different and legitimate case for multilateralism (in the
sense of free or freer trade for all), and thus could be seen as reinforcing
the case for multilateralism, the effect could also go the other way, and
did at times. One could thus argue, from the opposite counterfactual, that
if you believed that regionalism, in being discriminatory, was necessarily
inferior to non-discriminatory reduction of trade barriers, then this too
was wrong. Ironically, in view of the later shift of his views to multilateralism and free trade, reflecting perhaps the changed intellectual environment in Cambridge and Chicago and also further reflection, it is
interesting to quote Johnson (1967, pp. 163–4) in the context of proposals for trade preferences, for and among developing countries, for
manufactured goods:

Both proposals violate the non-discrimination principle of the General Agreement
on Tariffs and Trade and the GATT ban on new preferential arrangements other
than customs unions and free trade areas embracing the bulk of the trade of the
participating countries. This, however, does not mean that the proposed trading
arrangements would necessarily be economically disadvantageous. The postwar
development of the theory of customs unions and of commercial policy changes,
culminating in the theory of second best has shown that in a tariff-ridden world
economy there is no a priori reason for believing that nondiscrimination among
import sources is economically superior to discriminatory trading arrangements. It

has demonstrated also that the question of whether a discriminatory tariff reduction improves or worsens the efficiency and economic welfare of the countries involved and the world as a whole depends on the empirical circumstances of the particular case.

Both the theory of second best and modern welfare economics (as well as ordinary common sense) indicate that policy changes that secure desirable results in terms of income distribution or other objectives at the cost of reduced economic efficiency may constitute improvements on a balance of gain and loss, and may legitimately be recommended if no more efficient method of achieving the same objectives is feasible or acceptable.

In fact, Johnson was an active proponent of NAFTA, an acronym which then stood for the North *Atlantic* Free-Trade Area (inclusive of the United Kingdom) rather than for the present North *American* Free-Trade Area which is predicated on a conceptually narrower, geographically-defined regional basis. As it happened, the concept of NAFTA failed to get off the ground, though the ideas concerning regional blocs and trading arrangements remained seductive through much of the 1960s, only to be abandoned thereafter until the recent 1980s' revival.

The recent revival of regionalism, which I describe as the "Second Regionalism" in contrast to, and because it is a sequel to, the "First Regionalism" of the 1960s, raises several of the old issues anew. But the historically changed situation which has resurrected regionalism equally provides the context in which it must be analysed, raising several new issues.

In this chapter, I address these manifold questions, dividing the analysis into a discussion of six areas:

• Article XXIV of the GATT, which sanctions CUs and FTAs (section 1.1);

• the "First Regionalism," briefly reviewing the factors that led to it and the reasons why, in the end, it failed (section 1.2);

• the "Second Regionalism," the reasons for its revival and its differential prospects (section 1.3);

• the key issues that this renewed regionalism raises, distinguishing among two main questions (section 1.4);

• the first, relating to the static impact effect of regional trade blocs (section 1.5);

• the second, concerning the dynamic time-path that regionalism offers, in itself and vis-à-vis multilateralism when the objective is to reach (non-discriminatory) free trade for all, so that one asks "whether multilateralism is the best way to get to multilateralism," therefore distinguishing between "process multilateralism" and "outcome multilateralism" (section 1.6).

In the light of this analysis, I conclude by examining the current US trade-policy shift to regionalism and arguing for a change in its focus from "piecemeal" to "programmatic" regionalism, less antithetical to reaching the "outcome-multilateralism" objective of eventual free trade for all (section 1.7). Some final observations conclude the chapter (section 1.8).

1.1   Article XXIV of the GATT: Rationale

The principle of non-discrimination is central to the final conception of the GATT, signed on 30 October 1947 by representatives from 23 countries in Geneva. Article I embodies the strong support for non-discrimination, requiring (unconditional) MFN for all GATT members.

Aside from "grandfathering" provisions, the only significant exception to MFN is made in Article XXIV, which permits CUs and FTAs and therefore sanctions preferential trade-barrier reductions among a subset of GATT members, as long as they go all the way to elimination.[2]

It is an intriguing question as to why Article XXIV was accepted, and it is a question that also has significance for some of the issues raised by the "Second Regionalism." It is a bit odd that an exception to MFN should be allowed as long as it is total (going all the way to 100 percent) rather than partial (say, 20 percent preference for one's favoured friends): it is as if your cardinal told you that petting is more morally reprehensible than sleeping around. In fact the post-Vinerian theory of preferential trade areas suggests that 100 percent preferences are less likely to increase welfare than partial preferences.[3]

The rationale for Article XXIV's inclusion in the GATT must therefore be explained in other ways. Perhaps there was an inchoate, if strong, feeling that integration with 100 percent preferences was somehow special and consonant with the objective on multilateralism. Thus, Dam (1970, pp. 274–5) quotes the prominent US official Clair Wilcox as follows:

A Custom union (with 100% preferences) creates a wider trading area, removes obstacles to competition, makes possible a more economic allocation of resources and thus operates to increase production and raise planes of living. A preferential system (less than 100%) on the other hand, retains internal barriers, obstructs economy in production, and restrains the growth of income and demand ... A customs union is conducive to the expansion of trade on a basis of multilateralism and nondiscrimination; a preferential system is not.

Wilcox's statement was little more than assertion, however. But the rationale for inclusion of Article XXIV in the GATT appears to have been threefold, as follows:

• Full integration on trade, that is, going all the way down to freedom of trade flows among any subset of GATT members, would have to be allowed since it created an important element of single-nation characteristics (such as virtual freedom of trade and factor movements) among these nations, and implied that the resulting quasi-national status following from such integration in trade legitimated the exception to MFN obligation toward other GATT members.

• The fact that the exception would be permitted only for the extremely difficult case where all trade barriers would need to come down seemed to preclude the possibility that all kinds of preferential arrangements would break out, returning the world to the fragmented, discriminatory bilateralism-infested situation of the 1930s.

• One could also think of Article XXIV as permitting a supplemental, practical route to the universal free trade that GATT favoured as the ultimate goal, with the general negotiations during the many Rounds leading to a dismantling of trade barriers on a GATT-wide basis while deeper integration would be achieved simultaneously within those areas where politics permitted faster movement to free trade under a strategy of full and time-bound commitment. This is an argument that is not at centre stage: is regionalism truly a building, rather than a stumbling, bloc towards multilateral free trade for all: in other words, will it fragment, or integrate, the world economy?

The clear determination of 100 percent preferences as compatible with multilateralism and non-discrimination, and the equally firm view that anything less was not, meant that when Article XXIV was drafted, its principal objective was to close all possible loopholes by which it could degenerate into a justification for preferential arrangements of less than 100 percent; paragraphs 4–10 of Article XXIV were written precisely for this purpose. But, as is now commonly conceded, their inherent ambiguity and the political pressures for approval of substantial regional groupings of preferences of less than 100 percent have combined to frustrate the full import of the original desire to sanction only 100 percent preferences.

This tension between intention and reality has a direct bearing on the important question of strengthening Article XXIV today beyond even what its original drafters intended. I will therefore sketch briefly the important respects in which the original intention of Article XXIV was reasonably clear but was occasionally violated in spirit, to the point where the great expert on GATT law, Professor John Jackson, has gone so far as to observe that the accommodation of the European Common Market's imperfect union in disregard of the legal requirements of Article XXIV was the beginning of the breakdown of the GATT's legal discipline, which we now seek to repair.[4] Two issues suffice to demonstrate this contention.

First, in regard to the elimination of internal barriers down to 100 percent, there was enough scope within the language of Article XXIV, paragraph 8, for its intent to be successfully avoided. Ambiguities could be exploited on two main fronts.

The first ambiguity lay in the directive that "duties and other restrictive regulations on commerce" were (with specified exceptions permitted under Article XI, XII, XIII, XIV, and XX) to be "eliminated with respect to substantially all the trade between the constituent territories." Skilful lawyers and representatives of governments could work wonders with the concept of "substantially all the trade," and then, even if a percentage cutoff point was accepted for this purpose (for example, 75 percent of all initial trade), important issues remained ambiguous, such as whether across-the-board (75 percent) cut on everything were required or whether substantial sectors could be left out altogether from the scope of the cuts—the latter being evidently at variance with the intent of those who favoured (100 percent) CUs but opposed (less than 100 percent) preferential arrangements. With both interpretations possible, sectorally non-uniform preferential arrangements could evidently not effectively be ruled out.

An ambiguity of equal importance arose in regard to the problem of the speed with which the "100 percent preferences" would be implemented. Evidently, if they were stretched out over very long periods, one was de facto sanctioning "less than 100 percent" preferential arrangements. In GATT jargon, this was the problem of "interim arrangements." Paragraph 5 therefore addressed this issue, requiring "a plan and schedule," and asking for the CU or FTA to be fully consummated "within a reasonable length of time." Paragraph 7, in turn, laid down specific procedures for such interim arrangements to be approved. Needless to say, this nonetheless left the door open for substantial laxity in conception and execution of the CUs and FTAs under Article XXIV.

Dam's (1970, p. 290) overall judgement of the outcome is perhaps too harsh, but is certainly in the ballpark:

The record is not comforting ... Perhaps only one of the more than one dozen regional arrangements that have come before the GATT complied fully with Article XXIV criteria. That was the recent United Kingdom/Ireland Free-Trade Area, and even in that case certain doubts were expressed before the working party. In some cases, the regional arrangements were very wide off the mark. The European Coal and Steel Community, covering only two major product lines, could not even qualify for the special regional-arrangement waiver of Article XXIV: 10 but required a general waiver under Article XXV: 5. The New Zealand/Australia Free-Trade Agreement, although not purportedly an example of "functional integration," provided for the liberalization of an even smaller percentage of intermember trade. A strong tendency has also been manifested for interim agreements to provide for an even longer transitional period and to contain increasingly fewer detailed commitments for eventual completion of the customs union or free-trade area.

1.2   The "First Regionalism": Failure in the 1960s

In any event, one can correctly assert (based on the acceptance of Article XXIV into the GATT) that regionalism, in the shape of (100 percent) CUs and FTAs, was not generally considered, by the architects of the GATT or by the United States, which was the chief proponent of multilateralism and non-discrimination, as antithetical to the GATT and to these principles.

1. Nonetheless, the United States, long suspicious of discriminatory trade arrangements, restrained itself from resorting to Article XXIV. The formation of the European Community in 1958 marked a partial watershed. The United States puts its shoulder to the wheel and saw the Common Market through, negotiating around the different hoops of Article XXIV, emasculating the Article somewhat so as to seek GATT approval of an imperfect union (especially in regard to discriminatory preferences for the eighteen ex-colonies in Africa that the Europeans insisted on retaining, requiring therefore a waiver of GATT rules), all in the cause of what it saw as a *politically* beneficial union of the original six nations that formed the Community. But despite the enthusiasm of many to follow the European Community with a NAFTA, and even a Pacific Free-Trade Area (PAFTA), centred on the United States, nothing came of it: the United States remained indifferent to such notions.[5]

2. There was an outbreak of FTA proposals in the developing countries as well. While stimulated by the European examples, they were motivated by the altogether different economic rationale formulated by Cooper and Massell (1965a, 1965b), Johnson (1965) and Bhagwati (1968). This was that, given any targeted level of import-substituting industrialisation, the developing countries with their small markets could reduce the cost of this industrialisation by exploiting economies of scale through preferential opening of markets with one another.[6] By the end of the 1960s, however, the attempts at forming regional FTAs and CUs along these lines had also

collapsed. The problem was that, rather than use trade liberalisation and hence prices to guide industry allocation, the developing countries attempting such unions sought to allocate industries by bureaucratic negotiation and to tie trade to such allocations, putting the cart before the horse and killing the forward motion.

Thus, while the world was indeed filled with proposals for NAFTA, PAFTA, LAFTA (the Latin American Free-Trade Area, replaced by LAIA, the Latin American Integration Agreement, in 1980), and ever more in the 1960s, until one could be forgiven for imagining that a veritable chemical revolution had broken out, regionalism had virtually died by the end of the decade, except for the original European Community and EFTA.

1.3   The "Second Regionalism": Revival in the 1980s

But regionalism (i.e., preferential trade liberalisation) is now back. Those who do not know the history of the "First Regionalism" are doomed to extrapolate from the current political ferment in favour of FTAs and CUs and assume uncritically that regionalism is here to stay. Those who know the history may make the reverse mistake of thinking that regionalism will again fail. I believe that careful analysis of the causes of the resurrection of regionalism suggests that regionalism this time is likely to endure.

The main driving force for regionalism today is the conversion of the United States, hitherto an abstaining party, to Article XXIV. Beginning with the FTA with Israel (a reflection of the special relationship between the two nations and hence of little general value), the FTA with Canada marked a distinct change. Now the NAFTA is being negotiated with Mexico, and the Enterprise for the Americas' Initiative (EAI) envisages more FTAs with the nations of South America, with Chile at the head of the line.

The conversion of the United States is of major significance. As the key defender of multilateralism through the postwar years, its decision now to travel the regional route (in the geographical *and* the preferential senses simultaneously) tilts the balance of forces at the margin away from multilateralism to regionalism. This shift has taken place in the context of an anti-multilateralist ethos that has reflected alternative but nonetheless eventually reinforcing views:

• The "Memorial Drive" school[7] holds that the GATT is dead (Thurow: Davos) or that the GATT should be killed (Dornbusch).[8] Regionalism is then presented in effect as an *alternative* to multilateralism. This school, aptly named in view of its funereal approach to multilateralism, has influence in Democratic circles and plays to the prejudices that one finds in Congressional circles that mistakenly identify multilateralism with America's postwar altruism and regionalism (with its connotation of "exploiting our own markets for ourselves") with the presumed current necessity finally to "look after one's interests."

• An alternative view is that regionalism is a useful *supplement*, not an alternative, to multilateralism. "We are walking on only two legs" is the popular argument. That we may wind up walking on all fours is ignored.

• It is also often asserted that regionalism will not merely supplement multilateralism. It will also *accelerate* the multilateral process: the threat of going (unilateral and) regional will produce multilateral agreements that may otherwise be held up. (However, this may be an optimistic view since threats that have to be implemented and repeatedly made, as has been the case with US regionalism, are not efficient threats; and they change external perceptions about what US trade policy priorities are, quite regardless of what the United States asserts to be its true intentions. In fact, the taking of two roads simultaneously can affect adversely the travel down one, as I argue below at length.)

• The panic over the continuing payments deficit has also fed demands for "quick" results on trade (although the two issues are broadly delinkable: payments surpluses and deficits are macroeconomic phenomena that are not influenced in any predictable way by trade policy changes whose impact on the difference between domestic savings and investment, if any, can come in different ways that can go in opposing directions). Associated with this has been impatience with the pace of the multilateral trade-negotiating process and the non sequitur (examined below) that regionalism necessarily works faster.

• In addition, "Europe 1992" and the impending integration of Eastern Europe into the European Community have reinforced, as the formation of the Common Market did with many three decades ago, those in North America who feel that a countervailing bloc must be formed there as well. Indeed, the fear that European investments would be diverted to Eastern Europe, once it is integrated with the European Community, was cited by President Salinas of Mexico as a factor decisively pushing him toward the Mexico–US FTA: this would, he felt, enable Mexico to get the investment needed from America and Japan.

• There are strong non-economic, political and cultural factors also driving Mexico toward an FTA with its northern neighbour. Just as the Turks since Ataturk have tried to seek a European rather than an Arab (or Islamic) identity, the Mexicans clearly now seek an American future rather than one with their southern neighbours. The Hispanic (economic) destiny that many in America fear from illegal immigration and integration with Mexico has its flip side in the American (economic) destiny that Mexico's reforming elite, trained in the top universities in the United States, hope for.

• The offer in June 1990 by President Bush to get more nations from South America to join the United States in an FTA, as part of a general package of economic initiatives to assist these nations, reflects the compulsions that the debt crisis there imposes on American policy to respond in a regional framework to ensure that this crisis remains manageable and does not engulf the United States, whose banks are principally endangered by it.

• Then again, the response of South American nations to the prospect of FTAs with NAFTA, and in some cases with one another first and then joining up with NAFTA, has been enthusiastic. This time around, the prospects are better that in the 1960s. Quite simply, there is now a marked shift in economic thinking towards trade liberalisation and market forces. The macroeconomic crisis of the 1980s has fed the movement to microeconomic reforms, much as it is currently doing in India. The changed economic and political attitudes are comforting to those of us who went into the trenches to fight these battles as early as the 1960s. It is also amusing to see those who dismissed our arguments as "reactionary" or "ideological" then, now embracing these ideas and policies and the leaders who are implementing them, with no apologies to us and with a facade of independently-obtained wisdom. But, frankly, it is good to have them finally on the right side; and it is good to have been in the right.

• Finally, the conjunction of the two dramatic events, "Europe 1992" and the US–Canada FTA, even though fortuitous and prompted by different motivations and historical circumstances, certainly has created a sense elsewhere that regionalism is the order of the day, and that others must follow suit. In the Far East, for instance, there has been a sense that a Japan-centred regional bloc may be necessary in a bloc-infested world, and Malaysia has actively sought a Japan-centred Asian bloc to rival and confront the US-led Americas bloc.

1.4 Regionalism versus Multilateralism: Key Questions

I suspect therefore that the "Second Regionalism" will endure: it shows many signs of strength and few points of vulnerability. But if so, those of us who see virtue in a rule-based, open and multilateral trading system must ask searching questions as to its compatibility with such discriminatory trading arrangements. In particular, two major questions must be answered:

• Is the immediate impact effect of such preferential trade blocs, whether CUs or FTAs, to reduce rather than increase world welfare?

• Regardless of the immediate impact effect, will regionalism lead to non-discriminatory multilateral free trade for all, through continued expansion of the regional blocs until universal free trade is reached, or will it fragment the world economy? And will, in any event, such a dynamic time-path show that regionalism will get us closer to the *goal* of multilateral free trade for all than multilateralism as the *process* of trade negotiation will?

I shall now treat each of these two important, and distinct (if at times analytically interrelated), questions in turn.

1.5 The Static Impact-Effect Question

The question of the static impact effect of preferential trade arrangements such as FTAs and CUs is, quite simply, the question raised by Viner (1950): would not such discriminatory arrangements be trade-diverting rather than trade-creating?[9]

It is important to raise this question because, as Viner taught us, FTAs and CUs are two-faced: they liberalise trade (among members), but they also protect (against outsiders). The important issue therefore is: which aspect of an FTA or a CU is dominant? Or, to put it in the economist's language: is a particular FTA or CU trade-diverting (that is, taking trade away from efficient outside suppliers and giving it to inefficient member countries) or trade-creating (that is, generating trade from one more efficient member at the expense of another less efficient member)?

Sadly, one might have scanned the leading articles, the editorials, and the Congressional testimony when the renewal of fast-track authority for the extension of NAFTA to Mexico was being debated in 1991, looking for references to trade diversion—and find scarcely any. Astonishingly, it was not just the politicians and lawyers for Mexico's lobby who equated the FTA with (non-discriminatory) free trade; reputed economists did so too.[10]

What can we say about this issue? In particular, what can we propose to ensure that, if CUs and FTAs are to flourish, they do not become trade-diversionary? Article XXIV's injunction not to raise the CU's or the FTA's average external tariff can be interpreted as a precaution against trade diversion and harm to outside GATT members, though (as argued below) this is not a satisfactory way to do it.

In essence, there are three approaches to containing the fallout of trade diversion from CUs and FTAs.

1.5.1 Converting Preferential CUs and FTAs into (Geographically) Regional Blocs

It is occasionally argued that we should encourage geographically proximate countries to form CUs and FTAs, discouraging geographically distant countries from doing so since the latter would be more likely to be trade-diverting.[11] This is a misguided prescription in my view, for several reasons.

To see this, it must be first appreciated that it rests on a syllogism. The first premise is that a CU or FTA is more likely to create trade and thus raise welfare, given a country's volume of international trade, the higher is the proportion of trade with the country's CU or FTA partners and the lower is this proportion with the non-member countries. The second premise is that countries sharing borders, or closer geographically to one another, have higher proportions of trade with one another than countries further apart do.

The first premise is, of course, well known to trade economists from the early post-Vinerian theory, as developed by Lipsey (1958). But Lipsey's argument focuses on the relative sizes of imports from each source vis-à-vis expenditure on domestic goods as the key and decisive factor in determining the size of losses and gains from the preferential cuts in trade barriers.[12]

While the likelihood argument is valid within the Lipsey model, it must be noted that it is only that. Thus, for specific CUs and FTAs, the *actual* welfare effects will depend, not merely on the trade and expenditure shares à la Lipsey but also on the *substitution* at the margin between commodities. Thus, for instance, the substitution between non-member goods and domestic goods may be very high, so that the costs of discrimination would tend to be high as well, ceteris paribus. In short, it is important to guess at substitution elasticities among goods *as well as* trade shares, with and between members and non-members of CUs and FTAs, to arrive at a better picture of the likely effects of *specific* CUs and FTAs that may be proposed.

As for the second premise, I have problems with this too, as a policy guideline. If I had access to captive research assistance and funds, I could examine whether, for all conceivable combinations of countries and distances among them, and for several different time periods, the premise is valid. I do not, so I must rely on casual empiricism and a priori arguments. Compare, for instance, the trade throughout the 1960s between India and Pakistan with that between India and the United Kingdom or the then USSR. The former trade has been smaller than the latter. Borders can breed hostility and undermine trade, just as alliances among distant countries with shared causes can promote trade (Gowa and Mansfield, 1991). The flag follows trade; and trade equally follows the flag which, at least in the 19th-century European expansion, was not directly across the European nations' borders. Again, even if the premise is statistically valid for any set of observations, it may be a result of trade diversion itself: proximity may have led to preferential grant of concessions such as OAP and GSP at the expense of countries elsewhere.

In short, prescriptions to confine CUs and FTAs only to geographically proximate countries are not defensible because both premises have problems: the former is, at best, a likelihood proposition that should not be applied to specific situations where the welfare impact depends critically on other variables as well, whereas the latter does not have a firm empirical or conceptual basis.

But possibly the most damaging criticism that one can make of such a prescription is that it concentrates, at best, on the static impact-effect question and ignores the more important dynamic time-path question. By prescribing that we must rule out "distant" country unions, as between the United States and Israel and Chile, we would make the CUs and FTAs more exclusive and less open to new members, undercutting the objective of moving speedily towards the shared objective of (non-discriminatory) multilateral free trade for all. That would be tragic indeed.

1.5.2 *Designing Disciplines to Minimise Trade Diversion*

A different, and my preferred, approach is not to pretend to find rules of thumb to exclude CUs and FTAs "likely" to be trade-diversionary, but

rather to examine the different ways in which trade diversion could arise
and then to establish disciplines that would minimise its incidence.

1.5.2.1 Article XXIV In a sense, Article XXIV (paragraph 5) seeks to
do this by requiring that CUs, which must have a common external tariff,
should ensure that this common tariff "shall not on the whole be higher or
more restrictive than the general incidence of the duties and regulations
of commerce applicable ... prior to the formation of such a union." For
FTAs, the rule is that the 'duties and other regulations of commerce' are
not to be "higher or more restrictive" than those previously in effect.

Evidently, when tariffs change, as in CUs, and some increase and others
fall, the scope for skulduggery arises again, since Article XXIV leaves the
matter wholly ambiguous. As Dam (1970, p. 217) has noted: "these ambiguities plagued the review by the CONTRACTING PARTIES to the EEC
Treaty of Rome—The Six, having used an arithmetic average, refused to
discuss the best method of calculation, because in their view paragraph 5
did not require any special method."

Besides, it is evident to trade economists that maintaining external
tariffs unchanged is, in any event, not the same as eliminating trade diversion. What *can* be said is that, the lower the external barriers, the less
is the scope for diverting efficient foreign supplies to member countries. A
desirable discipline to impose on CUs and FTAs would thus be to require,
for Article XXIV sanction, that one price to be paid must be the simulta-
neous reduction of the external tariff (implicit and explicit), pro rata to the
progressive elimination of internal trade barriers.

Possible ways of ensuring this may be indirect disciplines. One way
would be to modify Article XXIV to rule out FTAs with diverse tariffs by
members[13] and to permit only CUs with common external tariffs (CETs).
With most tariffs bound, this would ensure that for the most part a sub-
stantial downward shift in tariffs would be a consequence—that, say,
Argentina or Brazil would be lowering her trade barriers, *not* that the
United States would be raising hers. Since regionalism is probably going
to be a matter of low trade barrier hubs such as the United States and
Japan, joining with their respective regional spokes, this insistence on
CUs could perhaps produce excellent results.

An alternative, and surer, way would be to insist on CUs but also
write into Article XXIV the requirement that the *lowest* tariff of any
union member on an item *before* the union must be part of the CET of the
union.

1.5.2.2 Articles VI and XIX: AD and VERs But none of this is enough today. For the trade economists who work in a sustained way on the problems of the world trading system are aware that protection today takes the form of unfair capture of fair trade mechanisms such as anti-dumping (AD) actions and of voluntary export restraints (VERs); countries today thus have access to selective and elastic instruments of protection.[14] Given this reality, even the modification of Article XXIV, to ensure that the external (implicit and explicit) tariff barriers come down as a price for CUs to be allowed under GATT rules, will leave open a gaping hole that would be tantamount to an open invitation to trade diversion by these preferential arrangements. In fact, trade creation can degenerate rapidly into trade diversion, when AD actions and VERs are freely used.

Imagine that the United States begins to eliminate (by outcompeting) an inefficient Mexican industry once the FTA goes into effect. Even though the most efficient producer is Taiwan, if the next efficient United States outcompetes the least efficient Mexico, that would be desirable trade creation (though the best course would be free trade so that Taiwan would take more of the Mexican market instead).

But what would the Mexicans be likely to do? They would probably start AD actions against Taiwan, which would lead to reduced imports from Taiwan as the imports from the United States increased, leaving the Mexican production relatively unaffected: trade diversion from Taiwan to the United States would have occurred. Similarly, the effect of Mexican competition against the United States could well be that the United States would start AD actions and even VERs against Taiwan.

My belief that FTAs will lead to considerable trade diversion (because of modern methods of protection, which are inherently selective and can be captured readily for protectionist purposes) is one that may have been borne out in the European Community. It is well known that the European Community has used AD actions and VERs profusely to erect "Fortress Europe" against the Far East. Cannot much of this be a trade-diverting policy in response to the intensification of internal competition among the member states of the European Community?[15]

Two conclusions follow: (1) If inherently discriminatory regionalism is to flourish, as seems likely, then we need greater discipline for AD actions and VERs; Article VI needs reform and Article XIX needs compliance alongside the elimination of VERs (as the Dunkel draft on the MTN recommends). (2) This also implies that regionalism means, not the redundancy of the GATT, but the need for a stronger GATT. Those who think of the two as alternatives are prisoners of defunct modes of thinking, based on the days when protection was a different beast.

1.5.2.3 Judging Trade Diversion Case by Case

While the foregoing analysis embraces a set of policy-framework and incentive-creating reforms to minimise trade diversion, an alternative approach to the problem could be in terms of a case-by-case approach where the approval by the GATT of a proposed CU or FTA would depend on the evaluation of its trade-creating and trade-diverting effects and the requirement that the net anticipated effect be trade-creating.

McMillan (1991) has argued this in an ingenious paper[16] which proposes a simple test of admissibility: "does the bloc result in less trade between member countries and outsider countries?" Based on the welfare economics of CU theory, this is an aggregative test and therefore has some obvious analytical problems. It is also subject to the problem of computing plausible trade outcomes. It is hard enough to apply it ex post; ex ante, as a test of admissibility, I see little prospect of its being effectively used to exclude any proposed CU or FTA.

Its main merit is its apparent simplicity and its better grounding in economic theory. I therefore endorse the advisability of *some* version of the McMillan test replacing in Article XXIV the current requirement not to raise the average external tariff. But I see it as doing little *in practice* to avoid trade diversion. For this, we will have to rely on changing the incentive structure, including through suitable constraints imposed by stricter discipline on selective and elastic targeting of foreign suppliers. The issue of constraining trade diversion from proliferating preferential groupings is so important that it may not be a bad idea to *combine* the proposals made by McMillan and myself, rather than to treat them as alternatives.

1.6   The Dynamic Time-Path Question

The question of the dynamic time-path is particularly difficult: it is almost virgin territory.

Perhaps the theoretical approach to CU theory that appears to be most relevant to this problem is that of Kemp and Wan (1976). In contrast to the Vinerian approach, Kemp and Wan make the external tariff structure endogenously determined for the CU such that it improves the CU members' welfare while maintaining the outsiders' welfare unchanged.

This restores the pre-Vinerian intuition that a CU should be welfare-improving. The problem with the operational significance of the Kemp–Wan argument is that it really is an existence argument, without any structure being put on it within the context of a specific model so that we can develop intuition about what the external tariff structure for such a Kemp–Wan CU would be.[17] But that *any* subset of countries *could* form an unambiguously (world) welfare-improving union is definitely established by Kemp and Wan.

This also implies that the time-path to U^* (see figure 2.9, this volume) achieved under multilateral free trade as the optimum optimorum, can be made monotonic.[18] But what it does *not* say is that the union will necessarily expand and, if so, in a monotonically welfare-improving manner. For *that* answer, we must turn to the *incentive structure* that any CU provides to relevant "groups" for further expansion of the CU.

The incentives in question need not be *economic* incentives. In fact, it is hard to imagine that the arbitrary groupings of countries that seek FTAs and CUs are dependent on economic arguments as their key determinants. Often, politics seems to drive these choices of partners, as in the case of the European Community, and now in the case of FTAs throughout the Americas. This also accounts for the occasional non-regionally proximate choices of partners in such blocs: e.g., the United States and Israel, and Pakistan, Iran and Turkey in the early 1960s. But that economic factors contribute to the incentives for such blocs to be formed is not implausible. Thus, for instance, Edward Mansfield, a Columbia University political scientist, has suggested that trade blocs will tend to be formed by security-driven allies because the gains from trade from them will accrue to friends rather than foes.[19]

A meaningful examination of the incentives to form and to expand trade blocs will therefore have to be in the new and growing field of political economy-theoretic analysis. I believe that the models within which we investigate these issues will have to distinguish among at least three kinds of "agents," which I will detail below with illustrations of the kinds of arguments which we would find relevant:

• *Governments of member countries:* whether a CU will expand or not will depend partly on the willingness of the CU authorities to do so. This will be affected by ideas and ideology. Here I worry that CUs will be under pressure *not* to expand because one possible reaction to a CU will be: "we are already a large market, so what do we really stand to gain by going through the hassle of adding more members?" This is what I call the "Our Market Is Large Enough" syndrome. I think, as Martin Wolf has often noted, that large countries tend to be more inward-looking for precisely this type of reason.

In addition, the expansion of the CU to include any specific set of outside countries will imply differential aggregate-welfare effects for current members, implying in turn differential incentives for member countries for and against the expansion.[20] In this context, a CU (which generally includes transfers among members) may be more expansionary (à la Kemp—Wan argumentation) than an FTA, though a CU that simultaneously seeks *political* integration may be less willing to expand.

• *Interest groups in member countries:* We need also to consider how interest groups, who lobby for or against CU expansion, will behave. Again, since CUs are a balance of trade-creating and trade-protecting forces, it is possible that the protectionists who profit from the diversion of trade away from efficient suppliers abroad to themselves will line up against CU expansion to include those suppliers. The problem then will be the "These Are Our Markets" syndrome.

This syndrome is not absent from the NAFTA scene, as many leader articles and media quote from business groups testified during the fast-track renewal. In fact, this syndrome was also present in the Eastman Kodak pamphlet (Dornbusch et al., 1989) that I cited earlier. It is also a sentiment that was beautifully expressed by Signor Agnelli of Fiat: "The single market must first offer an advantage to European companies. This is a message we must insist on without hesitation."[21] It is, of course, fine or Signor Agnelli to express such sentiments: after all, Fiat has run for years, not on gas, but on VERs against the Japanese. But should economists also embrace such sentiments?

• *Interest groups and governments of outside countries:* The third set of "agents" has to be the outside countries. Here, the example of a CU may lead others to emulate and seek entry. Otherwise, the fear of trade diversion may also induce outsiders to seek entry: Irwin's marvellous study on the historical experience with trade liberalisation in the 19th century (1993) shows that the Anglo—French Treaty may well have served this purpose. If so, this acts as an incentive to expand the CU.

This is clearly an uncharted area that is evidently the most interesting for further analysis.[22] I might add just one empirical—econometric study, by Mansfield (1992), which takes trade data for 1850—1965, estimates an

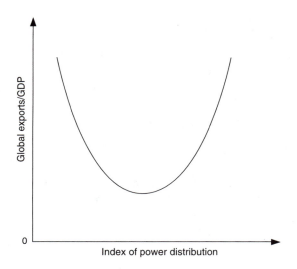

Figure 1.1
Concentration of power in the world and global exports. *Source*: Mansfield (1992).

index of "power distribution" (reflecting, among other things, trade blocs and economic power distribution) and comes up with figure 1.1. When power was centred in hegemons, during periods of British and American hegemony, and when there was "anarchy," the world economy was relatively liberalised (in the sense that global exports: GDP ratio was high); when there were a few middle-sized powers, as could happen with trade blocs, the result was a smaller ratio of trade to GDP (figure 1.1).

If Mansfield's analysis is accepted, and if it is considered to be a reasonable approximation to the question whether CUs will have expansionist or protectionist outlooks (mapping perhaps also into their attitudes to CU expansion or stagnation), then the presumption would be that historical experience suggests that trade blocs will fragment the world economy, not go on to unify it. Of course, history does not always repeat itself. But Mansfield's work certainly suggests caution in place of the gung-ho regionalism that has been urged by the Memorial Drive School.

To conclude, consider the following popular assertions by the regionalists:

- regionalism is quicker;
- regionalism is more efficient; and
- regionalism is more certain.

1.6.1   Is Regionalism Quicker?

The regionalists claim that the GATT is the "General Agreement to Talk and Talk," whereas regionalism proceeds quicker. But is this really so?

1. Historically, at least, the "First Regionalism" failed whereas the GATT oversaw the effective dismantling of prewar tariffs in the OECD countries and the enlargement of disciplines over NTBs at the Tokyo Round and beyond. A little caution, to say the least, is necessary before celebrating regionalism's quickfootedness.

2. For those who believe that regionalism offers a quick route to effective trade liberalisation, Dam's analysis quoted above needs renewed attention. There is a world of difference between announcing an FTA or a CU and its implementation, and the comparison is not pleasing if you are in the regional camp.

3. As for speed, even the best example of regionalism, the European Community, started almost four decades ago (1957) and is now into 1992. The "transition" has not therefore been instantaneous any more than negotiated reductions of trade barriers under the GATT Rounds. And this, too, despite the enormous political support for a united Europe.

4. Take agriculture. The record of regional trade blocs dealing with agricultural trade liberalisation is either non-existent or dismal; the CAP is not exactly the European Community's crowning achievement. In fact, if it were not for multilateralism (i.e., the Uruguay Round and the coalition of the Cairns Group that crystallised around the MTN), it is difficult to imagine that the process of unravelling the CAP could even have begun.

5. The (actual or potential) exercise of the regional option can also affect the efficacy of the multilateral one. The unwillingness of the European Community to start the MTN in 1982 and its largely reactive, rather than leadership, role at the Uruguay Round, are in some degree a reflection of its being less hungry for multilateralism given its internal market size and preoccupations. Then again, is it not evident that, were it not for the European Community, the capacity of the French (for whose political predicament one can only have sympathy, much as one deplores its consequence for the willingness to liberalise agriculture) to slow down the reform of the CAP and the liberalisation of world agriculture would have been significantly less?

6. Moreover, if regionalism is available as a realistic option, it will encourage exit rather than the seeking of voice and even the manifestation of loyalty to multilateralism:

• This may happen at the level of the bureaucrats who wind up preferring small-group negotiations among friends (code phrase: "like-minded people") to the intellectually and politically more demanding business of negotiating with and for the larger community of trading nations.

• Or else it may happen that, just as public choice theory à la Olson tells us in regard to the diffusion of consumer losses and concentration of producer gains that favour protectionist outcomes, the proponents of regionalism tend to be better focused and mobilised (they are often regional "experts" and partisans who ally themselves with the preferred policy options of the countries whose FTA cause they support), whereas the support for multilateralism is often more diffused and less politically effective and therefore takes second place when regionalism is on the political scene.

• Then again, regionalism may appeal to politicians since it translates more easily into votes: the wooing of the Hispanic voters, by urging them to identify with the FTA, was quite evident during the renewal of the fast-track authority in 1991 for the NAFTA negotiations with Mexico.

• The support of business groups for multilateralism may also erode with regional alternatives because of two different reasons: (i) If one can get a deal regionally, where one may have a "great deal of trade," then one may forget about the multilateral arena. Thus, if Canada could get the United States to agree to a fairer operation of the unfair trade mechanisms (a matter on which many Canadians today feel they were mistaken, with Prime Minister Mulroney and Mr. Riesman talking about Americans being "thugs" or like "third world dictators"[23]), why bother to fight the battles at the Uruguay Round where the powerful American manufacturing lobbies, zeroing in with the European Community against the Far East, seek instead to weaken the GATT rules? (ii) Again, one may get better protectionist, trade-diversionary deals for oneself in a preferential arrangement than in the non-discriminatory world of the GATT: e.g., Mexico's textile interests should benefit in the NAFTA relative to Caribbean and other external competitors in the US market, weakening the Mexican incentive to push for reform in the MFA forthwith.

7. Finally, it is true that the free-rider problem looks difficult as the number of GATT members increases steadily. Yet recent theoretical work on

GATT-style trade negotiations (Ludema, 1991) suggests that the free-rider problem may not be an effective barrier to freeing trade. Moreover, as Finger (1979) has pointed out, and as experience of inadequate GSP concessions underlines, developing countries have not been able to free-ride as much as their exemption from reciprocity under Special & Differential (S & D) treatment would imply: the trade concessions on commodities of interest to them have not gone as far as the concessions on commodities of interest to other GATT members without such an exemption. (Unconditional) MFN does not work in practice as well as it should from the free-riders' perspective.

1.6.2   Is Regionalism More Efficient?

Occasionally, one finds the regionalists arguing that regionalism is also more *efficient*: it produces *better* results. A typical argument is that, as part of the NAFTA negotiations, Mexico has accepted virtually all the US demands on intellectual property (IP) protection. A story, told in developing country circles, serves to probe this assertion critically: Ambassador Carla Hills was on a tour of South America, extolling the virtues of Mexico's "capitulation." At a dinner in her honour in Caracas, she apparently claimed: "Mexico now has world-class IP legislation." At this point, President Carlos Peretz supposedly turned to his left and remarked: "But Mexico does not have a world-class parliament."

The true moral of the story, however, is that, as part of the bilateral quid pro quos in an FTA or a CU, weak states may agree to specific demands of strong states,[24] in ways that are not exactly *optimal* from the viewpoint of the economic efficiency of the world trading system. In turn, however, these concessions can distort the outcome of the multilateral negotiations.

This may well have happened with TRIPs and TRIMs at the Uruguay Round.[25] As is now widely conceded among economists, the case for TRIPs for instance is *not* similar to the case for free trade: there is no presumption of mutual gain, world welfare itself may be reduced by any or more IP protection, and there is little empirical support for the view that "inadequate" IP protection impedes the creation of new technical knowledge significantly.[26] Yet the use of US muscle, unilaterally through "Special 301" actions, and the playing of the regional card through the NAFTA carrot for Mexico, have put TRIPs squarely and effectively into the MTN.

Again, a distorting impact on the multilateral trade rule from NAFTA negotiations can be feared from the fact that, as a price for the latter to be accepted by the Congress during the delicate renewal of fast-track authority, the US Administration had to accept demands for harmonisation in environment and labour standards by Mexico towards US standards. In political circles this effectively linked the case for free trade with the demands for "level playing fields" or fair trade (extremely widely interpreted),[27] legitimating these demands and weakening the ability of economists and of governments negotiating at the GATT (multilaterally for arm's length free trade) to resist this illegitimate constraint on freeing trade.[28]

1.6.3   Is Regionalism More Certain?

Much has been made, in the Mexican context, of the argument that the FTA will make trade liberalisation irreversible. But something needs to be added here:

• GATT also creates commitments: tariffs are bound. (This does not apply to concessions made under conditionality, of course, by the IMF or the IBRD.) Mexico *is* a member, if recent, of the GATT.

• Recall Dam (quoted above): Article XXIV is so full of holes in its discipline that almost anything goes. Reductions of trade barriers can be slowed down, as "circumstances" require, other bindings can be torn up by mutual consent (an easier task when there are only a few members in the bloc but more difficult under the GATT), etc.

• Recall, too, that regional agreements have failed (LAFTA) and stagnated (ASEAN) as well. The current mood in Canada over NAFTA is sour and the MTN looks better in consequence.[29] The sense, however, that the United States has let Canada down and failed to live by the spirit of the FTA agreements will probably not endure. But who knows?

1.7   The United States: From "Piecemeal" to "Programmatic" Regionalism

Let me conclude by considering more specifically the US shift to regionalism for the Americas in the perspective of the objective of arriving at (non-discriminatory) free trade for all.

US regionalism, when presided over by Ambassador William Brock, then the US Trade Representative, was *not* geographically-circumscribed

regionalism. Rather, it was truly open-ended. Brock was known to have offered an FTA to Egypt (along with the one to Israel) and to the ASEAN countries; indeed, he would have offered it to the moon and Mars if only life had been discovered there with a government in place to negotiate with. This regionalism was evidently motivated by a vision, even if flawed,[30] that saw regionalism as clearly the route to multilateralism: it would go on expanding, eventually embracing many, preferably all.

By contrast, today's regionalism, confined to the Americas by President Bush's men, lacks the "vision thing." In fact, when allied with Secretary Baker's recently reported admonition to the Japanese not to encourage an Asian trade bloc, as suggested by Malaysia as a necessary response to the European Community and US regionalism, the US policy appears to Asia also to be self-contradictory and self-serving: "regional blocs are good for us but not for you." And it simply won't wash, though Japan, fearing further bashing, will be deterred for a while.

If America's regionalism is not to turn into a piecemeal, world trading system-fragmenting force, it is necessary to give to it a programmatic, world trade system unifying format and agenda. One possibility is to encourage, not discourage, Japan to line up the Asian countries (all the way to the Indian subcontinent) into an AFTA, with the US lining up the South Americans into the NAFTA, on a schedule, say, of 10 years. Then, Japan and the United States, the two "hubs," would meet and coalesce into a larger FTA at that point,[31] finally negotiating with the European Community and its associate countries to arrive at the Grand Finale of multilateral free trade for all in Geneva.

Only such "programmatic" regionalism, in one of several possible variants, would ensure that US regionalism was not perceived by Asia to be hostile and fragmenting.[32] It alone would make regionalism less harmful to the MTN and the GATT and more supportive of the cause of multilateral free trade for all.

1.8   Concluding Remarks

The question of regionalism is thus both a difficult and delicate one. Only time will tell whether the revival of regionalism since the 1980s will have been a sanguine and benign development or a malign force that will serve to undermine the widely-shared objective of multilateral free trade for all.

My judgement is that the revival of regionalism is unfortunate. But, given its political appeal and its likely spread, I believe that it is important to contain and shape it in the ways sketched here so that it becomes max-

imally useful and minimally damaging, and consonant with the objectives of arriving at multilateral free trade for all.

Notes

This chapter reflects my personal views and bears no relationship to my position as Economic Policy Adviser to the Director-General, GATT. Thanks are due to Robert Baldwin, James Benedict, Richard Blackhurst, Christopher Bliss, Don Davis, Sunil Gulati, Douglas Irwin, John McMillan, Arvind Panagariya, T. N. Srinivasan and John Whalley for helpful conversations and suggestions.

Editorial Note: A figure and corresponding discussion that appeared in the original chapter have been omitted from section 1.4 to avoid overlap with chapter 2 (this volume).

1. The Vinerian approach to customs union theory has been carried forward by others more recently, chiefly by Berglas (1979) and Corden (1976). In addition, three alternative theoretical approaches can be distinguished: by Kemp and Wan (1976): by Cooper and Massell (1965a, 1965b), Johnson (1965) and Bhagwati (1968); and by Brecher and Bhagwati (1981). All four approaches are distinguished and discussed in the graduate textbook by Bhagwati and Srinivasan (1983, Chapter 27) and in Bhagwati (1991a). Each is touched upon later in this chapter.

2. Two points should be noted. First, there is a difference between intention and reality: as argued below, the Article XXIV-sanctioned FTAs and CUs have never gone "all the way." Second, GATT's MFN is universal only for its members, so it falls short of total universalism. but the important point to remember is that the GATT is open to membership to all who meet the criteria for admission, and has generally been inclusive rather than exclusive.

3. Of course, this theory developed *after* the incorporation of Article XXIV into the GATT. So its inconsistency with Article XXIV, on its own terms, is perhaps only an amusing observation. Note, however, that James Meade was a main actor in both. The argument is developed in two alternative ways in Lipsey (1960, p. 507) and in Johnson (1967, p. 203).

4. A substantially improved and more effectively functioning dispute settlement mechanism, aimed at restoring GATT's legal discipline, is an important part of the 1992 "Dunkel draft" of what the Uruguay Round should conclude.

5. Japan in fact, appears to have probed the possibility of going into such an arrangement with the United States as one of its partners in the 1960s but to no avail.

6. The question of "multilateralism" versus "regionalism" surfaced at a different level even within this preferential trade liberalisation among the developing countries. Thus, in the early 1960s, we were discussing whether the Cooper–Massell–Johnson–Bhagwati argument should not be considered on a G-77-wide basis rather than for much smaller groups of developing countries. This was the main issue before a 1962 UNCTAD Expert Group in New York, of which I was a member, which met over three weeks to draft the recommendation that preferential trade liberalisation among the developing countries be "multilateral," i.e., G-77-wide, rather than narrowly focused. Unfortunately, the preferential arrangements that were contemplated took the latter, narrower focus.

7. The MIT Economics Department is at 50 Memorial Drive in Cambridge, Massachusetts. I obviously exclude the diaspora, including myself! If the views expressed with Dornbusch in an Eastman Kodak publication (Dornbusch et al., 1989) are a guide. Krugman may hold one of the positions described above. This pamphlet makes somewhat odd and untenable

statements about what the GATT does and does not do. Cf. Finger's (1989) rather blunt analysis of these assertions in *The World Economy* and my own complaints about the confusions following from loose writing on trade-policy issues, and the resulting prostitution of an important debate, in Bhagwati (1991b). Whether the Memorial Drive school has by now under fire shifted its anti-multilateral stance and joined the more common view that regionalism is a useful supplement, not an alternative, to multilateralism is anyone's guess, given the conflicting reports one hears of its many oral pronouncements on the lecture circuit from its peripatetic members. But if it truly has abandoned its early vitriolic anti-GATT position, I would be delighted in its demise.

8. I rely upon oral presentation at the 1988 annual meeting of the American Enterprise Institute in Washington, DC.

9. Defined in Vinerian fashion, a trade-diverting FTA can still improve a member country's welfare but will generally harm outside countries. The focus below is on the impact on others, as is presumably the intention also of Article XXIV's injunction not to raise the average external tariff.

10. Aside from obfuscating the distinction between preferential and non-discriminatory trade liberalisation, the pro-FTA economists got carried away by the "battle for Mexico." Thus, while it is perfectly possible for Mexico to gain much while the United States gains little, a *Wall Street Journal* article by Dornbusch (1991) argued that trade with Mexico was already largely free because of OAP provisions and the GSP (so that the union fears of job losses, etc. were exaggerated), and simultaneously that Mexico would achieve prosperity thanks to the FTA. It is, of course, possible to argue each position separately in the "segmented markets" of Mexico City and Washington, DC, turning arguments on their head as necessary for one's case. But it takes chutzpah to make the contradictory arguments in the same article.

11. I must confess that I had not come across this prescription earlier. But in a report in the *Economic Focus* column in *The Economist* in 1991, of a Jackson Hole Conference on FTAs, it was attributed to Paul Krugman and Lawrence Summers.

12. See Lipsey (1960, pp. 507–8): "As far as the prices of the goods from a country's union partner are concerned, they are brought into equality with rates of transformation vis-à-vis domestic goods, but they are moved away from equality with rates of transformation vis-à-vis imports from the outside world. These imports from the union partner are thus involved in both a gain and a loss and their size is per se unimportant; what matters is the relation between imports from the outside world and expenditure on domestic commodities: the larger are purchases of domestic commodities and the smaller are purchases from the outside world, the more likely is it that the union will bring gain. Consider a simple example in which a country purchases from its union partner only eggs while it purchases from the outside world only shoes, all other commodities being produced and consumed at home. Now when the union is formed the 'correct' price ratio (i.e., the one which conforms with the real rate of transformation) between eggs and shoes will be disturbed but, on the other hand, eggs will be brought into the 'correct' price relationship with all other commodities—bacon, butter, cheese, meat, etc., and in these circumstances a customs union is very likely to bring gain, for the loss in distorting the price ratio between eggs and shoes will be small relative to the gain in establishing the correct price ratio between eggs and all other commodities. Now, however, let us reverse the position of domestic trade and imports from the outside world, making shoes the only commodity produced and consumed at home, eggs still being imported from the union partner, while everything else is now bought from the outside world. In these circumstances the customs union is most likely to bring a loss: the gains in establishing the

correct price ratio between eggs and shoes are indeed likely to be very small compared with the losses of distorting the price ratio between eggs and all other commodities."

13. In any event, by encouraging rules of origin because the trade-barrier walls everywhere are not equally high, FTAs encourage in turn the bureaucratic-cum-industry capture of the essentially arbitrary "local content" rules for protectionist purposes.

14. VERs are evidently selective by countries; AD actions are selective down to the level of the firm, as Brian Hindley has often noted.

15. Brian Hindley and Patrick Messerlin are investigating this hypothesis for the GATT Secretariat as part of a set of studies to support the 1992 GATT *Annual Report* on *Regionalism and Multilateralism*, following the 1991 *Annual Report* on *Trade and the Environment*.

16. This paper has also been commissioned by the GATT Secretariat for its 1992 *Annual Report*.

17. Christopher Bliss (1990) has recently made a valuable stab at this problem.

18. Such time-paths are clearly not unique. Thus, for instance, any number of such paths could be generated by relaxing the requirement that, at each stage, the non-union outside countries be left only as well off as before the new expansion of the CU.

19. This argument is being investigated in Mansfield's forthcoming paper for the 1992 GATT *Annual Report*.

20. This analysis must use the Brecher and Bhagwati (1981) approach to theorising about CUs since it relates to analysing the effects of changes in domestic and external policies and parameters on the distribution of income and welfare among member states.

21. Quoted by Wolf (1989).

22. Again, at the instance of the GATT secretariat, this question will be investigated in depth for the 1992 GATT *Annual Report*, by Bernhart Hoekman with Michael Leidy, and by Edward Mansfield.

23. Those who think that much of Japan-bashing is not prejudiced may want to think about the differential and exaggerated reaction in the United States to the far more innocuous remarks of Prime Minister Miyazawa and Speaker Sakarauchi.

24. In Mexico's case, President Salinas's political stake in getting an FTA with the United States is vastly disproportionate to President Bush's.

25. TRIPs are trade-related IP provisions and TRIMs are trade-related investment measures. The weakness of the case for their inclusion in the GATT, at least in the forms canvassed by many lobbies, is discussed in Bhagwati (1991a).

26. It is not surprising therefore that the spokesman for TRIPs have shifted from utilitarian methods of argumentation to "rights": they talk now of "theft" and "piracy."

27. That the environmental and labour standards' negotiations in NAFTA will be "parallel" rather than "integrated" is of no consequence, any more than running the services negotiations parallel to other negotiations at the Uruguay Round has been.

28. The danger posed by the proliferating demands for "level playing fields" or fair trade, chiefly in the United States but elsewhere too, is extremely serious. It is analysed, and the theoretical questions raised by it are noted, in Bhagwati (1992). The environment issue, in particular, has been discussed in this context in the 1991 GATT *Annual Report*.

29. Whalley's splendid study of the US–Canada FTA (1992) supports the sceptical views that I have advanced of the prospect and wisdom of the "Second Regionalism."

30. For reasons that I have already indicated above, regionalism is not quite the benign trade policy that it is now popularly believed to be.

31. This would require discarding the extreme Japanophobia that characterises the so-called "revisionists" who are really "regressionists" twice over: they use simple-minded regressions to condemn Japan for its "closed markets" (e.g., that Japan's manufactures' import share is stagnant and/or low compared to others') and they also wish to return the United States to the Japan-bashing of the prewar period that had given way to sense and sensitivity in the postwar years: cf. Bhagwati (1991a).

32. Saxonhouse's excellent study (1992) only complements and underlines what I argue here. I should add that while the United States signals a world trading system fragmenting message to Asia through NAFTA, Mexico by contrast signals a pro-world trade message. In joining in free trade with the colossus to its north, President Salinas boldly and effectively tells the developing countries that free trade is good and not to be feared.

References

Berglas, E. (1979) "Preferential Trading Theory: The *n* Commodity Case," *Journal of Political Economy*, **87**, pp. 315–31.

Bhagwati, J. N. (1968) "Trade Liberalization Among LDCs, Trade Theory and GATT Rules," in J. N. Wolfe (ed.), *Value, Capital, and Growth: Papers in Honour of Sir John Hicks*, Oxford: Oxford University.

——— (1991a) *The World Trading System at Risk*, Princeton: Princeton University Press and Harvester Wheatsheaf.

——— (1991b) "Revealing Talk on Trade," *The American Enterprise*, **2(6)**, pp. 72–8.

——— (1992) "Fair Trade, Reciprocity and Harmonization: The New Challenge to the Theory and Policy of Free Trade," Columbia University, Economics Department, *Discussion Paper Series*, **604** (April).

Bhagwati, J. N. and T. N. Srinivasan (1983) *Lectures on International Trade*, Cambridge, Mass.: MIT Press.

Bliss, C. (1990) "The Optimal External Tariff in an Enlarging Customs Union," CEPR, *Discussion Paper*, 368 (February), London: CEPR.

Brecher, R. and J. N. Bhagwati (1981) "Foreign Ownership and the Theory of Trade and Welfare," *Journal of Political Economy*, **89(3)**, pp. 497–512.

Cooper, C. A. and B. F. Massell (1965a) "A New Look at Customs Union Theory," *The Economic Journal*, **75**, pp. 742–7.

——— (1965b) "Towards a General Theory of Customs Unions for Developing Countries," *Journal of Political Economy*, **73(5)**, pp. 461–76.

Corden, W. M. (1976) "Customs Union Theory and the Nonuniformity of Tariffs," *Journal of International Economics*, **61(1)**, pp. 99–107.

Dam, K. (1970) *The GATT: Law and Intenational Economic Organization*, Chicago: University of Chicago Press.

Dornbusch, R. (1991) "If Mexico Prospers, So will We," *The Wall Street Journal* (April 11) Op.-Ed. section.

Dornbusch, R. et al. (1989) *Meeting World Challenges: United States Manufacturing in the 1990s*, Rochester, NY: pamphlet issued by the Eastman Kodak company.

The Economist (1991) Economics Focus column (July).

Finger, J. M. (1979) "Trade Liberalization: A Public Cholice Perspective," in R. C. Amachen, G. Haberler and T. Willett (eds.), *Challenges to a Liberal International Economic Order*, Washington, DC: American Enterprise Institute.

———— (1989) "Picturing America's Future: Kodak's Solution of American Trade Exposure," *The World Economy*, **12(3)**, pp. 377–80.

Gowa, J. and E. Mansfield (1991) "Allies, Adversaries, and International Trade," paper presented to the American Political Science Association Meetings, Washington, DC (mimeo).

Grandmont, J. M. and D. McFadden (1972) "A Technical Note on Classical Gains from Trade," *Journal of International Economics*, **2**, pp. 109–25.

Irwin, D. (1993) "Multilateral and Bilateral Trade Policies in the World Trading System: An Historical Perspective," chap. 4 in J. de Melo and A. Panagariya (eds.), *New Dimensions in Regional Integration*, Cambridge, UK: World Bank and Cambridge University Press.

Johnson, H. G. (1958a) "The Gains from Free Trade with Europe: An Estimate," *Manchester School of Economic and Social Studies*.

———— (1958b) "The Economics Gains from Free Trade with Europe," *Three Banks Review*.

———— (1965) "An Economic Theory of Protectionism, Tariff Bargaining, and the Formation of Customs Unions," *Journal of Political Economy*, **73** (June), pp. 256–83.

———— (1967) *Eonomic Policies Toward Less Developed Countries*, Washington, DC: Brookings Institution.

Kemp, M. C. (1972) "The Gains from International Trade," *The Economic Journal*, **72**, pp. 803–19.

Kemp, M. C. and H. Wan (1976) "An Elementary Proposition Concerning the Formation of Customs Unions," *Journal of International Economics*, **6** (February), pp. 95–8.

Lipsey, R. G. (1957) "The Theory of Customs Unions: Trade Diversion and Welfare," *Economica*, **24**, pp. 40–6.

———— (1958) "The Theory of Customs Unions: A General Equilibrium Analysis," University of London, Ph.D. thesis.

———— (1960) "The Theory of Customs Unions: A General Survey," *The Economic Journal*, **70**, pp. 498–513.

Lipsey, R. G. and K. J. Lancaster (1956–7) "The General Theory of Second Best," *Review of Economic Studies*, **24**, pp. 33–49.

Ludema, R. (1991) "International Trade Bargaining and the Most Favoured Nation Clause," *Economics and Politics*, **3(1)**, pp. 1–41.

Mansfield, E. (1992) "The Concentration of Capabilities and International Trade," *International Organization* (forthcoming).

McMillan, J. (1991) "Do Trade Blocs Foster Open Trade?," University of California at San Diego (mimeo).

Meade, J. E. (1956) *The Theory of Customs Unions*, Amsterdam: North-Holland.

Samuelson, P. A. (1939) "The Gains from International Trade," *Canadian Journal of Economics and Political Science*, **5(2)**, pp. 195–205.

Saxonhouse, G. R. (1992) "Trading Blocs and East Asia," chap. 12 in J. de Melo and A. Panagariya (eds.), *New Dimensions in Regional Integration*, Cambridge, UK: World Bank and Cambridge University Press.

Viner, J. (1950) *The Customs Union Issue*, New York: Carnegie Endowment for International Peace.

Whalley, J. (1993) "Regional Trade Arrangements in North America: CUSTA and NAFTA," chap. 11 in J. de Melo and A. Panagariya (eds.), *New Dimensions in Regional Integration*, Cambridge, UK: World Bank and Cambridge University Press.

Wolf, M. (1989) "European Community 1992: The Lure of the *Chasse Gardée*," *The World Economy*, **12(3)**, pp. 373–6.

2

Preferential Trading Areas and Multilateralism— Strangers, Friends, or Foes?

Jagdish Bhagwati and
Arvind Panagariya

The question of Preferential Trading Areas, as we should call them in preference to Free Trade Areas and customs unions, phrases that falsely equate them in the public mind and discourse with nonpreferential free trade, has not been distant from international economists' thoughts and concerns since the beginning of the postwar period when the architects of the General Agreement on Tariffs and Trade had to confront PTAs and accommodate them into the GATT via Article XXIV.[1]

Their wisdom became a center of analytical attention, especially at the time of the steps taken to form the European Community by the Treaty of Rome in 1957 and when, in what Bhagwati (1991) has called the period of First Regionalism, other Article XXIV-sanctioned PTAs were considered and even attempted in other areas.[2] The theory of PTAs of Viner (1950)—to which Meade (1955), Lipsey (1957, 1960), and other international economists at the time made important contributions—while preceding the formation of the European Community, developed more fully as a result of that singular event. The attempts at providing a more realistic rationale for the extension of such PTAs to developing countries, on the other hand, as a way of reducing the cost of any targeted level of industrialization, came from Cooper and Massell (1965a, 1965b), Johnson (1965), and Bhagwati (1968) at the time.[3]

It must be said that the First Regionalism was stillborn; beyond the European Community (and its offshoot, the European Free Trade Association), there was practically no successful emulation of the European developments elsewhere. At the same time, given the fact that it arose over the concerns that such PTAs were not the same as nondiscriminatory freeing of trade, the Vinerian theory was "static," concerning itself simply with the

Originally published, as chapter 1, in *The Economics of Preferential Trade Agreements*, ed. Jagdish Bhagwati and Arvind Panagariya (Washington, DC: American Enterprise Institute, 1996), 1–78. Reprinted with permission.

issue as to when such PTAs would be trade-diverting or trade-creating, thus diminishing or increasing welfare.

The recent revival of interest in the theory of Preferential Trading Areas, marking what Bhagwati (1991) has christened the Second Regionalism, has come instead from the conversion of the United States to preferential trading arrangements, starting with the Canada-U.S. Free Trade Agreement (CUFTA) and the later extension to include Mexico under the North American Free Trade Agreement (NAFTA). This time around, the movement has extended equally to other areas, involving again developing countries on their own, as in the Southern Cone Common Market (MERCOSUR), but with success rather than failure.

In 1982, the United States could not get multilateral trade talks started at Geneva and hence turned to ever-expanding PTAs as an alternative way of getting eventually to worldwide free trade. This has given the theory of PTAs a "dynamic time-path" dimension (Bhagwati 1993a). When would such an approach lead to a progressive freeing of trade barriers through expanding membership (and/or accelerating multilateral trade negotiations in a benign symbiosis)? This is also a political economy-theoretic question, fitting nicely into the modern preoccupation of economic theorists with questions relating to what policies emerge (that is, with "public choice") rather than what they should be (that is, with "social choice").

From a policy viewpoint also, this revival of PTAs is an important development. It was fed (if not led) by the U.S.-centered NAFTA and its proposed extension to Chile and beyond, and by Asia-Pacific Economic Cooperation (APEC), which some in the United States would like to see turn into another PTA, and by the call of European politicians such as Foreign Minister Klaus Kinkel of Germany at the outset, and by many others subsequently, to form TAFTA (a Transatlantic Free Trade Area). With WTO jumpstarted and multilateralism functioning, the theoretical and policy questions then must be confronted: should these proposals for proliferating PTAs, especially when inclusive of hegemonic powers such as the United States, be encouraged by economists?

In this chapter we undertake the following tasks. After reviewing key phrases and concepts, we extend the "static" analysis of PTAs. This enables us to examine several recent claims in favor of PTAs and persuades us to discard them as unpersuasive.

Specifically, our analysis enables us to examine and reject the much-cited claim that it is wrong to worry about trade diversion and that PTAs are generally as good as nonpreferential trade liberalization.

Our analysis gives added insight into why the usual argument made these days is mistaken. This is the argument that when countries joining a PTA have large shares of their trade with one another and are thus "natural trading partners," they need not fear losses. The nonhegemonic countries that are liberalizing with a hegemon that is generally open and offering few new reductions of trade barriers, as is the case with Mexico and with other potential NAFTA members outside of the United States and Canada, could face the prospect of significant "static" welfare losses.

Next, we turn to the dynamic time-path question. In the policy context, this necessitates our considering arguments as to why a proliferation of PTAs, despite their creating a harmful "spaghetti-bowl" phenomenon in the world economy, may be beneficial because of their helpful consequences for the progressive freeing of trade and moving the world economy to worldwide free trade.

We systematize the current analytical contributions on this problem and evaluate the current policy developments.[4] It is our view that PTAs that are hegemon centered, as NAFTA is, are not the desirable way to advance the cause of worldwide freeing of trade barriers and that it is better to focus on WTO-centered MFN trade liberalization. By contrast, we consider intradeveloping-country, non-hegemon-centered PTAs, such as MERCOSUR, in a more favorable light. First, however, we need to clarify a few central phrases and concepts.

Phrases and Concepts

Two phrases are frequently used: PTAs and regionalism. The two significant concepts are, first, trade creation and diversion and, second, stumbling and building blocks.

Preferential Trading Areas

This term refers to FTAs, CUs (which also have a common external tariff), and Common Markets (which additionally have freedom of internal factor movement within the area defined by member states). All these arrangements fall within the purview of GATT Article XXIV. Lesser forms have traditionally been permitted for developing countries and come under Economic Cooperation among Developing Countries (ECDC). We will have something to say about that too, though our chapter will be almost exclusively focused on Article XXIV-sanctioned PTAs and, within that category, on FTAs in particular.

Regionalism

This term has been loosely used by many, including us, as synonymous with PTAs. Strictly speaking, however, regionalism refers to PTAs defined by a geographic region. There is a school of thought (to which Lawrence Summers and Paul Krugman have subscribed) that considers regional PTAs to be a priori less likely to lead to static trade diversion than non-regional PTAs and such regional PTAs to be therefore ipso facto acceptable. This is a substantive issue that we will consider, as did Bhagwati (1993a) in a preliminary way. Our focus, however, will be on PTAs, not regional PTAs.

Trade Creation and Trade Diversion (Viner)

The concepts of trade creation and trade diversion as two possibilities that define the second-best nature of the static analysis of PTAs go back to Viner (1950), of course. While there are various ways in which these two concepts have subsequently been defined, we will use them (in the theoretical analysis below) in the original Vinerian sense to mean a shift of imports from an efficient to an inefficient source under trade diversion, and a shift from an inefficient to an efficient source under trade creation.[5]

"Stumbling Blocks" and "Building Blocks" (Bhagwati)

The phraseology and conceptualization of PTAs that, in a dynamic time-path sense, contribute to the multilateral freeing of trade either by progressively adding new members (down the PTA path to worldwide free trade) or by prompting accelerated multilateral trade negotiations and are thus *building blocks* toward the multilateral freeing of trade and those that do the opposite and hence are *stumbling blocks* to the goal of worldwide, multilateral freeing of trade, owes to Bhagwati (1991, 77) and has been adopted by Lawrence (1991) and others.[6] Insofar as Viner's trade creation and trade diversion concepts were designed to divide PTAs into those that were good and those that were bad in the static sense, Bhagwati's building block and stumbling block concepts are designed to divide PTAs into those that are good and those that are bad in the dynamic, time-path sense.

Rethinking Static Welfare Analysis

We now begin with the static analysis. Frankly, so much has been written on the static analysis since Viner's pioneering 1950 contribution, indeed by virtually every important international economist, that one may think that there is little to add.

The Issues Examined

Yet there is something to be gained by another, close look at the conventional static analysis in view of several presuppositions, mostly favorable to PTAs, which have recently been made by policy analysts.

It has been forcefully argued by Summers (1991, 299) in an influential paper that international economists should not be preoccupied by trade diversion: "I find it surprising that this issue is taken so seriously—in most other situations, economists laugh off second best considerations and focus on direct impacts."

Our first reaction is to deny the premise of his analogy: economists, faced with a second-best problem, typically *do* worry about that aspect of the problem. Indeed, if the world was first best, market prices would reflect social opportunity costs, and there would be no need for cost-benefit analysis for projects. The World Bank, where Summers served with distinction, would then have to close down most of its project-lending research and analysis aimed at determining the shadow prices to be used in judging the acceptability of projects.

Second, the problem of preferential trade liberalization is indeed an inherently second-best problem since nondiscriminatory trade liberalization is being ruled out. Ignoring this aspect is unwarranted.

Third, one should not confuse "second best" with "primary impact." First-best problems also are characterized by primary and total effects.

Fourth, if Summers implies that trade-diverting PTAs are a minor nuisance, he is misled presumably by the fact that efficiency losses are Harberger triangles and "small." But such PTAs impose losses on member countries also through tariff-revenue-*redistribution*, and these can be large: they are rectangles, while the efficiency effects are triangles.

We also consider the contention in the recent policy debate that countries that trade with each other in larger volume than with other nations are "natural" trading partners and hence that PTAs among them are likely to be welfare enhancing to their members for that reason.

This contention is further linked with the argument that "regional" PTAs are desirable (in the sense of being more likely to create welfare gains for their members) because geographically contiguous countries (particularly if they share common borders) have larger volumes of trade with one another than with others.

Our analysis here challenges the premise that large volumes of initial trade lessen the likelihood of loss from PTAs. Consequently, it also undermines the associated contention that regional PTAs are more desirable.

We also question the alternative but related "natural trading partners" hypothesis that regional PTAs are likely to improve welfare by conserving on transport costs. We show that transport costs by themselves do not provide a reason for discriminatory PTAs.[7]

The Theoretical Analysis

Since Viner's classic work in 1950, PTAs have been considered to be harmful both to member countries (whose imports are the subject of the trade diversion) and to the world when trade diversion arises, and to be welfare enhancing when trade creation occurs instead. This ambiguity of outcomes, depending on the relative strengths of the two effects when a PTA is formed, has been the principal reason for the debate among economists as to whether a specific PTA is desirable.

We will begin the theoretical analysis below by showing, however, that the conventional trade creation and trade diversion are not the entire story in deciding on the welfare outcome for an *individual* member of a PTA. Even if trade creation effects are larger than trade diversion effects so that the union as a whole benefits, an individual member could lose on account of adverse income distribution effects arising from tariff revenue redistribution.

The redistribution of tariff revenue between member countries arises, of course, from a shift in the terms of trade within the union. When a member country lowers its tariff on the partner without lowering it on the rest of the world, within-union terms of trade shift in favor of the partner (for both existing and new imports from it). The extent of the unfavorable redistributive effect on a member country is obviously determined by the degree of preferential access it gives to the partner country in relation to the preferential access it receives from the latter: the greater the margin of preference the country gives, the more it stands to lose. This implies that when a country with a high degree of protection forms a PTA with a country with relatively open markets, as in the case of Mexico and the

United States, the former may well be faced with a net welfare loss. We develop this theme and its ramifications, in the following analysis, using simple models from the literature and distinguishing clearly among the effects on member country and world welfare.

The Viner Model—Constant Costs

The natural starting point for explaining the economics of regional integration is Viner's partial equilibrium model. This model does not fully capture the effects noted above but is, nevertheless, an important step toward understanding them. Assume that there are three countries, A, B, and C. Countries A and B are potential union partners and C represents the rest of the world. In figure 2.1, panels a and b, let $M_A M_A$ represent A's import demand for a specific product and $P_B E_B$ and $P_C E_C$ the (export) supplies of the same product available from B and C, respectively. Following Viner, it is assumed that the supply prices of B and C are constant at P_B and P_C, respectively. In panel a, the supply price of C exceeds that of B and in panel b the opposite is true.

In panel a illustrating the case of a *trade-creating union*, with an initial nondiscriminatory specific tariff t, A imports OM_0 quantity of the good.[8] All imports come from B so that A raises areas 1 and 2 in tariff revenue. If A now forms an FTA with B, imports from B expand from OM_0 to OM_{FTA}. The tariff revenue disappears, but the price facing consumers declines by t; A's consumers capture the entire revenue in the form of increased surplus. Because B is the lower cost source of the product, there is positive trade creation and no trade diversion.[9] Working like nondiscriminatory free trade, the FTA yields to A and to the union a net gain represented by areas 3 and 4.[10]

Panel b illustrates the case of a *trade-diverting union*. Here B is the higher cost source of the product with the result that, given a nondiscriminatory tariff in A, all imports come from C. A imports OM_0 and collects areas 1 and 2 in tariff revenue. If A and B now form an FTA, imports expand to OM_{FTA}, but the source of their supply switches from C to B. Though the reduction in A's domestic price leads to some trade creation—increased imports lead to a displacement of some inefficient domestic production and increase in consumption in A—the switch to the higher cost source, B, leads to a large trade diversion of OM_0 quantity of imports from C to B. Thus, panel b shows a case where the union diverts trade from C, but it also creates some trade. The gains to A are given by area 3 and the losses by area 2. The loss of area 2 results from a deterioration in A's terms of

Panel A. Trade-creating Union of A and B

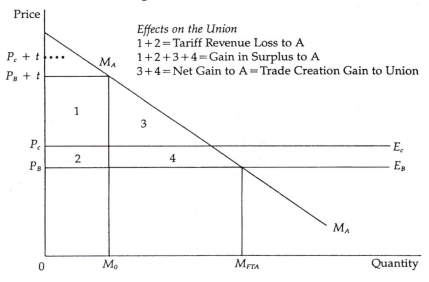

Panel B. Trade-Diverting Union of A and B

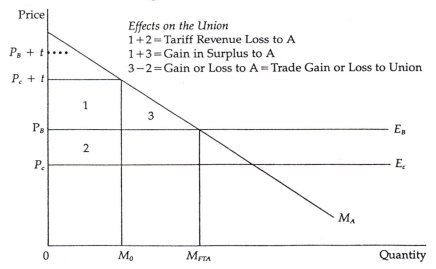

Figure 2.1 (panels A, B, and C)
Constant costs, according to strictly Vinerian analysis.

Panel C. General Equilibrium Analysis: Viner-Lipsey Model of Trade-Diverting Union

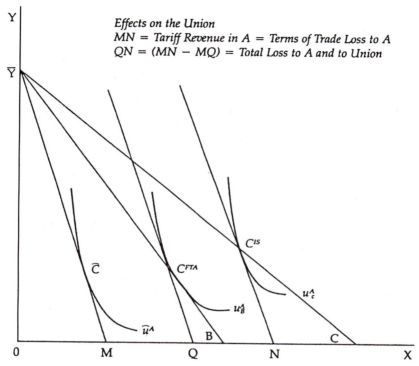

Effects on the Union
MN = *Tariff Revenue in A* = *Terms of Trade Loss to A*
QN = $(MN - MQ)$ = *Total Loss to A and to Union*

Figure 2.1 (continued)

trade from P_C to P_B and takes the form of the excess of the loss of tariff revenue $(1 + 2)$ over that which is captured partially (1) by A's consumers. Area 2 goes to pay for the higher cost of production in B than in C.

Now, unless cost differences between B and C are small, areas similar to area 2 will be large in relation to the triangular areas of gain. The welfare loss to A from the loss of revenue on diverted imports applies to the *entire* initial quantity of imports, whereas the gain applies only to the *change* in the quantity of imports. The FTA will be associated with trade creation in some sectors and trade diversion in others. But since losses the likely to be large in cases involving trade diversion, trade diversion in even a few sectors can more than offset the gains arising from trade creation in a large number of sectors.

The trade-diverting case of panel b can also be illustrated in general equilibrium by using the Lipsey (1958) version of the Viner analysis as in panel c. There, the economy of A is specialized in producing at $\bar{Y}$, with $\bar{Y}C$ and $\bar{Y}B$ the given, fixed terms of trade with C and B, respectively. With an initial nondiscriminating tariff, A trades with C and consumes at C^{IS}, winding up with welfare at U_C^A. With the FTA between A and B, the trade shifts to B. A winds up consuming at C^{FTA} and its welfare is reduced to U_B^A. The welfare loss QN can then be seen as the difference between the tariff-revenue or terms-of-trade loss MN and the gain MQ that comes from the ability to shift consumption from $\hat{C}$ to C^{FTA}.[11] (OM is the income at domestic prices in the initial situation, and tariff revenue is MN, the sum of the two yielding ON as national expenditure.)

A final and obvious point may be stressed concerning nondiscriminatory trade liberalization by country A. In both the cases shown in figure 2.1, A obtains maximum trade gains and its welfare is improved relative to the initial as well as the FTA equilibrium by a nondiscriminatory liberalization. Such liberalization leads to the same equilibrium in the trade-creating union in panel a (as a limiting case) and eliminates trade diversion in the case in panel b, amounting to free trade with the most efficient supplier for each commodity.

Partner Country's Supply Curve Is Upward Sloped

Because of the assumption that the export-supply curves of both B and C are perfectly elastic, the model in figure 2.1 leads to at least two unrealistic outcomes.[12] First, imports into A come from either B or C but not both. Second, in the trade diversion case, the losses of A represented by area 2 are used up entirely to finance B's higher costs of production: the partner country B makes no gain whatsoever. The model thus captures only one side of the possibly "mercantilist" nature of trade-diverting FTAs: country A can lose from its own (discriminatory) trade liberalization, but country B does not gain from it.

A more realistic model allows the supply curve of one or both countries B and C to slope upward. In the interest of simplicity, we will allow for an upward-sloped supply curve for only one country at a time. Figure 2.2 takes up the case when the partner country B's supply curve slopes upward and that of the outside country C is horizontal. This case captures the essence of the more general model in which the outside country's supply curve also slopes upward but is more elastic than the partner's. Figure 2.3 shows instead the case when the union is between A and C so that the partner country's supply curve is more elastic than that of the outside world.

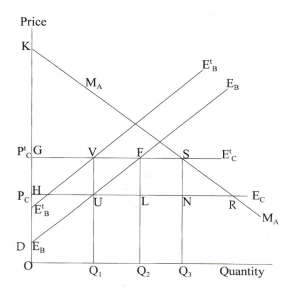

Figure 2.2
Effect of union (A + B) with rising costs from partner country.

In both figures 2.2 and 2.3, as before, we then let $M_A M_A$ represent the import demand for a product imported by A. The supply curve of the product available from B is upward sloped and is represented by $E_B E_B$. Country C's export supply curve, represented by $P_C E_C$, is horizontal. The tariff continues to be specific. Consider then figure 2.2 and three cases: an initial nondiscriminatory tariff, free trade, and an FTA.

Under a *nondiscriminatory tariff* at rate t per unit, supplies from B and C, as perceived by buyers in A, are given by $E_B^t E_B^t$ and $P_C^t E_C^t$, respectively. Total imports into A equal OQ_3 of which OQ_1 come from B and $Q_1 Q_3$ from C. Country A collects tariff revenue equivalent to rectangle GHNS. The gains from trade for A amount to the area under the import-demand curve and above the domestic price plus the tariff revenue, that is, triangle KSG plus rectangle GHNS. For country B, the gains from trade equal the area above $E_B E_B$ and below the net price received, P_C, that is, area HUD. Country C neither gains nor loses from trade. Table 2.1 summarizes this information in column 1.

Suppose instead the A decides to adopt a policy of *free trade* by eliminating the tariff on a nondiscriminatory basis. The price in A declines to P_C, imports from B do not change, and imports from C rise by NR. Tariff revenue disappears, but the gains from trade rise to KGS + GHNS + RSN:

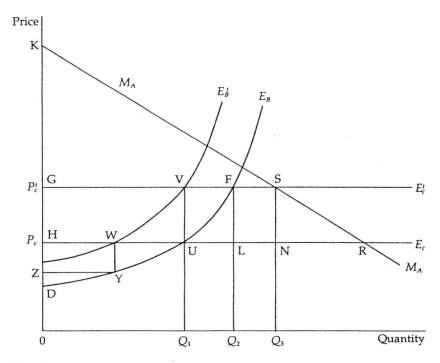

Figure 2.3
Effect of union (A + C) with rising costs from outside country.

there is a net welfare gain to A of RSN. The extra gain comes from
increased benefits to consumers and producers in A. The gains to country
B remain unchanged at HDU. Because of the perfectly elastic supply,
country C neither gains nor loses from trade before or after trade liberalization by A. Therefore, the world as a whole benefits by area RSN. These
changes are summarized in column 2 of table 2.1.

Next, assume that A forms an FTA with B by eliminating entirely the
tariff on B but retaining it on C. Imports from B rise to OQ_2, and those
from C decline to Q_2Q_3. Now B gains from the FTA due to an improvement in its terms of trade. The net price received by the exporters of
B increases from P_C to P_C^t, and the gains from trade to B rise to
HDU + GFUH. Country B gains from A's liberalization.

Because imports continue to come from C before as well as after the
FTA and C's supply is perfectly elastic, the price in A is unchanged. But
now that there is no tariff revenue on goods coming from B, A' gains
from trade decline by GFLH. Stated differently, A's within-union terms of

Table 2.1
Gains from Trade under Unilateral Liberalization and Free Trade Area (Country A plus Country B)

Country	Nondiscriminatory tariff (Initial situation) (1)	Free trade (FT) (2)	Free trade area (A and B) (FTA) (3)
A	KGS + GHNS	KGS + GHNS + RSN (A gains)	KGS + GHNS − GFLH (A loses)
B	HDU	HDU (no change)	HDU + (GFLH − FLU =) GFUH (B gains)
C	0	0 (no change)	0 (no change)
World	KGS + GHNS + HDU	KGS + GHNS + HDU + RSN (World gains)	KGS + GHNS + HDU − FLU (World losses)

Note: This table relates to figure 2.2 in the text.
a. World Welfare Loss from FTA compared with FT: FLU + RSN.
b. World Welfare Loss from FTA compared with Initial Situation: FLU.

trade worsen by the full amount of the tariff liberalization country A loses from its own liberalization. Because the FTA diverts imports Q_1Q_2 from the more efficient C to the less efficient B, A's loss exceeds B's gain by the area FLU. The world as a whole loses by the same area FLU. The last column in table 2.1 shows these changes.

It is now evident that Summers' earlier-cited argument that international economists should embrace PTAs because second-best "trade diversion" worries are "laughable," and that primary effects must be considered to be dominant, is misplaced when impacts on the welfare of specific countries are considered. The loss to A from its own preferential liberalization arises primarily from the primary effect of these.[13] If we assume that the initial imports from the union partner are large, the loss to A in this wholly trade-diverting union is substantial and reflects the tariff revenues lost on the original imports (plus these diverted imports) from the partner country B.

Clearly, FTAs can give rise to large redistributive effects (on original imports) between countries. The amount of trade diverted (Q_1Q_2) may be small, and the loss to the union from this trade diversion is small because it is a triangle, but all this really has no relevance to our critique of Summers as just concluded.

Next, our analysis casts doubt on the recent presumption that countries that trade with each other in large volume are "natural" trading partners and regional arrangements among them must therefore be beneficial to them. It is not entirely clear from the literature what it means to be "natural" trading partners.[14] A quotation from Summer[14] (1991, 297), however, should help: "Are trading blocs likely to divert large amounts of trade? In answering this question, the issue of natural trading blocs is crucial because to the extent that blocs are created between countries that already trade disproportionately, the risk of large amounts of trade diversion is reduced."[15]

Later we consider this entire question of natural trading partners and their desirability. But our analysis so far already provides a devastating critique of the presumption advanced in favor of such natural trading blocs. It is evident from figure 2.2 that the larger the initial quantity of imports from a trading partner, the greater (not smaller) the loss to the country liberalizing preferentially, ceteris paribus. That is to say, the more natural the trading partner according to Summers' definition, the larger the loss from a discriminatory trade liberalization with it!

Finally, it has been frequently argued that, given today's low levels of trade restrictions, preferential trading arrangements are unlikely to be harmful: trade creation effects should dominate the outcome, making PTAs as good as FT (free trade). But this argument, plausible as it sounds, is contradicted by our analysis. Thus in figure 2.2, if the initial non-discriminatory tariff is sufficiently high, an FTA between A and B can eliminate C as a supplier of the product. In this case, the FTA lowers the internal price in A and gives rise to trade creation. Under some (admittedly strong) conditions, this trade creation can outweigh the tariff-revenue loss and may improve welfare. By contrast, if the initial tariff is low, the chances are poor that the formation of the FTA will eliminate imports from C and lower the internal price.

The Outside Country's Supply Curve Is Upward Sloped

The conclusion that A's preferential liberalization hurts itself and benefits its union partner has been derived under the assumption that the supply of B is less than perfectly elastic and that of C is perfectly elastic. In this setting, the union partner is a less efficient supplier of the product than is the outside world. What will happen if the situation was reversed such that B's supply curve was perfectly elastic and C's less than perfectly elastic?

This case can be analyzed by letting A form a union with C rather than B. In this case, analyzed in figure 2.3, an FTA lowers the price in A to P_C. Though there is no gain to the union partner, A's gain from the FTA

Table 2.2
Gains from Trade under Free Trade Area (Country A plus Country C)

Country	Nondiscriminatory tariff (1)	FTA (A and C) (2)
A	KGS + GHNS	KGS + GHNS + RSN + HWYZ (A gains)
B	HDU	ZYD = HDU − WYU − HWYZ (B losses)
C	0	0 (no change)
World	KGS + GHNS + HDU	KGS + GHNS + HDU + RSN − WYU (World may gain or lose according as RSN $\gtrless$ WYU)

Note: This table relates to figure 2.3 in the text. Column 1 is identical to column (1) in table 2.1 and is reproduced here to facilitate comparison. The results under Free Trade are identical between the two FTAs, (A and B) and (A and C).

(= RSN + HWYZ) exceeds that under nondiscriminatory liberalization (that is, free trade) by the amount of tariff revenue (= HWYZ) collected on imports from the outside country.[16] This case brings us back to the conventional presumption that A's liberalization should benefit it (though the presumption that others should gain from the liberalization does not carry through for the outsider country B that loses). The precise welfare results, based on analysis of figure 2.3, are drawn together in table 2.2.

This case clearly undercuts the arguments about the dangers of PTAs to country A that were made in the previous section. Therefore, it is important to ask how relevant this case is empirically. It is perhaps reasonable to assert that a union partner is likely to resemble B in some products and C in other products, and therefore the effect of the FTA will be ambiguous in general.

A common claim has been that NAFTA is likely to benefit Mexico because the United States the Canada are very large and therefore the most efficient suppliers of a majority of Mexico's products. Our analysis suggests, however, at least two reasons why this conclusion is not warranted.

First, given that the outside world includes the European Union, Japan, China, Korea, Hong Kong, and numerous other outward oriented and highly competitive countries, the conclusion that the United States and Canada are the most efficient suppliers of a large majority of Mexico's products is highly suspect. Indeed, if it were true we would be hard-pressed to explain the persistent demands for antidumping and other forms of protection in the United States.[17] Second, recall that if the union partner is a large supplier of imports, the tariff redistribution losses to A in the case of trade diversion are large. Therefore, even if the union partner is the most efficient supplier of the majority of A's imports, losses may outweigh any gains. In the case of NAFTA, the United States does account for a sufficiently large proportion of Mexico's imports for us to conjecture plausibly that the tariff-redistribution losses in trade-diversion cases could outweigh the gains in trade-creation cases.

This analysis has an important qualification that will be discussed in the next section. Before doing so, we mention two additional possibilities that are worthy of brief consideration: first, export-supply curves are upward sloped for both B and C; second, the products of A, B, and C are imperfect substitutes. In either of these cases, the small-country and small-union assumptions are violated, and a complete elimination of the tariff by A, whether on a discriminatory or nondiscriminatory basis, is not the optimal policy.[18] We will look at the second case in detail [a bit later].

But here we note that our conclusions remain valid under the following circumstances. In case one, if the elasticity of supply of the outside country is high in relation to that of the union partner, B, a discriminatory tariff reduction is likely to hurt A itself while benefiting B. In case two, analyzed later in the chapter, if B's goods are poor substitutes for A's goods but not C's, as seems entirely plausible, discriminatory liberalization by A will hurt A itself and benefit the union partner, B, even at constant terms of trade, whereas the terms of trade effects will reinforce this outcome. Before we present this analysis in detail, an important qualification to figures 2.2 and 2.3 must be noted.

A Qualification and Modification

Figures 2.2 and 2.3 capture the essence of a large body of the literature on regional arrangements that emerged in the 1950s and 1960s. But these figures have an important limitation that has been ignored entirely in the literature until recently. They implicitly assume that either (1) the partner country maintains the same tariff as A on the product under consideration (that is, the arrangement is a Customs Union), or (2) the product is not consumed in the partner country. Let us explain why.

Consider first the case depicted in figure 2.2. The common practice in the literature, as in our foregoing analysis, has been to assume that post-FTA prices in a member country are determined by the price in the outside country, C, plus the country's own tariff. As Richardson (1994) has noted recently, however, this assumption is incorrect in general. It implies that, if tariffs in A and B are different, producer as well as consumer prices in A and B are different. But given duty-free movement of goods produced within the union, producer prices between A and B must equalize under an FTA.

Assume that the tariff on the product under consideration is lower in B than in A, violating condition one above. In figure 2.2, recall that $E_B E_B$ is B's supply curve for exports, that is, output supply net of domestic consumption. Under a nondiscriminatory tariff in A, B's producers sell OQ_1 in A. Because the net price received by exporters on sales in A is P_C, the domestic price in B will also be P_C. If A and B now form an FTA and the price in A remains P_C^t, producers in B have no incentive to sell anything in their domestic market unless the price there also rises to P_C^t. But given that the tariff in B is lower than that in A, the price in B cannot rise to P_C^t, and the entire quantity of the product previously sold in B is diverted to A. The rules of origin can forbid the diversion of goods *imported* from C to A but not of goods *produced* in B.[19] Unless domestic consumption of the product in B is zero (assumption two above), B's export-supply curve shifts to the right by the quantities demanded in B at each price, that is, B's export-supply curve coincides with its output-supply curve.

Figure 2.4 lays out how the allowance for the diversion of B's domestic sales to A after the formation of the FTA affects our conclusions. It reproduces figure 2.2, omitting $E_B^t E_B^t$. In the initial equilibrium, with a nondiscriminatory tariff in A, imports from B are OQ_1 as in figure 2.2. After the FTA is formed, the expansion of exports is larger than that given by point F. How much larger it is will depend on where B's total supply curve lies. There are three possibilities.[20]

First, if the total supply curve intersects $M_A M_A$ above point S as shown by $S_B S_B$, the results of the previous section hold with a vengeance.[21] Exports from B now expand more than in figure 2.2, and losses to A from the transfer of tariff revenue are larger. In this case, B's producers sell all of their output in A and receive the same price as A's producers, namely, P_C^t. The entire quantity consumed in B is imported from C, with consumers paying a price lower than P_C^t. Country A imports from countries B and C.

Second, suppose that B's supply curve intersects $M_A M_A$ between S and W, where the height of W is P_C plus the tariff in B. In this case, the price in A is determined by the height of the point of intersection of B's supply curve and $M_A M_A$. Because this price is below P_C^t, a part of the lost tariff revenue is now captured by A's consumers. But we still have a tariff-revenue transfer to firms in B. The transfer is larger the closer the intersection point of the two curves to S. Producers in B sell all their output in A, A does not import anything from C, and B imports everything from C.

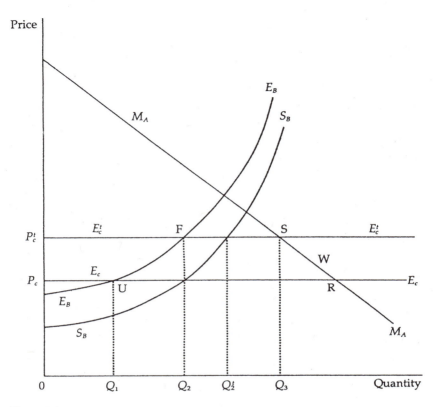

Figure 2.4
The consequences of differing external tariff rates in members of a free trade area.

Finally, if B's supply curve intersects $M_A M_A$ below point W, the price in A drops to the tariff-inclusive price in B given by the height of point W. All of A's imports come from B with producers in B selling in A as well as B. Both consumer and producer prices equalize between A and B. In this case, the redistributive effect is a declining function of the tariff in B. In the limit, if the external tariff in B is zero, the FTA leads to free trade in A (just as in B).

The case depicted in figure 2.3 is also modified along the lines of figure 2.4 if the good in question is consumed in the partner country (C) and the latter levies a tariff lower than that of A. To illustrate, assume that the tariff in C is zero, and the demand for the product in C at P_C is larger than B's supply at that price. Then, B can sell all it wants to export at P_C to C. In the post-FTA equilibrium, A's imports come entirely from C, while B sells all its exports to C. The tariff revenue raised by A on imports from B in figure 2.3 is no longer available, and A's gains from the FTA with C are reduced to triangle RSN, the same as under unilateral, nondiscriminatory liberalization.

An Imperfect-Substitutes Model

An unrealistic implication of the model just explored in figure 2.4 is that, under an FTA, either producers of B must sell all their output in A and none in their domestic market (the first two cases) or consumers in A must import everything from B and none from C (the last case). This conclusion does not require a complete FTA; it can hold true even in the presence of a small tariff preference as long as external tariffs in the two countries are different. A quick examination of the direction of trade data of member countries of preferential trading arrangements such as the Association of Southeast Asian Nations (ASEAN) and NAFTA shows that this outcome is inconsistent with reality.

A natural way to avoid these extreme results is to cast the analysis in terms of a model with product differentiation. A fully satisfactory model of this type requires the introduction of economies of scale and monopolistic competition or oligopoly. Such an elaborate model is beyond the scope of this chapter. But taking recourse to the Armington structure whereby products are distinguished by the country of origin and drawing on the Meade (1955) model, we take a first stab at the problem.

An important point to note at the outset is that when products are differentiated by the country of origin, the small-country or small-union assumption must be abandoned.[22] If the product originating in a country is not produced anywhere else, by definition, the country is a monopolist for that product and cannot be a price taker in the world market.[23] Our approach below is to first consider the implications of FTAs at constant border prices and then bring in the effects of changes in the terms of trade.

Assume that there are three products denoted a, b, and c. Countries A, B, and C specialize in and export a, b, and c, respectively. Choose the units of each product so that its international price is unity in the initial equilibrium. Focus as before on country A's welfare. In the initial equilibrium, let A impose a uniform tariff t per unit on imports from B and C.

In figure 2.5 we measure A's consumption of b to the right and that of c to the left of the origin, O. Because b and c are not produced in A, the demand curves also represent import demands. Given the tariff t on b and

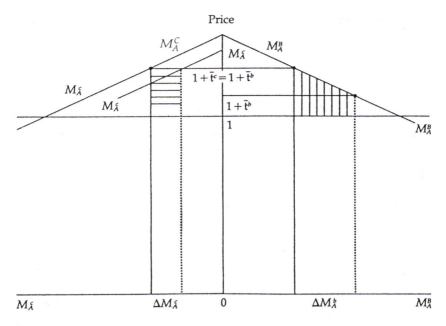

Figure 2.5
Effect of a small tariff preference by country A to country B.

c, (import) demand curves are represented by $M_A^b M_A^b$ and $M_A^c M_A^c$. The demand curve for each product is drawn given the tariff rate on the other product. Assuming substitutability, a reduction in the tariff on one product shifts the demand curve for the other product toward the vertical axis.

Let us now introduce preferential trading through a small reduction in the tariff on imports from B. Imports from B expand and generate a gain equal to $t_b \Delta M_A^b$ and approximated by the vertically shaded area in figure 2.5. This is trade creation. But the reduction in the tariff on b also causes an inward shift in the demand curve for c as shown by the dotted curve. There is trade diversion and a corresponding loss equal to $t_c \Delta M_A^c$ and approximated by the horizontally shaded area.[24]

Is there a net gain or loss to country A? The answer depends on the relative sizes of the two shaded areas. For a small change in the tariff, these areas are approximated by rectangles whose height equals t. Therefore, the gain is larger than the loss if and only if the increase in the value of imports of b at world prices is larger than the reduction in the value of imports of c.[25] If we now assume that the partner country's good, b, and A's export good, a, are substitutes in A's demand, the preferential reduction in the tariff lowers the consumption of good a and allows an expansion of exports. Working through the trade balance condition, we can see that the expansion of exports must expand total imports valued at world prices. That is to say, imports of b expand more than imports of c contract. The area associated with trade creation in figure 2.5 exceeds the area associated with trade diversion; the *introduction* of preferential trading is beneficial.

This result is attributed to Lipsey (1958) and hinges critically on substitutability between demands for the partner country's goods and exportables and constancy of the terms of trade. For the moment, let us make these assumptions and ask what happens as we continue to lower the tariff on good b, holding the tariff on good c unchanged. For each successive reduction in the tariff, the height of the rectangle associated with trade creation declines but that of the rectangle associated with trade diversion remains unchanged. Sooner or later, before the tariff on b goes to zero, the gain from extra trade creation becomes smaller than the loss from extra trade diversion. Further reductions in the tariff lead to a *reduction* in welfare.[26]

In sum, assuming constant terms of trade and substitutability between imports from B and exports, a preferential reduction in the tariff on B's goods first improves welfare and then lowers it. This relationship is shown in figure 2.6. As drawn, the level of welfare with a complete FTA is lower than that in the initial equilibrium. But in general, we cannot tell whether welfare rises or falls upon the establishment of an FTA.

The natural question then is whether we can establish a presumption one way or the other. To answer it, let us examine the second-best optimum tariff in the Meade model on B's goods given the tariff on C's goods. As shown in Panagariya (1996b), this tariff can be written as

$$\frac{t^b_{opt}}{1 + t^b_{opt}} = \frac{\bar{t}^c}{1 + \bar{t}^c} \cdot \frac{1}{1 + \frac{\eta_{ba}}{\eta_{bc}}}, \tag{1}$$

where η_{ba} and η_{bc} are country A's compensated, crossprice elasticities of demand for the partner country's good with respect to the price of its own good and that of the outside country's good, respectively. These elasticities respectively measure the degree of substitutability between the partner's and A's own goods and that between the partner's and outside country's goods.

If the two elasticities are equal, the optimum tariff on b is approximately half of the tariff on c. In applying this model and argument to the

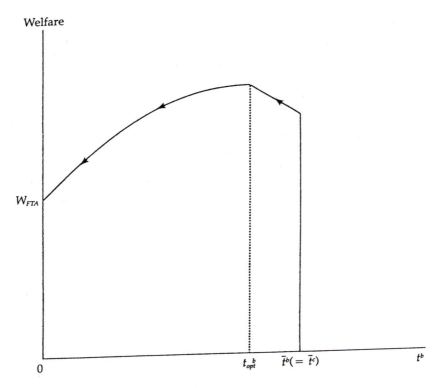

Figure 2.6
Effect of preferential tariff reduction and welfare.

real world, it is reasonable to expect, however, that the degree of substitutability is substantially higher between the imports from the two sources, B and C, than that between imports from B and A's exportables. For instance, Chile's imports from North America are likely to exhibit a much greater degree of substitutability with goods from the European Union or East Asia than with its own exports. Given this fact, the optimum tariff on b is higher than one-half of the tariff on the outside country's goods. In the limit, if the cross-price elasticity of demand for B with respect to the price of A is zero, the optimum tariff on b equals the initial tariff on c. In terms of figure 2.5, exports do not change at all when preferential trading is introduced and trade diversion exactly offsets trade creation. In terms of figure 2.6, welfare falls monotonically as we lower the tariff on b while holding the tariff on c constant.

The analysis up to this point has assumed that the terms of trade are constant, and it does not allow for the tariff-revenue-redistribution effect discussed earlier.[27] As already noted, with goods differentiated by the country of origin, the terms of trade cannot be assumed constant. The derivation of the effects of preferential trading on the terms of trade in the three-good model is complicated. Fortunately, in a neglected but important paper, these effects were worked out by Robert Mundell. To quote him,

1. A discriminatory tariff reduction by a member country improves the terms of trade of the partner country with respect to both the tariff reducing country and the rest of the world, but the terms of trade of the tariff-reducing country might rise or fall with respect to third countries.
2. The degree of improvement in the terms of trade of the partner country is likely to be larger the greater is the member's tariff reduction; this establishes the presumption that a member's gain from a free-trade area will be larger the higher are initial tariffs of partner countries (Mundell 1964, 8).

Not surprisingly, once the terms-of-trade changes are brought back into the analysis, the "mercantilist" bias in results noted earlier (that is, that A loses from its own liberalization) comes back even in the Meade model.[28] We are once again driven to the conclusion that a high-protection country (Mexico) forming an FTA with a low-protection country (United States) is likely to lose from the FTA. Observe that the terms-of-trade effects are in addition to the likely losses from second-best considerations at fixed terms of trade as discussed in figures 2.5 and 2.6.

Revenue Seeking

The conclusion that a country is likely to lose from its own preferential liberalization can break down in the presence of 100 percent, perfectly competitive, resource-using revenue-seeking activities.[29] Given this type of revenue seeking, each dollar's worth of tariff revenue will be matched by a dollar's worth of real resources used unproductively. The tariff revenue is represented by the rectangle GHNS in figure 2.2, where A and B form the FTA. This revenue is now lost in revenue seeking and will not contribute to the country's welfare. The introduction of preferential trading will then lead to a loss of tariff revenue in the amount GFLH, but it will generate an exactly equivalent gain from a release of resources employed in revenue seeking, leaving A's welfare unchanged. For the union as a whole, however, the reduced revenue seeking will generate a net gain equal to GFLH. A large part of this gain, trapezium GFUH, will go to the partner country B, while the remaining part, triangle UFL, pays for the cost of trade diversion. In sum, country A's welfare does not change while that of B rises.

Next, consider the case in figure 2.3 where A and C have the FTA instead. Once again, the rectangle GSNH now will not contribute to the country's welfare in the initial equilibrium. But when preferential liberalization is introduced, the internal price of A falls to the level shown by point R and the rectangle (plus triangle SNR) becomes a part of the consumers' surplus and hence A's welfare rises. Country B's welfare does not change.

Combining the two cases, we obtain the conclusion that, in the presence of 100 percent perfectly competitive revenue seeking, each partner benefits unambiguously (or at least does not lose) from preferential trading. This conclusion undermines our argument that preferential liberalization by a country with respect to its major trading partner is likely to hurt itself and benefit its partner.

We suggest, however, that there are at least two reasons why we should not take this conclusion seriously. First, even though revenue seeking is an important phenomenon in certain contexts and worthy of analysis in its own right, it is hardly invoked when making major policy decisions. We are not aware of a single reference to revenue seeking as a major reason for NAFTA in the public debate in either Mexico or the United States and Canada preceding its approval. Indeed, if we are to take revenue seeking seriously, we should take it and other types of directly unproductive profit-seeking (DUP) activities arising from all other policies into account as well. Second, the twin assumptions of 100 percent and perfectly competitive revenue seeking are unrealistic. Empirically, revenue seeking is likely for several reasons to be a small fraction of the total revenue. In particular, the operation of the "Brother-in-Law Theorem" and of settled rules for allocation of revenues will often turn potential DUP activities into transfers.

"Natural Trading Partners" Hypothesis and Regional PTAs

We now turn to the question of natural trading partners.[30] As we noted earlier, the "natural trading partners" phrasing and hypothesis (that PTAs among them are more likely to beneficial) originated in Wonnacott and Lutz (1989). Based on the work of Viner (1950), Lipsey (1960), and Johnson (1962), these authors provided detailed criteria for determining whether or not a given set of countries constituted natural trading partners:

Trade creation is likely to be great, and trade diversion small, if the prospective members of an FTA are natural trading partners. Several points are relevant:

• Are the prospective members already major trading partners? If so, the FTA will be reinforcing natural trading partners, not artificially diverting them.

• Are the prospective members close geographically? Groupings of distant nations may be economically inefficient because of the high transportation costs (Wonnacott and Lutz 1989, 69).

Wonnacott and Lutz offered two further criteria, one based on complementarity versus competitiveness of the economies and the other on the countries' relative levels of economic development. They noted, however, that these characteristics are "much more difficult to evaluate." Because subsequent advocates of FTAs have not included these criteria in defining natural trading partners, we will not discuss them.

For clarity, we will refer to the first two criteria spelled out in the above passage from Wonnacott and Lutz as the "volume-of-trade" and "transport-cost" criteria and examine them in turn.

The Volume-of-Trade Criterion   The volume-of-trade criterion for choosing natural trading partners and treating them as likely therefore to be welfare enhancing to their members seems plausible at first glance but is, in fact, treacherous for several reasons.

First, the criterion is neither symmetric nor transitive. A lack of symmetry implies that country A may be a natural trading partner of country B, but the reverse may not hold true. A lack of transitivity implies that even if A is a natural trading partner of B, and B is a natural trading partner of C, A may not be a natural trading partner of C. Lest this be viewed as a purely academic point, we note that the United States is Mexico's largest trading partner, but the reverse is not true. Similarly, the United States is the largest trading partner of both Canada and Mexico, but Canada and Mexico have little trade with each other.

Second, the volume-of-trade criterion is premised on the view that a larger initial volume of trade between potential partners implies a lower likelihood of loss because of trade diversion. In terms of figure 2.2, this implies that the larger is OQ_1, the smaller is Q_1Q_2.

This is, however, an unsupported inference from the fact that, for any given volume of initial imports (OQ_3), the higher is the partner country's initial share, the lower is the outside country's share and hence the smaller is the *scope* for diverting trade. Instead, what one needs to determine is how likely is the *actual* trade diversion. Thus, for example, between two alternate situations, one where Q_1Q_3 (the scope for trade diversion) is twice as large as in the other, $Q_1 Q_2$ (the actual trade diversion) could still be only half as much.

The underlying model that defines the trade volumes in different equilibriums may well imply then that the relationship between the initial volume of imports from the partner country and the trade to be diverted to it may be altogether tenuous.

Thus, consider the Lipsey (1958) analysis of the question, based on the small-union version of the Meade model we have discussed.[31] Lipsey, as Bhagwati recalled in his earlier critique of the volume-of-trade criterion, focused not on the initial volume of imports but "on the relative sizes of imports from each source vis-à-vis expenditure on domestic goods as the key and decisive factor in determining the size of losses and gains from the preferential cuts in trade barriers" (Bhagwati 1993a, 34). Of course, on the basis of equation 1 and the discussion of it, we can also conclude that, in general in this model, the higher is the compensated crossprice elasticity of its demand for the partner's good with respect to the price of its own good *relative* to the crossprice elasticity of its demand for the good with respect to the price of the outside country's good, the higher is the likelihood that an FTA improves a country's welfare. This general conclusion reduces to the Lipsey argument when the liberalizing country's preferences are of the CES variety.[32]

For a country such as Mexico joining the NAFTA with the United States, we may well expect in fact the former elasticity to be lower than the latter so that the welfare presumption for this "natural trading partner" of the United States from NAFTA is ironically likely to be in favor of trade-diversion effects dominating the outcome.

There is a further subtle point to be noted. In figure 2.6, starting from a nondiscriminatory tariff, as country A lowers the tariff on B, trade share shifts in favor of B at the expense of country C. That is, A and B become more natural trading partners according to the volume-of-trade criterion. Yet, once the tariff on B attains the second-best optimum, t_{opt}^b, further preferential liberalization is accompanied by a *reduction* in the welfare of A. Thus, to the left of t_{opt}^b, A and B are more natural trading partners than to the right of it, but preferential tariff reductions in that range reduce welfare.

Third, even this conclusion understates the folly of regarding a large initial volume of imports as a benign phenomenon. It ignores the crucial tariff-revenue-redistribution effect that we have highlighted. In FTAs involving countries with asymmetric levels of protection and a high volume of trade initially, the country with higher protection is likely to lose even if trade-creation effects dominate trade-diversion effects. Under such circumstances, the net gain from trade-creation and trade-diversion effects could likely be swamped by the loss from the tariff-revenue-redistribution effect. The case for Mexico gaining from joining NAFTA thus looks dismal on this account as well.

While, therefore, the volume-of-trade criterion for judging FTAs to be benign is clearly to be rejected, linking it to *regionalism* and thus declaring regional FTAs to be more benign than nonregional FTAs is additionally wrong. There is no evidence at all that pairs of contiguous countries, or countries with common borders, have larger volumes of trade with each other than do pairs that are not so situated or that trade volumes of pairs of countries, arranged by distance between the countries in the pair, will show distance to be inversely related to trade volumes.[33]

This is evident from the somewhat aggregated destination-related trade volume statistics for major regions in 1980, 1985, and 1990 in table 2.3.[34] Then again, take just one telling example.[35] Chile shares a common border with Argentina, but in 1993 it shipped only 6.2 percent of exports to Argentina and received only 5 percent of its imports from her (Panagariya 1995b, tables 3 and 4). By contrast, the United States does not have a common border with Chile but in 1993 accounted for 16.2 percent of her exports and 24.9 percent of her imports. The volume-of-trade criterion then would make the United States, *not* Argentina, the natural trading partner of Chile, clearly controverting the claim that the volume-of-trade criterion translates into a regional criterion.

As contended by Bhagwati (1993a), the equation by Krugman (1991a) and Summers (1991) of the two concepts of volume of trade and regionalism (whether of the distance or the common border or contiguity variety) is therefore simply wrong.

Nonetheless, Frankel and Wei (1995) have recently argued otherwise, claiming that their empirical work favors the Krugman-Summers assertion. They use the gravity model as their basic tool to conclude that "proximity is in general an important determinant of bilateral trade around the world, notwithstanding exceptions like India-Pakistan and other cases."

But this misses the point at issue. What is at stake is not whether distance, interpreted through the gravity model and/or common border modeled through a dummy, matters.[36] There does seem to be a *partial* correlation between distance, proximity, common border, and so on, on the one hand, and trade volumes on the other.[37] But what we have to look at is the *total* initial volume of trade, and this does not correlate simply with distance as the right-hand side variable, as required by the

Table 2.3
Direction of Exports by Major Regions, 1980, 1985, and 1990

Exporter	Year	Partner							
		North America	Western Europe	Europe	East Asia[a]	Latin America	Africa	Middle East	South Asia
North	1980	33.5	25.2	27.4	15.8	8.9	3.3	4.2	1.0
America	1985	44.4	19.3	21.0	15.5	5.9	2.5	3.2	1.0
	1990	41.9	22.3	23.4	20.4	5.0	1.7	2.6	0.8
Western	1980	6.7	67.1	71.9	2.9	2.4	7.2	5.5	0.7
Europe	1985	11.3	64.9	68.9	3.6	1.6	5.2	5.0	0.9
	1990	8.3	71.0	74.4	5.3	1.1	3.3	3.3	0.7
Europe	1980	6.3	63.7	72.7	2.7	2.3	6.9	5.5	0.7
	1985	11.0	63.5	69.2	3.4	1.6	5.1	5.0	0.9
	1990	8.2	70.6	74.5	5.2	1.1	3.3	3.3	0.7
East Asia	1980	26.0	16.8	18.9	29.9	4.1	4.4	7.4	1.8
	1985	37.8	13.6	15.5	25.3	2.8	2.2	5.1	2.0
	1990	31.9	19.8	20.7	32.3	1.9	1.6	3.0	1.5
Latin	1980	27.9	26.5	35.1	5.4	16.6	2.7	1.9	0.5
America	1985	35.8	25.9	30.4	7.1	12.1	3.7	3.0	0.7
	1990	22.9	25.3	27.6	10.3	14.0	2.1	2.4	0.4
Africa	1980	27.4	43.6	46.1	4.3	3.2	1.8	1.7	0.3
	1985	14.8	64.9	69.3	1.8	4.2	5.1	2.2	0.7
	1990	3.0	66.0	68.0	4.6	0.6	12.8	4.4	3.6
Middle	1980	11.5	40.3	41.5	28.7	5.0	1.5	4.1	2.5
East	1985	6.2	15.0	17.7	1.5	0.3	1.4	8.7	0.4
	1990	17.8	48.6	53.0	9.1	1.2	3.6	8.5	0.9
South	1980	10.9	24.6	39.4	14.5	0.5	6.8	14.5	5.6
Asia	1985	18.4	20.8	37.0	16.4	0.4	4.6	11.0	4.4
	1990	17.1	30.1	46.6	18.3	0.3	2.7	6.5	3.2

Source: Panagariya (1993). He cites U.N. COMTRADE data.
Note: This table broadly underlines the point that total trade volumes that matter do not show any relationship to proximity of countries geographically.
a. East Asia does not include China.

"natural trading partners" assertion of the volume-of-trade criterion for forming PTAs.

Next, we have the difficult problem of endogeneity of initial trade volumes with respect to preferences. If the large volumes are themselves attributable, in significant degree, to preferences granted earlier, then they are not "natural," nor is it proper to think that additional preferences are "therefore" harmless. The point is best understood by thinking of high trade barriers by a country leading to a larger within-country trade relative to external trade. To deduce that added barriers are harmless is to compound the harm done by existing barriers that are, of course, preferences in favor of trade within the country.

This is not an idle question. Offshore assembly provisions between the United States and Mexico and the longstanding GATT-sanctioned free trade regime in autos between Canada and the United States are certainly not negligible factors in pre-NAFTA U.S. trade with these NAFTA members. In granting preferences under the Generalized System of Preferences, the United States, EC, and Japan have all concentrated on their regions. Thus, the partial correlation between distance and trade volumes (in gravity models) may be a result of preferences granted to proximate neighbors, rather than a "natural" phenomenon justifying (new) preferences.[38]

Finally, we need to raise a different objection to the argument that a high initial volume of imports from a partner country will work to protect a country against trade diversion. Quite aside from the fact that aggregate volumes shift significantly in practice over time, the comparative advantage in specific goods and services often changes in different locations.[39] Consistent with a given aggregate trade volume, its composition may shift so as to yield greater trade diversion when a PTA is present.

Consider a case, based on constant costs for simplicity, in which the United States imports a product from Canada under a nondiscriminatory tariff. if a PTA is formed between the two countries, the product will continue to be imported from Canada. But suppose that, on a future data, Canada loses its comparative advantage to Taiwan ever so slightly so that the preferential advantage enjoyed by her outweighs this loss. There will be trade diversion, and imports into the United States will continue to come from Canada with the volume of trade remaining unchanged.[40] Observe that there is an asymmetry here between a shift in comparative advantage away from the partner and that toward it. If Canada experiences a reduction in the cost of production of a product imported by the United States from Taiwan under a PTA, there can still be trade diversion. Because of the preference, Canada will replace Taiwan as the supplier of this product even before Canada's costs fall below those of Taiwan. The volume of trade will rise, and at the same time there will be trade diversion.[41] The proponents of the complacent "high volume of imports" thesis are thus trapped in a static view of comparative advantage that is particularly at odds with today's volatile, "kaleidoscopic" comparative advantage in the global economy.

Transport-Cost Criterion   But if the volume-of-trade criterion is conceptually inappropriate and must be summarily rejected, what about the transport-cost criterion? This criterion maps directly into distance and hence into regionalism. However, the question to be analyzed is: should PTA partners be chosen on the basis of lower transport costs, and hence greater proximity, to maximize gains to members or to minimize losses to them?

The earliest reference we could find to transport costs in the context of trade liberalization is from Johnson (1962, 61): "If the separate markets of various members are divided by serious geographical barriers which require high transport costs to overcome them, the enlargement of the market may be more apparent than real." All he seemed to be arguing was the truism that trade liberalization may be meaningless if high transport costs prevented trade from breaking out.

But the natural trading partners hypothesis is altogether different and incorrect. There is, in fact, no reason to think that greater proximity increases the likelihood of gain for members in a PTA. This can be seen simply by constructing a counterexample where a union with a country (C) that is more distant produces more gain (for A) than a union with the country (B) that is less distant but otherwise identical (to C).

First note that as long as country A in figure 2.2 imports the good from both B and C in the pre- and post-FTA equilibrium, the presence of transportation costs has no effect whatsoever on the analysis based on that figure. All we need to do is to imagine that the supply price of C is inclusive of transport costs, while such costs are absent for the partner, B. This introduction of transport costs leaves the remainder of the analysis entirely unchanged.

To construct the counterexample noted above, consider a world consisting of three countries: A, B, and C. Country A has the option to form an FTA with either B or C. Countries B and C are identical in all respects except that the latter is located farther away. If the supply curves of B and C were horizontal, we would be in a world represented in panel a of figure 2.1 with $(P_C - P_B)$ representing transportation costs from C to A.

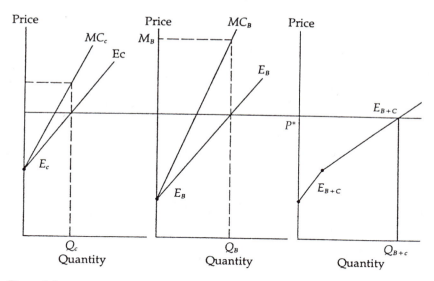

Figure 2.7
Example of positive effects of union with a more distant country.

Technically, in this case an FTA with the geographically proximate B improves A's welfare. But recall the limitation of such an FTA: country A does not trade with C before or after the union is formed; and in the post-FTA equilibrium, the external tariff does not matter so the FTA is really equivalent to nondiscriminatory free trade.

To make the example substantive, we must therefore assume that supply curves of B and C are upward sloped.[42] In figure 2.7, we draw three panels. In the first two panels, we show the export supply curves of C and B as $E_C E_C$ and $E_B E_B$, respectively. In the third panel, we have their combined supply obtained by summing horizontally the individual supplies from the first two panels. The supply curves of C and B are identical in all respects except that C's supply price includes a constant per-unit transportation cost. Thus, for each quantity, C's supply price exceeds that of B by the per-unit transportation cost.[43]

To avoid clutter, we do not draw A's demand curve. Instead, imagine that there is an arbitrary nondiscriminatory tariff initially that yields the total demand for imports as represented by point Q_{B+C}. The price paid for this quantity to B and C is P^*. Individual supplies of B and C can be obtained by intersecting their supply curves with P^* and are shown by Q_B and Q_C. Not surprisingly, imports are larger from the geographically proximate country B than from C.

Now consider the introduction of preferential trading. To see which way preferences should be given, draw the *marginal* cost curve associated with each supply curve. These are shown by MC_B and MC_C. It is then immediate that, at the initial nondiscriminatory tariff, the marginal cost of imports is higher on imports from B than from C. We then obtain the dramatic conclusion that if A wants to give a tariff preference, it should opt for the distant partner C rather than the proximate B! The transport-cost criterion for choosing partners in a PTA is exactly wrong in this instance.

The explanation of this result is straightforward. The discriminating monopsonist model says that for any quantity of total purchases, the supplier with higher elasticity should be paid a higher price. In the present problem, this prescription translates into a lower tax on the supplier with higher elasticity. And transportation costs make C's supply curve more elastic than that of B.

Endogenous Tariffs on the Outside Country

So far, we have assumed that when an FTA is formed, the tariff on the outside country is held at its original level. But this may not always be true. When an FTA begins to take a bite, lobbies representing declining domestic industries may be able to reassert themselves. Because the FTA ties the authorities' hands with respect to the union partner, they will have to respond by raising protection against outside countries. This, indeed, happened recently following the [1994] Mexican crisis when the country raised external tariffs on 502 products from 20 percent or less to 35 percent!

This possibility had been anticipated by Bhagwati (1993a, 36–37). He wrote:

Imagine that the United States begins to eliminate (by out competing) an inefficient Mexican industry once the FTA goes into effect. Even though the most efficient producer is Taiwan, if the next efficient United States out competes the least efficient Mexico, that would be desirable trade creation....

But what would the Mexicans be likely to do? They would probably start AD actions against Taiwan.

This possibility raises the questions whether, once we allow for endogenous policy response, welfare may actually decline relative to the FTA and, indeed, to the initial equilibrium. Answers to both questions are in the affirmative.

A simple example demonstrating welfare deterioration relative to the FTA can be given as follows. For a zero tariff on B, calculate A's optimum tariff on C. Suppose that A sets the initial, nondiscriminatory tariff on B and C at this level. Then, by construction, an FTA with B, holding C's tariff unchanged, not only improves A's welfare but actually maximizes it. If now lobbying pressure leads to a rise in the external tariff, A's welfare will necessarily fall.

The more interesting is the possibility that A's welfare can decline relative to the initial, pre-FTA equilibrium. To demonstrate it, note that A's welfare can be written as

$$W = CS + PS + t_B P_B^* M_B + t_C P_C^* M_C$$
$$= CS + PS + (P - P_B^*)M_B + (P - P_C^*)M_C$$
$$= CS + PS + P(M_B + M_C) - (P_B^* M_B + P_C^* M_C), \qquad (2)$$

where CS denotes A's consumers' surplus, PS its producers' surplus, P domestic price, $P_i^* (i = B, C)$ border price on imports from i, t_i the *ad valorem* tariff on imports from i, and M_i imports from i. The last two terms in these equalities represent tariff revenue on imports. Given a nondiscriminatory tariff initially, $P_B^* = P_C^*$.

Take the case favorable to an FTA with B by assuming that at each world price, B's supply is more elastic than C's. Assume further that the initial, nondiscriminatory tariff is sufficiently high that the FTA with no change in the tariff on C is welfare improving for A.[44] We will now show that if, because of lobbying pressure, the FTA is accompanied by a rise in the tariff on C such that *total* imports are unchanged, it is possible for its welfare to decline. Given that the FTA with no change in the tariff on C is welfare improving, this result shows that the endogenous tariff response can turn a welfare-improving FTA into a welfare-reducing proposition.

With no change in imports, the domestic price in A does not change and neither do CS and PS. From equation 2, it is then clear that welfare will rise or fall as the cost of imports, represented by the last term in the last equality, falls or rises. This property allows us to analyze the impact of the endogenous choice of the tariff by focusing on import supplies from B and C only.

In figure 2.8, as assumed, B's export-supply curve is more elastic than that of C at each price. This means that under a nondiscriminatory tariff, A's *private* marginal cost of obtaining imports from B is lower than that from C. Therefore, *at the margin*, A benefits by switching imports from C to B.

Initially, with a nondiscriminatory tariff, A buys the product at P^* per-unit from both B and C. Imports from the two countries are given by M_B and M_C, respectively. The marginal cost of obtaining imports from B is

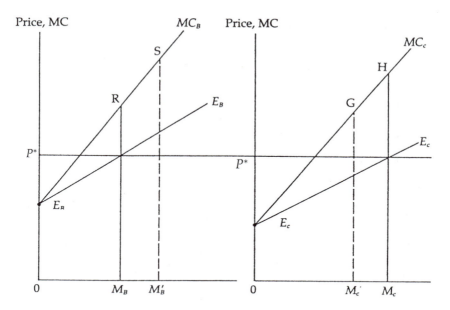

Figure 2.8
Welfare loss from endogenous increase in external tariff after formation of a free trade area.

less than that from C, $RM_B < HM_C$. As noted in the previous paragraph, at the margin, switching imports from C to B is beneficial to A: a small reduction in the tariff on B and increase in tariff on C which keeps total imports unchanged is welfare improving. But the FTA requires taking the tariff on B all the way to 0. As that is done, the marginal cost of obtaining imports from B rises, and as we correspondingly raise the tariff on C to keep the total imports unchanged, the marginal cost of imports from C falls. It is entirely possible that the two marginal costs cross and then reach levels such that the total cost of imports actually rises. Figure 2.8 is drawn on the assumption that the FTA increases imports from B by $M_B M'_B$. The tariff on C has to be raised to reduce imports from that country by an equivalent amount shown by $M_C M'_C$. As drawn, the net change in the cost of imports, $SRM_B M'_B$-$GHM_C M'_C$, is positive indicating that welfare declines.[45]

Welfare Loss without Trade Diversion

The general impression in the literature is that a welfare loss from an FTA can arise only if there is trade diversion. It is easy to show, however, that a welfare loss to an *individual* member (though not to the union as a whole nor to the world) can arise even if there is no trade diversion. The simplest example of this phenomenon can be gleaned from figure 2.2. Starting from a nondiscriminatory tariff, marginal costs of production in B and C are equal. Given that *at the margin* both B and C are equally efficient suppliers of the product, there can be no trade diversion if we lower the tariff on B by an infinitesimally small amount. Yet because A's terms of trade with respect to B deteriorate by the full amount of the tariff reduction, it will lose from such a change.

In figure 2.2, because the domestic price does not change after the introduction of preferential trading, there is no trade creation. But if we allow C's supply curve to slope upward, the introduction of a small tariff preference for B will also generate a trade-creation effect. This is because the preference improves A's terms of trade with respect to C, lowers the domestic price, and displaces some inefficient domestic production. For reasons explained in the previous paragraph, there is no trade diversion, however. Yet it is possible for the loss from the accompanying deterioration in the terms of trade vis-à-vis B to more than offset the gain from trade creation as well as the improvement in the terms of trade vis-à-vis C (a result that can be derived algebraically, of course).

Concluding against PTAs

Our analysis of the static effects of PTAs is far less sanguine than is customarily assumed by several policy economists, bureaucrats, and politicians today. It also challenges and undermines the validity of the claims made in behalf of "regional" PTAs, whether the regions are defined in terms of countries with relatively high intraregional trade or in terms of proximity with or without common borders.

Therefore, if we were to assume that PTAs result from a variety of noneconomic factors, we need not be complacent about the possibility of their resulting in harmful effects.[46] Nor would there be any good reason to be complacent even if those PTAs were to be essentially regional in scope, when "regional" means geographic proximity or higher volumes of trade among, rather than outside, members.

We add three final observations. First, the common usage by journalists and politicians of the word "regional" frequently includes "common-ocean" arrangements such as APEC. Remember that APEC includes both South Korea and Chile, countries whose mutual trade is characterized by smallness of volume *and* largeness of distance, so that neither of the two criteria of distance or volume of trade for sanctifying PTAs as desirable, inappropriate as we have shown it to be, holds for every member of APEC vis-á-vis every other.

Second, is the presence of common waters a new criterion for getting nations to form a PTA (the Pacific Ocean in the case of APEC)? We should not forget that the major oceans, and hence most of the trading nations of the world, are united by the world's water, and even more readily thanks to the Suez and Panama canals! In fact, the fullest-bodied common-waters "regional" area is clearly approximated by the membership of the WTO, as would have been appreciated by Ferdinand Magellan, who starting out from San Lucar in 1519 sailed from the Atlantic into the Pacific, an ocean unknown at the time.[47]

Third, the term "continental trading arrangements" has also been frequently used by Wei and Frankel (1995), who argue that "many [trading blocs] are along continental lines."[48] But this is at best misleading and at worst incorrect. Even if we confine ourselves to Article XXIV-sanctioned arrangements, we still must distinguish among PTAs that are continent-wide and hence "continental," those that cut across continents and are thus "intercontinental," and those that consist of members entirely *within*, but are not extended to *all* countries in, a continent and hence must be called "subcontinental."

Geographers and earth scientists divide the earth traditionally into four oceans (Arctic, Indian, Atlantic, and Pacific) and seven continents (Europe, Asia, Africa, Australia, North America, South America, and Antarctica). Only NAFTA and the PTA between Australia and New Zealand can then qualify as continental. And, the major new Article XXIV-sanctioned PTAs, which have been proposed by different groups in recent years (NAFTA extension into South America, APEC, and TAFTA) and which would clearly dwarf the continental PTAs clearly cut across continents.[49] Then again, MERCOSUR and ASEAN are clearly subcontinental. Of course, if one adds all the non-Article XXIV preferential trading arrangements, the matter looks even worse for those who claim that "many" of today's "trade blocs" are "continental."

Theoretical Analysis of the Dynamic Time-Path Question

Our analysis of the economics of PTAs would be seriously incomplete if, having analyzed the static effects, we did not go on to analyze the dynamic time-path question.

Formulating the Time-Path Question

Essentially, this question relates not to whether the immediate (static) effect of a PTA is good or bad, but whether the (dynamic) effect to the PTA is to accelerate or decelerate the continued reduction of trade barriers toward the goal of reducing them worldwide. This question may be formulated analytically in two separate ways.

Question I Assume that the time-path of MTN (multilateral trade negotiations) and the time-path of PTAs are separable and do not influence each other. The two policies are "strangers" to (that is, independent of) one another: neither hurts or helps the other. Will then the PTA time-path be characterized by stagnant or negligible expansion of membership? Or will we have expanding membership, with this even turning eventually into worldwide membership as in the WTO, thus arriving at non-discriminatory free trade for all? A similar question can be raised for the MTN time-path. And the analysis can be extended to a comparison of the two time-paths, ranking the efficacy of the two methods of reducing trade barriers to achieve the goal of worldwide free trade for all.

Question II Assume instead, as is more sensible, that if both the MTN and the PTA time-paths are embraced simultaneously, they will interact. In particular, the policy of undertaking PTAs will have a malign impact on (be a "foe" of) the progress along the MTN time-path, or it will have a benign effect on (be a "friend" of) the MTN time-path.[50]

Question I can be illustrated with the aid of figure 2.9, which portrays a sample of possibilities for the time-paths in question. World (rather than individual member) welfare is put on the vertical axis and time along the horizontal axis. For the PTA time-paths drawn, an upward movement along the path implies growing membership; for the MTN (or what are described as "process-multilateralism") time-paths, it implies non-discriminatory lowering of trade barriers among the nearly worldwide WTO membership instead. The PTA and MTN time-paths are assumed to be independent of each other; the PTA time-path neither accelerates nor decelerates the course of MTN (thus ruling out Question II-type issues). The goal can be treated as reaching U^*, the worldwide freeing of trade barriers on a nondiscriminatory basis at a specified time.

Question I can be illustrated by reference to the PTA paths I–IV. Thus, PTAs may improve welfare immediately, in the static sense, from U^0 to U_p^2 or reduce it to U_p^1. In either case, the time-path could then be stagnant

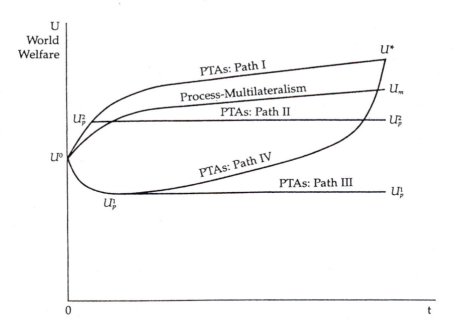

Figure 2.9
Alternative time-paths under multilateralism and under PTAs.

(as with time-paths II and III), implying a fragmentation of the world economy through no further expansion of the initial PTA. Else, it can lead (as in time-paths I and IV) to multilateral free trade for all at U^* through continued expansion and coagulation of the PTAs. Under "process multilateralism," that is, MTN as a multilateral process of reducing trade barriers as distinct from multilateralism as the goal desired, the time-path may fail to reach U^* and instead fall short at U_m because of free-rider problems.

As indicated, if the PTA and MTN time-paths are interdependent, we can address Question II. In that case, the MTN time-path becomes a function of whether the PTA time-path is traveled simultaneously.

Question Originating in Policy

The dynamic time-path question has arisen, just as the static one did, in policy concerns and political decisions that ran ahead of the theory. The post-Vinerian, in-depth analysis of the static question coincided with the movement that eventually created the European Community through the Treaty of Rome in 1957. The dynamic time-path question has arisen in the context of the U.S. failure to get an MTN Round started at the GATT Ministerial in 1982 and the U.S. decision to finally abandon its studied avoidance of Article XXIV-sanctioned PTAs. The policy choice made was initially Hobson's choice: if the MTN could not be used to continue lowering trade barriers, then PTAs would be used instead. If the turnpike could not be used, one had no option except to use the dirt road.

For several reasons that have been systematically explored in Bhagwati (1993b), the United States ended, however, becoming committed to "walking on both legs," embracing both the PTA and the MTN paths. Indeed, the United States has now become an active proponent of this view, continuing to do so even after the Uruguay Round of MTN had been successfully conducted and the WTO launched. And, in doing so, its spokespersons have frequently implied that PTAs will have a benign, beneficial impact on the worldwide lowering of trade barriers through induced acceleration of MTN.

The questions that we have posed above spring from this shift in U.S. policy, which has been manifest for several years, starting from the Bush administration and articulated as a distinct policy in the Clinton administration. In Bhagwati (1991, 1993), the challenge to international trade theorists to analyze these questions was identified and a preliminary set of arguments offered. We recapitulate briefly those arguments and then review the theoretical literature that has been developing since then on the dynamic time-path questions.

"Exogenously Determined" Time-Paths: A Diversion

First, however, it is necessary to consider and to turn aside certain theoretical approaches that are not meaningful for thinking about the dynamic time-path questions at hand, even though they have often been mistaken to be so.

Kemp-Wan The seminal approach of Kemp and Wan (1976) to Customs Union theory seems to be the most pertinent to our questions but, in fact, is not. Unlike the Vinerian approach, Kemp and Wan made the external tariff structure (of the Customs Union) endogenously chosen so that each member country's welfare would be improved, while that of the nonmembers was left unchanged. The beauty of this approach was that it restored, as it were, the commonsense intuition prior to Viner that a CU should be welfare improving for members and for the world. This is, of course, a "possibility" theorem, no more and no less.[51]

It is then immediately apparent that the PTA time-path to U^* in figure 2.9 can be made monotonic, provided expanding membership of a PTA always satisfies the Kemp-Wan rule for forming a Customs Union. But what this argument does not say, and indeed cannot say, is that the PTA will necessarily expand and, if so, in this Kemp-Wan fashion.

For that answer, to what is obviously Question I, we must turn to the *incentive structure* that any CU/PTA provides, through interests, ideology, and institutions, for expansion or stagnation of its membership.

Krugman   The same argument applies to the theoretical approach to the question of PTAs recently introduced by Paul Krugman (1991a, 1991b, 1993). Again the expansion of membership is treated as exogenously specified, as in Viner, and the welfare consequences of the world mechanically dividing into a steadily increasing number of symmetric blocs— clearly demarcated countries are then not even the natural constituents of these "blobs"-cum-blocs—are considered and, for particular specifications, the monotonicity of world welfare examined, including even calculations concerning the "optimal" number of such symmetric PTAs/blocs! This, in turn, has led to critiques, as of the symmetry assumption by Srinivasan (1993), who essentially shows that the specific Krugman conclusions are easily reversed by abandoning symmetry, and to further variations by a few others.[52] Yet it is hard to see the analytical interest of this approach or, more important, its relevance to the compelling (incentive-structure) questions today concerning the membership expansion of PTAs. In short, it fails to throw light on the analysis of the dynamic time-path questions of the type introduced above. For that analysis which is currently, quite correctly, on the top of the theoretical agenda, we must turn elsewhere.

Incentive Structure Arguments

At the April 1992 World Bank Conference on Regional Integration, Bhagwati (1993a), having reiterated the need to analyze the dynamic time-path question, advanced several arguments concerning the incentive structure within specific PTAs, once formed, to expand or to stagnate. Before we discuss the theoretical modeling of such ideas by Baldwin (1993), Krishna (1993), and Levy (1994), among others, it is worth recapitulating the principal arguments distinguished by Bhagwati.[53]

We need to recognize, of course, that the incentives may be political rather than (narrowly) economic. A PTA may be formed, and even expanded, to seek political allies by using trade as foreign policy and to target the benefits of trade to politically favored nations.[54] Politics is not a negligible factor in the discriminatory trade arrangements implemented by the EU via Association Agreements with the smaller countries on its periphery and beyond; and it certainly cannot be ignored in the transformation of the original Canada-U.S. Free Trade Agreement into NAFTA with Mexico and then into the Enterprise of Americas Initiative.

But that is clearly not the whole story, and we can learn much by thinking carefully about the incentive structure for membership expansion in political-economy-theoretic terms. To do this, Bhagwati (1993a) distinguished among three different types of "agents" and offered the following analysis.

Governments of Member Countries   PTAs will be under pressure not to expand because governments may feel that "we already have a large market, so what do we stand to gain by going through the hassle of adding more members?" This is the "our market is large enough" syndrome, emphasized by Martin Wolf, who has often noted that large countries have tended to opt for inward-looking trade and investment strategies, while the small ones have gone the outward-looking route.

Interest Groups in Member Countries   The interest groups in member countries may be for or against new members. The internationally oriented exporting firms may be expected to endorse new members whose markets then become preferentially available to them vis-à-vis nonmember exporters to these new members.[55] On the other hand, the firms that are profiting from access to preferential markets in the member (partner) countries will not want new members whose firms are also exporters of the same or similar products in the member markets. Both incentives reflect the preferential nature of the PTAs.

The former incentive was clear in the NAFTA debate in the United States and reflected in many pronouncements, including that of pro-NAFTA economists (and even President Clinton, who played the Japanophobic card that the United States would have preferential access to Mexico vis-à-vis Japan). It is also evident in the statement of Signor Agnelli of Fiat: "The single market must first offer an advantage to European companies. This is a message we must insist on without hesitation."

Interest Groups in Nonmember Countries   The third set of agents is in the nonmember countries. Here the example of a PTA may lead others to emulate, even to seek, entry. Then again, the fear of trade diversion may also induce outsiders to seek entry.[56]

Recent Theoretical Analyses

Subsequently, the analysis of the dynamic time-path question moved into formal political economy-theoretic modeling. We provide here a synoptic review of the few significant contributions to date, organizing the literature analytically in light of the two questions distinguished above and also in terms of whether the analysis models the incentives of nonmembers to join or those of the members to expand.[57]

Question I   The single contribution that focuses on Question I (the incentive to add members to a PTA) is by Richard Baldwin (1993), who concentrates, in turn, on the incentive of nonmembers to join the PTA. He constructs a model to demonstrate that this incentive will be positive: the PTA will create a "domino" effect, with outsiders wanting to become insiders on an escalator. The argument is basically driven by the fact that the PTA implies a loss of cost competitiveness by imperfectly competitive nonmember firms whose profits in the PTA markets decline because they must face the tariffs that member countries' firms do not have to pay. These firms then lobby for entry, tilting the political equilibrium at the margin toward entry demands in their countries. The countries closest to the margin will then enter the bloc, assuming that the members have open entry. This enlarges the market and thereby increases the cost of nonmembership and pulls in countries at the next margin. Given the assumptions, including continuity, this domino model can take the PTA time-path to U^* in figure 2.9.

   While Baldwin formalizes the incentive of nonmembers to get inside the PTA, interestingly there is no formalization of the incentives of members to add or reject new members that have been discussed in the literature, as by Bhagwati (1993a). Indeed, the Baldwin model itself shows, on the flip side, that member firms will gain from the cost advantage that they enjoy vis-à-vis the nonmember firms and hence will have an opposed interest in not admitting the nonmembers to the PTA: a full analysis of the political economy of both members and nonmembers in the Baldwin model could then lead to specific equilibrium outcomes that leave the PTA expansion imperiled.

Question II   The rest of the theoretical contributions address Question II, that is, whether the PTA possibility and/or time-path helps or harms the MTN time-path. Pravin Krishna (1993) and Philip Levy (1994) address directly and quite aptly this question and reach the "malign-impact" conclusion, unfavorable to the exhortation to "walk on both legs."

Krishna models the political process in the fashion of the government acting in response to implicit lobbying by firms, what Bhagwati (1990) has called "clearinghouse"—government assumption where the government is passive, as in Findlay and Wellisz (1982). Krishna shows in his oligopolistic-competition model that the bilateral PTA between two member countries reduces the incentive of the member countries to liberalize tariffs reciprocally with the nonmember world and that, with sufficient trade diversion, this incentive could be so reduced as to make impossible an initially feasible multilateral trade liberalization.

Levy models the political process instead in a median-voter model à la Mayer (1984); the government is not what Bhagwati (1990) has called "self-willed" with its own objectives but acts again as a clearing-house. Using a richer model with scale economies and product variety, Levy demonstrates that bilateral FTAs can undermine political support for multilateral free trade. At the same time, a benign impact is impossible in this model: if a multilateral free trade proposal is not feasible under autarky, the same multilateral proposal cannot be rendered feasible under any bilateral FTA.

The Krishna and Levy models throw light on the incentive-structure questions at hand when the agents are the lobbying groups and interests that are affected by different policy options. However, we might also note that there are contributions that take the more conventional view of governments, which act as agents maximizing social welfare (so that they may be regarded as acting as the custodians of the "general interest" as defined by economists), but then ask whether the effect of allowing PTAs to form affects outcomes concerning trade policy relating to the multilateral system. Rodney Ludema (1993) has analyzed the effect of PTAs on multilateral bargaining outcomes, arguing plausibly that the PTAs give strategic advantage to their members, whereas Kyle Bagwell and Robert Staiger (1993) have analyzed how the formation of a PTA—distinguishing between an FTA and a CU, as they yield different answers—will affect the (unbound) tariffs of the member countries on nonmembers.

The Sequential Bargaining Argument

In conclusion, we note that a different kind of model is implied, though not yet formalized, by the recent argument of Bhagwati (1994) that combines three separate notions.

The first is that even though a multilateral bargain *simultaneously* with a group of nonhegemonic powers is profitable and hence possible, a hegemonic power will gain a greater payoff by bargaining *sequentially* with them, using bilateral and plurilateral PTA approaches, picking the countries that are the most vulnerable and then moving on to the next one and so on.[58]

The second is that this insight has now been appreciated by several lobbies (for example, the intellectual property protection lobby, the environmental and labor standard groups), which are piggybacking on to trade liberalization and trade institutions to secure their maximalist objectives and which see that the PTA approach (which may be seen as an "incentive" strategy), combined with the occasional use of aggressive unilateralism à la punitive Section 301 actions (which may be seen as a "punishment" strategy), is more likely to procure their objectives at the WTO and multilaterally than if pursued directly there through MTN alone.

The third is that the two processes, the MTN and the PTA paths, are to be traveled in tandem since the ultimate goal is indeed to arrive at multilateral, universal obligations in the areas desired by these lobbies by the nonhegemonic powers.

If this "model" provides insight into the political process driving the legitimation of the PTA time-path, then no hegemonic power is likely to abandon the PTA path simply because the WTO exists and is jump-started. A "selfish hegemon," looking after its own narrowly defined interests, reflecting its own lobbying-derived needs, will indeed want to "walk on both legs." But the multilateral outcome, so affected and determined, need not then be considered to have been affected in the socially optimal direction unless one makes the assumption, made effortlessly by hegemonic spokesmen in their policy pronouncements, that "what is good for the hegemon (and its lobbies) is good for the world trading system." Indeed, when we see that the intellectual property protections that were built into the WTO are almost certainly excessive according to the analytical and empirical argumentation of many of the best international economists today, it is hard to regard the ability of the hegemon to induce such outcomes with the aid of PTAs (and aggressive unilateralism) as creating a "benign" effect of the PTAs on the MTN path.

Implications for Current Policy

The case for PTAs, whether on static or on dynamic grounds, appears far less compelling and attractive than many politicians and policy-makers now believe. In fact, it is likely that most of them, misled by the inevitable confusion between free trade and free trade areas that some economists have wittingly or unwittingly encouraged, are not even aware that the scholarly scene is rife today with serious opposition to PTAs.[59]

The Politics of PTAs

The current preoccupation with PTAs reflects overriding political factors. Recall our earlier discussion of the sequential-bargaining advantage to hegemonic powers. Or consider the fact that the leaders of the smaller, nonhegemonic powers get to play a more prominent role, with better photo-opportunities, with smaller summits, especially when a hegemonic power such as the United States features its own president, than would ever be the case at the WTO. Or consider that where the PTAs are regional, as is MERCOSUR (among Argentina, Brazil, Paraguay, and Uruguay), the discriminatory trade agreement can be depicted politically as an act of foreign policy statesmanship. Or consider simply the operation of Gresham's Law: PTAs by some encourage PTAs by others, especially when they are being continually misportrayed by other politicians and countries as statesmanlike moves to free trade. And, of course, there are always the amateur geopoliticians and geoeconomists. Like little boys playing Nintendo games on their computer screens, they think of playing the game of "trade blocs" to indulge their pet prejudices against Europe or Japan. Some want to make the APEC into a PTA to play off against a "protectionist" Europe, while others think of TAFTA as a weapon to play off against the "unfairly trading" Japan.[60]

The "Spaghetti Bowl" Phenomenon

Our view, for reasons explored fully in this chapter, is that the spread of PTAs is desirable only when two justifications obtain: you are building a Common Market with full-scale integration of factor markets and even political harmonization; or the multilateral MFN, MTN process is not working. As we argued earlier, neither rationale is operative today.

In fact, the proliferation of PTAs today poses the danger, indeed the certainty, that a veritable "spaghetti bowl" phenomenon, as Bhagwati has called it, will emerge where trade barriers, including duties, will vary depending on origin, and complex and protection-accommodating rules of origin will find their way into practice.[61] And this, too, at a time when multinationals are getting truly global, and the identification of "local content" and hence origin of traded goods and services is becoming increasingly meaningless and hence subject to inevitable arbitrariness. PTAs are just one, and indeed a gigantic, step backward from this reality: the need today is to intensify the commitment to the basic tenet of non-discrimination that the architects of GATT correctly saw as a principal virtue, not to undermine it.

PTAs with and among Hegemons

We would therefore suggest that Article XXIV-sanctioned PTAs that involve hegemonic powers should be actively discouraged. They involve NAFTA extension southward or overseas, EU free-trade-area agreements with non-EU countries, APEC's transformation into a PTA, and TAFTA.

Such a self-denial would appear anti-free-trade, given the current state of confused thinking and the political capital invested by many in the cause of the PTAs. But it would be speaking to a far more compelling, and truer, version of free trade. It would also require true statesmanship on the part of the leaders of the hegemonic powers, as against the political advantages of opting for what is an inefficient and indeed harmful option.

PTAs among the Nonhegemons

Our view of PTAs among the nonhegemons, principally developing countries, is just a trifle less critical.

To begin with, what MERCOSUR does, for example, has only a fraction of the significance that the United States and the European Union have individually. The trade policy choices of the nonhegemons have comparatively more consequences for themselves than for the world. This contrast is sufficient to regard what they are doing with a less fiercely critical eye than that directed at the hegemons.

Remember again that the impact on their own welfare of PTAs is not necessarily benign. Especially, when these countries get into a PTA with hegemonic powers (for example, Mexico joining the United States in NAFTA), the outcomes for them may be welfare worsening (in the static sense) because of the tariff-revenue-redistribution effect, among other reasons. Failure to understand the differential economics of PTAs, as contrasted with that of free trade, underlies many of the favorable assessments often advanced in behalf of the developing countries that seek to join PTAs with the hegemonic powers.[62] A similar caveat would be relevant to PTAs among the nonhegemons themselves.

We may still consider these PTAs, such as MERCOSUR, with some favor, although nondiscriminatory free trade is the best option. After all, the acceptance of Article XXIV discipline (imperfect as it is) is an improvement over protectionism or over the utterly chaotic and arbitrary ECDC (economic cooperation among developing countries) at the GATT under which these countries were free from such discipline and could indulge in any level and kind of preferences among themselves.

Conclusion

At present, the spread of hegemonic PTAs has been halted. The Osaka meeting of APEC in November 1995 witnessed the Asian members of APEC reaffirming their desire to stick to MFN and hence implicitly to reject the PTA approach even though the U.S. position on the issue apparently remained problematic and ambiguous (with several pro-PTA proponents in the administration). Equally, at Madrid, the idea of TAFTA has been deflected away from an Article XXIV agreement to the New Trans-Atlantic Agenda that merely seeks, and in a presumably nondiscriminatory fashion, the lowering of trade and investment barriers in the area. For the time being, the extension of NAFTA to the South has also been halted, for reasons that may not hold for long beyond the presidential election in 1996.

All this yields enough time to take a closer look at the dangerous drift to PTAs that has been aided by the unfortunate conversion of the United States to the thesis that any trade liberalization is as good as any other. Perhaps, as often happens in economic policy, what presently looks like a politically irreversible trend will yield to economic wisdom. We will see.

Appendix 2A1:   Varieties of PTAs within the World Trade Organization

There are three categories of PTAs within the World Trade Organization framework. First, under Article XXIV, countries can form Free Trade Areas or Customs Unions. Of the one hundred thirty-four arrangements notified to the GATT/WTO as of June 1, 1995, 108 fell under this category (see table 2A.1). Second, developing countries can form PTAs under the

Table 2A.1
134 Regional Trading Arrangements Notified to the GATT/WTO, 1949–1995

Official title	Usual reference	Date of entry into force	GATT cover
Interim Agreement for a Customs Union between the Union of South Africa and Southern Rhodesia	South Africa–South Rhodesia Customs Union	Apr. 1, 1949	Article XXIV
Free-Trade Treaty between the Republics of Nicaragua and El Salvador	El Salvador–Nicaragua Free Trade Area	Aug. 21, 1951	Article XXIV
Rome Treaty (European Economic Communities and European Atomic Energy Community)	EEC and EURATOM	Jan. 1, 1958	Article XXIV
Multilateral Central American Free Trade and Economic Integration Treaty (participation of Nicaragua)	Central American Free Trade Area	June 2, 1959	Article XXIV
Stockholm Convention (European Free Trade Association)	EFTA	May 3, 1960	Article XXIV
The Montevideo Treaty (Latin American Free Trade Area)	LAFTA	June 2, 1961	Article XXIV
Association of Finland with the European Free Trade Association	EFTA–Finland Association (FINEFTA)	June 26, 1961	Article XXIV
General Treaty for Central American Economic Integration (participation of Nicaragua)	Central American Common Market	Oct. 12, 1961	Article XXIV
The Borneo Free Trade Area	Borneo Free Trade Area	Jan. 1, 1962	Article XXIV
Trade Agreement between the Republic of Ghana and the Republic of Upper Volta	Ghana–Upper Volta Trade Agreement	May 9, 1962	Article XXIV
Regulation of Economic and Customs Relations between the Member States of the Equatorial Customs Union and the Federal Republic of Cameroon	Equatorial Customs Union—Cameroon Association	July 1, 1962	Article XXIV
Agreement setting up an association between the European Economic Community and Greece	EEC–Greece Association Agreement	Nov. 1, 1962	Article XXIV
African Common Market	African Common Market	June 1, 1963	Article XXIV
Convention of Association between the European Economic Community and the African and Malagasy States Associated with that community	Yaoundé I	Jan. 1, 1964	Article XXIV

Table 2A.1 (continued)

Official title	Usual reference	Date of entry into force	GATT cover
Agreement for Economic Unity among Arab League States	Arab Common Market	Apr. 30, 1964	Article XXIV
Association between the EEC and certain non-European Countries and Territories maintaining special relations with France and the Netherlands, "PTOM-I"	EEC–PTOM I	June 1, 1964	Article XXIV
Agreement creating an association between the European Economic Community and Turkey; "The Ankara Agreement"	EEC–Turkey Association Agreement of 1963	Dec. 1, 1964	Article XXIV
New Zealand/Australia Free Trade Agreement	Australia–New Zealand Free Trade Agreement	Jan. 1, 1966	Article XXIV
United Kingdom/Ireland Free Trade Area Agreement	Ireland–United Kingdom Free Trade Area	July 1, 1966	Article XXIV
Agreement Establishing the Caribbean Free Trade Association	CARIFTA	May 1, 1968	Article XXIV
Agreement establishing an association between the European Economic Community and the Kingdom of Morocco	EEC–Morocco Association Agreement of 1969	Sept. 1, 1969	Article XXIV
Agreement establishing an association between the European Economic Community and the Republic of Tunisia	EEC–Tunisia Association Agreement of 1969	Sept. 1, 1969	Article XXIV
European Free Trade Association; Accession of Iceland	EFTA/FINEFTA– Iceland Accession	Mar. 1, 1970	Article XXIV
Agreement between the European Economic Community and the State of Israel	EEC–Israel Agreement of 1970	Oct. 1, 1970	Article XXIV
Agreement between the European Economic Community and Spain	EEC–Spain Agreement of 1970	Oct. 1, 1970	Article XXIV
Agreement establishing an Association between the European Economic Community and the United Republic of Tanzania, the Republic of Uganda, and the Republic of Kenya	Arusha II Agreement	Jan. 1, 1971	Article XXIV
Association between the EEC and Certain Non-European Countries and Territories	EEC–PTOM II	Jan. 1, 1971	Article XXIV

Table 2A.1 (continued)

Official title	Usual reference	Date of entry into force	GATT cover
EEC; African and Malagasy states and overseas countries and territories agreements	Yaoundé II	Jan. 1, 1971	Article XXIV
Agreement Establishing an Association between Malta and the European Economic Community	EEC–Malta Association Agreement	Apr. 1, 1971	Article XXIV
Agreements between Austria and the European Communities	EC–Austria Agreements of 1972	Oct. 1, 1972	Article XXIV
Treaty concerning the accession of the Kingdom of Denmark, Ireland, the Kingdom of Norway, and the United Kingdom of Great Britain and Northern Ireland	EC–Accession of Denmark, Ireland and United Kingdom	Jan. 1, 1973	Article XXIV
Agreements between the European Communities and Portugal	EC–Portugal Agreements of 1972	Jan. 1, 1973	Article XXIV
Agreements between the European Communities and Sweden	EC–Sweden Agreements	Jan. 1, 1973	Article XXIV
Agreement between the European Economic Community and the Swiss Confederation	EC–Switzerland/ Liechtenstein Agreements	Jan. 1, 1973	Article XXIV
EEC; Turkey additional protocol to the Association Agreement	EEC–Turkey Additional Protocol to the Association Agreement	Jan. 1, 1973	Article XXIV
Agreement between the European Economic Community and the Republic of Iceland	EC–Iceland Agreements	Apr. 1, 1973	Article XXIV
Agreement between the European Economic Community and Cyprus	EEC–Cyprus Association Agreement	June 1, 1973	Article XXIV
Agreement between the European Economic Community and the Kingdom of Norway	EC–Norway Agreements	July 1, 1973	Article XXIV
Treaty establishing the Caribbean Community	CARICOM	Aug. 1, 1973	Article XXIV
Agreement between the European Economic Community and the Arab Republic of Egypt	EEC–Egypt Agreement of 1972	Nov. 1, 1973	Article XXIV

Table 2A.1 (continued)

Official title	Usual reference	Date of entry into force	GATT cover
Agreement between the European Economic Community and the Lebanese Republic	EEC–Lebanon Agreement of 1972	Nov. 1, 1973	Article XXIV
Agreements between the European Communities and Finland	EC–Finland Agreements	Jan. 1, 1974	Article XXIV
Supplementary protocol to the Association Agreement between the European Economic Community and Turkey consequent on the accession of new member states to the Community	EC–Turkey Association Agreement of 1973	Jan. 1, 1974	Article XXIV
Agreement between the Republic of Finland and the People's Republic of Bulgaria on the reciprocal removal of obstacles to trade	Bulgaria–Finland Agreement	Jan. 1, 1975	Article XXIV
Agreement between the Republic of Finland and the Czechoslovak Socialist Republic on the reciprocal removal of obstacles to trade	Finland–Czechoslovakia Agreement	Jan. 1, 1975	Article XXIV
Agreement between the Republic of Finland and the Hungarian People's Republic on the reciprocal removal of obstacles to trade	Finland–Hungary Agreement	Jan. 1, 1975	Article XXIV
Additional protocol to the agreement establishing an association between the European Economic Community and Greece consequent on the accession of new member states to the Community	EEC–Greece Additional Protocol	July 1, 1975	Article XXIV
Agreement between the European Economic Community and the State of Israel	EEC–Israel Agreement of 1975	July 1, 1975	Article XXIV
Agreement between the Republic of Finland and the German Democratic Republic on the removal of obstacles to trade on the basis of Reciprocity concerning advantages and obligations	Finland–German Democratic Republic Agreement	July 1, 1975	Article XXIV
ACP; EEC First Convention of Lomé	First Convention of Lomé	Apr. 1, 1976	Article XXIV
Interim agreement between the European Economic Community and the Peoples Democratic Republic of Algeria	EC–Algeria Agreements of 1976	July 1, 1976	Article XXIV

Table 2A.1 (continued)

Official title	Usual reference	Date of entry into force	GATT cover
Interim agreement between the European Economic Community and the Kingdom of Morocco	EC–Morocco Agreements	July 1, 1976	Article XXIV
Interim agreement between the European Economic Community and the Republic of Tunisia	EC–Tunisia Agreements of 1976	July 1, 1976	Article XXIV
Interim agreement between the European Economic Community and the Portuguese Republic	EEC–Portugal Interim Agreement	Nov. 1, 1976	Article XXIV
Australia–Papua New Guinea Trade and Commercial Relations Agreement (PATCRA)	Australia–Papua New Guinea Agreement (PATCRA)	Feb. 1, 1977	Article XXIV
Interim cooperation agreement between the European Communities and the Arab Republic of Egypt	EEC–Egypt Interim Agreement of 1977	July 1, 1977	Article XXIV
Agreement between the European Economic Community and Jordan	EEC–Jordan Interim Agreement of 1977	July 1, 1977	Article XXIV
Agreement between the European Economic Community and Lebanon	EEC–Lebanon Interim Agreement of 1977	July 1, 1977	Article XXIV
Agreement between the European Economic Community and Syria	EEC–Syria Interim Agreement of 1977	July 1, 1977	Article XXIV
Agreement between the Republic of Finland and the Polish People's Republic on the reciprocal removal of obstacles to trade	Finland–Poland Agreement	Apr. 1, 1978	Article XXIV
EFTA–Spain Agreement	EFTA–Spain Agreement	May 1, 1980	Article XXIV
Interim agreement between the European Economic Community and the Socialist Federal Republic of Yugoslavia on trade and trade cooperation	EEC–Yugoslavia Interim Agreement	July 1, 1980	Article XXIV
EEC–Greece Accession Agreement	EEC–Greece Accession Agreement	Jan. 1, 1981	Article XXIV
ACP; EEC Second Convention of Lomé	Second Convention of Lomé	Jan. 1, 1981	Article XXIV

Table 2A.1 (continued)

Official title	Usual reference	Date of entry into force	GATT cover
Australia–New Zealand Closer Economic Relations Trade Agreement (ANZCERTA)	Australia–New Zealand (ANZCERTA)	Jan. 1, 1983	Article XXIV
Agreement on the establishment of a free trade area between the Government of the United States of America and the Government of Israel	Israel–United States Free Trade Area Agreement	Aug. 19, 1985	Article XXIV
Accession of Portugal and Spain to the European Communities	EEC–Portugal and Spain Accessions	Jan. 1, 1986	Article XXIV
ACP; EEC Third Convention of Lomé	Third Convention of Lomé	Mar. 1, 1986	Article XXIV
Canada–United States Free Trade Agreement	Canada–U.S. Free Trade Agreement	Jan. 1, 1989	Article XXIV
Agreement between the European Community, of the one part, and the Government of Denmark and the Home Government of the Faroe Islands, of the other part	EC–Denmark and Faroe Islands Agreement	Jan. 1, 1992	Article XXIV
Interim agreement on trade and trade-related matters between the European Economic Community and the ECSC, of the one part, and the Czech and Slovak Federal Republic (CSFR), of the other part	EC–Czech and Slovak Federal Republic Interim Agreement of 1991	Mar. 1, 1992	Article XXIV
Interim agreement on trade and trade-related matters between the European Economic Community and the European Coal and Steel Community, of the one part, and Hungary, of the other part	EC–Hungary Interim Agreement of 1991	Mar. 1, 1992	Article XXIV
Interim agreement on trade and trade-related matters between the European Economic Community and the European Coal and Steel Community, of the one part, and Poland, of the other part	EC–Poland Interim Agreement of 1991	Mar. 1, 1992	Article XXIV
Agreement between the EFTA states and Turkey	EFTA–Turkey Agreement	Apr. 1, 1992	Article XXIV
Free trade agreement between the Kingdom of Norway and the Republic of Estonia	Estonia–Norway Free Trade Agreement	June 15, 1992	Article XXIV

Table 2A.1 (continued)

Official title	Usual reference	Date of entry into force	GATT cover
Free trade agreement between the Kingdom of Norway and the Republic of Latvia	Latvia–Norway Free Trade Agreement	June 16, 1992	Article XXIV
Free trade agreement between the Kingdom of Norway and the Republic of Lithuania	Lithuania–Norway Free Trade Agreement	June 16, 1992	Article XXIV
Agreement between the EFTA states and the Czech and Slovak Federal Republic	Czech and Slovak Federal Republic–EFTA Agreement	July 1, 1992	Article XXIV
Free trade agreement between the Kingdom of Sweden and the Republic of Estonia	Estonia–Sweden Free Trade Agreement	July 1, 1992	Article XXIV
Free trade agreement between the Kingdom of Sweden and the Republic of Latvia	Latvia–Sweden Free Trade Agreement	July 1, 1992	Article XXIV
Free trade agreement between the Kingdom of Sweden and the Republic of Lithuania	Lithuania–Sweden Free Trade Agreement	July 1, 1992	Article XXIV
Estonia–Finland protocol regarding temporary arrangements on trade and economic cooperation	Estonia–Finland Agreement	Dec. 1, 1992	Article XXIV
Czech Republic and Slovak Republic Customs Union	Czech Republic and Slovak Republic Customs Union	Jan. 1, 1993	Article XXIV
EFTA–Israel Free Trade Agreement	EFTA–Israel Free Trade Agreement	Jan. 1, 1993	Article XXIV
Central European Free Trade Agreement concluded by the Czech Republic, the Republic of Hungary, the Republic of Poland and the Slovak Republic	CEFTA	Mar. 1, 1993	Article XXIV
Free Trade Agreement between the Swiss Confederation and the Republic of Estonia	Estonia–Switzerland Free Trade Agreement	Apr. 1, 1993	Article XXIV
Free Trade Agreement between the Swiss Confederation and the Republic of Latvia	Latvia–Switzerland Free Trade Agreement	Apr. 1, 1993	Article XXIV
Free Trade Agreement between the Swiss Confederation and the Republic of Lithuania	Lithuania–Switzerland Free Trade Agreement	Apr. 1, 1993	Article XXIV

Table 2A.1 (continued)

Official title	Usual reference	Date of entry into force	GATT cover
Interim agreement on trade and trade-related matters between the European Economic Community and the European Coal and Steel Community, of the one part, and Romania, of the other part	EEC–Romania Interim Agreement	May 1, 1993	Article XXIV
Agreement between the EFTA states and Romania	EFTA–Romania Agreement	May 1, 1993	Article XXIV
EFTA–Bulgaria Free Trade Agreement	EFTA–Bulgaria Free Trade Agreement	July 1, 1993	Article XXIV
Finland–Latvia protocol regarding temporary arrangements on trade and economic cooperation	Finland–Latvia Protocol	July 1, 1993	Article XXIV
Finland–Lithuania Protocol regarding Temporary arrangements on trade and economic cooperation	Finland–Lithuania Protocol	July 1, 1993	Article XXIV
Cooperation agreement between the European Economic Community and the Republic of Slovenia	EEC–Slovenia Cooperation Agreement	July 19, 1993	Article XXIV
Agreement between the EFTA states and the Republic of Hungary	EFTA–Hungary Agreement	Oct. 1, 1993	Article XXIV
Agreement between the EFTA states and the Republic of Poland	EFTA–Poland Agreement	Nov. 15, 1993	Article XXIV
Interim agreement on trade and trade-related matters between the European Economic Community and the ECSC, of the one part, and the Republic of Bulgaria, of the other part	EEC–Bulgaria Interim Agreement	Dec. 31, 1993	Article XXIV
Free trade agreement between the Czech Republic and the Republic of Slovenia	Czech Republic– Slovenia Free Trade Agreement	Jan. 1, 1994	Article XXIV
North American Free Trade Agreement	NAFTA	Jan. 1, 1994	Article XXIV
Free trade agreement between the Slovak Republic and the Republic of Slovenia	Slovak Republic– Slovenia Free Trade Agreement	Jan. 1, 1994	Article XXIV
Austria, Finland, Sweden–EU accession agreement	Austria, Finland, Sweden–EU Accession Agreement	Jan. 1, 1995	Article XXIV

Table 2A.1 (continued)

Official title	Usual reference	Date of entry into force	GATT cover
Czech Republic–Romania Free Trade Agreement	Czech Republic–Romania Free Trade Agreement	Jan. 1, 1995	Article XXIV
Agreement on free trade and trade-related matters between the European Community, the European Atomic Energy Community and the ECSC, of the one part, and the Republic of Estonia, of the other part	EC–Estonia Agreement	Jan. 1, 1995	Article XXIV
Agreement on free trade and trade-related matters between the European Community, the European Atomic Energy Community and the ECSC, of the one part, and the Republic of Latvia, of the other part	EC–Latvia Agreement	Jan. 1, 1995	Article XXIV
Agreement on free trade and trade-related matters between the European Community, the European Atomic Energy Community and the ECSC, of the one part, and the Republic of Lithuania, of the other part	EC–Lithuania Agreement	Jan. 1, 1995	Article XXIV
Free trade agreement between the Republic of Hungary and the Republic of Slovenia	Hungary–Slovenia Free Trade Agreement	Jan. 1, 1995	Article XXIV
Slovak Republic–Romania Free Trade Agreement	Slovak Republic–Romania Free Trade Agreement	Jan. 1, 1995	Article XXIV
EFTA–Slovenia Free Trade Agreement	EFTA–Slovenia Free Trade Agreement	June 1, 1995	Article XXIV
The Unified Economic Agreement among the countries of the Gulf Cooperation Council	Gulf Cooperation Council		Enabling Clause
Additional protocol on preferential tariffs among members of the organization for economic cooperation (ECO)	Preferential Tariffs among ECO-members		Enabling Clause
South Asian Association for Regional Cooperation; Preferential Trade Arrangement (SAPTA)	SAPTA		Enabling Clause

Table 2A.1 (continued)

Official title	Usual reference	Date of entry into force	GATT cover
Protocol relating to trade negotiations among developing countries	Protocol relating to Trade Negotiations among Developing Countries	Feb. 11, 1973	Enabling Clause
First agreement on trade negotiations among developing member countries of the Economic and Social Commission for Asia and the Pacific	Bangkok Agreement	June 17, 1976	Enabling Clause
Association of South-East Asian Nations ASEAN declaration	ASEAN Preferential Trading Arrangements	Aug. 31, 1977	Enabling Clause
South Pacific Regional Trade and Economic Cooperation Agreement	SPARTECA	Jan. 1, 1981	Enabling Clause
Second Treaty of Montevideo	Latin American Integration Association, "LAIA"	Mar. 18, 1981	Enabling Clause
Cartagena Agreement	Andean Group	May 25, 1988	Enabling Clause
Global System of Trade Preferences among developing countries (GSTP)	GSTP	Apr. 19, 1989	Enabling Clause
Trade agreement between the government of the Kingdom of Thailand and the government of the Lao People's Democratic Republic	Lao–Thailand Trade Agreement	June 20, 1991	Enabling Clause
Treaty of Asunción, Treaty Establishing a Common Market between the Argentine Republic, the Federal Republic of Brazil, the Republic of Paraguay, and the Eastern Republic of Uruguay	MERCOSUR	Nov. 29, 1991	Enabling Clause
Common effective preferential tariff scheme for the ASEAN Free Trade Area	Preferential Tariff Scheme for the ASEAN Free Trade Area	Jan. 28, 1992	Enabling Clause
Common Market for Eastern and Southern Africa	COMESA	Dec. 8, 1994	Enabling Clause
Bolivia-Mexico Free Trade Treaty	Bolivia-Mexico Free Trade Treaty	Jan. 1, 1995	Enabling Clause
Mexico-Costa Rica Free Trade Area	Mexico–Costa Rica Free Trade Area	Jan. 1, 1995	Enabling Clause

Table 2A.1 (continued)

Official title	Usual reference	Date of entry into force	GATT cover
Colombia, Mexico, and Venezuela Free Trade Agreement	Treaty of the Group of Three (G3)	Jan. 1, 1995	Enabling Clause
Australian treatment of products of Papua New Guinea	Australian Treatment of Products of Papua New Guinea		Waiver–Art. I : 1
French trading arrangements with Morocco	France–Morocco Trading Arrangements		Waiver–Art. I : 1
	Australia–Federation of Rhodesia and Nyasaland Agreement	July 1, 1955	Waiver–Art. I : 1
United States Caribbean Basin Economic Recovery Act	U.S.–Caribbean CBERA	Jan. 1, 1984	Waiver–Art. I : 1
Canadian tariff treatment for commonwealth Caribbean countries	CARIBCAN	May 12, 1986	Waiver–Art. I : 1
ACP—EEC Fourth Convention of Lomé	Fourth Convention of Lomé	Sept. 1, 1991	Waiver–Art. I : 1
Andean Trade Preference Act	U.S.–Andean Trade Preference Act	Dec. 4, 1991	Waiver–Art. I : 1
Trade agreement between the governments of the Federation of Rhodesia and Nyasaland and the Union of South Africa	Federation of Rhodesia/ Nyasaland–South Africa Agreement of 1955	July 1, 1955	Waiver–Art. I : 2
	Federation of Rhodesia/ Nyasaland–South Africa Agreement of 1960	July 1, 1960	Waiver–Art. I : 2

Enabling Clause. Here a full FTA or CU as defined in Article XXIV is not required, and partial preferences are allowed. Seventeen arrangements fall under this category. Finally, within the Generalized System of Preferences (GSP), a waiver from the MFN Article I may be given for preferences granted by developed countries to developing countries. Nine agreements fall under this category.

Notes

We thank Jeffrey Frankel, Philip Levy, T. N. Srinivasan, Robert Staiger, and participants in the CIE-AEI Conference in June 1995, as well as Pravin Krishna, for many helpful conversations and comments on an earlier draft. We have also benefited from suggestions made at seminars at Harvard and Osaka universities, the University of Maryland, and the Stockholm School of Economics. Special appreciation is expressed to Maria Pillinini of the Development Division of the World Trade Organization for providing the list of PTAs at the end of this chapter in appendix table 1A-1.

1. The focus of our chapter will be on Article XXIV-sanctioned PTAs, rather than on every kind of preferential arrangement among any subset of World Trade Organization (WTO) members. PTAs, often grouped together into a single category, actually fall into three different WTO categories: Article XXIV arrangements involving FTAs and CUs, Enabling Clause arrangements limited to developing countries and permitting partial preferences, and Generalized System of Preferences (GSP) arrangements permitted via a grant of an exception to Article I. Appendix table 1A-1 provides a complete list of PTAs reported to WTO to date according to the WTO category within which they fall.

2. The reasons why these did not succeed are discussed in Bhagwati (1991).

3. These different approaches, and the later approaches to the static theory of preferential trading areas by Kemp and Wan (1976) and Brecher and Bhagwati (1981), have been distinguished and discussed in the graduate textbook by Bhagwati and Srinivasan (1983). The Cooper-Massell-Johnson-Bhagwati argument has also been formalized recently, using the Kemp-Wan approach and combining it with the theory of noneconomic objectives, by Krishna and Bhagwati (1994).

4. Our analytical synthesis draws on Bhagwati, Krishna, and Panagariya (1996) and also on our paper for the 1996 American Economic Association meetings in San Francisco, Bhagwati and Panagariya (1996).

5. In Viner's analysis, reproduced in figure 2.1, with constant costs everywhere, the concepts translate immediately into a shift of imports from the outside to the partner country as trade diversion and a shift from the home country production to imports from the partner country as trade creation. This translation does not hold fully in figure 2.3, for example.

6. In a generous introductory footnote to his article entitled "Emerging Regional Arrangements: Building Blocks or Stumbling Blocks?" Lawrence (1991) writes, "I owe this phrase to Jagdish Bhagwati." Bhagwati (1991, 77) refers to the expansion of membership as a test of PTAs serving as "building blocks" for worldwide freeing of trade: this concept is illustrated in figure 2.9, reproduced from Bhagwati (1993a). Evidently, if going down the PTA path can trigger multilateral negotiations and their successful conclusion, that too can be a way in which PTAs may serve as building blocks, as discussed here.

7. The "natural trading partners" hypothesis comes therefore in two forms. In the first form, the emphasis is on a large initial volume of trade that may result, inter alia, from geographical proximity. In the second form, the emphasis is on transport costs that are assumed to be low between countries within the same region. We have been firmly informed by Paul Wonnacott that the term "natural trading partner" originated in Wonnacott and Lutz (1989). Many authors have attributed the term instead to Krugman (1991a), who, along with Summers, should nevertheless be credited with popularizing it.

8. We assume a specific rather than an ad valorem tariff for geometric simplicity when supply curves are rising. Nothing in the analysis hangs on it.

9. Because imports expand, some of the inefficient domestic production is replaced by imports from B. A also gains from an increase in the consumers' surplus in excess of the tariff revenue.

10. B gains nothing and C loses nothing, given the constant-cost assumptions on their supply curves in trade.

11. The measure used is the conventional Hicksian equivalent variation: keeping the initial nondiscriminatory tariff, how much income can A withdraw to yield the same welfare loss as the FTA imposes?

12. Many of the points in this and the following section have been made earlier in Panagariya (1995a, 1995b). The tariff-revenue-transfer effect central to our analysis is normally present in all models characterized by flexible terms of trade. Thus, see the three-good, three-country general-equilibrium analyses of Berglas (1979) and Riezman (1979), which are neatly summarized within a unified framework by Lloyd (1982). Both Berglas and Riezman find, as we do, that when intra-union terms of trade are flexible, a large volume of imports from the partner country is inversely related to the welfare effect of a preferential liberalization. Neither of these authors makes many of the points we make or looks at the problem as we do, however.

13. There is no trade creation in the example as the FTA leaves the domestic price and therefore total imports into A unchanged.

14. We discuss the natural trading partners hypothesis in the alternative context of transport costs later in the chapter.

15. In a similar vein, Krugman (1991a, 21) notes, "To reemphasize why this matters: if a disproportionate share of world trade would take place within trading blocs even in the absence of any preferential trading arrangement, then the gains from trade creation within blocs are likely to outweigh any possible losses from external trade diversion."

16. Ceteris paribus, the less A trades with the outside country, the less tariff revenue it collects and the less is its gain. Thus, in the spirit of our previous discussion, a high proportion of trade with the partner implies smaller gains from preferential liberalization.

17. In addition, a fraction of the large imports from the United States could well be a result of preferential policies rather than competitiveness.

18. It is a common practice in the computable general-equilibrium (CGE) models to differentiate goods by the country of origin and yet impose the small-country assumption. To a general equilibrium theorist, this is not correct. If a country is the sole producer of its exports, it necessarily has market power.

19. Rules of origin can and do, of course, restrict trade in other ways. For a recent analysis of how rules of origin can lead to welfare-worsening outcomes, see Krueger (1993, 1995).

20. See Grossman and Helpman (1995) in this context.

21. Note that the horizontal difference between $E_B E_B$ and $S_B S_B$ declines as price rises. This is because the demand in B must fall with a rise in the price.

22. This simple point seems to have escaped a number of CGE-modelers of NAFTA who distinguish products by the country of origin and continue to impose the small-country assumption.

23. The same would also hold true if we were to use a monopolistic-competition or oligopoly model.

24. In a small, open economy with tariffs as the only distortion, the change in welfare (real income) from an infinitesimally small change in any set of tariffs equals the change in tariff revenue evaluated at initial tariff rates (Eaton and Panagariya 1979). For an infinitesimally small change in the tariff on B, the vertically shaded area in figure 2.5 is the increase and the horizontally shaded area the decrease in tariff revenue measured at the original tariff rates.

25. Observe that the world price of each product is unity. Therefore, the base of the rectangle represents both the quantity and value of imports at world prices.

26. To make this point another way, start with a zero tariff on good b and a positive tariff on c. The introduction of a small tariff on b will not lead to an efficiency loss in the b market but will generate an efficiency cost in the c market.

27. The effects shown in figure 2.5 do not arise in the partial equilibrium model of figures 2.2 and 2.3. Because these effects require the presence of at least two importables, they do not arise even in a two-good general equilibrium model.

28. Recall that in figures 2.1 and 2.2, the *internal* terms of trade are variable. Country A's terms of trade with respect to country B deteriorate by the full amount of the tariff reduction. But because of the small-union assumption, the external terms of trade do not change there.

29. One hundred percent revenue seeking means that the entire revenue is available for those who wish to seek it. Perfectly competitive revenue seeking leads to a dollar's worth of resource loss for a dollar of revenue sought. The two assumptions together imply that the resources used up in revenue seeking equal the tariff revenues in equilibrium. For rent seeking, see Krueger (1974) and for revenue seeking, see Bhagwati and Srinivasan (1980).

30. A detailed, general equilibrium analysis of this issue is provided in Panagariya (1996a, 1996b).

31. We assumed earlier that each country is the sole producer of its export good. This assumption necessarily makes the terms of trade variable. In the conventional analysis, as also in the present discussion, the outside country is assumed to produce all goods and is large. The terms of trade are then determined in the outside country, and the only effects that arise are those depicted in figure 2.5. In arriving at the conclusions discussed in this paragraph, Lipsey also assumed that preferences are Cobb-Douglas. For further details, see Panagariya (1996a, 1996b).

32. As quoted in footnote 12 of Bhagwati (1993a), according to Lipsey, "the larger are purchases of domestic commodities and the smaller are purchases from the outside world, the more likely is it that the union will bring gain." If the liberalizing country's preferences are of the CES variety, the compensated crossprice elasticity of its demand for the partner's good with respect to the price of its own good reduces to the product of the expenditure share of its own good and the elasticity of substitution. A similar statement applies to the compensated crossprice elasticity of the country's demand for the partner's good with respect to the

price of the outside country's good. Thus, under CES preferences, our condition in the text reduces to Lipsey's. As noted in the previous footnote, Lipsey himself had relied on Cobb-Douglas preferences to derive the conclusion quoted at the beginning of this footnote.

33. This would not be generally true even if we were to take the measure just for one individual country with every other country instead of pooling all possible pairs together.

34. Thus, intra-African exports were only 12.8 percent of total African exports in 1990.

35. There are countless other examples. Bhagwati (1993a) cites India-Pakistan versus India-United Kingdom and India-USSR as an example.

36. Although Frankel and Wei find that a common border increases trade volumes, Dhar and Panagariya (1994), who estimate the gravity equation on a country-by-country basis for twenty-two countries, find the common-border effect to be negative in six cases. This conflict of results underlies the serious reservations we have about the use of these gravity models to infer "trade diversion," and so on: the coefficients vary considerably depending on the dataset, and sometimes the signs do as well.

37. We note, however, that the recent critique of gravity models by Jacques J. Polak (1996) casts serious doubt on even this conclusion. Polak estimates a gravity equation for total imports as a function of income, population, and a location index measuring how favorably a country is located for purposes of international trade. He finds that, for 1960 trade data, the location index yields a statistically significant effect, as in Frankel-Wei regressions. But for the 1990 sample used by Frankel and Wei, the effect is statistically insignificant.

38. Of course, even if the relationship was "natural," it does not justify preferences as argued already by us.

39. Bhagwati, in several writings, for example, Bhagwati and Dehejia (1994) and Bhagwati (1996a), has argued that comparative advantage has become "kaleidoscopic," that is, thin and volatile, as technical know-how has converged, multinationals have become global, interest rates have become closer across nations, and access to different capital markets has become more open. More and more industries are thus footloose.

40. In this paragraph, we abstract from the demand effects. The inclusion of demand effects will modify the discussion but not the fundamental point.

41. And if costs indeed fall below those of Taiwan, there is no extra gain from the PTA since in that case Canada would have replaced Taiwan as the supplier even under a nondiscriminatory tariff.

42. This makes the analysis complicated because the countries now wield market power, and unilateral free trade is no longer optimal.

43. The point can also be made under "iceberg" type transport costs that are frequently employed in international trade literature. In this formulation, a constant fraction of the good melts away in transit.

44. If the initial tariff is above the optimum tariff, given the elasticity assumption, a small preferential reduction in the tariff on B is welfare improving. For a complete removal of the tariff on B to be welfare improving, the initial tariff must be substantially higher than the optimum tariff.

45. De Melo, Panagariya, and Rodrik (1993) note a similar possibility when the country faces a revenue constraint.

46. We discuss these noneconomic factors later in the chapter. Our analysis, which has focused mainly on the effects on the member countries, has not addressed adequately the issue of the effects on nonmembers. However, there is a revival of interest in that issue as well. See, in particular, Srinivasan (1995) and Winters (1995a, 1995b).

47. The common-water definition, of course, excludes land-locked countries such as Nepal and countries with shores only on land-locked seas such as the Caspian. These, however, add up to only a small fraction of world trade. See Bhagwati (1996b) for more on common-waters FTAs.

48. Also see Frankel, Stein, and Wei (1995a, 1995b). Interestingly, Haberler (1943) appears to have been the first to use the term *continental blocs*.

49. As matters stand currently, however, APEC and TAFTA are extremely unlikely to become Article XXIV-sanctioned PTAs, despite the U.S. obsession with PTAs, whereas the extension of NAFTA to the South looks like a long-term process.

50. Similarly, the MTN path may facilitate or obstruct the expansion of PTA membership, so that the interaction between the two paths may be mutual.

51. Christopher Bliss (1994) has tried to give the argument some structure. More recently, T. N. Srinivasan (1995) has done so in the context of examining the question of the impact of PTAs on nonmember welfare.

52. See Deardorff and Stern (1994).

53. Bhagwati (1993a, 40—44) also discussed skeptically the claims that PTA formation is quicker, more efficient, and more certain than MTN.

54. For an early analysis of the political factors underlying the formation of PTAs, see the work by the political scientist Edward Mansfield (1992) cited and discussed in Bhagwati (1993a). Other political scientists, such as Miles Kahler and Joseph Grieco, have written in this area recently

55. In comparing incentives for export-oriented firms, for lobbying for a PTA (for example, NAFTA) as against MTN (for example, the Uruguay Round), a dollar's worth of lobbying would go a longer way in the former case because any preferential opening of the Mexican market would be better for the U.S. exporter than such an opening on an MFN basis that yields the benefits equally to U.S. rivals in Japan, the EU, and elsewhere. This argument applies only to the extent that the MTN process simultaneously does not open other markets to the U.S. exporter on a reciprocal basis.

56. Bhagwati (1993a) cites Irwin's (1993) study of trade liberalization in the nineteenth century, which shows that the Anglo-French Treaty may well have served this purpose. Richard Baldwin's (1993) subsequent formalization of this basic idea in what he calls the "domino" theory of PTA expansion is discussed below.

57. In this review, we do not include the important contributions to the political economy-theoretic analysis of PTAs that do not directly address either of the two dynamic time-path questions at issue in the text. For example, Grossman and Helpman (1995) have modeled the formation of PTAs, demonstrating the critical role played by the possibility of trade diversion in the outcome, a conclusion also arrived at independently by Pravin Krishna (1993) in a different model. Similarly, Panagariya and Findlay (1996) have formalized the endogeneity argument that reduced protection between members in a PTA can lead to increased protection against nonmembers. Using a political process consisting of lobbying by owners of specific factors, they also investigate the external tariffs that emerge under an FTA and a CU.

For answers to a similar set of questions, but under the assumption of a welfare-maximizing government, see our discussion of Bagwell and Staiger (1993).

58. As noted in Bhagwati (1993a, 1994), this is exactly what the United States achieved, in terms of intellectual property protection and even concessions on environmental and labor standards enforcement, by getting then president Carlos Salinas into a one-on-one bargaining situation in NAFTA. And now Chile is poised to accept these obligations as the price of getting into NAFTA. On the other hand, as the virtually unanimous developing country objections to labor standards demands at the WTO show, neither Mexico nor Chile would have agreed to these demands in the purely WTO context.

59. This was stated to be the case for Washington, D.C., by a well-placed trade economist in the Clinton administration, at a recent conference on the subject of PTAs. The first author, at a Stockholm conference on WTO issues in 1996, organized by the Swedish trade minister, Mats Hellström, found a similar unawareness among some of the trade ministers and bureaucrats present, even as the response of the attending economists to his critical remarks about the current obsession with PTAs was enthusiastic.

60. And then there are also those who think that the APEC, turned into a PTA that excludes the extension of trade barrier reductions to Europe, will prompt Europe to its own tariff cuts in a benign outcome. This viewpoint, ascribed in the media to C. F. Bergsten, is premised on his view that the Seattle APEC summit pushed the Europeans into settling the Uruguay Round. The latter view is unpersuasive since, in the end, it was the U.S. administration that decided to accept the advice of many to close the Round with whatever it could get and to proceed to build on that in future negotiations. For a critique of similar, special pleading to justify NAFTA, see Bhagwati (1995, 11–12).

61. For a detailed statement of this critique, see Bhagwati (1995).

62. Unfortunately, this comment also applies to many of the numerical models, including the computable general-equilibrium models, estimating the gains from PTAs, as discussed by Panagariya in a forthcoming essay. And then there are the more elementary conceptual errors that afflict the numerical estimates of gains in *employment* from NAFTA. These errors were widely repeated by the media at the time.

References

Bagwell, Kyle, and Robert Staiger. "Multilateral Cooperation During the Formation of Free Trade Areas." NBER Working Paper no. 4364, 1993.

Baldwin, Richard. "A Domino Theory of Regionalism." CEPR Working Paper no. 857, November 1993.

Berglas, Eitan. "Preferential Trading: The n Commodity Case." *Journal of Political Economy*, vol. 87, 1979, pp. 315–31.

Bhagwati, Jagdish. "Trade Liberalization Among LDCs, Trade Theory and GATT Rules." In J. N. Wolf, ed., *Value, Capital, and Growth: Papers in Honour of J. R. Hicks*. Oxford: Oxford University Press, 1968.

———. "The Theory of Political Economy, Economic Policy, and Foreign Investment." In M. Scott and D. Lal, eds., *Public Policy and Economic Development*, Essays in Honor of I.M.D. Little, pp. 217–30. Oxford: Clarendon Press, 1990.

————. *The World Trading System at Risk*. Princeton, N.J.: Princeton University and Harvester Wheatsheaf, 1991.

————. "Regionalism and Multilateralism: An Overview." In Jaime de Melo and Arvind Panagariya, eds., *New Dimensions in Regional Integration*. Cambridge: Cambridge University Press, 1993a.

————. "Beyond NAFTA: Clinton's Trading Choices." *Foreign Policy*, Summer 1993b, pp. 155–62.

————. "Threats to the World Trading System: Income Distribution and the Selfish Hegemon." *Journal of International Affairs*, vol. 48, Spring 1994, pp. 279–85.

————. "U.S. Trade Policy: The Infatuation with Free Trade Areas." In Jagdish Bhagwati and Anne O. Krueger, *The Dangerous Drift to Preferential Trade Agreements*. Washington, D.C.: AEI Press, 1995.

————. "Trade and Wages: A Malign Relationship?" In Susan Collins, ed., *The American Worker: Exports, Imports and Jobs*. Washington, D.C.: Brookings Institution, forthcoming (1996a).

————. "Watering of Trade." *Journal of International Economics*, forthcoming (1996b).

Bhagwati, Jagdish, and Vivek Dehejia. "Trade and Wages: Is Marx Striking Again?" In Jagdish Bhagwati and M. Kosters, eds., *Trade and Wages: Leveling Wages Down?* Washington, D.C.: AEI Press, 1994.

Bhagwati, Jagdish, Pravin Krishna, and Arvind Panagariya. "Introduction." In Jagdish Bhagwati and Pravin Krishna, eds., *Contributions to the Theory of Preferential Trading Areas*. Cambridge, Mass.: MIT Press, forthcoming.

Bhagwati, Jagdish, and Arvind Panagariya. "The Theory of Preferential Trade Agreements: Historical Evolution and Current Trends." *American Economic Review*, vol. 86, pp. 82–87.

Bhagwati, Jagdish, and T. N. Srinivasan. "Revenue Seeking: A Generalization of the Theory of Tariffs." *Journal of Political Economy*, vol. 88, December 1980, pp. 1069–87.

————. *Lectures in Trade Theory*. Cambridge, Mass.: MIT Press, 1983. Bliss, Christopher. *Economic Theory and Policy for Trading Blocs*. Manchester and New York: Manchester University Press, 1994.

Brecher, Richard, and Jagdish Bhagwati. "Foreign Ownership and the Theory of Trade and Welfare." *Journal of Political Economy*, vol. 89, June 1981, pp. 497–511.

Cooper, C. A., and B. F. Massell. "A New Look at Customs Union Theory." *Economic Journal*, vol. 75, 1965a, pp. 742–47.

————. "Towards a General Theory of Customs Unions for Developing Countries." *Journal of Political Economy*, vol. 73, 1965b, pp. 461–76.

Deardorff, Alan V., and Robert M. Stern. "Multilateral Trade Negotiations and Preferential Trading Arrangements." In Alan V. Deardorff and Robert M. Stern, eds., *Analytical and Negotiating Issues in the Global Trading System*. Ann Arbor: University of Michigan Press, 1994.

de Melo, Jaime, and Arvind Panagariya, ed. *New Dimensions in Regional Integration*. Cambridge, Great Britain: Cambridge University Press, 1993.

de Melo, Jaime, Arvind Panagariya, and Dani Rodrik. "The New Regionalism: A Country Perspective." In Jaime de Melo and Arvind Panagariya, eds., *New Dimensions in Regional Integration*, chap. 6. Cambridge, Great Britain: Cambridge University Press, 1993.

Dhar, Sumana, and Arvind Panagariya. "Is East Asia Less Open than North America and the European Economic Community? No." Policy Research Working Paper no. 1370. Washington, D.C.: World Bank, 1994.

Eaton, Jonathan, and Arvind Panagariya. "Gains from Trade under Variable Returns to Scale, Commodity Taxation, Tariffs and Factor Market Distortions." *Journal of International Economics*, vol. 9, 1979, pp. 481–501.

Findlay, Ronald, and Stanislaw Wellisz. "Endogenous Tariffs, the Political Economy of Trade Restrictions and Welfare." In Jagdish Bhagwati, ed., *Import Competition and Response*. Chicago and London: University of Chicago Press, 1982.

Frankel, Jeffrey, and Sheng-Jin Wei. "The New Regionalism and Asia: Impact and Options." Paper presented at the Asian Development Bank Conference on Emerging Global Trading Environment and Developing Asia, May 29–30, 1995.

Frankel, Jeffrey, E. Stein, and Shing-Jin Wei. "Trading Blocs and the Americas: The Natural, the Unnatural and the Supernatural." *Journal of Development Economics*, vol. 47, June 1995a, pp. 61–96.

―――. "Continental Trading Blocs: Are They Natural or Super-Natural?" NBER Working Paper no. 4588, 1995b.

Grossman, Gene, and Elhanan Helpman. "The Politics of Free Trade Agreements." *American Economic Review*, September 1995, pp. 667–90.

Haberler, Gottfried. "The Political Economy of Regional or Continental Blocs." In Seymour. E. Harris, ed., *Postwar Economic Problems*. New York. 1943.

Irwin, Douglas. "Multilateral and Bilateral Trade Policies in the World Trading System: An Historical Perspective." In Jaime de Melo and Arvind Panagariya, eds., *New Dimensions in Regional Integration*. Cambridge, Great Britain: Cambridge University Press, 1993.

Johnson, Harry. *Money, Trade and Economic Growth*. Cambridge, Mass.: Harvard University Press, 1962.

―――. "An Economic Theory of Protectionism, Tariff Bargaining, and the Formation of Customs Unions." *Journal of Political Economy*, vol. 73, June 1965, pp. 256–83.

Kemp, Murray C., and Henry Wan. "An Elementary Proposition Concerning the Formation of Customs Unions." *Journal of International Economics*, vol. 6, February 1976, pp. 95–98.

Krishna, Pravin. "Regionalism and Multilateralism: A Political Economy Approach." Economics Department, Columbia University, mimeo, December 1993. Presented to the NBER Universities Research Conference on International Trade and Regulations, Cambridge, Mass., 1993.

Krishna, Pravin, and Jagdish Bhagwati. "Necessarily Welfare-Enhancing Customs Unions with Industrialization Constraints: A Proof of the Cooper-Massell-Johnson-Bhagwati Conjecture." Columbia University Working Papers, April 1994.

Krueger, Anne O. "The Political-Economy of the Rent Seeking Society." *American Economic Review*, vol. 69, 1974, pp. 291–303.

————. "Rules of Origin as Protectionist Devices." NBER Working Paper no. 4352. April 1993. [Forthcoming] in J. Melvin, J. Moore, and R. Riezman, eds. *International Trade Theory: Essays in Honour of John Chipman*. United Kingdom: Routledge, 1996.

————. "Free Trade Agreements versus Customs Unions." NBER Working Paper no. 5084, April 1995.

Krugman, Paul. "The Move to Free Trade Zones." In Symposium sponsored by the Federal Reserve Bank of Kansas City, *Policy Implications of Trade and Currency Zones*, 1991a.

————. "Is Bilateralism Bad?" In E. Helpman and A. Razin, eds., *International Trade and Trade Policy*. Cambridge, Mass.: MIT Press, 1991b.

————. "Regionalism versus Multilateralism: Analytical Notes." In Jaime de Melo and Arvind Panagariya, eds., *New Dimensions in Regional Integration*. Cambridge, Great Britain: Cambridge University Press, 1993.

Lawrence, Robert Z. "Emerging Regional Arrangements: Building Blocks or Stumbling Blocks?" In Richard O'Brien, ed., *Finance and the International Economy*, Amex Bank Prize Essays. Oxford: Oxford University Press for the Amex Bank Review, 1991.

Levy, Philip. "A Political Economic Analysis of Free Trade Agreements." *American Economic Review*, forthcoming.

Lipsey, Richard. "The Theory of Customs Unions: Trade Diversion and Welfare." *Economica*, vol. 24, 1957, pp. 40–46.

————. *The Theory of Customs Unions: A General Equilibrium Analysis*. University of London, Ph.D. Thesis, 1958.

————. "The Theory of Customs Unions: A General Survey." *Economic Journal*, vol. 70, 1960, pp. 498–513.

Lloyd, Peter J. "3 × 3 Theory of Customs Unions." *Journal of International Economics*, vol. 12, 1982, pp. 41–63.

Ludema, Rodney. "On the Value of Preferential Trade Agreements in Multilateral Negotiations." Mimeo. 1993.

Mansfield, Edward. "The Concentration of Capabilities and International Trade." *International Organization*.

Mayer, Wolfgang. "Endogenous Tariff Formation." *American Economic Review*, vol. 74, December 1984, pp. 970–85.

Meade, James E. *The Theory of Customs Unions*. Amsterdam: North-Holland, 1955.

Mundell, Robert A. "Tariff Preferences and the Terms of Trade." *Manchester School of Economic and Social Studies*, vol. 32, 1964, pp. 1–13.

Panagariya, Arvind. "Should East Asia Go Regional? No, No and Maybe." WPS 1209. Washington, D.C.: World Bank, 1993.

————. "East Asia and the New Regionalism." *World Economy*, vol. 17, November 1994, pp. 817–39.

————. "Rethinking the New Regionalism." Paper presented at the Trade Expansion Program Conference of the United Nations Development Programme and World Bank, January 1995a.

————. "The Free Trade Area of the Americas: Good for Latin America?" Working Paper no. 12, *World Economy*, forthcoming. Center for International Economics, University of Maryland, 1995b.

————. "Preferential Trading and the Myth of Natural Trading Partners." Working Paper no. 200, Center for Japan-U.S. Business and Economic Studies, Stern School of Business, New York University, New York, 1996a.

————. "The Meade Model of Preferential Trading: History, Analytics and Policy Implications." Mimeo, University of Maryland, Department of Economics, 1996b.

Panagariya, Arvind, and Ronald Findlay. "A Political Economy Analysis of Free Trade Areas and customs Unions." In Robert Feenstra, Gene Grossman, and Douglas Irwin, eds., *The Political Economy of Trade Reform*, Essays in Honor of Jagdish Bhagwati. Cambridge, Mass.: MIT Press, 1996.

Polak, Jacques J. "Is APEC a Natural Regional Trading Bloc? A critique of the 'Gravity Model' of International Trade." Mimeo (revised version to appear in the *World Economy*).

Richardson, M. "Why a Free Trade Area? The Tariff Also Rises." *Economics & Politics*, vol. 6, March 1994, pp. 79–95.

Riezman, Raymond. "A 3 × 3 Model of Customs Unions." *Journal of International Economics*, vol. 9, 1979, pp. 341–54.

Srinivasan, T. N. "Discussion." In Jaime de Melo and Arvind Panagariya, eds., *New Dimensions in Regional Integration*. Cambridge, Great Britain: Cambridge University Press, 1993.

————. "Common External Tariffs of a Customs Union: The Case of Identical Cobb-Douglas Tastes." Mimeo, Yale University, 1995.

Summers, Lawrence. "Regionalism and the World Trading System." Symposium Sponsored by the Federal Reserve Bank of Kansas City, *Policy Implications of Trade and Currency Zones*, 1991.

Viner, Jacob. *The Customs Union Issue*. New York: Carnegie Endowment for International Peace, 1950.

Wei, Sheng-Jin, and Jeffrey Frankel. "Open Regionalism in a World of Continental Trade Blocs." Revised version of NBER Working Paper no. 5272, November 1995.

Winters, L. A. "Regionalism and the Rest of the World: The Irrelevance of the Kemp-Wan Theorem." Mimeo. Washington, D.C.: World Bank, 1995a.

————. "European Integration and Economic Welfare in the Rest of the World." Mimeo. Washington, D.C.: World Bank, 1995b.

Wolf, Martin. "Comments." In Jeffrey J. Schott, ed., *Free Trade Areas and U.S. Trade Policy*, pp. 89–95. Washington, D.C.: Institute for International Economics, 1989.

Wonnacott, Paul, and Mark Lutz. "Is There a Case for Free Trade Areas?" In Schott, Jeffrey J., ed., *Free Trade Areas and U.S. Trade Policy*, pp. 59–84. Washington, D.C.: Institute for International Economics, 1989.

II

"Static" Analysis: Issues Relating to Single PTAs

Trade Creation and Trade Diversion

3 The Customs Union Issue

Jacob Viner

3.1 Customs Union as an Approach to Free Trade

The literature on customs unions in general, whether written by economists or non-economists, by free-traders or protectionists, is almost universally favorable to them, and only here and there is a sceptical note to
be encountered, usually by an economist with free-trade tendencies. It is a
strange phenomenon which unites free-traders and protectionists in the
field of commercial policy, and its strangeness suggests that there is
something peculiar in the apparent economics of customs unions. The
customs union problem is entangled in the whole free-trade–protection
issue, and it has never yet been properly disentangled.

The free-trader and the protectionist, in their reasoning about foreign
trade, start from different premises—which they rarely state fully—and
reach different conclusions. If in the case of customs unions they agree in
their conclusions, it must be because they see in customs unions different
sets of facts, and not because an identical customs union can meet the
requirements of both the free-trader and the protectionist. It will be
argued here that customs unions differ from each other in certain vital but
not obvious respects, and that the free-trade supporter of customs union
expects from it consequences which if they were associated in the mind of
the protectionist with customs union would lead him to oppose it. It will
also be argued, although with less conviction because it involves judg-
ments about quantities in the absence of actual or even possible measure-
ment, that with respect to most customs union projects the protectionist
is right and the free-trader is wrong in regarding the project as something, given his premises, which he can logically support.

Originally published, as chapter 4, in *The Customs Union Issue*, Jacob Viner (New York:
Carnegie Endowment for International Peace, 1950), 41–56. Reprinted with permission.

To simplify the analysis, it will at first be confined to perfect customs unions between pairs of countries; and the "administrative" advantages of customs unions, such as the shortening of customs walls, and the "administrative" disadvantages, such as the necessity of coordinating customs codes and of allocating revenues by agreed formula, will be tentatively disregarded. Also, to separate the problem of customs unions per se from the question of whether in practice customs unions would result in a higher or in a lower "average level" of duties[1] on imports into the customs union area from outside the area, it will be assumed that the average level of duties on imports from outside the customs area is precisely the same for the two countries, computed as it would be if they had not formed the customs union. It will at first be assumed that the duties are of only two types:[2] (a) "nominal duties," that is, duties which have no effect on imports because there would be no imports of commodities of the kind involved even in the absence of any import duties on them;[3] and (b) "effective protective duties," that is, duties which operate to reduce imports not only by making commodities of the specific kind involved more expensive to potential consumers and so lessening their consumption, but also, and chiefly, by diverting consumption from imported commodities to the products of corresponding domestic industries. The analysis will be directed toward finding answers to the following questions: in so far as the establishment of the customs union results in change in the national locus of production of goods purchased, is the net change one of diversion of purchases to lower or higher money-cost sources of supply, abstracting from duty-elements in money costs: (a) for each of the customs union countries taken separately; (b) for the two combined; (c) for the outside world; (d) for the world as a whole? If the customs union is a movement in the direction of free trade, it must be predominantly a movement in the direction of goods being supplied from lower money-cost sources than before. If the customs union has the effect of diverting purchases to higher money-cost sources, it is then a device for making tariff protection more effective. None of these questions can be answered a priori, and the correct answers will depend on just how the customs union operates in practice. All that a priori analysis can do, is to demonstrate, within limits, how the customs union must operate if it is to have specific types of consequence.

The removal of "nominal" duties, or duties which are ineffective as barriers to trade, can be disregarded, and attention can be confined to the consequences of the removal, as the result of customs union, of duties which previously had operated effectively as a barrier, partial or complete, to import.

There will be commodities, however, which one of the members of the customs union will now newly import from the other but which it formerly did not import at all because the price of the protected domestic product was lower than the price at any foreign source plus the duty. This shift in the locus of production as between the two countries is a shift from a high-cost to a lower-cost point, a shift which the free-trader can properly approve, as at least a step in the right direction, even if universal free trade would divert production to a source with still lower costs.

There will be other commodities which one of the members of the customs union will now newly import from the other whereas before the customs union it imported them from a third country, because that was the cheapest possible source of supply even after payment of duty. The shift in the locus of production is now not as between the two member countries but as between a low-cost third country and the other, high-cost, member country. This is a shift of the type which the protectionist approves, but it is not one which the free-trader who understands the logic of his own doctrine can properly approve.[4]

Simplified as this exposition is, it appears to cover most of the basic economic issues involved. The primary purpose of a customs union, and its major consequence for good or bad, is to shift sources of supply, and the shift can be either to lower- or to higher-cost sources, depending on circumstances. It will be noted that for the free-trader the benefit from a customs union to the customs union area as a whole derives from that portion of the new trade between the member countries which is wholly new trade, whereas each particular portion of the new trade between the member countries which is a substitute for trade with third countries he must regard as a consequence of the customs union which is injurious for the importing country, for the external world, and for the world as a whole, and is beneficial only to the supplying member country. The protectionist, on the other hand, is certain to regard the substitution of trade between the member countries for trade with third countries as the major beneficial feature of customs union from the point of view of the participating countries and to be unenthusiastic about or even to regard as a drawback—at least for the importing country—the wholly new trade which results from the customs union.

From the free-trade point of view, whether a particular customs union is a move in the right or in the wrong direction depends, therefore, so far as the argument has as yet been carried, on which of the two types of consequences ensue from that custom union.

Where the trade-creating force is predominant, one of the members at least must benefit, both may benefit, the two combined must have a net benefit, and the world at large benefits; but the outside world loses, in the short-run at least, and can gain in the long-run only as the result of the general diffusion of the increased prosperity of the customs union area. Where the trade-diverting effect is predominant, one at least of the member countries is bound to be injured, both may be injured, the two combined will suffer a net injury, and there will be injury to the outside world and to the world at large. The question as to what presumptions can reasonably be held to prevail with respect to the relative importance in practice of the two types of effects will be examined subsequently.

To the reasoning presented above, there is one qualification in favor of customs union which needs to be made, on which both free-traders and protectionists can with reason find some common ground, although, in the opinion of the writer, they both tend to exaggerate its importance for the customs union problem. It has here been assumed hitherto that in so far as a customs union has effects on trade these must be either trade-creating or trade-diverting effects. This would be true if as output of any industry in a particular country increases over the long-run relative to the national economy as a whole, its money costs of production per unit relative to the general level of money costs also tended to rise. Economists are generally agreed, however, that there are firms, and consequently also industries, where this rule does not hold but instead unit costs decrease as output expands. From this they conclude that where a small country by itself, because of the limited size of its domestic market (and, it should be added, the prevention by foreign tariffs of its finding a market outside), may be unable to reach a scale of production large enough to make low unit-costs of production possible, two or more such countries combined may provide a market large enough to make low unit-cost production possible. If an industry which thus expands, whether from zero or from a previous small output, is in country A, and the other member of the customs union is country B, the diversion of B's imports from a country, C, outside the customs union to country A, may be a beneficial one for B as well as for A, and, moreover, there may be suppression of trade, namely, of the imports of A from C of the commodity in question, which may also be beneficial to A. Whether such diversion—and suppression—of trade will, from the free-trade point of view, be beneficial or injurious to A will depend on several circumstances. The cost of production in A of the commodity in question is now lower than it was before. There is gain, therefore, for A as compared to the precustoms-union situation with respect to that portion of its present output which corresponds to its previous output (which may have been zero), and there is clear gain on such of its additional output as is now exported to B. On additional output beyond this, however, there is loss to A if the new cost, though lower than the previous one, is higher than the cost (before duty) at which it is obtainable from C, but there is additional gain to A if the new cost is lower than the cost (before duty) at which it is obtainable from C. For B, there is loss by the amount imported by B times the per unit amount by which A's price exceeds the price at which B's import needs could be supplied by C; there is gain to B only if A's price is now lower than C's price (before duty). There is thus a possibility—though not, as is generally taken for granted in the literature, a certainty—that if the unit-cost of production falls as the result of the enlarged protected market consequent upon customs union there will be a gain from customs union for one of the members, for both the members, and/or for the union as a whole, but there is also a possibility—and often a probability—that there will be loss in each case.

It does not seem probable that the prospects of reduction in unit-costs of production as the result of enlargement of the tariff area are ordinarily substantial, even when the individual member countries are quite small in economic size. The arguments for substantial economies from increased scale of industry presented by economists rest wholly or mostly on alleged economies of scale for *plants* or *firms*, and on the assumption that large-scale plants or firms are not practicable in small *industries* and therefore in small countries. It seems to the writer unlikely, however, that substantial efficiency-economies of scale of plant are common once the plants are of moderate size, and he is convinced that in most industries plants can attain or approach closely their optimum size for efficiency even though the industries are not large in size. Were it not for trade barriers, moreover, even small countries could have large industries.

There are few industries, even in countries where large-scale production is common, in which there are not plants of moderate size which are as efficient, or nearly as efficient, measured in unit-costs, as the giant plants; and there are few giant firms which do not maintain some of their plants, presumably at a profit, on a moderate scale. There are few manufacturing industries—and the economies of scale of plant or industry are generally conceded to be confined mainly or only to such industries—which have not been able to maintain themselves on a low-cost basis in one or more small countries, such as Switzerland, Sweden, Denmark, or Belgium. If the applicability of this argument is confined to products which nowhere are produced at a low unit-cost from plants which are quite small, either absolutely or as compared to the maximum size elsewhere, the scope of the argument is much more limited than is commonly taken for granted. It may be asked in rebuttal, how then explain the existence of giant plants and giant firms? It is at least a partial answer: (1) as to size of plants, that the survival of plants of moderate size in competition with the giant plants calls equally for explanation; and (2) as to size of firms, that there are in an imperfectly competitive world many incentives to growth in size of firm even at the cost of efficiency in production—firms of quite undistinguished records in efficiency of production have been known to grow by absorption of more efficient smaller firms and by the use of monopoly power in buying and in retention of customers, and, generally speaking, growth in size is more often the result of efficiency than contributory to efficiency.

The general rule appears to be that once an industry is large enough to make possible optimum scale—and degree of specialization of production—in plants, further expansion of the industry in a national economy of constant over-all size is bound to be under conditions of increasing unit-costs as output increases, in the absence of new inventions. To expand, the industry must draw away from other industries increased amounts of the resources it uses, and consequently must pay higher prices per unit for resources of the type which it uses more heavily than does industry at large, and must reduce the extent to which it uses them relative to other types of resources, thus bringing into operation the law of diminishing returns. It may be objected that this will not hold true in the case of a customs union, since this in effect increases the over-all size of the "national" economy. It is the supply conditions of factors of production, however, which are the relevant restrictive factor on expansion of output of an industry without increase of unit-costs, and unless customs union appreciably increases the inter-member mobility of factors of production it does not in this sense increase the "scale" of the "national" economy from the point of view of production conditions even if it does increase it from the point of view of the size of the protected market for sales.

Few free-traders have dealt with the economics of customs unions in any detail, and one must resort in some measure to inference from the implications of brief dicta to find the explanation for their general support of customs union as constituting an approach to their ideal of the territorial allocation of production in accordance with comparative costs of production. The major explanation seems to lie in an unreflecting association on their part of any removal or reduction of trade barriers with movement in the direction of free trade. Businessmen, however, and governments which have had to try simultaneously to satisfy both special interests seeking increased protection and voters hostile to protection, have long known of ways of making increased protection look like movement in a free-trade direction. They have known how, under suitable circumstances, protection against foreign competition could be increased by *reducing* duties and reduced by increasing duties. Let us suppose that there are import duties both on wool and on woolen cloth, but that no wool is produced at home despite the duty. Removing the duty on wool while leaving the duty unchanged on the woolen cloth results in increased protection for the cloth industry while having no significance for wool-raising. Or suppose that the wool is all produced at home, and sold to domestic cloth makers at the world price plus duty, but would be all pro-duced at home even if there were no duty on wool, but would then be sold at the world price. Removal of the duty on wool again increases the protection for the woolen industry without reducing the volume of domestic production of wool.

When the customs union operates to divert trade from its previous channels rather than to create new trade, the partial removal of duties which it involves operates in analogous manner to increase the protective effect for high-cost producers of the duties which remain, not, however, by reducing imports into their own national territory but by extending the operation in their favor of the protective duty to the territory of the other partner of the customs union. It would in theory be possible that if two areas were joined in customs union, the customs union would have no trade-creating effect and only trade-diverting effect, i.e., no industry in either area would meet with new competition from the other area, while some high-cost industries, existing or potential, in each area would acquire a new set of consumers in the other area who would be placed at their mercy because the customs union tariff will now shut them off from low-cost sources of supply. A set of connected tariff walls can give more market-dominance to high-cost producers than a set of independent tariff walls, if the former set has had its internal sections knocked out.

This is well, though ingenuously, brought out in one of the leading treatises in favor of customs unions, where the author, after arguing that free-traders should like them because they eliminate trade barriers, pro-ceeds to argue that protectionists should also like them because of the extension of the (protected) market area which they provide for producers within the territory of the customs union; "as for the internal competition, it will not be formidable if care is exercised in choosing as partners in customs unions countries which are complementary [in production] rather than competitive."[5]

Free-traders sometimes in almost the same breath disapprove of preferential reductions of tariffs but approve of customs unions, which involve 100 percent preference, and this is the position at present of the United States Government and the doctrine of the Havana Charter.[6] If the distinction is made to rest, as often seems to be the case, on some supposed virtue in a 100 percent preference, which suddenly turns to maximum evil at 99 percent, the degree of evil tapering off as the degree of preference shrinks, it is a distinction as illogical, the writer believes, as this way of putting it makes it sound.[7] On the legal side, the discussion of the bearing of the *degree* of preference on its compatibility with most-favored-nation obligations has sometimes led to the opposite conclusion, namely, that, on the principle a majori ad minus, if a customs union with its 100 percent preferences is compatible with the most-favored-nation principle, still more must fractional preferences be compatible.[8] This seems plausible enough until it is realized that acceptance of this reasoning would have the practical consequence that 100 percent preferences would be legal if incident to customs union and lesser preferences would be legal because greater ones were, so that *all* preferences would be legal. The moral is that on both the economic and legal side the problem is too complex to be settled by simple maxims.[9] A 50 percent preference is economically either less desirable or more desirable than a 100 percent preference according only as preference at all is under the circumstances desirable or undesirable.[10]

There is one ground only on which, aside from administrative considerations, it can consistently be held that preferences are economically bad and are increasingly bad as they approach 100 percent, but that customs union is an economic blessing. Customs union, if it is complete, involves a cross-the-board removal of the duties between the members of the union; since the removal is non-selective by its very nature, the beneficial preferences are established along with the injurious ones, the trade-creating ones along with the trade-diverting ones. Preferential arrangements, on the other hand, can be, and usually are, selective, and it is possible, and in practice probable, that the preferences selected will be predominantly of the trade-diverting or injurious kind. But aside from possible administrative economies, cross-the-board 100 percent preferences without customs union are economically as good—or as bad—as customs union.

From the free-trade point of view, that is, the point of view that movement in the direction of international specialization in production in accordance with comparative costs is economically desirable, there can be formulated in accordance with the preceding analysis a series of propositions as to the conditions which need to be met to justify the presumption that the establishment of a particular customs union will represent a movement toward free trade rather than away from it.

A customs union is more likely to operate in the free-trade direction, whether appraisal is in terms of its consequence for the customs union area alone or for the world as a whole:

1. the larger the economic area of the customs union and therefore the greater the potential scope for internal division of labor;

2. the lower the "average" tariff level on imports from outside the customs union area as compared to what that level would be in the absence of customs union;

3. the greater the correspondence in kind of products of the range of high-cost industries as between the different parts of the customs union which were protected by tariffs in both of the member countries before customs union was established, i.e., the *less* the degree of complementarity —or the *greater* the degree of rivalry—of the member countries with respect to *protected* industries, prior to customs union;[11]

4. the greater the differences in unit-costs for protected industries of the same kind as between the different parts of the customs union, and therefore the greater the economies to be derived from free trade with respect to these industries within the customs union area;

5. the higher the tariff levels in potential export markets outside the customs union area with respect to commodities in whose production the member countries of the customs union would have a comparative advantage under free trade, and therefore the less the injury resulting from reducing the degree of specialization in production as between the customs union area and the outside world;

6. the greater the range of protected industries for which an enlargement of the market would result in unit-costs lower than those at which the commodities concerned could be imported from outside the customs union area;

7. the smaller the range of protected industries for which an enlargement of the market would not result in unit-costs lower than those at which the

commodities concerned could be imported from outside the customs union area but which would nevertheless expand under customs union.

Confident judgment as to what the over-all balance between these conflicting considerations would be, it should be obvious, cannot be made for customs unions in general and in the abstract, but must be confined to particular projects and be based on economic surveys thorough enough to justify reasonably reliable estimates as to the weights to be given in the particular circumstances to the respective elements in the problem. Customs unions are, from the free-trade point of view, neither necessarily good nor necessarily bad; the circumstances discussed above are the determining factors. As has been pointed out earlier, it would be easy to set up a hypothetical model where customs union would mean nothing economically except an intensification of uneconomic protection, an increase in the effectiveness of trade barriers as interferences with international division of labor. A universal customs union, on the other hand, would be the equivalent of universal free trade. Actual customs unions must fall somewhere between these two extremes.

The non-technical reader is again warned that this analysis not only takes for granted the validity—at least when only purely economic considerations are taken into account—of the argument for free trade from a cosmopolitan point of view, but that its results are much less favorable to customs union in general than the position taken by most free-trade economists who have discussed the issue.[12] One of the few exceptions is Lionel Robbins, whose formulation of the issue as here quoted is, in the opinion of the writer, excellent:

... The purpose of international division of labour is not merely to make possible the import of things which cannot be produced on the spot; it is rather to permit the resources on the spot to be devoted wholly to the production of the things they are best fitted to produce, the remainder being procured from elsewhere....

It follows, therefore, that the gain from regional regrouping or wider units of any kind is not a gain of greater self-sufficiency, but a gain of the abolition of so much self-sufficiency on the part of the areas which are thus amalgamated....[13]

... From the international point of view, the tariff union is not an advantage in itself. It is an advantage only in so far as, on balance, it conduces to more extensive division of labour. It is to be justified only by arguments which would justify still more its extension to all areas capable of entering into trade relationships.... No doubt if we could coax the rest of the world into free trade by a high tariff union against the produce of the Eskimos that would be, on balance, an international gain. But it would be inferior to an arrangement whereby the Eskimos were included. The only completely innocuous tariff union would be directed against the inaccessible produce of the moon.[14]

Another exception, however, seems to go further than is justified. R. G. Hawtrey writes as follows:

> The most-favoured-nation clause has been criticised in that it prevented a relaxation of tariffs between adjacent countries, by which at any rate a beginning might have been made in the removal of obstacles to trade. A reduction of import duties by Belgium and Holland in favour of one another's products would have involved discrimination against other countries, such as Great Britain....
>
> But to suppose that agreements of that kind would be a move towards free trade is a delusion. The preferential treatment that would have been given by Belgium and Holland to one another would have made their existing protective tariffs more exclusive against other countries. In fact the wider the extent of economic activity encircled by a tariff barrier of given height, the greater is its effect in excluding the goods of foreign producers. The break-up of the Austro-Hungarian Empire resulted in the creation of new frontiers, and the new tariff barriers obstructed trade between one succession State and another. But if the import duties had remained at the same level as before, the markets which the succession States lost in one another would have been more accessible than before to outside producers.[15]

Reduction of the extent of division of labor between the customs union area and the outside world is the major objective and would be a major consequence of most projected customs unions, and would be a consequence in some degree of *any* customs union with protective duties, unless the duties on imports from outside the customs union were drastically cut upon establishment of the union. But Hawtrey should not leave out of consideration the increase in the extent to which division of labor *within* the customs union area prevails as the result of customs union.

3.2   Customs Union and the "Terms of Trade"

There is a possibility, so far not mentioned, of economic benefit from a tariff to the tariff-levying country which countries may be able to exploit more effectively combined in customs union than if they operated as separate tariff areas. This benefit to the customs area, however, carries with it a corresponding injury to the outside world. A tariff does not merely divert consumption from imported to domestically produced commodities—this is, from the free-trade point of view, the economic disadvantage of a tariff for the tariff-levying country and one of its disadvantages for the rest of the world—but it also alters in favor of the tariff-levying country the rate at which its exports exchange for the imports which survive the tariff, or its "terms of trade," and within limits—which may be narrow and which can never be determined accurately—an improvement in the national "terms of trade" carries with it an increase in the national total benefit from trade. The greater the economic area of the tariff-levying unit, the greater is likely to be, other things being equal, the improvement in its terms of trade with the outside world resulting from its tariff.[16] A customs union, by increasing the extent of the territory which operates under a single tariff, thus tends to increase the efficacy of the tariff in improving the terms of trade of that area vis-à-vis the rest of the world.

Notes

1. Whether it is possible to give this concept of an "average level" of duties both some degree of precision of definition and economic significance is taken up later. See infra, pp. 66–68.

2. "Revenue duties" are dealt with subsequently. See infra, pp. 65–66.

3. Such duties, while they have no effect on imports, can have other effects of some economic importance, though these are not directly relevant here. In countries where an approach to perfect competition does not prevail, which means most countries, import duties may protect monopolistic or government-supported domestic price levels instead of protecting domestic production.

4. A third possibility should be mentioned. The import duty on a particular commodity may be so high in one of the countries that it is prohibitive of import, but domestic production may be impossible or excessively costly, so that there is no consumption. Upon formation of the customs union, the commodity in question may be imported from the other member country, where its cost of production may be high or low as compared to costs elsewhere but is assumed to be lower than outside costs plus the duty on imports from outside the customs union. The original duty thus served as a sumptuary measure rather than as a protective or revenue measure. Whether the removal of a sumptuary measure is of benefit for the country particularly concerned as potential consumer is not a type of question which the economist has any special capacity to answer. But if as the result of customs union country A removes a duty of this kind preferentially for imports from the other member country, B, there is a clear loss for A as compared to the removal of duty regardless of source if B is a high-cost source of supply. There is an unquestionable benefit here, however, for the supplying country, and it does not injure outside countries in any direct way.

5. L. Bosc, op. cit., p. 98. He moves on to a perfect non sequitur: "Thanks to this judicious choice, *there will be established within the customs union a fecund division of labor*, while the customs frontiers thus extended further territorially will protect the internal market against the superiority of other countries." (Italics supplied.)

6. Cf. Clair Wilcox, *A Charter for World Trade* (New York, 1949), p. 70:

Preferences have been opposed and customs unions favored, in principle, by the United States. This position may obviously be criticized as lacking in logical consistency. In preferential arrangements, discrimination against the outer world is partial; in customs unions, it is complete. But the distinction is none the less defensible. A customs union creates a wider trading area, removes obstacles to competition, makes possible a more economic allocation of resources, and thus operates to increase production and raise planes of living. A preferential system, on the other hand, retains internal barriers, obstructs economy in production, and restrains the growth of income and demand. It is set up for the purpose of conferring a privilege on producers within the system and imposing a handicap on external competitors. A customs union is conducive to the expansion of trade on a basis of multilateralism and nondiscrimination; a preferential system is not.

There would seem to be little or nothing in what is said here about the *evils* of preference which is not potentially true also for customs unions; and equally little in what is said here about the *benefits* of customs unions which is acceptable further than as being potentially true if circumstances are right, and which, where true at all, is not also potentially true, if circumstances are right, of preferences.

7. One is reminded of Dryden's "My wound is great because it is so small," and Saint-Evremond's rejoinder, "Then 'twould be greater, were it none at all."

8. Sandor von Matlekovits, *Die Zollpolitik der österreichisch-ungarischen Monarchie und des Deutschen Reiches seit 1868 und deren nächste Zukunft* (Leipzing, 1891).

9. The following illustration of the ambiguous working in practice of the a majori ad minus principle is not, it is hoped, wholly without relevance:

"It being made felony by an act of parliament to steal *horses*, it was doubted whether stealing *one horse only* was within the statute: in construction of penal law, the less number may not be included under the greater, but the reverse can never follow. Cf. the King of Prussia's error when he comments that, an English law prohibiting bigamy, a man accused of having five wives was acquitted, as not coming under the law." Daines Barrington, *Observations on the More Ancient Statutes*, 4th ed. (London, 1755), p. 547. (Italics in the original.)

10. It is to be remembered that administrative economies are here disregarded. If they were to be taken into account, a 100 percent preference could be held more desirable than say a 99 percent one on the ground that it made the economic wastes of customs formalities unnecessary—if it did—even though otherwise the smaller the preference the less objectionable it would be.

11. In the literature on customs union, it is almost invariably taken for granted that rivalry is a disadvantage and complementarity is an advantage in the formation of customs unions. See infra, pp. 73 ff., with reference to the Benelux and Franco-Italian projects.

12. For conclusions, by economists sympathetic to free trade, more favorable to customs union, see especially: Gottfried von Haberler, *The Theory of International Trade* (London, 1936), pp. 383–91 and idem, "The Political Economy of Regional or Continental Blocs," in Seymour E. Harris, *ed., Postwar Economic Problems* (New York, 1943), especially pp. 330–34, and other writings of Haberler; John de Beers, "Tariff Aspects of a Federal Union," *Quarterly Journal of Economics* (1941), 49–92; and *Customs Unions, 1947*, pp. 75 ff., which follows Haberler's treatment closely and uncritically.

The more favorable conclusions with respect to customs unions reached by these writers are the consequence, mainly: (1) of failure to give consideration, or to give adequate consideration, to the effect of customs union in extending the area over which preexisting import duties exercise a protective effect; (2) of confusing the problem of the effect on location of production of customs union with the different, and for present purposes inconsequential, problem of the "incidence of import duties," or the location of impact of burden of payment of import duties actually collected; and (3) of applying the standard techniques of partial equilibrium analysis, traditionally applied to the analysis of the determination of prices of particular commodities taken one at a time, to foreign trade as a whole and to the tariff problem where its findings are either totally without significance or of totally indeterminable significance.

The present writer's own questioning in print of the usual arguments for customs union began in 1931: see "The Most-Favoured-Nation Clause," *Index*, VI (1931), p. 11. Haberler and de Beers have in the writings cited above found fault with the present writer's treatment as unduly critical of customs union, in part on the basis of reasoning of the type commented on in the preceding paragraph, and in part on the ground that the possibility of increased division of labor within the area of the customs union was denied or over-looked. In the few sentences devoted to the problem in the above-mentioned *Index* article, the writer asserted only the *possibility* that preferential duties would mean a greater diversion of trade from its free-trade pattern than uniform protection. He did not discuss the possibilities more favorable to customs union. Nor can he find in that article anything corresponding to the proposition attributed to him by de Beers, that an increase of imports must come from the same sources as under free trade, if there is to be gain. De Beers, however, cites a statement made by the present writer in 1933: "... if a regional agreement, preferential as between the countries within that region, is beneficial to both those countries, it must necessarily follow that had it been extended to the entire world no substantial change would have resulted in the effect of the agreement." This *is* a faulty statement. It is taken from a non-verbatim report of an extemporaneous discussion which the writer had no opportunity to edit—and, may add, did not know until some years later to have been put into print. (See International Studies Conference, *The State and Economic Life* [Paris, 1934], p. 50). He makes no claim, however, to have been misreported, and is not now in a position to deny that it correctly represented the state of his thinking at that time.

13. Under customs union, there would be a decrease in the degree of self-sufficiency of each member area, but an increase in the degree of self-sufficiency of the customs union area as a whole.

14. Lionel Robbins, *Economic Planning and International Order* (London, 1937), pp. 120–22.

15. R. G. Hawtrey, *Economic Destiny* (London [1944]), pp. 135–36.

16. The greater the economic area of the tariff unit, other things equal, the greater is likely to be the elasticity of its "reciprocal demand" for outside products and the less is likely to be the elasticity of the "reciprocal demand" of the outside world for its products, and consequently the greater the possibility of improvement in its terms of trade through unilateral manipulation of its tariff.

4

The Theory of Customs Unions: Trade Diversion and Welfare

Richard G. Lipsey

In his book *The Customs Union Issue* Professor Viner draws the distinction between the trade-creating and the trade-diverting effects of a customs union. In any theory of customs unions this must be a fundamental distinction. However, after defining the two terms, Professor Viner goes on to conclude that, in some sense, trade creation may be said to be a "good thing" and trade diversion a "bad thing."[1]

When a customs union is formed, relative prices in the domestic markets of the member countries are changed because the tariffs on some imports are removed. These price changes are likely to have two important initial effects. First, they may influence the world location of production in the several ways carefully analysed by Viner. Secondly, they will have a parallel effect on the location of world consumption. Usually one would expect to find the union members increasing their consumption of each other's products while reducing imports from the rest of the world.[2] Changes of the first type will be classified under the general heading, *production effects of union*, and changes of the second type as *consumption effects of union*. It must be emphasised that even if world production is fixed, a customs union will cause some changes in patterns of consumption due to changes in relative prices in the domestic markets of the member countries. The consumption effect, therefore, may operate even if there is no production effect.

The proposition that a change brought about by a customs union is, in general, good or bad necessarily implies a welfare judgement. But the effect of a customs union on welfare must be a combination of its effects on the location, and hence the cost of world production and on the location, and hence the "utility," of world consumption. In this chapter it will be shown that when consumption effects are allowed for, the simple

Originally published in *Economica* 24 (February 1957): 40–46. Reprinted with permission.

conclusions that trade creation is "good" and trade diversion is "bad" are no longer valid. Although the distinction between trade creation and trade diversion is fundamental for classifying the changes in production consequent on the formation of a customs union, it is not one on which welfare conclusions can be based.

4.1

The problem of the welfare effects of trade diversion will be isolated by using an extremely simple model. The model will be used to show that an increase in welfare may follow from the formation of a customs union which results solely in the diversion of trade from lower—to higher—cost sources of supply. Furthermore, it will be shown that this welfare gain may be enjoyed by the country whose import trade is diverted, by the customs union area considered as a unit and by the world as a whole.

The analysis will be based on the following simple model: The world is divided into three countries, A, B, and C. The effects of various trade policies on the welfare of country A only is first considered. A is a small country whose inhabitants consume two commodities, wheat and clothing. A specialises in the production of wheat and obtains her clothing by means of international trade. Being small, she cannot influence the price of clothing in terms of wheat. Country C offers clothing at a lower wheat price than does B, so that, in the absence of country-discriminating tariffs, A will trade with C, exporting wheat in return for clothing. It is assumed that A levies a tariff on imports but that the rate is not high enough to protect a domestic clothing industry, so that she purchases her clothing from C. Now let country A form a customs union with country B, as a result of which B replaces C as the supplier of clothing to A. B is a higher cost producer of clothing than is C but her price without the tariff is less than C's price with the tariff. Hence, the union causes trade diversion, A's trade being diverted from C to B.

Indifference curves are used in the analysis but the conclusions reached do not depend on the assumption of a unique community welfare function. For this reason it is first assumed that in country A there is only one consumer, whose indifference map is, ipso facto, country A's community indifference map. Later the analysis is extended to a community of more than one individual.

Figure 4.1 illustrates the conditions existing in country A. OD measures A's production of wheat. The price ratio between wheat and clothing when trade is with C is shown by the slope of the price line DE. The free-trade equilibrium position is at point G. It is assumed that A levies a tariff on clothing imports of (EF/OF) percent. If the tariff revenue were destroyed, the new equilibrium would be at H where an indifference curve is tangent to the domestic price line, DF. However, if the usual assumption is made that the tariff revenue is returned to the consumer, then the point of final equilibrium must be located on DE. It will be where an indifference curve has a slope equal to that of DF at the point where it cuts DE. In Figure 4.1 the equilibrium is at point K, where the curve through that point is tangent to D'F' which is drawn parallel to DF.[3] At this point it is impossible for the consumer to trade along his domestic price line D'F' and reach a higher indifference curve.[4] The tariff has the expected result of lowering imports of clothing and raising consumption of domestic wheat.

It is assumed that A now forms a trade-diverting customs union with country B. The line indicating the terms of trade with B must lie between DE and DF.[5] Since there is no tariff levied on A-B trade, the equilibrium position must be located on the price-consumption line WHGZ. The effects of the union on country A's welfare may now be considered. In figure 4.1, starting from the point D, draw a line tangential to the indifference curve I'' (the curve through K) and extend it to cut the clothing axis at some point V. The slope of this line DV indicates terms of trade with country B which leave A as well off as when trade was with country C. If A obtains any terms of trade with B worse than DE but better than DV, the trade-diverting customs union must result in an increase in A's welfare. If she obtains any terms of trade better than DF but worse than DV, trade diversion will occur but it will result in a loss of welfare for A.[6] It can be concluded, therefore, that country A might gain by entering a customs union whose sole production effect was to divert her import trade from lower—to higher—cost sources of supply.

The above conclusion may not have an immediate common-sense appeal,[7] yet the explanation is easily seen with the help of a diagram. The possibility stems from the fact that whenever imports are subject to a tariff, the position of equilibrium must be one where an indifference curve cuts (not is tangent to) the international price line. From this it follows that there will exist an area where indifference curves higher than the one achieved at equilibrium lie below the international price line. In figure 4.1 this is the area above I'' but below DE. As long as the final equilibrium position lies within this area, trade carried on in the absence of tariffs, at terms of trade worse than those indicated by DE, will increase welfare. In a verbal statement this possibility may be explained by referring to the

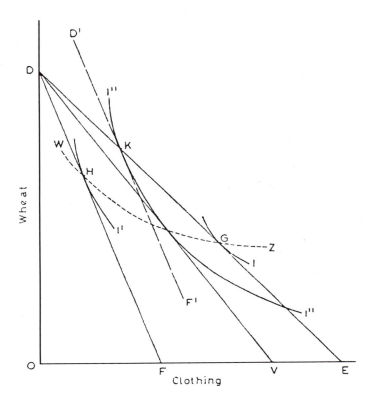

Figure 4.1

two opposing effects of the trade-diverting customs union. First, A shifts
her purchases from a lower—to a higher—cost source of supply. It now
becomes necessary to export a larger quantity of goods in order to obtain
any given quantity of imports. Second, the divergence between domestic
and international prices is eliminated when the union is formed. The removal of the tariff has the effect of allowing the consumer in A to adjust
his purchases to a domestic price ratio which now is equal to the rate at
which wheat can be transformed into clothing by means of international
trade. The final welfare effect of the trade-diverting customs union must
be the net effect of these two opposing tendencies; the first working to
lower welfare and the second to raise it.

If, to take a limiting case as an example, country B's price of clothing
exceeds country C's price by only an infinitesimal amount, then the union
would allow A to return to a position only an infinitesimal distance below

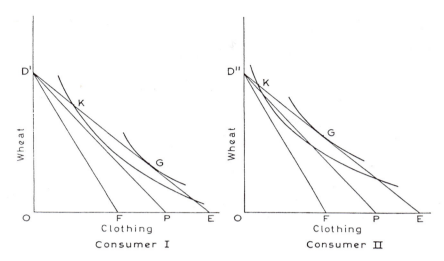

Figure 4.2

the free trade position, G. In this case the only effect operating is the consumption one and the trade-diverting customs union raises welfare virtually to the free trade level.[8]

4.2

It must now be shown that the conclusions reached do not depend on the existence of a unique community indifference map for country A. This will be done by considering a case where country A is a community of two individuals. Figure 4.2 is a repetition of figure 4.1, all the lettering is the same except that the distribution of income in terms of wheat is shown by OD' for consumer I and by OD'' for consumer II (OD' + OD'' = OD in figure 4.1). For each individual the free-trade equilibrium position will be at the point where the international price line, DE, is tangent to one of his indifference curves. Similary, when a tariff is placed on imported clothing, each consumer will move to an equilibrium position (K' and K'') which will satisfy the conditions for the location of the point K in figure 4.1.

Once allowance is made for the existence of more than one consumer in country A, two problems arise in connection with the trade-diverting customs union between A and B. First, there will be some prices of clothing which will permit one consumer to reach an indifference curve higher than the one he achieved at K while the other consumer is forced to a curve lower than the one he attained at K. Such a price is shown by the lines D'P and D''P in Figure 4.2.[9] Thus, the clear distinction between gains and losses disappears as there will be some prices for which some consumers gain while others lose. Second, the union may cause a redistribution of wheat income[10] such that one consumer always suffers a reduction in welfare. However, there will always be some prices of clothing higher than the one offered by country C which will allow all consumers to reach higher indifference curves than the ones they achieved when trade was with C. Therefore, the conclusion still stands that a country may form a trade-diverting customs union and yet gain an increase in welfare in the sense that every consumer moves to a higher indifference curve.

4.3

Finally, it may be objected that in considering the welfare of only one country, a parochial point of view has been adopted. The objection would run somewhat as follows: Surprising though it is that one country can increase its welfare by forming a trade-diverting customs union, the world as a whole must surely suffer a loss when this occurs.[11] The complex problem of how to measure changes in world welfare when there are many countries, each pursuing a different tariff policy, cannot be discussed in a short paper. However, for the present argument, it is sufficient to show that a case is possible where there is no doubt that world welfare is raised by the creation of a trade-diverting customs union.

Assume that B and C, the two countries that constitute the rest of the world in the previous model, are both large and that each produces wheat and clothing under conditions of constant rates of transformation. B and C levy prohibitive tariffs on trade with each other so that the only trade before the union is that between A and C. But C produces both wheat and clothing and, therefore, trade is carried on at a relative price which is equal to her domestic price ratio. After the union is formed, A trades with country B. C suffers no loss from the elimination of the trade to which she was indifferent in any case. Country B continues to produce both wheat and clothing so that she gains nothing from the new trade with A. Thus, all the gains from trade accrue to A both before and after the union. If the trade-diverting customs union raises A's welfare—and this possibility has already been demonstrated—then it raises the world's welfare.

Notes

I am greatly indebted to Mr. K. Klappholz, Doctor H. Makower and Professor J. E. Meade for their many valuable comments and suggestions.

1. The relevant passage from Viner is as follows:

There will be commodities, however, which one of the members of the customs union will now newly import from the other but which it formerly did not import at all because the price of the protected domestic product was lower than the price at any foreign source plus the duty. This shift in the locus of production as between the two countries is a shift from a high-cost to a lower-cost point, *a shift which the free trader can properly approve* ...

There will be other commodities which one of the members of the customs union will now newly import from the other whereas before the customs union it imported them from a third country, because that was the cheapest possible source of supply even after payment of the duty. The shift in the locus of production is now not as between the two member countries but as between a low-cost third country and the other, high-cost, member country. This is a shift which the protectionist approves, but *it is not one which the free trader who understands the logic of his own doctrine can properly approve*. (Viner, Jacob, *The Customs Union Issue*, Carnegie Endowment for International Peace, New York, 1950, p. 43.) Italics not in the original.

2. But this is not necessarily so. See note 3 below.

3. If neither wheat nor clothing is an inferior good, the point K must lie between G and H in relation to the clothing axis.

4. It will be noted that, if projected to the axes, D'F' would have a Y intercept above the point D. This illustrates the fact that whatever bundle of wheat and clothing the consumer may be consuming at K, it will appear to him that he could trade all his clothing for more wheat than there is in existence. This illusion results from the fact that the tariff makes the price of wheat appear to the consumer lower than the price at which the two commodities can in fact be traded in the international market.

5. By assumption, B's price of clothing in terms of wheat is higher than C's price. Therefore, the line must lie to the left of DE. However, if trade diversion is to occur, B's clothing price must be less than C's price plus the tariff. Therefore, the line must lie to the right of DF.

6. The figure also illustrates the effect of the customs union on the volume of A's trade. Since K lies between G and H in relation to the clothing axis (see note 3) and since the post-union equilibrium point must be located on the price-consumption line, WHGZ, between the points G and H, it follows that A's imports of clothing may either rise or fall as a result of the trade-diverting customs union.

7. The conclusion represents but another application of the general theory of second best to problems of international trade. See: Lipsey, R. G., and Lancaster, Kelvin, "The General Theory of Second Best," *The Review of Economic Studies*, Vol. XXIV, No. 1, 1956–57. The trade-diversion problem is, in fact, a very simple application of the theory of multiple-layer second-best optima (op. cit., Section X). Given the existence of price distortion by tariffs, the maximization of production is no longer necessarily desirable. An "inefficient" production solution may provide an efficient welfare solution. (e.g. In figure 4.1, welfare is increased by moving from point K to some point *below* DE.)

8. A word of warning about the present model: The two-commodity model is a simplification adopted for the present analysis where it is desired to demonstrate only the possibility

that trade diversion may raise the welfare of a single country and of the world. Further analysis based on so simple a model might lead to the conclusion that the consumption effect always works to raise welfare. This is not so. The important peculiarity of the present model is that country A has only one import. For any detailed analysis of the consumption effect, a three-commodity model is required. Consider, for example, a case where country A produces commodity X while importing commodity Y from country B and commodity Z from country C. Now if A forms a customs union with country B the consumption effect on welfare is complex. This is so even if there is neither trade creation nor trade diversion, so that A continues to buy Y from B and Z from C. In this case, the removal of tariffs from imports of Y changes two price ratios. On the one hand, A's domestic price ratio between X and Y is made equal to the rate at which these two commodities can be transformed into each other by means of international trade. On the other hand, the domestic price ratio between Y and Z is now made to diverge from their rate of transformation by international trade. The X–Y change works to raise welfare while the Y–Z change works to lower it. The consumption effect on welfare is now the net effect of these two opposing tendencies.

This is not the place for a detailed discussion of this example. The case is mentioned only to show that a two-commodity model obscures many of the most important problems in the theory of customs unions. An example of this type is analysed in some detail in: Lipsey & Lancaster, op. cit., Section 4.5.

9. D'P and D''P have identical slopes indicating some single price facing both consumers.

10. I.e. the points D' and D'' may shift after the union is formed.

11. Where the trade-diverting effect is predominant, one at least of the member countries is bound to be injured, both may be injured, the two combined will suffer a net injury, and there will be injury to the outside world and to the world at large." Viner, op. cit., p. 44.

5

The Economic Theory of Customs Union

Harry G. Johnson

The economic theory of customs union is of great practical relevance.[1] It has an obvious immediate bearing on the formation of regional blocs of countries, such as the European Common Market, the Free Trade Area, and the India-Pakistan-Ceylon customs union which has sometimes been suggested; this is especially so because, quite irrationally, international convention condemns preferential systems except when the degree of preference is 100 percent, as it is within national boundaries or in customs unions. It also has a direct bearing on the internal affairs and politics of countries containing economically distinct regions, particularly if these regions correspond with political or other cultural distinctions; in such countries, the question of regional gains or losses from participation in the national economy may be an important, and chronic, source of political discord—witness the problem of the maritime provinces in Canada, the Scottish and Welsh nationalist movements in the United Kingdom, and the position of East Pakistan in Pakistan.

The economic theory of customs union is also, unfortunately, complicated. The reason, as Viner pointed out in his pioneer analysis of the problem,[2] is that it combines elements of freer trade with elements of greater protection. While it provides freedom of trade between the participating countries, it also provides more protection for producers inside the customs union area against competition from outside the area, since the protected market available to these producers is enlarged by the creation of a protected position in the markets of other countries partner to the union in addition to their protected position in their domestic market. This is the main reason for much of the confusion of popular thought on the subject of customs union: a particular customs union may be

Originally published in *Pakistan Economic Journal* 10, no. 1 (March 1960): 14–32. Reprinted, as chapter 3, in *Money, Trade and Economic Growth*, Harry Johnson (London: Allen & Unwin, 1962), 46–62. Reprinted with permission.

advocated by both free traders and protectionists, and conversely may be condemned by both, for opposite reasons.

The fact that a customs union is a mixture of freer trade and more protection means that it cannot be analysed by established welfare economics theory, which is concerned with the conditions for maximum welfare— the optimum conditions. Instead, the analysis of customs union requires the development of a theory capable of dealing with the conditions for improving welfare, for making things better rather than achieving the best possible, for maximizing welfare subject to arbitrary constraints which preclude the technically possible maximum—sub-optimum conditions or, to coin a phrase, *melior* conditions. The elements of such a theory were originated by Jacob Viner, with specific reference to the customs union problem.[3] More recently, James Meade,[4] drawing on a seminal article by Marcus Fleming,[5] has developed the general theory of such problems, "the theory of second-best," which still more recently has been re-stated and further generalized by Richard Lipsey and Kelvin Lancaster.[6] "The general theorem of second-best" at which these authors arrive may be stated simply as follows: if an economy is prevented from attaining *all* the conditions for maximum welfare simultaneously, the fulfilment of one of these conditions will not necessarily make the country better off than would its non-fulfilment. The achievement of the maximum *attainable* welfare will generally require violation of the conditions for maximum welfare; and the effect on welfare of a movement towards fulfilment of one of the optimum conditions will depend on the precise circumstances of the case.

Before proceeding to the customs union problem let me illustrate the difference between traditional optimum theory and second-best theory by reference to the familiar proposition that a tax on a specific commodity imposes an excess burden. In so doing I assume (what is not always so) that money prices and costs represent real social values and costs; and I employ Marshallian consumers' surplus analysis, even though in its crude form this entails certain well-known difficulties associated with changes in the marginal utility of income. For simplicity, I also assume constant costs in production.

The traditional argument is illustrated in Fig. 5.1, where DD is the demand curve, PQR the constant-cost supply curve, and P'Q' the supply curve including the tax. The tax shifts the equilibrium point from R to Q', imposing a loss of consumer surplus P'Q'RP, of which P'Q'QP is balanced by tax revenue accruing to the government, leaving Q'QR as the net loss of consumers' surplus due to the taxation of the commodity, or the "ex-

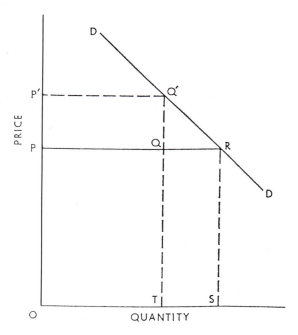

Figure 5.1

cess burden" of the tax; so that if the tax were removed and replaced by, for example, a lump sum tax, there would be a gain Q'QR of consumers' surplus.

This analysis rests on the assumption that value to consumers is equal to production cost at the margin elsewhere in the economy.[7] But value may exceed cost for other commodities, either because of imperfections in the markets for these commodities, or, as I shall assume, because they also bear taxes. The analysis of the effects on welfare of replacing the specific tax on the original commodity by a lump sum tax in this case can be carried out on two alternative lines, depending on whether the Government is assumed to maintain tax rates unchanged, or to adjust the amount of lump sum taxation so as to maintain an unchanged total revenue.[8]

On the first assumption, in order to expand consumption from OT to OS, consumers must reduce expenditure on other goods by QTSR. To the extent that other goods are taxed, reduction of expenditure on them releases resources which were not required to produce consumer satisfaction but instead were being used by the Government for its own purposes; the corresponding reduction in the amount of Government tax

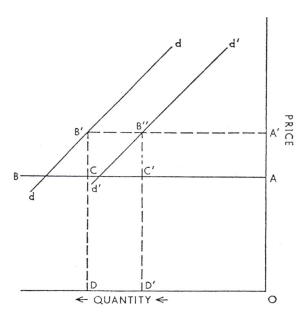

Figure 5.2

revenue and activity must be counted as a loss, against the gain in consumers' surplus on the commodity freed from taxation. This loss is illustrated in Fig. 5.2, where AB is the constant-cost supply curve of other
commodities (treated as an aggregate for convenience), A'B''B' is the
supply curve including taxes, dd is the demand curve when the original
commodity is taxed, and d'd' the demand curve when the tax on the
original commodity is replaced by a lump sum tax.[9] The replacement of
the tax on the original commodity reduces expenditure on other commodities by B'DD'B'' (equal to QTSR in Fig. 5.1) but of this amount, only
CDD'C' was required to produce the initial quantity of other commodities
consumed, B'CC'B'' going to the Government as tax revenue financing
Governmental services. In diverting expenditure from other commodities
to the commodity on which the tax is replaced, the community must
sacrifice not only the consumption of other commodities, but also the
consumption of the Governmental services previously financed by taxes
levied on the sacrificed consumption. There is a net gain only if this latter
sacrifice is less than the gain in consumers' surplus on the increased consumption of the tax-freed commodity, that is, if Q'QR in Fig. 5.1 exceeds
B'CC'B'' in Fig. 5.2.

On the second assumption, for production of the tax-freed commodity to increase from OT to OS resources to the value QTSR must shift out of other lines of production. To the extent that other lines of production bear taxes, expenditure on other goods must fall by more than the value of the resources required to expand production of the tax-freed commodity, the excess corresponding to the additional lump sum taxes required to compensate the Government for the loss of tax revenue due to reduced consumption of these other goods; the corresponding reduction in total consumer expenditure on commodities is a loss which must be counted against the gain in consumers' surplus on the commodity freed from taxation. This loss can also be illustrated by Fig. 5.2, if the definitions of its construction are slightly modified, so as to equate CDD'C', the reduction in the quantity of resources employed in other industries due to the tax replacement, with QTSR in Fig. 5.1. The diversion of resources to production of the tax-freed commodity entails a reduction of expenditure on other commodities of B'DD'B", a net reduction of expenditure of B'CC'B" which corresponds to the increase in lump sum taxes required to compensate the Government for the loss of tax revenue B'CC'B". There will be a net gain only if the reduction of consumer expenditure is less than the gain in consumers' surplus on the tax-freed commodity, that is, if QQ'R in Fig. 5.1 exceeds B'CC'B" in Fig. 5.2.

The two alternative lines of analysis I have just expounded correspond to two ways of looking at the excess of value to consumers over cost of production of the other commodities than the one freed of tax. The first emphasizes the fact that it costs less to produce a given amount of (marginal) satisfaction in the taxed than in the untaxed industry, so that to maintain satisfaction unchanged while switching consumption to the latter industry it is necessary to obtain additional resources by reducing Government activity. The second emphasizes the fact that a given amount of resources produces more (marginal) satisfaction in the taxed than in the untaxed industry, so that a reallocation of production towards the untaxed industry must reduce the total of consumers' satisfaction obtained.

There is a further, important complication to the analysis. The foregoing argument assumes that other commodities than the tax-freed good can be treated as an aggregate, subject to a common rate of taxation, expenditure on which is simply diverted to the commodity on which the tax is replaced. In fact, some of these commodities will be substitutional, and others complementary, with the good on which the tax is replaced; and they will bear taxes at different rates. The effect of the replacement of the tax on a particular commodity by a lump sum tax will be to divert expenditures from the substitutes for that commodity to its complements, as well as to the commodity itself; insofar as the complements are subject to higher taxes than the substitutes, this diversion will involve a gain (which may be reckoned in either of the two ways discussed previously) additional to the increase in consumers' surplus on the tax-freed good; and conversely, insofar as complements are subject to lower taxes than substitutes, there will be an additional loss. There will be a net gain or loss to the economy from the replacement of the tax by a lump sum subsidy, according as the net reduction in the amount of taxes collected on other commodities is less or greater than the increase in consumers' surplus on the commodity on which the tax is replaced.

Let us now turn to the application of this kind of analysis to the problem of tariffs and commercial policy. To avoid the problem of welfare changes associated with the re-shuffling of internal production between goods bearing different tax rates, let us assume that there are no taxes on domestically produced goods;[10] and to avoid the complications arising from the fact that in practice the rate of tariff on an imported good often depends on the particular country from which it comes, let us assume that the tariff does not discriminate between imports of the same commodity according to their country of origin.

The effect of tariffs is to foster production of domestic goods which meet the consumers' demands at a higher real cost than would imports from abroad. This is because the consumer chooses between domestic and imported goods on the basis of their price inside the country: in the case of a domestically-produced good this price is equal to cost at the margin, whereas in the case of an import this price is above cost by the amount of the tariff collected on the good. The higher cost of want-satisfaction brought about by tariffs has two aspects: on the one hand, it takes the form of higher-cost domestic production of goods identical with those that would otherwise be imported; on the other hand, it takes the form of domestic production of other goods which meet the same need as imports would, but which cost more to produce. In both ways, the tariff promotes the choice of more expensive domestic as compared with cheaper foreign means of satisfying demand. But as between alternative sources of foreign goods, the tariff does not interfere with the choice of the cheaper source: because the tariff rate on imports is (by assumption) the same whatever their source, the import from the cheapest source will have the lowest price after the tariff has been paid and the commodity landed in the importing country.

A customs union involves eliminating the tariff on imports from some foreign sources ("the partner country" for short) but not from others ("the foreign country" for short). One effect of this is to promote a shift from consumption of higher-cost domestic products to consumption of lower-cost foreign products originating in the partner country. This shift has two aspects, paralleling the two aspects of the effects of tariffs just discussed: domestic production of goods identical with those produced abroad is reduced or eliminated, the good now being imported from the partner country; and there is increased consumption of partner-country substitutes for domestic goods which formerly satisfied the need at a higher cost. In short, the demand for imports increases for two reasons: the replacement of domestic by partner production of the same goods— "the production effect"—and increased consumption of partner substitutes for domestic goods—"the consumption effect"; the production effect and the consumption effect together constitute "the trade creation effect" of the customs union.[11] Corresponding to its two components, trade creation entails an economic gain of two sorts; the saving on the real cost of goods previously produced domestically and now imported from the partner country; and the gain in consumers' surplus from the substitution of lower-cost for higher-cost means of satisfying wants.

The gain from trade creation is illustrated diagrammatically in Fig. 5.3. In the diagram, DD is the domestic demand curve for a commodity, SS its domestic supply curve, PQR the partner supply curve (assumed to be constant-cost) and P'Q'R' the partner supply curve with the tariff added to the partner price. With the tariff, the country consumes OS' of which OT' is supplied by domestic production and T'S' imported. When the tariff is eliminated, domestic production falls to OT and consumption rises to OS. The saving of cost on domestic production replaced by imports is QQ'M, and the gain in consumers' surplus from substitution of imports for other goods previously domestically produced is R'NR, so that the total gain from trade creation is the sum of these two areas, approximately equal to half the product of the change in the quantity of imports (TT' plus S'S) and the money amount of the tariff per unit of imports (PP'). (The area P'PQQ' represents a transfer of producers' surplus to consumers, and the area Q'MNR' a transfer of tax proceeds to consumers' surplus, both of which cancel for the country as a whole.)

In addition to the trade creation effect, however, the elimination of the tariff on imports from partner but not from foreign sources has the effect of promoting shifts in the source of imports from lower-cost foreign to higher-cost partner sources. As before, such shifts have two aspects: an

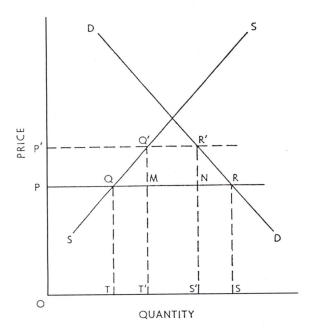

Figure 5.3

increase in the cost of identical goods owing to the shift from foreign to
partner sources; and substitution of higher-cost partner goods for lower-
cost foreign goods of a different description but suitable for satisfying the
same needs. Such shifts constitute "the trade diversion effect" of customs
union. The loss to the country from this source is measured by the difference in cost between the two sources of imports multiplied by the amount
of trade diverted.

The loss from trade diversion is illustrated diagrammatically in Fig. 5.4.
DD is the demand curve, PT and πR the foreign and partner supply
curves (assumed to be constant-cost) and P'Q' and π'Q" these curves after
the tariff. These supply curves can be thought of either as relating to
physically identical products, or as relating to the quantities of different
products required to produce the same consumer satisfaction. With the
tariff applied to both sources of imports, the country imports OS' from
the foreign country at a total cost of OPTS'. When the tariff on partner
imports is eliminated, the country shifts to importing OS from the partner
country; for its previous consumption OS' it now pays a total cost OπRS',
representing an increase in cost (a loss) of πRTP. This loss must be

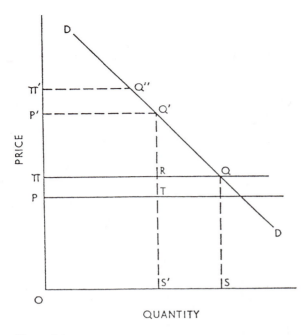

Figure 5.4

weighed against the gain from trade creation (increased total consumption) of Q'RQ.

The foregoing argument assumes perfect foreign and partner elasticity of supply of importable goods. If supplies are not perfectly elastic, the trade diversion effect has two further consequences.[12] In the first place, as trade is diverted from foreign to partner sources the foreign supply price falls. In consequence, the country enjoys a terms-of-trade gain on any trade with the foreign country which survives the formation of the customs union. In addition, any such survival of trade with the foreign country reduces the amount of, and loss from, trade diversion. This has an important implication: the greater the exploitation of the foreigner through a favourable movement of the terms of trade, the less the loss from trade diversion. This implication is to be contrasted with the argument often put forward in favour of customs union by protectionists, that a customs union is a means of favouring the partner country at the expense of the foreigner (rather than of domestic industry)—to the extent that imports from the partner expand at the expense of the foreigner, it is the domestic consumer who loses. The second consequence of imperfectly elastic supplies is that the partner supply price rises as trade is diverted. This means that the loss to the country per unit of trade diverted is greater than it would have been with constant costs; on the other hand, it implies that part of this loss is not a net loss to the domestic and partner economies taken together, but simply a transfer from domestic consumers' surplus to partner producers' surplus.

In addition to the consequences of customs union previously analysed, there may also be various secondary repercussions. For example, if some particular foreign goods are complementary to imports from partner country sources, the trade creation effect of elimination of tariffs on partner imports will also create trade with the foreign country, thereby resulting in additional gains. Similarly, if the country's exports to the partner country which are stimulated by the customs union are substitutes in domestic consumption for foreign goods, the country may increase its imports from the foreign country and so enjoy a gain measured by the tariff revenue on the increased imports. Conversely, complementarity-substitutionary relations between goods might accentuate the country's loss from trade diversion.

Similar gains and losses to those discussed above would result from the elimination of partner duties on the country's exports resulting from customs union. Most of these would accrue to the partner country; but insofar as domestic supply of exports was inelastic, the country would enjoy a terms of trade gain from elimination of the partner country's import duties.

A full analysis of the factors which determine the gains and losses from the formation of a customs union accruing to the individual members would require more time than is available.[13] But the foregoing analysis does indicate certain general principles relevant to this question. In the first place, a country is more likely to gain from the creation of trade resulting from a customs union the higher the initial level of its tariffs, and the more elastic the domestic demand for and supply of goods which the partner country is capable of producing. In the second place, a country is less likely to lose from trade diversion the smaller are the initial differences in cost between the partner and the foreign sources of supply for goods which both can produce, the more elastic is the partner supply of such goods, and the less elastic is the foreign supply of them; also, the less the degree of substitutability in consumption between goods from partner and from foreign sources. Thirdly, the country is more likely to gain on its terms of trade with the foreign country the more inelastic is the foreign supply of imports to it, and the more inelastic the foreign demand for its exports. Further, since a customs union usually involves some change in the level of the tariff on imports from foreign sources, the loss from trade diversion will tend to be less, and the possibility of gains on the terms of trade with foreign sources also less, the lower the tariff on foreign sources after the formation of the customs union as compared with the level of that tariff before the formation of the union.

These general principles can be summarized, very roughly, in the form of a statement about the relation between the natures of the countries embarking on a customs union and the probable gains from such a union. Statements of this kind, however, must be recognized as dangerous, since a general description of the nature of a country is not an adequate substitute for detailed analysis of the probabilities of trade creation, trade diversion and terms of trade effects. With that qualification, it can be said that a country is more likely to reap a gain from entering on a customs union, the more it and its partner country (countries) are initially similar in the products they produce but different in the pattern of relative prices at which they produce them. This is especially true if the products both produce are things which are consumed in rapidly increasing quantities as the standard of living rises, since in this case the income-raising effect of trade creation is self-reinforcing. Further, members are more likely to gain the more different they are from the rest of the world, since this implies that the possibility of losses from trade diversion is less; and the more dependent the rest of the world is on member countries for the import of products in inelastic supply in the rest of the world or the export of products in inelastic demand in the rest of the world, since these imply the possibility of gains on the terms of trade with the rest of the world. (There is some conflict between these last two criteria since exploitation of the foreigner through a favourable movement of the terms of trade requires the possibility of some diversion of imports or exports away from the foreigner towards members of the union.)

This general statement implies that a customs union between heavily protected manufacturing countries, such as the European Common Market, is likely to lead to considerable gain, especially if each has been using some of the income derived from its manufacturing skill to protect its agriculture from foreign competition. Similarly, agricultural areas of a similar kind each bent on industrialization are likely to gain from entering a customs union.

To reverse the statement, a country is less likely to gain from entering a customs union, the more different it is from its partners, the more the partners produce close substitutes for goods produced in foreign countries, and the greater the difference in real costs between foreign and partner supplies of such products; also the more elastic is the foreign supply of such products, and the more the country concerned is a producer for the world market rather than for the market of one or more of the partner countries. An example of a country unlikely to gain from participation in a customs union is an economy with strong advantages in agricultural production uniting with a manufacturing region. The usual objection to such a union is that an agricultural region is unlikely to industrialize without substantial protective tariffs on manufactures. This argument is not particularly cogent, because the comparative advantage of the economy may well lie in agricultural production and the effect of tariffs be to reduce its real income; the fundamental objection in this case is that the customs union renders it subject to exploitation by the inefficient manufacturing partner country, so that it loses its comparative advantages without compensation. This may have been the case, for example, with the maritime and western provinces of Canada in the past, when both could compete on a world market for their products but through their participation in Confederation were forced to buy manufactures from central Canadian manufacturing industry.

The argument so far has been concerned with possible gains and losses from the effects of customs union on the efficiency of specialization and division of labour within the customs union and between it and the outside world. There are other economic aspects of customs union which may also be important. In particular, the enlargement of the internal market brought about by customs union may bring economic advantages besides those of more efficient allocation of production and consumption between countries on the basis of costs of production of commodities before the formation of customs union. For one thing, formation of a customs union may bring about more widespread and effective competition between firms and industries, with a consequent elimination of monopolistic distortions of the economy. In the argument presented so far, it has been assumed that competition prevailed within national markets, so that prices conformed to the minimum real costs technically attainable; if this is untrue, increased competition brought about by customs union may have significant effects in increasing the efficiency of production, apart from specializing production on producers with the lowest real production costs in the pre-union situation. Second, and possibly of greatest long run importance, formation of a customs union may increase the average rate of growth of the member economies, since the larger size of the internal market available to individual industries may both make it safer for the individual firm to invest resources and effort in the introduction of innovations and the deliberate pursuit of expansion, and put increased competitive pressure on individual firms to exploit whatever opportunities they have for expanding their share of the market and their absolute level of sales.[14] Third, formation of a customs union may permit individual firms, and also industries, to exploit the possibilities of economies of scale in production. The possibility of exploiting economies of scale does not, however, necessarily mean that each partner, or all members together, will be better off with the customs union than without; for even though such economies reduce cost of production inside the union that cost may still be higher than the cost of supplies formerly imported from outside the union.

This point is illustrated in Fig. 5.5. In the diagram $S_h S_h$ is the long-run Marshallian supply curve of domestic output in the home country, and $D_h D_h$ the home demand curve; $S_f S_f$ is the foreign supply curve, and $S_f' S_f'$ that supply curve with the tariff initially levied by the home and partner

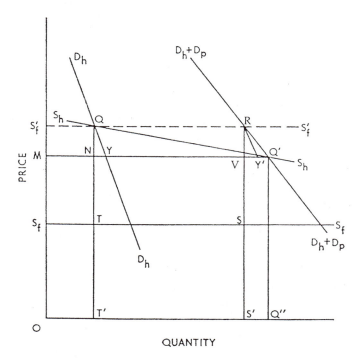

Figure 5.5

countries; $D_h + D_p D_h + D_p$ is the demand curve of the home and partner countries together. Before union, the home country consumes OT' of domestically-produced output at a total cost of OT'QS$_f'$; while the partner country consumes T'S' of imports, at a cost of T'S'ST.[15] With the formation of the customs union, partner consumption is diverted to home-country supply, which expands and in so doing lowers cost, the final equilibrium entailing production and consumption in the market as a whole of OQ" at a cost of OQ"Q'M. The two countries together enjoy a gain of consumers' surplus from expanded consumption of RVQ', of which RVY' (= QNY) accrues to the home country; on its previous level of consumption the home country enjoys a reduction of the real cost in the amount MNQS$_f'$; the partner country, however, suffers an increase in the real cost of its previous consumption in the amount TSVN, which may outweigh its gain of consumers' surplus from expanded consumption RY'Q' and may be large enough to outweigh the home country's gains from lower real cost and expanded consumption as well—as shown by the magnitudes in the diagram. This case, it should be noted, requires that the partner country previously met its wants by imports: if both previously met their wants from protected domestic production, concentration of production in one country where it was subject to economies of scale would necessarily be beneficial to both.

The three possible favourable effects of the enlargement of the market brought about by customs union just discussed all assume that the enlargement of the market will be of the right type to promote such favourable effects. Whether this will be so or not depends on the nature of the existing markets in the member countries and the effects of enlargement through customs union on the nature of the resulting market. If the separate markets of the various members are divided by serious geographical barriers which require high transport costs to overcome them, the enlargement of the market may be more apparent than real; similarly, cultural differences may preserve the separation of member markets despite the removal of tariffs. Again, the Canadian case, at least in its early stages, offers an example of the limitations of removal of taxation barriers in the presence of important physical and cultural barriers to a mass market. This problem is obviously even more acute in the case of Pakistan.

Let me conclude by turning from the economic theory of customs union to some of the problems which arise in the negotiation of them. In discussing these, I shall draw in a general way on the recent experience of the Common Market and Free Trade Area negotiations. The motivation towards the formation of a customs union is often political rather than economic; the economic urge may spring either from a desire for more effective protection, or from a desire for the advantages of greater freedom of trade. In the latter case, the formation of a customs union appears to offer a way around the difficulties of bargaining for mutual tariff reductions within the framework of the most-favoured-nation clause, a framework which impedes progress after a certain point because much of the benefit of a tariff concession goes to third countries, and even more because commodity-by-commodity bargaining accentuates the influence of vested interests in protection in the bargaining countries. The vested interests in protection, however, keep reasserting themselves in the negotiations. The central problem of establishing a customs union is to determine the height and the pattern of the common tariff. Both offer scope for conflict between the protectionist interests of various countries, as well as between protectionists and free traders. One problem which has been important in the Common Market negotiations concerns the treatment of components and materials, where there is a conflict between countries which rely on imports and find their comparative advantage in the processing and advanced stages of production, and those which protect domestic production of such things from imported substitutes; the fixing of the common tariff level determines the distribution of loss between the materials-using industries of the former group and the materials-producing industries of the latter group. Needless to say, the straight averaging of rates which is sometimes resorted to to solve such problems, and is also often taken as a standard ensuring that the degree of protection against outside countries is not increased, has no simple economic rationale—as can be readily inferred from the foregoing analysis of welfare effects.

Two problems which may be of considerable practical importance, particularly for customs unions among underdeveloped countries, are the division of the revenue from the common tariff—especially difficult if certain ports carry on entrepôt activity—and the replacement of lost tariff revenue by other taxes, which may easily have equivalent protective effects. Again, the practical rules of thumb which tend to suggest themselves are often difficult to rationalize in terms of the theory of the welfare effects of customs union and of taxation.

Finally, since freedom of trade between countries both increases the risks of competitive enterprise and reduces the autonomy of domestic economic policy, negotiations for establishment of a customs union (or a free trade area, for that matter) tend to encounter demands for the co-ordination of national economic policies and in particular for the "harmonization" of laws, regulations and other practices affecting the competitive position in the common market area of producers in different countries. Such demands, particularly those for "harmonization," can generally be shown to rest on fallacious arguments stemming from ignorance of the principle of comparative cost, or from an implicit assumption that domestic wage-price levels and the exchange rate are both absolutely rigid; but they may nevertheless cause misunderstanding and bedevil negotiations.

Notes

Editorial Note: The Appendix in the original article has been deleted.

1. A customs union is defined as an agreement between members of a group of countries to remove tariffs levied by each on imports from the others, while establishing a tariff at common rates on imports into the member countries from non-member countries. It is to be distinguished from a free trade area, which allows members to fix their own separate tariff rates on imports from non-members, though they remove tariffs on trade among themselves. Both are narrower than an economic union, which may involve agreement on many other matters of international economic relations, including particularly freedom of factor movements between members. The economic theory of all three has much in common, and the analysis of the present chapter is generally applicable to a free trade area as well as a customs union.

2. Jacob Viner, *The Customs Union Issue* (New York: Carnegie Endowment for International Peace, 1950), Chap. 4, 41–78.

3. Op. cit.

4. J. E. Meade, *The Theory of International Economic Policy, Volume II: Trade and Welfare* (London: Oxford University Press, 1955); also ibid., *The Theory of Customs Unions* (Amsterdam: North Holland Publishing Company, 1956).

5. J. M. Fleming, "On Making the Best of Balance of Payments Restrictions on Imports," *Economic Journal*, LXI, no. 241, March 1951, 48–71.

6. R. G. Lipsey and Kelvin Lancaster, "The General Theory of Second Best," *Review of Economic Studies*, XXIV(1), no. 63, 1956–57, 11–33; M. McManus, "Comments on the General Theory of Second Best," *Review of Economic Studies*, XXVI(3), no. 71, June 1959, 209–24; Kelvin Lancaster and R. G. Lipsey, "McManus on Second Best," *Review of Economic Studies*, XXVI(3), no. 71, June 1959, 225–6.

7. The assumption is implicit in the cancellation of the production cost QRST against the corresponding part of the marginal utility Q'RST of the difference in consumption TS between the taxed and untaxed situations to arrive at the net loss Q'QR; this procedure assumes that resources worth QRST would produce QRST worth of utility in other industries.

8. It is assumed that the location of DD is not affected by the difference between thd two assumptions. This, as well as the implicit assumption of the ensuing analysis that changes in

Government revenue can be cancelled against consumers' surplus, implies that the level of Government expenditure is optimal and that changes in it can be treated as small.

9. Movement from dd to d'd' involves no loss of consumers' surplus; all changes in consumers' surplus are already taken into account in Fig. 5.1.

10. We also abstract from divergences between price and marginal cost due to imperfect competition.

11. It should be noted that the use of the concept of trade creation in this lecture differs from that of other writers (such as Meade and Lipsey) who, following Viner, use it (and the corresponding concept of trade diversion) to refer solely to changes in the location of production, dealing with consumption changes in a rather different fashion, as part of the problem of optimizing trade. The present usage, which lumps production and consumption effects together in the categories of trade creation and trade diversion, seems more easily manageable, particularly when (as below) imperfectly elastic supplies and incomplete specialization are considered.

12. A formal analysis of the effects of discriminatory tariff elimination when partner and foreign supplies are imperfectly elastic is appended to this lecture.

13. For a full discussion, see J. E. Meade, op. cit.

14. This point is stressed by Tibor Scitovsky in relation to European integration; see his *Economic Theory and Western European Integration* (London: Allen and Unwin, Stanford: Stanford University Press, 1958), especially Chap. I, Sec. A, par. 2, 19–48, and Chap. III, 110–35.

15. For diagrammatic simplicity it is assumed that the home tariff rate is just sufficient to protect domestic output from foreign competition, i.e. the difference between the cost at which domestic demand can be satisfied and the foreign cost is just equal to the tariff rate.

6

Tariff Preferences and the Terms of Trade

Robert Mundell

The impact of tariff preferences on resource allocation and welfare has been the subject of notable theoretical advances in the past decade,[1] but there is a gap in the literature on the closely-related question of their effect on the terms of trade, changes in which might significantly affect the distribution of the gains or losses among members, and between the preference area as a whole and the rest of the world. The purpose of this chapter is to fill part of this gap by establishing what appear to be the main propositions valid for an arbitrary number of countries, and to contrast the results with those which derive from the traditional theory of non-discriminatory tariffs.

6.1

I make three simplifying assumptions: (1) initial tariffs are low; (2) the contemplated tariff reductions are small; and (3) all exports are gross substitutes in world consumption in the sense that a rise in the price of any country's exports, all other prices remaining constant, creates an excess demand for the exports of every other country.[2] The significance of these assumptions will be dealt with later.

Consider a three-country system in which A and B denote the prospective member countries and C, the rest of the world. The problem is to deduce the changes in the world (relative) prices of the three countries when the tariff concessions are initiated. The simplest approach to the solution is to investigate, for each tariff reduction in isolation, the changes in the balances of trade on the tentative supposition that international prices remain constant.

Originally published in *Manchester School of Economics and Social Studies* 32 (1964): 1–13. Reprinted with permission.

Let us examine first the reduction in A's tariff on B's exports. At constant international prices the price of B's goods in A falls by the amount of the tariff reduction. This *price* effect, assuming for now that all goods are substitutes in A's consumption,[3] shifts demand in A away from home goods and C's goods onto B's goods, occasioning an improvement in B's balance and a worsening of C's balance. It can also be shown, however, that A's balance worsens since the difference between the improvement in B's balance and the worsening of C's balance must equal the change in A's balance (by Cournot's law that the sum of all balances is identically zero), and because the improvement in B's balance must exceed the worsening of C's balance by the reduced spending in A on home goods (by Walras's law that all excess demands sum to zero within any country).[4] The price effect thus induces an improvement in B's balance and deteriorations in A's and C's balances.

The price effect, however, is partly offset by the *budgetary* effect—A's government experiences a budget deficit equal to the reduced tariff proceeds, and this deficit must be corrected by decreased government spending or increased taxes. The final result therefore depends on whether or not the change in spending due to the method by which the government restores balance in its budget is sufficient to offset the initial price effect. In principle either result is possible depending on which taxes are increased or how the government reduces spending, but there is a strong presumption that the initial price effect will dominate. For example, if income taxes are raised the reduced level of disposable income of the community means that consumers in A will spend less on all goods (in the absence of inferior commodities), but this budgetary effect is exactly equal, for small tariff changes, to the income effect implicit within the initial price effect,[5] leaving only pure substitution terms which work in the same direction as the original price effect. Only in exceptional cases where reduction in government spending is the method used to balance the budget and where it is heavily biased against one of the goods, can the budgetary effect dominate. In what follows I ignore these exceptional cases.

The tariff reduction, then, tends to improve B's balance and worsen A's and C's balances at constant international prices. The latter must therefore move, if equilibrium is to be restored, in a direction which worsens B's balance and improves the balances of A and C. Figure 6.1 provides a method of determining this direction.

The lines AA', BB' and CC' trace the loci of the world prices of A and B, relative to the world prices of C, which permit equilibrium (before the tariff changes) in the balances of A, B and C respectively. The following characteristics of these curves are implied by the assumption that all goods are substitutes in world markets:

1. AA' and BB' have positive slopes.[6] This follows because a rise in A's price (relative to C's price) must be associated with a rise in B's price (relative to C's price) along any iso-balance line, since a c.p. rise in A's price worsens A's and improves B's balance, while a c.p. rise in B's price worsens B's and improves A's balance. Similarly, CC' has a negative slope because a rise in A's price (relative to C's price) would improve C's balance and must therefore be associated, along C's iso-balance schedule, with a fall in B's price which would worsen C's balance (the assymmetrical position of C's curve derives from the (unimportant) assumption that C's goods serve as numeraire).

2. The slope of AA' must exceed, and the slope of BB' must fall short of the slope of a line from O to Q. This follows because a movement along this line is a proportionate movement of B's and A's prices, and is therefore the same (in a "homogeneous" price system) as a c.p. movement of C's price. Any point on OQ must therefore be a point of balance-of-payments surplus for A and B and balance-of-payments deficit for C, while any point along OQ *extended* must be a point of surplus for C and deficit for A and B.

3. When the system is not in equilibrium at the point Q the situations of deficit or surplus in the balances of the three countries must be those indicated by the inequalities in the six sectors.

The diagram can now be used to establish the direction of change in the terms of trade. From the initial equilibrium Q the tariff reduction in A causes the three schedules to shift. At constant international prices, i.e., at the point Q, the tariff reduction causes B's balance to be in surplus and A's and C's balances to be in deficit, so world prices must move in a direction which worsens B's balance and improves those of A and C. In other words, the new point of equilibrium must lie in Quadrant I where, from the point of view of the situation before the tariff change, A's and C's balances are in surplus and B's is in deficit. The characteristics of Quadrant I therefore outline the changes in relative prices which must take place as a result of the tariff reduction; in this quadrant B's price has risen relative to the prices of A and C. This establishes the most important proposition about discriminatory tariff reductions: *a tariff reduction in a member country unambiguously improves the terms of trade of the partner country.*

Notice that it cannot be determined, a priori, whether the terms of trade of the tariff-reducing country (A) rise or fall relative to the foreign country; an equilibrium in Quadrant I is consistent with either result. But given the elasticities of demand in A for the goods of B and C (these elasticities determine the change in the balances at constant international prices), there exists a line which determines the new equilibria for successively larger tariff reductions in A. Thus, if the point a represents the new equilibrium as a result of a small tariff reduction in A, then the point a' would indicate that for a slightly larger tariff reduction. The line Qaa' I shall call A's "tariff-reduction line." Its slope as drawn is negative but in fact all that can be definitely established is that it must lie between the slopes of QC and QA'.

Now let us consider the effect of reduction in B's tariff on A's goods and the combined effect of both A's and B's tariff reductions. B's tariff reduction creates a surplus in A's balance and deficits in the balances of B and C, necessitating an improvement in A's terms of trade relative to both other countries. In the diagram the new equilibrium, as a result of B's tariff reduction alone, must be in Quadrant III following the same line of reasoning as in the analysis of A's tariff reduction. B's tariff-reduction line is described by Qbb', with any slope between that of QB' and QC'.

The final effect of any given set of mutual discriminatory tariff reductions can be determined by adding the results. If A's tariff reduction results in a new equilibrium at, say, a, and B's tariff reduction results in a new equilibrium at, say, b, the combined effect is determined by completing the parallelogram formed by the two tariff-reduction lines Qa and Qb, establishing the point T_1 as the new equilibrium. Similarly, the points T_2, T_3 and T_4 are the new equilibria for the respective sets of points on the tariff-reduction lines, (a', b'), (a, b') and (a', b).

6.2

All the attainable points lie northeast of CC' but they might lie in any of the three Quadrants, I, II and III. The characteristics of these quadrants indicate the general conclusions which follow from discriminatory tariff reductions: in Quadrant I, B's terms of trade have unambiguously improved; in Quadrant III, A's terms of trade have unambiguously improved; and in Quadrant II, C's terms of trade have unambiguously worsened (the indicated change in the terms of trade is unambiguous in the sense that the improvement or deterioration is with respect to both the other countries). In all three quadrants the terms of trade of the rest of the world worsens with respect to at least one and perhaps both of the member countries.

The entire area northeast of CC, however, is not attainable by given tariff reductions; given the elasticities of demand in the two member

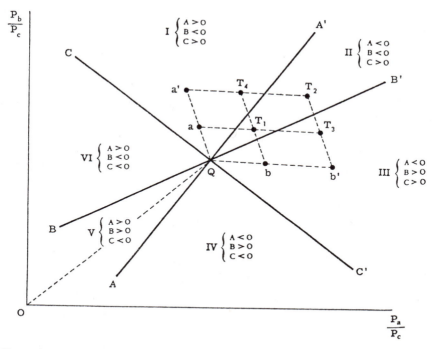

Figure 6.1

countries, only the area east of *A*'s and north of *B*'s tariff-reduction line encloses the point of final equilibrium, and this area is necessarily smaller than the area northeast of *CC*. But the attainable area must nevertheless enclose all of Quadrant II, yielding another important conclusion: *some sets of tariff reductions necessarily improve the terms of trade of both member countries with respect to the rest of the world* (this might not include the specific tariff reductions implied by a free-trade area, however) A special case is where the members lower tariffs in a ratio which preserves the original intra-union terms of trade resulting in a new equilibrium along *OQ* extended; in this case it is obvious that the terms of trade of the outside world unambiguously fall since the balance of payments of each individual country in the union improves while that of the outside world worsens, as a result of the tariff reductions at constant world prices. But this special case is only one of many instances in which the terms of trade of the outside world fall with respect to both members; indeed, there is a general presumption that this is the normal case since the balance of payments of the union as a whole necessarily improves (at constant prices) while that of each country in the rest of the world worsens.

Finally, one can consider the possibility of independence or complementarity in national (but not in world) consumptions. The smaller are the cross elasticities of demand in member countries between the exports of the partner country and the exports of third countries, the greater is the likelihood that the terms of trade of one of the member countries will deteriorate with respect to foreign countries. At the limit—where A's tariff reduction does not reduce imports into A from foreign countries, and where B's tariff reduction does not reduce imports into B from foreign countries—the terms of trade of one of the member countries is likely to improve, while that of the other member country is likely to fall, since the tariff reductions cause a deficit in one member and a surplus in the other member, whereas the balance of the rest of the world is unaltered (there is an exception if the tariffs are reduced in a way which preserves the intra-union balance; in that case world prices remain unchanged). As we pass the limit—as some complementarity appears in the consumptions of member countries—there arises the possibility that the terms of trade of the rest of the world improve with respect to both member countries. Thus, if B's and C's goods were complementary and, similarly, if A's and C's goods were complementary in B's consumption, B's tariff reduction alone would prompt a fall in B's terms of trade. Then the combined tariff reductions would stimulate, at constant world prices, a surplus in foreign countries and a deficit in the union as a whole, occasioning an improvement in the terms of trade of the outside world relative to the union.

6.3

The following generalizations now emerge from this study of tariff preferences:

1. A discriminatory tariff reduction by a member country improves the terms of trade of the partner country with respect to both the tariff-reducing country and the rest of the world, but the terms of trade of the tariff-reducing country might rise or fall with respect to third countries.

2. The degree of improvement in the terms of trade of the partner country is likely to be larger the greater is the member's tariff reduction; this establishes the presumption that a member's gain from a free-trade area will be larger the higher are the initial tariffs of partner countries.

3. It cannot be established, a priori, that arbitrary sets of discriminatory tariff reductions by member countries must improve the terms of trade of

both member countries; it is possible that the terms of trade of one of the members deteriorate relative to third countries.

4. Nevertheless, there exists a presumption that the terms of trade of both member countries improve relative to the outside world. This presumption is established by the fact that the balance of trade of the preference area as a whole must improve, while that of each country in the rest of the world must deteriorate. It follows immediately that the terms of trade of one of the members improve relative to third countries; if, for example, the balance of trade of a member country deteriorates as a result of the tariff reduction (at constant world prices) the terms of trade of the partner country must improve.

5. Moreover, there are numerous sets of tariff reductions that must improve the terms of trade of both member countries. A special case is where tariffs are reduced so as to leave the intra-union terms of trade unaltered.

6. The above propositions hold where all goods are substitutes in national consumptions. If complementarity is present between the goods of partner countries and the outside world there arises the possibility that the terms of trade of the latter improve relative to both member countries.

6.4

It remains now to indicate briefly the significance of the three assumptions made at the beginning, and to contrast the results with those which derive from traditional tariff theory. The assumption that initial tariffs are low ensures that the tariff reductions reduce the value of tariff proceeds and create deficits in the government budgets; our conclusions would not hold if, for example, initial tariffs were prohibitive. The assumption that the tariff changes are small is necessary for similar reasons, because large tariff changes would be likely to change the composition of imports and exports; and because the proposition relating to the equality of the budgetary effect (when income taxes are raised) and the income effect implicit within the price change would not be exact. The assumption of substitution in world markets, however, is one which requires more intensive examination.

If complementarity is present in the world economy the conclusions reached in this paper might be fundamentally changed; in general terms (even if the requirement that the system is dynamically stable be imposed) almost any result can occur. Analysis of complementarity would therefore deteriorate into a difficult exercise in taxonomy, and one which is probably unrewarding unless actual statistics can be introduced. The assumption of substitution seems to be necessary in order to get definite results, and to establish a useful "normal" case with which more complicated examples can be compared.

It must not be thought, however, that the restrictive assumption of universal substitution is any less necessary in analysis of the traditional theory of tariffs or, indeed, in any of the other branches of international trade theory. The certain results which appear to derive from traditional theory are equally based on the assumption of substitution, but the assumption is hidden by the usual two-country model employed in that branch of analysis; whereas an analysis of discriminatory tariffs logically requires at least a three-country model of the world economy and thus explicit recognition of the problem of complementarity. Only if complementarity is assumed to be slight or absent does the proposition of traditional tariff theory, that an (undiscriminatory) tariff reduction worsens the terms of trade of the tariff-reducing country, hold, just as this assumption is necessary to establish that an undiscriminatory tariff reduction improves the terms of trade of the partner country.

6.5   Appendix

The propositions now established for three countries hold also for an arbitrary number of countries. Suppose that there are $n + 1$ countries, numbered 0, 1, 2, ..., n and that the exports of country 0 are numeraire. Let B_i be the balance of trade (or payments) of the i-th country, expressed in terms of the numeraire, and let p_j denote the price of the exports of the j-th country, with p_j initially equal to unity (by appropriate choice of units). The system can be written as follows:

$$B_i(p_1, \ldots, p_n; t) = 0 \tag{1}$$

where t is a parameter representing the combined tariff reductions. By differentiation we obtain

$$\sum_{j=1}^{n} \frac{\delta B_i}{\delta p_j} \frac{dp_j}{dt} = -\frac{\delta B_i}{\delta t} \ (i = 1, 2, \ldots, n). \tag{2}$$

The solution for $\dfrac{dp_i}{dt}$ is

$$\frac{dp_i}{dt} = -\sum_{j=1}^{n} \frac{\delta B_j}{\delta t} \frac{\Delta_{ji}}{\Delta} \tag{3}$$

where Δ is the Jacobian $\dfrac{\delta(B_l, \ldots, B_n)}{\delta(p_l, \ldots, p_n)}$ and Δ_{ji} is the co-factor of its j-th row and i-th column. The assumption of gross substitution in world markets implies that Δ_{ii} and Δ are of opposite sign, so that the ratio of the two is negative.[7]

Suppose that countries 0 and 1 are the member countries. Then it follows immediately that a tariff reduction in *one* of the member countries, say country 1,[8] improves the terms of trade of the partner country since, in that case, $\dfrac{\delta B_j}{\delta t} < 0$ for *every* $j = 1, 2, \ldots, n$; the expression on the right of (3) is negative.

Taking the tariff changes in both countries into account, it is not definite that a member country's terms of trade rise. This can be seen by separating the first term in (3) from the other to get

$$\frac{dp_i}{dt} = -\frac{\delta B_l}{\delta t}\frac{\Delta_{li}}{\Delta} - \sum_{j=2}^{n}\frac{\delta B_j}{\delta t}\frac{\Delta_{ji}}{\Delta} \tag{4}$$

The first term might be positive or negative depending on the elasticities of demand in the two member countries and on the size of the relative tariff reductions. But if a member's balance worsens as a result of the tariff reductions, it follows that partner's terms of trade must improve; the uncertainty as to sign only appears to apply if the balances of both members improve.

It is readily shown, however, that the terms of trade of both members cannot deteriorate. To see this, consider the intra-union terms of trade, and note that this might change in any direction. But if the intra-union terms of trade of one of the members improve, then the terms of trade of that member must improve relative to third countries. Suppose, for instance, that the intra-union terms of trade of country 0 improve so that

$$\frac{dp_l}{dt} = -\frac{\delta B_l}{\delta t}\frac{\Delta_{ll}}{\Delta} - \sum_{j=2}^{n}\frac{\delta B_j}{\delta t}\frac{\Delta_{jl}}{\Delta} < 0. \tag{5}$$

It follows, from (5) that

$$\frac{\delta B_l}{\delta t} = -\zeta - \sum_{j=2}^{n}\frac{\delta B}{\delta t}\frac{\Delta_{jl}}{\Delta_{ll}} \tag{6}$$

where ζ is a positive number. Substituting (6) in (4) we get

$$\frac{dp_i}{dt} = \left[\zeta + \sum_{j=2}^{n} \frac{\delta B_j}{\delta t} \frac{\Delta_{jl}}{\Delta_{ll}} \right] \frac{\Delta_{li}}{\Delta} - \sum_{j=2}^{n} \frac{\delta B_j}{\delta t} \frac{\Delta_{ji}}{\Delta}$$

$$= \zeta \frac{\Delta_{li}}{\Delta} + \sum_{j=2}^{n} \frac{\delta B_j}{\delta t} \frac{\Delta_{jl}\Delta_{li} - \Delta_{ji}\Delta_{ll}}{\Delta\Delta_{ll}} \tag{7}$$

Now the first term is obviously negative. The second term will be negative provided the numerator and the denominator of the term containing determinants are of the same sign; this is readily shown to be the case, making use of Mosak's theorem and another theorem about determinants.[9] This is sufficient to prove that one of the member country's terms of trade must improve.

There are a number of special cases in which the terms of trade of both members improve, relative to outside countries. The case considered in the text is where the intra-union terms of trade are unchanged; the proof in the general case follows readily by setting the expression in (5) equal to zero, and substituting in (4) to get the same results as in (7) without the first term.

Notes

1. Three main works on the theory of customs unions are: Jacob Viner, *The Customs Union Issue* (Carnegie Endowment for International Peace: New York, 1950); James E. Meade, *The Theory of Customs Unions* (North Holland: Amsterdam 1956); and Tibor Scitowsky, *Economic Theory and Western European Integration* (Stanford University Press: Stanford 1958); but mention should also be made of H. Makower and G. Morton, "A Contribution Towards a Theory of Customs Unions," *Economic Journal*, Vol. LXIII No. 249 (March 1953); R. G. Lipsey, "The Theory of Customs Unions: Trade Diversion and Welfare," *Economica*, Vol. XXIV No. 93 (February 1957); H. G. Johnson, "Discriminatory Tariff Reduction: A Marshallian Analysis," *Indian Journal of Economics*, Vol. XXXVIII No. 148 (July 1957); and R. G. Lipsey, "The Theory of Customs Union: A General Survey," *Economic Journal*, Vol. LXX No. 279 (September 1960), 496–513.

2. In "The Pure Theory of International Trade," *American Economic Review*, Vol. L No. 1 (March 1960) I compared the traditional two-country model of international trade with a multiple-country system, and found (for tariffs, income transfers, productivity changes, consumption and production taxes) that the two models yield practically identical qualitative results provided that all exports are gross substitutes.

3. Some goods might be complements in a nation's consumption without interfering with the assumption that all goods are gross substitutes in world markets. I assume here that all goods are *net* and *gross* substitutes in A's consumption, but the implications of relaxing this assumption will be discussed later.

4. Let A, B, and C be the balances of the three countries, and dt the change in A's tariff. With units chosen to make each price initially unity, the change in B's balance at constant terms of trade, as a proportion of the tariff change, is

$$\left(\frac{\delta B}{\delta t}\right)' = \left(\frac{\delta I_{bu}}{\delta t}\frac{1}{I_{bu}}\right)I_{bu} = -\eta_{bu\cdot b}I_{bu}$$

where I_{bu} is the level of imports from B to A and $\eta_{bu\cdot b}$ is the negative (own) elasticity of demand for B's goods in A due to a change in the price of B's goods; and the change in C's balance can be written

$$\left(\frac{\delta C}{\delta t}\right)' = \left(\frac{\delta I_{cu}}{\delta t}\frac{1}{I_{cu}}\right)I_{cu} = -\eta_{cu\cdot b}I_{cu}$$

where $\eta_{cu\cdot b}$ is the positive (cross) elasticity of demand for C's goods in A due to the change in price of B's goods. Now by Cournot's law we have

$$\left(\frac{\delta A}{\delta t}\right)' + \left(\frac{\delta B}{\delta t}\right)' + \left(\frac{\delta C}{\delta t}\right)' = 0$$

so

$$\left(\frac{\delta A}{\delta t}\right)' = (\eta_{ba\cdot b}I_{ba} + \eta_{cd\cdot b}I_{ca}).$$

On the other hand, from Walras' law, we have

$$\eta_{aa\cdot b}I_{aa} + \eta_{ba\cdot b}I_{ba} + \eta_{ca\cdot b}I_{ca} = 0$$

where $\eta_{aa\cdot b}$ is the positive (cross) elasticity of A's demand for home goods due to a change in B's price, and I_{aa} is home consumption. It follows that

$$\left(\frac{\delta A}{\delta t}\right)' = -\eta_{aa\cdot b}I_{aa} < 0$$

5. The price effects treated in the preceding note can be split into pure substitution elasticities and income propensities as follows:

$$-\eta_{ba\cdot b}I_{ba} = -\eta'_{ba\cdot b}I_{ba} + m_{ba}I_{ba}$$

and

$$-\eta_{ca\cdot b}I_{ca} = -\eta'_{ca\cdot b}I_{ca} + m_{ca}I_{ba}$$

where m_{ba} and m_{ca} are the marginal propensities to spend in A on imports from B and C, and the primes denote that the elasticities have no income effects.

The increased income taxes reduce disposable income in A by $I_{ba}dt$ so that the budgetary effects alter B's and C's balances as a proportion of the tariff change, according to the equations

$$\left(\frac{\delta B}{\delta t}\right)'' = -m_{ba}I_{ba}$$

and

$$\left(\frac{\delta C}{\delta t}\right)'' = -m_{ca}I_{ba}.$$

The combined impact of the price and budgetary effects, before world prices change, is therefore

$$\frac{\delta B}{\delta t} = \left(\frac{\delta B}{\delta t}\right)' + \left(\frac{\delta B}{\delta t}\right)'' = -\eta'_{ba\cdot b}I_{ba} > 0$$

and

$$\frac{dC}{\delta t} = \left(\frac{\delta C}{\delta t}\right)' + \left(\frac{\delta C}{\delta t}\right)'' = -\eta_{ca \cdot b} l_{ca} < 0.$$

In "The Pure Theory of International Trade: Comment," *American Economic Review*, Vol. L No. 4 (September 1960), 721–2, Professor H. G. Johnson corrected a conclusion of my earlier paper (Mundell, op. cit., n. 30) where the income effect implicit within the tariff reduction was wrongly weighted; his *Comment* has helped to clarify my present analysis of income effects.

6. The three schedules are drawn as straight lines to emphasize that the analysis is exact for small changes only.

7. By Mosak's theorem that: if the off-diagonal elements of Δ are positive (implied by the assumption of gross substitution) and *if* the matrix of Δ is Hicksian, then *all* the elements of Δ^{-1} are negative; and by the stability theorems of Arrow and Hurwicz, Hahn, Negishi and Uzawa that: if all the off-diagonal elements of Δ are positive and the row- or column-sums are negative, the matrix of Δ *is* Hicksian. References are given in my article previously cited.

8. The proof that: if a country o lowers its tariff, the terms of trade of country l improve, is slightly more difficult, and requires the introduction of a theorem developed by Metzler for the Keynesian case (Lloyd Metzler, "A Multiple-Country Theory of Income Transfers," *Journal of Political Economy*, Vol. LIX, No. 1 (February 1951), p. 21 and applied to the classical case in my article (no. 29); but the reader's intuition should persuade him that the analysis in the text is sufficient since the choice of numeraire cannot affect *relative* prices.

9. The following identity is true for any determinant:

$$\Delta\Delta_{ll,ii} = \Delta_{ll}\Delta_{ii} - \Delta_{ii}\Delta_{li}:$$

but from Mosak's theorem, and the stability theorems, it follows that the two terms on the left have the same sign, so that the difference on the right is positive. This means that the ratio of the determinants in the second equation is negative.

See Metzler (op. cit., p. 26) for a previous application to the generalized Keynesian system.

7

The Meade Model of Preferential Trading: History, Analytics, and Policy Implications

Arvind Panagariya

Though the theory of preferential trading had its birth in Jacob Viner's (1950) celebrated work for the Carnegie Endowment, *The Customs Union Issue*, the first complete general-equilibrium model of preferential trading was provided by James Meade (1955) in the de Vries Lectures, delivered at the Netherlands School of Economics while the Benelux union was in progress and published as *The Theory of Customs Unions*.[1] Remarkably, at a time when two-good models dominated the thinking of international trade theorists, Meade constructed a complete three-good, three-country model and even went on to extend it to a multicountry, multicommodity context. The model has proved as durable as Viner's concepts of trade creation and trade diversion with Lipsey (1958, chaps. 5–6, 1960), Mundell (1964), Vanek (1965, Appendix), Corden (1976), Collier (1979), McMillan and McCann (1981), and Lloyd (1982) making significant contributions to its further development.[2] Insights emerging out of the model have also shaped the policy debate on regional integration (see Bhagwati and Panagariya, 1996a).

Peter Kenen has much in common with Meade. Like Meade, he has the unusual distinction of having advanced both branches of international economics: pure trade and finance. Those of us who had the opportunity to sit through his lectures on international trade can also recall his clever use of geometry, as was done by Meade (1952) in *A Geometry of International Trade*. Indeed, Peter was once a student of Meade and, in the 1950s, alongside him, helped build the area of trade and welfare as we know it today (Kenen 1957 and 1959).

This essay honors Peter Kenen by bringing together the history, analytics, and policy implication of *The Theory of Customs Unions*. The essay

Originally published in *International Trade and Finance: New Frontiers for Research, Essays in Honor of Peter B. Kenen*, ed. Benjamin Cohen (New York: Cambridge University Press, 1997), 57–88. Reprinted with permission.

is an appropriate tribute to Peter's scholarship not only because Meade was a major intellectual influence for him but also because he has himself made important contributions to the monetary theory of economic integration. Thus, whereas Meade (1955) gave us the first welfare theoretic analysis of customs unions in a general-equilibrium model, Peter Kenen (1969) pioneered the theory of optimum currency areas.

Though all contributors to the Meade model listed above, except Mundell (1964), used the term "customs unions" in their titles, only Viner (1950) and Vanek (1965) explicitly distinguished them as unions involving internal free trade and a *common* external tariff. Almost all other authors, including Meade himself, used the term more broadly for what is best described generically as a preferential trading area (PTA) involving only internal free trade and hence including free trade areas (FTAs). Thus, Lipsey explicitly defined the theory of customs unions as "the theory of geographically discriminatory reductions in tariffs." Meade and subsequent writers on "customs unions" almost never considered the implications of harmonization of external tariffs to a common level across member countries and generally focused on the effects of tariff preferences or free trade areas with external tariffs held at their original levels in each country.[3]

Because so much has been written on the Meade model during the past three decades, it may seem that there is little new to be added. Yet, there is a good deal to be gained by examining the original text, which has remained poorly understood in the literature. Thus, I will begin by establishing that the post-Meade literature on the Meade model has been in error in two important respects: (i) unlike the predominant impression in the literature, Meade evaluated preferential trading and free trade areas from the viewpoint of the world as a whole rather than the union or a union member, and (ii) unlike the modern versions of the "Meade Model," Meade himself did not assume fixed terms of trade between either union members or the union and the rest of the world.

I also provide a formal treatment of Meade's original analysis and unify it with the help of a few algebraic expressions. Among other things, this formalization will help us bring out clearly the importance Meade attached to tariffs in the outside country in evaluating the desirability of preferential trading arrangements. The subsequent literature has almost completely disregarded the importance of this factor. I also offer an analysis of the effects of preferential liberalization by a country on its welfare in the presence of flexible terms of trade.

A further contribution of this essay lies in providing a concise treatment of the small-union Meade model and offering some new results in this overcrowded field. In particular, I show that Lipsey's (1958) result that the larger the expenditure on home goods relative to that on the outside country's good the more likely that preferential liberalization will benefit a small country can be extended to the case of CES preferences. Lipsey had derived this result for Cobb–Douglas preferences.

Finally, I offer a detailed analysis of the implications of the Meade model for "natural trading partners" hypothesis, according to which the larger the initial volume of trade between union members the greater the likelihood that the union will be welfare improving. I conclude that the Meade model does not support this hypothesis.

In Section 7.1, I discuss *The Theory of Customs Unions* in detail. This discussion is divided into three subsections: history, analytics, and policy implications. In Section 7.2, I consider the small-union Meade model, extending the existing analysis. In particular, I derive an expression for the second-best optimum tariff that is far more transparent and intuitive than that in the existing literature. In Section 7.3, the issue of "natural trading partners" is examined critically in the context of the Meade model. Here I generalize Lipsey's result as mentioned above and discuss briefly the implications of fully flexible terms of trade for it. I conclude the essay in Section 7.4.

7.1   James Meade's Theory of Customs Unions

There are eight chapters and two appendices in *The Theory of Customs Unions*. Chapter 1 discusses policies to maintain full employment and balance of payments within the context of a customs union. This chapter is not central to the analysis of customs unions but perhaps reflects the general preoccupation of economists with balances of payments and full employment issues at the time. In Chapter 2, Meade provides a formal interpretation and critique of Viner's theory of customs unions. He takes the view that Viner's (1950) analysis is based on a model characterized by infinite supply elasticities and zero demand elasticities in all countries.[4]

In Chapter 3, he introduces his basic model, which has three goods and three countries. Taking the opposite extreme of his formulation of the Viner model, Meade postulates zero supply elasticities and positive demand elasticities. These properties are obtained by restricting the analysis to the pure exchange model and by assuming that demands behave in the normal fashion. Some of Meade's key conclusions are stated in this chapter.

In Chapter 4, Meade extends his model to many commodities and allows all commodities to be produced in all countries. The key contribution of this chapter is to develop a measure of a change in the world welfare due to a policy change. In Chapter 5, he applies this measure to preferential liberalization by a union member and offers a rich analysis under alternative assumptions of substitutability and complementarity between the liberalized and other goods.

To proceed in steps, Meade limits the analysis in Chapter 5 to the effects that accompany a reduction in the price of the liberalized good in the country granting the preference and an increase in the price of the same good in the country receiving the preference. Noting that these effects leave imbalances in the countries' trade accounts, in Chapter 6, Meade turns to the effects on welfare that will arise from policies aimed at restoring trade balance in each country. Here, in the spirit of Chapter 1, he launches into a discussion of monetary and exchange-rate policies to restore trade balance. In my view, this is the least satisfactory chapter in the book, for two reasons. First, as we will see explicitly below, the welfare measure used by Meade requires equality of income and expenditure or, equivalently, balance in trade for each country. What is left out of balance in Chapter 5 is not the trade accounts of different countries but of world markets in goods. Meade's technique involves deriving the changes in imports and exports due to certain price changes, assumed to have been induced by preferential liberalization by one of the countries, and then evaluating the effects of these changes on world welfare. But because the price changes are themselves not fully endogenized, there is no guarantee that the changes in exports and imports of different countries will be just right to clear the world markets. Second, the natural instrument to restore full equilibrium in pure trade models is not macroeconomic policies, to which Meade resorted, but the terms of trade.

In Chapter 7, Meade discusses the limitation of his analysis. Interestingly, here he provides an important result, in the presence of quantitative restrictions, that has been identified incorrectly by Baldwin and Venables (1995) as what has come to be known as the Kemp–Wan theorem. In Chapter 8, Meade summarizes his main conclusions. Appendix 1 offers the rules of the game for the balance of payments of an economic union that partner countries may wish to adopt, and Appendix 2 derives an expression for the change in welfare in a closed economy. Apart from Appendix 2, the entire book is written in straight prose with no diagrams or equations.

7.1.1 History: Some Common Confusions

Economists familiar with post-Meade (1955) writings on the Meade model but not *The Theory of Customs Unions* will be surprised to know that the latter said little about the impact of preferential trading on union members themselves. With rare exceptions, the focus of Meade's original text was exclusively on the impact of preferential trading on world welfare.[5] He set the stage for his analysis on the second page of Chapter 1 thus,

> The problem which I want to discuss in these lectures is whether this removal of barriers to trade between the two partner countries is likely to lead to a more or less economic use of the world's economic resources. It is not my intention to inquire into the possible effects of the formation of the union upon the level of economic activity within the various parts of the world.

Throughout the book, unless otherwise noted, whenever Meade uses the term "welfare effects" or "effects on standards," he means world welfare. In Chapter 7, which is devoted primarily to a discussion of the limitations to his analysis, Meade notes,

> A third important way in which my analysis has been restricted up to this point is that it has made no allowance for the effects of the customs union upon the distribution of income between the trading countries concerned. (94)

Despite these clear statements, the post-Meade literature has attributed to Meade results derived for an individual union member or the union as a whole.[6]

A related confusion in the literature concerns the treatment of the terms of trade. Though Meade did not explicitly solve his model for changes in the terms of trade, nowhere in the book did he assume that the terms of trade are fixed. Indeed, his analysis explicitly considers the effects of the change in the international price of the product on which the tariff preference is granted. Nevertheless, the Meade model, as we know it today, assumes that union members are price takers in the world market (Lloyd 1982, table 1). As far as I am able to trace, the switch was made by Lipsey (1958, chaps. 5 and 6) without explicit recognition and adopted by virtually all subsequent analysts of the model.[7] Unlike Meade (1955), the small-union model focuses naturally on the welfare of the union or individual union members rather than the world.

Why has this confusion persisted in the literature? We will see below that the results obtained by Meade *for world welfare under flexible terms of trade* are qualitatively similar to those obtained for *the union or an*

individual union member under fixed terms of trade. In the spirit of two nega-
tives turning into a positive, the *double switch* in assumptions—one making
the union or a union member the object of analysis and the other fixing the
terms of trade—leads to no change in results. It is this fact that perhaps
led Lipsey (1958, 1960) and others to equate erroneously their model and
results to those of Meade.[8] But, of course, each switch in assumptions by
itself is important. Thus, if Lipsey had made only one switch by focusing
on the welfare of a union member but retaining the assumption of fully
flexible terms of trade, his results would have been drastically different
from those of Meade.

7.1.2 Analytics and Main Results

Let us set up the problem in the most general form as Meade would have
ideally liked and, indeed, implicitly did in Chapter 4 of his book.[9] Assume
there are n goods indexed by i and m countries indexed by j. We use a
subscript to identify a commodity and superscript to distinguish a country. Denote by p_i^* the international price of good i, p_i^j the (domestic) price
of good i in country j and t_i^j the corresponding ad valorem trade tax. Per-
unit trade tax on good i in country j is $t_i^j \cdot p_i^* \equiv p_i^j - p_i^*$ in the case of an
importable and $t_i^j \cdot p_i^* \equiv p_i^* - p_i^j$ in the case of an exportable. If trade tax
on a commodity is zero, its domestic price equals the international price.

For any country j, the expenditure-income equality implies

$$e^j(p_1^j, p_2^j, \ldots, p_n^j; u^j) = r^j(p_1^j, p_2^j, \ldots, p_n^j)$$
$$+ \sum_i (p_i^j - p_i^*)(e_i^j - r_i^j) \qquad j = 1, \ldots m \qquad (7.1)$$

where $e^j(\cdot)$ and $r^j(\cdot)$ are, respectively, the standard expenditure and rev-
enue functions for country j. In addition, $e_i^j \equiv \partial e^j / \partial p_i^j$ and $r_i^j \equiv \partial r^j / \partial p_i^j$.
Defining $m^j(p_1^j, p_2^j, \ldots, p_n^j; u^j) \equiv e^j(\cdot) - r^j(\cdot)$, we can rewrite (7.1) as

$$m^j(p_1^j, p_2^j, \ldots, p_n^j; u^j) = \sum_i (p_i^j - p_1^*)m_i^j(\cdot) \qquad (7.1')$$

where $m_i^j \equiv \partial m^j / \partial p_i^j$ is the compensated import-demand function for
good i in country j. The market-clearing condition for good i requires

$$\Sigma_j m_i^j = 0, \qquad i = 1, \ldots n \qquad (7.2)$$

The relationship between the domestic and international prices may be
written

$$t_i^j \cdot p_i^* \equiv p_i^j - p_i^* \qquad \text{if } m_i^j > 0 \text{ and}$$

$$t_i^j \cdot p_i^* \equiv p_i^* - p_i^j \qquad \text{if } m_i^j < 0 \qquad i = 1, \ldots n; \quad j = 1, \ldots m \qquad (7.3)$$

Note that m_i^j is positive or negative as country j imports or exports good i. In (7.1'), (7.2), and (7.3), we have $m + n + mn$ equations in m utilities, n international prices, and mn domestic prices. We can choose one international price arbitrarily by the choice of a numeraire and drop one of the corresponding market-clearing conditions in (7.2). The remaining system defines an equilibrium in the world economy of the kind envisioned by Meade.

To obtain the key expression that serves as the basis of all of Meade's analysis, let us suppose that there is a small change in the tariff rates of various goods in different countries. Later, we will focus on the change in just one tariff rate, but that is not necessary at this stage. Differentiating (7.1) totally, we can obtain

$$e_u^j du^j = - \sum_i m_i^j dp_i^* + \sum_i (p_i^j - p_i^*) \, dm_i^j \qquad i = 1, \ldots n; j = 1, \ldots m \qquad (7.4)$$

where $e_u^j \equiv \partial e^j / \partial u^j$ and we make use of the fact that $r^j(\cdot)$ does not depend on u. Because e_u^j is the reciprocal of the marginal utility of income, the left-hand side of (7.4) represents the change in utility in terms of the numeraire good and may be thought of as the change in the real income of country j. Looking at the right-hand side, the change in the real income equals the import-weighted sum of the change in the terms of trade plus the change in tariff revenue valued at the initial tariff rates. This is now a standard result in trade models.

Because Meade assesses the desirability of preferential trading from the viewpoint of the world, we need to develop an expression for the world welfare. This Meade did by summing the changes in real incomes across countries. Thus, letting w stand for the world welfare,

$$dw = \sum_j e_u^j du^j = - \sum_j \sum_i m_i^j dp_i^* + \sum_j \sum_i (p_i^j - p_i^*) \, dm_i^j$$

$$i = 1, \ldots n; \quad j = 1, \ldots m$$

$$= - \sum_i dp_i^* \sum_j m_i^j + \sum_j \sum_i (p_i^j - p_i^*) \, dm_i^j \qquad (7.5)$$

Recalling, however, that $\Sigma_j m_i^j = 0$ by the market-clearing condition (7.2), we obtain[10]

$$dw = \sum_j \sum_i (p_i^j - p_i^*) \, dm_i^j \qquad i = 1, \ldots n; \quad j = 1, \ldots m \qquad (7.6)$$

If we assume that there are no export taxes in any of the countries, the second equality in (7.3) yields $p_i^* = p_i^j$, where p_i^j is the price of good j in the country exporting that product. Similarly, for an importable, using the first equation in (7.3), we have $p_i^j - p_i^* \equiv t_i^j \cdot p_i^*$. We can rewrite equation (7.6) as

$$dw = \sum_j \sum_i t_i^j \cdot p_i^* dm_i^j \qquad i = 1, \ldots n; \quad j = 1, \ldots m \qquad (7.6')$$

where p_i^* is the supply price of good i in the exporting country. Equation (7.6′) constitutes the key to all of Meade's results. Though Meade does not derive it explicitly in the book, he states it in precise terms as follows:

What we need to do, therefore, is to take all the changes in international trade which are due directly or indirectly to the reduction in the Dutch duty on Belgian beer; value each change at its supply price in the exporting country and weight it by the *ad valorem* rate of duty in the exporting country; add up the resulting items for all increases of trade and do the same for all decreases of trade; if the resulting sum for the increases of trade is greater than that for the decreases of trade, then there is an increase in welfare; and vice versa. (66)

A key point to note is that the changes in real incomes of individual countries arising out of shifts in the terms of trade play no role in the determination of the change in the real income of the world. Being redistributive in nature, the welfare effects due to changes in the terms of trade cancel one another entirely when summed across countries. By focusing on the world welfare, Meade is able to work with a model with fully flexible terms of trade without having to deal with the complications arising out of such changes. According to (7.6′), irrespective of how the terms of trade change, an expansion of imports of good i in country j increases world welfare if such imports are restricted initially by a tariff.

This is not to suggest that the changes in the terms of trade do not matter. If we were to carry equation (7.6′) any further by decomposing the total change in the $m_i^j(\cdot)$ into those arising from changes in the various arguments of the latter—tariffs, terms of trade, and utility—the terms of trade effects will come back to haunt us. The terms of trade determine (and are determined by) how exactly the $m_i^j(\cdot)$ change.

Equation (7.4), which underlies equation (7.6′), requires that the income-expenditure equality, shown in (7.1) or (7.1′), holds at all times. This equality is, of course, equivalent to the trade balance condition for coun-

Table 7.1
Domestic Prices in the Meade Model, Chapter 3 (Good 1 is exported by Country A, 2 by B and 3 by C)

	Good 1	Good 2	Good 3
Country A	$p_1^A \equiv p_1^*$	$p_2^A \equiv p_2^*(1 + t_2^A)$	$p_3^A \equiv p_3^*(1 + t_3^A)$
Country B	$p_1^B \equiv p_1^*(1 + t_1^B)$	$p_2^B \equiv p_2^*$	$p_3^B \equiv p_3^*(1 + t_3^A)$
Country C	$p_1^C \equiv p_1^*(1 + t_1^C)$	$p_2^C \equiv p_1^*(1 + t_2^A)$	$p_3^C \equiv p_3^*$

try j.[11] If $(7.6')$ is to be used as a measure of the change in welfare, trade balance is required in each country. Therefore, Meade is in error when he begins Chapter 6 under the premise that the changes discussed in Chapter 5 leave the countries out of trade balance. What are left out of balance are goods markets. For, in deriving $(7.6')$, we do not require that the goods market be cleared in the postpreference equilibrium, that is, we do not impose the condition $\Sigma_j dm_i^j = 0$ $(i = 1, 2, 3)$.[12]

The conclusion quoted following equation $(7.6')$ is stated by Meade in Chapter 4 in the context of a multicountry, multicommodity model. But prior to considering this general model, he discusses, in Chapter 3, the special case of a three-country, three-commodity model. It is useful to consider that model in detail here. Meade assumes that each country is specialized completely in the production of its export good and imports the other two goods. His objective is to focus on the effects arising out of shifts in demand, in contrast to Viner, who had focused on shifts in supply.

Denote the three countries by A, B, and C and the commodities produced and exported by them by 1, 2, and 3, respectively. Each country exports the good it produces to the other two and imports the goods produced by them. Because each country levies tariffs but no export taxes, the pattern of domestic prices takes the form shown in Table 7.1. In this setting, assuming that goods are substitutes, Meade offers the following conclusions at the end of Chapter 3:

We can conclude that from the point of view of our present simple model where the advantages of trade consist solely in satisfying demands better out of given fixed supplies, a customs union is more likely to raise standards: (i) the higher are the initial duties of the countries forming the union, (ii) the lower are the duties in the outside countries, (iii) the more substitutable for each other are the products of the countries forming the union, and (iv) the less substitutable are the products of the outside world with the products of the countries forming the union. We can add to these conclusions the observation that the first stages of mutual tariff reduction on the Dutch–Belgian trade are likely to do more good (or less harm) than the later stages. (52)

To see how and under what conditions these results emerge, let us re-write equation (7.6') for the present three-good model. Remembering that countries A, B, and C export goods 1, 2, and 3, respectively, and do not produce imported goods, (7.6') reduces to

$$dw = \sum_{i=2,3} t_i^A p_i^* de_i^A + \sum_{i=1,3} t_i^B p_i^* de_i^B + \sum_{i=1,2} t_i^C p_i^* de_i^C \qquad (7.7)$$

where e_i^j is the demand for commodity i in country j.

A complete analysis of this model requires us to solve for the changes in the terms of trade and utility and use these, in turn, to solve for the de_i^j. Meade does not undertake this complicated exercise but instead bases his results on the following observations:

i. Mutual tariff preferences by countries A and B will expand their imports from each other; that is, de_2^A, $de_1^B > 0$. In Vinerian terms, these changes represent trade creation.

ii. Countries A and B will import less from country C; that is, de_3^A, $de_3^B < 0$. These changes constitute trade diversion.

iii. Country C will import less from A and B; that is, de_1^C, $de_2^C < 0$. These changes can also be called trade diversion.[13]

A tariff preference by each member country lowers the domestic price of the good imported from the partner relative to those of other goods, giving rise to observation (i). Given substitutability, a reduction in the relative price of the partner's good reduces the demand for the outside country's good, leading to observation (ii). Finally, because the supplies of 1 and 2 are redirected toward A and B due to preferences, these goods become more expensive to C, which gives rise to observation (iii).[14]

Given observations (i)–(iii), the results appearing in the quotation following equation (7.6') are straightforward. The more substitutable are goods 1 and 2 for each other and the less substitutable are these goods for good 3, the larger will be the changes in (i) relative to those in (ii) and (iii) in absolute terms. The presumption then is that the first two terms in (7.6') are positive while the third one is negative. *Given this result*, the higher the initial tariffs in A and B relative to those in C, the more likely that the right-hand side of the equation will be positive.

Suppose now that the initial tariffs in all countries are nondiscriminatory. Then, if the effects in (i) are large relative to those in (ii) and (iii), the initial tariff preference will raise world welfare. Moreover, the larger the tariffs in A and B relative to that in C, the larger will be the gain. As further tariff preferences are granted, however, the t_i^j multiplying the changes in demands in (i) will decline while those multiplying the changes in demands in (ii) and (iii) will remain unchanged; that is, as more and more preferences are granted, the weights on the positive terms in (7.7) become smaller relative to those on the negative terms. As stated in the last sentence of Meade's statement quoted above, the gains are likely to be smaller or losses larger on the later stages of tariff preferences.

We can conclude this subsection with an interesting result that appears in Chapter 7 almost as a "throw away." Noting that an important limitation of his analysis in the preceding chapters is the exclusion of quantitative restrictions (96–99), Meade deals briefly with the implications of these restrictions and offers the following result:

We can, therefore, conclude that if all trade barriers take the form of fixed and unchanged quantitative restrictions, then a customs union must increase economic welfare. The primary expansion of trade between the partner countries will, as we have seen, invariably increase welfare, and there can be no secondary or tertiary changes in trade except in markets in which either there are no quota restrictions or existing quota restrictions have become ineffective. In either case the secondary and tertiary changes have no effect upon economic welfare. (98)

This result, stated with respect to world welfare, can be derived from equation (7.6′). With quotas in place, the t_i^j must now be interpreted as implicit ad valorem quota rents. For products subject to an effective import quota, this quota rent is positive. A relaxation of effective import quotas between union members expands trade between them but has no effect on trade in other products subject to effective quotas. It is then immediate that such a change improves world welfare. Intuitively, the relaxation of a quota generates a positive, trade-creation effect in the sector subject to the change but, because imports of other products subject to effective quotas do not decline, there is no trade diversion. In sum, freeing up of trade between members in the presence of quantitative restrictions gives rise to the effects in (i) above but not those in (ii) and (iii).

This result must be distinguished from another important result in the literature, stated originally by Kemp (1964), proved formally by Ohyama (1972) and Kemp and Wan (1976), and known in the literature as the Kemp–Wan theorem.[15] Because, in their recent important survey of the literature on regional integration, Baldwin and Venables (1995) have identified the two results as essentially the same, it is worthwhile to consider the distinction between them in some detail. It is best to begin by quoting Kemp's original statement of the result:

Thus, suppose that the union sets its common external tariffs at levels calculated to achieve the same volume and composition of trade with the rest of the world as occurred before the union was formed. The improved productive and distributive efficiency of the union ensures that the union and, after compensation if necessary, all member countries are better off after the union than before. And, obviously, the nonmember countries are not worse off. It follows that the world as a whole is better off. (1964: 176)

Next, let us quote Baldwin and Venables:[16]

Inspection of eq. (2.2) reveals that internal trade is the optimal policy for the RIA if, as its internal trade policy is changed, the external trade of the RIA remains constant (i.e., $dm_{31} = dm_{32} = 0$). This is the Meade–Ohyama–Kemp–Wan theorem. Meade (1955, p. 98) showed that if all external trade barriers are "fixed and unchanging" quantitative restrictions, then the RIA must increase the sum of the economic welfare of member nations. Ohyama (1972), and Kemp and Wan (1976) rediscovered and extended Meade's result by showing that a sufficiently intricate change in the CU's external tariffs could be used to freeze external trade, so that standard gains from trade arguments could be applied to trade within the RIA. (1995: 1605)

In my view, this statement is in error for both understating and overstating Meade's contribution. It understates Meade's contribution by suggesting that his result requires freezing the rest of the world's trade vector and, hence, its terms of trade. As we have already seen, Meade required no such assumption. The statement overstates Meade's contribution by suggesting that he showed that "if all external trade barriers are 'fixed and unchanging' quantitative restrictions, then an RIA must increase the sum of the economic welfare of member nations." Meade neither showed nor claimed to have shown an improvement in the welfare of the union; his analysis and claim were confined to an improvement in the welfare of the world as a whole. Indeed, to guarantee Kemp's result of an improvement in the welfare of the union with no change in the welfare of the rest of the world, it is not sufficient to assume that all external trade *barriers* are fixed and unchanging as *stated* by Baldwin and Venables in the third sentence of the above excerpt; instead, the result requires that all external *trade* be fixed and unchanging as actually *assumed* by them in the first sentence. The distinction is important because Meade makes only the former assumption: although all trade barriers must take the form of quantitative restrictions, they need not apply to all trade. As is clear from the second half of the excerpt from Meade (1955) reproduced above, he explicitly allows for changes in the rest of the world's trade in the products that are either free from trade barriers or become free because the formation of the union renders the restrictions on them redundant.

Under Meade's assumption, following a regional integration agreement, trade in some products with the rest of the world can change, which, in turn, implies that the terms of trade between the union and the rest of the world can change. And because we cannot rule out the possibility that the terms of trade can turn against the union, an improvement in its welfare cannot be guaranteed even though an improvement in global welfare is guaranteed.[17]

But this is not all. There is another subtle difference between the results of Meade and Kemp. The Kemp result deals specifically with a customs union in which all external barriers are replaced by a *common* external tariff. There is no such requirement in Meade's result. Thus, Meade's result, focusing as it does exclusively on world welfare, does not require the union members to adopt an (implicit) common external tariff by turning the initial country-specific quotas on the rest of the world into union-wide quotas in the post-union equilibrium. Each member's quotas on trade with outside countries are kept *individually* at their original levels and, therefore, tariffs implied by those quotas can be different. For example, take Meade's three-country, three-commodity model with complete specialization. Suppose countries A and B have import quotas on each other's goods initially, B has a quota on imports from C, and A does not restrict imports from C. If A and B now form a free trade area, eliminating import quotas on each other, the implicit tariff on C's product will be zero in A but positive in B. This is entirely consistent with Meade's general approach, which focused on FTAs rather than customs unions.

It is tempting to think that if all of A's and B's imports from C are subject to quotas in the initial equilibrium and if, upon the formation of the union, the quotas are unified at the union level to hold total commodity-wise imports from C fixed, the Meade result will coincide with the Kemp result. But even this correspondence will fail to obtain in a multi-commodity world, since there is no guarantee that this will leave *commodity-wise* exports to the rest of the world unchanged.[18] Free trade within the union will, in general, lead to changes in exports to the rest of the world even if the union's *import* vector is unchanged. Note that Kemp fixes the entire trade vector, including exports.

Though the Kemp result is, thus, distinct from the Meade result, the latter does anticipate a different result in the literature on piecemeal trade reform. According to this latter result, established formally by Corden and Falvey (1985), the relaxation of an effective import quota by a small open economy is necessarily welfare improving. The mechanism underlying this result is the same as that underlying Meade's result: the relaxation of a quota generates a direct welfare gain but brings no losses due to a contraction of imports of other products subject to positive quota rent. And within a small country, there are no terms-of-trade effects.

7.1.3 Policy Implications: Further Results

Is preferential trading or an FTA likely to improve or worsen world welfare? In Chapter 3, Meade sidesteps this question by confining himself to stating the conditions under which the change is welfare improving and not taking a position on whether these conditions are likely to be met. After generalizing the model to many commodities and production of all goods in all countries in Chapter 4, he takes up this question in Chapter 5. He first presents a relatively complete taxonomy of possible effects of an infinitesimally small tariff preference by one of the member countries and then offers his judgment on which of the various effects are more likely in practice.

Suppose that country A gives a small tariff preference to country B on good 2. As already noted, Meade does not solve the model fully. Instead, he focuses on the effects that arise from the changes in the price of the product subject to the tariff preference. The preference lowers p_2^A and raises p_2^B and increases imports of good 2 into A from B. Meade calls this expansion of trade between A and B the *primary effect* of the tariff preference. The change is necessarily beneficial.

The primary effect is accompanied by what Meade calls *secondary effects*: the changes in international trade in products that, in A or B, are close substitutes for or close complements to good 2. He distinguishes eight cases, four involving substitutability and four complementarity.

Case 1 In A, good 2 exhibits substitutability with good 3, which is imported from C. The decline in p_2^A in this case diverts A's demand away from good 3; that is, there is a *secondary contraction of A's imports* from C, which is harmful.

Case 2 In A, good 2 is a close substitute for its own exportable, good 1. In this case, the decline in p_2^A lowers the demand for good 1 and releases it for exports. There is a *secondary expansion of A's exports* which is beneficial.

Case 3 In B, good 2 exhibits substitutability with a product exported to C. The rise in p_2^B leads to a contraction of this product and reduces B's exports to the latter. This is a harmful *secondary contraction of B's exports*.

Case 4   In B, good 2 exhibits substitutability with a good imported by B. Then a rise in p_2^B leads to a beneficial *secondary expansion of imports* into B.

Corresponding to each of these cases, Meade notes a case involving complementarity and, therefore, giving rise to the opposite welfare effect. For instance, corresponding to case (i), suppose that in country A, good 2 exhibits complementarity with a good imported from C. This could happen if good 2 (e.g., beer) is consumed jointly with the good imported from C (e.g., beer bottles). In this case, the reduction in p_2^A leads to a beneficial *secondary expansion of imports* into A. Other cases of complementarity can be constructed similarly.

From a policy standpoint, the critical issue is which of these cases are most plausible. Meade takes the following view:

> Then two cases which may perhaps most commonly occur are those in which the primary commodity is a close substitute with other imports in the country of imports (Case 1 above) and with other exports in the country of exports (Case 3 above). (1955: 73)

Meade provides a detailed analysis of why these two cases are important in practice. Space constraints do not permit me to reproduce this most interesting discussion, though I recommend it strongly to the reader. It is worthwhile, however, to reproduce one other paragraph summarizing the implications of Cases 1 and 2:

> If we allow for the possibility that there is trade diversion on the demand side in the importing country and on the supply side in the exporting country it is clear that the removal of the duties on imports from one country might do very considerable damage. The Netherlands removes its duties on imports from Belgium. The Netherlands may now purchase from Belgium the sort of things which it previously purchased from elsewhere, and at the same time Belgium may now sell to the Netherlands the sort of things which she was previously selling elsewhere. If there is any presumption that any country's imports are likely to be highly competitive with each other, since the country is likely to import the same class of products, and that any country's exports are likely to be highly competitive with each other, because it is likely to export the same general class of products,—then this is the sort of result which we should expect. The Netherlands will import from Belgium instead of from outside countries and Belgium will sell to the Netherlands rather than to outside countries. The losses from the combined trade diversion of Dutch imports and of Belgian exports may well much outweigh the advantages to be gained from the net trade expansion between the Netherlands and Belgium. (Meade 1955: 77–78)

This discussion suggests that Meade is skeptical of trade preferences or FTAs leading to net benefits for the world as a whole. It must be noted, however, that his skepticism is not as unequivocal as that of Viner.[19] Meade's arguments for why a tariff preference might do "very considerable damage," and suggestions on how Viner "might still further have strengthened his case against customs unions" are invariably followed by qualifications and examples in which trade diversion effects may not occur. But, at a minimum, we can safely conclude that he does not attempt to make a persuasive case in favor of preferential trading and that, on balance, his analysis is unfavorable to FTAs as an instrument of enhancing world welfare.

7.2   The Small-Union Model

Let me now turn to what is popularly known as the "Meade Model." The main results are due to Lipsey (1958, chaps. 5 and 6) with McMillan and McCann (1981) reformulating the model in terms of compensated demands. I first derive the results derived by Lipsey (1958) in chapter 5 (conclusions #1–#4, Lipsey 1970: 38) and then consider McMillan and McCann's formulation. In chapter 6, Lipsey provides a further important result relating welfare results to expenditure shares on domestic and outside country's goods. This result, its possible generalizations, and its limitations are discussed in Section 7.3 below.

Assume that there are three countries, A, B, and C, and three goods, 1, 2, and 3. Countries A and B are completely specialized in 1 and 2, respectively, whereas C produces all three commodities. Countries A and B are potential union members and are small in relation to C. Assuming that there are no trade taxes in C, border prices facing A and B coincide with those prevailing in C. The structure of prices in the three countries is summarized in Table 7.2.

An obvious but important point to note is that in any model with union members specialized completely in the export commodity and all border prices determined outside the union, a union member will be

Table 7.2
Domestic Prices in the Small-Union Meade Model (Good 1 is exported by Country A, 2 by B, and 3 by C; prices in C are fixed)

	Good 1	Good 2	Good 3
Country A	$p_1^A = p_1^*$	$p_2^A \equiv p_2^*(1 + t_2^A)$	$p_3^A \equiv p_3^*(1 + t_3^A)$
Country B	$p_1^B \equiv p_1^*(1 + t_1^B)$	$p_2^B = p_2^*$	$p_3^B \equiv p_3^*(1 + t_3^A)$
Country C	p_1^*	p_2^*	p_3^*

affected by its own policy changes only and not by policy changes in the partner country. Thus, in the small-union Meade model outlined in the previous paragraph, preferential liberalization by country A will affect itself but not country B. The reason for this property is that domestic prices which guide economic activity in each country are determined by the border price plus the country's own tariff, and the border price is entirely unaffected by policy changes in the partner country. In order for preferential liberalization by A to affect B, its policy changes must have an influence on the latter's internal prices.[20]

Given that each country is unaffected by changes in tariffs in the partner country, we can analyze the effects of a preferential trading agreement in exactly the same way as we analyze (unilateral) trade reform by a small open economy in isolation. Moreover, because of the symmetry between union members, it suffices to analyze the effects of preferential trading by one union member. The effects on the other member and the union as a whole can be inferred by symmetry. The rest of the world is, of course, unaffected due to the fact that the union is too small to affect the prices there.

Let us consider country A. Because the only relevant variables other than world prices are those relating to country A, we drop the country superscript and distinguish world prices by an asterisk. The equilibrium in country A is given by

$$e(p_1^*, (1+t_2)p_2^*, (1+t_3)p_3^*; u) = p_1^* \tilde{q}_1 + t_2 p_2^* e_2(\cdot) + t_3 p_3^* e_3(\cdot) \qquad (7.8)$$

where $\tilde{q}_1$ is the quantity of good 1 produced. Because of complete specialization, this quantity is fixed. As before, $e_i(\cdot)(i = 1, 2, 3)$ is the partial derivative of $e(\cdot)$ with respect to the ith argument and p_i^* is the international price (i.e., the price in country C) of good i and is constant.

We are now interested in the effect of a small reduction by A in the tariff on the good imported from B. Differentiate equation (7.8) with respect to t_2, and we have

$$e_u du = t_2 p_2^* de_2(\cdot) + t_3 p_3^* de_3(\cdot) \qquad (7.9)$$

This equation is analogous to equation (7.7) for the world welfare in the presence of endogenous terms of trade. Thus, the equation obtained for a single country under the small-country assumption matches closely that obtained for the world as a whole under flexible terms of trade. This will not be true if we assumed A to be large, as is verified readily by comparing (7.7) to (7.4).

Equation (7.9) immediately yields Lipsey's (1970: 38) result #4: a sufficient (but not necessary) condition for a preferential liberalization to improve a country's welfare is that it increase the quantity of all imports. Intuitively, tariffs restrict imports below the optimal level. Any change which increases imports is a move toward the optimum.

Next, observe that the trade balance condition implies $\Sigma_i p_i^* e_i = p_i^* \tilde{q}_1$. Given fixed terms of trade, total differentiation of this condition yields

$$p_3^* de_3 = -(p_1^* de_1 + p_2^* de_2) \tag{7.10}$$

Substituting (7.10) into (7.9), we obtain,

$$e_u du = -(t_3 - t_2) p_2^* de_2(\,\cdot\,) - t_3 p_1^* de_1(\,\cdot\,) \tag{7.11}$$

Because $t_3 - t_2 \geq 0$ by assumption and a reduction in t_2 increases the imports of good 2, the first term on the right-hand side is nonpositive. This gives us Lipsey's (1970: 38) result #3: a necessary condition for preferential liberalization to improve a country's welfare is that it lowers the country's expenditure on its domestic good, thereby increasing the volume of imports, both measured at world prices. Intuitively, suppose the expenditure on the domestic good and, hence, the total volume of imports, at world prices, is unchanged. Then the expansion in the imports of good 2 is exactly offset by the contraction of imports of good 3. With $t_3 \geq t_2$, the beneficial effect of the former change is at most as large as the harmful effect of the latter.

From (7.11), starting with a nondiscriminatory tariff, we have $t_3 = t_2$ initially. Therefore, for the initial tariff preference, a reduction in the expenditure on the domestic good, measured at the world price, is necessary and sufficient for an improvement in country A's welfare. Assuming gross substitutability, a reduction in t_2 increases the imports of good 2 and reduces those of good 3. Therefore, it follows from (7.9) that, ceteris paribus, for each subsequent reduction in t_2, the lower is t_2, the less likely that the reduction will improve welfare. Under gross substitutability, once t_2 reaches a certain level, further tariff reductions will be associated with welfare deterioration. As Lipsey (1970: 36) noted, this value of the tariff can be called the *second-best optimum tariff*. We now have Lipsey's (1970: 38) result #1: a union that reduces the tariff on the partner country's good is more likely to be beneficial than the one which removes the tariff entirely.

Finally, suppose we assume that the initial level of tariff on the partner country exceeds that on the outside country. Then it is straightforward from (7.11) that a decline in the expenditure on the domestic good, measured at the world price, is no longer necessary for welfare improvement. For example, a reduction in t_2 improves welfare even if it leaves the expenditure on the domestic good unchanged. This is the main result derived by Corden (1976).

Alternatively, ceteris paribus, the gain from initial tariff reductions will be larger the higher the initial tariff on the partner in relation to that on the outside country. Moreover, the higher t_2 is in relation to t_3 initially, the more tariff reductions it will take before we get to the point where the reductions begin to yield welfare losses. These facts give rise to Lipsey's (1970: 38) result #2: an FTA is more likely to raise welfare the higher is the level of tariff on the partner initially in relation to that on the outside country.

So far, we have derived the results in terms of ex post responses of expenditures in country A. But we can push the analysis one step further by solving the model in terms of ex ante responses imbedded in the expenditure function.[21] Thus, since $de_2 = e_{22}p_2^*dt_2 + e_{2u}du$ and $de_3 = e_{32}p_2^*dt_2 + e_{3u}du$, we can rewrite equation (3.9) as

$$S \cdot du = p_2^*(t_2p_2^*e_{22} + t_3p_3^*e_{32}) \, dt_2 \tag{7.12}$$

where $S \equiv e_u - t_2p_2^*e_{2u} - t_3p_3^*e_{3u}$. Because e_u is linear homogeneous in domestic prices, we have $e_u = p_1^*e_{u1} + (1+t_2)p_2^*e_{u2} + (1+t_3)p_3^*e_{u3}$ and, hence, $S = p_1^*e_{u1} + p_2^*e_{u2} + p_3^*e_{u3}$. Assuming all goods to be normal in consumption, $S > 0$ and the sign of du corresponds to the sign of the right-hand side of (7.12). Because $e_{22} < 0$ by concavity of the expenditure function, a sufficient condition for a reduction in t_2 to improve welfare is that goods 2 and 3 be independent or net complements in country A's demand (i.e., $e_{32} \leq 0$). This result is similar to Lipsey's result #4, noted above, and can be found in McMillan and McCann (1981).

We can derive results similar to Lipsey's results #1–3 in terms of net substitutability. But I will leave this task to the reader and focus, instead, on the role of the *relative* degree of substitutability between good 2 on the one hand and 1 and 3 on the other. To study this relationship, it is useful to transform (7.12) further. Remembering that $e_2(\cdot)$ is homogeneous of degree zero in domestic prices, we have

$$p_1^*e_{21} + (1+t_2)p_2^*e_{22} + (1+t_3)p_3^*e_{23} = 0 \tag{7.13}$$

Solving this equation for e_{22}, substituting the resulting value into (7.12), and simplifying, we obtain

$$S \cdot du = -\frac{p_2^*}{1+t_2} [t_2 p_1^* e_{21} + (t_2 - t_3) p_3^* e_{32}] \, dt_2 \qquad (7.14)$$

Denote by $\eta_{2i} \equiv (p_i/e_2) e_{2i}$ ($i = 1, 3$) the compensated cross-price elasticity of demand for good 2 with respect to the (domestic) price of good i in country A where $p_1 = p_1^*$ and $p_3 = (1 + t_3) p_3^*$. We can rewrite (7.14) as

$$S \cdot du = -p_2^* e_2 \left[\frac{t_2}{1+t_2} \eta_{21} + \left(\frac{t_2}{1+t_2} - \frac{t_3}{1+t_3} \right) \eta_{23} \right] dt_2 \qquad (7.14')$$

If good 2 exhibits substitutability with both 1 and 3, the η_{2i} are positive. Assuming further that $t_3 \geq t_2$, the first term in brackets on the right-hand side is positive and the second one is negative. In the spirit of Meade's results for the world welfare, we see that the more substitutable is B's good for A's and the less substitutable it is for C's, the more likely that an increase in tariff preference will improve welfare. Also, ceteris paribus, as t_2 is reduced relative to t_3, the gain is smaller and smaller until it becomes negative. The second-best optimum tariff where this switch takes place can be obtained by setting $du = 0$ in (7.14'). Denoting this tariff by t^{opt}, we have[22]

$$\frac{t_2^{\mathrm{opt}}}{1+t_2^{\mathrm{opt}}} = \frac{t_3}{1+t_3} \cdot \frac{1}{1 + \dfrac{\eta_{21}}{\eta_{23}}} \qquad (7.15)$$

Not surprisingly, the optimum tariff is related positively to the tariff on the outside country. The higher the latter, the greater the loss from trade diversion caused by preferential liberalization. Moreover, the greater the degree of substitutability between the two importables relative to that between the partner's good and the home good, the higher the second-best optimum tariff.

So far, we have assumed that countries A and B are completely specialized in their export goods. We may ask whether the model can be generalized to allow for the production of imported goods in A and B. On the face of it, this seems simple enough and Lloyd (1982: 54), indeed, notes that the "results carry over if one allows production of all commodities and replaces the net substitution or independence in demand relations with net substitution or independence in excess demand."

Yet, the generalization is tricky on account of a point made by Richardson (1994). Suppose A and B produce all goods, including good 3. Suppose further that the tariff on good 3 is higher in A than in B, yielding $p_3^A > p_3^B$ where $p_3^j = (1 + t_3^j) p_3^C$ ($j = A, B$). If A and B form an FTA, however, producer prices in the two countries must necessarily equalize. There are no restrictions on the movement of goods *produced* within an FTA. This means that producers of good 3 in country B will want to sell all their output in country A and buyers there will have to import everything they consume from C. The producer price for good 3 will become p_3^A throughout the union while consumers in B will be subject to p_3^B.[23]

This complication arises whenever a good imported from outside the union is also produced by the union member with the lower external tariff on it.[24] In particular, the analysis in Meade's Chapters 4 and 5 can be subject to this critique. The implicit assumption that validates the analysis when all goods are produced in all locations is that the goods imported from the outside country remain subject to a nondiscriminatory tariff.[25] Thus, the generalization suggested by Lloyd will be valid only if it is assumed that A and B subject each other to the same tariff on good 3 that they impose on C. A weaker restriction is that the level of preference on good 3 by a union member does not exceed the other union member's tariff on that good. Alternatively, we can assume that good 3 is not produced in the country with the lower tariff on that good on the outside country.

7.3 "Natural Trading Partners" and the Meade Model

Wonnacott and Lutz (1989), Krugman (1991), and Summers (1991) have argued that countries that trade disproportionately large amounts with each other are "natural trading partners" and FTAs between them are likely to be welfare improving. For example, Krugman asserts,

To reemphasize why this matters: if a disproportionate share of world trade would take place within trading blocs even in the absence of any preferential trading arrangement, then the gains from trade creation within blocs are likely to outweigh any possible losses from external trade diversion. (29)

In a similar vein, Summers argues,

Are trading blocs likely to divert large amounts of trade? In answering this question, the issue of natural trading blocs is crucial because to the extent that blocs are created between countries that already trade disproportionately, the risk of large amounts of trade diversion is reduced. (297)

Bhagwati (1993), Panagariya (1996a), and Bhagwati and Panagariya (1996a) have subjected this view to a systematic critique. The main issue in the present context is whether we can find support for the natural trading partners hypothesis in the Meade model. There are two references in the literature that may appear to offer an affirmative answer and, therefore, deserve a careful scrutiny. The first reference is in Meade's Chapter 8 and the second in Lipsey (1960). In Chapter 8, summarizing his conclusions, Meade notes:

> Fourth, a customs union between two countries will be the more likely to raise economic welfare, if each is the principal supplier to the other of the products which it exports to the other and if each is the principal market for the other of the products which it imports from the other. Thus if the Netherlands makes up the main external market for Belgium for the sort of things *which she imports from Belgium*, there is less *scope for* the diversion of Belgian exports from other markets to the Dutch market. Similarly, if Belgium makes up the main external source for the Netherlands of the sort of things *which she exports to the Netherlands*, there is *less scope* for the diversion of Dutch imports from other countries' products onto Belgian products. (1955: 108–9; emphasis added)

Two points can be made against any possible support for the natural trading partners hypothesis in this paragraph. First, it does not relate the extent of *total* intraregional trade to the likelihood of welfare improvement from preferential trading. The member countries may trade very little with each other and yet they may be principal sources of and destinations for the products *which they trade with each other* and vice versa. Second, if the partner is the major source of the types of products it supplies a member, there is less *scope for* trade diversion. But the actual trade diversion depends, not on the *scope for* trade diversion, but on the degree of substitutability between the partner's goods and those of outside countries. And there is no hint anywhere in the book that the degree of substitutability depends on the extent of intraregional trade in the products traded by member countries with each other. The same point applies to the criterion that if a partner is the main destination for the types of products exported by a member, there is less scope for trade diversion.

The second reference bearing on natural trading partners hypotheses appears in Lipsey (1960), who, drawing on Lipsey (1958), notes:

> This argument gives rise to two general conclusions.... The first is that *given a country's volume of international trade*, a customs union is more likely to raise welfare the higher is the proportion of trade with the country's union partner and the lower the proportion with the outside world. The second is that a customs union is more likely to raise welfare the lower is the total volume of foreign trade, for the lower is foreign trade, the lower must be purchases from the outside world relative to purchases of domestic commodities. (emphasis in the original)

Several points must be noted with respect to these two conclusions. First, though Lipsey (1960) states them as general conclusions without any qualifications whatsoever, they are actually derived, in Lipsey (1958, chapter 6), under two highly restrictive conditions: (i) the country is specialized completely in the export good, and (ii) preferences are Cobb–Douglas. I show at the end of this section that the conclusions can be generalized to CES preferences, but that, too, is highly restrictive, especially when taken in conjunction with the complete specialization assumption.

Recall that the general criterion for welfare improvement from a tariff preference, emerging from equation (7.14'), is based on substitutability: the more substitutable are home goods for imports from the partner relative to the substitutability between the two types of imports, the more likely that preferential liberalization will improve welfare. In the context of the North American Free Trade Agreement (NAFTA), the more substitutable are U.S. goods for Mexican goods relative to those coming from outside countries, the more likely that Mexico will benefit from preferential liberalization. But, as Meade himself argued, the relative substitutability is likely to go the other way: the U.S. goods are likely to be better substitutes for outside countries' goods than those of Mexico.

Second, these conclusions also require the small-country assumption. But, in general, preferential liberalization by a country is likely to worsen its terms of trade vis-à-vis the union partner. This is particularly true when the initial degree of openness in the member countries is highly uneven. In such a situation, the more open member of the union undertakes far less preferential liberalization than the less open partner. For example, prior to NAFTA, the United States had much lower external tariffs than Mexico. Therefore, NAFTA involves far more preferential liberalization by Mexico than the United States and is likely to result in a deterioration of the former's terms of trade vis-à-vis the latter. And when the terms of trade deteriorate, the larger the initial volume of imports from the partner, the larger the loss. This point will also be developed formally below.

Finally, as Bhagwati (1993) noted in his original critique of the natural trading partners hypothesis, even if we swallow Lipsey's (1958) highly restrictive assumptions, his conclusions point to a small expenditure on the outside country's good relative to that on *home goods* as the key criterion for welfare improvement rather than a low expenditure on the partner country's goods relative to the *outside country's goods*. Thus, a country buying 20 percent of its total imports from the outside country but devoting only 10 percent of its expenditure to home goods will likely fail the Lipsey test, whereas a country buying 80 percent of its imports from the outside country but devoting 80 percent of its expenditure to home goods will likely pass it.

The inevitable conclusion is that the Meade model provides no support for natural trading partners hypothesis. In the remainder of this section, I generalize Lipsey's result to CES utility function and indicate briefly the implications of endogenous terms of trade for natural trading partners hypothesis.

Let the utility function be

$$u(c_1, c_2, c_3) = \left[\sum_{i=1}^{3} a_i c_i^\alpha \right]^{1/\alpha} \tag{7.16}$$

where c_i is the consumption of good i $(i = 1, 2, 3)$ and a_i and α are constants such that $a_i > 0$ and $-\infty < \alpha < 1$. The expenditure function associated with this utility function is

$$e(p_1, p_2, p_3; u) = \left[\sum_{i=1}^{3} a_i^\sigma p_i^{1-\sigma} \right]^{1/(1-\sigma)} u \tag{7.17}$$

where $\sigma \equiv 1/(1 - \alpha)$ is the elasticity of substitution between any pair of goods. Given (7.17), simple manipulations allow us to obtain

$$\eta_{2k} = \frac{p_k}{e_2} \frac{\partial e_2}{\partial p_k} = \sigma \left(\frac{p_k e_k}{e} \right) \equiv \beta_k \qquad k = 1, 3 \tag{7.18}$$

where β_k is the proportion of total expenditure devoted to product k. Substituting from (7.18) into (7.15), the second-best optimum tariff in the present CES case becomes

$$\frac{t_2^{\text{opt}}}{1 + t_2^{\text{opt}}} = \frac{t_3}{1 + t_3} \cdot \frac{1}{1 + \dfrac{\beta_1}{\beta_3}} \tag{7.19}$$

It is immediately clear from this equation that the larger the share of expenditure devoted to the home good relative to that to the outside country's good, the smaller is the second-best optimum tariff on the partner and hence the more likely that an FTA between countries A and B will be beneficial to A. Lipsey (1958) established this result for the special case of Cobb–Douglas preferences, that is, $\sigma = 1$.

Finally, let us consider the large-union case.[26] Focus, once again, on country A. Set $p_1^* \equiv 1$ by the choice of numeraire. Differentiating (7.8) totally, allowing t_2 and the terms of trade to change, we have

$$S \cdot du = -e_2 dp_2^* - e_3 dp_3^*$$

$$+ [t_2 p_2^* e_{22} + t_3 p_3^* e_{32}](1 + t_2) \, dp_2^*$$

$$+ [t_2 p_2^* e_{23} + t_3 p_3^* e_{33}](1 + t_3) \, dp_3^*$$

$$+ [t_2 p_2^* e_{22} + t_3 p_3^* e_{32}] p_2^* dt_2 \qquad (7.20)$$

Note that, as we saw in equation (7.12) under the small-union assumption, we obtain only the last term of equation (7.20). This term is the sole source of the results considered so far in the present section. But with intra-union as well as extra-union terms of trade variable, we have four additional terms. The first two terms, shown in the top row of equation (7.20), capture the direct effects of changes in the intra- and extra-union terms of trade, respectively.[27] The magnitude of these effects depends on the initial volume of imports times the change in the relevant price. Mundell (1964) shows that preferential liberalization by a country worsens its intra-union terms of trade, that is, a reduction in t_2 by A leads to a rise in p_2^*. Mundell also shows that the effect of preferential liberalization on the country's extra-union terms of trade is ambiguous in general, but the presumption is in favor of an improvement in them: the diversion of demand toward the partner's good and away from the outside country's good is likely to lower p_3^*. Evidently, the larger the initial imports from the partner, the greater the loss to A from the deterioration in its intra-union terms of trade (i.e., the rise in p_2^*). Moreover, since this loss accrues on the entire quantity of imports, even if the rise in p_2^* accounts for half of the reduction in t_2, the loss to A can be large in relation to any gain that will accrue on account of the last term in (7.20), on which Lipsey's results rest.[28] Thus, ceteris paribus, a large volume of trade with the partner is associated with a welfare loss, not gain, from preferential liberalization. According to the second term in (7.20), accepting Mundell's presumption that country A's extra-union terms of trade improve, the smaller the initial volume of trade with the outside country, the smaller the gain on this account.

What can we say about the terms in the last three rows in equation (7.20)? The terms in the second and third rows represent the effects on tariff revenue attributable to *changes in imports* resulting from shifts in the terms of trade. The term in the last row, analyzed by Lipsey, Lloyd, and others, represents the change in tariff revenue resulting from the change in imports attributable to the change in t_2, holding all terms of trade constant. To find out the signs of these terms, we need to use the zero-degree homogeneity of e_2 shown in equation (7.13) and a similar property for e_3.

Recall that, using (7.13), we were able to transform the term in parentheses in equation (7.12) as shown in (7.14). This same transformation for the second and fourth rows and an analogous transformation, using zero-degree homogeneity of e_3, for the third row allows us to rewrite (7.20) as

$$S \cdot du = -e_2 dp_2^* - e_3 dp_3^*$$
$$- [t_2 p_1^* e_{12} + (t_2 - t_3) p_3^* e_{32}] \, dp_2^*$$
$$- [t_3 p_1^* e_{13} + (t_3 - t_2) p_2^* e_{23}] \, dp_3^*$$
$$- [t_2 p_1^* e_{12} + (t_2 - t_3) p_3^* e_{32}] p_2^* dt_2 \qquad (7.20')$$

Assuming goods 1 and 2 are net substitutes, at $t_2 = t_3$, the term in the second row is negative. Thus, the effect of the change in terms of trade with respect to the partner country is unambiguously negative. The rise in p_2^* by itself reduces imports and hence tariff revenue. Assuming that p_3^* falls, the third row is positive. The reduction in p_3^* leads to increased imports from country C, which is unambiguously beneficial. Finally, given $dt_2 < 0$ by assumption, the last term is positive at $t_2 = t_3$, but ambiguous in general.

It may be noted that I have considered here the effect of a reduction in the tariff by A only. To the extent that B lowers its tariff on A's good, the latter's terms of trade with the former may not deteriorate. But in situations such as NAFTA, where the extent of preferential liberalization is asymmetric, the effects discussed above will predict the results correctly.

7.4 Concluding Remarks

Rather than restate the results of the essay, which have already been summarized in the introduction, I conclude with suggestions for future research. Though much has been written on the Meade model, there is clearly need for further work. Despite Mundell's (1964) seminal contribution, little has been written on the welfare implications of the model for union members in the presence of endogenous terms of trade. This essay has made a beginning but fallen short of solving the problem completely. The problem of the world welfare can also be analyzed further by solving the model in terms of the expenditure function rather than ex post, total changes as in equation (7.6). Finally, because the assumption of complete specialization is arbitrary, it may be worthwhile to formulate the model in terms of the Dixit–Stiglitz–Krugman model of monopolistic competition. These are some of the directions in which my current research is moving.

Notes

I am grateful to Jagdish Bhagwati for his generous comments which, in particular, helped sharpen the distinction between one of Meade's results and the Kemp–Wan theorem. Thanks are also due to Jerry Cohen and Dani Rodrik for comments on an earlier draft.

1. Sadly, James E. Meade passed away on December 22, 1995, while this essay was still in process.

2. Also see the more general treatment of the theory of the second best in Lipsey and Lancaster (1956–57). Lipsey (1958), the author's Ph.D. thesis, was subsequently published under its original title, with minor corrections, as Lipsey (1970). To keep the chronology of the development of the Meade model straight, I have referred to this key contribution as Lipsey (1958) in most of this essay, but, where page numbers had to be specified due to a lack of availability of the thesis, I have used Lipsey (1970). By doing so, I have avoided the error made by Collier (1979) in identifying Lipsey (1970) as a post-Lipsey (1960) development.

3. Bhagwati (1995) has urged, and Bhagwati and Panagariya (1996a, 1996b) have adopted, the use of the term PTA to include *both* customs unions and FTAs.

4. This interpretation has subsequently become synonymous with the "Viner model." There has been a controversy in the literature on whether or not Viner actually assumed infinite supply elasticities and zero demand elasticities (Bhagwati 1971, 1973; Johnson 1974; Kirman 1973). In a letter to Max Corden dated March 13, 1965, and published subsequently in the *Journal of International Economics*, Viner (1965) himself disagreed vehemently with Meade's interpretation of his model. Michaely (1976) provides a fuller account of the controversy. On zero demand elasticities, which essentially amount to ignoring consumption effects, Michaely rejects Johnson's (1974) contention that these effects were incorporated by Viner in his trade creation effect and essentially agrees with Bhagwati's (1973) view that Viner had simply "not thought through the question completely." On the supply side, Michaely concludes that though Viner explicitly assumed increasing costs and, hence, finite supply elasticities, his conclusion that, in any one industry, preferential liberalization leads to either trade creation or trade diversion, but not both, does require infinite supply elasticities.

5. On pages 46 and 48, Meade does refer to welfare effects of preferential trading on the member countries' welfare. But such references are rare.

6. Thus, see Lloyd (1982: 52). There also exists some ambiguity concerning the object of welfare analysis in Lipsey's (1960) discussion of Meade. Lipsey introduces a figure 3 to explain Meade's welfare analysis. In discussing this figure, he does not make explicit whether it is the welfare of the world or of the union that is being considered. From the context of the paper, a casual reader is likely to be misled into thinking that the discussion applies to the union's welfare, though it actually applies to world welfare.

In print, I have been able to find only Corden (1965: 55) as explicitly recognizing that Meade's analysis applies to global rather than the union's welfare. Interestingly, Corden sees this fact as the "principal limitation" of Meade's work.

7. The sole exception is the important but neglected paper by Mundell (1964), which focuses directly on the terms of trade effects of preferential liberalization. Though Lipsey

(1958) also deals with flexible terms of trade in chapters 7 and 8, there he switches to a two-good model.

8. Interestingly, in footnote 8, Lloyd (1982) notes, "Meade did not make the small country assumption." But, in the text, he attributes results based on the small-country model to Meade. From an individual member's viewpoint, these results cannot obtain in a model with flexible terms of trade and, therefore, could not have been obtained by Meade.

9. Thus, in the concluding paragraph of Chapter 4, describing the problem in terms of a union between Netherlands and Belgium, with Germany representing the rest of the world, Meade notes, "We need, therefore, to consider the direct and indirect effect of a small reduction in the Dutch duty on Belgian beer upon all trades in all products between the Netherlands, Belgium and Germany. Now at this point one should, perhaps, try to build a complicated model in which every economic quantity in the world is made to depend upon every other quantity.... I am not able to handle the mathematics which would be necessary for such an analysis. We shall have to be content with a more rough and ready method." (1955: 66)

10. This expression is also derived by Kowalczyk (1990) in passing.

11. Because $m^j(\cdot)$ is linear homogeneous in the goods prices, we have $m^j = \Sigma_i p_i^j m_i^j$. Making use of this equality, (7.1') reduces to $\Sigma_i p_i^* m_i^j = 0$, which is the trade balance condition.

12. Of course, we do require that goods markets be cleared in the initial equilibrium. Recall that we do use equation (7.2) in deriving (7.6').

13. Though the post-Meade literature has generally focused on the effects of preferential trading on union members, there has been some revival of interest in studying the effects of this change on the rest of the world. Thus, see Bliss (1994), Srinivasan (1996), and Winters (1995).

14. Although observations (i)–(iii) are plausible, they are not infallible. Income effects due to shifts in the terms of trade could easily reverse some of these results. Meade himself does not represent these results as the only possibility. Moreover, in Chapter 5, where he analyzes the multicountry, multicommodity model, he offers a wide array of possibilities.

15. Vanek (1965, chap. 7) also states this result, along with a proof, for the special case of a three-country, two-commodity model. There is no reference to Kemp (1964) in Vanek (1965) or vice versa.

16. In the following quotation, RIA stands for regional integration agreement.

17. For instance, if the products on which union members remove quotas against each other exhibit complementarity with those imported from the rest of the world freely, the terms of trade can turn against the union.

18. Recall here that throughout the book, Meade works only with import restrictions. Indeed, Meade himself did not even think in terms of a union-wide quota or quantitative restrictions on all imports from the rest of the world. On pp. 96–99, nowhere does Meade indicate that union members adopt a union-wide quota in the post-union equilibrium. Furthermore, as a careful reading of the passage quoted in the text of this paper will reveal, Meade's result requires only that "all trade barriers take the form of fixed and unchanged quantitative restrictions" rather than that all trade be subject to quantitative restrictions.

19. In the concluding paragraph of his book, Viner offered the following verdict on the role of customs unions as a solution to the existing problems in the field of international economics: "Whether used as a mere incantation against the evils resulting from present-day

economic policy or vigorously prosecuted, it will in either case be unlikely to prove a practical and suitable remedy for today's economic ills, and it will almost inevitably operate as a psychological barrier to the realization of the more desirable but less desired objective of the Havana chapter—the balanced multilateral reduction of trade barriers on a non-discriminatory basis."

20. Mundell (1964), Berglas (1979), and Riezman (1979), as well as Meade (1955) allow for endogenous terms of trade. As a result, in these models, policy changes in one country do affect other countries. Berglas works with what appears to be a small-union model but manages to link the price of one of the commodities in a member country to that in the partner country by assuming that the former cannot trade this commodity with the rest of the world.

21. McMillan and McCann (1981) also analyze the small-union Meade model in terms of net substitutability, but do not make many of the points made below.

22. McMillan and McCann (1981) also derive this second-best optimum tariff, but their expression is more complex and does not lend itself to as clear an interpretation as that in equation (7.15).

23. This outcome assumes that A continues to import some of good 3 from country C. It is possible that B will eliminate C as a supplier, in which case both the consumer and producer prices in A will fall below $(1 + t_3^A)p_3^C$.

24. The problem arises whenever the tariff on a good in a member country is smaller than the margin of preference given by the partner country. Thus let A have the higher external tariff on good 3 than B. Denote by t_3^A A's tariff on C and by τ_3^A its tariff on country B with $t_3^A - \tau_3^A$ representing the tariff preference. The net price received by B's producers in A equals $(1 + t_3^A - \tau_3^A)p_3^C$. If this price exceeds $(1 + t_3^B)p_3^C$, that is, if the tariff preference in A exceeds the tariff in B, all supplies of good 3 in B will be diverted to A. Thus, for $t_3^A - \tau_3^A = t_3^B$, our calculus method will break down.

25. Strictly speaking, we must also assume that each good exported by a union member to the partner is also exported to the outside country.

26. Here I draw on Panagariya (1996b).

27. From country A's viewpoint, a rise in p_2^* and p_3^* is equivalent to a deterioration in the intra- and extra-union terms of trade, respectively.

28. This point is emphasized in Bhagwati and Panagariya (1996a).

References

Baldwin, Richard, and Anthony Venables (1995), "Regional Economic Integration." In Gene Grossman and Ken Rogoff, *Handbook of International Economics*, Vol. III, pp. 1597–1644. Amsterdam: North Holland.

Berglas, Eitan (1979). "Preferential Trading: The *n* Commodity Case," *Journal of Political Economy* 87(21), 315–31.

Bhagwati, Jagdish (1971). "Trade-Diverting Customs Unions and Welfare Improvement: A Clarification," *Economic Journal* 81, 580–7.

Bhagwati, Jagdish (1973). "A Reply to Professor Kirman," *Economic Journal* 83, 895–7.

Bhagwati, Jagdish (1993). "Regionalism and Multilateralism: An Overview." In Melo and Panagariya, 1993, pp. 22–51.

Bhagwati, Jagdish (1995). "U.S. Trade Policy: The Infatuation with Free Trade Areas." In J. Bhagwati and Anne O. Krueger, eds., *The Dangerous Drift to Preferential Trade Agreements*, pp. 1–18. Washington, DC: American Enter-prise Institute for Public Policy Research.

Bhagwati, Jagdish, and Arvind Panagariya (1996a). "Preferential Trading Areas and Multi-lateralism: Strangers, Friends or Foes?" In Jagdish Bhagwati and Arvind Panagariya, eds., *The Economics of Preferential Trade Agreements*, Washington, DC: AEI Press, pp. 1–78.

Bhagwati, Jagdish, and Arvind Panagariya (1996b). "The Theory of Preferential Trade Agreements: Historical Evolution and Current Trends." *American Economic Review: Papers and Proceedings* 86(2) (May), 82–7.

Bliss, Christopher (1994). *Economic Theory and Policy for Trading Blocks*, Manchester, V. K., and New York: Manchester University Press.

Collier, Paul (1979). "The Welfare Effects of Customs Union: An Anatomy," *Economic Journal* 89 (March), 84–95.

Corden, W. M. (1965). *Recent Developments in the Theory of International Trade*. Special Papers in International Economics 7, International Finance Section, Princeton University, March.

Corden, Max (1976). "Customs Unions Theory and the Nonuniformity of Tariffs," *Journal of International Economics* 6, 99–106.

Corden, Max, and Rodney Falvey (1985). "Quotas and the Second Best," *Economics Letters*, 18, 67–70.

Johnson, H. G. (1974). "Trade Diverting Customs Union: A Comment," *Economic Journal* 84, 618–21.

Kemp, Murray C. (1964). *The Pure Theory of International Trade*. Englewood Cliffs, NJ: Prentice-Hall, 176–7.

Kemp, Murray C., and Henry Wan (1976). "An Elementary Proposition Concerning the Formation of Customs Unions," *Journal of International Economics* 6 (February), 95–8.

Kenen, Peter B. (1957). "On the Geometry of Welfare Economics," *Quarterly Journal of Economics* 71(3) 426–47.

Kenen, Peter B. (1959). "Distribution, Demand and Equilibrium in International Trade: A Diagrammatic Analysis," *Kyklos* 12(4), 629–38.

Kenen, Peter B. (1969). "The Theory of Optimum Currency Areas: An Eclectic View." In R. A. Mundell and A. K. Swaboda, eds., *Monetary Problems of the International Economy*, pp. 41–60. Chicago: Chicago University Press, 1969.

Kirman, A. P. (1973). "Trade Diverting Customs Unions and Welfare Improvement: A Comment," *Economic Journal* 83, 890–4.

Kowalczyk, Carsten (1990). "Welfare and Customs Unions," NBER Working Paper No. 3476, October.

Krugman, P. (1991). "The Move to Free Trade Zones." In *Policy Implications of Trade and Currency Zones*, pp. 7–41. Symposium Sponsored by the Federal Reserve Bank of Kansas City.

Lipsey, Richard (1958). "The Theory of Customs Unions: A General Equilibrium Analysis," Ph.D. thesis, University of London.

Lipsey, Richard (1960). "The Theory of Customs Unions: A General Survey," *Economic Journal* 70, 498–513.

Lipsey, Richard (1970). *The Theory of Customs Unions: A General Equilibrium Analysis*, LSE Research Monographs 7. London: London School of Economics and Political Science.

Lipsey, Richard, and Kelvin Lancaster (1956–57). "The General Theory of Second Best," *Review of Economic Studies* 24, 11–32.

Lloyd, Peter J. (1982). "3 × 3 Theory of Customs Unions," *Journal of International Economics* 12, 41–63.

McMillan, John, and Ewen McCann (1981). "Welfare Effects in Customs Union," *Economic Journal* 91 (September), 697–703.

Meade, James E. (1952). *A Geometry of International Trade*. London: Allen and Unwin.

Meade, James E. (1955). *The Theory of Customs Unions*. Amsterdam: North-Holland.

Melo, Jaime de, and Arvind Panagariya, ed. (1993). *New Dimensions in Regional Integration*. Cambridge University Press.

Michaely, Michael (1976). "The Assumptions of Jacob Viner's Theory of Customs Unions," *Journal of International Economics* 6, 75–93.

Mundell, Robert A. (1964). "Tariff Preferences and the Terms of Trade," *Manchester School of Economic and Social Studies*, 1–13.

Ohyama, M. (1972). "Trade and Welfare in General Equilibrium," *Keio Economic Studies* 9, 37–73.

Panagariya, Arvind (1996a). "The Free Trade Area of the Americas: Good for Latin America?" *World Economy* 19(5) (September), 485–515.

Panagariya, Arvind (1996b). "Preferential Trading and the Myth of Natural Trading Partners," Working Paper No. 200. New York University: Center for Japan–U.S. Business and Economic Studies, Stern School of Business.

Richardson, M. (1994). "Why a Free Trade Area? The Tariff Also Rises," *Economics and Politics* 6(1) (March), 79–95.

Riezman, Raymond (1979). "A 3 × 3 Model of Customs Unions," *Journal of International Economics* 9, 341–54.

Srinivasan, T. N. (1996). "Common External Tariffs of a Customs Union: Alternative Approaches," New York University: Working Paper No. 200. Center for Japan–U.S. Business and Economic Studies, Stern School of Business.

Summers, Lawrence (1991). "Regionalism and the World Trading System," In *Policy Implications of Trade and Currency Zones*, pp. 295–301. Symposium Sponsored by the Federal Reserve Bank of Kansas City.

Vanek, Jaroslav (1965). *General Equilibrium of International Discrimination. The Case of Customs Unions*. Cambridge: Harvard University Press.

Viner, Jacob (1950). *The Customs Union Issue*. New York: Carnegie Endowment for International Peace.

Viner, Jacob (1965). "A Letter to W. M. Corden," published in *Journal of International Economics* (1976) 6(1), 107–8.

Winters, L. A. (1995). "European Integration and Economic Welfare in the Rest of the World," mimeo., The World Bank.

Wonnacott, Paul, and Mark Lutz (1989). "Is There a Case for Free Trade Areas?" In Jeffrey Schott, ed., *Free Trade Areas and U.S. Trade Policy*, pp. 59–84. Washington, DC: Institute for International Economics.

8

Economies of Scale and Customs Union Theory

W. Max Corden

Orthodox customs union theory assumes constant or increasing costs for each industry and is frequently criticized for failing to allow for economies of scale. The aim of this article is to incorporate economies of scale systematically in customs union theory. In particular, we want to see whether the familiar concepts of *trade creation* and *trade diversion* are still relevant.[1]

The approach will initially be partial equilibrium and static, this being also the way in which the principal propositions of established customs union theory were originally expounded. The economies of scale will be assumed to be *internal* to firms, so that the traditional assumption of perfect competition cannot be maintained. A crucial simplification will be the assumption that the countries forming the union face given prices from the outside world, economy-of-scale effects in the outside world as a result of the formation of the union being insignificant. We shall assume three countries, countries *A* and *B*, which form the union, and country *C*, representing the rest of the world.

8.1 Simple Model: Two New Effects Introduced

We begin with a single homogeneous product which is produced in country *C* and is at least capable of being produced in the two union countries. There is a single actual or potential producer in each of the union countries. He has a declining average cost curve which indicates private and social average costs. He is assumed to pay constant prices for his factors of production whatever the scale of output, so that there are no factor rents. The average cost curve is assumed to include normal profits.

Originally published in *Journal of Political Economy* 80 (1972): 465–475. Reprinted with permission.

Each union country faces a given c.i.f. import and f.o.b. export price set by country C; because of transport costs and C's tariff, the export price is below the import price. It is convenient, though not essential, to assume that the two countries face the same import and export prices for the product. The average cost curve in each country is assumed to reach its minimum at a level above the export price, so that exporting the product to country C is ruled out. We also assume that, because of their tariffs and their relatively high costs, neither country initially exports to the other.[2]

We must now introduce tariffs. We have a choice of two simple assumptions. (1) We could assume that the two countries have the same tariff rate on the product before the union is formed. This is not a very realistic assumption, but it is implicit in much of orthodox customs union theory and means that one can focus on the effects of the freeing of trade within the union and need not be concerned with the establishment of a common external tariff, since such a tariff already exists. Since we want to define precisely what has to be added to orthodox theory when economies of scale are introduced, we should explore this case. (2) Alternatively, we could assume that tariff rates are "made to measure" at levels designed to make the tariff-inclusive import price just equal to average costs, including normal profits, hence avoiding any excess profits. If there is no domestic production, there will be no tariff. This may be a more realistic assumption, and we consider it in the next section. But we begin with assumption 1.

Subject to a qualification to be considered below, in each country the domestic price is determined by the cost of imports from C plus the given tariff on imports from C. At this price there is a given quantity of domestic demand, and at this quantity there will be an average cost of actual or potential production. If this average cost is less than the domestic price, there will be domestic production and no imports; and if the average cost of the potential domestic producer exceeds the domestic price at that quantity, there will be imports and no domestic production.[3] The qualification is that the price of imports from C, including tariff, sets only an upper limit to the price a domestic producer can charge. It might pay a profit-maximizing producer to charge less. But we assume at this stage that he maximizes profits by charging right up to the "import-preventing" price. The same analysis applies once the customs union is formed, provided we assume no transport costs within the union. Either the union demand will be supplied wholly by imports from C, or there will be a single domestic producer within the union. In the latter case he might price below the price set by imports from C, but we shall assume at this stage that he prices up to the limit price. This has the important implication that the prices facing consumers are not affected by the establishment of the union: hence (*a*) the total market for the product in each country remains unchanged and (*b*) there are no welfare effects on consumers. This assumption will be removed in the next section.

Now we come to the main analysis, which can be very brief. Initially there may be production of the product in both countries, in one only, or in neither. We consider each of these three cases briefly.

8.1.1   Initial Production in Both Countries

When the union is formed, one of the two producers, say country *A*'s, will capture the whole union market, the other going out of business. Hence the average costs of country *A*'s producer fall. Total costs of producing the product in the union thus decline because of specialization. This effect can be decomposed into two parts. (*a*) Country *B*'s expensive domestic production is replaced by imports from *A* which are cheaper to produce; hence there has, in a sense, been a movement to a cheaper source of supply through the opening up of trade between *A* and *B*, and hence an orthodox *trade-creation effect*. But it must be remembered that the domestic price in *B* is assumed to be given at this stage. So none of the gain will go to *B*; it will all go to excess profits in *A*, and indeed *B* may lose, since its expelled producer may have earned excess profits. (*b*) Country *A* obtains its domestic supplies at lower cost of production. This can be called the *cost-reduction effect*. While it is a consequence of the creation of trade with *B*, it is not an orthodox trade-creation effect, since it is the result not of a movement to a cheaper source of supply but rather of the cheapening of an existing source of supply. Country *A*'s consumers will gain nothing (because they face the same price as before), and the whole gain will go in profits to the producer.

8.1.2   Initial Production in Country A Only

There are two possibilities now. The most likely is that country *A*'s producer captures the whole union market.[4] The effects can again be decomposed. (*a*) Country *B* replaces imports from *C* with imports from *A*. The latter are dearer than imports from *C*, since otherwise *A* would not have needed the formation of the union to break into *B*'s market. Hence *B* loses from *trade diversion*, a dearer source of imports replacing a cheaper source of imports. The trade diversion loss to *B* will be equal to the loss of tariff revenue on imports from C. For the union as a whole the trade diversion loss may be less, since A's producer may earn some excess profits on imports to B. (b) As in our earlier example, A obtains its own product at lower cost now, so that there is a *cost-reduction effect* equal to the extra profits earned on sales at home.

The other possibility—*production reversal*—seems less likely. When the union is formed, production in B may start, and B's producer may drive A's producer out of business and capture the whole union market. His costs will be less than A's were before the union was formed, so that this time there is a trade-creation gain through A obtaining its needs from a cheaper source (though this gain will go wholly to B), while B loses through the replacement of cheap imports from C with somewhat dearer domestic production. The costs of its newly established producer when he is supplying the whole union market must be greater than the cost of imports from C, for otherwise he could have become established even before the union was formed. When imports from C are replaced by domestic production, there is a *trade-suppression effect*.[5] It is akin to the trade-diversion effect, since a dearer source replaces a cheaper source, but this time the dearer source is a newly established domestic producer, not the partner country.

8.1.3 Initial Production in Neither Country

When the union is established, production in, say, country A may begin for the first time, since its average costs may not fall below the given domestic price. They will still be above the costs of imports from C, excluding duty, for otherwise A could have broken into B's market even without the union and so obtained the benefits of the combined market. In this case there is a *trade-suppression effect* for A (more expensive domestic production replaces cheaper imports from C) and a *trade-diversion effect* for B (more expensive imports from the partner replace cheaper imports from C). In both countries the whole loss is reflected in the loss of tariff revenue; this revenue loss will exceed the combined real income loss if the new producer earns excess profits.

Our conclusion is that the trade-creation and trade-diversion concepts are still relevant but that they must be supplemented by two other concepts, the "cost-reduction effect" and the "trade-suppression effect." This is the main conclusion of this paper and remains even when some of the awkward or limiting assumptions are removed. Our examples suggest that the cost-reduction effect is likely to be the more important of the two.

8.2   Made-to-Measure Tariff Making: Consumption Effects Introduced

The assumption that the tariffs in country A and country B are the same initially, so that a common external tariff already exists, and that domestic producers always price up to the tariff-inclusive price, has conveniently eliminated any consumption effects but has led to the peculiar result in our first example that the trade creation gain through B getting its product from a cheaper source goes wholly to country A. It seems more sensible to assume that the purpose of tariffs is protection, not revenue, and that either a tariff will be high enough to bring domestic production into being (with imports wholly excluded) or it will not be imposed at all. Furthermore, we can now assume, as an interesting limiting case, that if a tariff is provided, it is just high enough to allow the domestic producer to cover his costs plus normal profits. These are the two components of what can be called *made-to-measure tariff making*.[6] Thus there are now no tariff revenues and no excess profits. All gains and losses will be borne by consumers. With this revised approach let us look at two of our cases.

8.2.1   *Initial Production in Both Countries*

The average costs of country A's producer when he supplies the whole union will be less than his costs when he supplied only his home market, and less than the costs of the former producer in B when he was supplying *his* own market. Thus the union domestic price can be less than the domestic price ruling initially in either country. Given made-to-measure tariff making, the common external tariff will thus be less than the two initial tariffs and consumers in both countries will gain from the establishment of the union. (*a*) In country B there is a familiar trade-creation gain having two components: the production effect results from the replacement of dearer domestic production by cheaper imports from A, and the consumption effect results from the increased consumption induced by the lower domestic price. (*b*) In country A there is a cost-reduction gain going to its consumers; this has also a production and a consumption component. The production effect is that the original amount of production sold domestically is now obtained at a lower price, while the consumption effect is that at the lower price an extra amount is purchased on which consumer's surplus is obtained.

The fact that the made-to-measure policy requires the common external tariff to be less than both initial tariffs suggests that made-to-measure

tariff making may not be a wholly realistic assumption. In practice the result may be intermediate to that of this model and the previous one: the
tariff may fall in at least one country, the gain going mainly or wholly
to consumers there, while in the other country the gain goes in excess
profits to the union producer (who may not belong to that country).

8.2.2 Initial Production in Country A Only

The made-to-measure model is applied quite easily to this case. Only one
point need be noted here. If country B initially did not have domestic
production, then its tariff will have been zero. If country A is to capture
B's market—which A is assumed not to have captured before—this will
result not from the freeing of trade within the union but from country B
imposing a tariff—that is, from the establishment of the common external
tariff at a positive level. The price to domestic consumers in B will then
rise, and their losses can be divided into production- and consumption-
effect components: the new, lower, amount consumed is now obtained at
a higher cost than before, this being a shift to a dearer source of supply—
the familiar trade-diversion effect—and in addition there is a loss in consumer's surplus on the reduced amount of consumption induced by the
higher price. This latter consumption effect of trade diversion does not
emerge in orthodox partial-equilibrium customs union theory.

   *We can conclude that our four effects—trade creation, trade diversion, cost
reduction, and trade suppression—each have a production and a consumption
component. In a limiting case (the model of Section 8.1) the consumption components disappear. In another limiting case (the present section) all the gains and
losses (whether from production or consumption effects) are borne by consumers.*
One can conceive of intermediate cases where there are some consumption effects and where some of the gains go in excess profits and some of
the losses are borne by the government through loss of customs revenue.
The extent of consumption effects and of excess profits depends on the
extent to which the tariff system permits monopolists to exploit their
position and whether they choose to do so. The distribution of gains
and losses among government, producers, and consumers is crucial, since it
affects the distribution of the gains and losses between the partner countries.

8.3 Oligopoly and Product Differentiation

We now depart from the assumption of a single producer in each country
and in the union and allow for oligopoly and product differentiation.

8.3.1   Initial Production in Both Countries

Suppose that there are initially *two* producers in each country. It can no longer be assumed that the increased size of the market must lead to scale economies; if the two firms in each country did not amalgamate originally, or one of them did not attempt to out-compete the other, there is no strong reason to assume that amalgamation or competition would operate in the larger area. Of course, in the world of oligopoly anything is possible, but it is conceivable that the four producers all stay in business, dividing up the market of the union among them. They may do this by differentiating their products, and since there can now be four versions of each product available to each consumer instead of two, there will be a welfare gain; this is essentially a trade-creation effect. There need be no cost-reduction effect, since the increased trade in differentiated products need not necessarily be associated with increased output by any firm.

There may initially have been more than one firm in each country because the potentially dominant producer was reluctant to swallow up the weaker firms for fear of public hostility to monopoly, leading possibly to public intervention. When the customs union is established, it becomes possible to preserve the semblance of competition while eliminating all but one producer in each country; indeed, a government may urge the national firms to amalgamate so as to strengthen the competitive power of domestic production. The two remaining firms—one in each country —may not combine either because of fear of antimonopoly action or because of the difficulty of arranging amalgamations of firms across countries, combined with hostility to, or legislation against, takeovers by foreign firms. The reduction in the number of producers will then lead to a cost-reduction gain. In addition, trade across the borders may increase, or start for the first time, as a result of product differentiation. This may or may not represent a trade-creation gain. On the one hand, the number of firms the consumer can choose to purchase from is the same as before, so he may have no more choice in variety of product; but, on the other hand, he can now choose between products made in different countries.

8.3.2   Initial Production in Country A Only

There may be several producers in country *A*; when the union is formed, they all enter *B*'s market, and there is the usual cost-reduction gain for *A* and trade-diversion loss for *B*. Two complications can be noted. (*a*) If the expansion of output by the various producers has brought them all closer to scales of output where average costs are at the minimum, the joint loss that they incur by failing to amalgamate is reduced; hence it becomes likelier that the oligopolistic situation will persist. (*b*) Some of the cost-reduction gains may be lost because producers in *B* may enter the field for the first time, since they now have a larger potential market available.

8.4 General Equilibrium

A really satisfactory general-equilibrium customs union model with economies of scale is difficult to produce. Some of the propositions of orthodox customs union theory have been expounded in terms of the two-good model, and this has led to results similar to those that emerge from the partial-equilibrium exposition. Models with more goods become rather complicated and tend to be expounded in a piecemeal way. There seems little point in developing the economies-of-scale argument in terms of a two-good model; it generally leads to the result that a country produces only one product, though no doubt many of the results produced so far in partial-equilibrium terms could be obtained. Here an alternative approach will be sketched out. It should be borne in mind that the aim is to isolate economy-of-scale effects.

There are many import-competing products; each product is produced, or potentially produced, in each country by only one firm. For each product the average cost curve is downward sloping up to a point, the curve turning upward eventually, so as to rule out exports of the product to country *C*. In addition, there is an export product with constant costs. There is a single mobile factor of production—labor—and its money wage is given. The cost curves for each product are thus independent of each other, since they depend only on the given money wage and the relevant production functions. In the initial situation each country has a made-to-measure tariff structure, leading to domestic production of some products and imports of others. Our partial-equilibrium analysis can now be applied directly. When the union is formed, production of some products will expand as the partner's market is taken over (cost reduction), production of others will cease as the domestic market is vacated for the partner (trade creation), and imports from *C* may cease because they are replaced either by imports from the partner (trade diversion) or by domestic production (trade suppression). All our four effects will happen at the same time.

Are there any general equilibrium complications? First, the demand curves for different products may shift because real income as a whole and income distribution may change, and because there are cross-elasticities. A fall in the price of one product would shift the demand curve for another product to the left. For any particular product the level of demand is crucial in determining either the tariff rate required to sustain a domestic industry or, alternatively, whether a domestic industry can be sustained with a given tariff rate. Furthermore, it determines the actual volume of output. Because of these demand relationships one cannot look at each product separately as if the general-equilibrium story were just made up of a set of separable partial-equilibrium stories. But it remains true that there are our four effects.

A second general-equilibrium complication is the need to maintain balance-of-payments equilibrium, which (with constant money wages) would be brought about through exchange-rate adjustment. In the first instance, with a given exchange rate, many of country A's industries might expand into B's market, while many of B's industries close down. Such a situation will then provoke appreciation of A's and depreciation of B's currency, and hence declines in the prices facing A's producers and increases in the prices facing B's producers (each in terms of their own currencies). This will then cause some of A's industries to go out of business and some of B's industries to revive again. In considering our effects in a general-equilibrium model, we should compare the initial preunion situation with the situation after the union is formed, each situation having its own equilibrium exchange rate.

8.5   Dynamic Considerations

There is nothing essentially "dynamic" about economies of scale. The whole of the analysis so far has been comparative static. But it is true that in a comparative-static model when there are economies of scale it is not possible to describe precisely the equilibrium that will be reached in a customs union. If initially our product is produced in both partner countries, we can say that when the union is formed one country might take over the whole market. But we cannot say which country it will be: that depends on dynamic considerations—on the nature of oligopolistic competition, the relative rates of gross investment in the two countries, and so on.[7] In the comparative-static model it is clear that, if only one firm survives, there will be trade-creation and cost-reduction effects, both of which represent gains to someone, but one cannot say which country will obtain the trade-creation and which the cost-reduction effect.

More generally, customs union theory may not tell us much about the reallocation of existing resources, owing to their immobility, but it can tell us something about the allocation and productivity of new investment. In the short run capital is immobile and industries do not just "take over" the whole market in another country or "close down" as neatly as a comparative-static model might suggest. Assuming a "putty-clay" model, the more gross investment there is in proportion to existing output, the more outputs will respond over a given period to price changes. Hence the effects described in this paper will take time, how much depending on the rate of gross investment.

Appendix

In figure 8.1 DD' is country A's demand curve for the product, and LL' is the horizontal sum of country A's and country B's demand curve. The c.i.f. import price (when importing from C) is OP_m, and the f.o.b. export price (to C) is P_x. These prices are identical for countries A and B. We illustrate the argument of Section 8.1 of this chapter. The given tariff is P_mT. Before the union is formed B has to pay this tariff on imports from A as well as from C, so that the combined demand curve facing

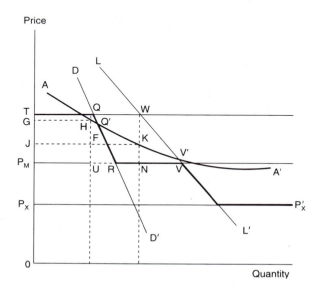

Figure 8.1

A's producer is $TQRVZP'_x$. Once the union is formed, the demand curve facing him is $TWZP'_x$.

Curve AA' is country A's average-cost curve. If it cuts DD' below Q (as drawn) then there is domestic production in A before the union is formed; if it cuts DD' above Q, the whole amount of domestic consumption TQ will be imported (unless there are exports to B). If AA' cuts LL' above V (as drawn), there will be no exports to B in the absence of the union (unless there are exports to C) because B will find imports from C cheaper, while with the union production will depend on a positive common external tariff. If AA' cuts LL' below V there will be exports to B even in the absence of the union, and with the union production will not depend on a positive common tariff; furthermore, there will be production in A even if AA' happens to cut DD' above Q. If AA' cuts LL' above W (which it can do only if there is no production initially, AA' also cutting DD' above Q), then there will be no production even with the union. Provided the minimum-cost point on AA' is above $P_xP'_x$ (as drawn), there will be no exports to C.

The diagram assumes (a) that even though B may have produced initially, it vacates production once the union is formed, and (b) that there are no transport costs within the union.

If (1) the producer prices right up to the import-preventing price OT and (2) B imported from C before the union, then the cost-reduction effect is $GHFJ$ and the trade-diversion effect for the union as a whole is $FKNU$ (both shaded). The loss of customs revenue to B, and hence the total loss to B, is $UQWN$, of which the trade-diversion effect $FKNU$ is a net loss to the union countries combined and $FQWK$ is a redistribution toward A's producer, who gains $FQWK$ plus the cost-reduction effect. From the point of view of B alone, one would describe the customs revenue loss $UQWN$ as the "trade-diversion effect."

If the made-to-measure system operated, the price to A's consumers before the union is formed would be given by the point Q', and the price to A's and B's consumers after the union is formed, by V'. Bearing this in mind, the diagram could be used to illustrate the various arguments of Section 8.2.

Notes

1. Viner (1950, pp. 45–46) has a substantial discussion of economies of scale, but this has not been followed up in the literature. Some of his conclusions differ from those in this chapter, possibly because his (unspecified) assumptions differ. See also Johnson (1962, pp. 60–61).

2. The requirements for this condition emerge precisely from the diagram in the Appendix.

3. See Corden (1967). The present article is essentially an extension of the analysis of this earlier paper to customs union theory.

4. See the Appendix for a geometric exposition of this case. This case is also expounded geometrically in Johnson (1962, p. 59) and is described in Viner (1950, pp. 45–46).

5. The term comes from Viner (1950, p. 45).

6. The term comes from Australia; the complicated structure of the Australian tariff system can be explained partly by an attempt to apply (not entirely consciously) the made-to-measure principle.

7. One might envisage a process of cutthroat competition to decide which of the two firms will survive. The firm that would have the relatively lower average costs if it supplied the union market on its own will have an advantage; this may depend on relative factor intensities, and so on. If "learning by doing" counts for anything, and provided it is related to output, one might expect (other things being equal) the firm that initially enjoyed the larger home market to have the lower costs after the union is formed, and so to survive. Relative financial resources to bear temporary losses are also relevant. During the process of "sorting out," the union price may fall substantially, so that there may be a temporary income redistribution from producers to consumers.

References

Corden, W. M. "Monopoly, Tariffs and Subsidies." *Economica* 34 (February 1967): 50–58.

Johnson, H. G. *Money, Trade and Economic Growth.* London: Allen & Unwin, 1962.

Viner, J. *The Customs Union Issue.* London: Carnegie Endowment Internat. Peace, 1950.

Making a Necessarily
Welfare-Improving
Customs Union

9

An Elementary Proposition Concerning the Formation of Customs Unions

Murray C. Kemp and
Henry Y. Wan Jr.

9.1 Introduction

In the welter of inconclusive debate concerning the implications of customs unions, the following elementary yet basic proposition seems to have been almost lost to sight.[1]

Proposition Consider any competitive world trading equilibrium, with any number of countries and commodities, and with no restrictions whatever on the tariffs and other commodity taxes of individual countries, and with costs of transport fully recognized. Now let any subset of the countries form a customs union. Then there exists a common tariff vector and a system of lump-sum compensatory payments, involving only members of the union, such that there is an associated tariff-ridden competitive equilibrium in which each individual, whether a member of the union or not, is not worse off than before the formation of the union.[2]

A detailed list of assumptions, and a relatively formal proof, may be found in section 9.2. Here we merely note that there exists a common tariff vector which is consistent with pre-union world prices and, therefore, with pre-union trade patterns and pre-union levels of welfare for nonmembers.

The proposition is interesting in that it contains no qualifications whatever concerning the size or number of the countries which are contemplating union, their pre- or post-union trading relationships, their relative states of development or levels of average income, and their propinquities in terms of geography or costs of transportation.

The proposition is interesting also because it implies that an incentive to form and enlarge customs unions persists until the world is one big

Originally published in *Journal of International Economics* 6 (February 1976): 95–98. Reprinted with permission.

customs union, that is, until world free trade prevails. More precisely, given any initial trading equilibrium, there exist finite sequences of steps, at each step new customs unions being created or old unions enlarged, such that at each step no individual is made worse off and such that after the last step the world is free-trading. (In general, at each step some individual actually benefits.) Indeed, on the basis of these observations one might attempt to rehabilitate the vague pre-Vinerian view that to form a customs union is to move in the direction of free trade.

Evidently the incentive is latent and insufficiently strong; tariffs and other artificial obstacles to trade persist. That the world is not free-trading must be explained in terms of:

1. the game-theoretic problems of choosing partners, dividing the spoils and enforcing agreements;

2. the noneconomic objectives of nations; and

3. the possibility that the "right" common tariff vector and system of compensatory payments might be associated with the "wrong" post-union equilibrium, that is, an equilibrium in which some members are worse off than before the union.[3]

A role may be found also for:

4. inertia and ignorance concerning the implications of possible unions (in particular, concerning the long list of lump-sum compensatory payments required) and, in the short run, for

5. the restraint exercised by international agreements to limit tariffs and other restrictions on trade.

However (5) can form no part of an explanation of the persistence of trading blocks in the long run.

Topics (1)–(4) form a possible agenda for the further study of customs unions. For a preliminary analysis of (1) the reader may consult Caves (1971); and for suggestive work on (2) he is referred to Cooper and Massell (1965), Johnson (1965) and Bhagwati (1968).

9.2   Proof of the Proposition

Suppose that (ia) the consumption set of each individual is closed, convex and bounded below, (ib) the preferences of each individual are convex and representable by a continuous ordinal utility function, (ic) each individual can survive with a consumption bundle each component of which is somewhat less than his pre-union consumption bundle, (ii) the production set of each economy is closed, convex, contains the origin and is such that positive output requires at least one positive input (impossibility of free production).

Consider a fictitious economy composed of the member economies but with a net endowment equal to the sum of the member endowments plus the equilibrium pre-union net excess supply of the rest of the world. In view of (i) and (ii), the economy possesses an optimum and any optimum can be supported by at least one internal price vector (Debreu (1959, pp. 92–93, 95–96)). Either the pre-union equilibrium of the member countries is a Pareto-optimal equilibrium of the fictitious economy (that is, corresponds to a maximal point of the utility possibility set), or it is not; in the latter case, a preferred Pareto-optimal equilibrium can be attained by means of lump-sum transfers among individuals in the fictitious economy. That essentially completes the proof. It only remains to note that the required vector of common tariffs may be computed as the difference between the vector of pre-union world prices and the vector of internal union prices.

Commodities can be indexed by location. Hence the resource-using activity of moving commodities from one country to another is accommodated in the several production sets; no special treatment of cost of transportation is needed.

Notes

We acknowledge with gratitude the useful comments of Jagdish Bhagwati, John Chipman and two referees.

1. A crude version of the proposition, together with an indication of the lines along which a proof may be constructed, can be found in Kemp (1964, p. 176). A geometric proof for the canonical three-countries, two-commodities case has been furnished by Vanek (1965, pp. 160–179). Negishi (1972, p. 187) has provided an algebraic treatment of the same canonical case.

2. With the same common tariff vector and system of lump-sum payments there may be associated other competitive equilibria which are not Pareto-comparable to the pre-union equilibrium. For this reason, the assertion is worded with care.

3. See footnote 2.

References

Debreu, G., 1959, Theory of value (John Wiley, New York).

Kemp, M. C., 1964, The pure theory of international trade (Prentice-Hall, Englewood Cliffs, NJ).

Cooper, C. A. and B. F. Massell, 1965, Towards a general theory of customs unions for developing countries, Journal of Political Economy 73, 461–476.

Johnson, H. G., 1965, An economic theory of protectionism, tariff bargaining, and the formation of customs unions, Journal of Political Economy 73, 256–283.

Vanek, J., 1965, General equilibrium of international discrimination: The case of customs unions (Harvard University Press, Cambridge, MA).

Bhagwati, J., 1968, Trade liberalization among LDCs, trade theory, and GATT rules, in: J. N. Wolfe, ed., Value, capital, and growth: Papers in honour of Sir John Hicks (Edinburgh University Press, Edinburgh) 21–43.

Caves, R. E., 1971, The economics of reciprocity: Theory and evidence on bilateral trading arrangements, Harvard Institute of Economic Research, Discussion Paper No. 166 (Harvard University, Cambridge, MA).

Negishi, T., 1972, General equilibrium theory and international trade (North-Holland, Amsterdam).

10

The Comparison of Second-Best Equilibria: The Case of Customs Unions

Murray C. Kemp and
Henry Y. Wan Jr.

10.1 Introduction

In Kemp and Wan (1976) we stated a proposition concerning the formation of customs unions:[1]

Proposition Consider any competitive world trading equilibrium, with any number of countries and commodities, with no restrictions whatever on the tariffs and other commodity taxes of individual countries, and with costs of transport fully recognized. Now let any subset of the countries form a customs union, defined to exclude commodity taxes other than tariffs. Then there exists a common tariff vector and a system of lumpsum compensatory payments, involving only members of the union, such that there is an associated tariff-ridden competitive equilibrium in which each individual, whether a member of the union or not, is not worse off than before the formation of the union.

The proposition is remarkable for its generality. Thus it contains no qualifications concerning the number or size of countries which are contemplating union, their pre- or post-union trading relationships, their relative states of development or levels of average income, their preferences or relative factor endowments, or their propinquities in terms of geography or costs of transportation.

The proposition is remarkable also for its decisiveness. For, generally speaking, welfare comparisons of second-best equilibria are inconclusive.

Finally, as noted in our earlier paper, the proposition is interesting because it implies that an incentive to form and enlarge customs unions persists until the world becomes one big union, that is, until world free trade

Originally published in *Journal of Economics* (Zeitschrift für Nationalökonomie), Suppl. 5 (1986): 161–167. Reprinted with permission.

prevails. More precisely, given any initial world trading equilibrium, there exists finite sequences of steps, at each step new customs unions being created or old unions enlarged, such that at each step no individual is made worse off and such that after the last step the world is free trading. (In general, at each step some individual actually benefits.) Indeed, on the basis of these observations one might attempt to rehabilitate the vague pre-Vinerian view that to form a customs union is to move in the direction of free trade.

However the proposition lacks proof. The assumptions listed by Kemp and Wan (1976) are now seen to be not quite strong enough to support the conclusions of the theorem. In particular, they do not rule out "Arrow's corner"[2] and thus do not guarantee that optimal allocations can be decentralized by prices; and they do not ensure the existence of a utility frontier. To overcome the first of these difficulties we now propose a revised form of our assumption (ic) and to overcome the second difficulty we offer a modified form of assumption (ii):

(ic′)   each individual can survive with somewhat less of every component of any consumption bundle which is not worse than his pre-union consumption bundle;

(ii′)   the union-wide aggregate production set is closed and convex and is such that positive output requires at least one positive input (impossibility of free production).

10.2   Proof of Proposition

The union-wide economy is the vector[3] $((X_i, \lesssim_i), (Y_j), (\omega_i), (\theta_{ij}))$, where Y_j is the production set of country j and X_i, $\lesssim_i$, ω_i and (θ_{ij}) are the consumption set, preferences, endowment and vector of profit shares of household i. The pre-union state of the economy is $a^0 = ((x_i^0), (y_j^0))$, where x_i^0 is the consumption vector of household i and y_j^0 is the output vector of country j; it belongs to the set of attainable states

$$A = \left(\prod_i X_i \right) \left(\prod_j Y_j \right) \cap \left\{ ((x_i), (y_j)) : \sum_i x_i - \sum_j y_j = \sum_i \omega_i + z^0 \right\}$$

where z^0 is the vector of pre-union net imports from the rest of the world at world prices p^0.

In terms of the above notation, the complete set of revised assumptions is as follows:

(ia) X_i is closed, convex and lower-bounded for $\leq$;

(ib) $\precsim_i$ is convex and can be represented by a continuous utility function u_i;

(ic')   if $x_i \succsim_i x_i^0$ then there is $\underline{x}_i \in X_i$ with $\underline{x}_i \ll x_i$;[4]

(ii') $Y \equiv \sum_j Y_j$ is closed and convex, and $Y \cap \Omega = \{0\}$.

(In (ii'), Ω is the non-negative orthant.)

Given these assumptions, it can be verified that conditions (a)–(d) of 6.2 (i) of Debreu (1959) are satisfied. Thus condition (a) follows from our (ia) and Debreu's 1.9 (13), (b) is implied by our (ib) and Debreu's 1.7 (3'), (c) is reproduced in our (ii') and (d) follows from the fact that $a^0 \in A$. From a statement in the proof of Debreu's 6.2 (i), the set of all attainable vectors of utility levels, $u(A)$, is compact, with its subset of maximal elements being the "utility frontier". Therefore there is some $a^* \in A$ which is *both* Pareto-optimal *and* such that a^* is Pareto-not-worse than a^0 (that is, $a^* \succsim a^0$ in Debreu's notation). Either all households are satiated at a^* and none is worse off than at a^0, so that one can set the intra-union price $p^* = 0$; or one household is not satiated and it can be verified that the conditions of Debreu's 6.4 (1) are satisfied.[5] In the latter event, a^* is an equilibrium relative to an intra-union price $p^* \geq 0$; hence, from (ic'), $p^* x_i^* > \min_{X_i} p^* x_i$ and (a^*, p^*) is a competitive equilibrium. The lumpsum transfer for i, $p^* x_i^* - p^* (\omega_i + \sum_j \theta_{ij} y_j^*)$, and the external tariff, $p^0 - p^*$, are then straightforwardly derived.[6] $\square$

We offer two brief remarks designed to amplify the proof.

Remark 1   We have constructed a fictitious union-wide economy with an aggregate endowment equal to the true collective endowment $\sum_i \omega_i$ modified by the collective net import z^0 from the rest of the world. The sum $\sum_i \omega_i + z^0$ need not be non-negative; indeed Theorem 6.2 (i) of Debreu (1959) imposes no such requirement. The compact image of the attainable set under u has an outer "frontier" which either contains the initial utility vector $u(a^0)$ or lies to its north-east, as illustrated by Figs. 10.1 and 10.2, respectively. That part of the frontier which is Pareto-not-worse than $u(a^0)$ is either $u(a^0)$ itself or a continuum of points NE of $u(a^0)$. The corresponding efficient attainable states can then be associated with intra-union price vectors to constitute compensated equilibria.

Remark 2   Suppose one household is unsatiated at p^*. Without loss of generality we may assume that the world price vector p^0 is a member of the natural simplex

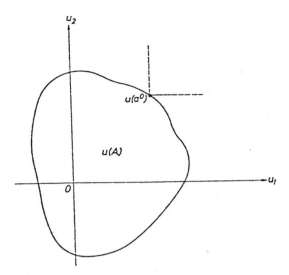

Figure 10.1

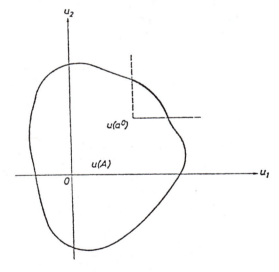

Figure 10.2

$$P \equiv \left\{ p \in \mathbb{R}^n_+ : \sum_k p_k = 1 \right\}.$$

Any equilibrium intra-union price vector p^* is then semi-positive but need not satisfy the restriction

$$\sum_k p_{k^*} = 1.$$

If p^* is an equilibrium intra-union price vector then, for any $\lambda > 0$, so is λp^*. The change from p^* to λp^* causes nominal profits and incomes in the customs union to change proportionately and causes the vector of tariff rates $p^* - p^0$ to change in an affine way to $\lambda p^* - p^0$, thus causing the net tariff revenue

$$(p^* - p^0)z^0 = p^* z^0 - p^0 z^0$$
$$= p^* z^0$$

to change in the proportion λ, together with all transfer payments.

10.3 The Necessity and Informational Requirements of Lumpsum Compensation

In the Proposition of Section 10.1 it is stipulated that intra-union compensation be by lumpsum transfers. We offer two defensive comments.

On the one hand, it seems to be part of the folklore of trade theorists that any scheme of lumpsum compensation requires detailed knowledge of individual preferences and production sets and thus imposes on the policy-maker a practically impossible informational burden. In fact it has been shown by Grinols (1981) that, in the context of customs unions, there always exists a scheme of lumpsum compensation the application of which requires only observable data from the initial equilibrium (roughly, the data required by the income-tax authority) and which, in particular, requires no knowledge of preferences or production sets. Thus let the i-th individual receive, as compensation, the commodity vector

$$\sigma_i \equiv x_i^0 - \omega_i^0 - \sum_j \theta_{ij} y_j^0.$$

Under any vector p^* of post-union equilibrium prices, this translates into a price-dependent transfer of $p^* \sigma_i$ and, therefore, an income of

$$w_i^* = p^*(\sigma_i + \omega_i^0) = p^*x_i^0 - \sum_j \theta_{ij}p^*y_j^0$$
$$= p^*x_i^0 + \sum_j \theta_{ij}p^*(y_j^* - y_j^0).$$

Now $y_j^0 \in Y_j^0 \subseteq Y_j^*$ and $p^*y_j^* = \max p^* Y_j^*$; hence $p^*(y_j^* - y_j^0) \geqq 0$ and $w_i^* \geqq p^*x_i^0$. It follows that the compensation is adequate.

On the other hand, it is widely believed that the stipulation that compensation be lumpsum is inessential, that if there is a Pareto-improving customs union with lumpsum compensation then there is a Pareto-improving customs union without lumpsum transfers but with compensation effected by means of country-specific commodity taxes and subsidies. The basis of this belief is a passage in Dixit and Norman (1980, pp. 192–194). However, a careful examination of their argument reveals that not even the existence of a compensated post-union equilibrium is established. And we now have several counterexamples to the proposition that, in general, compensation need not be lumpsum; see Kemp and Wan (1986)[7].

Notes

Thanks are due to J. Bhagwati, M. Yano, and E. Grinols for encouragement and advice.

1. The proposition was first stated by Kemp (1964, p. 176). It may be found also in Vanek (1965) and Ohyama (1972).

2. For "Arrow's corner," see Arrow (1951) and Chipman (1965).

3. Our notation closely follows Debreu (1959).

4. It follows from (ic′) that the entire set $X^{x_i^0} \equiv \{x_i \in X_i : x_i \gtrsim_i x_i^0\}$ is in the interior of X_i.

5. Specifically, Debreu's (a), (b.1–2) and (c) follow respectively from our (ia), (ib) and (ii′); and his assumption that some individual i' is non-satiated is fulfilled in the present case.

6. Professor Earl Grinols has kindly pointed out that there is an alternative way of correcting our earlier (1976) proof. This consists in retaining (ia), (ib) and (ic), and adding the assumption (id) that all individual preferences are non-satiable. Then one can specify a particular scheme of lumpsum transfers, similar to that of Grinols (1981), to prove the existence of a compensated equilibrium in which no-one is worse off than before.

7. The examples of Kemp and Wan were devised to counter the single-country proposition that if free trade is Pareto-beneficial when compensation is by means of lumpsum transfers then it is Pareto-beneficial when compensation is effected by means of commodity taxes and subsidies. However, the examples can be re-interpreted as applying to customs unions with each member initially applying prohibitive tariffs.

References

K. J. Arrow (1951): An Extension of the Basic Theorems of Classical Welfare Economics, in: J. Neyman (ed.): Proceedings of the Second Berkeley Symposium on Mathematical Statistics and Probability, Berkeley, pp. 507–532.

J. S. Chipman (1965): A Survey of the Theory of International Trade: Part 2, The Neoclassical Theory, Econometrica 33, pp. 685–760.

G. Debreu (1959): Theory of Value, New York.

A. K. Dixit and V. Norman (1980): Theory of International Trade, Cambridge and Welwyn.

E. L. Grinols (1981): An Extension of the Kemp-Wan Theorem on the Formation of Customs Unions, Journal of International Economics 11, pp. 259–266.

M. C. Kemp (1964): The Pure Theory of International Trade, Englewood Cliffs, N.J.

M. C. Kemp and H. Y. Wan, Jr. (1976): An Elementary Proposition Concerning the Formation of Customs Unions, Journal of International Economics 6, pp. 95–97.

M. C. Kemp and H. Y. Wan, Jr. (1986): Gains from Trade With and Without Lumpsum Compensation, Journal of International Economics 21, pp. 99–110.

M. Ohyama (1972): Trade and Welfare in General Equilibrium, Keio Economic Studies 9, pp. 37–73.

J. Vanek (1965): General Equilibrium of International Discrimination, Cambridge, Mass.

11

An Extension of the Kemp–Wan Theorem on the Formation of Customs Unions

Earl L. Grinols

11.1 Introduction

In August of 1961, the British government applied for membership in the European Economic Community. After an initial rejection and further years of hard bargaining, Britain became a full member on January 1, 1973 in accordance with the treaty of accession signed the previous year. The entire process, therefore, took eleven years and five months from first negotiations to final entry.

The intriguing aspect of the British experience is that in spite of the supposed advantages to free trade, the negotiations were as difficult as they were and opposition to British entry came from within Britain as well as the Common Market. The question under what conditions a nation will benefit from the formation of a customs union, however, is not new. It dates back at least to the publication of Viner's *The Customs Union Issue* (1950). Further, in 1976 Kemp and Wan showed that as long as perfect competition prevails inside the union a compensation scheme between members can always be found whereby every individual is made better off or no worse off after the formation or enlargement of the customs union than he was before. The fact that the world does not freely trade, therefore, must be explained on other grounds. One obstacle, suggested by Kemp and Wan, which seems to be borne out by the British experience, is the difficulty of settling upon a compensation scheme. Either the venality and self-interest of the member nations make it impossible to reach an early agreement, or the technical problems of calculating mutually beneficial terms have overwhelmed the various negotiators. We address the latter issue here.

Originally published in *Journal of International Economics* 11 (1981): 259–266. Reprinted with permission.

We show that a simple compensation scheme yielding the Kemp–Wan result can always be defined in terms of observable trade flows and market prices. Moreover, there are circumstances in which the proposed scheme is the only feasible one. Using world prices for evaluation each and every country "breaks even" under the proposed scheme, receiving a transfer which has zero value. Thus, from the point of view of world prices the transfer is financially neutral. Using post-union internal prices for valuation, member nations may have to pay or receive a net transfer. The sum of such transfers can be shown to equal the union's total tariff revenue from the rest of the world, thus providing a serendipitous revenue-sharing rule for the tariff yields.

Section 11.2 below provides an intuitive discussion of the compensating scheme and its existence proof, the formal derivation being relegated to the appendix. Section 11.3 describes the two properties of the scheme mentioned above and concluding remarks are contained in section 11.4.

11.2   The Compensation Scheme

At the micro-level, no individual will become worse off if he is offered the option of consuming exactly the same bundle that he consumed before the formation of the union. If there were no production this could be accomplished by redistributing existing endowments to every individual in the union as a subsidy-in-kind which is equal to the difference between his true endowment vector and the pre-union consumption vector. Summing over all consumers in each nation and canceling the intra-national trade, the scheme promises each member nation a subsidy equal to its pre-union trade vector. Summing over all member nations and canceling out the intra-union trade, the scheme promises the union a subsidy equal to the net trade vector with the rest of the world at the pre-union level according to pre-union world prices. If the resultant economy after redistribution has an equilibrium leaving world prices at their initial level with competitive equilibrium within the union we have succeeded in making all individuals no worse off than before. This is so since in a competitive equilibrium no consumer can be worse off than consuming his endowment, and the 'endowment' in our contrived equilibrium is the pre-union consumption vector. For the union as a whole the shortfall in needed endowments is obtained from the rest of the world through trade.

When production is present allowance needs to be made for the distribution of firm profits and the possibility that pre-union consumption of some goods may be greater than their availability in the post-union equilibrium. A simple redistribution of existing endowments and trade flows will no longer work. Instead each individual can be assured the ability to purchase his pre-union consumption bundle at the prices he faces in the post-union equilibrium.[1] The resources needed by each country to cover these commitments will exceed the value of its domestic production and endowments by no more than its pre-union trade flows evaluated at post-union prices.[2] Summing over all member nations and canceling out the intra-union trade, the union needs income above the value of its own production and endowments no greater than the value of its pre-union trade vector with the rest of the world. If after the various transfers are made to each consumer and production is chosen in each firm to maximize profits, the economy has a competitive equilibrium, then we have succeeded in making each individual no worse off than before for the same reasons given in the pure trade case.

In proving the existence of an equilibrium Kemp and Wan rely on the second fundamental theorem of welfare economics, which says that every Pareto optimum can be supported by a competitive equilibrium with appropriate redistributions including the possibility of redistribution across national borders. Their proof is "existential" rather than "constructive," however, and gives no clue about the compensation scheme which has to be employed. In our case we have specified the necessary distribution to each nation as its pre-union trade vector and need a theorem showing that any Pareto noninferior allocation can be supported as a competitive equilibrium without further redistributions across national borders.[3] We therefore appeal to the Grandmont–McFadden theorem, which satisfies these requirements, to obtain the following propositions.

Proposition 1 Consider a world trading equilibrium, with any number of countries and commodities and with no restrictions whatever on the tariffs and other commodity taxes of individual countries and with costs of transport fully recognized. Let the subset $1, \ldots, K$ of countries form a customs union with competitive free trade internally. Then there exists a common tariff barrier and well-defined distribution policy of lump-sum compensatory payments such that each individual, whether a member of the union or not, is not worse off than before the formation of the union. The compensatory payments across national borders have zero value when valued at world prices and add to union tariff revenues with the rest of the world when valued at internal post-union prices.

A description of the exact compensations referred to and the proof of proposition 1 is given in the appendix. Applied to the world as a whole, proposition 1 implies the following:

Proposition 2 Given the conditions of proposition 1, let countries 1, ..., K represent the entire world. Let the world move to competitive free trade. Then there exists a well-defined distribution policy of lump-sum compensatory payments such that each individual is not worse off than before the move to free trade. Furthermore, compensatory payments across national borders have zero value when valued at pre-free-trade prices, and add to zero when valued at post-free-trade prices.[4]

The proof of proposition 2 is given in the appendix. We turn now to the implications of propositions 1 and 2 on a national level and a description of the implied financial arrangements.

11.3 Properties of the Compensation Scheme

We said in section 11.2 that the only compensations which are needed allow all households and firms the option of continuing their pre-union consumption and production plans if they so choose. In the post-union equilibrium, however, they will generally recontract to new positions representing different consumption and higher profits at the post-union prices.[5] The union countries keep world prices at their pre-union level by creating a common tariff to bridge the gap between world prices and the post-union equilibrium prices. The compensation to each country is given by its pre-union trade vector. Since trading is assumed to be balanced at world prices, the world-price valuation of such compensation must always be zero.

For the union as a whole the tariff revenues equal the difference between the union trade vector valued at domestic prices and at the world prices. Since the external trade vector of the union has zero value at world prices (trade being balanced) the magnitude of tariff receipts is equal to the value of the union's trade at domestic prices. But, the union's trade with the rest of the world is equal to its pre-union trade, thus the sum of compensations to member nations equals tariff receipts. The compensation scheme therefore yields as a by-product a revenue-sharing rule for the common tariff.

The proposed scheme is always feasible since by proposition 1 there exists an equilibrium when the necessary promises are made which is

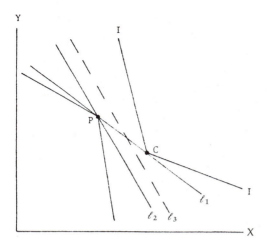

Figure 11.1
Compensation in a one-person, two-good economy.

consistent with them being carried out. We now show that there are situations in which the proposed compensations are the only ones which
will work. This follows since there are demand structures and production
sets such that if the country got anything less it could not make everyone
better off. For example, consider the one-person, two-good economy of
country A in fig. 11.1, where P is the pre-union vector of production and
C is the pre-union vector of consumption. Proposition 1 implies that
country A is given income equal to the value of the vector $P - C$ at post-
union prices corresponding to the line l_2. (Balanced trade implies $P - C$
has zero value at world prices corresponding to line l_1.) Anything less
would leave it with a budget line such as the dotted l_3 which lies to the
left of C. In other situations, of course, substitutability in production and
consumption might imply each country could be able to get by with
somewhat less. Verifying this would require knowledge of preferences,
however, and would be difficult to check. In the absence of restrictions on
production and consumption, the above arrangements are the only ones
which will work in all cases.[6]

11.4   Conclusions

We have described compensation arrangements for uniform welfare
improvement from the formation of customs unions which are always

feasible and depend only on the information contained in prices and pre-union trade flows. As a final comment, we note that should there exist two sectors of a given region such as two geographic locations in the world, or two well defined sets of consumers and firms within a nation, that proposition 1 can be applied to those subsets as easily as to nations. What is required is the ability to transfer the net value of production to consumers inside the respective subsets. If a nation cannot eliminate all barriers to free trade, it may be able to make welfare gains by doing so in some sectors. This is possible without hurting any consumer.

Appendix

Let countries $1, \ldots, K$ be the countries considering forming a customs union. Consider next the fictitious economy where each nation's endowment consists of its usual endowment plus its share of the pre-union net excess supply of the rest of the world. Let Y_k denote the net production set of country K (production plus endowment). Following Grandmont and McFadden, suppose that:

(Y.1) Y_k is a closed subset of R^N,

(Y.2)   Inaction is possible: $0 \in Y_k$,

(Y.3) Y_k is convex,

(Y.4)   There is free disposal, $y \in Y_k$, $y' \leq y$ implies $y' \in Y_k$,

(Y.5)   The set of efficient points in Y_k is bounded.[7]

Assumption (Y.2), in the context of net production, implies that each nation is able to meet its pre-union trading commitments.

On the demand side, define the set of goods as N and the subset N_k as $\{n \in N \mid y_n > 0 \text{ for some } y \in Y_k, y \geq 0\}$. Prices on N and N_k are $P = \{(p_1, \ldots, p_n) \mid 0 \leq p_n < +\infty \text{ for } n \in N\}$ and $P_k = \{(p_1, \ldots, p_n) \mid 0 \leq p_n < +\infty \text{ for } n \in N_k, p_n = +\infty \text{ for } n \notin N_k\}$. $\bar{P}_k$ will denote PUP_k. Suppose:

(D.1)   Consumer i of nation k can subsist on goods in N_k, i.e. there is a vector x with $x_n = 0$ for $n \notin N_k$ upon which consumer i can subsist.

(D.2)   Values of the demand function are non-empty for positive prices and incomes above subsistence level.

(D.3)   Consumer i's demand correspondence is positively homogeneous of degree zero on prices and income, is a closed upper hemicontinuous correspondence for prices in P and incomes above subsistence, is a convex subset of individual i's budget set, and all income is spent.

(E.1)   The pre-union allocation of goods in nation k is such that the value of each consumer's commodity vector exceeds his subsistence income at each non-zero price vector in P_k for which $p \cdot y_k$ is maximized. For each $p \in P_k$ with $\sum_{n \in N_k} P_n > 0$ national income exceeds the sum of minimum incomes needed for subsistence of its citizens.[8]

(E.2)   There is at least one commodity which can be supplied in every nation, and at least one consumer in each nation who, when given an income above his subsistence level and a price vector with a zero price for that good, will demand an unbounded amount of some commodity.

Assumption (E.2) is an assumption of convenience to rule out the possibility of fragmented equilibria where subeconomies have no dealings with one another. (E.1) in turn, rules out the possibility of starvation for any individual.

Given the above definitions, the following theorem adapted from Grandmont and McFadden applies to the formation of customs union:

Theorem   Suppose that nations $1, \ldots, K$ with the fictitious endowments satisfy conditions (Y.1)–(Y.5), each consumer in nation k satisfies (D.1)–(D.3), (E.1) and (E.2) hold. Then there exists a free trade competitive equilibrium for the distribution policy whereby each nation gives income to each consumer equal to the value of his pre-union consumption at post-union prices and a non-negative fraction of the remaining national income. This equilibrium is Pareto non-inferior for the consumers of each nation $1, \ldots, K$ when compared to their initial allocation. Further, if the prices and initial allocations were not a competitive equilibrium and if every consumer is locally nonsatiated at the pre-union allocation, then the allocation achieved under union is Pareto preferable for the union's consumers to their initial allocation.

This nearly completes the proof of proposition 1.

The required vector of common tariffs in proposition 1 may be computed as the vector of pre-union world prices less the vector of internal union prices. Proposition 2 follows from the application of the above theorem to every nation simultaneously. On a national level the income $p \cdot y_k$ is distributed for post-union equilibrium prices p. Since this differs from the value of domestically produced goods and services by the value of pre-union trade flows, each country must receive a portion of the union's tariff revenues equal to its pre-union trade flows valued at internal post-union prices.

Notes

I would like to thank Henry Wan and Murray Kemp for their insightful and helpful comments.

1. A precise description of such arrangements can be found in Grandmont and McFadden (1972). Following them, each individual is given an income function, $I^i = P^*c^i + \theta^i[I - \sum_i P^*c^i]$, where P^* is the vector of equilibrium prices, c^i is individual i's vector of pre-union consumption, θ^i are scalars between zero and one summing to unity, and I is total income available on the national level for distribution. Individuals know their income for any set of prices in the same way that a Debreu consumer endowed with labor, for example, knows his income for any given price of labor. The plan is feasible if the government can assure in equilibrium that I^i is large enough to purchase c^i. This, of course, is equivalent to $I - \sum_i P^*c^i$ greater than or equal to zero.

2. Since $c = y + e + x$, where c is consumption, y is production, e endowments and x is trade with the rest of the world all listed in vector terms, income needed to purchase c at the post union price vector P^* will be $P^*y + P^*e + P^*x$, where y^* is the profit maximizing production at prices P^*. Since P^*y is at most equal to P^*y^*, $P^*(y^* + e)$ needs to be augmented by no more than P^*x.

3. The usual proof is also based on Debreu (1959) which describes a private ownership economy, whereas the present paper describes an economy with government determination of incomes. The Debreu theorem would therefore require certain other minor modifications.

4. This last property is added for completeness relative to the statement of proposition 1. It follows trivially from the fact that the "union" represents the entire world and trade with the "outside" is a null vector.

5. The latter follows from profit maximization by firms at the new set of prices.

6. Changes in member compensations can easily be related to profits if one desires. Let c_k, y_k, e_k, and x_k be the vectors of aggregate pre-union consumption, production, endowments, and trade for country k, respectively, and let y_k^*, P^* be the vectors of post-union production and prices. If y_k^* is known, country k's subsidy can be as little as $P^* \cdot x_k - P^*(y_k^* - y_k)$ and leave it enough income to fulfil its promises to be able to purchase pre-union consumption. This follows since $P^*(y_k^* + e_k) + P^*x_k \geqq P^*(y_k^* + e_k) + [P^*x_k - P^*(y_k^* - y_k)] = P^*(y_k + e_k + x_k) = P^*c_k$. The first relation follows from the fact that $P^*(y_k^* - y_k) \geqq 0$ by firm profit maximization. The second is cancellation of terms and the third follows from the definition of consumption. Thus P^*x_k is a high enough subsidy in all cases while $P^*x_k - P^*(y_k^* - y_k)$ is the least that will work for commitments P^*c_k.

7. See Grandmont and McFadden for a discussion of weaker conditions than (Y.5).

8. A mild sufficient condition for (E.1) is that each consumer have an allocation on which he can survive which is strictly smaller than his given allocation in every component. See Grandmont and McFadden (1972, p. 119) for other conditions.

References

Debreu, Gerard, 1959, Theory of value (Cowles Foundation for Research in Economics, New Haven, CT).

Kemp, M. and H. Y. Wan, 1976, An elementary proposition concerning the formation of customs unions, Journal of International Economics 6, 95—97.

Grandmont, J. M. and D. McFadden, 1972, A technical note on classical gains from trade, Journal of International Economics 2, 109—125.

Viner, Jacob, 1950, The customs union issue (Carnegie Endowment for International Peace, New York).

12

The Common External Tariff of a Customs Union: Alternative Approaches

T. N. Srinivasan

12.1 Introduction

The most favoured nation principle (or MFN principle as it is usually called) is enshrined in Article I of the General Agreement on Tariffs and Trade (GATT) concluded in 1947 and is considered by all to be the foundation of the agreement. Yet GATT has allowed several exceptions to MFN principle such as, for example, its "grandfathering" of pre-existing preferential trade arrangements, the notorious regime of discriminatory quantitative restrictions on trade in textiles called the Multi-Fibre Arrangement, and the waiver granted to developing countries under the "enabling clause" of the Tokyo Round Agreement of 1979 for providing preferential access to other developing countries to their markets. However, the most prominent exception is in its Article XXIV relating to the CUs and FTAs, since by their definition both clearly involve preferential treatment of the trade among members of such arrangements as compared to their trade with non-members. Two essential features of the article as it relates to a Customs Union are:

(i) ... with respect to a customs union, or an interim agreement leading to a formation of a customs union, the duties and other regulations of commerce imposed at the institution of any such union or interim agreement in respect of trade with contracting parties not parties to such union or agreement shall not on the whole be higher or more restrictive than the *general incidence* of the duties and regulations of commerce applicable in the constituent territories prior to the formation of such union or the adoption of such interim agreement (ii) duties and other restrictive regulations of commerce (except, where necessary, those permitted under Articles XI, XII, XIII, XIV, XV and XX) are eliminated with respect to *substantially all the trade* between the constituent territories of the union or at least with respect

Originally published in *Japan and the World Economy* 9 (November 1997): 447–465.
Reprinted with permission.

to *substantially all the trade* in products originating in such territories... (GATT, 1994, pp. 523–524, emphasis added)

The article made it clear that any contracting party of the GATT deciding to enter into a CU or FTA or an interim agreement towards that end shall promptly notify the other contracting parties of their intentions to do so and, presumably, to agree to abide by the requirements of Article XXIV.

It has been suggested that by insisting on the departure from MFN being extreme with respect to trade among members in view of the fact that, substantially, all of it had to be free and also requiring that the general incidence of barriers on trade with non-members is not raised, the intention of the drafters of GATT was to make it very difficult to form a CU or FTA. Yet the history of consideration of notifications of such arrangements and actions on them by the contracting parties is one of evasion, rather than strict enforcement, of the provisions of Article XXIV. For example, in the case of the most celebrated such agreement, namely the Rome Treaty of the European Economic Community, the GATT "blinked," according to Finger (1993, p. 137). He quotes from a report of a GATT (1959, p. 70) committee that considered the issue:

[T]he Committee felt that it would be more fruitful if attention could be directed to specific and practical problems, leaving aside for the time being questions of law and debates about the compatibility of the Rome Treaty with Article XXIV of the General Agreement.

It is clear that even if the contracting parties wished to enforce Article XXIV they would have run into difficulties. As Jackson (1989, p. 141) points out, the requirements that substantially all trade among members be free and the common external tariff

be not "on the whole" more restrictive than the "general incidence of" duties and regulations before the CU was formed ... however, [are] difficult legal concepts to apply, and have caused much controversy in the GATT. In addition, the GATT exception allows an "interim agreement"—one which leads to a CU or FTA within a reasonable time—to depart from MFN. This has opened a loophole of considerable size, since almost any type of preferential agreement can be claimed to fall within the exception for "interim agreement," and "reasonable time" is exceedingly imprecise.

The agreement concluding the Uruguay Round of multilateral trade negotiations signed in April 1994 at Marrakesh included an understanding with respect to the interpretation of Article XXIV. It clarified that for purposes of comparison,

... the general incidence of the duties and other regulations of commerce applicable before and after the formation of a customs union shall in respect of duties and charges be based upon an overall assessment of weighted average tariff rates and of customs duties collected. This assessment shall be based on import statistics for a previous representative period to be supplied by the customs union, on a tariff-line basis and in values and quantities, broken down by WTO country of origin. For this purpose, the duties and charges to be taken into consideration shall be the applied rates of duty.

The substitution of the vague phrase "general incidence" by a much more precise criterion for comparison of pre- and post-union tariff structures is to be welcomed. However no rationale for proposed criterion is offered. Nor is it established that one can infer how the interests of non-members are affected by the formation of CU by using the suggested comparison.

The reform of Article XXIV began to attract scholarly attention because of a revived interest since the late eighties in free trade areas and other preferential trading arrangements (PTAs).[1] Between the initiation of the Uruguay Round in 1986 and the establishment of the World Trade Organization (WTO) on January 1, 1995 as many as 30 agreements were notified as compared to 68 agreements notified in the previous four decades (WTO, 1995a, Appendix Table 1.A). The belief that such a revival was a passing phenomenon reflecting primarily a gloomy assessment (at the time of its mid-term review in December 1988) of the prospect of successfully concluding the Uruguay Round negotiations, and the fear that the global trading system will break up into warring trade blocs, turned out to be mistaken. The interest in PTAs gathered further steam, rather than wane, even after the successful conclusion of the UR negotiations. In fact, since the establishment of WTO, 12 more agreements have been notified (WTO, 1995b, p. 12). As such, the reform of Article XXIV continues to be a matter of concern. Among the issues currently being raised is the central question of the common external tariffs of a customs union. What should be the structure of such tariffs?

In what follows, I first briefly describe alternative approaches to this central question, in particular, whether the relevant issue should be one of the height of the post-union barriers on trade with non-members or one of post-union *welfare* of non-members (Section 12.2). Kemp and Wan (1976) in their celebrated article take the latter approach and show the existence of a post-union tariff structure for a customs union (of any arbitrary collection of members of a global trading system) that is global welfare improving, as long as lump sum income transfers among members of the union are feasible.[2] Such a tariff structure, in comparison to the pre-union world equilibrium, maintains the welfare of each resident of non-union members while increasing the welfare of at least one resident of a member of the union. The Kemp–Wan proposition is of importance in that it shows the existence of a *dynamic path* to global free trade through successive enlargements of customs unions, each enlargement being Pareto-improving over its predecessor. Along such a path, the regional approach towards trade liberalization through the formation of customs unions becomes a "building block" rather than a "stumbling block," to use Bhagwati's (1991) apt phrases, in the march towards global free trade. I go beyond the Kemp–Wan proof of the existence of such a *common* tariff structure by characterizing it for two benchmark examples in terms of an appropriately defined average of *different* pre-union tariffs of members. Such an average is not only as well-defined as the average specified in the Uruguay Round version of Article XXIV, but unlike the latter it has a welfare content in addition. I show this using a Ricardian model of a three-country trading world in Section 12.3. In Section 12.4, I show analogous results hold in a model with a more complex production technology as long as all countries have identical Samuelson social utility functions of the Cobb–Douglas type. I also address the issue of the intra-union transfers associated with the Kemp–Wan tariff, an issue which is elegantly illustrated for a special case in Donald Davis's discussion of this chapter [not included in this volume].

12.2 Alternative Approaches to Common External Tariffs

Jacob Viner (1950), in his justly celebrated analysis of Customs Unions (CU), distinguished between trade-creating and trade-diverting unions and implied that the former enhance, and the latter lessen, global welfare. Although such a welfare implication was shown not to hold in general, the idea that the formation of a customs union should be judged in terms of its impact on global welfare is widely accepted. The GATT was negotiated and entered into in 1947 well before Viner's analysis (and long before that of Kemp and Wan) was published. It is therefore hard to say whether the negotiators of the GATT had, without using the Viner's terminology, the same concerns about trade diversion as Viner or indeed whether like Kemp and Wan they had global welfare in mind, in insisting that the common tariffs of a CU be no higher than the general incidence of tariffs of the member countries in the pre-union situation. Indeed, if they did, they (and as some, including economists, still do) failed to appreciate that the height of barriers in a CU on its trade with non-members need not necessarily indicate how global welfare would be affected by the formation of the CU.

Two of the proposals for reform of Article XXIV are by Bhagwati (1991) and McMillan (1993). Bhagwati proposed that a CU should be approved only when its common external tariff is set at the minimum of the pre-union import tariffs of the member countries. An implication of this is that the CU will engage in free trade with *all* non-members, if at least one member has a zero pre-union tariff for each of the traded commodities! Even if this were not the case, as I show in Section 12.3, the Bhagwati proposal could *lower* the welfare of some members of the CU and *raise* that of non-members.[3] Since such a possibility could deter the formation of a union, the Bhagwati proposal may still be treated as a desirable reform which in effect sets a price or hurdle on WTO members who wish to enter a customs union and thus compromise the MFN principle.

McMillan (1993) also points out that in Article XXIV of GATT (1947)

... nowhere is it specified how the "general incidence" of a set of tariffs is to be measured. Are before and after tariffs to be compared item by item, or are average tariffs to be compared? If the latter, is it a simple average, or a weighted average with trade volumes as weights? (p. 299)

He suggests that

Article XXIV could be made more workable by phrasing its requirements not in terms of the height of tariffs but in terms of trade volumes; that is, by looking at the trade consequences of the restrictions rather than trying to measure their effect on domestic prices ... A proposed RIA (Regional Integration Agreement), in order to get GATTs imprimatur, would have to promise not to introduce policies that result in external trade volumes being lowered. And, if after some years the RIA is seen to have reduced its imports from the rest of the world, it would be required to adjust its trade restrictions so as to reverse their fall in imports. (p. 300)

Measuring trade volumes is certainly more workable. But changes in *aggregate* volumes of trade with non-members need not necessarily indicate changes in global welfare. Besides, by substituting *outcome* variables (viz. trade volumes for *instrument* variables, viz. tariff rates), the McMillan proposal sanctifies the malodorous "managed-trade" approach to trade policy.[4] On the other hand, the Kemp–Wan approach is based on tariffs that maintain the terms of trade of unchanged. As such, each non-member, as long as it maintains its trade barriers unchanged, will maintain its welfare at the same level as it was prior to the formation of the CU. Thus, global welfare has to increase, since at least one member can be made better off with the formation of the union without hurting others. Strictly speaking, the adoption of a Kemp–Wan structure (which is in general not unique) keeps the prices faced by non-members unchanged.[5] This in turn ensures that no one in any non-member country is adversely affected by the formation of the CU as long as each such country does not alter its tariffs. As such, adoption of a Kemp–Wan tariff structure by a CU is *sufficient* to ensure that the welfare of non-members is not adversely affected by its formation. It is certainly not necessary—after all, one cannot rule out the possibility that in spite of the change in the prices faced by non-members incidental to the adoption by a CU of a tariff structure that differs from a Kemp–Wan structure, welfare of non-members is not adversely affected. Also, as Winters (1996) rightly cautions, the Kemp–Wan approach cannot be used as a benchmark to evaluate any proposed tariff structure. There is no way in general of determining how a deviation from a Kemp–Wan tariff structure by a CU affects welfare of consumers in any non-member country relative to its level prior to the formation of the Union.

12.3   Customs Unions in a Ricardian World: Two Examples

I now turn to the characterization of Kemp–Wan tariffs. Let labour be the single factor of production with the labour endowment (inelastically supplied) of country i being $\bar{L}_i$ ($i = 1, 2, 3$). Let a_j^i be the unit labour requirement of commodity j in country i ($i = 1, 2, 3; j = 1, 2$) so that the maximum possible output $\bar{Q}_j^i$ of good j in country i is $\bar{L}^i / a_j^i$. Let the Samuelson social utility function be $\alpha \operatorname{Log} C_1 + (1 - \alpha) \operatorname{Log} C_2$ (with $0 < \alpha < 1$) in all three countries. In autarky the domestic relative price of good 2 (with good 1 as numeraire) in country i is $\pi^i(A) = a_2^i / a_1^i$. Let the ranking of comparative advantage be $\pi^1(A) < \pi^2(A) < \pi^3(A)$.

Suppose that, in the initial trading equilibrium, country 1 is specialized in and exports good 2 to the other two countries which are both specialized in good 1. Let the world relative price of good 2 with good 1 as numeraire be $\pi(T)$. Let t^i be the rate of ad valorem import tariff in country i so that the prices are as follows:

	Good 1	Good 2
World price	1	$\pi(T)$
Domestic price:		
Country 1	$1 + t^1$	$\pi(T)$
Country 2	1	$(1 + t^2)\pi(T)$
Country 3	1	$(1 + t^3)\pi(T)$

Let tariff revenues be returned to consumers in a lump sum fashion. Let $E^i(T)$ be the total expenditure in country i in *domestic* prices. Then country 1 spends $\alpha E^1(T)$ on imports of good 1 from the other two and country i $(i = 2, 3)$ spends $(1 - \alpha)E^i(T)$ on imports of good 2 from country 1. As such, the tariff revenue $R^i(T)$ in country i is given by

$$R^1(T) = \frac{\alpha E^1(T)}{1 + t^1}t^1 \quad R^i(T) = \frac{(1 - \alpha)E^i(T)}{\pi(T)(1 + t^i)}t^i\pi(T)$$

Expenditure $E^i(T) \equiv$ Value of Production + Tariff Revenue. Hence

$$E^1(T) = \pi(T)\bar{Q}_2^1 + R^1(T) \Rightarrow E^1(T) = \frac{(1 + t^1)\pi(T)\bar{Q}_2^1}{[1 + (1 - \alpha)t^1]}$$

$$E^i(T) = \bar{Q}_1^i + R^i(T) \Rightarrow E^i(T) = \frac{(1 + t^i)}{(1 + \alpha t^i)}\bar{Q}_1^i \quad \text{for } i = 1, 2$$

Market clearance for good 2 (by Walras' law the market for good 1 clears if the market for good 2 clears) implies that exports from country 1 equal the sum of imports of countries 2 and 3. Now

$$\text{Exports of good 2 by country } 1 \equiv \left[\frac{\alpha \bar{Q}_2^1}{1 + (1 - \alpha)t^1}\right]$$

$$\text{Imports of good 2 by country } i = \frac{(1 - \alpha)\bar{Q}_1^i}{\pi(T)(1 + \alpha t^i)}$$

Thus, market clearance requires

$$\frac{\alpha \bar{Q}_2^1}{1 + (1 - \alpha)t^1} = \frac{1 - \alpha}{\pi(T)}\sum_{i=2}^{3}\left(\frac{\bar{Q}_1^i}{1 + \alpha t^i}\right)$$

or

$$\pi(T) = \left(\frac{1 - \alpha}{\alpha}\right)\frac{[1 + (1 - \alpha)t^1]}{\bar{Q}_2^1}\sum_{i=2}^{3}\left(\frac{\bar{Q}_1^i}{1 + \alpha t^i}\right) \tag{12.1}$$

For the assumed pattern of specialization and trade to be consistent, we must have $\pi^1(A) < \pi(T)/(1 + t^1)$ and $\pi(T)(1 + t^i) < \pi^i(A)$ for $i = 2, 3$.

Having characterized the initial trading equilibrium, the first example that I consider is a CU of countries 2 and 3. I assume that the outside country, namely country 1, leaves its tariff unchanged at the same level as it was prior to the formation of a CU by the other two countries. The objective is to derive the Kemp–Wan post-union common tariff and characterize it as a function of pre-union tariffs. By definition, such a tariff will leave country 1's welfare unchanged at its pre-union level while improving the welfare of at least one of the members without reducing that of the other. Since the tariff of country 1 is unchanged, for its welfare to be unchanged, its terms of trade *after* the formation of the CU should be the same as before. With its terms of trade and tariff remaining unchanged, the net exports of country 1, which in a balanced-trade equilibrium equals the net imports of the CU, also remains unchanged. Given the net import vector, the CU countries can choose a production vector that ensures that at least one gains without the other losing or both gain as compared to the pre-union equilibrium. Thus, the essential step in deriving the Kemp–Wan tariff is to look for a tariff that leaves post-union terms of trade at their pre-union level.

Suppose the pattern of specialization and trade is unaffected by the formation of CU. Any *common external* tariff t to be consistent with the vague provisions of Article XXIV of GATT (1947) presumably has to satisfy $t \leq \text{Max}(t^2, t^3) = t^3$ (say). Let the new world relative price of good 2 be $\pi(\text{CU})$. It is easy now to see that, with a common external tariff t, and identical tastes in the two-member countries, imports of good 2 into the union will be $(1 - \alpha)E(\text{CU})/\pi(\text{CU})(1 + t)$ where $E(\text{CU})$ is the total expenditure of the union. Hence, tariff revenue will be

$$\frac{t(1 - \alpha)E(\text{CU})}{(1 + t)}.$$

By definition $E(\text{CU}) \equiv$ value of production + tariff revenue, or

$$E(\text{CU}) = \sum_{i=2}^{3} \bar{Q}_1^i + \frac{t(1 - \alpha)E(\text{CU})}{1 + t}$$

so that

$$E(\text{CU}) = \frac{1 + t}{(1 + \alpha t)} \sum_{i=2}^{3} \bar{Q}_1^i.$$

Substituting this in the expression for imports of good 2, and equating it to the exports of good 2 from country 1, i.e.

$$\frac{\alpha \bar{Q}_2^1}{1 + (1 - \alpha)t^1},$$

we get

$$\bar{Q}_2^1 \pi(CU) = \left[\frac{1-\alpha}{\alpha}\right][1 + (1-\alpha)t^1]\left(\frac{1}{1+\alpha t}\right)\sum_{i=2}^{3}\bar{Q}_1^i \qquad (12.2)$$

From Eq. (12.1) and Eq. (12.2), we get the critical relationship between the post-CU terms of trade $\pi(CU)$ and the pre-CU terms of trade $\pi(T)$:

$$\frac{\pi(CU)}{\pi(T)} = \frac{1}{(1+\alpha t)}\left(\sum_{i=2}^{3}\bar{Q}_1^i\right)\Bigg/\left(\sum_{i=\alpha}^{3}\frac{\bar{Q}_1^i}{1+\alpha t^i}\right) \qquad (12.3)$$

Now clearly the common tariff t will not be set below $Min(t^2, t^3) = t^2$ so that $(1 + \alpha t^2) < (1 + \alpha t^3)$. If the weighted harmonic mean of $(1 - \alpha t^i)$ with weights $\bar{Q}_1^i$, i.e.

$$\left(\sum\bar{Q}_1^i\right)\Bigg/\sum\left(\frac{\bar{Q}_1^i}{1+\alpha t^i}\right)$$

is greater than (respectively, equal to or less than) $(1 + \alpha t)$, then $\pi(CU)$ will be greater than (respectively, equal to or less than) $\pi(T)$.

Compare, more intuitively, the import-weighted average $\bar{t}$ of t^2, t^3 in the pre-union situation with the post-union common tariff t. Now

$$\bar{t} = \left(\sum\frac{t^i\bar{Q}_1^i}{1+\alpha t^i}\right)\Bigg/\sum\left(\frac{\bar{Q}_1^i}{1+\alpha t^i}\right) \qquad (12.4)$$

so that

$$(1 + \alpha\bar{t}) = \left(\frac{\sum\bar{Q}_1^i}{\sum\bar{Q}_1^i/(1+\alpha t^i)}\right) \qquad (12.5)$$

In fact, since there is no domestic production of good 2 in either country, $\bar{t}$ is also a *domestic consumption* weighted average of t^1 and t^2. Put differently, the tariffs t^i are simply consumption taxes. It is appropriate then that consumption weights are used to average them.

Comparison of Eqs. (12.3) and (12.5) shows that $\pi(CU) \gtreqless \pi(T)$ according as $\bar{t} \gtreqless t$. Of course, if $\pi(CU) > \pi(T)$ then country 1 outside the union gains from the formation of the union since its terms of trade $\pi(CU)$ are better compared to the pre-union situation and its tariff t^1 is unchanged.

Now, I am in a position to analyse the implications, for the welfare of non-members, of the common external tariffs proposed by Bhagwati and Kemp and Wan.

(1) The *Kemp–Wan tariff*, of course, has no impact on the non-member country's (i.e. country 1) welfare by assumption. For this to happen $\pi(CU)$

has to equal $\pi(T)$. The common tariff that brings this about is clearly $\bar{t}$ which is unique in this example; the reason being that all consumers within the union have identical homothetic tastes so that lump-sum income transfers within the union have no effect on aggregate demand in the union and, for the assumed tastes, the competitive equilibrium is unique. Being a positive weighted average of t^2 and t^3, $\bar{t}$ lies between the two.

(2) The *Bhagwati-tariff*, which would be at t^2 (the lower of the two member tariffs in the pre-CU situation), will lead on the other hand to welfare gain for the country outside the CU. If there are no internal transfers within the union, country 2 will lose since the terms of trade worsen and its tariff post-union is the same as the tariff pre-union. Country 3 experiences two effects relative to its pre-union situation—a terms of trade loss but a lowering of import tariff. This means that if there are no transfers, it may gain or lose. Thus, without transfers, the union will not come about since country 2 will lose from the union.

(3) It was noted earlier that Article XXIV of GATT (1947) was vague in specifying how the general incidence of tariffs on trade with non-members in the pre-CU situation is to be assessed. The Uruguay Round version does require that it should be based on an import weighted average of applied tariffs. In the present model, $\bar{t}$ is the weighted average of the applied tariffs t^2 and t^3 before the CU, using the imports (or equivalently consumption, since there is no production of the imported good) as weights. It was shown that as long as the post-union common external tariff does not exceed $\bar{t}$, the welfare of the outside country does not go down. Thus, in the present model the test proposed in the Uruguay Round version of Article XXIV applies exactly.

Consider now the issue of internal transfers within the CU. With a Kemp–Wan tariff in place, the terms-of-trade of the union is the same as that in the pre-union situation, viz. $\pi(T)$. Also, the trade-vector of the union is the unchanged trade-vector of the country outside the union. Thus, given that the aggregate production vector of the union is unchanged, it follows that the *aggregate consumption vector* of the union is unchanged as compared to the pre-union situation. Hence, the feasible allocation of post-union aggregate consumption between the two members can be shown in an Edgeworth Box as in Fig. 12.1. The length of the horizontal (respectively, vertical) side of the box equals the aggregate consumption of good 2 (respectively, good 1) in the pre-union situation. Given identical homothetic preferences, the Pareto optimal allocations of the aggregate consumption between the two countries lie on the diagonal $O^2 O^3$ with O^i representing the origin for measuring consumption of

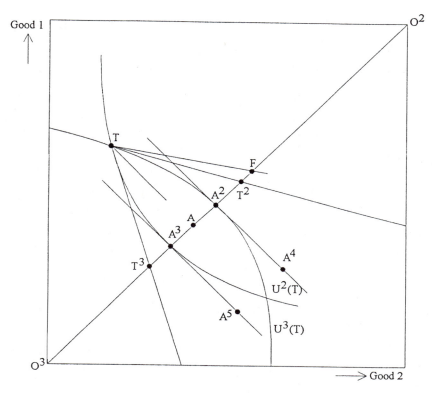

Figure 12.1
Consumption allocation in a CU of countries 2 and 3.

country i $(i = 2, 3)$. The pre-union allocation is at point T, with the indifference curves $U^i(T)(i = 2, 3)$ passing through that point. The slope of the tangent TT^i to $U^i(T)$ at T represents the pre-union domestic price $\pi(T)(1 + t^i)$ in country i $(i = 1, 2)$. The terms of trade $\pi(T)$ is represented by the slope of TF. The Pareto optimal allocations that are not inferior to T for either country lie between A^2 and A^3. Of course, along any point on the diagonal $O^2 O^3$ including the stretch $A^2 A^3$, the indifference curves of the countries not only are tangent to each other, but also have the same common slope, i.e. the slope of $A^2 A^4$ or $A^3 A^5$. The difference between the slope of the terms of trade TF and that of $A^2 A^4$ or $A^2 A^5$ equals the Kemp–Wan tariff $\bar{t}$ times the terms of trade $\pi(CU)$ and this does not depend on the post-union allocation of consumption. Since T lies to the left of A^i on $U^i(T)$, $i = 2$, 3, it follows that $t^2 < \bar{t} < t^3$. If the post-union allocation is at A^2, the welfare of country i $(i = 2, 3)$ remains at its pre-union situation while the other member of the union gains. If the post-union allocation is at some point A between A^2 and A^3 both countries gain from the union. The consumption expenditure of country i is the value of its consumption bundle at the post-union tariff inclusive price A, i.e. the slope of A^2A^4 (or A^2A^5). This is financed by its income at factor cost (i.e. the value of its production at the same price), the tariff revenue from its imports and any transfer it receives from the other country.

The second example relates to a CU between countries 1 and 2 instead of between countries 2 and 3. This case is interesting to analyze since, in the pre-union situation, the two countries are specialized in, and import-ing, *different* commodities. This is a situation typical of many real world CUs in which the pre-union trade patterns of members are often very dif-ferent with some members exporting commodities which others import. For concreteness, let the common external tariff of the CU be the Kemp–Wan tariff. By definition it keeps the trade vector of the non-member country 3 unchanged. Since country 3 is assumed not to change its tariff t^3, this means its pattern, volume and terms of trade have to remain unchanged. In particular it will continue to export (respectively, import) good 1 (respectively, good 2). Thus, post-union world relative price of good 2 has to be $\pi(T)$, i.e. $\pi(\text{CU}) = \pi(T)$ and the union will export good 2 and import good 1. The interesting issue is its post-union pattern of production. Clearly country 1 will continue to produce good 2. What about country 2 and what would be the domestic relative price of good 2 in terms of good 1 in the union?

Given a common post-union Kemp–Wan import tariff t on good 1, its domestic price in the union (in units of world numeraire) will be $(1 + t)$. The domestic price in the union of its export good 2 is its world price (in units of world numeraire) $\pi(T)$. Since $\pi(T)(1 + t^2) < \pi^2(A)$ (the autarky price), a fortiori $\pi(T)/1 + t < \pi^2(A)$ so that country 2 continues to be specialized in good 1 after its joining a customs union with country 1. Thus, the post-union production pattern of the union is the same as its pre-union pattern: country 1 specializes in and produces $\bar{Q}_2^1$ units of good 2 and country 2 specializes in and produces $\bar{Q}_1^2$ units of good 1.

Let $E(\text{CU})$ be the aggregate expenditure of the union (in world numer-aire units). Then its demand for its import good, i.e. good 1, is $\alpha E(\text{CU})/(1 + t)$, given identical Cobb–Douglas tastes in the union coun-tries (with α as the share of expenditure on good 1) and $(1 + t)$ being the domestic price of good 1. The domestic supply of good 1 in the union is $\bar{Q}_1^2$ so that imports are $\alpha E(\text{CU})/(1 + t) - \bar{Q}_1^2$. Tariff revenue on these imports is $t[\alpha E(U)/(1+t) - \bar{Q}_1^2]$. The value of domestic production $(\bar{Q}_1^2, \bar{Q}_2^1)$ at domestic prices is $(1+t)\bar{Q}_1^2 + \pi(T)\bar{Q}_2^1$. Hence by definition

$$E(CU) = (1+t)\bar{Q}_1^2 + \pi(T)\bar{Q}_2^1 + t\left[\frac{\alpha E(CU)}{(1+t)} - \bar{Q}_1^2\right]$$

or

$$E(CU) = \left[\frac{1+t}{1+(1-\alpha)t}\right][\bar{Q}_1^2 + \pi(T)\bar{Q}_2^1] \tag{12.6}$$

This in turn implies imports of $[\alpha/(1 + (1-\alpha)t^3)][\bar{Q}_1^2 + \pi(T)\bar{Q}_2^1] - \bar{Q}_1^2$ units of good 1. Equating this with exports $(1-\alpha)/(1-\alpha t^3)\bar{Q}_1^3$ units of good 1 from country 3 yields

$$\left[\frac{\alpha}{1+(1-\alpha)t}\right][\bar{Q}_1^2 + \pi(T)\bar{Q}_2^1] - \bar{Q}_1^2 = \frac{(1-\alpha)\bar{Q}_1^3}{(1+\alpha t^3)}$$

or

$$t = \frac{1}{1-\alpha}\frac{\left[-(1-\alpha)Q_1^2 + \alpha\pi(T)\bar{Q}_2^1 - \left(\frac{1-\alpha}{1+\alpha t^3}\right)\bar{Q}_1^3\right]}{\bar{Q}_1^2 + \left(\frac{1-\alpha}{1+\alpha t^3}\right)\bar{Q}_1^3} \tag{12.7}$$

Once again the Kemp–Wan tariff t turns out to be unique in this example for the same reason as mentioned earlier. Now $\alpha\pi(T)\bar{Q}_2^1 = (1-\alpha)[1 + (1-\alpha)t^1](\sum_{i=2}^{3}\bar{Q}_1^i/(1+\alpha t^i))$. Hence

$$\left[\bar{Q}_1^2 + \left(\frac{1-\alpha}{1+\alpha t^3}\right)\bar{Q}_1^3\right]t$$

$$= \left[-\bar{Q}_1^2 + \frac{[1+(1-\alpha)t^1]}{(1+\alpha t^2)}\bar{Q}_1^2 + \frac{[1+(1-\alpha)t^1]}{(1+\alpha t^3)}\bar{Q}_1^3 - \frac{1}{(1+\alpha t^3)}\bar{Q}_1^3\right]$$

$$= \frac{[-\alpha t^3 + (1-\alpha)t^1]}{(1+\alpha t^2)}\bar{Q}_1^2 + \frac{(1-\alpha)t^1}{(1+\alpha t^3)}\bar{Q}_1^3$$

$$= \frac{-\alpha t^2}{1+\alpha t^2}\bar{Q}_1^2 + (1-\alpha)t^1\sum_{i=2}^{3}\bar{Q}_1^2/(1+\alpha t^i)$$

Thus,

$$t = \frac{-\alpha t^2/(1+\alpha t^2)\bar{Q}_1^2 + t^1(1-\alpha)\sum_{i=2}^{3}\bar{Q}_1^i/(1+\alpha t^i)}{\alpha(1 t^2)/(1+\alpha t^2)Q_1^2 + (1-\alpha)\sum_{i=2}^{3}Q_1^i/(1+\alpha t^i)} \tag{12.8}$$

$$t - t^1 = \frac{-(\alpha Q_1^2/(1 + \alpha t^2))(t^2 + t^1)}{\alpha(1 + t^2)Q_1^2/(1 + \alpha t^2) + (1 - \alpha)\sum_{i=2}^{3} \bar{Q}^i/(1 + \alpha t^i)} < 0 \qquad (12.9)$$

Now since country 1 does not produce good 1, it imports it from the other two countries both of whom export it. Thus, the pre-union consumption of good 1 in country 1 equals the sum of exports of good 1 by countries 2 and 3, viz. $(1 - \alpha)\sum_{i=2}^{3} \bar{Q}_1^i/(1 + \alpha t^i)$. Country 2 produces only good 2 and exports $(1 - \alpha)\bar{Q}_1^2/(1 + \alpha t^2)$ units of it. Hence, it consumes $\alpha(1 + t^2)/(1 + \alpha t^2)$ units of it. Now a tariff at the rate t^2 on imports of good 2 is equivalent to a tax $t^2/(1 + t^2)$ on exports of good 1 or a *subsidy* on its domestic consumption. As such it is seen from Eq. (12.7) that the Kemp–Wan tariff (or equivalently, a tax on consumption) of good 1 in the post-union situation is the *consumption-weighted* average of the *tax* of $t^2/(1 + t^2)$ (or *subsidy* of $t^2/(1 + t^2)$) on its consumption in country 2 and the tax t^1 on its consumption in country 1 in the pre-union situation.

It should be noted that since the two countries forming the CU (countries 1 and 2) were taxing and importing *two different* commodities in the pre-union equilibrium, and in the post-union equilibrium the union imports only one of the two (viz. good 1), the union's tariff (i.e. the Kemp–Wan tariff) cannot be expressed as an average with pre-union import weights of pre-union tariffs on good 1. By contrast, in a CU of countries 2 and 3, since both countries did not produce and imported the same good (viz. good 2) in the pre-union equilibrium and continue to do so after they form a union, the Kemp–Wan tariff could be equivalently expressed as consumption-weighted as well as an import-weighted average of pre-union tariffs on good 2.

Fig. 12.2 illustrates the algebra. As in Fig. 12.1, O^1O^2 with O^i representing the origin for measuring country i ($i = 1, 2$), is the locus of Pareto Optimal allocations of aggregate consumption between the two members. The pre-union allocation is at T. The slope TT^1 of $U^1(T)$ at T is the pre-union domestic relative price of good 2, $\pi(T)/1 + t^1$, in country 1. Slope TT^2 of $U^2(T)$ at T is the pre-union domestic price $\pi(T)(1 + t^2)$ in country 2. The terms of trade $\pi(T)$ is the slope of TF. The post-union Pareto optimal allocations not inferior to T for either country are between A^1A^2. At any of these allocations the domestic relative price of good 2 (i.e. $\pi(T)/(1 + t)$) is the slope of $U^1(T)$ at A^1, i.e. the slope of A^1A^4 which is also the slope of $U^2(T)$ at A^2, i.e. the slope of A^2A^5. From the diagram it is obvious that $t < t^1$ and $1 + t^2 > 1/1 + t$ since T lies to the left of A^i on $U^i(T)$, $i = 1, 2$. If the post-union allocation is at A^i ($i = 1, 2$), the welfare of country i remains as in the pre-union situation and that of the

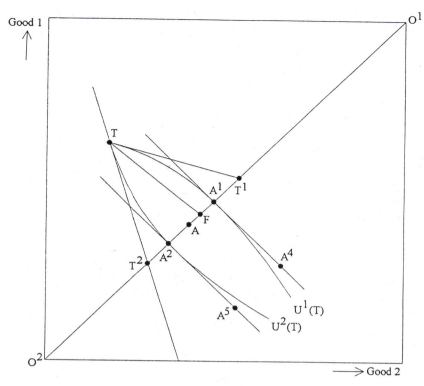

Figure 12.2
Consumption allocation in a CU of countries 1 and 2.

other country increases. At any point in between, such as A, both gain whatever be the chosen allocation between A^1 and A^2, the net transfer received by country i is the difference between the cost of its consumption (valued at post-union domestic prices) and the sum of the value of its production at the same prices and the tariff revenue from its imports. The sum of the net transfers of the two countries equals zero by definition.

The message from the two examples is that the common, post-CU Kemp–Wan tariff is the *pre-union-consumption weighted* average of the *pre-union* taxes (or subsidies) on the commodity imported in the post-union equilibrium. In the case where this commodity is imported and not produced in the pre-union equilibrium by both countries forming the union, the Kemp–Wan tariff is also the pre-union, import-weighted average of pre-union import tariffs. It is shown below that a version of the

consumption-weighted average characterization of Kemp–Wan tariffs
emerges when we generalize the Ricardian model.

12.4   A General Production Model

The Ricardian model of production in Section 12.3 together with identical
Cobb–Douglas social utility functions in the three countries enabled the
explicit computation of pre- and post-union equilibria algebraically. Since
the Ricardian production technology is very special, it is worth examining
the robustness of the characterization of the Kemp–Wan tariff as the
consumption-weighted average of pre-union consumption taxes to changes
in production technology. In this section, a general production technology
(possibly different in different countries) involving the production of
n ($n \geq 1$) commodities in each country from an inelastically supplied factor
endowment of that country is implicitly assumed. However, all countries
are assumed to have the same Cobb–Douglas social utility function.

Let $Q^i(T)$ and $Q^i(CU)$ denote the output vectors of the ith member of
the union ($i = 1, 2, \ldots, I$) in the pre- and post-union equilibria, respectively. Let $\pi(T)$ be the equilibrium world prices and $M(T)$ the net imports
of the union in the pre-union equilibrium. Let t^i be the vector of ad valorem tariffs in country i in the pre-union equilibrium so that the domestic
price $\pi_j^i(T)$ of good j in country i is $\pi_j(T)(1 + t_j^i)$. Clearly if commodity j
is imported (respectively, exported) by country i, a positive t_j^i is to be
viewed as an import tax (respectively, export subsidy). A negative t_j^i
(which cannot be less than minus one) is an import subsidy (respectively,
export tax) by the same token. Let tariff revenue be returned to consumers
in a lump sum fashion. Given identical Cobb–Douglas tastes, aggregate
demand in each country depends only on prices and aggregate expenditure $E^i(T)$. Now $E^i(T)$ is the sum of the value of production at domestic
prices and tariff revenues. The net imports $M_j^i(T)$ of commodity j in
country i is by definition the difference between domestic consumption
$C_j^i(T)$ and output $Q_j^i(T)$. With α_j denoting the share of expenditure on
commodity j in each country,

$$C_j^i(T) = [\alpha_j E^i(T)/\pi_j(T)(1 + t_j^i)] \tag{12.10}$$

Hence tariff revenue $R^i(T)$ is given by

$$R^i(T) = \sum_{j=1}^{n} t_j^i \pi_j(T) M_j^i(T) \tag{12.11}$$

$$= \sum_{j=1}^{n} t_j^i \pi_j(T) \left[\frac{\alpha_j E^i(T)}{\pi_j(T)(1 + t_j^i)} - Q_j^i(T) \right] \tag{12.12}$$

Now

$$E^i(T) = \sum_{j=1}^{n} Q_j^i(T) \pi_j(T)(1 + t_j^i) + R^i(T) \tag{12.13}$$

Substituting Eq. (12.12) into Eq. (12.13) and solving for $E^i(T)$,

$$E^i(T) = (1 + \bar{t}^i) V^i(T) \tag{12.14}$$

where

$$\frac{1}{1 + \bar{t}^i} = \sum_{j=1}^{n} \frac{\alpha_j}{1 + t_j^i} \tag{12.15}$$

$$V^i(T) = \sum_{j=1}^{n} \pi_j(T) Q_j^i(T) \tag{12.16}$$

Using Eq. (12.16),

$$M_j^i(T) = \frac{\alpha_j (1 + \bar{t}^i) V^i(T)}{\pi_j(T)(1 + t_j^i)} - Q_j^i(T)$$

so that aggregate imports of union members is

$$M_j(T) = \sum_{i=1}^{I} M_j^i(T) = \frac{\alpha_j}{\pi_j(T)} \sum_{i=1}^{I} \left(\frac{1 + \bar{t}^i}{1 + t_j^i} \right) V^i(T) - Q_j(T) \tag{12.17}$$

where

$$Q_j(T) = \sum_{i=1}^{I} Q_j^i(T).$$

With the formation of the union, let the Kemp–Wan common external tariff on commodity j be t_j. Given identical Cobb–Douglas tastes and common domestic prices in all members of the union, domestic demand of the union depends only on the aggregate expenditure of $E(CU)$ of the union as a whole. As earlier, aggregate expenditure is the sum of the value of production in the union at domestic prices and tariff revenues. With unchanged terms of trade $\pi(T)$ and common tariffs t_j, imports $M_j(CU)$ of the union will be

$$\frac{\alpha_j E(\text{CU})}{\pi_j(T)(1+t_j)} - Q_j(\text{CU})$$

where $Q_j(\text{CU})$ is the sum $\sum_{i=1}^{I} Q_j^i(\text{CU})$. Using the analogue of Eq. (12.13) now for the CU, it is easy to show that

$$E(\text{CU}) = (1+\bar{t})V(\text{CU}) \tag{12.18}$$

where

$$V(\text{CU}) = \sum_{i=1}^{I} V^i(\text{CU}) = \sum_{i=1}^{I} \sum_{j=1}^{n} \pi_j(T)Q_j^i(\text{CU}) \tag{12.19}$$

and

$$\frac{1}{1+\bar{t}} = \sum_{j=1}^{n} \frac{\alpha_j}{1+t_j} \tag{12.20}$$

Substituting for $E(\text{CU})$ in $M_j(\text{CU})$,

$$M_j(\text{CU}) = \frac{\alpha_j(1+\bar{t})}{\pi_j(T)(1+t_j)} V(\text{CU}) - Q_j(\text{CU}).$$

By definition of Kemp–Wan tariffs t_j, net imports $M_j(\text{CU})$ of the union is the same as its pre-union imports $M_j(T)$. Hence,

$$\frac{\alpha_j(1+\bar{t})\sum_{i=1}^{I} V^i(\text{CU})}{\pi_j(T)(1+t_j)} - Q_j(\text{CU}) = \frac{\alpha_j}{\pi_j(T)} \sum_{i=1}^{I} \left(\frac{1+\bar{t}^i}{1+t_j^i}\right) V^i(T) - Q_j(T) \tag{12.21}$$

Let $\Delta_j^i \equiv Q_j^i(\text{CU}) - Q_j^i(T)$ and $\Delta_j = \sum_{i=1}^{I} \Delta_j^i$. Then

$$\sum_{i=1}^{I} V^i(\text{CU}) = \sum_{i=1}^{I} V^i(T) + \sum_{k=1}^{n} \pi_k(T)\Delta_k \tag{12.22}$$

Substituting Eq. (12.21) in Eq. (12.22) and rearranging

$$\frac{\alpha_j(1+\bar{t})}{(1+t_j)} = \frac{\sum_{i=1}^{I} \alpha_j(1+\bar{t}^i)/(1+t_j^i)V^i(T) + \pi_j(T)\Delta_j}{\sum_{i=1}^{I} V^i(T) + \sum_{k=1}^{n} \pi_k(T)\Delta_k} \tag{12.23}$$

From Eqs. (12.14) and (12.19) it is seen that

$$\tau_j \equiv \alpha_j \frac{(1+\bar{t})}{1+t_j} = \frac{(\alpha_j/1+t_j)}{\sum_{k=1}^{n}(\alpha_k/1+t_k)} \quad \text{and} \quad \tau_j^i \equiv \frac{\alpha_j(1+\bar{t}^i)}{1+t_j^i} = \frac{(\alpha_j/1+t_j^i)}{\sum_{k=1}^{n}(\alpha_k/1+t_k^i)}$$

$$(12.24)$$

Since $\sum_{j=1}^{n}\tau_j = \sum_{j=1}^{n}\tau_j^i = 1$, τ_j and τ_j^i represent appropriately weighted and normalized tariff structures, respectively, of the union and of country i in the pre-union situation. In fact it can be shown using Eqs. (12.10) and (12.14) that τ_j and τ_j^i equal, respectively, the share of the value (at unchanged world prices) of *consumption* of commodity j in the total value of consumption in the union and country i (prior to the union).

Let

$$w^i(T) = \frac{V^i(T)}{\sum_{i=1}^{I}V^i(T)} \qquad w_j = \frac{\pi_j(T)\Delta_j}{\sum_{k=1}^{n}\pi_k(T)\Delta_k}.$$

$$(12.25)$$

Thus, $w^i(T)$ is the share of country i in the value at unchanged world prices of the output of the union in the pre-union equilibrium and w^j is the share of the change in value (at unchanged world prices) of output of commodity j in the change in the value of output of all commodities brought about by the formation of the union and the induced change in domestic price structure in each of the countries. Substituting these in Eq. (12.24),

$$\tau_j = \frac{V(T)\sum_{i=1}^{I}w^i\tau_j^i + \Delta V w_j}{V(T) + \Delta V}$$

$$(12.26)$$

or

$$\tau_j - \bar{\tau}_j = \frac{\Delta V[w_j - \bar{\tau}_j]}{V(T) + \Delta V}$$

$$(12.27)$$

where $\bar{\tau}_j = \sum_{i=1}^{I}w^i\tau_j^i$, $V(T) = \sum_{i=1}^{I}V^i(T)$, $\Delta V = \sum_{k=1}^{n}\pi_k(T)\Delta_k$. $\bar{\tau}_j$ is the weighted average of pre-union τ_j^i. Now $V(T) + \Delta V = \sum_{i=1}^{I}V^i(CU) > 0$. If $\Delta > 0$, $\tau_j \gtreqless \bar{\tau}_j$ according as $w_j \gtreqless \bar{\tau}_j$. Thus, if after the formation of the union, the value of output of the union at unchanged world prices is higher than in the pre-union equilibrium, then the Kemp–Wan normalized tariff factor τ_j will exceed (respectively, fall short of) the weighted average $\bar{\tau}_j$ of the normalized tariff factors τ_j^i on commodity j in the union countries prior to the formation of the union, if the share w_j exceeds (respectively, falls short of) the same weighted average $\bar{\tau}_j$. In particular, if $w_j < 0$, i.e. the value of output of commodity j is lower in the post-union situation, then $\tau_j < \bar{\tau}_j^i$.

If $\Delta V < 0$, then $\tau_j \gtreqless \bar{\tau}_j$ according as $w_j \gtreqless \bar{\tau}_j$. In particular, if $w_j < 0$, then $\tau_j > \bar{\tau}_j$. Of course $\Delta V < 0$ does not necessarily imply $w_j < 0$.

It is clear from Eq. (12.27) that in the case of a world of pure exchange economies in which by definition $Q_j^i(T) = Q_j^i(\text{CU})$, ΔV will be zero and hence $\tau_j = \bar{\tau}_j$. Although one cannot compute Kemp–Wan τ_j from the pre-union data of τ_j^i and $V^i(T)$ for general production economies, if there are reasons to suggest that changes in output following the formation of the union are unlikely to make $|\Delta V / V(T) + \Delta V|$ large, then as a first order of approximation $\tau_j = \bar{\tau}_j$.

An alternative, but equivalent, approach to characterizing τ_j is to note that under the assumption of balanced trade $V^i(T) = \sum_{j=1}^{n} \pi_j(T) C_j^i(T)$ where $C_j^i(T)$ is consumption of good j in country i in the pre-union situation. Also, with unchanged net imports of good j in the union compared to the sum of net imports of member countries in the pre-union situation, the change in value of output Δ_j = change in value of consumption. Thus, the weight w^i is also the share of the value of consumption in country i to the sum of the value of consumption in the member countries (both valued at unchanged world prices) in the pre-union situation. Similarly, w_j is the share of the change in value of consumption of commodity j in the sum of the changes in the value of consumption of all commodities, again at unchanged world prices, between the post- and pre-union situation. One can therefore interpret Eq. (12.27) using "consumption" weights for averaging. Thus, the Kemp–Wan normalized tariff factor τ_j on commodity j will exceed, equal or fall short of the consumption weighted average $\bar{\tau}_j$ of the normalized tariff factors τ_j^i on the same commodities in the union countries in the pre-union situation according as w_j (the share of the change in value of consumption of commodity j in the sum of changes in the value of all commodities between the post- and pre-union equilibria) exceeds, equals or falls short of the same $\bar{\tau}_j$. In other words, if the formation of the union does not lead to a significant change in the value of consumption of all commodities, the Kemp–Wan normalized tariff factor τ_j on *each* commodity j will equal the *consumption weighted* average $\bar{\tau}_j$. While this is the exact analogue of the characterization of Kemp–Wan tariffs in the simple Ricardian model, in a more complex model the analogy holds only locally, i.e. for small changes in consumption.

Acknowledgements

Thanks are due to Jagdish Bhagwati, Donald Davis, Kala Krishna, Philip Levy, Richard Snape, Costas Syropoulos, Henry Wan, Jr. and Alan Winters for their comments and to the Economic Development Institute, World Bank, for their support during the summer of 1995 when much of this research was completed.

Notes

1. Among recent contributors to the literature related to Article XXIV are Bhagwati (1991), Bhagwati (1993), Bond et al. (1995), Finger (1993), Jun and Krishna (1996), McMillan (1993), Roessler (1993), Snape (1993), Syropoulos (1995a), Syropoulos (1995b) and Winters (1996).

2. For comparing alternative trading equilibria from a global welfare perspective, Pareto ranking is used.

3. The analysis of Syropoulos (1995a) of Nash equilibria of tariff games (in a symmetric three-country−three commodity world in which two countries form a CU while still maintaining some tariffs on internal trade) is of interest in this context. Internal liberalization (i.e. reduction of internal tariffs) could result in trade deflection and, as such, even if the CU sets its common tariffs à la Bhagwati's proposal so that there is *external* trade liberalization, nonetheless non-members could lose if the adverse trade deflection effect of internal trade liberalization outweighs the beneficial effects of external liberalization. Jun and Krishna (1996) analyze free trade areas without rules of origin. Since this is in effect equivalent to the adoption of the Bhagwati proposal, their analysis is also relevant. In a FTA formed by a developing country which (prior to the formation of the FTA) has higher tariffs on all imports, especially on final goods, they show that the welfare of FTA countries is likely to rise, and that of the rest of the world to fall, if the FTA imposes no rules of origin. Bond et al. (1995) consider a three-country−multicommodity endowment model with countries having identical preferences with a constant elasticity of substitution. Two of the countries form a CU while still maintaining some barriers on internal trade. They ask whether, in the context of internal trade liberalization in the two countries forming a CU, adjustments in their common external tariff to keep unchanged the terms of trade faced by the outside countries (which they call Kemp−Wan adjustments) are incentive-compatible for member and non-member countries. They show that they are not, if the elasticity of substitution between member and non-member goods in consumer preferences exceeds unity.

4. I thank Alan Winters for chiding me for not recognizing this feature of the McMillan proposal.

5. Kemp and Wan (1993) note that their proposed tariff structure is not necessarily unique. This can be seen by noting that a Kemp−Wan tariff on a commodity, being the difference between its domestic price in the CU and its unchanged world price, will in general depend on which of the many possible post-union Pareto Optimal allocations within the union is to be sustained as a competitive equilibrium through intra-union lump sum transfers. Of course, if all consumers have identical homothetic tastes, within union lump sum transfers will not affect aggregate demand. In such a case, we can treat the union as if it is populated by a single consumer, and provided its competitive equilibrium is unique, so will be its Kemp−Wan tariff structure.

References

Bhagwati, J., 1993. Regionalism and Multilateralism: An Overview, in: Jaime de Melo and Arvind Panagariya, eds., New Dimensions in Regional Integration (Cambridge University Press, Cambridge).

Bhagwati, J., 1991. The World Trading System at Risk (Princeton University Press, Princeton).

Bond, E., Syropoulos, C., Alan Winters, L., 1995. Deepening of Regional Integration and External Trade Relations: When are Kemp–Wan Tariff Adjustments Incentive-Compatible? processed.

Finger, J. M., 1993. GATT's Influence on Regional Arrangements, in: Jaime de Melo and Arvind Panagariya, eds., New Dimensions in Regional Integration (Cambridge University Press, Cambridge).

General Agreement on Tariffs and Trade (GATT), 1994. The Results of the Uruguay Round of Multilateral Trade Negotiations–The Legal Texts (GATT Secretariat, Geneva).

General Agreement on Tariffs and Trade, 1959. Basic Instruments and Selected Documents, 7th Supplement (GATT, Geneva).

Jackson, J., 1989. The World Trading System: Law and Policy of International Economic Relations (MIT Press, Cambridge, Mass.).

Jun, J., Krishna, K., 1996. Market Access and Welfare Effects of Free Trade Areas Without Rules of Origin, NBER Working Paper 5480 (National Bureau of Economic Research, Cambridge Massachusetts).

Kemp, M. C., H. Wan, Jr., 1993. The Welfare Economics of international Trade (Harwood Academic Publishers, Chur, Switzerland; Philadelphia, Pennsylvania).

Kemp, M. C., Wan, H., 1976. An elementary proposition concerning the formation of customs unions, Journal of International Economics, 6, 95–98.

McMillan, J., 1993. Does Regional integration Foster Open Trade? Economic Theory and GATT's Article XXIV, in: Kym Anderson and Richard Blackhurst, eds., Regional Integration and the Global Trading System (Harvester-Wheatsheaf, New York).

Roessler, F., 1993. The Relationship Between Regional Integration Agreements and the Multilateral Trade Order, in: Kym Anderson and Richard Blackhurst, eds., Regional Integration and the Global Trading System (Harvester-Wheatsheaf, New York).

Snape, R., 1993. History and Economics of GATT's Article XXIV, in: Kym Anderson and Richard Blackhurst, eds., Regional Integration and the Global Trading System (Harvester-Wheatsheaf, New York).

Syropoulos, C., 1995a. Customs Unions and Comparative Advantage, Pennsylvania State University, processed.

Syropoulos, C., 1995b, External Tariff Preferences in Customs Unions, Pennsylvania State University, processed.

Viner, J., 1950. The Customs Union Issue (Carnegie Endowment for International Peace, New York).

Winters, L. A., 1996. Regionalism and the Rest of the World: The Irrelevance of the Kemp–Wan Theorem, CEPR Discussion Paper No. 1316 (Centre for Economic Policy Research, London).

WTO, 1995a. Regionalism and the World Trading System (World Trade Organization, Geneva).

WTO, 1995b. Focus Newsletter, No. 7 (World Trade Organization, Geneva).

*Welfare-Improving
Customs Unions among
Developing Countries
Seeking Industrialization*

13

Toward a General Theory of Customs Unions for Developing Countries

C. A. Cooper and B. F. Massell

During the past fifteen years, economists have constructed an impressive theoretical apparatus for viewing the effect on a group of economically advanced nations of forming a customs union (CU). But there is no comparable body of analysis dealing with customs unions among less developed countries. To an important degree, such a theory must focus on economies of scale, changes in the terms of trade, balance of payments problems, externalities, capital imports, and underemployment—factors that have received isolated treatment in the literature but that have not been successfully woven into an integrated analytical framework. However, before one can construct a general model that takes these "dynamic" factors into account, it is useful to lay a foundation whose blocks are the ordinary static efficiency considerations dealt with in the CU literature relating to developed countries.

A fundamental difficulty in building on existing theory as developed by Viner, Meade, Lipsey, and others,[1] relates to what may be regarded as a dilemma of CU theory. Except for the terms-of-trade argument,[2] the very grounds on which a CU is said to be superior to non-discriminatory protection are precisely those grounds on which the union is necessarily inferior to free trade. A "good" CU is one that raises income through trade creation—that is, a move toward free trade. A "bad" union, on the other hand, reduces income through trade diversion—that is, a more protectionist policy. But, if a country accepts a "good" union as desirable, why does it not move all the way to free trade? And conversely, if a country is willing to reject the full benefits of free trade for the sake of unilateral protection, why should it be willing to give up its sheltered industries for

Originally published in *Journal of Political Economy* 73, no. 5 (1965): 461–476. Reprinted with permission.

the partial benefits of a CU? These questions are not dealt with systematically in the literature.[3]

This issue is especially relevant to the analysis of a CU formed by less developed countries. Whereas existing CU theory is, essentially, a disguised argument for free trade, what is needed is an analysis of alternative policies of protection. The mere fact that preunion protection exists suggests that free trade is not viewed as desirable by many countries, notably by a majority of the less developed countries. Although present CU theory leads to the conclusion that a world-wide union would be optimal, few of these countries would accept this view. Indeed, a principal objective of economic integration among less developed countries is to foster industrial development and to guide such development along more economic lines. Yet, the considerations that lead such a country to favor economic integration and to prefer one country to another as a prospective union partner lie outside traditional analysis. For example, what insight does CU theory provide regarding whether Mexico would be anxious to form a CU with the United States? Would trade creation provide Mexico with a welfare gain? Or would the blow to Mexican industry more than offset any rise in non-industrial income?

Just as increases in protection may have their cost, so may decreases in protection. Protection is justified, or rationalized, on many grounds, political as well as economic. It can be used to alter a country's terms of trade, to increase domestic employment, to raise revenue, or to foster local industry. It is certainly true that many less developed countries have accepted the arguments put forward by Prebisch, Seers, and others, in support of an accelerated industrialization policy.[4] Much of the work of the United Nations Economic Commission for Latin America and the Economic Commission for Africa, for example, is concerned with outlining such a policy.

The present study attempts to lay a cornerstone for a more general theory of CU's in less developed countries. We do not attempt to examine the conditions under which a protectionist policy makes good sense; rather, we accept industrialization as a legitimate policy goal and consider how membership in a CU may enable a less developed country to achieve more economically the ends served by protection. We emphasize, again, that we do not attempt here the complete dynamic theory that must ultimately form the basis for decision-making.[5] Our objective is the more modest one of weaving together into a single analytical strand the fragments relating to the static impact of a CU.

Preference for Industry

Our analysis is based on the simple assumption that there may be a social preference for particular types of economic activity—which we shall call "industry"—compared with other forms of activity. Specifically, we assume that economic planners in a less developed country may be willing to accept some reduction in national income to achieve an increase in industrial production.[6] Industrial production must, therefore, be introduced as a new dimension of the analysis. To compare alternative production possibilities, not only the national income but also the level of industrial production associated with each must be taken into account. This is shown in Figure 13.1 by the planners' "demand" curve, DD', which expresses the "price" (in terms of national income foregone) that planners are willing to pay for each increment to industrial production. It is assumed that, at a higher price, planners will typically choose less protection. It is further assumed that planners are indifferent to a choice between

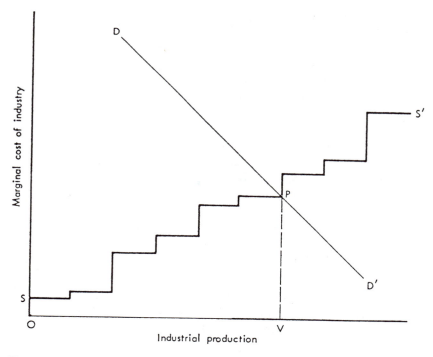

Figure 13.1
Demand for industry.

any two different industries and that diversification within the industrial sector is not an objective.[7] Therefore, the planners satisfy their demand for industrial production by selecting the lowest cost industries.

The "supply" side in Figure 13.1 is represented by the stepped curve SS'. To simplify the exposition, we assume full employment, constant costs, competitive pricing, and constant terms of trade.[8] Consider that initially only a single agricultural export good (corn) is produced and that corn production is more profitable in this country than any other economic activity. It is cheaper to import all other goods in exchange for corn exports than to produce them locally. The average "cost" of a local industry is then defined as the amount by which the average cost of producing the industry's output exceeds the price of a comparable imported good.[9] This cost is a measure of national income foregone by producing each unit of the good, where income is measured in purchasing power at world-market prices. It is assumed that industries under consideration by the planners are separable—that production in one does not require the presence of another, either as a market or as a source of supply.

To obtain the supply-of-industry (hereinafter referred to as "supply") curve, industries are ranked in ascending order according to their cost. As all industry is by assumption uneconomic and only corn is exported,[10] domestic demand places a constraint on the level of production in each industry. As a result, an expansion in industrial output involves moving up the steps in the curve, each step corresponding to a successively higher-cost industry.[11]

The optimal level of industrial production, as determined by the intersection of the demand and supply curves, is OV in Figure 13.1. Corresponding to this level of industrial production is an efficient tariff,[12] that is, a set of tariff rates that provide enough protection in each industry to the left of V to induce local production in that industry and that provide no protection for industries to the right of V. With constant costs, industries either supply the entire domestic market or do not operate at all. An industry will operate if (and only if) protected by a tariff rate no lower than the industry's cost.[13] In Figure 13.1, VP is the marginal cost of protection to the economy, that is, the cost of protecting the marginal industry. The total cost of protection is the area $OSPV$.

The welfare implications of this analysis can be seen more clearly in Figure 13.2. The technological trade-off between national income and industrial production is described by MN, which can be derived from the supply curve SS' in Figure 13.1. Curve MN shows how much national income must be foregone to achieve alternative levels of industrial produc-

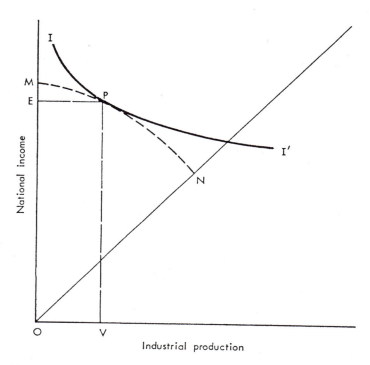

Figure 13.2
Preference for industry.

tion, subject to the constraint that all industrial production is consumed domestically. We shall term this curve a production-consumption locus.[14] Moving down curve MN corresponds to moving up the hierarchy of industries and increases the marginal cost of protection in discrete steps. Thus MN is stepwise convex. At point N, the economy would be producing only industrial goods, all for domestic consumption. National income would then equal industrial production. Under the present assumptions, then, MN cannot cross the 45° ray from the origin.

The indifference curve II' in Figure 13.2 expresses the planners' preference for industrial production and is related to the demand curve DD' in Figure 13.1.[15] If planners were indifferent between producing corn and industrial goods, the indifference curve would be horizontal, providing a corner optimum at point M, with all of the economy's resources devoted to corn production. With a negatively sloped indifference curve, as shown in Figure 13.2, the optimal position is at point P and includes a mixture of OV industrial goods and corn output equal to OE − OV.

Specialization and Efficiency

Now consider two countries, North and South, each with a development plan that consists simply of a list of industries to be developed during the plan period. Assume, for expository convenience, that the domestic demand is the same for each industrial product and is equal in the two countries.[16]

Next, consider the formation of a CU between North and South. As contrasted with a common market, a CU does not permit a free flow of resources between member countries. But, while resources are not pooled, markets are; and the pooling of markets permits specialization. Unless the two countries have identical economic structures, they will be able to produce a given level of combined industrial output at a lower cost in terms of income foregone.

The level of industrial production, its composition, and its distribution between the two countries is fully determined by a common external tariff[17]—that is, a set of tariff rates, one for each item. In principle, any tariff can be chosen. Thus the level, composition, and (within limits)[18] distribution of industrial production is subject to manipulation by the economic planners. For this reason it is of little interest to ask whether a CU is "good" or "bad" without specifying the tariff to be chosen. The question to which this chapter is principally addressed can now be formulated: Is there *any* tariff that will make *both* countries better off relative to individually optimal policies of non-preferential protection?[19]

One class of tariffs that deserves consideration is the set of "efficient" tariffs, where an efficient tariff is defined as one that provides any specified level of industrial production in the CU—irrespective of the composition and distribution of this production—at the lowest cost in terms of combined national income foregone by the two countries.

The gains from specialization, under assumed tariff efficiency, can be seen in Figure 13.3a. The curves S_n and S_s represent the supply curves for North and South, respectively, before forming the CU. With the CU, there is a new hierarchy of industries for the CU as a whole; corresponding to this hierarchy is a new supply curve, S_u. The new supply curve will lie below the old curves for two reasons.[20] First, if any item is produced at all in the CU, it will be produced in the lower-cost country;[21] second, the lowest cost industries can be operated at twice the pre-CU level of output (to supply both markets), so that any given level of industrial production can be obtained without resort to the higher-cost industries. There is an

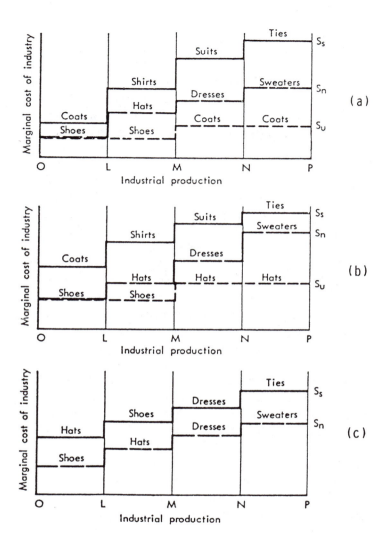

Figure 13.3
Effects of specialization.

efficient tariff corresponding to each point on the combined supply curve. Industries to the left of that point are protected; industries to the right are not.

The tariff that is chosen will depend on the preferences of the planners in the two countries. If the planners are indifferent as to the distribution of industrial production between the countries, they will choose an efficient tariff.[22] The initial lists contained industries that the planners were willing to pay for. In the CU, planners can obtain satisfaction more efficiently by pooling markets. There is, consequently, an income effect; the countries can produce the same combined industrial output with the CU that was planned initially and will have resources to spare. The income effect will tend to lead to an increase in both industrial production and national income. There is also a substitution effect, due to the lower marginal cost of protection, which will lead to an increase in industrial production at the cost of national income. Both effects will combine to increase industrial production; national income will increase as well, if the income effect outweighs the substitution effect.

As an example of the gains, consider that, in Figure 13.3a, each country initially planned industrial production equal to OM, so that planned industrial production of the two countries combined was equal to OP. North planned to produce shoes and hats, and South planned to produce coats and shirts. With a CU, the same combined industrial production, OP, can be obtained at a lower cost by producing twice as many shoes and coats and by foregoing production of higher-cost hats and shirts.

It may be more realistic to drop the assumption that planners are indifferent to the distribution of gains between countries, and to assume instead that planners in each country are primarily or solely interested in gains *to that country*.[23] Each country's level of social welfare (as reflected by the planners' indifference-curve map) is determined by that country's level of industrial production and income and is, therefore, completely specified by a common external tariff, together with a *rule* for distributing income between the countries.

If the tariff and the rule for distributing income are chosen by the two planning boards in collaboration, and if the two groups of planners act rationally,[24] they will choose a tariff and a rule that jointly result in a Pareto-optimal situation, that is, that result in a pair of levels of industrial production and national income such that neither country's social welfare can be increased without decreasing the social welfare of the partner country. But, as the following example illustrates, an efficient tariff may be non-Pareto optimal for *any* distributive rule.

Figure 13.3b is similar to Figure 13.3a, except that North's hat industry is now cheaper than South's coat industry. If, as before, combined industrial production is to be equal to OP, then an efficient tariff will protect shoes and hats, both of which will locate in North. North gets twice as much industry with the CU than without, but South gets no industry at all.

Now, make the further illustrative assumption that the planners' demand curve in each country is a vertical line passing through point M. Then South will willingly give up an arbitrarily large amount of income to obtain industrial production equal to OM. For South to reach this position with an efficient tariff requires North to produce both shoes and hats, with North's total industrial production then amounting to OP. North's hat industry causes both countries an income loss and, given North's planners' demand curve, there is no commensurate gain. Then, whatever the distribution of income between the two countries, this efficient tariff is non-Pareto optimal. The welfare of both countries could be raised by eliminating North's hat production. There is no efficient tariff that will enable each country to produce exactly OM units of industrial output.[25]

By considering only efficient tariffs one throws away degrees of freedom. The level of the tariff can be changed, and income can be redistributed between the countries; but industrial production *cannot* be redistributed. Additional degrees of freedom can be gained by considering a wider class of tariffs. And, as we shall see below, still more freedom can be obtained by considering either a *partial* CU or subsidization.

Quasi-Pareto Optimality

Given a national preference for industry, the evaluation of the impact of a CU on a member country must take into account not only changes in the country's national income but also changes in the size of the country's industrial sector. A gain in either dimension, if offset by a sufficiently large loss in the other dimension, will render the economy worse off. It is not sufficient to look at the joint income of the participants; to assess the welfare effects of a CU requires examining the two indifference-curve maps.

Specifying a common external tariff determines the level of industrial production in each country and the joint national income. But, because there is scope for redistributing this income without changing the tariff, the income of each country is not specified. Now, let us define a quasi-Pareto-optimal tariff as a tariff with the following property: Given the level of industrial production *in each country*, joint national income is maximized.

An efficient tariff is necessarily quasi-Pareto optimal, but not all quasi-Pareto-optimal tariffs are efficient. An example of an inefficient quasi-Pareto-optimal tariff can be seen in Figure 13.3b; as noted above, an efficient tariff corresponding to joint industrial production of OP is one that protects shoes and hats. This is also quasi-Pareto optimal. However, a tariff that protects only shoes and coats is not efficient but is quasi-Pareto optimal—there is no other tariff, providing each country with industrial production equal to OM, that will yield a higher joint income. Even though coat production is more expensive than hat production, coat production is South's most economic (least uneconomic) industry. A quasi-Pareto-optimal tariff is designed to permit *each* country to produce any specified level of industrial production in the cheapest way. It follows that genuine Pareto optimality must require choosing a quasi-Pareto-optimal tariff.[26]

It follows from the "rules" underlying CU's that neither country is permitted to produce a good that can be produced more cheaply in the other country. This may create problems, as can be seen in Figure 13.3c. Here South has an intra-union comparative *dis*advantage in its three cheapest industries—hats, shoes, and dresses—and hence cannot produce them in a CU with North. If these industries are protected at all, they will locate in lower-cost North. However, of those goods that South can produce, quasi-Pareto optimality requires that the cheapest are selected for protection. Thus the lowest cost industry in which South has an intra-union comparative advantage—ties—would be the first industry on South's list.

It follows from the discussion above that, under quasi-Pareto optimality, membership in a CU will result in a new hierarchy of industries for each country and, consequently, in new supply curves. The new hierarchy will include only industries in which the country has an intra-union comparative advantage. The ranking of these industries will remain unchanged, but each industry, if established at all, will operate at twice the planned pre-CU level of production, to supply the whole CU market.

If the distribution of income is left to market forces, the "cost" of each protected industry is shared equally by the two countries. Consequently, from each country's point of view, the cost of establishing an industry is reduced by one-half. This raises an interesting point. Because half the cost of a country's uneconomic industry is paid by consumers in the partner country, there is a divergence between private (which in this case means "national") and social (meaning "CU") costs of industry. In other words, there are external diseconomies associated with industrialization. If each country ignores these diseconomies and determines its level of industrial production with regard to private cost considerations alone, then a quasi-Pareto-optimal tariff will produce results that are non-Pareto optimal. We shall develop this point in the following section.

Production-Consumption Locus in a Customs union

Corresponding to each country's new supply-of-industry curve is a new production-consumption locus. If South increases its level of industrial production, it moves out along its locus. But if industrial production increases in North, South's locus is shifted toward the origin. This is illustrated in Figure 13.4. South's preunion locus is *MN*. The new locus is *ML*, assuming there to be no industrial production in North.[27] This new locus originates at point *M* because, assuming South to buy no products

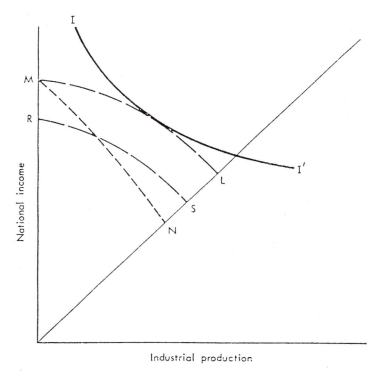

Figure 13.4
Impact of a customs union on the production-consumption locus.

from North, South retains the pre-CU option of producing at point M. Beyond point M, the new locus may lie wholly above the old one (as drawn in Figure 13.4); alternatively, the new locus may lie wholly below or may intersect the old locus.[28]

If North produces industrial goods, then South can no longer attain point M. South's locus then shifts down by an amount equal to South's share of the difference between North's cost of production and world-market prices of all goods produced by North (shown in Figure 13.4 by the distance MR).[29] Thus the position of South's locus will depend on North's level of industrial production and on how uneconomic this production is.[30]

Pareto Optimality

Let us define a Pareto-optimal tariff as a set of common external tariff rates with the following property: Given some rule for redistributing income, the tariff results in levels of industrial production in each country such that neither country's welfare can be raised without a reduction in the other country's welfare.

If the distribution of income is left to market forces, then each country will equate the marginal gain from industrial production to the marginal *private* cost, and a Pareto-optimal tariff will not be chosen. This can be seen as follows: An increase in industrial production in South will, up to a point, move South to a higher social indifference curve, as can be seen in Figure 13.4. But, for the reasons outlined above, an increase in North's industrial output will force South onto a lower production-consumption locus and, consequently, a lower indifference curve. By selecting a tariff that puts each country at the point at which an indifference curve is tangent to the production-consumption locus, both countries will be ignoring external diseconomies of industrialization. Although a unilateral reduction in industrial production will make either country worse off, a negotiated joint reduction in industrial production will make both countries better off.[31] Thus, the result is not Pareto optimal.

A genuine Pareto-optimal solution requires each country to take account of external diseconomies generated by its industrial production. One way to do this is to require each country to pay full income compensation to its partner for the relatively high-cost industrial goods sold in the partner's market. We can then construct a new curve—call it an "adjusted production-consumption locus." Each point on South's adjusted locus shows the income and industrial production available to South, after

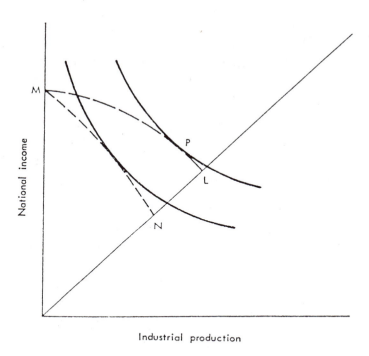

Figure 13.5
The adjusted production-consumption locus.

deducting from South's income an amount equal to the increased cost imposed on North. South pays no compensation if it has no industrial production, so the adjusted locus, *ML*, originates at point *M* (figure 13.5) as did the old locus, *MN*. But as South's industrial output expands, the required compensation increases, so that the divergence between the adjusted locus and the unadjusted locus widens.

South can select any point on its adjusted locus without affecting North's welfare. In Figure 13.5, South would choose point *P*, which represents a tangency solution. South can do no better, and North is indifferent between this point and any other point on the same locus. There is a comparable point on North's adjusted locus. The two countries can be maintained at this pair of points by a Pareto-optimal tariff.[32]

Although the present construct leads to a unique Pareto-optimal solution, other Pareto-optimal situations exist. To demonstrate this, modify the rules as follows: Each year, North makes some specified lump-sum income payment to South. Then South's locus shifts up, and North's locus shifts down. Unless the planners' demand for industry is wholly income inelastic, each country will choose a new level of industrial production, and there will be a new Pareto-optimal tariff.[33]

Each country's adjusted production-consumption locus will lie outside its pre-CU locus if the country has an intra-union comparative advantage in its lowest cost industries (so that the cost of a given level of industrial production is reduced). On the other hand, the adjusted locus will lie inside the pre-CU locus if the country has a comparative *dis*advantage in its cheapest industries (so that it is forced to move up the hierarchy of industries). Another possibility is that a country's adjusted locus *cuts* the pre-union locus. Then some levels of protection will be cheaper but other levels more costly, compared with the pre-CU situation.

If, at the relevant[34] part of the curve, each country's adjusted production-consumption locus lies outside its pre-union locus, then a CU necessarily permits both countries to gain.[35] Each country can produce at its preunion level of industrial output and will have resources to spare. But if the relevant part of either country's adjusted locus lies inside the pre-CU locus, that country is made worse off by the CU—at least under the tariff and set of rules discussed in this section.[36] In this case it may be possible for the more favored country to offer sufficient additional compensation to the less favored country in order to leave both countries better off. If this fails, then departure from the principle of free trade *within* the CU may still permit gains to both countries. We shall take up these possibilities in the two following sections.

Compensation

In figure 13.6, South's adjusted production-consumption locus is *ML*, compared with a pre-CU locus of *MN*. South is therefore forced onto a lower indifference curve in the CU. The amount of additional income compensation necessary to make South at least as well off with as without the union is shown in Figure 13.6 as *EF*. If North gains more than this amount, North will be able to compensate South fully and still be better off.[37] In this case, a CU is potentially beneficial. It is possible, however, that North will not gain enough to pay sufficient compensation to South, even if North's income gains exceed South's income losses.[38]

Partial Customs Unions

Allowing protection *within* a CU may increase the gains obtainable from one. A *partial* CU can be defined as an arrangement whereby two or more

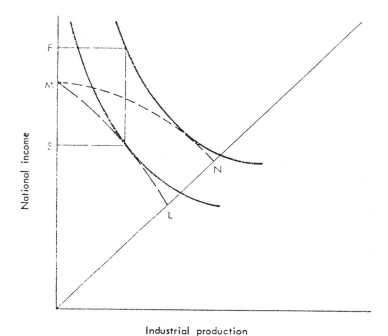

Figure 13.6
Compensation.

countries have a common external tariff—but not internal free trade. For example, some of South's manufactured goods could be protected against North's industry. South would have unrestricted access to North's market, but the reverse would not hold.

To take a simple but extreme case, suppose South is allowed to establish all the industries on its list, even though these industries are more economic in North. Assume also that North produces other industrial goods and sells them in the combined CU market, compensating South for the higher cost of these goods, compared to world-market prices. South is no worse off (indeed, South has not been affected by the union); and North gains, since the total cost of producing a given amount of industry in North is less than before the CU was formed.

It might even be desirable to allow South to export some of its higher-cost industrial goods to North. Suppose for example that, although South's most efficient industry can produce more cheaply in North, it nevertheless ranks far down on North's list, so that North chooses not to establish this industry. Then South can establish the industry, supply the combined market, and compensate North. In this case, North is clearly no worse off and South gains by being able to specialize on a low-cost industry instead of having to also develop a higher cost industry to serve the local market. These arrangements insure that each country's adjusted production-consumption locus lies outside the pre-CU locus.

Subsidies

In the analysis above, we have ruled out export subsidies. In principle, subsidizing exports offers greater scope for expanding the industrial sector than does a CU. If subsidization opened up world markets to a less developed country, the cost of protection would be lower still than in a CU. Subsidizing exports would permit more effective specialization. But "real-world" complications are such that an industrial sector based on production for export may be exceedingly difficult to establish and maintain. Not only are the industrial markets of advanced economies difficult to enter economically, but obtaining the necessary political co-operation would be very unlikely.[39]

But subsidization can be used *within* a CU. For example, each government can provide a sufficient subsidy to firms otherwise unable to compete in order to enable these firms to sell in the CU market at world-market prices. All intra-union trade then takes place at world prices, the purchasing country suffers no loss, and the producing country bears the entire cost of its industry. In terms of national accounts, a system of subsidies is equivalent to compensation. But with subsidization, compensation is automatic, and the prices of industrial goods within the CU remain equal to the prices of comparable imports.

Comparison with Existing Theory

It is of some interest to compare our results with those obtained by Viner and other CU theorists. In the Vinerian world, trade creation is good and trade diversion bad; a CU is more likely to result in a net welfare gain "the greater is the degree of overlapping between the class of commodities produced under tariff protection in the two countries."[40] With substantial overlapping, trade creation is likely to "outweigh" trade diversion. If, however, the two countries are complementary, different industries are likely to be protected in each country, and a CU will tend on balance to be trade-diverting, with the loss in efficiency (and hence in welfare) that Vinerian theory associates with this result.[41]

Our model differs in two respects. First, we allow a possible preference for industry; second, we regard the tariff as a policy instrument rather than an exogenous variable. The gains from a CU depend on what happens to both income and industrial output; this, in turn, depends on the common external tariff that is chosen. A CU involves the establishment of conditions under which the tariff can be used more effectively. Our conclusions have been based on the assumption that an appropriate tariff is always chosen. The emphasis is, in other words, on the *potential* gains. In Viner's world, the choice of tariff is sidestepped; it is often implied that a non-optimal tariff policy is adopted.[42]

In our model, either trade creation or trade diversion can be good and either can be bad. With a trade-diversion case, each economy expands its industrial production to supply the other's market. While this may reduce each economy's national income, industrial production is expanded. Without knowing more about the countries' indifference curves, one cannot say whether this raises or lowers welfare. Similarly, consider trade creation. Say that North is a lower-cost producer than South for all industrial products, so that with a CU, production shifts from South to North. Although South now pays less for its industrial goods, its industrial sector has been lost in the bargain. Is South necessarily better off? Again, one cannot answer without some knowledge of South's preferences. If either country loses income *or* industry, it must gain enough of the other to be adequately compensated.

The potential gain from a CU will be larger if: (1) There is a steeply rising marginal cost of protection in the two countries, (2) the countries have a strong preference for industry, (3) the countries are complementary, and (4) neither country dominates the other in industrial production generally.[43] Even if the fourth condition does not obtain, gains can still, in principle, be obtained from forming a partial union or from some other device that interferes with free trade within the CU. The impact of a CU will depend on the precise rules under which it is formed—the rules governing the location of industry, intra-union trade, and compensation. In general, the greater the flexibility of these rules, the larger are the potential gains.

But the real moral goes beyond these considerations. Economic integration may enable two or more economies to protect a given amount of industry at a lower real cost. Whether or not his result is effected depends on the preferences of the participants and, much more important, on the degree to which they co-operate. In many cases detailed cooperative effort will be needed if one country is not to lose more in the industry dimension than it gains in the income dimension or, worse still, to lose in both dimensions. A CU may make it technically possible for both countries to gain; a CU combined with subsidization or comparable policies will guarantee a potential gain. But neither set of policies will insure that the gains are realized.

In ideal cases there will be no conflict. By following their own bents, each country will gain. Even if no explicit compensation is granted, gains may be roughly distributed to each. But in other cases not only will explicit compensation agreements be required but there will have to be detailed agreement on intra-union division of industry.

Notes

The authors are indebted to Richard N. Cooper and Harry G. Johnson for their very helpful comments.

1. See Jacob Viner, *The Customs Union Issue* (New York: Carnegie Endowment for International Peace, 1950); James E. Meade, *The Theory of Customs Unions* (Amsterdam: North-Holland Publishing Co., 1955); Richard G. Lipsey, "Trade Diversion and Welfare," *Economica*, XXIV (February, 1957), 40–46, and "The Theory of Customs Unions: A General Survey," *Economic Journal*, LXX (September, 1960), 496–513; John Spraos, "The Condition for a Trade-Creating Customs Union," *Economic Journal* (March, 1964), pp. 101–8; Bela Balassa, *The Theory of Economic Integration* (Homewood, Ill.: Richard D. Irwin, 1961).

2. We have ruled out terms-of-trade effects in this paper for three reasons: (1) They are probably not an important source of gain from economic integration among a group of less developed countries. (2) In those cases where a terms-of-trade effect is important (for example, the European Economic Community), it is not especially interesting to evaluate a CU without considering also the effects of retaliation by those excluded from the club. (3) Our concern here is with the pure (static) theory of CU's among less developed countries; it is convenient to simplify the analysis as far as possible.

3. We have discussed this issue elsewhere; see our "A New Look at Customs Union Theory" (Santa Monica, Calif.: RAND Corporation, P-2972-2, April, 1965).

4. See Raul Prebisch, "Commercial Policy in the Underdeveloped Countries," *American Economic Review*, XLIX (May, 1959), 251–73; Dudley Seers, "A Model of Comparative Rates of Growth in the World Economy," *Economic Journal*, LXXIII (March, 1962), 45–78.

5. Some elements of a dynamic theory of less developed countries are contained in Sidney Dell, *Trade Blocs and Common Markets* (New York: Alfred A. Knopf, 1963); R. S. Bhambri, "Customs Unions and Underdeveloped Countries," *Economia Internazionale*, XV (March, 1962), 235–58; Massell, "The Distribution of Gains in a Common Market" (in preparation).

6. Throughout this analysis we shall identify social choice with the choice of the national economic planners. It is important to note that their concern is with the choice between industrial and other types of economic *activity* (or, equivalently, between industrial *activity* and national *income*). They are indifferent with respect to how consumers spend their income. Note also that we do not assume that planners *do* prefer industry, only that they *may*. The limiting case, where planners have no preference for industry, is discussed briefly in the text below.

7. The model can be generalized easily to take these factors into account, but the exposition becomes cumbersome.

8. These assumptions are in the spirit of existing CU theory.

9. By assumption, all industries have a cost greater than zero.

10. We shall discuss export subsidies later in the text; for now, they are ruled out.

11. In Fig. 13.1 the steps have been drawn the same length. This need not be the case but was done for ease of exposition—see text below. Note that the diagram ignores any changes in quantities consumed that may result from the adverse income effects to consumers of increased protection.

12. Throughout the chapter, we use the term "tariff" as shorthand for a *set* of tariff rates, one for each industry (some of which may be zero). Note also that we are focusing on *potential* gains; whether these gains are realized depends, of course, on whether an appropriate tariff is actually chosen.

13. With constant costs, a protective tariff on a particular industry's product is either ineffective or prohibitive. Provided the tariff is prohibitive, because of assumed competitive pricing it makes no difference how high the tariff rate is raised.

14. The production-consumption locus is not to be confused with either a production-possibilities or a consumption-possibilities locus; in a sense, it is a blend of the two.

15. If the planners' demand for industry is income elastic, the demand curve in Fig. 13.1 will shift to the right if MN shifts up. Strictly speaking, therefore, we should begin with the analysis contained in Fig. 13.2 and then derive the Fig. 13.1 results. But for clarity of exposition, it appears better to proceed as we have.

16. Then the steps in Fig. 13.1 are all of the same length. Moreover, the steps in one country's supply curve are the same length as those in the other country's curve.

17. To avoid cumbersome phases, we shall refer to the common external tariff in a CU as simply the "tariff."

18. The "limits" will become clear presently.

19. A limiting case of which is free trade. There may be more than one such tariff in which case we are also faced with the problem of choosing from among a set of tariffs. See text below.

20. Assuming S_n and S_s not to be horizontal.

21. That is, the country with the intra-union comparative advantage.

22. We have already assumed planners to be indifferent with respect to the composition of the industrial sector. Indifference with respect to the distribution between countries can be visualized most easily in terms of the formation of a joint economic planning board with responsibility for the economic development of the CU as a whole (although, in practice, even such a board is always subject to pressures from each of the countries).

23. As countries are decision-making units, it is important that each member country is convinced that it gains from joining the CU; otherwise it can refuse to join.

24. As we assume throughout the analysis.

25. In this situation the only efficient tariff that results in Pareto optimality is a tariff protecting shoes only. But then the gains all go to North. Compensation (in the form of income) paid by North to South would have no effect. Admittedly, this example is extreme, but it illustrates a more general point about tariff efficiency, as defined here.

26. There will be a quasi-Pareto-optimal tariff corresponding to each pair of levels of industrial production.

27. With a CU, the production-consumption locus is no longer constrained not to cross the 45° ray from the origin. South's value of industrial production may exceed its income, if some of the industrial goods are sold in North. Similarly, if South buys uneconomic industrial goods from North, South may be unable to reach the 45° ray. Whether the locus falls short of or crosses the 45° ray depends on how the CU affects South's terms of trade.

28. The fact that South's industrial production is partly supported by North's consumers tends to make South's new locus lie outside the old one (as a given industry costs South only one-half the pre-union price). In addition, specialization on the lowest cost industries (if South has an intra-union comparative advantage in these industries) will tend to make South's new locus lie above the old one. The new locus may lie below the old one only if South has an intra-union comparative *dis*advantage in its cheapest industries and must turn to higher-cost industries in order to have an industrial sector at all.

29. In other words, because South buys North's uneconomic goods at a price above the world market price, South's terms of trade deteriorate.

30. If North has an intra-union comparative advantage in all industries (and South consequently a comparative advantage only in corn production), then South's new locus will consist simply of one point on the vertical axis.

31. This is a common characteristics of two-person—non-zero sum games; an interesting parallel is the issue of disarmament.

32. We wish to emphasize that this tariff is not necessarily Pareto optimal (as defined above) with any other set of rules for distributing income between the countries.

33. A Pareto-optimal tariff is necessarily, quasi-Pareto optimal, but the converse does not hold. Also, a Pareto-optimal tariff need not be efficient, nor need an efficient tariff result in Pareto optimality.

34. This is admittedly a question-begging word.

35. That is, if the distributive rules and the tariff are chosen as outlined here.

36. One might think that a readjustment of exchange rates would enable both countries to specialize. But remember that each country produces corn for export; exchange rates are determined by the average cost of producing corn.

37. This transfer of income will shift South's locus out and North's locus in, so that a new tariff will be chosen.

38. If South loses industry as well as (or instead of) income, the amount of income compensation South requires depends on the shape of South's indifference curves, which bears no relation to the amount of North's income gains. For many developing nations, the indifference curves may be sufficiently steep in the relevant range that income compensation alone will not work.

39. Harry G. Johnson has suggested to us that general production subsidies could be used to evade the international rules against export subsidies.

40. R. G. Lipsey, "The Theory of Customs Unions," op. cit., p. 499, Lipsey goes on to qualify these results by considering intercommodity substitution. He maintains that, given a sufficiently inappropriate set of revenue tariffs, prior to the formation of the CU, trade diversion can raise welfare. (See the two papers by Lipsey cited above.) For a critique of Lipsey's analysis, see our paper described in n. 3.

41. Given that trade creation predominates, the magnitude of the gain will be greater (according to existing theory) the more complementary the two economies are—that is, the greater the difference in their costs of producing industrial goods. (See Lipsey, "The Theory of Customs Unions," op. cit.; H. Makower and G. Morton, "A Contribution towrds a Theory of Customs Unions," *Economic Journal*, LXII [March, 1953], 33–49; H. G. Johnson, *Trade and Economic Growth* [Cambridge, Mass.: Harvard University Press, 1962], p. 44.) But two situations must be distinguished. First, perhaps North has a substantial comparative advantage in industrial production generally, so that appreciable gains result from shifting production from South to North. In this case, the gains are simply a reflection of the highly uneconomic character of industrial production in South. But one is led to ask whether, in practice, South will be prepared to yield its protected industries to North. A quite different situation is one in which the industries on the lower half of North's supply curve are quite different from the industries on the lower half of South's curve. But this is a peculiar set of circumstances. If two countries produce identically the same batch of goods, one would be surprised to find grossly different structures of costs in producing these goods.

42. To be fair to Viner we should point out that GATT rules constrain the member countries' ability to select an optimal tariff. Viner's analysis is, of course, based on an entirely different conception of tariff policy.

43. That is, neither country has an intra-union comparative advantage in all or most industries (the case shown in Fig. 13.3c).

14

Necessarily Welfare-Enhancing Customs Unions with Industrialization Constraints: The Cooper–Massell–Johnson–Bhagwati Conjecture

Pravin Krishna and
Jagdish Bhagwati

14.1 Introduction

The conventional "static," "benign government" theory of Customs Unions was pioneered by Jacob Viner's (1950) pathbreaking work.[1] He essentially argued, counter-intuitively to those who thought that even preferential tariff cuts would necessarily be welfare-improving, that a subset of countries reducing tariffs on one another to zero would not necessarily be improving their own, or world welfare. In short, such Free Trade Areas or Customs Unions (with common external tariffs) could either be trade-diverting and harmful or trade-creating and beneficial.

Although there have been numerous important developments within this analytical framework, including by Lipsey (1957), Lipsey and Lancaster (1956), Johnson (1962) and Meade (1955), interesting developments in new directions have been made in two other contributions:

1. Bhagwati and Brecher (1980) have considered a rather different type of problem: if a Customs Union with internal factor mobility and a common external tariff is already in place, how would parametric and policy changes (e.g. factor accumulation and tariff change, respectively) affect the welfare of individual members countries? This question is clearly of analytical importance for the European Union and indeed for a federal state like the United States, if the regional welfare effects of such changes are at issue.

2. Kemp and Wan (1976) have remained more properly within the Viner–Lipsey type of question and have restored the original intuition that any subset of countries could improve their welfare, while not lowering that of others by forming an *appropriate* Customs Union.[2]

Originally published in *Japan and the World Economy* 9 (November 1997): 441–446. Reprinted with permission.

There is an interesting conjecture attributable to Cooper and Massell (1965), Johnson (1965) and Bhagwati (1968) that states that:

Any subset of countries can always form a welfare-enhancing Customs Union, while ensuring that they can maintain the degree of industrialization that they had achieved through protective tariffs.[3]

In this short note, we prove the proposition. In doing so, we re-prove the Kemp—Wan proposition using an optimization framework and then we readily extend it, by adapting the Bhagwati and Srinivasan (1969) analysis of non-economic objectives or constraints, to the problem at hand.

14.2 The Kemp—Wan Theorem

As in Kemp and Wan (1976), consider a competitive world trading system with any number of countries and with no restrictions whatever on the initial tariffs of individual countries. Let any subset of countries form a Customs Union. To see how aggregate gains for the member countries can be achieved, we use the familiar Samuelson (1956) social indifference curves, which enable us to write a well-behaved social utility function. We allow for the use of lump sum transfers between individuals in the member countries.[4] This allows us to neglect distributional issues between the member countries and to assert that, as we move up to higher social indifference curves, Pareto-superior outcomes can be achieved. The formulation of the problem closely parallels that of Bhagwati and Srinivasan (1969). Let $i = 1 \ldots n$, index goods and $j = 1 \ldots m$, index member countries.

Let the net import vector of the member countries from the rest of the world be denoted as

$$I = (I_1 \ldots I_n).$$

where, I_i would be positive if the ith good was a net import from the rest of the world and negative if it was a net export. Using the Kemp—Wan strategy, we freeze the net import vector of the union at the pre-union level and maximize the social utility function,

$$U = U(C_1 \ldots C_n) \tag{14.1}$$

subject to:

$$C_i = \Sigma_j X_i^j(L_i^j, K_i^j) + I_i \quad \forall i \tag{14.2}$$

$$\Sigma_i L_i^j = L^j \quad \forall j \tag{14.3}$$

$$\Sigma_i K_i^j = K_j \quad \forall j \tag{14.4}$$

$$I_i = I_i^F \quad \forall i \tag{14.5}$$

where C_i stands for the aggregate availability of good i in the union, X_i^j stands for production in country j of good i using a factor combination of L_i^j and K_i^j, respectively. L^j and K^j denote the total availability of these factors in country j. Although we only choose two factors of production, it will become clear that the results generalize to any number of factors. Note that the vector, $I^F = I = (I_1 \ldots I_n)$, is the pre-union net import vector and is fixed throughout the analysis. The maximization problem above simply recasts the Kemp and Wan (1976) problem[5] in welfare maximization terms. We can normalize the pre-union foreign prices of all goods to unity. It is important to note that we are not assuming a fixed foreign price vector. Since, as in Kemp and Wan (1976), we freeze the net import vector at the pre-union level, trade at the same foreign prices will obtain after the union is formed and the welfare of the rest of the world is not reduced. Eq. (14.3) and Eq. (14.4) are the resource constraints. Eq. (14.5) fixes imports at the pre-union level.

To solve this problem, we now form the Lagrangian:

$$= U - (\Sigma_i \lambda_i [C_i - (\Sigma_j X_i^j (L_i^j, K_i^j)) + I_i]) - (\Sigma_j \omega_j [\Sigma_i L_i^j - L^j])$$
$$- (\Sigma_j \rho_j [\Sigma_i K_i^j - K^j]) - (\Sigma_i \eta_i (I_i - I_i^F))$$

Maximization of the Lagrangian subject to the import vector constraint yields the necessary conditions for a constrained optimum. These are:

$$U_i = \lambda_i \quad \forall i \tag{14.6}$$

$$\lambda_i = \eta_i \quad \forall i \tag{14.7}$$

$$\lambda_i X_{i1}^j = \omega_j \text{ or } L_i^j = 0 \quad \forall i, j \tag{14.8}$$

$$\lambda_i X_{i2}^j = \rho_j \text{ or } K_i^j = 0 \quad \forall i, j \tag{14.9}$$

Eq. (14.6) along with Eqs. (14.8) and (14.9) implies that for an interior solution, the marginal rate of substitution between any two goods, say good 1 and good 2, in consumption as well as production is the same value, λ_1/λ_2. Also, from Eq. (14.6), we know that $\lambda_i > 0$, $\forall i$. We could conveniently choose $\lambda_1 = 0$. Finally, from Eq. (14.7), we then know that,

$$1 = \eta_1$$

implying that

$$\lambda_i/\lambda_1 = \eta_i \quad \forall i$$

that is, that the marginal rate of substitution in consumption as well as production is different from the foreign price ratio. For instance, the marginal rate of substitution in consumption as well as production between goods i and 1 is $\lambda_i/\lambda_1 = \eta_i$, whereas the foreign price ratio is simply 1 (by construction). This implies a tariff imposed against the rest of the world on imports of good i. Note that at an optimum all other first-order conditions are to be met. In other words, given the import constraint, the second-best optimum is obtained by the use of suitable tariffs on imports from the rest of the world and with all other Paretian conditions being met. Since the optimal way to achieve the net import vector I_1^F is as is described above, we can obviously conclude that any other way of achieving I_1^F can be (weakly) improved upon. Since I was actually achieved before the union, the pre-union situation can be (weakly) improved upon by the removal of all intra-union tariffs and by the use of a common external tariff (as is implied by the solution to the maximization problem above). This is simply the Kemp and Wan (1976) result.[6]

14.2.1 The Cooper–Massell–Johnson–Bhagwati Conjecture

We now take a non-economic production objective into account. Thus, for instance, let us assume that each country j within the union wants the level of its production of good i to be maintained at the pre-union level. This would imply additional constraints in the maximization exercise of the type,

$$X_i^j = \tilde{X}_i^j \quad \forall j \tag{14.10}$$

where $\tilde{X}_i^j$ is the pre-union level of production of good i in country j.

The inclusion of this additional constraint alters the first-order conditions corresponding to L_i^j and K_i^j. The new first-order conditions are,

$$(\lambda_i + \delta)X_{i1}^j = \omega_j \quad \forall j \tag{14.8a}$$

and

$$(\lambda_i + \delta)X_{i2}^j = \rho_j \quad \forall j. \tag{14.9a}$$

From Eqs. (14.8a) and (14.9a), the marginal rates of substitution in production between good i and all the other goods are different from the corresponding marginal rates of substitution in consumption between good i and the other goods, implying that a production tax-cum-subsidy policy in each country is optimal. Also, from Eq. (14.8a) and Eq. (14.9a), the marginal rate of substitution between L and K is the same in the production of the good i as it is in the production of all other goods. Thus, there is no factor subsidy involved (except in the trivial sense of an equi-proportionate subsidy on L and K used in the production of good i, which, after all, is equivalent to a production subsidy on good i). Importantly, all other Paretian conditions should still be met for a constrained optimum, implying that the intra-union tariffs should be kept at zero. Any other way of achieving $X_i^j = \tilde{X}_i^j$ can be (weakly) improved upon. Since $X_i^j = \tilde{X}_i^j$ was actually achieved before the union, the pre-union situation can be (weakly) improved upon and a (weakly) Pareto-superior outcome can be achieved.

Equally, it follows that the feasible welfare level of this union would be even greater if the constraint $X_i^j = \tilde{X}_i^j \, \forall j$ was weakened and rewritten as

$$\Sigma_j X_i^j = \Sigma_j \tilde{X}_i^j ,$$

so that the constraint is only an aggregate union-wide constraint (as originally in Cooper and Massell (1965)).

This result can also be readily extended to other 'non-economic' constraints. A welfare-enhancing Customs Union which does not harm or benefit non-members can be formed even if each member requires, for instance, that its manufacturing employment not fall. The 'supporting policy,' complementing the common external tariff, then will be an employment-tax-cum subsidy (exactly as in Bhagwati and Srinivasan (1969)).

14.3   Conclusions

This chapter demonstrates that welfare-improving Customs Unions can be guaranteed even if we are constrained by specific non-economic government objectives. We have considered a "production" objective here, but it is straightforward to show that this result can be extended to other non-economic objectives as well. As we would expect from the insights of both the Kemp–Wan theorem and the theory of non-economic objectives, the necessarily welfare improving Cooper–Massell–Johnson–Bhagwati union requires both an appropriate common tariff and an appropriate domestic tax-cum-subsidy addressed to the non-economic objective desired.

Acknowledgements

We are grateful to Earl Grinols and the seminar participants at NYU's Japan–US Center symposium on 'Bilateral and Multilateral Trade Negotiations' for helpful comments.

Notes

Using a technique very similar to the one adopted in this paper and following the unified intuition regarding second best problems developed in Krishna and Panagariya (1996)—that removal of some pre-existing distortions, if all remaining distortions are quantitative ones, is always (weakly) welfare improving, Krishna and Panagariya (1997) show that we can also always construct necessarily welfare improving *free trade areas* (in contrast to the necessarily welfare improving *customs unions* that the Kemp–Wan theorem delivers instead).

1. The Viner approach is "static" because it concerns only the welfare effects of a once-and-for-all FTA or CU formation instead of considering "time-path" questions. It is a "benign-government" approach because the formation of the FTA or CU is exogenously specified and the incentives to form them so that they are endogenously determined (as in Krishna (1993)) are not modeled. See Bhagwati (1993) for these analytical distinctions.

2. In doing so, they solved for the common external tariff, therefore using it as an endogenously-determined policy variable, unlike in the Viner–Lipsey approach.

3. For instance, Cooper and Massell (1965) ask, "Why should a country be willing to give up its sheltered industries for the partial benefits of a Customs Union?" and "Is there a tariff that would make both countries (in a CU) better off relative to optimal policies of non preferential tariff protection?" and Bhagwati (1968) states that "If LDCs could be allowed to reduce tariff barriers among themselves, this could permit the given trade diversion (implicit in each LDC's decision to industrialize) to be carried out at a lower cost."

4. Lump sum transfers to ensure Pareto superior outcomes are also used in the original Kemp–Wan framework. For an illuminating discussion of how such compensation schemes can be constructed, see Grinols (1981).

5. Kemp and Wan (1976) are not explicit about their need for a complete indexation of goods and factor endowments by their location. However, on closer examination, it is clear that their proof fixes the trade vector of *each* country to arrive at a welfare-improving customs union. the framework that is used in this paper relaxes the Kemp–Wan import constraint by only requiring that the pre-union net import vector be fixed for the union as a *whole*. By allowing for further substitution in production and consumption within the union, we can therefore achieve even greater levels of welfare than are possible under the corresponding Kemp-Wan construction.

6. The original proof of the theorem considers a fictitious economy composed of member countries but with a net endowment equal to the sum of the member countries' endowment plus the equilibrium preunion net excess supply of the rest of the world. The economy then possesses an optimum and any optimum can be supported by at least one internal price vector. If the pre-union equilibrium of the member countries is a Pareto-optimal equilibrium of the fictitious economy or it is not; in the latter case, a preferred Pareto-optimal equilibrium can be attained by means of lump sum transfers among individuals of the fictitious economy.

It must also be mentioned that the framework used in this paper is less general that the Kemp–Wan framework which, inter alia, allows for heterogenous preferences across consumers and for transport cost considerations.

References

Bhagwati, J., 1968. Trade liberalization among LDCs, Trade theory and GATT rules, in: J. N. Wolfe ed., Value, Capital and Growth: Papers in honor of Sir John Hicks, (Edinburgh University Press, Edinburgh) Chap. 2, pp. 21–43.

Bhagwati, J., 1993. Regionalism and multilateralism: An overview, in: A. Panagariya and J. De Melo, eds., New Dimensions in Regional Integration, World Bank.

Bhagwati, J., Brecher, R. A., 1980. 'National welfare in the presence of foreign-owned factors of production', Journal of International Economics, 10, 103–115.

Bhagwati, J., Srinivasan, T. N., 1969. Optimal intervention to achieve non-economic objectives, Review of Economic Studies 36 (1).

Cooper, C. A., Massell, B. F., 1965. Toward a general theory of Customs Unions for developing countries, Journal of Political Economy, 73, 256–283.

Grinols, E., 1981. An extension of the Kemp–Wan theorem on the formation of Customs Unions', Journal of International Economics, 11, 259–266.

Johnson, H. G., 1962. The economic theory of Customs Unions, in: Money, Trade and Economic Growth, (George Allen and Unwin, London), Chap. 3, pp. 46–74.

Johnson, H. G., 1965. An economic theory of protectionism, tariff bargaining, and the formation of Customs Unions, Journal of Political Economy, 73, 256–283.

Kemp, M. C., Wan, Henry Jr, 1976. An elementary proposition concerning the formation of Customs Unions, in: Murray Kemp, Three Topics in the Theory of International Trade: Distribution, Welfare and Uncertainty, (North Holland, Amsterdam).

Krishna, P., 1993. Regionalism vs. multilateralism: a political economy approach, Quarterly Journal of Economics, forthcoming.

Krishna, P., Panagariya, A., 1996. A Unification of the Theory of Second Best. Mimeo, Brown University.

Krishna, P., Panagariya, A., 1997. On the Existence of Necessarily Welfare Improving Free Trade Areas, Mimeo, Brown University.

Lipsey, R. G., 1957. The theory of Customs Unions: Trade diversion and welfare, Economica, 24, 40–46.

Lipsey, R. G., Lancaster, K., 1956. The general theory of second best, Review of Economic Studies, 24, 11–32.

Meade, J. E., 1955. The Theory of Customs Unions, North-Holland, Amsterdam.

Samuelson, P. A., 1956. Social indifference curves, Quarterly Journal of Economics, 70, 1–22.

Viner, J., 1950. The Customs Unions Issue, (Carnegie Endowment for International Peace, New York).

Impact on Members of Policy and Parametric Variations in a Common Market

15

Foreign Ownership and the Theory of Trade and Welfare

Richard A. Brecher and
Jagdish N. Bhagwati

15.1 Introduction

This chapter reconsiders a number of standard topics in the theory of
international trade by taking explicit account of the distinction between
national and aggregate income when fixed supplies of foreign-owned
inputs are present within the domestic economy. Extending the work of
Bhagwati and Brecher (1980),[1] the following analysis takes a new look at
welfare-theoretic aspects of international transfer, economic expansion,
and tariff policy, while it emphasizes significant departures from conventional wisdom that arise in the presence of foreign ownership. As these
selected departures suggest, many standard results are open to serious
question when part of the domestic product accrues to factor inputs from
abroad.

Originally, the motivation for the present two-group analysis (based
on the national-foreign distinction) came from a recent concern in Latin
America, where policymakers have been worried about the impact of
trade liberalization on national welfare, given the domestic presence of
foreign-owned multinational corporations. After further reflection, however, it is clear that the treatment below has much greater applicability to
a broad range of analytically similar cases. For example, it is possible
to treat in much the same way a wide variety of alternative domestic distinctions, including those based on race, sex, age, or ethnicity. The following techniques and results, moreover, are directly relevant for the fully
analogous two-group issue relating to the distribution of gains (or losses)
between trading partners in a customs union (such as the European
Economic Community) with factor mobility. While these other policy

Originally published in *Journal of Political Economy* 89, no. 3 (1981): 497–511. Reprinted with
permission.

problems are of considerable importance and interest as well, only the national-foreign distinction is pursued explicitly here for the sake of brevity.

Section 15.2 reviews the basic model of an open economy, in which foreign-owned and national supplies of two homogeneous factors are combined to produce two commodities. As Section 15.3 then shows, a transfer-receiving country might suffer a loss in national welfare, even under the usual conditions which would ensure a welfare gain if foreign ownership were absent. As established next by Section 15.4, a country experiencing economic expansion (due to factor-endowment growth or technological advance) might encounter a deterioration in national welfare, even under well-known conditions which would preclude this possibility of "immiserizing growth" in the absence of foreign ownership. Afterward, Section 15.5 explains why free trade might be inferior to *both* no trade and subsidized trade, as far as national welfare is concerned.[2] Section 15.6 summarizes the chapter's main results, based on the possibility of aggregate and national welfare moving in opposite directions.

Needless to say, this possibility would not arise if foreign-owned factors were taxed to the nationally optimal extent. Indeed, with these factors in perfectly inelastic supply, the optimal tax on each foreign input clearly would be 100 percent, thereby removing the after-tax distinction between aggregate and national welfare. Assuming that this type of optimal taxation of factors is politically infeasible, however, the present analysis cautions nationally oriented policymakers against the usual, automatic adoption of the standard welfare conclusions which reflect an aggregate point of view. More specifically, this paper shows precisely how the traditional (aggregate) propositions must be modified for a truly national perspective, when political constraints eliminate optimal taxation of inputs from abroad.

15.2   The Basic Model

Following the analysis of Bhagwati and Brecher (1980), the present section summarizes the basic two-commodity, two-factor model of an open economy (large or small), which plays host to given quantities of inputs from abroad. The aggregate factor endowments of the country are fixed at $\bar{K}^a$ units of capital and $\bar{L}^a$ units of labor, while the given amounts $\bar{K}^n$ and $\bar{L}^n$ are the national endowments of capital and labor, respectively. (Thus, the fixed supplies of foreign-owned capital and labor within the home country are $\bar{K}^a - \bar{K}^n$ and $\bar{L}^a - \bar{L}^n$, respectively.) It is assumed that

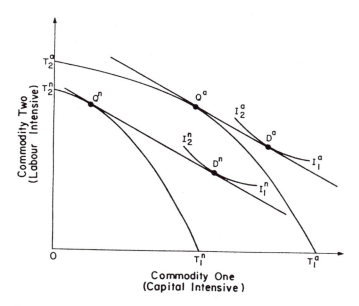

Figure 15.1
Differential trade-volume phenomenon.

$\bar{K}^a > \bar{K}^n > 0$ and $\bar{L}^a > \bar{L}^n > 0$, excluding the possibility that either factor within the home economy is owned wholly by nationals or completely by foreigners.[3] Commodity two is always labor intensive relative to capital-intensive commodity one, and the well-behaved technology exhibits constant returns to scale.

In figure 15.1, the home country is depicted in free-trade equilibrium. Aggregate production is at point Q^a on production-possibility frontier $T_2^a T_1^a$ (corresponding to $\bar{K}^a$ and $\bar{L}^a$), aggregate income is represented by budget line $Q^a D^a$, and aggregate consumption occurs at point D^a on indifference curve $I_2^a I_1^a$. (For simplicity of exposition, it is assumed that all income earned by factors from abroad is consumed locally, to avoid having to show repatriation of such income within the diagram.) By the reasoning of Bhagwati and Brecher (1980), national consumption takes place at point D^n on indifference curve $I_2^n I_1^n$, with national income given by budget line $Q^n D^n$ (parallel to $Q^a D^a$), *as if* nationals produced separately at point Q^n on production-possibility frontier $T_2^n T_1^n$ (drawn for $\bar{K}^n$ and $\bar{L}^n$).[4] To emphasize that the main results of this chapter qualitatively do *not* require any differences in consumer preferences between nationals and foreigners within the home country, assume throughout the text that the same set of indifference curves with unitary income elasticities of demand represents both national and aggregate tastes in consumption, although this simplification of the exposition could be dropped (as in footnotes to this chapter) without detracting from the essence of the analysis.[5]

The model may be summarized conveniently as follows:

$$X_i^j = F_i^j(p), \quad i = 1, 2, \quad j = a, n; \tag{15.1}$$

$$Y^j = X_1^j + pX_2^j, \quad j = a, n; \tag{15.2}$$

$$W^j = U^j(C_1^j, C_2^j), \quad j = a, n; \tag{15.3}$$

$$C_1^j + pC_2^j = Y^j, \quad j = a, n; \tag{15.4}$$

where p denotes the relative price of the second commodity in terms of the first; X_i^j denotes output of commodity i on frontier $T_2^j T_1^j$; each F_i^j is a conventional function of p, given $\bar{K}^j$, $\bar{L}^j$ and the (uniform) technology for commodity i; Y^a and Y^n denote the real value of aggregate and national income, respectively, in terms of the first commodity; C_i^a and C_i^n denote aggregate and national consumption, respectively, of commodity i ($i = 1, 2$); W^a and W^n denote aggregate and national welfare, respectively; and each U^j is a concave function of C_1^j and C_2^j, with positive partial derivatives denoted by $U_i^j \equiv \partial U^j / \partial C_i^j$ ($i = 1, 2$).

Later in the chapter when a change in relative prices is induced by various parametric shifts, either of the following phenomena might lead to a fall in national, despite a rise in aggregate, welfare, depending on the strength of other induced effects. The differential trade-volume phenomenon is shown in figure 15.1, where the aggregate (actual) volume of trade (defined by line segment $Q^a D^a$) is less than the national (hypothetical) volume of trade (defined by line segment $Q^n D^n$), implying (ceteris paribus) that a terms-of-trade deterioration worsens national welfare by more than aggregate welfare. Figure 15.2 (labeled similarly) illustrates the Bhagwati and Brecher (1980) differential trade-pattern phenomenon, which arises when the aggregate and national patterns of trade differ (in direction), so that an aggregate terms-of-trade improvement (tending to raise W^a) means a national terms-of-trade deterioration (tending to lower W^n). The national (relative to the aggregate) endowment of factors is labor abundant in figure 15.1 (with $\bar{K}^a / \bar{L}^a > \bar{K}^n / \bar{L}^n$) but capital abundant in figure 15.2 (with $\bar{K}^a / \bar{L}^a < \bar{K}^n / \bar{L}^n$), as suggested by the relative shapes of frontiers $T_2^a T_1^a$ and $T_2^n T_1^n$, in accordance with the reasoning of Rybczynski (1955).

To understand the possibility of a fall in national welfare despite a rise in aggregate welfare, it might be tempting to go no further than the fol-

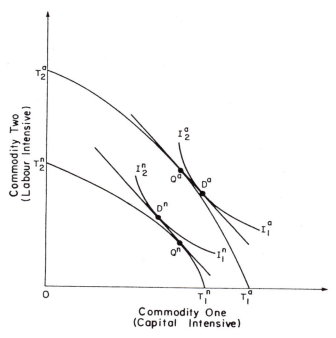

Figure 15.2
Differential trade-pattern phenomenon.

lowing simple observation. Whenever the national and aggregate endowments exhibit different capital/labor ratios, the domestic distribution of income might deteriorate for nationals, as a change in relative commodity prices alters the wage/rental ratio for reasons expounded by Stolper and Samuelson (1941). It is important to recognize, however, that generally this income-redistribution effect will not be strong enough to produce the differential responses in national and aggregate welfare if the relative factor-endowment discrepancy is too small to create either the differential trade-volume or the differential trade-pattern phenomenon. Even when either of these phenomena arises, moreover, a fall in national welfare despite a rise in aggregate welfare can occur if and only if certain specific conditions (derived below) are satisfied.

15.3 International Transfer

According to a standard result in the literature (see Mundell 1960), a transfer-receiving country cannot suffer a loss in aggregate welfare despite any possible deterioration in the aggregate terms of trade, as long as international commodity-market equilibrium is stable. In other words, the transfer-induced change in W^a cannot be negative, assuming that an excess demand for or supply of the second good in world markets can be cleared by a rise or fall in p, respectively. As the following argument demonstrates, however, a (large) transfer-receiving country might suffer a deterioration in national welfare, even under the assumption (maintained throughout the present chapter) that commodity markets are stable. This demonstration of a transfer-induced fall in W^n, moreover, does not even require a rise in the relative price of home importables.

If it is assumed that the transfer is given only to nationals, equations (15.2) are modified as follows:

$$Y^j = X_1^j + pX_2^j + \tau, \quad j = a, n, \tag{15.5}$$

where τ is the real value of the transfer in terms of the first commodity. If any part of the transfer were given to foreigners within the home country, the chances for a decline in W^n would simply be enhanced, thereby strengthening the argument below.

To examine the welfare implications of the transfer, differentiate equations (15.1), (15.3), (15.4), and (15.5) totally with respect to τ—assuming (without loss of generality) that initially $U_1^j = 1$, while noting that $U_2^j/U_1^j = p = -(dF_1^j/dp)/(dF_2^j/dp)$ from the first-order conditions for maximizing utility and profit. In this way, it is a straightforward exercise to derive

$$dW^j/d\tau = 1 + (E^j dp/d\tau), \quad j = a, n, \tag{15.6}$$

where $E^j = X_2^j - C_2^j$. Consistent with figures 15.1 and 15.2, which depict the home country exporting the second good, $E^a > 0$ by assumption throughout this chapter. As illustrated above, however, E^n can be either positive (in fig. 15.1) or negative (in fig. 15.2).

As equations (6) confirm, $dW^a/d\tau$ is the familiar sum of the following two components: the primary gain ($= 1$) from the transfer-induced increase in aggregate income, at the initial (pretransfer) set of relative prices; plus the secondary effect ($= E^a dp/d\tau$) from the possible increase or decrease in the real exchange value of the initial volume of home exports, in the event of a transfer-induced change (if any) in relative prices. The expression for $dW^n/d\tau$ is analogous. If foreign inputs were entirely absent from the home country, the distinction between national and aggregate variables would disappear, thereby implying that $E^n = E^a$ and (hence) that $dW^n/d\tau = dW^a/d\tau$. Given the actual presence of factor inputs from abroad, however, $dW^n/d\tau$ generally differs from $dW^a/d\tau$, except in the special case where either $E^n = E^a$ (despite the foreign presence) or $dp/d\tau = 0$.

To determine precise conditions for the direction of change in welfare, consider the standard transfer-induced terms-of-trade response, analyzed previously by Samuelson (1952, 1954) and subsequently by Mundell (1960). Thus, by well-known reasoning,

$$dp/d\tau = (1 - m - m^*)/(e + e^* - 1)E^a, \tag{15.7}$$

where e (>0) and m denote the relative-price elasticity of import demand and the marginal propensity to consume the importable, respectively, for the home country; e^* (>0) and m^* denote the corresponding variables for the rest of the world; and $\tau = 0$ in the initial (pretransfer) equilibrium.[6] Given the assumption above that world commodity-market equilibrium is stable, $e + e^* > 1$ throughout the present paper.

If equation (15.7) is substituted into equations (15.6), simple manipulation confirms that

$$dW^a/d\tau = (\varepsilon + \varepsilon^*)/(e + e^* - 1) > 0, \tag{15.8}$$

but shows that

$$dW^n/d\tau \gtreqless 0 \text{ as } (e + e^* - 1)E^a \gtreqless (m + m^* - 1)E^n, \tag{15.9}$$

where ε (>0) and ε^* (>0) denote the compensated (constant-utility) relative-price elasticity of import demand for the home country and the rest of the world, respectively, while $e = \varepsilon + m$ and $e^* = \varepsilon^* + m^*$, according to a standard decomposition.[7] Although $dW^a/d\tau > 0$ unambiguously, it is evidently possible to have $dW^n/d\tau < 0$ nevertheless.[8]

To highlight the important role of the differential trade-pattern and differential trade-volume phenomena, it is helpful to revert to equations (15.6), which imply that a fall in national, despite the rise in aggregate, welfare can occur only if $(E^n - E^a)dp/d\tau < 0$. This necessary condition for a fall in W^n holds if either $dp/d\tau < 0$ in the presence of the differential trade-volume phenomenon of figure 15.1 (where $E^n > E^a > 0$) or $dp/d\tau > 0$ in conjunction with the differential trade-pattern phenomenon of figure 15.2 (where $E^n < 0 < E^a$).[9] Correspondingly, if home exportables were relatively intensive in their use of capital (rather than labor), a transfer-induced deterioration in national (though not in aggregate) welfare would still be possible, provided that either the aggregate terms of trade improve in the case of labor-abundant nationals or an aggregate terms-of-trade decline occurs in the presence of capital-abundant nationals.

Consequently, the basic results of this section can be summarized generally in the following terms. When the home exportable uses intensively the factor that is relatively abundant in the national (as compared with the aggregate) endowment, the national and aggregate patterns of trade are the same, in which case a fall in national welfare might occur through a differential trade-volume phenomenon if the (national and aggregate) terms of trade worsen unambiguously. Alternatively, when the home exportable uses intensively the factor that is relatively scarce in the national (as compared with the aggregate) endowment, the aggregate and national patterns of trade could differ, in which case the differential trade-pattern phenomenon might give rise to a deterioration in national welfare if the national terms of trade worsen through an aggregate terms-of-trade improvement. These general results, moreover, hold equally well for changes in p induced by economic expansion and tariff policy, as will be clear from the analysis below.

15.4 Economic Expansion

As Bhagwati (1958a) has demonstrated, a once-and-for-all increase in a factor endowment or in a technological level might deteriorate the aggregate terms of trade enough to worsen aggregate welfare of the home country, but this immiserizing growth can occur only if either the rest of the world has an inelastic offer curve or growth would decrease the production of home importables at the initial product-price ratio. In other words, if the offer-curve elasticity for the rest of the world is not less than unitary and economic expansion is not "ultrabiased" against the production of home importables, the growth-induced change in W^a cannot be negative. Even under these circumstances (assumed throughout the present section) which preclude a fall in aggregate welfare, however, the following analysis demonstrates that a (large) country might suffer a loss in national welfare. This demonstration of a growth-induced decline in W^n, moreover, does not even require a rise in the relative price of home importables.

To allow for factor-endowment expansion or technological advance, equations (15.1) may be rewritten as follows:

$$X_i^j = F_i^j(p, \theta), \quad i = 1, 2, \quad j = a, n, \tag{15.10}$$

where θ is a general shift parameter, a rise in which indicates either a factor-endowment increase (for $\bar{K}^j$ or $\bar{L}^j$) or a disembodied technological improvement for an industry (one or two). It is assumed that any addition to the aggregate supply of capital or labor is owned fully by nationals. If any part of such addition were foreign owned, the likelihood of a decline in W^n would simply be enhanced, thereby strengthening the argument below. However, the ability of domestically located producers to take advantage of disembodied technological progress should be independent of the source of ownership of the inputs used, as assumed here.

Differentiating equations (15.2), (15.3), (15.4), and (15.10) totally with respect to θ, while recalling that $U_1^j = 1$ initially and that $U_2^j/U_1^j = p = -(\partial F_1^j/\partial p)/(\partial F_2^j/\partial p)$, we readily obtain the following result:

$$dW^j/d\theta = Y_\theta^j + (E^j dp/d\theta), \quad j = a, n, \tag{15.11}$$

where $Y_\theta^j \equiv \partial Y^j/\partial \theta > 0$. Thus, each $dW^j/d\theta$ is the sum of a primary growth effect (Y_θ^j) plus a secondary relative-price effect ($E^j dp/d\theta$), which are analogous to the welfare-related effects of the transfer mentioned above in Section 15.3. Although national and aggregate welfare again would remain equal if foreign inputs were entirely absent from the home country, the actual presence of foreign ownership gives rise to the possibility of having $dW^n/d\theta < 0$ when $dW^a/d\theta > 0$, except in the special case where $dp/d\theta = 0$.

Turning to the standard growth-induced terms-of-trade response, analyzed previously by Bhagwati (1958b) and subsequently by Kemp (1969, p. 110), we see that it is a well-known fact that

$$dp/d\theta = (\beta - m)Y_\theta^a/(e + e^* - 1)E^a, \tag{15.12}$$

where $\beta \equiv (\partial X_1^a/\partial \theta)/Y_\theta^a$. When this result is substituted into equations (15.11), straightforward manipulation confirms that

$$dW^a/d\theta = (\varepsilon + \beta + e^* - 1)Y_\theta^a/(e + e^* - 1) > 0 \tag{15.13}$$

but shows that

$$dW^n/d\theta \gtreqless 0 \text{ as } E^a(e + e^* - 1)Y_\theta^a \gtreqless E^n(m - \beta)Y_\theta^n, \tag{15.14}$$

where $\beta \geqq 0$, which recalls the assumption that growth would not reduce production of home importables at the initial commodity-price ratio; and $e^* \geqq 1$, which recalls the assumption that the rest of the world's offer curve is not inelastic. Thus, despite the fact that $dW^a/d\theta > 0$ unambiguously under these circumstances, it is still possible to have $dW^n/d\theta < 0$ nevertheless.[10]

Equations (15.11) imply that a fall in national (despite the rise in aggregate) welfare can occur only if $(E^n - E^a)dp/d\theta < Y_\theta^a - Y_\theta^n$. As could be

shown readily, this necessary condition for a fall in W^n can result from
each of the following alternative events, for example: an increase in either
the national endowment of capital or the technological level of industry
one, with $dp/d\theta > 0$ in the presence of the differential trade-pattern phenomenon (fig. 15.2); and an increase in either the national endowment of
both factors or the technological level of both industries, if $dp/d\theta < 0$
with the differential trade-volume phenomenon (fig. 15.1).[11] Correspondingly, if home exportables were relatively capital intensive, it would be
possible to have an expansion-induced deterioration in national (though
not in aggregate) welfare under a variety of circumstances, including the
following: an increase either in the national stock of labor or in the level
of technology for the production of importables, when the national endowment is labor abundant; or an increase either in the national endowment of both factors or in the level of technology for both sectors, when
nationals are capital abundant.

15.5 Tariff Policy

According to a standard result in the literature (see Bhagwati 1968), free
trade is ranked superior to both no trade and subsidized trade (assuming
that both offer curves are well behaved),[12] from the viewpoint of aggregate welfare. In other words, the home country cannot increase W^a above
the free-trade level either by using an import (or export) tax to eliminate
trade or by imposing an export (or import) subsidy to encourage trade.
From the national-welfare point of view, however, the ranking above may
be reversed. Since Bhagwati and Brecher (1980) already demonstrated the
possibility of such a reversal for free trade versus autarky, the following
analysis concentrates on free versus subsidized trade.

To allow for tariff policy, equations (15.2) may be modified as follows:

$$Y^j = X_1^j + pX_2^j + [(C_1^a - X_1^a)\alpha/(1-\alpha)], \quad j = a, n; \tag{15.15}$$

where α denotes the ad valorem tariff, which is an import tax (if $\alpha > 0$) or
an import subsidy (if $\alpha < 0$); the domestic relative price of the second
good is still denoted by p, so that the relative price of this good in world
markets is now equal to $p(1 + \alpha)$; and $(C_1^a - X_1^a)\alpha/(1 + \alpha)$ equals the real
value (in terms of the first good) of tax revenues or subsidy payments,
evaluated at domestic prices.[13] In writing equations (15.15), it is assumed
(for the sake of simplicity) that all tax revenues or subsidy payments, respectively, are returned to or collected from *national* consumers in lump-

sum fashion. If foreigners within the home country were to receive or finance any part of these revenues or payments, respectively, comparison of the free-trade and autarkic equilibria (which generate no tax revenues) clearly would be unaffected, while the chances of having free trade inferior to subsidized trade simply would be enhanced (thereby strengthening the analysis below).

To show that free trade might be inferior to subsidized trade from the national point of view, it is sufficient to establish the possibility of having $dW^n/d\alpha < 0$ in free-trade equilibrium. Consequently, throughout the following discussion, let $\alpha = 0$ in the initial (pretariff) equilibrium.

Differentiating equations (15.1), (15.3), (15.4), and (15.15) totally with respect to α and again recalling that $U_1^j = 1$ initially and that $U_2^j/U_1^j = p = (dF_1^j/dp)/(dF_2^j/dp)$, we may verify readily that

$$dW^j/d\alpha = pE^a + (E^j dp/d\alpha), \quad j = a, n; \tag{15.16}$$

note that $pE^a = C_1^a - X_1^a$ when (balanced) trade is initially free (with $\alpha = 0$). By well-known reasoning (see Kemp 1969, p. 96),

$$dp/d\alpha = p(1 - m - e^*)/(e + e^* - 1); \tag{15.17}$$

note that $1 - m$ equals the home country's marginal propensity to consume the exportable and recall that $\alpha = 0$ initially. When this result is substituted into equations (15.16), simple manipulation confirms that[14]

$$dW^a/d\alpha = \varepsilon pE^a/(e + e^* - 1) \gtreqqless 0 \tag{15.18}$$

but shows that

$$dW^n/d\alpha \lesseqqgtr 0 \text{ as} (e + e^* - 1)E^a \lesseqqgtr (m + e^* - 1)E^n. \tag{15.19}$$

Thus, despite the fact that $dW^a/d\alpha \gtreqqless 0$, it is evidently possible to have $dW^n/d\alpha < 0$ nevertheless.[15]

As implied by the equations (15.16), it is possible to have $dW^n/d\alpha < 0$ (even though $dW^a/d\alpha$ cannot be negative) if either a differential trade-volume phenomenon arises (fig. 15.1) when $dp/d\alpha < 0$ (the "normal" price response) or a differential trade-pattern phenomenon occurs (fig. 15.2) when $dp/d\alpha > 0$. (The "perverse" price response [$dp/d\alpha > 0$] can occur only in the large-country case, under conditions discussed by Metzler [1949].) Correspondingly, if home exportables were relatively capital intensive, it would be possible to have $dW^n/d\alpha < 0$ (even though $dW^a/d\alpha$ cannot be negative) if either nationals are labor abundant when $dp/d\alpha > 0$ or nationals are capital abundant when $dp/d\alpha < 0$.

Thus a trade subsidy might raise national (but not aggregate) welfare above the free-trade level. This analysis of a small subsidy (tax) on trade, moreover, complements the discussion of Bhagwati and Brecher (1980), who concentrate on prohibitive taxes on trade and thus are able to avoid the issue of tariff revenues.

The analysis of this section has an important implication for the traditional method of estimating the cost (benefit) of tariff protection or trade liberalization. Since the conventional method (as outlined by Johnson [1960]) ignores the source of ownership of domestically located inputs, the concept measured (in present notation) is clearly $dW^a/d\alpha$ rather than $dW^n/d\alpha$. Thus, the traditional estimate of the impact of protection or liberalization is an aggregate measure, which overstates or understates the national cost (benefit) if $(E^n - E^a)dp/d\alpha \lessgtr 0$, respectively, as suggested by equations (15.16). This misstatement arises because the conventional estimate simply sums the three standard components (namely, the external terms-of-trade effect and the costs of distortion in both production and consumption), while it fails to exclude the foreign-factor portion of the tariff-induced change in aggregate welfare.[16]

15.6 Summary

As demonstrated by this chapter, welfare aspects of international trade theory need to be reconsidered, when national and aggregate income differ in the presence of foreign ownership. Examples of this need are provided by the analysis of international transfer, economic expansion, and tariff policy. For a country receiving a transfer from abroad, national (but not aggregate) welfare might deteriorate even when international commodity-market equilibrium is stable, regardless of the direction of change in the world product-price ratio. In the case of economic expansion from factor-supply growth or technological advance, national (but not aggregate) welfare might worsen even when the rest of the world does not have an inelastic offer curve and domestic expansion is not ultrabiased against production of home importables, no matter what the direction of change in the world commodity-price ratio. As for tariff policy, free trade might be ranked inferior to both no trade and subsidized trade (in either direction), from the viewpoint of national (but not aggregate) welfare. Moreover, the conventional empirical estimates of the cost of protection à la Johnson's (1960) methodology are generally seen to be in need of correction if the economy has foreign-owned factors of production. In fact, many economies typically do have substantial labor inflows under *gas-tarbeiter* or other programs defined by immigration-quota policies, and, of course, equally there are substantial flows of capital among nation states.[17]

Notes

Thanks are due to the National Science Foundation grant no. SOC79-07541 for partial financial support of the research underlying this paper. The comments and suggestions of Alan Deardorff, Jacob Frenkel, Alasdair Smith, and anonymous referees are gratefully acknowledged.

1. Their work, in turn, extends the analysis of Bhagwati and Tironi (1980), who concentrate on a special case mentioned in n. 3 below.

2. This result is obtained also by Bhagwati and Tironi (1980), for a special case identified in n. 3 below. In addition, since Bhagwati and Brecher (1980) compare free-trade equilibrium with autarky, this chapter will emphasize instead the comparison of free versus subsidized trade.

3. For the special case in which $\bar{K}^a > \bar{K}^n = 0$ and $\bar{L}^a = \bar{L}^n > 0$, see Bhagwati and Tironi (1980).

4. The discussion could be extended readily to allow for the possibility of complete specialization, following the analysis of Bhagwati and Brecher (1980).

5. Nn. 6–8, 10, and 15 below extend the discussion to let tastes differ between nationals and foreigners within the home country. These extensions bring out the essentially "three-country" flavor of the analysis, in which nationals, domestically located foreigners, and the rest of the world can be treated as three distinct components of the international economy.

6. If preferences in consumption were allowed to differ between nationals and foreigners within the home country, it would be necessary to rewrite eq. (15.7) as follows, to reflect the present assumption that the entire transfer goes exclusively to nationals:

$$dp/d\tau = (1 - m^n - m^*)/(e + e^* - 1)E^a, \tag{15.7'}$$

where m^n denotes the national marginal propensity to consume the home importable.

7. Alternatively, if eq. (15.7') from n. 6 above were substituted into eq. (15.6), simple manipulation could show that

$$dW^a/d\tau = [(\varepsilon + \varepsilon^*) + (1 - \gamma)(m^f - m^n)]/(e + e^* - 1) \tag{15.8'}$$

and

$$dW^n/d\tau = [(\varepsilon + \varepsilon^*) + (1 - \gamma)(m^f + m^* - 1)]/(e + e^* - 1), \tag{15.9'}$$

where m^f denotes the marginal propensity to consume the home importable for foreigners within the home country; $\gamma \equiv (C_1^n - X_1^n)/(C_1^a - X_1^a) = E^n/E^a$; and use is made of the fact that $m = \gamma m^n + (1 - \gamma)m^f$. Eq. (15.8') indicates that $dW^a/d\tau$ can be decomposed into two comparative-static components. As could be shown readily, the first component $[(\varepsilon + \varepsilon^*)/(e + e^* - 1)]$ is the transfer-induced change in W^a that would occur initially if the transfer were given temporarily to nationals and domestically located foreigners in the respective amounts $\gamma\tau$ and $(1 - \gamma)\tau$, whereas the second component $[(1 - \gamma)(m^f - m^n)/(e + e^* - 1)]$ is the subsequent change in W^a that would occur as the portion $(1 - \gamma)\tau$ was passed from domestically located foreigners to nationals (the ultimate recipients of the entire transfer). Eq. (15.9′) could be interpreted analogously, since $-dW^n/d\tau$ equals the worldwide sum of transfer-induced changes in welfare for everyone excluding home-country nationals, as could be shown readily.

8. Under the present assumption that $m^f = m^n = m$, eq. (15.8′) of n. 7 above is equivalent to eq. (15.8), while eq. (15.9′) leads directly to condition (15.9). Alternatively, if it were the case that $m^f \neq m^n$, there would arise the new possibility of having $dW^a/d\tau < 0$ in eq. (15.8′). Also if it were supposed that $m^f = 1 - m^*$, it would be the case that $dW^n/d\tau > 0$ unambiguously in eq. (15.9′). This last result can be understood intuitively as follows: If foreign tastes are uniform throughout the world, the reasoning behind eq. (15.8) shows equally well that the transfer must lower worldwide foreign welfare; that is, $-dW^n/d\tau < 0$, recalling n. 7 above. Incidentally, in view of the fact that worldwide foreign welfare otherwise can rise (when $dW^n/d\tau < 0$) if $m^f \neq m^*$, international aid might be especially attractive for a donor country with investments in the aid-receiving economy.

9. Although $(E^n - E^a)dp/d\tau < 0$ also if $0 < E^n < E^a$ when $dp/d\tau > 0$, $dW^n/d\tau > 0$ in this case, as implied by eq. (15.6). The reader may also see alternatively that, from condition (15.9), $dW^n/d\tau < 0$ if and only if $(\varepsilon + \varepsilon^*)E^n + (E^a - E^n)(e + e^* - 1) < 0$. Therefore, national welfare *may* decline despite the increase in aggregate welfare if $E^n < 0 < E^a$ (i.e., the differential trade-pattern phenomenon holds) or if $E^n > E^a > 0$ (i.e., the differential trade-volume phenomenon holds).

10. Along lines suggested by nn. 6–8 for the case of international transfer, the analysis of economic expansion could be extended readily to distinguish between m^n and m^f. It is worth noting, however, that it would still be possible to have $dW^n/d\theta < 0$ even if it were the case that $m^f = 1 - m^*$.

11. Although $Y_\theta^a = Y_\theta^n$ with a national factor-endowment increase, it is possible that $Y_\theta^a > Y_\theta^n$ for a technological advance. Thus, with the latter (but not the former) type of economic expansion, a fall in national welfare despite the rise in aggregate welfare might occur even without the differential trade-volume and differential trade-pattern phenomena—if both industries experience the technological advance and $dp/d\theta < 0$.

12. I.e., the offer curve is assumed to represent imports as a monotonic decreasing function of their relative price in world markets. For the significance of this assumption in tariff analysis, see Bhagwati and Kemp (1969).

13. Although the corresponding value at *world* prices would be $(C_1^a - X_1^a)\alpha$, consumers respond directly to *domestic* (tariff-inclusive) prices instead.

14. Note that $dW^a/d\alpha = 0$ only in the small-country case where $e^* = \infty$, and even then the change in W^a does not equal zero for any discrete change in α, by well-known reasoning.

15. Along lines suggested by nn. 6–8, the analysis of tariff policy could be extended readily to let $m^f \neq m^n$, without eliminating the possibility of having $dW^n/d\alpha < 0$ even if $m^f = 1 - m^*$.

16. The foreign-factor portion of the change in aggregate welfare is represented by the expression $(E^a - E^n)dp/d\alpha$, which must be excluded from $dW^a/d\alpha$ to give $dW^n/d\alpha$, as suggested by eq. (15.16). Also by repeating the procedure of Bhagwati, Ramaswami, and Srinivasan (1969), it is possible to write (in present notation) that $dW^a/d\alpha = (E^a dp^*/d\alpha) + [(p^* - p)dX_2^a/d\alpha] + [(p - p^*)dC_2^a/d\alpha]$, where the relative price of the second good in world

markets is denoted p^*, which equals $p(1 + \alpha)$. The components $E^a dp^*/d\alpha$, $(p^* - p)dX_2^a/d\alpha$, and $(p - p^*)dC_2^a/d\alpha$ are the effects due to the terms-of-trade change, the production distortion, and the consumption distortion, respectively. When evaluated in free-trade equilibrium (where $\alpha = 0$ and $p = p^*$), the latter two (distortion-related) components disappear, leaving only the first (terms-of-trade) component. This remaining (first) component, moreover, is equivalent to the right-hand side of eq. (15.16) for $j = a$, since (in free-trade equilibrium) $dp/d\alpha = (dp^*/d\alpha) - p$.

17. Variations in protection may, in turn, lead to variations in the presence of foreign factors in the economy. Thus, for instance, Bhagwati (1980) has considered linkages between reduction in protection and reduction in the restrictiveness of immigration quotas. However, the analysis in the text has taken the endowment of *both* national and foreign-owned factors to be invariant to policy changes.

References

Bhagwati, Jagdish N. "Immiserizing Growth: A Geometrical Note." *Rev. Econ. Studies* 25 (June 1958): 201–5. (*a*)

———. "International Trade and Economic Expansion." *A.E.R.* 48 (December 1958): 941–53. (*b*)

———. "The Gains from Trade Once Again." *Oxford Econ. Papers* 20 (July 1968): 137–48.

———. "Shifting Comparative Advantage, Protectionist Demands, and Policy Response Options." Paper presented at a Ford-NBER conference on Import Competition and Adjustment: Theory and Policy, Cambridge, Mass., May 1980.

Bhagwati, Jagdish N., and Brecher, Richard A. "National Welfare in an Open Economy in the Presence of Foreign-owned Factors of Production." *J. Internat. Econ.* 10 (February 1980): 103–15.

Bhagwati, Jagdish N., and Kemp, Murray C. "Ranking of Tariffs under Monopoly Power in Trade." *Q.J.E.* 83 (May 1969): 330–35.

Bhagwati, Jagdish N.; Ramaswami, V. K.; and Srinivasan, T. N. "Domestic Distortions, Tariffs, and the Theory of Optimum Subsidy: Some Further Results." *J.P.E.* 77 (November/December 1969): 1005–10.

Bhagwati, Jagdish N., and Tironi, Ernesto. "Tariff Change, Foreign Capital and Immiserization: A Theoretical Analysis." *J. Development Econ.* 7 (March 1980): 71–83.

Johnson, Harry G. "The Cost of Protection and the Scientific Tariff." *J.P.E.* 68 (August 1960): 327–45.

Kemp, Murray C. *The Pure Theory of International Trade and Investment*. Englewood Cliffs, N.J.: Prentice-Hall, 1969.

Metzler, Lloyd A. "Tariffs, the Terms of Trade, and the Distribution of National Income." *J.P.E.* 57 (February 1949): 1–29.

Mundell, Robert A. "The Pure Theory of International Trade." *A.E.R.* 50 (March 1960): 67–110.

Rybczynski, T. M. "Factor Endowment and Relative Commodity Prices." *Economica* 22 (November 1955): 336–41.

Samuelson, Paul A. "The Transfer Problem and Transport Costs: The Terms of Trade When Impediments Are Absent." *Econ. J.* 62 (June 1952): 278–304.

———. "The Transfer Problem and Transport Costs, II: Analysis of Effects of Trade Impediments." *Econ. J.* 64 (June 1954): 264–89.

Stolper, Wolfgang F., and Samuelson, Paul A. "Protection and Real Wages." *Rev. Econ. Studies* 9 (November 1941): 58–73.

*Political-Economy-Theoretic
Analysis of the Formation
of PTAs and Their External
Tariffs*

16

The Politics of Free-Trade Agreements

Gene M. Grossman and
Elhanan Helpman

Governments have been meeting frequently of late to discuss the possibility of their forming bilateral or regional trading arrangements. The United States has concluded bilateral agreements with Israel, Canada, and Mexico and will pursue talks with Chile and perhaps other Latin American nations. The European Union expanded its membership to include Greece, Portugal, and Spain and has discussed preferential arrangements with many Central and Eastern European countries. Some members of the Association for South East Asian Nations (ASEAN) have been calling for the formation of a Pacific free-trade area. And Argentina, Brazil, Paraguay, and Uruguay have banded together to form the Southern Common Market (MERCOSUR).

These trade negotiations have never been easy, nor have they always been successful. One need only reflect on the recent debates in the United States concerning the NAFTA or those in Europe over accession to the EU to recognize the political hackles raised by prospective trade agreements. In this paper we attempt to analyze some of the political pressures that are brought to bear on a government as it contemplates whether to enter into a new trading arrangement. In particular, we address the following problem. Suppose that an opportunity arises for two countries to negotiate a free-trade agreement (FTA) among themselves. Will an FTA between these countries be politically viable? If so, what form will the agreement take?

These questions take us into the realm of international relations. Traditionally, studies of international relations in both political science and economics have adopted a "statist" mode of analysis (see the discussion of this point in Peter F. Cowhey [1990]). In this approach, states are seen as

Originally published in *American Economic Review* 85, no. 4 (September 1995): 667–690.
Reprinted with permission.

unified rational actors pursuing some well-defined objective. In economic analysis, for example, it is common to assume that the state seeks to maximize aggregate national welfare. Then the analysis focuses on the nature of the game between governments. We, like Robert Putnam (1988), would rather regard international relations as involving two distinct stages of strategic interaction. First, there is an initial stage during which political competition between the different interests in each country determines the government's policy preferences. Then there is a subsequent stage of give-and-take that determines international equilibrium. We would argue, moreover, that neither stage can be meaningfully analyzed without reference to the other. Inevitably, international interdependence sets the parameters for the domestic political contest, while the domestic political environment constrains the actions that governments can take internationally. Here and in a companion piece which examines multilateral negotiations over levels of nondiscriminatory tariffs (Grossman and Helpman, 1995), we implement this perspective, by incorporating the two stages of strategic interaction into a single, sequential game.

In treating the rivalry between competing interests in a single country we use the analytical framework that we developed in Grossman and Helpman (1994a). This framework emphasizes the interaction between lobby groups representing industry special interests and an incumbent government. In our model, lobby groups offer policy-contingent campaign contributions to politicians, who make decisions that serve their own political objectives. In this setting, a country's policy stance reflects the relative political power of its organized special interests and also the extent of the government's concern for the plight of the average voter.

The chapter is organized as follows. Section 16.1 develops the analytical framework, describing both the economic and political interactions and the effects of an FTA on the welfare of the various agents. In Section 16.2 we focus on "the initial stage," asking when the government of one country might be willing to endorse an agreement calling for complete and immediate liberalization of all bilateral trade with some partner. This forms the basis for our discussion in Section 16.3 of the outcome of a bilateral negotiation between two countries. In Section 16.4 we allow for the possibility that an FTA may exclude a few especially sensitive sectors, or that it may allow for some extended periods of adjustment. We show how a more liberal interpretation of GATT rules about the types of permissible FTA's may enhance political viability and examine the politics that determine which industries gain exemptions under the agreement. The concluding section summarizes our findings.

16.1   Analytical Framework

We examine the trade policy of two small countries that interact with one another and the rest of the world. The countries produce and trade many goods, all of whose international prices are normalized to 1. Initially, each country imposes the same tariff on all imports of a good regardless of source, in keeping with the "most favored nation" (MFN) clause of the GATT Articles of Agreement. The two countries now have the opportunity to discuss an FTA. Our aim is to identify the political and economic conditions in the two countries that would make it possible for their politically minded governments to conclude such an agreement.

We suppose that there is a numeraire good 0 that is untaxed in each country and n other goods. Some of these goods are imported by one or both of the small countries in the initial equilibrium, while others may be exported. In recognition of GATT rules, we exclude the possibility that the countries subsidize their exports. We also ignore export taxes, which are unconstitutional in the United States and rarely used elsewhere. Thus, we assume that the initial domestic price in either country of any good that is exported by that country is 1. As for import goods, these may be subject to arbitrary import tariffs. We let τ_i^j represent 1 plus the initial tariff rate on good i in country j, for $j = A, B$. With our normalization of international prices, these are also the domestic prices in country j for the import goods.[1]

Article XXIV of the GATT Articles of Agreement permits certain exceptions to the principle of MFN. Countries may enter bilateral or regional agreements if they eliminate "duties and other regulations of commerce" on "substantially all trade" among themselves. The GATT rules allow for both *customs unions*, in which member countries impose a common external tariff on trade with the rest of the world, and *free-trade areas*, in which the countries maintain separate external tariffs and enforce them with rules of origin. In this chapter we study only the latter type of agreement. GATT rules further stipulate that the external tariffs imposed after the conclusion of an FTA must be no higher than those that were in force beforehand. While the practical meaning of this requirement remains in doubt (see John McMillan, 1993), we appeal to it as loose justification for supposing that the initial tariffs τ_i^j continue to apply to imports from the rest of the world under any FTA that might be formed.[2]

The phrase "substantially all trade" in GATT Article XXIV has been interpreted to allow some latitude in the structuring of trade agreements. Regional and bilateral trade agreements typically exclude a few politically sensitive sectors and specify prolonged phase-in periods for some others. At first, we shall ignore this limited degree of flexibility and interpret the GATT rules as requiring that all goods be freely traded between the parties to any agreement. But later we will relax this assumption and suppose that the countries can exclude some sectors from the agreement. Then we will have the initial MFN tariffs remain in force on trade between A and B in the excluded goods.

16.1.1   Objectives of Economic and Political Agents

The qualitative features of the two small economies are similar. We describe the structure of one of these countries but omit, for the time being, the country superscripts which implicitly are attached to every function and variable.

The country has a voting population of size 1. Individuals within the country have identical preferences $u(c) = c_0 + \Sigma_{i=1}^{n} u_i(c_i)$, where c_i denotes consumption of good i and $u_i(\cdot)$ is an increasing and concave function. These preferences give rise to the per capita demands $D_i(q_i)$ for goods $i = 1, \ldots, n$ and the demand $y - \Sigma_{i=1}^{n} q_i D_i(q_i)$ for good 0, where q_i is the domestic consumer price of good i and y is the individual's spending. The same demands apply in the aggregate, except that individual spending is replaced by aggregate spending in the demand for good 0.

The production of good 0 uses only labor, with one unit of labor required per unit of output. Each other good is manufactured with constant returns to scale by labor and a sector-specific factor. Since the domestic price of good 0 has been normalized to 1, the competitive wage must equal 1 in any equilibrium in which this good is produced. Then the specific factor used in industry i earns the reward $\Pi_i(p_i)$, where p_i is the domestic producer price. Aggregate supply of good i is $X_i(p_i) = \Pi_i'(p_i) > 0$ for $i = 1, \ldots, n$.

We assume that the ownership of the specific factors is highly concentrated in the population. In fact, we take an extreme case where these factor owners comprise a negligible fraction of the total number of voters. The owners of a particular factor have a common interest in seeing a high domestic price for the good they produce and so favor protection from foreign competition. We assume, perhaps because they are few in number, that they can overcome the "collective-action problem" described by Mancur Olson (1965) and that they work together for their common political goals. The owners of the factor used in sector i form a special-interest group which takes political action in order to maximize joint welfare.[3]

As in Grossman and Helpman (1994a, 1995), we suppose that the incumbent government is in a position to set trade policy, which means here that it can either work toward a free-trade agreement or terminate the discussions. The politicians may receive contributions from the various interest groups, hoping to influence their decision. The politicians value these contributions—because they can help them to get reelected or for other reasons—but they may also care about the well-being of the average voter. Per capita welfare will enter the incumbent government's objective function if, for example, some voters are well informed about the effects of trade policy and base their votes partly on their standard of living. We assume that the government's objective has a simple linear form, $G \equiv \Sigma_i C_i + aW$, where C_i is the campaign contribution of the lobby representing industry i, W is aggregate (and per capita) welfare, and a is a parameter (possibly zero) reflecting the government's sensitivity to the average voter's well-being relative to its taste for campaign contributions.[4]

Each individual enjoys surplus of $S_i(q_i) \equiv u_i[D_i(q_i)] - q_i D_i(q_i)$ from consuming good i, $i = 1, \ldots, n$. He or she also receives a lump-sum transfer from the government, representing a share of the total tariff revenue, which is rebated to the public on an equal, per capita basis. Aggregate welfare of voters is given by

$$W = L + \sum_{i=1}^{n} \Pi_i(p_i) + \sum_{i=1}^{n} (\tau_i - 1)M_i + \sum_{i=1}^{n} S_i(q_i) \tag{16.1}$$

where L is aggregate labor supply and the right-hand side of (16.1) therefore represents the sum of labor income, profits, tariff revenues, and total consumer surplus. In the initial situation with MFN tariffs, $p_i = q_i = \tau_i$ and $M_i = D_i - X_i$, so W is maximized when $\tau_i = 1$ for all i. As usual, the small country suffers an aggregate welfare loss whenever its politics generate a deviation from free trade.

The small number of owners of the input used in industry i capture a negligible fraction of the consumer surplus in the economy and receive only a negligible fraction of the rebated tariff revenue. Thus, the objective of these factor owners can be closely approximated by $\Pi_i(p_i) - C_i$, their profits net of political contributions. We will use Π_{iN} to represent gross industry profits in the event that no agreement is reached, in which case output continues to sell for $p_i = \tau_i$. Similarly, we let Π_{iF} denote industry profits under an FTA, which depend of course on the producer prices that would prevail in the event of an agreement. In a moment, we will consider what these prices must be. But first we describe the nature of the political game.

16.1.2   The Political Game

Interest groups move first in the political game. They offer financial support to incumbent politicians in their home country but link their contributions to the actions taken by the government with respect to the trade agreement.[5] This follows Grossman and Helpman (1994a), where we applied Douglas B. Bernheim and Michael D. Whinston's (1986) notion of a menu auction to the problem of tariff formation. In our earlier paper, we allowed interest groups to design *contribution schedules* that made each campaign gift a function of the trade tax vector chosen by the government. Here the government has only two options: to pursue an agreement or not. It follows that a policy-contingent contribution schedule need only comprise two numbers, C_{iF} and C_{iN}, which are the gifts associated with the realization of an FTA and with a continuation of the status quo, respectively.

In fact, it is never optimal for a lobby to promise positive gifts for both policy outcomes, because then it could cut back equally on both of its offers without affecting the government's decision. And a lobby surely does not wish to give the government added incentive to choose the outcome that is contrary to its interests. Thus, each lobby need only quote a single number, representing its donation in the event that its preferred outcome is chosen. We limit each lobby to offer no more than what it stands to gain in profits if the government were to follow its bidding.[6]

The lobbies set their contributions non-cooperatively (although we will at times allow them to communicate first). Then, faced with the set of offers, the government takes a position on the trade accord. The government endorses the FTA if and only if $\Sigma_i C_{iF} + aW_F \geq \Sigma_i C_{iN} + aW_N$ (where W_R is aggregate welfare under regime R, $R = (F, N)$. Otherwise, it rejects the agreement.

16.1.3   Economic Equilibrium Under an FTA

Before we proceed to characterize the outcome of this political game, we discuss what effects the FTA would have on the voters and special-

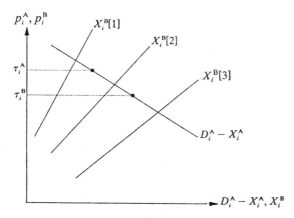

Figure 16.1
Industry effects of an FTA.

interest groups in each country. Our economic analysis builds on Martin Richardson (1992).

We focus on one particular product i. If both countries happen to export this good in the initial equilibrium, then each has a domestic price equal to 1, and the FTA will have no effect on outputs, profits, or consumption levels. The more interesting cases arise when at least one of the countries initially imports the good subject to a positive MFN tariff. Without loss of generality we consider an industry in which $\tau_i^A > \tau_i^B \geq 1$.

Figure 16.1 depicts the demand for imports by country A and three possible locations of the *total* supply curve for country B. Suppose that B's endowment of the specific factor is relatively small, as with $X_i^B[1]$, so that the total amount of that country's supply at price τ_i^A does not suffice to satisfy A's import demand at that price. Then A must continue to import from the rest of the world under an FTA, and its domestic price must remain at τ_i^A. The producers in B prefer to sell in A's market at the high price τ_i^A rather than to sell at the lower price τ_i^B (which may equal 1, if this is initially an export good) prevailing at home. These producers divert all of their output to country A after the conclusion of the FTA, and consumers in B satisfy all of their demands by importing from the rest of the world. The FTA has no effect on producer or consumer prices in country A, or on consumer prices in country B. It serves only to raise the prices paid to producers in the low-tariff country, who in effect would capture the protection of the high-tariff country (see Anne O. Krueger [1993] on a related point). We will refer to this as the case of *enhanced protection*.

At the opposite extreme, the endowment of the specific factor in B may be so large that this country's output would satisfy A's import demand at the lower price τ_i^B. In this case, represented by $X_i^B[3]$ in the figure, the domestic price in country A falls to τ_i^B. Now B is the source for all of A's imports, and producers in country B also sell in their home market. Consumers in B pay τ_i^B for the good just as they did before the agreement, and producers there continue to receive this sum. But producers in A receive less than before. This is a case of *reduced protection*.

Finally, the curve $X_i^B[2]$ represents an intermediate case in which B's supply curve intersects A's import demand at a price between τ_i^A and τ_i^B. In this case, when producers in B divert their output to the higher-priced market, this output is just sufficient to meet import demand at a price where there is no residual demand for imports from the rest of the world. Producers in B receive the equilibrium price in A's market, which is higher than τ_i^B but lower than τ_i^A. Consumers in B import from the rest of the world, paying the same price τ_i^B as they did before the agreement.

The main point here is that, depending on the size of B's potential output, the marginal good produced there may be sold in A's protected market, in B's less protected market, or possibly even on the world market. The price that B's producers receive and that all agents face in country A varies accordingly. Table 16.1 summarizes these findings.

16.1.4   Effects of an FTA on Economic Interests

We are now ready to describe how an FTA affects the profits of specific factor owners and the welfare of the average voter in each country. We continue to focus on a single industry in which $\tau_i^A > \tau_i^B \geq 1$. Of course

Table 16.1
Outcomes under an FTA ($\tau_i^A > \tau_i^B$)

Outcome	Enhanced protection	Intermediate case	Reduced protection
A imports from rest of world?	yes	no	no
B consumes own output?	no	no	yes
Producer price in A Consumer price in A Produce price in B	τ_i^A	$>\tau_i^B$ $<\tau_i^A$	τ_i^B
Consumer price in B	τ_i^B	τ_i^B	τ_i^B

the effect of an agreement on aggregate welfare reflects the sum of its effects in the various industries, including those in which $\tau_i^B > \tau_i^A \geq 1$.

Consider first an industry that experiences *enhanced protection*. Producers in country B benefit from their preferential access to A's highly protected market. Their gain amounts to $\Delta\Pi_i^B = \Pi_i^B(\tau_i^A) - \Pi_i^B(\tau_i^B)$. Producers in A are unaffected, since the domestic price there does not change. As for welfare, the only effect in A is the loss of tariff revenue. This country, which collects duties on all of its imports in this industry under the MFN tariff, does not collect any on its imports of $X_i^B(\tau_i^A)$ from its partner under the FTA. The welfare change in A amounts to

$$\Delta W_i^A = -(\tau_i^A - 1)X_i^B(\tau_i^A).$$

This welfare loss corresponds, of course, to the adverse effects of *trade diversion*, which are familiar from the literature on customs unions.

In country B the contribution of the industry under consideration to aggregate welfare rises. There are two components of this gain. First, as we have noted, profits in the industry increase. Second, the country imports from the rest of the world to replace sales formerly made by domestic producers. Assuming that $\tau_i^B > 1$, the country collects added tariff revenue on these new imports. The change in welfare equals $\Delta W_i^B = \Delta\Pi_i^B + (\tau_i^B - 1)X_i^B(\tau_i^B)$. We note that A's welfare loss exceeds B's welfare gain, reflecting the global efficiency cost associated with trade diversion.

For an industry that experiences *reduced protection*, the price obtained by producers in the low-tariff country does not change. These exporters gain nothing from the agreement, while the producers in country A suffer from the increased import competition. The expression for the profit change is $\Delta\Pi_i^A = \Pi_i^A(\tau_i^B) - \Pi_i^A(\tau_i^A) < 0$. Tariff proceeds in the industry fall to zero in country A, as all imports now originate in the partner country. But voters gain qua consumers from the fall in the domestic price of the good. The contribution of the industry to the change in aggregate welfare is $\Delta W_i^A = \Delta\Pi_i^A - (\tau_i^A - 1)M_i^A(\tau_i^A) + S_i^A(\tau_i^B) - S_i^A(\tau_i^A)$, which may be positive or negative, depending on the relative sizes of the gains from trade creation and the losses from trade diversion. Country B captures only the extra tariff revenue in this case $[\Delta W_i^B = (\tau_i^B - 1)M_i^A(\tau_i^B)]$, but joint welfare gains for the two countries are assured.

The intermediate case combines elements of the other two. Producers gain in country B and lose in country A. Aggregate welfare rises in B and may rise or fall in A. The effect on joint welfare of the two countries is ambiguous. As there is nothing new in this case, we will not consider it any further.

To summarize, an FTA can have any of several combinations of impacts on the economic actors with interests in a particular industry. Producers in the country that exports to its partner under an FTA sometimes gain and never lose. These producers are one potential source of political support for an agreement. On the other hand, the producers in the country that imports from its partner under the agreement never gain and sometimes lose. Here we find potential resistance. The stake of the general public in an FTA is less clear-cut. If most goods will be exported to the partner country, then aggregate welfare must rise, as consumer surplus never falls in the exporting country, and tariff revenues generally increase. If most goods will be imported, the aggregate welfare effect depends on the relative strength of the forces of trade creation and trade diversion, as is well known from the theory of discriminatory tariffs.

16.2   Unilateral Stances

We are ready to begin our search for equilibrium outcomes. We focus first on the political interactions in a single country. These determine the nation's *unilateral stance*, that is, the position that the government would adopt if it believed its decision would determine the fate of the agreement. We aim to describe the policy positions that can be supported as optimal government responses to equilibrium behavior by the country's interest groups. To this end, we propose the following definition.

Definition 1   A choice of regime $R \in \{N, F\}$ is a *unilateral stance* if there exists a set of political contributions $\{C_{iN}, C_{iF}\}$, one for each lobby i, such that:

a. $C_{iK} \geq 0$ for $K = N, F$ and for all i;

b. $C_{iK} \leq \max(0, \Pi_{iK} - \Pi_{iJ})$ for $J = N, F$; $K = N, F$; $J \neq K$;

c. $\Sigma_i C_{iR} + aW_R \geq \Sigma_i C_{iK} + aW_K$ for $K = N, F$;

d. for every lobby i there exist no contributions $\hat{C}_{iN} \geq 0$ and $\hat{C}_{iF} \geq 0$ and no regime $\hat{R}_i \in \{N, F\}$ such that:

$$\hat{C}_{i\hat{R}_i} + \sum_{j \neq i} C_{j\hat{R}_i} + aW_{\hat{R}_i} \geq \hat{C}_{iK} + \sum_{j \neq i} C_{jK} + aW_K \quad \text{for } K = N, F \tag{i}$$

and

$$\Pi_{i\hat{R}_i} - \hat{C}_{i\hat{R}_i} > \Pi_{iR} - C_{iR}. \tag{ii}$$

The definition stipulates that the political contributions supporting a unilateral stance must be nonnegative and no greater than what a lobby stands to gain under its preferred regime. The contributions induce the government to take the position R rather than the alternative, in the light of its own political objectives. And there are no alternative offers available to any lobby that, given the contribution schedules of the other lobbies and the anticipated optimization by the politicians, would leave the lobby with greater net welfare.

We will find that there are two generic types of unilateral stances that may exist for a given set of parameter values. We refer to a stance as *unpressured* if the government takes the chosen position despite there being no offers of contributions that encourage it to do so. By contrast, a *pressured* stance is one that the government takes partly in response to offers of interest-group support. We now derive the following result.

Result 1   There exists an unpressured stance in support of regime R if and only if

$$a(W_R - W_{\tilde{R}}) \geq \max\left[0, \max_i(\Pi_{i\tilde{R}} - \Pi_{iR})\right] \tag{16.2}$$

where $\tilde{R}$ is the alternative to regime R.

The result says that, in an unpressured stance, the government prefers the regime R to the alternative on grounds of public welfare. Moreover, there is no single lobby favoring the alternative policy that stands to lose so much under R that it would unilaterally sway the government from its concern for the plight of the average voter.

The proof is straightforward. First, suppose that all contribution offers are zero (i.e., $C_{iR} = C_{i\tilde{R}} = 0$ for all i). Then the government chooses the socially preferred position and, if (16.2) is satisfied, no single lobby finds it profitable given the zero offers of the others to induce the government to change its stance. This establishes that (16.2) is sufficient for an unpressured stance in favor of R. As for necessity, it is obvious that we must have $W_R - W_{\tilde{R}} \geq 0$ if the government is to choose R in the absence of any contributions in support of that position. And if $a(W_R - W_{\tilde{R}}) < \Pi_{i\tilde{R}} - \Pi_{iR}$ for any i, then lobby i could profitably deviate by bidding something more than $a(W_R - W_{\tilde{R}})$ but less than $\Pi_{i\tilde{R}} - \Pi_{iR}$, thereby inducing the government to choose $\tilde{R}$.

Next we examine stances that feature campaign giving by the prospective beneficiaries of the chosen regime. When $C_{iR} > 0$ for at least one lobby i, the government must be left indifferent between the two policy choices (i.e., $\Sigma_i C_{iR} + aW_R = \Sigma_i C_{i\tilde{R}} + aW_{\tilde{R}}$). Otherwise, one of the lobbies offering a positive contribution in support of R could reduce its offer without affecting the final outcome, thereby increasing its net income. Once we know that the government is left indifferent, we also know that every lobby on the losing side (i.e., those preferring $\tilde{R}$ to R) bids for $\tilde{R}$ the full amount of what it stands to lose under R; otherwise one such lobby would find it profitable to raise its offer for $\tilde{R}$ slightly, thereby tipping the balance to that policy. Of course, no lobby on the winning side offers more than the extra profits it earns under R, and each lobby contributes nothing if the government's choice is counter to its interests. Together, these considerations establish our second result.

Result 2   If there exists a pressured stance in support of regime R, then

$$\sum_i \Pi_{iR} + aW_R \geq \sum_i \Pi_{i\tilde{R}} + aW_{\tilde{R}}. \tag{16.3}$$

Condition (16.3) states that the regime supported in a pressured stance maximizes the sum of aggregate profits and a times average welfare. It follows that, if such a stance exists, the policy outcome it selects is (generically) unique. Existence requires

$$aW_R < aW_{\tilde{R}} + \sum_{i \in \mathscr{S}_{\tilde{R}}} (\Pi_{i\tilde{R}} - \Pi_{iR})$$

where $\mathscr{S}_{\tilde{R}}$ is the set of lobbies that prefer regime $\tilde{R}$, and R is the regime that satisfies (16.3). In other words, a pressured stance exists whenever positive contributions by the supporters of regime R are needed to induce the government to choose this stance when each opponent of R bids its maximum willingness to pay for the alternative. When this inequality fails, the proponents of R can refrain from offering any contributions with the assurance that the government will nonetheless choose their preferred stance.

It is possible that both a pressured and an unpressured stance will exist for some parameter values. In that event, the two stances may select the same policy outcome. But this need not be the case. Whereas the unpressured stance always endorses the socially preferred regime, the pressured stance may select the regime that harms the average voter. This happens any time the aggregate profit gain from R relative to $\tilde{R}$ exceeds a times the social welfare loss.

In cases where pressured and unpressured stances both exist and support different policy positions, there may be compelling reasons to focus primarily on the pressured stance. In these circumstances, the unpressured stance does not survive as an equilibrium when we allow a limited degree of coordination among the lobbies. In particular, consider the notion of a *coalition-proof equilibrium*, as discussed by Douglas B. Bernheim et al. (1987). This refinement of Nash equilibrium rejects any outcome for which there exists a set of actions by some coalition of players such that (i) each member of the coalition attains a payoff as high or higher than in the Nash equilibrium, given the actions of nonmembers of the coalition; and (ii) the proposed action of each coalition member is a best response to the proposed or given actions of the others. The refinement applies best to situations where players can communicate but cannot make binding agreements. The communication could be used to spell out the entire list of proposed plays by coalition members, so that each would realize that it could gain by following the proposal and that it and the others have no incentive to cheat, assuming that all members do as proposed.

The unpressured stance will fail to be coalition-proof whenever it selects a regime different from the pressured stance. To see why, suppose that (16.2) is satisfied for R and (16.3) is satisfied for $\tilde{R}$. In the unpressured stance, all supporters of R contribute nothing. An industry that is harmed by R could propose a coalition comprising all such industries. It could propose that the members jointly contribute enough so that the total contributions just overcome the government's sensitivity to voter opposition, with no member being asked to contribute more than what it has to gain. Then, given the zero contributions of the nonmembers of this coalition, the government would be induced to choose $\tilde{R}$. Each member of the coalition would benefit from this deviation, and each would see itself as pivotal and so would have no incentive to cheat. Since we have assumed that (16.3) is satisfied for $\tilde{R}$, the collective gains of the coalition members are large enough to allow such a proposal to be designed. Evidently, the unpressured stance rests in these circumstances on the inability of opponents of the chosen regime to coordinate their political activity.

Bernheim and Whinston (1986) have shown that all coalition-proof equilibria in menu auctions select an action from among the set of actions that maximizes the joint welfare of the principals and the agent, and also that any element in this set can be supported as a coalition-proof equilibrium. Here, the government acts as agent for the many interest groups, and condition (16.3) expresses the requirement for joint welfare maximization. Since the regime that maximizes joint welfare always exists, we have proved the following.

Result 3 A coalition-proof stance always exists. This stance supports regime R if and only if condition (16.3) is satisfied.

Results 2 and 3 imply immediately that *all pressured stances are coalition-proof.*

This completes our discussion of the equilibrium interactions in a single polity. To summarize, there always exists at least one unilateral stance. This stance may be pressured or unpressured. When a pressured stance exists, it always supports the (generically) unique regime that maximizes the joint welfare of lobbies and politicians. When an unpressured stance exists, it supports the regime that benefits the average voter. When both exist, they may or may not endorse the same outcome. If they do not, then only the pressured stance will be coalition-proof. In these situations, it will be possible for a coalition of lobbies to upset the unpressured stance by minimal coordination of their political activities.

16.3 Equilibrium Agreements

We turn now to the international negotiation. Our prohibition on exclusions leaves the two governments with little to negotiate about. In principle, they could discuss compensation payments that would be made from one treasury to the other under the terms of a potential agreement. Such compensation schemes do play a part in some regional trade agreements, such as the European Common Market. But transfers still seem the exception rather than the rule (for example, they are not included in the terms of the North American Free Trade Agreement), and even where they are used, they often are limited in scope. While we could include (limited or full) opportunities for compensation in our analysis of FTA's, we choose to focus on the case where such opportunities are unavailable in order to avoid a cumbersome taxonomy.

In the absence of transfers, an FTA requires the unilateral support of both governments. If the lobbies in each country anticipate that the other government will pursue the agreement, they will expect that their own country's political deliberations will determine its fate. Then they will act exactly as described in our analysis of unilateral stances in Section 16.2.[7] In a subgame-perfect Nash equilibrium, all expectations about the behavior of the other government are fulfilled. This justifies the following definition.

Definition 2 An FTA is an *equilibrium agreement* if and only if $R = F$ is a unilateral stance in both countries.

Our objective in this section is to characterize the economic and political conditions in the two countries under which an FTA can arise as an equilibrium outcome.

A central theme will emerge from our analysis. We will argue that the political viability of an FTA requires sufficient "balance" in the potential trade between the parties to the agreement. To motivate this idea, it helps to begin with an extreme case. Suppose that all goods exported by country A in the status quo ante are also exports of country B and that country A has the higher MFN tariff in all of its import-competing sectors. Then country A would not export to country B at all in the event of an agreement. This means that none of the lobbies in A would support the agreement. If most industries would experience enhanced protection, then welfare in A would be likely to fall, in which case there could be no unilateral stance in A in support of the FTA. On the other hand, if most industries would experience reduced protection, then the potential opposition to the agreement from the special interests would be great. The only chance for an FTA in this case of extreme imbalance in potential trade would be if the agreement happened to be welfare-improving and the opposing interests failed to coordinate their lobbying activities or if they were unable to muster enough opposition to block the accord. And even this last scenario would be unlikely, if the initial MFN tariffs also were the outgrowth of a political process.[8]

In order to be more precise about what we mean by balance and also to see how industry conditions influence the political outcome, we turn to a special (but less extreme) case with particular functional forms. We suppose now that the households in both countries share identical utility functions wherein all of the nonnumeraire goods enter symmetrically and each $u_i(\,.\,)$ is quadratic. Then aggregate demand for any good i in country j has the linear form

$$D_i^j(q_i^j) = D - bq_i^j \quad \text{for } i = 1, 2, \ldots, n \quad \text{and} \quad j = A, B. \tag{16.4}$$

Also, aggregate world supply of every good is the same, and the supply in each country is inelastic. We assume that $X_i^A = \theta X$ and $X_i^B = (1 - \theta)X$ in a fraction s of the industries, while $X_i^A = (1 - \theta)X$ and $X_i^B = \theta X$ in the remaining fraction $1 - s$ of the industries. In other words, all industries are mirror images, with country A having the larger supply in some industries and country B the larger supply in the others. Here s measures the extent of imbalance in the number of potential export industries and θ measures the imbalance in output in any one sector. Without further loss of generality we take $\theta > 1/2$ and $s \geq 1/2$.

The viability of an FTA also depends, of course, on the structure of the initial MFN tariffs. So far we have taken these as arbitrary. But it is reasonable to suppose that they too are an equilibrium outcome of a political process. For the purposes of our illustrative example, we will now assume that the MFN tariffs initially protecting the import-competing industries in each country are those that would result from a contribution game similar to the one described here. Assuming that both sets of politicians place the same weight a on aggregate welfare in their objective functions, application of Proposition 1 in Grossman and Helpman (1994a) gives

$$\tau_i^j = 1 + \frac{X_i^j}{ab} \quad \text{for } j = A, B \tag{16.5}$$

for all sectors i that have positive imports in the initial equilibrium.

In this example, different types of outcomes emerge depending on the configuration of parameter values. We will examine three different sets of parameter restrictions. While these possibilities do not exhaust the entire parameter space, they do illustrate all of the different considerations that may come into play.

Restriction 1:

$$\frac{D-b}{X} > 1 + \frac{\theta}{a}.$$

With this restriction on the parameters, all of the nonnumeraire goods are imported in both countries in the initial equilibrium, when the MFN tariffs given in (16.5) apply. Country A has the higher import tariff in the fraction s of industries where its supply is θX, while country B has the higher tariff in the remaining fraction $1 - s$ of industries. This is because the political processes are similar in the two countries, and the special interests in each country are willing to contribute more in their initial bids for MFN protection when they have more output at stake.

Under an FTA, each country would import from its partners all of those goods on which its MFN tariff is higher. This means that A would import a fraction s of the nonnumeraire goods from B, and B would import the remaining fraction $1 - s$ of these goods from A. Moreover, under Restriction 1, the output in the low-tariff country would not suffice to satisfy import demand in the high-tariff country at the latter country's pre-agreement domestic price. Therefore, recalling Table 16.1, all industries would experience enhanced protection under the proposed FTA. It is straightforward to calculate the contribution of sector i to the change in aggregate welfare in each country using the formulas from Subsection 16.1.4. We find

$$
\Delta W_i^j = \begin{cases} -\dfrac{\theta(1-\theta)X^2}{ab} & \text{if } X_i^j = \theta X \\[2ex] \dfrac{\theta(1-\theta)X^2}{ab} & \text{if } X_i^j = (1-\theta)X \end{cases}
\tag{16.6}
$$

for $j = A$, B. Notice that what one country gains in aggregate welfare, the other loses.[9]

We can also calculate the profit changes that would result from the FTA. With all industries experiencing enhanced protection, the various import-competing interests in the high-tariff sectors would not suffer any profit losses. Meanwhile, the factor owners in industries that would export under the agreement would all gain. We have

$$
\Delta \Pi_i^j = \begin{cases} 0 & \text{if } X_i^j = \theta X \\[2ex] \dfrac{(2\theta - 1)(1-\theta)X^2}{ab} & \text{if } X_i^j = (1-\theta)X \end{cases}
\tag{16.7}
$$

for $j = A$, B.

We are now ready to examine the unilateral stances. From (16.6) we see that an unpressured stance can favor an FTA in country A only if $s = 1/2$ (i.e., if the number of potential export industries is exactly the same in each country). If $s = 1/2$, the FTA is welfare-neutral, and the government in A could (marginally) support an agreement without any lobbying on its behalf. But if $s > 1/2$, the welfare loss from the fraction s of high-tariff industries in country A would exceed the welfare gain from the fraction $1 - s$ of low-tariff industries. Some political activity on the part of the beneficiaries would be necessary for the FTA to materialize.

What about the pressured stances? Using (16.6) and (16.7) we find that condition (16.3) indicates pressured support for an agreement in country B for all $s \geq 1/2$ and that the government of country A will be induced to favor the accord if and only if

$$
s \leq \frac{1}{2} + \frac{\theta - \frac{1}{2}}{2\theta - 1 + 2a\theta} < 1.
\tag{16.8}
$$

The inequality in (16.8) will be satisfied for s sufficiently close to 1/2. Then the potential profit gains to the owners of the fraction $1 - s$ of the specific factors will be sufficiently large in the aggregate to outweigh the ·

cost to the average voter. On the other hand, if s is close to 1, then the contributions by supporters of the agreement will not be sufficient to sway the government in the light of the prospective harm to the average voter. For a given value of s, a pressured stance in A is more likely to support the FTA the smaller is the weight a that the government attaches to aggregate welfare, since welfare in A surely falls under the agreement. Finally, the political viability of a potential agreement increases with the extent of supply imbalance in a representative industry, because the potential profit gains for exporters grow more rapidly with θ than do the social welfare losses in the import sectors.

Restriction 2:

$$1 + \frac{1-\theta}{a} > \frac{D-b}{X} > \theta + \frac{\theta}{a}.$$

When this restriction holds, all nonnumeraire goods again are imported by both countries in the preagreement equilibrium. But now, using the tariff formula (16.5), we find that the supply of output in the low-tariff country in each industry is enough to satisfy all demand by the other country at the low-tariff country's price. This means that all industries would experience reduced protection under the agreement.

Again we can calculate the contribution of each sector to the change in aggregate welfare in each country. We find that, for the high-tariff sectors, where there are the offsetting effects of trade creation and trade diversion, the answer depends on the parameter values.[10] Meanwhile, the contribution of the low-tariff sectors in each country to social welfare increases under an FTA, as these all become export sectors.

Summing over all industries, we find that an FTA may increase or decrease aggregate welfare in country A. If the potential export industries are evenly divided ($s = 1/2$), aggregate welfare must rise. Then an unpressured stance favors an FTA in both countries as long as no single import-competing industry has sufficient reason to block it. For this, it is sufficient that the total number of specific factors exceeds four. On the other hand, if $s = 1$, aggregate welfare rises in country A only if the beneficial effect of trade creation in the import-competing sectors is sufficiently large. Thus, even if the special interests that will be hurt by an FTA fail to coalesce into a (noncooperative) coalition, the fate of the agreement remains in doubt.

What if the special-interests groups do become active in the political battle over the FTA? In this case of reduced protection, it is the most politically powerful producers in each country (i.e., those that succeeded in securing high barriers in the initial political equilibrium) that would be harmed by an agreement. Moreover, the potential exporters stand nothing to gain. When we calculate the profit losses for the import-competing industries, we find that for $s = 1/2$ the aggregate profit loss in the $n/2$ high-tariff industries exceeds a times the total welfare gain. Therefore, the pressured stance in each country rejects the FTA. As s increases, industry opposition to the FTA grows in country A, while the potential social benefit from the agreement may rise or fall. But even if it rises, the profit losses grow faster with s than a times the welfare gain. It follows that the pressured stance in A rejects the FTA not only when the industries are evenly divided between the countries, but for all values of $s \in [1/2, 1]$. The international outcome must be a continuation of the status quo if the special interests in A induce a coalition-proof stance.

Restriction 3:

$$\theta > \frac{D - b}{X} > (1 - \theta)\left(1 + \frac{1}{a}\right).$$

In this case the producers in each country with output θX export their product in the initial equilibrium. Since we rule out export subsidies, they receive only the international price for their goods. Meanwhile, the producers with output $(1 - \theta)X$ cannot satisfy domestic demand at the tariff-inclusive domestic price, when the tariff is given by (16.5). These sectors are protected in the initial equilibrium. It can be shown that all industries experience reduced protection under the FTA, so that international prices would prevail in all sectors under a trade agreement.

The export sectors again gain nothing from an FTA. But this time, these sectors also contribute nothing to the change in aggregate welfare, as no tariff revenue is collected on the imports that replace diverted sales. The factor owners in import-competing sectors sacrifice profits under an agreement, while the contribution of these sectors to aggregate welfare expands. We must as usual evaluate the sum of $\Delta\Pi_i^j$ and $a\Delta W_i^j$, but now the sum need only be taken over the import-competing industries in country j. In each such industry, tariff revenue falls due to trade diversion, and a politically motivated tariff is removed. Since the MFN tariffs in (16.5) were themselves set to maximize a political objective function, their elimination must reduce the joint welfare of the lobby and the government. It follows that the pressured stance rejects the agreement in both countries.

Let us summarize what we have learned from this example and comment on how the lessons might extend to more general settings. First, we find that the political viability of an FTA requires s to be close to $1/2$. This is the sense in which potential trade between the countries must be balanced: there must be a sufficient number of potential exporters in each country who will lobby for the agreement, or a sufficient number of sectors with assured welfare gains, to offset the potential losses from trade diversion. This result does not rely on the particulars of our example. Any time an FTA would have most trade flows in one direction, political viability in the importing country will be very much in doubt. Viability then requires a predominance of industries facing reduced protection and also that trade creation would outweigh trade diversion in many of these, so that aggregate gains would be generated by the agreement. Moreover, since reduced protection implies losses for import-competing industries, it requires a coordination failure among the lobbies who would wish to block the accord. Trade imbalances may explain, for example, why the United States has had more difficulty in concluding trade agreements with several Asian trade partners than it has with partners in North America.

Second, the example suggests that political viability may require a sufficient number of industries that would experience enhanced protection as compared with the number facing reduced protection. In the example, an FTA can emerge as a coalition-proof equilibrium for some parameters satisfying Restriction 1, but not for any that satisfy Restrictions 2 or 3. In the first of these cases, enhanced protection is in store for all, and the would-be exporters represent a potential source of support for an agreement. In the second and third cases, the import-competing industries face the prospect of reduced protection and are willing to contribute to block it. Recall that enhanced protection generally means joint welfare losses as a consequence of trade diversion (although such losses do not arise in the example with completely inelastic supplies), while reduced protection generally means joint welfare gains stemming from trade creation. The example thus suggests a more far-reaching conclusion: the conditions needed for the political viability of an FTA may contradict those that ensure its social desirability.[11]

The example delivers this message too starkly. Even in our model, there can be efficiency-enhancing agreements that pass political muster if demand curves are nonlinear. And our model neglects some additional sources of joint welfare gain that need not imply an absence of extra profits for exporters. We have assumed, for example, that all markets are globally integrated and that international prices set the terms of trade prior to any agreement. If, instead, we allowed some goods to have high transport costs (or high trade barriers in the rest of the world), the markets in A and B might initially be segmented from those abroad. Then exporters in one country could gain from bilateral tariff reductions even as prices fell for consumers in the other (see Paul Wonnacott and Ronald Wonnacott, 1981). Similarly, if products were differentiated by country of origin, the importing country could realize welfare gains while the exporters saw their profits rise. Still, there is an important lesson here that is general. Whenever a trade agreement gives rise to trade diversion, there will be narrow interests that enjoy private gains, while costs will be shared by all taxpayers. To the extent that industry interests are better represented in the political process than are taxpayer's interests, trade diversion will enhance political viability while contributing to an inefficient allocation of resources in the two partner countries.

16.4   Industry Exclusions

Governments that are considering a free-trade agreement have some ability to make a pact palatable to opposing interests. They can do so by providing long periods of adjustment to some sectors and by excluding others from the agreement entirely. However, the national governments are bound to clash on the issue of exceptions, because each seeks to preserve protection for some of its politically powerful industries, while each tries to gain market access for all of its potential exporters. An equilibrium agreement is one that reflects the political pressures on each government and also the give-and-take of the bargaining process.

In this section, we show how industry exclusions might make an otherwise impossible FTA politically viable. We also examine the determinants of the number and identity of excluded sectors. We use "exclusions" here to represent not only the granting of permanent exemptions from an agreement, but also as a metaphor for long phase-in periods. The number of such exclusions should not be so large as to violate the GATT stipulation that an FTA must liberalize "substantially all trade."

16.4.1   Unilateral Stances

We begin as before by focusing on the political interactions in a single country. We investigate what type of agreement (if any) a government would choose in response to domestic political pressures, assuming that it could dictate terms to its FTA partner. Of course, an equilibrium agreement need not look anything like the *unilateral stance*; but it helps to understand the political process in one country before turning to the two-country bargaining problem.

The lobbies' contribution schedules now must reflect the various positions that their government might take. A government can choose to reject an agreement entirely, it can pursue an agreement calling for the exclusion of certain sectors, or it can seek an agreement with completely free bilateral trade. In principle, the lobbies might link their contributions to the identities of all entries on the list of excluded sectors. However, in our model, the owners of a specific factor care only about the fate of their own industry. An industry facing the prospect of increased competition from partner imports will prefer that its protection be preserved for as long as possible, while an industry that hopes to find a new or expanded export market will not want to see its products among those excluded from the agreement. We can assume without loss of generality that the special interests distinguish their contribution offers only among outcomes that affect their profits. Each lobby i specifies exactly three numbers, denoted C_{iN}, C_{iE}, and C_{iI}, that represent its campaign gift in the event that the government rejects the FTA, in the event that it concludes an FTA but with industry i excluded from the agreement, and in the event that it concludes an FTA with industry i included in the agreement, respectively.[12] Excluded sectors retain their MFN tariffs once an FTA is enacted.

We define a unilateral stance in much the same way as we did in Section 16.3. In particular, the unilateral stance supports some regime; either the government rejects the agreement entirely ($R = N$) or it opts for an agreement ($R = F$) with a particular set (perhaps empty) of excluded sectors. In an equilibrium stance, the government achieves greater political welfare G than it could under any alternative regime satisfying GATT rules on exclusions. Furthermore, no lobby is able to redesign its offer triplet, given the offers of the other lobbies and the anticipated optimization by the politicians, in such a way as to increase its profits net of contributions.

As McMillan (1993) has argued, GATT rules on the admissibility of free-trade agreements are anything but clear. The requirement that an agreement must liberalize "substantially all trade" can be interpreted to place a limit on the number of industries that can be excluded from an agreement, on the fraction of bilateral trade excluded, on the fraction of total trade excluded, or perhaps on something else. We can cover all of the various possibilities by representing the rule as $\int_{i \in \mathscr{E}} T_i \, di \leq T$, where $\mathscr{E}$

is the set of excluded industries, T_i is the size of sector i according to the indicated measure, and T is the exogenous limit imposed by the constraint. If, for example, the rule places a limit on the number of excluded industries, then $T_i = 1$ for all i, whereas if it places a limit on the fraction of excluded trade, then T_i is the share of industry i in total preagreement trade. By writing the rule as an integral, we of course assume a continuum of sectors. This allows us to avoid "integer problems," which would complicate the exposition without furthering understanding.[13]

In describing the unilateral stances that can emerge as equilibrium government responses to political pressures, it will prove convenient to refer to the *politically optimal set of exclusions*, $\mathscr{E}(T)$. We define this set as follows. First, we order the industries so that $i \in [0, n]$ and $g_i \equiv (\Delta\Pi_i + a\Delta W_i)/T_i$ increases with i. Second, we assign the label i_0 to the sector with the lowest index such that $g_i = 0$. If $g_i > 0$ for all i, then $i_0 = 0$. Finally, we define $\hat{i}$ so that

$$\int_0^{\hat{i}} T_i \, di = T.$$

Definition 3 The set of *politically optimal exclusions* $\mathscr{E}(T)$ is the set of sectors i such that $i \in [0, \min(i_0, \hat{i})]$.

This definition requires that, for any industry in the set $\mathscr{E}(T)$, the joint gain to the government and the factor owners from liberalizing bilateral trade in good i must be nonpositive and in fact more negative (when normalized by the "size" of the sector) than for any sector not in the set.

Our first result concerns coalition-proof stances.

Result 4 There exists a coalition-proof stance with $R = F$ if and only if

$$\int_{i \in \mathscr{E}(T)} (\Pi_{iN} + aW_{iN}) \, di + \int_{i \notin \mathscr{E}(T)} (\Pi_{iF} + aW_{iF}) \, di \geq \int_i (\Pi_{iN} + aW_{iN}) \, di.$$

$$(16.9)$$

In this stance, the sectors $i \in \mathscr{E}(T)$ are excluded from the agreement.

The left-hand side of (16.9) gives the joint welfare of all lobbies and the government under an FTA with excluded sectors $\mathscr{E}(T)$, while the right-hand side gives the joint welfare of these parties in the status quo. The result follows from theorem 3 of Bernheim and Whinston (1986), which states that every coalition-proof equilibrium in a menu auction selects an action from among those that maximize the joint welfare of the principals and the agent.[14] In the coalition-proof unilateral stance, the constraint on the size of the excluded set will bind if and only if there exists more than a measure T of industries (measured in the relevant way; i.e., by number, trade volume, etc.), in which the factor owners would lose more in profits from being included in the agreement than a times what the average voter would gain. The excluded industries are those that are most politically sensitive, in the sense that their inclusion imposes the greatest cost to specific factor owners and politicians taken together.

The coalition-proof stance can be supported by "truthful offers" in which (i) each lobby bids the same amount for an exclusion as for an outright rejection of the agreement ($C_{iE} = C_{iN} \geq 0$ for all i); (ii) all industries $j \notin \mathscr{E}(T)$ bid for an exclusion exactly what they stand to lose (if anything) by being included in the agreement; and (iii) all industries $i \in \mathscr{E}(T)$ bid for an exclusion at most what they stand to save by having their trade barriers preserved, and exactly what is needed to ensure that they are among those excluded. This stance may be *pressured*, in the sense that at least some of the industries that stand to gain from the FTA contribute actively on its behalf (i.e., $C_{il} > 0$ for some i). The joint contributions of these (export) industries then are just sufficient to overcome the political resistance to the agreement.

Inequality (16.9) may hold even when inequality (16.4) fails for $R = F$. That is, the coalition-proof stance may endorse an FTA with exclusions in cases where the agreement would be defeated in the absence of exclusions. The exclusions allow the government to avoid the biggest political costs associated with an FTA, and the net political gain may be positive once these particularly exposed sectors are sheltered from the agreement.

When inequality (16.9) does fail, a coalition of industries can form to block any proposed FTA. Moreover, the contributions that block a given proposal require no monitoring (they are best responses) and leave each coalition member at least as well off as under the agreement. However, as before, the interests that oppose the FTA may fail to achieve the required degree of coordination. In this event, the politics may give rise to a unilateral stance in support of an FTA, even though the interests that stand to benefit from the agreement contribute nothing to further its cause. We will refer to such a stance with all $C_{il} = 0$ as *unpressured*.[15] The next result gives the necessary and sufficient conditions for the existence of such a stance.

Result 5   There exists an unpressured stance with $R = F$ if and only if

$$\int_{i \in \mathscr{E}(T)} a W_{iN} \, di + \int_{i \notin \mathscr{E}(T)} a W_{iF} \, di + C \geq \int_{i} a W_{iN} \, di \qquad (16.10)$$

where $C = \int_{i \in \mathscr{E}(T)} \max[0, a(W_{iF} - W_{iN}) + \max_{j \notin \mathscr{E}(T)}(-T_j g_j)]\, di.$ In   this
stance, the sectors $i \in \mathscr{E}(T)$ are excluded from the agreement.

The proof of this result is available from the authors upon request.[16]
Intuitively, C represents the total amount of contributions by lobbies that
are excluded from the agreement when each such lobby gives the minimum amount that ensures it a place on the list of exclusions (given the
equilibrium bids of the others). Each excluded lobby must compensate the
government for the political cost of any loss in aggregate welfare that
results from its placement on the list of exclusions. This is reflected in the
term $a(W_{iF} - W_{iN})$. It must also bid enough to overcome the offers of
those lobbies that fail to secure a place on the list. Each lobby j not
included in $\mathscr{E}(T)$ bids $C_{jE} = \Pi_{jN} - \Pi_{jF}$ for a potential exclusion, so $-T_j g_j$
reflects the opportunity cost to the government of leaving lobby j off of
the list. If for lobby i, $a(W_{iF} - W_{iN}) + \max_{j \notin \mathscr{E}(T)}(-T_j g_j) < 0$, then the
government would wish to exclude this lobby even without any positive
inducement, in which case the lobby contributes nothing (i.e., $C_{iE} = 0$).

Result 5 is analogous to Result 1. In each case, the unpressured stance
in favor of F can exist because the opponents of the agreement fail to coordinate their political activities to further their common cause. When
each lobby expects others to offer little or nothing for a total rejection of
the agreement, no single lobby among those slated for inclusion may
have enough at stake to warrant its acting unilaterally. Of course, in the
case of Result 5, the stake of any single lobby is assumed to be small, and
so the unpressured stance exists whenever the agreement coupled with
the minimal contributions from the excluded sectors is palatable to the
politicians.

From Results 4 and 5 we see that all unilateral stances in support of an
FTA share the same set of (politically optimal) exclusions. It is easy to see
why. Suppose, to the contrary, that there existed a unilateral stance in
which some mass of sectors $i \in \mathscr{E}(T)$ were not exempted and that perhaps
some others $j \notin \mathscr{E}(T)$ were excluded in their place. First, if there were no
such j's, then each such i would be willing to bid up to $\Pi_{iN} - \Pi_{iF}$ in order
to secure an exclusion. The government would add i to the exclusion list
if the contribution offer were large enough to compensate for the political
cost, $a(W_{iF} - W_{iN})$. But according to the definition of $\mathscr{E}(T)$, we must have
$\Pi_{iN} - \Pi_{iF} \geq a(W_{iF} - W_{iN})$, because $g_i < 0$ for all $i \in \mathscr{E}(T)$. Second, if
there were some mass of j's on the list of exclusions in the place of the i's,
choose some subsets of the i's (say $\tilde{I}$) and the j's (say $\tilde{J}$) such that
$\int_{i \in \tilde{I}} T_i\, di = \int_{j \in \tilde{J}} T_j\, dj.$ The j's in $\tilde{J}$ would have bid at most $\int_{j \in \tilde{J}}(\Pi_{jN} - \Pi_{jF})\, dj$

for their places on the list of exemptions. Again, the definition of $\mathscr{E}(T)$ ensures that the lobbies $i \in \tilde{I}$ could have bid something less than their potential profit gain, and this would have been enough to induce the government to exclude these sectors instead of those in $\tilde{J}$.

16.4.2 Bargaining over Industry Exclusions

We turn now to the international negotiation of an FTA that might exclude certain industries. We will argue first that the ability to issue some exemptions can save an FTA that otherwise would not be politically viable.[17] Then we will discuss the considerations that determine the number and identity of the excluded sectors.

The fact that exemptions can save an FTA follows almost immediately from the analysis in the previous section. We have seen that the prospects for a unilateral stance in support of an FTA improve when a government has the flexibility to issue exemptions. The exemptions allow the government to capture the support of some potential losers, while at the same time winning the favor of exporters (and perhaps voters) who would benefit from the agreement. Of course, in a negotiating situation, neither country is likely to be in a position to dictate the terms of an agreement. Yet the logic of our argument continues to apply. A successful negotiation requires that *some* agreement be identified that both governments prefer on political grounds to the status quo ante. Exclusions improve the prospects for this, because they can by "sold" to some powerful import-competing interests in exchange for their support.

Which sectors will be granted exclusions in an equilibrium agreement? The answer depends on the particulars of the negotiating process. We appeal here to the simple and familiar Nash bargaining solution in order to illustrate some of the considerations that come into play.[18]

Suppose that the equilibrium agreement is designed to maximize a geometric weighted average of the "surpluses" of the two negotiating governments. Moreover, let the lobbies anticipate this bargaining outcome at the time that they make their contribution offers. Since the governments always have the option to walk away from the negotiating table, their surpluses are calculated with reference to the political welfare they would achieve by setting $R = N$. More formally, the equilibrium agreement can be represented by a set of indicator variables, α_i, where $\alpha_i = 0$ implies that sector i is included in the FTA ($i \in I$) while $\alpha_i = 1$ implies that sector i is excluded from the agreement ($i \in \mathscr{E}$). The Nash bargaining solution solves expression (16.11), below, subject to the constraint that $\int \alpha_i T_i \, di \leq T$, where

β^J is the Nash weight attached to the surplus of government J and $\bar{G}^J \equiv \int (a^J W_{iN}^J + C_{iN}^J)\, di$ is the political welfare that accrues to government J if it chooses to stay with the status quo.

$$\max_{\{\alpha_i\}} \sum_{J=A,B} \beta^J \log\left\{ \int_i [(1 - \alpha_i)(a^J W_{iF}^J + C_{i1}^J) + \alpha_i(a^J W_{iN}^J + C_{iE}^J)]\, di - \bar{G}^J \right\}$$

(16.11)

To find the solution to this problem, we can treat the α_i's for the moment as if they could vary continuously between 0 and 1. Then the first-order conditions for maximizing (16.11) imply

$$\sum_{J=A,B} \frac{\beta^J}{G^J - \bar{G}^J} \left[\frac{(a^J W_{iF}^J + C_{i1}^J) - (a^J W_{iN}^J + C_{iE}^J)}{T_i} \right] \geq -\lambda \quad \text{when } \alpha_i = 0$$

$$\sum_{J=A,B} \frac{\beta^J}{G^J - \bar{G}^J} \left[\frac{(a^J W_{iF}^J + C_{i1}^J) - (a^J W_{iN}^J + C_{iE}^J)}{T_i} \right] \leq -\lambda \quad \text{when } \alpha_i = 1$$

and $\lambda \geq 0$, where $G^J \equiv \int_{i \in \mathcal{E}} (a^J W_{iN}^J + C_{iE}^J)\, di + \int_{i \in I} (a^J W_{iF}^J + C_{i1}^J)\, di$ is the equilibrium political welfare of government J in the Nash bargain, and λ is the Lagrange multiplier associated with the limited-exclusions constraint. It follows that if industries are ordered according to the term on the left-hand side of the first two inequalities, then the Nash agreement excludes all sectors with indexes less than or equal to some critical cutoff value.

These conditions give the decision rule in terms of the industry-specific contribution offers. It would be more revealing to have an ordering that depends only on aggregates and on the supply and demand conditions in the various industries. To this end, we will establish the following result.

Result 6 Let the industries be ordered so that $\omega^A g_i^A + \omega^B g_i^B$ is increasing with i, where $\omega^J \equiv \beta^J/(G^J - \bar{G}^J)$ and $g_i^J \equiv (\Delta\Pi_i^J + a\Delta W_i^J)/T_i$. Then the FTA that solves the Nash bargaining problem excludes all industries $i \in [0, i^*]$, for some $i^* \geq 0$.

The proof relies on the fact that each small lobby takes G^J and $\bar{G}^J$ as constant in constructing its contribution offer. Each industry expects to be included in the FTA if its offer and that of the same industry in the other country are such that

$$\sum_{J=A,B} \omega^J [a^J (W_{iF}^J - W_{iN}^J) + C_{i1}^J - C_{iE}^J]/T_i < -\lambda$$

and to be excluded if the direction of inequality is reversed. There are several cases to consider.

First consider an excluded industry ($j \in \mathscr{E}$), where the special interests in the importing country (say A, for concreteness) make a positive contribution to secure the exclusion ($C_{jE}^A > 0$). We know that these contributions must be lowered to the point where the negotiators are just marginally willing to exclude the sector, that is, where

$$\sum_{J=A,B} \omega^J [a^J(W_{jF}^J - W_{jN}^J) + C_{jI}^J - C_{iE}^J]/T_j = -\lambda.$$

The industry's payment does not exceed its profit differential; $C_{jE}^A \leq \Pi_{jN}^A - \Pi_{jF}^A$. We know also that the export interest in country B, which would rather not see its product on the list of exclusions, must bid up to the full profit differential to avoid this outcome ($C_{jI}^B = \Pi_{jF}^B - \Pi_{jN}^B$). Otherwise, a slight increase in its offer will be profitable for this lobby. Combining these facts, we have $\omega^A g_j^A + \omega^B g_j^B \leq -\lambda$ for this excluded industry.

Next consider an included industry ($k \in I$), where the special interests in the exporting country (again A, for concreteness) contribute positively to ensure that their product is not among those excluded ($C_{kI}^A > 0$). Again, the negotiators must be left indifferent between including this sector in the agreement and not. This time we must have $C_{kI}^A \leq \Pi_{kF}^A - \Pi_{kN}^A$, and (by a similar argument as before) $C_{kE}^B = \Pi_{kN}^B - \Pi_{kF}^B$. So now we find $\omega^A g_k^A + \omega^B g_k^B \geq -\lambda$ for this included industry.

Third consider an excluded industry ℓ, where the import-competing interests in (say) A make no contribution; $C_{\ell E}^A = 0$. Since this is an import-competing industry, we must have $\Pi_{\ell N}^A - \Pi_{\ell F}^A \geq 0$. Also, we know that the export industry in B does not find it profitable to bid what it would take to ensure that its product is not among those excluded. That is, the bid $C_{\ell I}^B$ that would make

$$\omega^B C_{\ell I}^B + \sum_{J=A,B} \omega^J a^J (W_{\ell F}^J - W_{\ell N}^J) = -\lambda T_\ell$$

exceeds $\Pi_{\ell F}^B - \Pi_{\ell N}^B$. These facts again imply that $\omega^A g_\ell^A + \omega^B g_\ell^B \leq -\lambda$ for this excluded industry.

Finally, the argument for an included industry in which the export interests do not make any positive contribution is analogous to the previous one. So, in each case, if $\omega^A g_i^A + \omega^B g_i^B$ exceeds $-\lambda$, the industry is covered by the FTA, whereas if this magnitude falls short of $-\lambda$ the industry appears on the list of exclusions. Result 6 follows immediately.

The result reveals that the same factors that dictate the politically optimal set of exclusions in a single country also enter into the determination of the set of exclusions in a Nash bargain. In each country, a sector's political "clout" depends upon the effect that the FTA would have on the sum of profits and a times aggregate welfare, normalized for the sector's size (as measured by T_i). If this number (represented by g_i^J) is positive, it means that there is a potential political gain for country J from having the sector included in any free-trade agreement. If it is negative, then it would be politically desirable to leave it out. In the unilateral stance, the government excludes only those sectors whose inclusion would be politically damaging and, among those, the ones that would generate the greatest political harm. In the Nash bargain, on the other hand, the politics in both countries must be taken into account.

The Nash solution takes a weighted sum of the political cost/benefit measures for the two countries. The same weights apply in comparing all of the different industries. They reflect the relative bargaining abilities of the two sets of negotiators (as captured in the Nash framework by the weighting parameters β^A and β^B) and the relative surpluses that the two governments attain under the FTA as compared to the status quo. As usual, a government that has a relatively stronger threat point (a high $\bar{G}^J$) finds its interests weighted more heavily in the final bargain. So, for example, the harm that an FTA might bring to some import-competing industries in country A will be given greater consideration, and the gains from improved market access for country-B exporters will receive less consideration, the greater is $\bar{G}^A$ and the smaller $\bar{G}^B$. The $\bar{G}^J$'s in turn reflect the aggregate welfare that country J achieves in the status quo with no FTA and the contributions that the government would receive from its import-competing sector if it rejected the agreement entirely. If $\bar{G}^A$ is very large, for example, then ω^A will be large, and only import-competing industries in country A (which may have $g_i^A < 0$) will be candidates for exclusion from the agreement. The same would be true if β^A were large.

When the two governments' bargaining situations are relatively symmetric ($\omega^A \cong \omega^B$), then the agreement compares the political benefit to one country from having an exporting sector included with the possible cost to the other in terms of lost profits and forgone tariff revenue. If, for example, the sector would experience enhanced protection, the potential gains to the exporting industry may be large, while the import-competing industry would suffer no losses at all. Such a sector would probably not find its way onto the list of exclusions, unless the prospective welfare loss for the importing country due to the trade diversion were exceptionally large. By contrast, a sector that would experience reduced protection may well be considered for the exclusion list, especially if the prospective consumer-surplus gains the importing country are modest. Then the political benefit to the exporting country from including the sector would be small (because the export industry reaps no extra profits) while the fallout from losses that would befall the import-competing producers may be great. Finally, note that only industries with $\omega^A g_i^A + \omega^B g_i^B < 0$ are candidates for exclusions, and the constraint on the size of the exclusion set binds only if there is a sufficient mass (appropriately measured) of such sectors.

16.5   Conclusions

We have examined the conditions under which a free-trade agreement might emerge as an equilibrium outcome of a negotiation between politically minded governments. The governments, we imagine, respond to political pressures from industry special interests but also pay some heed to the plight of the average voter.

If an FTA must completely liberalize trade among the partner countries, a particular government might endorse an agreement in two types of situations. The first arises when the FTA would generate substantial welfare gains for the average voter and adversely affected interest groups fail to coordinate their efforts to defeat the accord. The second arises when the agreement would create profit gains for actual or potential exporters in excess of the losses that would be suffered by import-competing industries, plus the political cost of any welfare harm that might be inflicted on the average voter.

A free-trade agreement requires the assent of both governments. We have found that this outcome is most likely when there is relative balance in the potential trade between the partner countries and when the agreement affords enhanced protection rather than reduced protection to most sectors. With enhanced protection, an exporting industry captures the benefits of the high domestic prices in the partner country. With reduced protection, an import-competing industry sees its domestic price fall as a result of the duty-free imports from the partner. Whereas reduced protection may involve some trade creation, enhanced protection gives rise only to trade diversion. Thus, the conditions that enhance the viability of a potential agreement also raise the likelihood that the agreement would reduce aggregate social welfare.

If some industries can be excluded from an FTA, the prospects for an agreement improve. Each government would wish to exclude those sectors whose inclusion would impose on it the greatest political costs. Political costs reflect either the fierce opposition of the import-competing interests or the harm that would be suffered by the average voter in the face of inefficient trade diversion. By excluding some sensitive sectors, a government may be able to diffuse the opposition to an FTA.

In a bargaining situation, the equilibrium agreement reflects the political pressures felt by both negotiating governments. We examined the Nash bargaining solution and found that exclusions are granted to industries for which a weighted sum of the political benefit of market access in the exporting country and the (possible) political cost of more intense import competition in the importing country is most negative. Both the political benefit and the political cost are measured by a weighted sum of the change in industry profits and the change in average welfare in going from the status quo to bilateral free trade. The weights on benefits in one country and costs in the other reflect the negotiating abilities of the two governments (i.e., the "Nash weights") and the political welfare that would accrue to the two governments if they rejected the agreement entirely.

We conducted all of our analysis under the restrictive (but somewhat realistic) assumption that governments cannot offer direct, treasury-to-treasury, transfer payments as compensation for any political costs associated with an agreement. It would be a simple matter to redo our analysis for the case in which such transfers are feasible. The more interesting and difficult question in the political economy of international relations concerns the reasons why compensation payments have played such a limited role in most trade negotiations.

Appendix

Contributions to Foreign Governments

In the main text we maintained the assumption that an interest group can offer contributions only to its own, native government. Now we relax this assumption and allow lobbies in each country to seek influence over the other's policy. We examine the conditions under which an FTA without exclusions can emerge as an equilibrium outcome, and we compare the scope for such agreements with the case when politicians are prohibited from accepting gifts from abroad.

An FTA can emerge as an equilibrium outcome in one of three different ways. First, both governments may support the agreement as an unpressured stance. Second, both may support it as a pressured stance. Third, one government may favor the FTA as an unpressured position, while the other is being pressured into such support. We discuss each of these possibilities in turn.

An FTA can result without pressure in either country if and only if

$$a^J(W_F^J - W_N^J) \geq \max[0, \max_i(\Pi_{iN}^A - \Pi_{iF}^A), \max_i(\Pi_{iN}^B - \Pi_{iF}^B)]$$

$$\text{for } J = A \text{ and } J = B. \tag{16.A1}$$

In words, the FTA must offer aggregate welfare gains to both electorates; and there can be no single import-competing industry in either country that stands to lose so much under the agreement that it could profitably block the accord with contributions to one government *or the other*. Clearly, this condition is more restrictive than the analogous one in the situation without cross-country contributions [compare (16.2)]. Without foreign contributions, we required only that it be unprofitable for any lobby to turn its own government against the accord. Now an import-competing industry may succeed politically by offering a big enough gift to the foreign politicians, even if it is unwilling to pay what it would take to win over its own government.

If an FTA emerges as a pressured stance in both countries, then both governments will be left indifferent to the pact. Also, each lobby that will lose under the agreement offers contributions to each government that exhaust its potential to benefit by preserving the status quo. This is because each such lobby could block the pact by swaying either one of the two governments, and no such lobby needs to ante up its offer when both governments actually endorse $R = F$. Finally, no lobby that will benefit from the agreement pays the two governments combined more than what it stands to gain under the FTA. Combining the three equalities and the inequality, we find that an equilibrium outcome with pressured stances in both countries in support of the regime F requires

$$a^A W_F^A + a^B W_F^B + \sum_{i,J} \Pi_{iF}^J \geq a^A W_N^A + a^B W_N^B + \sum_{i,J} \Pi_{iN}^J$$

$$+ \sum_{i \in \mathscr{S}_{N,J}} (\Pi_{iN}^J - \Pi_{iF}^J). \tag{16.A2}$$

There are offsetting considerations at play when comparing this condition to the analogous one that applied before. On the one hand, the export interests in each country can enter into the political battle abroad and possibly help their allies to overcome resistance to the agreement that the latter could not defeat alone. The force of this can be seen by noting that, even if (16.3) does not hold separately for both $J = A$ and $J = B$, the left-hand side of (16.A2) may nonetheless exceed the sum of the first three terms on the right-hand side. On the other hand, the import-competing interests in each country have the opportunity to voice their opposition in both. Thus, even if (16.3) does hold for both $J = A$ and $J = B$, condition (16.A2) may fail due to the presence of the fourth term on the right. In short, an ambiguity arises in comparing the alternative political situations: the presence of foreign contributions may make an FTA politically viable that would not otherwise be so, but it also may negate the viability of an agreement that could emerge as a political equilibrium without foreign influences.

The final outcome to consider is one where government J supports the agreement as an unpressured stance, while government K supports the agreement as a result of political pressure. In country J, a condition like (16.A1) must be satisfied: the FTA must improve national welfare there; and no single lobby representing an import-competing industry in either country should be able to reverse the government's unpressured stance. Again, this condition is somewhat more stringent than the corresponding one that applied without foreign contributions. In country K, the government is left indifferent, the import-competing interests in both countries offer their full profit differential in an effort to block the pact, while the export interests offer at most what they stand to gain. These requirements imply

$$a^K W_F^K + \sum_{i,J} \Pi_{iF}^J \geq a^K W_N^K + \sum_{i,J} \Pi_{iN}^J \tag{16.A3}$$

which may be more or less stringent than the corresponding condition in the absence of foreign contributions. Suppose, for example, that government A would support the agreement in an unpressured stance, and consider the outcome of the political contest in country B. Allowing foreign contributions enhances the prospect for a pressured stance with $R^B = F$ if $\Sigma_i \Pi_{iF}^A \geq \Sigma_i \Pi_{iN}^A$ and reduces it otherwise. The cross-border contributions bring foreign interests into play in country B's political battle, which strengthens one side or the other depending upon which interests in country A have more at stake in the decision.

Notes

Financial support was provided by the National Science Foundation, the U.S.–Israel Binational Science Foundation, and the CEPR. Grossman also gratefully acknowledges the John S. Guggenheim Memorial Foundation, the Sumitomo Bank Fund, the Daiwa Bank Fund, and the Center of International Studies at Princeton University. We thank Raquel Fernandez, Paul Krugman, Torsten Persson, Dani Rodrik, and two anonymous referees for helpful comments.

1. We adopt the convention that $\tau_i^j = 1$ for the numeraire good 0 and for any goods that are exported by country j in the initial equilibrium.

2. We recognize that this assumption is not without fault. Martin Richardson (1993) has shown, for example, that countries may have reason to *lower* their external tariffs after completing a trade agreement. A more complete analysis—which would allow for an additional stage of tariff-setting after the FTA issue was resolved—would certainly be desirable but is beyond the scope of this chapter.

3. In Grossman and Helpman (1994a, 1995) we allow for the possibility that some sectors may fail to organize for political action, although we take the set of organized lobbies as exogenous in our analysis. Here, for simplicity, we assume that all sectors are organized.

4. Alternatively, we could use the welfare of the median voter, rather than that of the mean voter, as an argument in the government's objective function. The difference is that the median individual owns none of any industry-specific factor. The analysis would proceed similarly, except that W would be defined in (16.1) to exclude aggregate profits. See Grossman and Helpman (1994a) for further discussion of the government's objective function.

5. We choose to ignore in the main text the possibility that interest groups may offer contributions to a foreign government. Although such contributions do sometimes occur, the scope for interest groups to influence foreign government's decisions generally is quite limited. This may be because politicians regard foreign gifts as tainted money and so place a lower value on them in their political objective function. In any event, we discuss the differences that arise when interest groups can give to either government in the Appendix.

6. For each lobby, the strategy of bidding zero for all outcomes weakly dominates any strategy with a bid in excess of what the lobby stands to gain under its preferred regime. Our assumption serves to rule out weakly dominated strategies.

7. If the Nash equilibrium entails a continuation of the status quo, then lobbies in at least one country must expect that the other government will oppose the FTA at the international talks. These lobbies will contribute nothing to block the agreement, because they will believe it to be doomed in any case. This means that a pressured stance against an FTA will be observed in an international equilibrium in at most one country.

8. We will see that, if the MFN tariffs are the result of a political process similar to the one assumed to precede the negotiation of the FTA, then the joint welfare of the government and the lobby must fall in any import-competing industry where a tariff rate is lowered. This means that no pressured stance could support an FTA if all industries were import-competing and all experienced reduced protection under an FTA.

9. Joint social welfare in the two countries does not change, because outputs are fixed in each country and consumer prices do not change, so neither do demands. With a fixed allocation of resources in each country, only the distribution of the industry surplus can be affected by the FTA.

10. The details of this and succeeding calculations may be found in Grossman and Helpman (1994b).

11. Albert O. Hirschman (1981) made a similar point in his prescient discussion of the dynamics of the European Community.

12. In a world with differentiated products and two-way trade, we would need to allow for the possibility that an agreement removes one country's barrier to imports of good i, but not the other's. Here, trade in any one good is unidirectional, with imports going from the low-tariff country to the high-tariff country. In this context, an industry exclusion means that the high-tariff country retains its barrier to imports from its FTA partner.

13. Integer problems may arise, because sectors must be excluded wholly or not at all. With large sectors, a ranking of industries according to their (size-adjusted) political clout would not fully determine the list of exclusions, because some potential "last" entry on the list might cause the constraint to be violated while another (smaller) sector would not.

14. Note that $\mathscr{E}(T)$ maximizes $\int_{i \in \mathscr{E}} (\Pi_{iN} + aW_{iN})\, di + \int_{i \notin \mathscr{E}} (\Pi_{iF} + aW_{iF})\, di$ among all sets $\tilde{\mathscr{E}}$ that have $\int_{i \in \tilde{\mathscr{E}}} T_i\, di \leq T$.

15. It is unpressured in the sense that the government's decision to pursue the agreement elicits no contributions from beneficiaries. The government may, however, collect contributions from some or all of the industries that are granted exclusions.

16. In Grossman and Helpman (1994b) we proved a similar result for the case of a finite number of sectors, where GATT rules are taken to imply a restriction on the number of elements in the set of excluded sectors. With sectors of finite size, we must allow for the possibility that a single sector may be able to block the agreement even if it does not coordinate its political activities with the others.

17. It appears, for example, that the NAFTA was saved by last-minute concessions granted to U.S. sugar producers and citrus growers in the form of exclusions from the agreement.

18. In Grossman and Helpman (1994b) we used an alternating-offer bargaining model to establish two propositions. First, we showed that an FTA with exclusions can be an equilibrium outcome in an explicit bargaining model, even if the unique equilibrium when exclusions are prohibited entails a continuation of the status quo. Second, all exclusions may apply to the imports of a single country, if that country's government is the only one that would reject an all-inclusive FTA.

References

Bernheim, B. Douglas; Peleg, Bezalel and Whinston, Michael D. "Coalition-Proof Nash Equilibria I: Concepts." *Journal of Economic Theory*, June 1987, *42*(1), pp. 1–12.

Bernheim, B. Douglas and Whinston, Michael D. "Menu Auctions, Resource Allocation, and Economic Influence." *Quarterly Journal of Economics*, February 1986, *101*(1), pp. 1–31.

Cowhey, Peter. "'States' and 'Politics' in American Foreign Economic Policy," in J. S. Odell and T. D. Willett, eds., *International trade policies: Gains from exchange between economics and political science*. Ann Arbor: University of Michigan Press, 1990, pp. 225–51.

Grossman, Gene M. and Helpman, Elhanan. "Protection for Sale." *American Economic Review*, September 1994a, *84*(4), pp. 833–50.

————. "The Politics of Free Trade Agreements." Discussion Paper in Economics No. 166, Woodrow Wilson School of Public and International Affairs, Princeton University, 1994b.

————. "Trade Wars and Trade Talks." *Journal of Political Economy*, 1995 (forthcoming).

Hirschman, Albert O. *Essays in trespassing: Economics to politics and beyond.* Cambridge: Cambridge University Press, 1981.

Krueger, Anne O. "Free Trade Agreements as Protectionist Devices: Rules of Origin." National Bureau of Economic Research (Cambridge, MA) Working Paper No. 4352, 1993.

McMillan, John. "Does Regional Integration Foster Open Trade? Economic Theory and GATT's Article XXIV," in K. Anderson and R. Blackhurst, eds., *Regional integration and the global trading system.* London: Harvester Wheatsheaf, 1993, pp. 292–310.

Olson, Mancur. *The logic of collective action,* Cambridge, MA: Harvard University Press, 1965.

Putnam, Robert. "Diplomacy and Domestic Politics: The Logic of Two level Games." *International Organization,* Summer 1988, 43(3), pp. 427–60.

Richardson, Martin. "Some Implications of Internal Trade in a Free Trade Area." Working Paper No. 92-01, Georgetown University, 1992.

————. "Endogenous Protection and Trade Diversion." *Journal of International Economics,* May 1993, 34(3–4), pp. 309–24.

Wonnacott, Paul and Wonnacott, Ronald. "Is Unilateral Tariff Reduction Preferable to a Customs Union? The Curious Case of the Missing Foreign Tariffs." *American Economic Review,* June 1981, 71(3), pp. 704–14.

17

A Political-Economy Analysis of Free-Trade Areas and Customs Unions

Arvind Panagariya and
Ronald Findlay

Following Viner's (1950) lead, trade theorists have generally treated trade policy as exogenous in evaluating the welfare effects of preferential trading arrangements. The general approach has been to start with a tariff-distorted equilibrium and ask whether a particular set of preferential tariff reductions between union partners is welfare-improving for each participating country, the union, and the world as a whole.[1]

The recent revival of regionalism around the world, particularly the North American Free Trade Agreement (NAFTA), has led trade theorists to take a fresh look at the theory of regional economic integration. Today the world trading system is far more complex than that represented in the stylized, Vinerian models. An important dimension of this complexity is the endogeneity of trade policies.[2] In most countries trade policies are the result of complex interactions between the government and interest groups. Sometimes governments themselves are not benign, welfare-maximizing entities and pursue objectives other than welfare maximization. This endogenous nature of trade policy, richly analyzed in a large number of contributions under the rubric of "political economy of trade policy," has important implications for the theory of regional economic integration.[3]

This chapter honors Jagdish Bhagwati by examining formally two ideas espoused by him in the area of economic integration and endogenous trade policy. These ideas, contained in Bhagwati (1993), can be summarized as follows: First, if trade policy is endogenous, reduced protection between member countries within a regional integration scheme is likely to be accompanied by increased protection against outside countries. As a corollary, a regional arrangement that appears welfare improving at first

Originally published, as chapter 13, in *The Political Economy of Trade Reform: Essays in Honor of Jagdish Bhagwati* (Cambridge, MA: MIT Press, 1996), 265–287.

sight may turn out to be a welfare-reducing proposition. Second, between a free-trade area (FTA) and customs union (CU), the latter is likely to be less protectionist and welfare superior.

We examine these ideas within the three-good, three-country, small-union Meade (1955) model with the modification that trade policy is endogenous. We demonstrate that, as conjectured by Bhagwati (1993), the introduction of preferential trading can indeed raise protection against imports from the rest of the world. We also examine Meade's original result on welfare implications of preferential trading within our model. According to that result the introduction of preferential trading is welfare improving provided that the excess demand for the union partner's good exhibits substitutability with respect to the excess demand for the exportable. The substitutability assumption ensures that a reduction in the tariff on imports from the partner leads to an expansion of exports and hence a reduction in the anti-trade bias in the economy. In our model, since preferential trading leads to increased protection against the outside country, the substitutability assumption is no longer sufficient to guarantee trade expansion or welfare improvement.

Turning to a comparison of FTAs and CUs, suppose that the two countries are symmetric in the sense that they choose the same external tariff under a FTA. We show that in this case the common external tariff is lower and welfare higher for both countries under a CU than FTA. This result follows from the free-rider problem in lobbying under a CU not present under a FTA. In the asymmetric case with different tariffs in the two countries under a FTA, the common external tariff under a CU is lower than the higher tariff under the FTA but may or may not be lower than the lower tariff. The country with the higher tariff under the FTA is better off under a CU than under the FTA. But the same may or may not hold true for the other country. Under a CU the larger the number of members in the union the more acute the free-rider problem and the lower the common external tariff. Ceteris paribus, the larger the number of members in the union the more likely that all members enjoy a higher welfare under a CU than FTA.

Recently Grossman and Helpman (1995a), de Melo, Panagariya, and Rodrik (1993) and Richardson (1993a, 1993b, 1994) have considered economic integration in models of endogenous policy formulation. Of these, Richardson (1994) is most directly relevant to our study. Richardson compares FTAs and CUs and arrives at results similar to ours. A key limitation of his model is that it allows for only two goods. Given the nature of the problem, this forces him to assume that the potential members export and import the same goods. Within this setup there is no trade between the two countries in the absence of a FTA and hence no compelling reason for economic integration. In our model there are three goods and each potential member exports to as well as imports from the other in the absence of economic integration. Therefore economic integration serves as a natural instrument for a mutual exchange of market access.

On the positive side, Richardson introduces an important new element into the analysis of FTAs not present in the previous literature. The conventional practice in the literature, such as by Meade (1955), Lipsey (1960), Berglas (1979), Riezman (1979), and Lloyd (1982), is to assume that in the post-FTA equilibrium the domestic price of a good imported from the outside country in each member country equals the border price plus the tariff levied by it. Richardson points out that though the consumer prices can differ in member countries of a FTA producer prices must be equalized by internal free trade. The rules of origin forbid the lower-tariff country from importing the outside country's goods and reexporting them to the higher-tariff country. This restriction prevents arbitrage between consumer prices in member countries. But producers in the lower-tariff country can sell *their* output in the higher-tariff country at the latter's higher price leading to arbitrage in producer prices across the union.[4] This feature leads to a lobbying equilibrium in Richardson's model under a FTA such that the lobby in potentially lower-tariff country chooses to free-ride the lobby in the other country. The outcome is a zero tariff in the former.

In this chapter, though initially we maintain the conventional assumption, for purposes of comparing FTAs and CUs, we work with both sets of assumptions. Because the conventional assumption is analytically more convenient, we derive our results first under this assumption and later point out how they change when arbitrage is allowed in producer prices. Under the conventional assumption the producer price in each country is determined by its own tariff. This feature eliminates the free-rider problem present in Richardson's model and leads to lobbying and positive tariffs in both countries under a FTA.[5]

The chapter is organized as follows: In section 17.1 we reformulate the Meade model by making trade policy endogenous. In section 17.2 we analyze the effects of preferential trading. In section 17.3 we compare FTAs and CUs. As just noted, though we maintain the conventional assumption with respect to domestic prices in the initial part of the chapter, we also deal with the case where producer prices are equalized across the union under a FTA. This task is performed in section 17.4. Concluding remarks are offered in section 17.5.

Before we begin, it may be noted that following the standard practice in the literature on economic integration, our analysis is cast in terms of tariffs. But tariffs should be viewed as representing protection resulting from various trade policy instruments such as voluntary export restraints, anti-dumping actions, and other mechanisms. We are aware that tariff increases are generally limited or ruled out by GATT bindings and GATT Article XXIV. Therefore, when our model predicts any tariff increases, they should be viewed as increases in the level of overall protection rather than tariffs per se.

17.1   The Meade Model with Endogenous Trade Policy

Let there be three countries A, B, and C and three goods x, y, and z. By assumption, each country exports one good and imports the other two. We let goods x, y, and z be export goods of A, B, and C, respectively. A and B are potential partners in a regional arrangement and C represents the rest of the world. A and B are small in relation to C such that the terms of trade are determined in C.

We outline the equilibrium in country A in detail. Equilibrium in country B can be outlined symmetrically. The role of country C is simply to absorb any excess demands and supplies from A and B at the fixed terms of trade. Each good is produced using a sector specific factor and a common factor. The factor specific to sector i ($i = x, y, z$) is labeled "sector i capital" and that common to all sectors is referred to as labor. Output, capital, and labor in sector i are denoted Q_i, K_i, and L_i, respectively. Each good is produced via a conventional constant-returns-to-scale technology,

$$Q_i = F_i(\bar{K}_i, L_i), \quad i = x, y, z, \tag{17.1}$$

where Q stands for output and a bar over a variable is used to indicate that the variable is fixed. Goods y and z are imported, and good x is exported by A. We choose the units of goods in such a way that the world price of each good is 1. Denoting by t_i the tariff on good i, the domestic price of good i is $1 + t_i$. Because A exports good x, we have $t_x = 0$ and $t_y, t_z > 0$. Acting competitively in the goods and factor markets, firms in sector i choose L_i to maximize profits given by $(1 + t_i)F_i(\bar{K}_i, L_i) - wL_i$. The outcome is a profit function $\pi^i(1 + t_i, w)$ which is linear homogenous in its arguments. Moreover,

$$\pi_i^i(1 + t_i, w) = F_i(\bar{K}_i, L_i) = Q_i, \tag{17.2}$$

$$\pi_w^i(1 + t_i, w) = -L_i, \tag{17.3}$$

where $\pi_i^i(\cdot)$ and $\pi_w^i(\cdot)$ denote partial derivatives of $\pi^i(\cdot)$ with respect to the domestic price of good i and w, respectively.

In (17.2) and (17.3), we have six equations in seven variables $F_i(\cdot)$, L_i, and w. Adding the full-employment constraint, we can obtain an exactly determined system of equations. We can then study the effects of exogenous changes in tariffs induced by the introduction of preferential trading. This is the standard Meade exercise.

Our objective is to make tariffs endogenous, however. To accomplish this in a simple way, we adopt the Findlay-Wellisz (1982) approach as simplified by Rodrik (1986) and also used by Panagariya and Rodrik (1993). Thus, we write

$$t_i = g_i(l_i), \quad g_i(0) = 0, g_i' > 0, g_i'' < 0; i = y, z, \tag{17.4}$$

where l_i is the amount of labor employed in lobbying.

Observe that we do not allow for lobbying by factors in one import-competing industry against protection in the other import-competing industry. Nor do we allow for lobbying against protection by the owners of capital in the export sector. These assumptions can be defended partially on grounds that political process is more responsive to an industry's demands of protection for itself rather than against other industries and that the balance of political power is usually stacked against export industries. But admittedly, the assumptions are extreme, and more work on the elaboration of lobbying process as outlined, for example, in Grossman and Helpman (1994), will be fruitful.

The level of lobbying is chosen so as to maximize the return to the sector-specific factor. That is so say, lobbyists maximize $\pi^i[1 + g_i(l_i), w] - wl_i$ with respect to l_i. This yields the first-order condition

$$g_i'(l_i) \cdot \pi_i^i(1 + g_i(l_i), w) = w, \quad i = y, z, \tag{17.5}$$

where $g_i'(l_i)$ is the derivative of $g_i(\cdot)$ with respect to l_i. Recalling that $\pi_i^i(\cdot) = F_i(\cdot) = Q_i$, the left-hand side of (17.5) can be interpreted as the revenue generated by employing an additional unit of labor in lobbying or the marginal revenue product (MRP$_i$) of lobbying. The right-hand side of (17.5) is the marginal cost of lobbying. Thus (17.5) says that lobbyists equate the marginal revenue and marginal cost of lobbying. Note that we assume that lobbyists take the wage rate as given. This is a standard assumption in models of lobbying.

The second-order condition associated with the lobbyists' problem requires that the marginal revenue product of labor given by the left-hand side of (17.5) be negative function of l_i. That is to say,

$$\frac{\partial(\mathrm{MRP}_i)}{\partial l_i} \equiv S_i = g_i''(l_i)\pi_i^i(\,\cdot\,) + [g_i'(l_i)]^2\pi_{ii}^i(\,\cdot\,) < 0, \quad i = y, z. \tag{17.6}$$

The first term on the right-hand side is negative, while the second term is positive. Therefore the right-hand side is not automatically negative. In the following, S_i will be used to denote the expression on the right-hand side of (17.6).

We can now introduce the full-employment constraint,

$$L_x + L_y + L_z + l_y + l_z = \bar{L}, \tag{17.7}$$

where $\bar{L}$ is the total endowment of labor.

The model for country A is now fully specified. Imbedded in equations (17.2)–(17.5) and (17.7), we have eleven equations in eleven variables, L_i, $F_i(= Q_i)$, l_y, l_z, t_y, t_z, and w. We can specify country B's model analogously with the modification that it exports good y rather than x.

Before we proceed to introduce preferential trading, it is useful to make the model more compact and provide a diagrammatic representation of it. Taking advantage of (17.3), we can rewrite the full-employment condition as

$$-[\pi_w^x(1, w) + \pi_w^y(1 + g_y(l_y), w) + \pi_w^z(1 + g_z(l_z), w)] + l_y + l_z = \bar{L}. \tag{17.7'}$$

This equation, along with (17.5), can be solved for l_y, l_z, and w. Given solution values of these variables, (17.4) gives the t_i, (17.3) the L_i and (17.2) and Q_i.

Equation (17.5) gives us l_i ($i = y, z$) as a function of the wage w. Assuming the second-order condition (17.6) holds, l_i declines as w rises. From (17.3), at constant l_i and hence a constant t_i, an increase in w lowers L_i directly. In addition, because the increase in w lowers l_i and hence t_i, it also lowers L_i indirectly. The combined demand for labor in sector i, $L_i + l_i$, is an inverse function of w.

In figure 17.1, O_yO_x represents the total endowment of labor in the economy. Measuring $L_y + l_y$ to the right from O_y, D^y_{L+l} represents the total demand (including that in lobbying) for labor in sector y. Analogously, measuring L_x to the left from O_x, D^x_L represents the demand for labor in sector x. This demand function is downward sloped for the usual reasons.

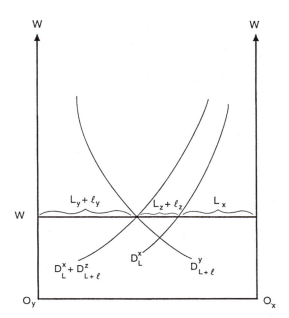

Figure 17.1
Labor market equilibrium.

Finally, $D_L^x + D_{L+l}^z$ shows the combined demand for labor in sectors x and z, $L_x + L_z + l_z$. At the intersection of D_{L+l}^y and D_{L+l}^z, the full-employment condition (17.7) is satisfied. The intersection determines equilibrium w and the allocation of labor among the three sectors. Thus we obtain the total quantity of labor in sector i, $L_i + l_i$ $(i = y, z)$. To determine L_i and l_i separately, we use (17.5) which yields l_i given w. Given L_i and l_i and L_x, (17.2) determines the Q_i.

17.2 Preferential Trading

Let us now introduce preferential trading between A and B. In the traditional models of preferential trading, this is done by lowering intra-union tariffs exogenously. In our model, tariffs are endogenous. Therefore the essence of preferential trading must be captured through a shift in the lobbying function for good 2. Following Hillman and Moser (1995) and Grossman and Helpman (1995b), this shift can be viewed as the result of a recognition by member governments that they can enjoy political gains by exchanging market access.

We will assume that the lobbying function for good 2 shifts in such a way that a given level of lobbying yields a lower level of tariff without affecting the *marginal* return on lobbying. This is accomplished most simply by replacing $g_y(l_y)$ by $-\beta_y + g_y(l_y)$ and letting β_y rise. Making this substitution into (17.5) for $i = y$, differentiating the resulting equation and evaluating it at $\beta_y = 0$, we obtain

$$S_y dl_y = g_y' \pi_{yy}^y d\beta_y + (1 - g_y' \pi_{yw}^y)\, dw. \tag{17.8}$$

Similarly, substituting for t_y from (17.4) into (17.3) with $g_y(\cdot)$ replaced by $-\beta_y + g_y(\cdot)$ and differentiating, we obtain

$$dL_y = \pi_{wy}^y(-d\beta_y + g_y' dl_y) + \pi_{ww}^y\, dw. \tag{17.9}$$

Given $S_y < 0$ and g_y', $\pi_{yy}^y > 0$, (17.8) implies that at a given w, preferential trading lowers l_y. Then, because $\pi_{wy}^y < 0$, (17.9) says that at a given w, preferential trading lowers L_y. In figure 17.1 preferential trading leads to a leftward shift in D_{L+l}^y. We immediately see that the wage must fall. Intuitively, at the original wage, a downward shift in the lobbying function makes lobbying in sector y less attractive and lowers l_y. The decline in l_y reduces t_y and makes sector y less profitable and lowers L_y. The reduction in L_y as well as l_y at the original wage puts a downward pressure on the wage.

The decline in wage makes lobbying in sector z more profitable. Assuming that the second-order condition in (17.6) holds, we can deduce from (17.5) that the introduction of preferential trading, by reducing the wage, raises l_z and hence t_z. Thus we have the interesting result that trade liberalization vis-à-vis the partner country is accompanied by increased protection against the rest of the world. Reduction in opportunities to lobby against one trading partner makes lobbying against the other partner more attractive. Assuming that goods 2 and 3 are close substitutes, this result captures the spirit of Bhagwati's (1993) fears regarding pernicious effects of FTAs on trade policies toward third countries. To quote him:

Imagine that the United States begins to eliminate (by outcompeting) an inefficient Mexican industry once the FTA goes into effect. Even though the most efficient producer is Taiwan, if the next efficient United States outcompetes the least efficient Mexico, that would be desirable trade creation.... But what would the Mexicans be likely to do? They would probably start AD actions against Taiwan, which would lead to reduced imports from Taiwan.

If we think of A, B, and C as Mexico, the United States, and Taiwan and of goods 2 and 3 as textile products imported from B (United States) and

C (Taiwan), respectively, our result is in close conformity with this example.[6]

The effect of the introduction of preferential trading on t_y can be obtained formally by differentiating (17.4) for $i = y$ after replacing $g_y(l_y)$ by $-\beta_y + g_y(l_y)$ and using (17.8) above. We have

$$\frac{dt_y}{d\beta_y} = -\left[1 - \frac{g_y'^{\,2}\pi_{yy}}{S_y}\right] + \frac{g_y'}{S_y}(1 - g_y'\pi_{yw}^y)\frac{dw}{d\beta_y} \qquad (17.10)$$

In (17.10) the first term is negative, while the second term (including $dw/d\beta_y$) is positive. The first term captures the effect of the increase in β_y while holding the wage constant. This effect lowers t_y by reducing the marginal revenue product directly as well as through a reduction in the output of good y. The second term captures the effect on t_y due to a change in the wage rate. Because the wage declines, profitability of lobbying rises solely on this account. The net effect depends on the relative strengths of these two effects, and it may seem that t_y may actually rise if the indirect wage effect is sufficiently strong. We demonstrate in the appendix, however, that this cannot happen; the direct effect of the rise in β_y necessarily dominates.

We next turn to the effect of preferential trading on welfare. Meade's original result is that if we have $t_y = t_z$ initially, and the excess demand for good y exhibits substitutability with the excess demand for the exportable, the introduction of preferential trading is necessarily welfare improving. Intuitively, an exogenous reduction in t_y increases the imports of that good but may increase or reduce the imports of good z. If the imports of good z rise, deleterious effects of tariffs are reduced in both goods and welfare improves necessarily. If imports of good z decline as is likely, however, the harmful effect of distortion in that sector increases. The question then is whether the loss due to this change is smaller than the gain from the rise in the imports of good y. If excess demands for goods y and x exhibit substitutability, exports of good x rise in response to a reduction in t_y. Given balanced trade, this means that there is a net expansion of imports, that is, imports of good y expand more than the decline in the imports of good z. If we now also assume that $t_y = t_z$ initially, the welfare gain due to the larger expansion of imports of good y must exceed the welfare loss due to a contraction of imports of good z. On balance, welfare improves.

In view of the results already derived, it should not be surprising that this important Meade result may not hold in the presence of endogenous trade policy. We have already seen that the introduction of preferential trading is accompanied by increased protection against third countries. Therefore there is no guarantee that substitutability between excess demands for good y and good x will be sufficient to lead to a net expansion of imports. The combined effect of a reduction in t_y and increase in t_z may well be to reduce total trade. Moreover we must take into account the effect of the introduction of preferential trading on real resources used in lobbying.

In the remainder of this section we present a formal proof of these results. We assume that preferences can be represented by a well-defined social welfare function. We can then obtain the expenditure function in the usual way. The budget constraint or, equivalently, the trade balance condition requires that expenditure and income be equal. Letting U denote utility and $E(\cdot)$ represent the expenditure function, we have

$$E(1, 1 + t_y, 1 + t_z; U) = \sum_{i=x}^{z} \pi^i (1 + t_i, w) - w \sum_{i=x}^{z} \pi_w^i (1 + t_i, w)$$

$$+ t_y(E_y - \pi_y^y) + t_z(E_z - \pi_z^z), \qquad (17.11)$$

where E_i is the partial derivative of $E(\cdot)$ with respect to the domestic price of good i $(i = x, y, z)$. On the right-hand side, the first term represents profits plus wages to workers employed in lobbying, the second term wages to workers employed in production activity, and the third and fourth terms tariff revenue that is redistributed. Because good x is exported, $t_x = 0$ and the domestic price of good x is 1. Tariff rates t_y and t_z are endogenous though we keep this fact in the background.

Differentiating (17.11) totally, allowing t_y and t_z to change, we have

$$M \, dU = -w(dl_y + dl_z) + [t_y(E_{yy} - \pi_{yy}^y) + t_z E_{zy}] \, dt_y$$

$$+ [t_y E_{yz} + t_z(E_{zz} - \pi_{zz}^z)] \, dt_z - [t_y \pi_{yw}^y + t_z \pi_{zw}^z] \, dw. \qquad (17.12)$$

where $M \equiv E_U - t_y E_{Uy} - t_z E_{Uz}$ is positive as long as all goods are normal in consumption. The next step is to exploit the zero-degree homogeneity of E_y and E_z in price variables. Zero-degree homogeneity of E_y in prices allows us to write

$$E_{yx} + (1 + t_y)E_{yy} + (1 + t_z)E_{yz} = 0. \qquad (17.13)$$

Equation (17.13), in turn, yields

$$t_y E_{yy} + t_z E_{zy} = -\frac{1}{1+t_y}[(t_y - t_z)E_{yz} + t_y E_{yx}]. \tag{17.13'}$$

Making use of (17.13) and an analogous expression for $t_y E_{zy} + t_z E_{zz}$, we can rewrite (17.12) as

$$M \, dU = -w(dl_y + dl_z) - (t_y \pi_{yw}^y + t_z \pi_{zw}^z)\, dw$$

$$-\frac{1}{1+t_y}[(t_y - t_z)E_{yz} + t_y E_{yx} + t_y(1+t_y)\pi_{yy}^y]\, dt_y$$

$$-\frac{1}{1+t_z}[(t_z - t_y)E_{zy} + t_z E_{zx} + t_z(1+t_z)\pi_{zz}^z]\, dt_z. \tag{17.12'}$$

Consider first the Meade result. In the absence of lobbying, $dl_y = dl_z \equiv 0$, and since t_z is exogenous, $dt_z = 0$. We also assume that tariffs on goods from B and C are equal initially, $t_y = t_z$. Taking into account these factors, (17.12') can be rewritten as

$$M \, dU = -\frac{t_y E_{yx}}{1+t_y} dt_y - t_y[\pi_{yy}^y\, dt_y + (\pi_{yw}^y + \pi_{zw}^z)\, dw]. \tag{17.14}$$

With no lobbying, the full-employment constraint yields $dw = -[\pi_{wy}^y / \sum_i \pi_{ww}^i]\, dt_y$. Substituting this into (17.14) and making use of zero degree homogeneity of $\pi_y^i(\cdot)$ and $\pi_w^z(\cdot)$, we can reduce (17.14) to

$$M \, dU = -\frac{t_y}{1+t_y}\left[E_{yx} - \frac{w\pi_{yw}^y \pi_{ww}^x}{\sum_{i=x}^z \pi_{ww}^i}\right] dt_y. \tag{17.14'}$$

From (17.14'), if we lower t_y, holding t_z fixed exogenously (i.e., $dt_y < 0$) at $t_y = t_z$, we see the right-hand side is positive provided that $E_{yx} > 0$, that is, the demand for goods y and x exhibit net substitutability.[7] This is the standard Meade result.

Next, suppose that tariffs are endogenous. In this case $dt_z > 0$ and $dl_y + dl_z \neq 0$. We can no longer go from (17.12') to (17.14'). In (17.12') the first term captures the welfare effect of the change in the overall level of lobbying activity. Because w falls, l_z rises necessarily. But the decline in the profitability of lobbying in sector y (i.e., the rise in β_y) is likely to lower l_y. Thus the net effect on $l_y + l_z$ is ambiguous. The second term in (17.12') is positive, while the third one is negative under the substitutability assumption. The last term, given that dw is negative for a reduction in t_y, is also negative. Thus, $t_y = t_z$ is no longer sufficient to yield an improvement in welfare under substitutability between import-competing goods and the exportable.

17.3   FTA versus Customs Union

We now assume that countries A and B have decided to eliminate trade restrictions between themselves but must choose between FTA and CU. The former allows the external tariff to be determined at the national level, while the latter requires them to be determined at the regional level. Formally, we can imagine that under a FTA, tariffs on third countries in each union member continue to be determined via the lobbying function introduced in (17.4), while under a customs union an institutional change requires the determination of a common external tariff. Note that under a FTA, we are assuming that both producer prices and consumer prices of the good imported from the outside country are different in A and B. The possibility of the producer-price arbitrage is introduced in the next section.

A key question is, How should the lobbying function be formulated in the case of a customs union? We know that if this choice is made arbitrarily, we can obtain any ranking of FTA and CU that we like. Therefore we opt for as neutral a choice as possible.[8] In the case of a customs union, we write the lobbying function for good z as

$$t_z^c = h_z(l_z^c) \equiv h_z(l_z + l_z^*), \quad h' > 0, h'' < 0, \tag{17.15}$$

where an asterisk is used to distinguish country B's variables and superscript c is used to indicate unionwide variables under a customs union. Accordingly, t_z^c is the common external tariff and $l_z^c = l_z + l_z^*$. We assume that the regional institution is equally responsive to lobbying by agents of the two members. Who invests into lobbying is not important. What matters is how much.

Under a FTA, lobbying is done at the national level, and tariffs in the two member countries may be different. We write

$$t_z^F = g_z(l_z), \quad t_z^{F*} = g_z(l_z^*). \tag{17.4'}$$

For ease of comparison, we assume that the lobbying *functions* under a FTA are identical in the two countries.

To maintain neutrality, we assume that functions $h_z(\cdot)$ and $g_z(\cdot)$ are related with each other according to

$$h_z(l_z + l_z^*) = g_z\left(\frac{l_z + l_z^*}{2}\right), \tag{17.16a}$$

$$h_z'(l_z + l_z^*) < g_z'(l_z + l_z^*). \tag{17.16b}$$

According to (17.16a), if $l_z = l_z^* = \bar{l}_z$ so that the lobbies in each of A and B invest $\bar{l}_z$ amount of resources, the external tariff under a FTA and CU is the same. Under a FTA we have

$$t_z^F = g_z(\bar{l}_z), \quad t_z^{F^*} = g_z(\bar{l}_z),$$

and under a customs union we have

$$t_z^c = h_z(\bar{l}_z + \bar{l}_z) = h_z(2\bar{l}_z) = g_z\left(\frac{2\bar{l}_z}{2}\right) = g_z(\bar{l}_z) = t_z^F, t_z^{F^*}.$$

Thus lobbying functions themselves are neutral with respect to the type of regional arrangement chosen.

Another way to compare $h_z(\cdot)$ and $g_z(\cdot)$ is that under a CU, if lobbying is done by agents of a single country, say A, they will have to invest twice as much resources to obtain a given level of tariff as under a FTA. Under a CU, the tariff granted to A is also granted to B. Therefore the effort required to obtain a given tariff is twice as much. Viewed in this way, it is clear that our formulation captures the free-rider problem which is often associated with the formation of a CU. In policy discussions, it is commonly asserted that a customs union can be an instrument of weakening the interest groups seeking protection. A surrender of tariff-making power to the regional institution means less influence of interest groups within a member nation.

According to (17.16b), for a given amount of labor employed in lobbying, the *marginal* product of lobbying is higher under a FTA than under a CU. Equation (17.16a) is not sufficient to yield this condition. But the condition is plausible and is satisfied by function $g_z(\cdot) = \lambda l_z^\phi$, where λ and ϕ are constants and the value of ϕ lies between 0 and 1.

The question we wish to address now is, can FTA and CU be ranked, and what does this ranking depend on? To answer, we must first determine equilibrium tariffs under the two regimes. Under FTA, the tariff will be determined as in the previous section. Under CU, the problem is trickier.

Protection is a private good under a FTA. But under a CU it becomes a public good subject to the free-rider problem. As we demonstrate below, this feature yields the usual outcome associated with the private provision of public goods: Only the "most desperate" buyer chooses to pay for it while the others choose to free ride.[9]

Consider the problem of the lobby in country A. Its problem is to maximize $\pi^z[1 + h_z(l_z + l_z^*), w] - wl_z$ with respect to l_z taking w as given. At the optimum, the marginal revenue product of l_z must be larger than or equal to the marginal cost of l_z. That is,

$$h_z'(l_z^c)\pi_z^z(1 + h_z(l_z^c), w) \geq w, \tag{17.17}$$

where $l_z^c = l_c + l_z^*$ is the total amount of labor employed in lobbying. An analogous condition can be written for country B's lobby. The question then is whether (17.17) and the analogous condition for B's lobby can simultaneously holds as equalities. The answer is that only by a sheer coincidence is this possible. Treating (17.17) as an equality, we can determine l_z^c as a function of w. Likewise the condition for B gives us another equation determining l_z^c as a function of w^*, the wage in B. It is unlikely that the two equations will yield the same value of l_z^c.

To explain what is going on here, assume that the wage is constant in each country. For example, we could assume that the exportable in each country (i.e., good x in A and good y in B) uses only labor. We can then represent the marginal revenue product of l_z net of the marginal cost, given by the left-hand side of (17.17) minus the right-hand side (i.e., wage), as a function of l_z^c alone. This is done in figure 17.2. By virtue of the second-order condition this curve, labeled NMRP (net MRP), is downward sloped.

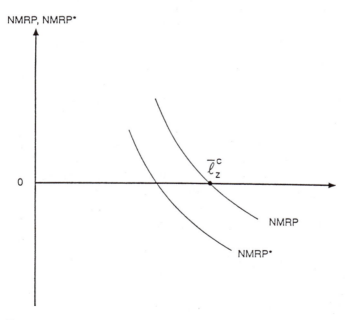

Figure 17.2
Nash equilibrium in lobbying.

Next, draw country B's net marginal revenue product curve measuring it in the same units as A's. Suppose that it lies below country A's curve, as shown by NMRP*. In this case the lobby in B will choose to free-ride the lobby in country A. The reason for this outcome is that for $l_z^* = 0$, A's best choice is $l_z = \bar{l}_z^c$, and for $l_z = \bar{l}_z^c$, B's best response is $l_z^* = 0$. Thus the solution $l_z^* = 0$ and $l_z = \bar{l}_z^c$ is a Nash equilibrium. Analogously, if NMRP* were to lie above NMRP, $l_z = 0$ and $l_z^* = \bar{l}_z^c$ would be a Nash solution. If the two curves were to coincide on the horizontal axis, the total lobbying would still be $\bar{l}_z^c$ but how it is divided between A and B would be indeterminate.

Observe that given $\pi_z^z(\cdot) = Q_z$, the level of output of the good imported from country C plays a key role in the determination of which lobby supplies the common external tariff. In view of (17.17), the larger the ratio of this output to the wage rate in a country, the more likely lobbying will be concentrated there. For instance, given the relative sizes of import-competing industries in the United States and Mexico, despite the lower wage in Mexico, under a customs union arrangement, one will expect the United States to be the "supplier" of the common external tariff.

For concreteness, assume that all lobbying is done in country A. To get a fix on some additional results, assume further that the exportable uses only labor. Then the wage in terms of the exportable is fixed and, hence, the same under a FTA and CU. Following Panagariya and Rodrik (1993), we now show that the level of lobbying and hence the tariff is lower under a customs union than that in A under a FTA. Letting $\bar{l}_z^c$ be the level of lobbying under a CU, we evaluate the marginal revenue product of lobbying under a FTA, given by the left-hand side of (17.5), at $\bar{l}_z^c$. Given (17.16a), $g_z(\bar{l}_z^c) > h_z(\bar{l}_z^c)$, and given (17.16b), $g_z'(\bar{l}_z^c) > h_z'(\bar{l}_z^c)$. Since (17.17) holds as an equality at $\bar{l}_z^c$ under a CU and w is the same under a CU and FTA, these inequalities imply that the marginal revenue product of lobbying under a FTA [the left-hand side of (17.5)] exceeds w at $\bar{l}_z^c$. The level of lobbying and the tariff on z in country A will be higher under a FTA than a CU.

The common external tariff can, however, be higher than the tariff in B under a FTA. We distinguish B's variables by an asterisk (*). Letting $\bar{t}_z^c$ be the common external tariff, we solve the equation $g_z(l_z^*) = \bar{t}_z^c$.[10] The solution, denoted $\tilde{l}_z^*$, gives the level of lobbying that will generate the tariff $\bar{t}_z^c$ under a FTA in B. Then, if $g_z'(\tilde{l}_z^*)\pi^{z^*}(1 + g_z(\tilde{l}_z^*), w^*)$ exceeds w^*, the tariff in B under a FTA will be higher than that under a CU. A crucial factor determining the outcome is the potential output of z or, equivalently, the amount of z-specific factor, K_z^*, available. The smaller the potential output of z, the more likely the tariff under a CU will be higher than under a FTA.

An additional result that may be derived is that as the number of members in the potential regional arrangement rises, assuming that A remains the supplier of the common external tariff, the level of the external tariff declines. This is because the increase in the number of members in the union exacerbates the free-rider problem. Formally, in (17.16a) and (17.16b), $l_z + l_z^*$ and $(l_z + l_z^*)/2$ are replaced by $\sum_j l_z^j$ and $\sum_j l_z^j/m$, where j denotes a union member and m is the total number of members in the union. An implication of this result is that countries will be better off entering into a customs union with larger number of countries than with small number of them. But it also implies that lobbies will likely resist the enlargement of a customs union more than of a FTA.

Finally, the welfare ranking of FTA and CU is not unique except in the specific case when the tariff chosen by the two countries under a FTA is the same and the exportable uses only labor. In this case the common external tariff under a CU is lower than the FTA tariff in both countries. Moreover each country invests less resources in lobbying under CU than under a FTA. Welfare is necessarily higher under the former arrangement. In the asymmetric case, though the country that supplies the external tariff under a CU is better off under this arrangement than under a FTA, the other country may be worse off. This is because the latter may end up with higher tariffs under a CU than under a FTA. The larger the number of members, the more likely that a CU will dominate a FTA from the view-point of all members.

17.4   The Producer-Price Arbitrage under a FTA

So far we have assumed complete segmentation of the price of z, the good imported from C, across A and B under a FTA. We now introduce the possibility of producer-price arbitrage under a FTA as in Richardson (1993b, 1994). There are three possible price configurations. We use figure 17.3, adapted from Grossmam and Helpman (1995a) whose analysis of FTAs also incorporates the producer-price arbitrage, to discuss these configurations. We take a partial equilibrium setting and begin by assuming that tariffs are exogenous. Without loss of generality, let $t_z > t_z^*$; that is, assume that the tariff on z is higher in A than B.

In case 1 shown in figure 17.3, $M_z M_z$, represents A's *import-demand* for good z while $Q_z^* Q_z^*$ represents B's *total supply* of good z. Values $1 + t_z$ and $1 + t_z^*$ denote the border price plus tariff in A and B, respectively. As

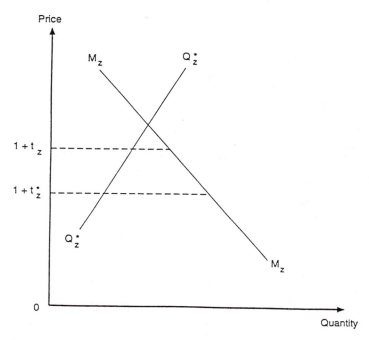

Figure 17.3
Producer-price arbitage.

drawn, B's supply curve intersects A's import-demand curve *above* $1 + t_z$. Both the consumer and producer price in A settle at $1 + t_z$. Because imports can enter B at $1 + t_z^*$, z cannot be sold there at a price higher than $1 + t_z^*$. But given internal free trade, B's producers can sell their output in A at the higher price $1 + t_z$. B sells all of its output in A, receiving A's price $1 + t_z$. All of B's consumption comes from C at the consumer price $1 + t_z^*$. A's consumption comes from all three sources, domestic, B and C.

In case 2, not shown in figure 17.3, B's supply curve lies so far to the right that it intersects A's import-demand curve below $1 + t_z^*$. In this case all of A's imports come from B. B's producers sell a part of their output in the home market. The price settles at $1 + t_z^*$ for both producers and consumers throughout the union.

Finally, in case 3, B's supply curve intersects A's import-demand curve between $1 + t_z$ and $1 + t_z^*$. The price in A facing producers and consumers in this case is determined by the point of intersection of the two curves. Producers in B sell all of their output in A. A's imports come entirely from B and B's consumers are supplied solely by C at price $1 + t_z^*$.

To analyze the implications of producer-price arbitrage for the analysis of FTAs, we focus on case 1 only. We begin by assuming that in the absence of the producer-price arbitrage, country A chooses a higher tariff than B. If we now introduce producer-price arbitrage, it is evident that producers in B will choose to sell good z in A. If we further assume that A's demand for imports at its tariff inclusive price is larger than the total quantity B's producers want to sell at that price—the situation depicted in figure 17.3—the lobby in B will choose not to lobby at all! In this equilibrium producers in B sell nothing in their home market and hence do not need to lobby for protection there. They simply free-ride the high tariff in A. The entire quantity of good z consumed in B comes from the outside country at the world price.

The free-rider problem characterizing this equilibrium is different than in the CU equilibrium considered earlier in one fundamental respect. While country B benefits from A's lobbying, such free-riding generates no negative externality for the lobby in A. Formally, the marginal revenue product of lobbying continues to be given by equation (17.5). Therefore, ceteris paribus, the lobby in A chooses the same tariff in the presence of producer-price arbitrage as in its absence in section 17.3. What is different is that the lobby in B chooses not to lobby at all.

Turning to a welfare comparison, it is evident that country B is unambiguously better off in the present FTA equilibrium than in the CU equilibrium of section 17.3. This result holds because consumers in B now face world prices in all products and producers have access to A's superior terms of trade in product z. As regards country A, its equilibrium is the same as that in the absence of producer-price arbitrage. This means that the common external tariff under CU will be lower than its FTA tariff, and it will be better off under the former arrangement (see the proof in the previous section). Thus, whereas in the absence of producer-price arbitrage, it is *possible* for both A and B to be better off under a CU than a FTA, in the presence of such arbitrage, one country (B) is necessarily worse off and the other necessarily better off.

17.5   Summary of Results

In this chapter we have analyzed the welfare effects of regional integration in a model of endogenous protection. We have shown that in this setting, the introduction of preferential trading leads to an increase in protection against countries outside the preferential trading area. We have also demonstrated that the important Meade result on preferential trading breaks down when protection is endogenous. According to the Meade result, if the excess demand for the good being liberalized exhibits substitutability with respect to the exportable, the introduction of preferential trading is welfare improving. In the presence of endogenous protection, because preferential trading is accompanied by increased protection against non-partners, its effect on welfare is ambiguous.

We have also compared free-trade areas and customs unions. Here we have provided a formal treatment of the argument that a customs union is more effective than a free-trade area in diluting the power of interest groups. Under a customs union the tariff available to one country becomes available to all countries in the union. This introduces a free-rider problem in lobbying, and all lobbying takes place in one country. The lobby chooses a lower (common) external tariff under a customs union than under a free-trade area. This means that welfare in the country where lobbying takes place is higher under a customs union than under a free-trade area. If producer-price arbitrage is ruled out, the other country may or may not be better off under a FTA than a CU. If that country chooses a lower tariff under a free-trade area than the common external tariff under the customs union, its welfare under the former arrangement is higher. If producer-price arbitrage is taken into account, since this country chooses not to lobby at all under a FTA, its welfare in the FTA equilibrium is necessarily higher than under a CU. Finally, the level of the common external tariff declines as the number of members in the union increases. Therefore the larger the number of partners in a customs union, the more likely it will improve welfare of member countries. By the same token, due to the free-rider problem, lobbies are likely to resist the enlargement of a customs union.

17.6   Appendix

We demonstrate that the effect of a rise in β_y on t_y, shown in (17.10), is negative. We first solve for $dw/d\beta_y$. The change in L_y and l_y is given by (17.8). and (17.9), respectively. The change in L_z and l_z is given by analogous equations with $d\beta_y$ set to 0. Finally, the change in L_x is $-\pi^x_{ww}\, dw$. Substituting these changes in labor demands into the full-employment constraint and solving, we obtain

$$\frac{dw}{d\beta_y} = \frac{1}{H}\left[\pi^y_{wy} + \frac{1}{S_y}(1 - g'_y\pi^y_{wy})g'_y\pi^y_{yy}\right],\qquad (17.A1)$$

where H is defined as follows:

$$H \equiv \sum_{i=x}^{z} \pi_{ww}^{i} - \frac{1}{S_y}(1 - g_y' \pi_{wy}^{y})^2 - \frac{1}{S_z}(1 - g_z' \pi_{wz}^{z})^2. \tag{17.A2}$$

From equations (17.10) and (17.A1), $dt_y/d\beta_y < 0$, if and only if

$$-(S_y - g_y'^2 \pi_{yy}^{y})H > g_y'(1 - g_y' \pi_{yw}^{y}) \left[\pi_{wy}^{y} + \frac{1}{S_y}(1 - g_y' \pi_{wy}^{y})g_y' \pi_{yy}^{y} \right].$$

Taking (17.A2) into account and canceling terms with $1/S_y$ as a factor, this inequality holds true if and only if

$$- (S_y - g_y'^2 \pi_{yy}^{y}) \left[\sum_{i=x}^{z} \pi_{ww}^{i} - \frac{1}{S_z}(1 - g_z' \pi_{wz}^{z})^2 \right] + (1 - g_y' \pi_{wy}^{y})^2$$

$$> -g_y'(1 - g_y' \pi_{yw}^{y})\pi_{wy}^{y},$$

or, equivalently, if and only if

$$-(S_y - g_y'^2 \pi_{yy}^{y}) \left[\sum_{i=x}^{z} \pi_{ww}^{i} - \frac{1}{S_z}(1 - g_z' \pi_{wz}^{z})^2 \right] + (1 - g_y' \pi_{wy}^{y}) > 0.$$

Given the signs of various partial derivatives, this inequality necessarily holds true.

Notes

We thank Gene Grossman and Poonam Gupta for many helpful comments.

1. For instance, see Meade (1955), Lipsey (1960), Berglas (1979), Riezman (1979), and Lloyd (1982).

2. Another dimension, not addressed in this chapter, is the increased interdependence of different regional arrangements. Today the world is dividing *simultaneously* into a few large trading blocs. This means that regional arrangements can no longer be analyzed in isolation as has been the case with much of the Vinerian literature. Krugman (1991) and Deardorff and Stern (1991) provide models of trading blocs that emphasize this interdependence.

3. Among key contributions to this literature are Krueger (1974), Brock and Magee (1978), Bhagwati and Srinivasan (1980), and Findlay and Wellisz (1982). Two book-length treatments of the subject are Magee, Brock, and Young (1989) and Hillman (1989). Models of regional integration with endogenous policy are discussed later in the text.

4. If the supply in the lower-tariff country is sufficiently large, arbitrage in producer prices can also lead to arbitrage in consumer prices. See Grossman and Helpman (1995a) and section 17.4 for more details.

5. Of course, we do have a free-rider problem in the CU equilibrium as does Richardson.

6. Observe that the Bhagwati result can arise through alternative mechanisms. For instance, if the government wishes to maintain a certain level of output in the industry, it will increase protection against the third country as it liberalizes trade with respect to the partner.

7. As noted earlier, the general condition in the Meade model is that the *excess* demands for the product whose tariff is reduced and the exportable exhibit substitutability. Because all goods exhibit substitutability in production in our model, the substitutability in demand ensures that excess demands exhibit substitutability.

8. We draw heavily on Panagariya and Rodrik (1993), who in turn draw on Rodrik (1986).

9. For a review of the literature on private provision of public goods, see Cornes and Sandler (1986). Also see Hillman (1989, 1991) and Ursprung (1990) in this regard.

10. Recall that the lobbying function is assumed to be the same in B as A. Therefore no asterisk is used to distinguish the lobbying function in B from that in A.

References

Berglas, E. 1979. Preferential trading: The *n* commodity case. *Journal of Political Economy* 87:315–31.

Bhagwati, Jagdish. 1993. Regionalism and multilateralism: An overview. In J. de Melo and A. Panagariya, eds., *New Dimensions in Regional Integration*. Cambridge: Cambridge University Press.

Bhagwati, Jagdish, and T. N. Srinivasan. 1980. Revenue-seeking: A generalization of the theory of tariffs. *Journal of Political Economy* 88:1069–87.

Brock, William A., and Stephen P. Magee. 1978. The economics of special interest policies: The case of the tariff. *American Economic Review* 68:246–50.

Cornes, Richard, and Todd Sandler. 1986. *The Theory of Externalities, Public Goods and Club Goods*. Cambridge: Cambridge University Press.

Deardorff, Alan, and Robert Stern. 1991. Multilateral trade negotiations and preferential trading arrangements. Mimeo.

de Melo, Jaime, and Panagariya, Arvind, eds. 1993a. *New Dimensions in Regional Integration*. Cambridge: Cambridge University Press.

de Melo, Jaime, Dani Rodrik, and Arvind Panagariya. 1993b. The new regionalism: A country perspective. In J. de Melo and A. Panagariya, eds., *New Dimensions in Regional Integration*. Cambridge: Cambridge University Press.

Findlay, Ronald, and Stanislaw Wellisz. 1982. Endogenous tariffs, the political economy of trade restrictions, and welfare. In J. Bhagwati, ed., *Import Competition and Response*. Chicago: University of Chicago Press.

Grossman, Gene, and Elhanan Helpman, 1994. Protecion for sale. *American Economic Review* 84:833–50.

Grossman, Gene, and Elhanan Helpman. 1995a. The politics of free trade agreements. *American Economic Review* 85, forthcoming.

Grossman, Gene, and Elhanan Helpman. 1995b. Trade wars and trade talks. *Journal of Political Economy* 103:675–708.

Hillman, Arye. 1989. *The Political Economy of Protection*. Chur, Switzerland: Harwood Academic Publishers.

Hillman, Arye. 1991. Protection, politics, and market structure. In E. Helpman and A. Razin, eds., *International Trade and Trade Policy*. Cambridge: MIT Press.

Hillman, Arye, and Peter Moser. 1995. Trade liberalization as politically optimal exchange of markets. In Mathew Canzoneri et al., eds., *The New Transatlantic Economy*. Cambridge: Cambridge University Press.

Krueger, Anne O. 1974. The political economy of the rent-seeking society. *American Economic Review* 64:291–303.

Krugman, Paul. 1991. Is bilateralism bad? In E. Helpman and A. Razin, eds., *International Trade and Trade Policy*. Cambridge: MIT Press.

Lipsey, Richard. 1960. The theory of customs unions: A general survey. *Economic Journal* 70:498–513.

Lloyd, Peter. 1982. 3×3 theory of customs unions. *Journal of International Economics* 12:41–63.

Magee, Stephen P., William A. Brock, and Leslie Young. 1989. *Black Hole Tariffs and Endogenous Policy Theory*. Cambridge: Cambridge University Press.

Meade, James E. 1955. *The Theory of Customs Unions*. Amsterdam: North-Holland.

Panagariya, Arvind and Dani Rodrik. 1993. Political economy arguments for a uniform tariff. *International Economic Review* 34:685–704.

Richardson, Martin. 1993a. Endogenous protection and trade diversion. *Journal of International Economics* 34:309–34.

Richardson, Martin. 1993b. Tariff revenue competition in a free trade area. Mimeo. Forthcoming in *European Economic Review*.

Richardson, Martin. 1994. Why a free trade area? The tariff also rises. *Economics and Politics* 6:79–95.

Rodrik, Dani. 1986. Tariffs, subsidies and welfare with endogenous policy. *Journal of International Economics* 21:285–99.

Riezman, Raymond. 1979. A 3×3 model of customs unions. *Journal of International Economics* 72:820–29.

Ursprung, Heinrich. 1990. Public goods, rent dissipation, and candidate competition. *Economics and Politics* 2:115–32.

Viner, Jacob. 1950. *The Customs Union Issue*. New York: Carnegie Endowment for International Peace.

18

Why a Free Trade Area?
The Tariff Also Rises

Martin Richardson

18.1 Introduction

Why would two countries ever form a free trade area (FTA)? Woodland (1982, pp. 348–350) demonstrates that the optimal form of preferential trading agreement amongst countries, when international transfers exist, is one with a common external tariff; i.e. a customs union (CU). By a simple application of the results of Dixit and Norman (1980, pp. 191–194), this is also true if member countries have only commodity and factor taxation available and coordinate these taxes (see Richardson (1992)). One reason free trade areas are the preferential trading agreement of choice for many countries may be that this degree of coordination is lacking. This chapter highlights another reason: we demonstrate that a country may choose a FTA rather than a CU if tariffs are set endogenously through the lobbying efforts of interested industries. In a FTA a domestic industry need lobby only the domestic government for a particular external tariff whereas, in a CU, a given tariff requires that a larger legislative group be courted. Of course, there are also more firms involved in lobbying as those in the partner country also seek protection but there is correspondingly a greater degree of free-riding in the lobbying process within a CU than within a FTA; this lessens the attractiveness of the former to firms.[1,2]

This approach also bears upon the merits of preferential trading arrangements (PTAs) versus unilateral tariff reductions. In our analysis we consider two small countries combining in some agreement excluding a large third country (the rest of the world) which trades in every commodity. Accordingly, there are no terms of trade gains associated with the union and, if governments were traditional aggregate welfare maximizers, the question would arise as to why there is any external tariff at all. This

Originally published in *Economics and Politics* 6, no. 1 (March 1994): 79–96. Reprinted with permission.

problem plagues many traditional analyses of CUs[3] but in our set-up a non-zero tariff occurs as an equilibrium lobbying outcome.

One question not dealt with here is why a PTA is entered into at all. Richardson (1993a) discusses a number of reasons why the formation of a PTA may be more likely, in general models of endogenous policy, than either small tariff changes or multilateral reforms. In brief: regarding the latter, there is no presumption that Pareto-improving multilateral changes in tariffs even exist in models of endogenous policy. Also, in such models, bilateral agreements might prevail where unilateral tariff reductions would not as they bring more interested producer groups (namely exporters) into the process by virtue of the reciprocal nature of tariff reductions. Essentially, PTAs "package" tariff reductions that might individually be rejected as harmful to an interested sector but which are, on aggregate, welfare improving. Finally, a political equilibrium might be disturbed by large bilateral changes in tariffs when small changes would be rejected if there are costs of participation in the political process—large changes then might yield welfare gains that exceed the participation "threshold."

Further, the political determination of the *form* of PTA is easily intro-duced as the outcome of an earlier lobbying process in which the industry group, anticipating the effects of a FTA and a CU as described in this chapter, lobbies for one form of PTA or the other. Adding this stage of lobbying explicitly serves only to obscure our central point and is there-fore omitted.

The remainder of the chapter is organized as follows. In the next Section we turn to an analysis of tariff-setting in a FTA and a CU where internal producer prices are equated in the FTA. Firms lobby for tariff protection and we show that free-riding problems amongst lobbying firms may lead them to favor a FTA over a CU. We show that the same results hold in a more standard model of a FTA and we also show that they hold regardless of whether or not there is free-riding amongst lob-bying firms *within* a country. We demonstrate that the traditional welfare consequences of CU formation are positive, however. A final Section summarizes and concludes.

18.2   A Political Economy Model of Tariff-Setting

18.2.1   The Model

The results of Dixit and Norman (1980) and Richardson (1992)[4] suggest that formation of a FTA is suboptimal for members compared to a CU and yet preferential trading arrangements in the world are very commonly FTAs. One explanation for this is that either commodity taxes themselves, or the degree of cooperation in tax-setting needed to guarantee gains from a CU, are not present in most PTAs. The former possibility is irrelevant for any moderately developed country and the latter, while perhaps explaining why countries pursue completely independent trade policies rather than forming PTAs of any sort, seems to be less credible in explaining why countries that *do* cooperate to the extent of forming a FTA do not go the extra yard to a CU.

In this Section we argue that one potential reason for this apparently mysterious behavior is that tariffs are not chosen in the national interest but rather are the outcome of lobbying by interested parties. We consider two countries starting in a FTA and deciding whether to move to a CU, and we suppose that firms in an industry lobby their government for protection, if the good is an importable, or for export subsidies if an exportable.[5] The issue of the formation of a FTA in a model of endogenous policy is discussed in Richardson (1993a) and we do not pursue it here, taking the FTA as a starting point and considering the decision to form a CU instead. We consider two countries, A and B, in a FTA excluding the rest of the world, C. A and B are small relative to C and so face fixed trading prices with C. This highlights the role of lobbying in determining the tariff—the traditional optimal tariff for each country is zero, given internal free trade, but in our model each country chooses a non-zero external tariff in FTA equilibrium.

We consider a simple two-good general equilibrium model involving lobbying by firms. The model we use is similar to that of Rodrik (1986) but we suppress internal free-riding within a country and our tariff-setting function is a little different in order to capture the effects on lobbying of creating a CU. As Lloyd (1982) has argued, a truly satisfactory analysis of preferential trading arrangements must include at least three goods to avoid either asymmetries or a lack of trade between member countries. Our purpose here, however, is not to establish the generality of particular results but rather to provide an illustration of a particular intuition. Accordingly, we consider a model in which there is no trade between the member countries[6] but each trades the same goods with the rest of the world. As demonstrated in Richardson (1992) these are the only categories of goods in which the two partners might face different internal prices in a FTA.

Consider typical member country A. The country produces numeraire good Y according to a constant returns to scale production function in labor alone. It also produces good X according to a constant returns to scale production function in labor and sector-specific capital. Labor is intersectorally mobile and the country exports Y to country C from which it imports X. We assume that A is incompletely specialized at all relevant prices. The domestic consumer price of X is $p = p^* + t^A$ where p^* is the world price which is given and t^A is a specific tariff set according to the lobbying activity of the specific factor in the X sector. Without loss of generality, we normalize p^* to unity henceforth. The X industry consists of n identical owners (firms) of the X-specific total capital stock, K, each with $k = K/n$.

The main challenge in modeling the FTA/CU choice here is in specifying the mechanism by which tariffs are set in such a way that comparisons can be made between tariff-setting in an individual country and tariff-setting for a pair of countries in a CU. We adopt a model of representative democracy in which the political system is assumed to be identical in both member countries, yielding a reduced-form tariff-setting function which applies both at a country level and at the CU level.

We suppose that firms devote real resources to lobbying the tariff-setting authority. The latter is modeled, according to a very simplistic (and somewhat cynical) view of representative democracy, as a collection of automata. The level of tariff protection is determined by the votes of political representatives, each of whom can be "bought off" through lobbying activities.[7] All representatives are identical, each representing an identical constituency, and each has an identical, positive monotonic "cost" function mapping per-representative lobbying expenditures into the level of the tariff they will support. That is, each representative resists protection, in the interests of the consumers she represents, but lobbying can overcome that resistance according to a deterministic function wherein a given amount of lobbying will persuade a representative to support a certain tariff. This can be thought of as a reduced-form political-support function à la Hillman (1982) except that the relative weight placed on producers versus consumers is endogenous. All other things being equal, greater lobbying yields greater protection.[8] However, the greater the number of voters in the economy the more representatives there are and thus the more lobbying the industry will need to undertake in order to secure a given level of protection. This interpretation provides a solid foundation for the intuitive proposition that a million dollars spent on lobbying will secure a higher level of protection for an industry in a small economy than the same sum spent in a much larger economy.[9] Also, this specification enables the direct comparison of FTA and CU equilibria as the form of the tariff-setting function is unchanged when countries form a CU; however, the number of representatives to be lobbied increases.

For concreteness, letting L be the total labor force of the economy (and, for neatness, the total electorate)[10] and L^S the total amount of resources put into lobbying by interested producers, we suppose that the domestic consumer price $p = 1 + t$ is determined by some function $p[L^S, L]$.[11] We make the following assumptions about this function: where numerical subscripts denote appropriate partial derivatives of a function, $p[0, L] = 1$, $p_2 < 0$, $p_{22} > 0$, $p_1 > 0$, $p_{11} < 0$ and $p_{12} < 0$. That is, with no lobbying, no protection is granted. The greater the number of representatives (the greater the size of the electorate), the lower is the tariff, ceteris paribus. The impact of a greater number of representatives on the tariff decreases, in absolute magnitude, as the number rises. The greater the amount of lobbying, the higher is the tariff but this also has a decreasing effect and, finally, an increase in lobbying reduces the marginal effect of an increase in L on the tariff. Further, we suppose that to obtain any given tariff in a larger economy requires greater lobbying effort in equal proportion—this captures the idea that it is the number of representatives that must be lobbied that is critical in determining the effectiveness of lobbying and embodies the fact that all representatives have identical preferences and represent identical electorates. Thus $p[.]$ is homogeneous of degree zero in L^S and L.

As we wish to concentrate on the effect of forming a CU, we suppose initially that the X industry within each country is perfectly cohesive. So lobbying efforts are coordinated and there is no domestic free-riding problem. This simplification of Rodrik's model is not essential (and is relaxed later) but makes our notation tidier.

One final aspect of our model deserves some attention as we differ from the usual approach taken in the literature on FTAs. It is usually supposed that if two members of a FTA have different external tariffs on an imported good then their internal prices will differ. This stems from the enforcement of rules-of-origin to prevent the erosion of any such price differences through re-exporting (or trade "deflection"). However, Richardson (1992) and (1993b) points out that such rules can only maintain differences in consumer prices: while re-exporting of external goods can be prohibited, the export of goods produced within a FTA partner cannot. Thus, producer prices within a FTA must be equalized regardless of tariff (and consumer price) differences. This simple observation has a number of serious consequences for the analysis of FTAs; in particular it will affect the equilibrium level of external tariffs, possibly quite dramatically as the following example shows.

If one partner has a higher domestic price, *all* intra-FTA production will be sold in that country. For instance, suppose that $t^B < t^A$. To keep matters simple, suppose that total production of X in A and B combined is less than demand in one of the countries at all relevant prices;[12] in such a case all production of X is sold in A at a price $1 + t^A$ (recalling the normalization of the world price to unity) and all of B's consumption (at $p^B = 1 + t^B$) is imported from C. In this model of endogenous tariff-setting there is no incentive to expend *any* resources on lobbying in B in such a case as the tariff is completely redundant in protecting the industry in B so long as the partner's tariff is higher. However, the free-riding by B's producers has no consequences for the industry in A (even though it costs country A in terms of tariff revenues foregone) as the price faced by producers in A is still $1 + t^A$. Note that a CU is *not* affected by this problem as both partners' tariffs are then equal.

To complete the description of the model, we specify the problem facing the X industry. In the Y sector, production occurs according to $Y = wL_Y$ where w is a positive constant and L_Y denotes total labor employed in the Y sector. So long as the country is incompletely specialized, as assumed above, this guarantees that the wage rate in the economy is constant at w. Denoting industry values with upper-case letters and firm values with lower-case letters, the typical X-sector firm in country A (suppressing A superscripts for clarity) has a profit function given by π^i:

$$\pi^i = p^{max}f[l^{xi}, k] - w(l^{xi} + l^{si})$$

where $p^{max} \equiv max\{p[L^{s, -i} + l^{si}, L], 1 + t^B\}$

where l^{si} and l^{xi} denote labor devoted to lobbying and production respectively, $L^{s, -i} = \sum_{k \neq i}^n l^{sk}$ and $f[.]$ is the firm's linear homogeneous production function. Given the assumed cohesion of the industry lobby, the aggregate amount of labor to devote to lobbying, L^S, and the amount to employ in production, L^X, are chosen in order to maximize profits given by $\Pi^* = n\pi^i$. We seek a Nash equilibrium in lobbying expenditures so that each country's lobby group takes the level of lobbying in the other country as given. The industry's problem is then described in (18.1):

$$\underset{\{L^S, L^X\}}{Max} \ \Pi^* = p^{max}F[L^X, K] - w(L^S + L^X) \tag{18.1}$$

where $p^{max} = max\{p[L^S, L], 1 + t^B\}$ and $F[.] = nf[.]$.

Suppose first that $t^B = 0$ so that $p^{max} = p[L^S, L]$. First-order conditions (FOCs) for problem (18.1), assuming an interior solution, are then given in (18.2) and (18.3) where subscripts denote partial derivatives and asterisks denote optimal levels of L^X and L^S in the FTA regime. Each firm then sets $l^{xi} = L^{X*}/n$ and $l^{si} = L^{S*}/n$.

$$p[L^{S*}, L]F_1[L^{X*}, K] - w = 0 \qquad (18.2)$$

$$p_1[L^{S*}, L]F[L^{X*}, K] - w = 0 \qquad (18.3)$$

Second-order conditions (SOCs) for a maximum require, dropping function arguments for clarity, that $F_{11}^* < 0$, $p_{11}^* < 0$ and $p^* F_{11}^* p_{11}^* F^* - (p_1^* F_1^*)^2 > 0$. We also assume $p_{111} = F_{111} = 0$.

However, suppose instead that $1 + t^B \geq p[L^{S*}, L]$. In this case $p^{max} = 1 + t^B$ and the industry in A would be better served by free-riding on B's tariff, selling all its output in B, doing no lobbying and so saving on lobbying expenses.

18.2.2 FTA or CU?

The effect of a lobbying externality on the choice between a CU and a FTA is most clearly seen when A and B are identical. We start with a FTA between the two, with the external tariff in each set by optimal lobbying by firms in that country alone. The Appendix shows that a FTA in this context may be characterized by one of three Nash equilibria: two asymmetric outcomes in which one partner sets a zero tariff and free-rides on the other's lobbying and one mixed strategy equilibrium in which each industry sometimes lobbies and sometimes does not, attempting to free-ride.[13] In all cases, when an industry does lobby its optimal level is determined by (18.2) and (18.3).

Consider now the formation of a CU. While the level of protection depends on the resources devoted to lobbying by both countries, production still depends on resource allocation at the *national* level. In lobbying for protection in a CU the firm is faced with a larger anti-protection group, modeled here as the innate resistance to protection of a greater number of policy-makers representing a larger number of voters, than in the single-country case. On the other hand, there is also a greater number of firms lobbying for protection as the CU tariff affects firms in *both* countries. Were a CU to be formed, the tariff would be set according to $p[L^{SA} + L^{SB}, L^A + L^B]$ where L^{Si} and L^j denote the total amount of labor used in lobbying and the total size of the electorate respectively in country j, j = A, B. In this case, the industry in A, for example, faces problem (18.4), where tildes denote the CU regime:

$$\underset{\{L^{SA},L^{XA}\}}{\text{Max}} \ \tilde{\Pi} = p[L^{SB} + L^{SA}, 2L]F[L^{XA}, K] - w(L^{SA} + L^{XA}) \qquad (18.4)$$

FOCs for an interior solution to this problem are given in (18.5) and (18.6) where tildes denote optimal levels of L^X and L^S in the CU. Each firm sets $\tilde{l}^{xi} = \tilde{L}^X/n$ and $\tilde{l}^{si} = \tilde{L}^S/n$.

$$p[L^{SB} + \tilde{L}^S, 2L] \ F_1[2\tilde{L}^X, 2K] - w = 0 \qquad (18.5)$$

$$p_1[L^{SB} + \tilde{L}^S, 2L] \ F[2\tilde{L}^X, 2K] - 2w = 0 \qquad (18.6)$$

In writing (18.5) and (18.6) we have used the fact that both A and B are identical and so have aggregated the FOCs over 2n firms. While total lobbying may rise from the FTA to the CU (as one industry does no lobbying at all in the pure strategy FTA equilibrium) *effective* lobbying—in the sense of determining the producer price—will fall in the CU. There will be free-riding between the two countries' industries and so a lower level of lobbying by an active firm and thus a lower level of protection than is jointly optimal for the industry, but the free-riding is of a different nature to, and is not as extreme as, that in the FTA case.

We now show that the price received by producers in the CU is less than that received in the FTA pure strategy equilibria.[14] In the latter, firms in both A and B receive a price $p[L^{S*}, L]$, regardless of which country is activity lobbying. This price will only emerge in the CU if both industries expend L^{S*} on lobbying. It is clear that (18.5) and (18.6) cannot be solved by $\tilde{L}^S$ equal to L^{S*} and $\tilde{L}^X$ equal to L^{X*}: if this were the case then $F_1[\tilde{L}^X, K]$ would equal $F_1[L^{X*}, K]$ so that $p[L^{SB} + \tilde{L}^S, 2L]$ equals $p[L^{S*}, L]$ also, by (18.5). But then (18.6) and (18.3) would be inconsistent: $p_1[2\tilde{L}^S, 2L]F[\tilde{L}^X, K]$ equals $(1/2)p_1[L^{S*}, L]F[L^{X*}, K]$ by the homogeneity properties of $p[.]$.

To see that L^S and L^X would both fall were a CU to be formed note that, for (18.5) to hold, L^S and L^X must both either rise or fall $((dL^S/dL^X)|_{(18.5)} = -(pF_{11}/p_1F_1) > 0)$. This is shown as an upward-sloping locus (18.5) in L^S/L^X space in Figure 18.1. Equation (18.6) also defines a locus of L^S and L^X which is upward-sloping: $((dL^S/dL^X)|_{(18.6)} = -(p_1F_1/p_{11}F) > 0)$. By SOCs, (18.5) is steeper than (18.6). While (18.5) is satisfied at $L^S = L^{S*}$ and $L^X = L^{X*}$, the LHS of (18.6) is less than the RHS at this point. The value of the LHS of (18.6) is increasing in L^X, given L^S, thus the FTA point L^{S*}, L^{X*} must lie to the left of the locus satisfying (18.6), as drawn. So the values of L^S and L^X that jointly satisfy (18.5) and (18.6) must both be less than the FTA values.

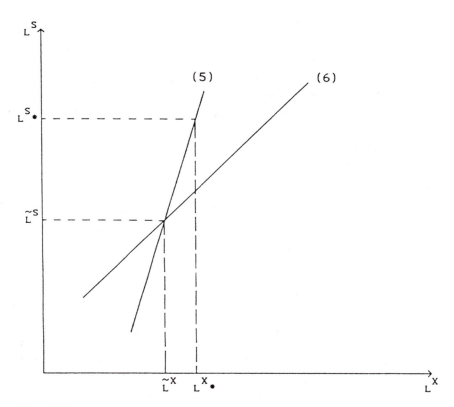

Figure 18.1

Hence firms in the X industry would be less profitable under a CU than under the FTA. This is true for both the industry not lobbying in the FTA (as it now incurs lobbying expenditures *and* receives a lower price than in the FTA) and for that which is lobbying.[15] In the mixed strategy FTA equilibrium the results are similar: the Appendix shows that expected profits are equal to those of the industries when *both* lobby in an amount L^{S*}. Again, this exceeds the profit that would ensue in a CU.

In the model exposited here we have established that firms in the import-competing sector would prefer a FTA to a CU (in fact, in this model with no trade between partners, our model implies that firms prefer independent external tariff-setting in general to a CU). We have not specified either how the choice between a CU and FTA is actually made or, indeed, how a preferential trading agreement gets onto the political agenda at all. In a model of endogenous policy, however, these are important issues. As noted in the Introduction, I have argued elsewhere (Richardson (1993a)) that there are a number of reasons that a preferential trading arrangement may succeed where marginal tariff reductions will not in models of endogenous tariffs. As far as the *form* of that arrangement is concerned, however, just as firms lobby for tariff levels, presumably they also lobby for their preferred arrangement. Our results above suggest firms would have a preference for a FTA in which the equilibrium external tariff will be higher.

Beyond the case of identical countries, it is clear that the externality effect will be more of a disincentive to forming a CU for a small country than for a large one. This is particularly true if internal lobby groups are *not* cohesive: a large country will then have a lower tariff in a FTA than a small country, as the externality problem is more extreme. Upon formation of a CU, the common external tariff will then be lower for *both* countries, thus the smaller partner will favor a FTA over a CU even more than the larger partner.

18.2.3 Some Modifications

Our results have been framed in a model with two prominent features. First, we assumed that lobbying firms were cohesive within a country but not within a CU and it might seem that the results follow from the presence of free-riding at the international level but not intranationally. Second, we have cast our analysis in a model in which producer prices are always equated within a FTA. While we argue that this is the correct context for analysis of a FTA, it might also seem that our results are a consequence of this framework in that, for example, only one industry lobbies in the pure strategy FTA equilibrium. This Section demonstrates that our conclusions are robust to both of these features of the model. Briefly, the presence of internal free-riding does not change the qualitative results as the free-riding problem is still exacerbated by the formation of a CU (with 2n firms lobbying as opposed to n.) Nor is the equality of producer prices in a FTA qualitatively significant here: in the standard approach we have *both* industries lobbying in the amount L^{S*} in the FTA as opposed to just one in the pure strategy equilibrium above.

In this set-up, each of n firms lobbies independently, taking the efforts of the others as given, and the producer price in the FTA is simply the outcome of domestic lobbying, regardless of the partner country's efforts. Typical firm i chooses l^{si} and l^{xi} to maximize $\pi^i = p[L^{S,\,-i} + l^{si}, L]\, f[l^{xi}, k] - w(l^{xi} + l^{si})$. FOCs are (18.7) and (18.8):

$$p_1[.]f[.] - w = 0 \tag{18.7}$$

$$p[.]f_1[.] - w = 0 \tag{18.8}$$

As $f[.]$ is hom(1) (and so $f_1[.]$ is hom(0)) so adding (18.7) and (18.8) up over n symmetric firms gives (18.9) and (18.10), where double asterisks denote FTA equilibrium values:[16]

$$p_1[.]f[nl^{xi}, nk] - nw = 0 \quad \text{or} \quad p_1[L^{S**}, L]F[L^{X**}, K] = nw \tag{18.9}$$

$$p[.]f_1[nl^{xi}, nk] - w = 0 \quad \text{or} \quad p[L^{S**}, L]F_1[L^{X**}, K] = w \tag{18.10}$$

For a CU, L is doubled and each of the 2n firms lobbies the same tariff-setting agent. Deriving FOCs as before, using carets to denote optimal aggregate levels in one country, aggregating over 2n firms and invoking symmetry, we get (18.11) and (18.12):

$$p_1[2\hat{L}^S, 2L]F[2\hat{L}^X, 2K] = 2nw \tag{18.11}$$

$$p[2\hat{L}^S, 2L]F_1[2\hat{L}^X, 2K] = w \tag{18.12}$$

If the CU were to leave optimal labor employment in each use unchanged, so that $\hat{L}^S = L^{S**}$ and $\hat{L}^S = L^{S**}$, then (18.12) would hold as both $p[.]$ and $F_1[.]$ are hom(0) in their arguments. However, while the RHS of (18.11) is twice that of (18.9), the LHS is the same, from the homogeneity properties of $F[.]$ and $p_1[.]$. Inspection of (18.11) and (18.12), as earlier, demonstrates that both L^S and L^X must fall when the CU is formed.[17] Further, it is clear that firms' profits must fall when the CU is formed—the internal free-riding which leads to lobbying and output both being too low already in the FTA is worsened by international free-riding in the CU which leads output and lobbying to fall even further. To see this formally, note first that per-firm profits are simply $\pi^i = \Pi/n$ so if Π falls so too does π^i. Then,

$$d\Pi = (p_1[.]F[.] - w) dL^S + (p[.]F_1[.] - w) dL^X = (n-1)w dL^S > 0$$

when evaluated at the FTA outcome L^{X**}, L^{S**}: (18.9) implies that $p_1[L^{S**}, L]F[L^{X**}, K]$ equals nw and (18.10) that $p[L^{S**}, L]F_1[L^{X**}, K] - w$ equals 0. That is, aggregate profits would rise if L^S were increased (and L^X too: as we go from a FTA to a CU, L^X continues to be chosen optimally, for each L^S, so (18.10) gives L^X as an implicit function of L^S and implies that $dL^X/dL^S = -(p_1[.]F_1[.])/(p[.]F_{11}[.]) > 0$.) Thus the *decrease* in L^S and L^X that the CU induces only serves to lower profits further.

18.2.4   Welfare

We turn now to analysis of the welfare consequences of changes in the external tariff. As these are small countries it is clear that consumers must lose from any tariff. However, tariff reductions yield additional gains here in that they occur as a consequence of decreased lobbying, an activity that uses real resources. As Rodrik (1986) notes, it is not clear exactly what interpretation can be placed upon the standard welfare calculus in this sort of model as policy-makers are automata who do not attempt to maximize any particular measure of social welfare. Furthermore, policy-makers may themselves derive some welfare from lobbying activities and this is not considered in the following analysis. Nevertheless, it is instructive to examine the effects on the representative consumer of any change in lobbying here, using the model of Section 18.2.3 above.[18]

Intuitively, the ideal is to have free trade and waste no resources in lobbying. With a positive tariff too much of the importable is produced from the point of view of an efficient allocation of resources *and* there is wasteful lobbying. The CU, in reducing the level of lobbying, improves welfare on both these fronts.

Letting u denote the utility level of the aggregate consumer we can describe consumers' behavior by an aggregate expenditure function $E[1, p, u]$ which has all of the usual properties (see Dixit and Norman (1980)). National income in this economy is the sum of the values of output of X and Y plus any tariff revenue earned on imports of X. Thus the economy's budget constraint is given by:

$$E[1, p, u] = p[L^S, L]F[L^X, K] + w(L - L^S - L^X) + (p - p^*)m^X \qquad (18.13)$$

where m^X denotes imports of X. We use the following facts to totally differentiate (18.13) and rearrange to get (18.14) which measures welfare effects of any small changes in L^S or L^X. First, the partial derivative of $E[.]$ with respect to p, E_p, gives the compensated demand for X. Second, imports are consumption minus production, so $m^X = E_p[.] - F[.]$. Third, $t = p - p^*$, $dp^* = 0$ (small country) and $dp = p_1 dL^S$.

$$(E_u - tE_{pu}) du = (tE_{pp}p_1 - w) dL^S - tF_1 dL^X \qquad (18.14)$$

We make the usual stability assumption that the Hatta term, $(E_u - tE_{pu})$, is positive. Expression (18.14) identifies three channels through which an increase in L^S or L^X will affect welfare. The coefficient on dL^S on the right hand side is comprised of two effects. As E_{pp} is negative ($E[.]$ is concave in prices) so the term $tE_{pp}p_1\,dL^S$ represents lost tariff revenue on decreased imports of X resulting from a higher consumer price as increased lobbying raises the tariff. An extra unit of labor devoted to lobbying decreases Y production by w, hence the second term—$w\,dL^S$ is a welfare loss due to this lost output and represents the real resource cost of lobbying. The final term in (18.14) captures the loss of tariff revenues from increased output of the importable at home if more labor is devoted to its production.

We demonstrated in 18.2.3 above that $dL^S < 0$ and $dL^X < 0$ as we go from a FTA to a CU. From (18.14), therefore, these changes are unambiguously welfare-improving.[19]

18.3   Summary and Conclusion

In this chapter we have argued that, when policy is set for reasons other than traditional welfare considerations—specifically, when it is the outcome of a particular endogenous political process—there may be reasons a FTA is preferred to a CU. In particular, in our model of lobbying, a CU entails a lobbying externality and leads to lower tariffs and decreased profitability of firms. We have shown that this conclusion holds whether or not producer prices are equated in a FTA and whether or not lobbying is plagued by free-riding at the national level.

One final comment on the model used here is in order. We have taken a very simple two-good framework in which to exposit our main result. As noted, a more satisfactory treatment of preferential trading arrangements requires at least three goods in order to motivate the formation of a FTA with internal trade whilst also featuring goods traded by both partners with the non-partner. Adding another good, however, greatly complicates the analysis of the political market—another fixed factor, for example, would also indulge in lobbying against the tariff on X and results on the desirability of a CU would hinge critically upon which industry is more plagued by the free-riding externality. Nevertheless, the basic results of this chapter should carry over to more sophisticated models with appropriate modifications.

Appendix

This Appendix works through the analysis of Section 18.2.1 when producer prices are equated within a FTA even if external tariffs differ. We confine our attention to the case wherein total demand for X in A and B exceeds total intra-FTA supply at all relevant prices; thus the free-riding effect has no impact on consumer prices.

As a FTA cannot restrict the location of sales of firms from either member country, so producers in both countries face the same price as each other even if external tariffs (and thus consumers' prices) differ. Accordingly, given a world price 1, if consumer prices in country $i = A$, B are denoted $p^i = 1 + t^i$ then producers in i face a price $p_p^i = p^m \equiv \max\{p^A, p^B\}$. Let the tariff that results from the solution to the industry's problem in Section 18.2 of the chapter be denoted t^*. That is, t^* is the tariff that results when each industry lobbies for its own protection—this is not only the FTA equilibrium in the analysis of Section 18.2.3 (and the pure strategy equilibrium level of FTA tariff in the country that lobbies in the model of 18.2.1) but, in this model of identical countries, is also the tariff that would result if A and B were to have no FTA but were to set tariffs unilaterally instead. As a last piece of notation, let $\Pi^i[t^A, t^B]$ now denote the derived profit function of the industry in country $i = A$, B in a FTA, written as a function of external tariffs. Profits depend directly on the choice of L^S and L^X but the former maps monotonically into a tariff rate. Let $L^{Xi}[L^{Si}]$ denote the solution to the following partial maximization problem, *given* L^{Si}:

$$\underset{\{L^{Xi}\}}{\text{Max}} \; p[L^{Si}, L^i]F[L^{Xi}, K] - w(L^{Si} + L^{Xi})$$

Then, where $t^i[L^{Si}]$ is the tariff that results from lobbying of L^{Si}, we define:

$$\Pi^A[t^A, t^B] \equiv \Pi^A[t^A[L^{SA}], t^B[L^{SB}]]$$

$$= p^{max}F[L^{XA}[L^{SA}], K] - w(L^{SA} + L^{XA}[L^{SA}])$$

where $p^{max} \equiv 1 + \max\{t^A[L^{SA}], t^B[L^{SB}]\}$. The industry's problem is then to choose L^{SA} to maximize Π^A but, as $p_1 < 0$ and L^i is fixed, each level of L^{Si} is associated with a unique t^i; thus we can write profits in terms of tariffs rather than the more fundamental lobbying levels.

A useful way to view this problem is to consider Π^A as a composite function:[20]

$$\Pi^A[t^A, t^B] = \max\{\Pi^{A1}[t^A], \Pi^{A2}[t^B]\}$$

$$\text{where} \begin{cases} \Pi^{A1} = (1 + t^A[L^{SA}])F[.] - (wL^{SA} + L^{XA}[L^{SA}]) \\ \Pi^{A2} = (1 + t^B)F[L^{XA}, K] - wL^{XA} \end{cases}$$

This is generically illustrated in Figure 18.2 for some $t^B = t''$ where profits from doing no lobbying and free-riding on B's tariff are shown as $\Pi^{A2}[t'']$,

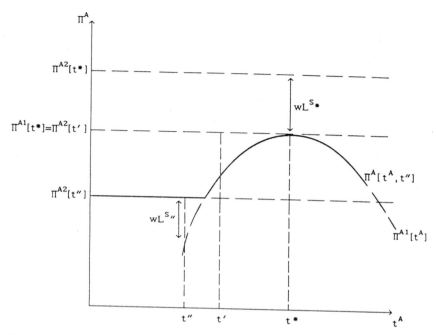

Figure 18.2

profits from lobbying for one's own tariff are shown as $\Pi^{A1}[t^A]$ and the composite upper envelope of the two is shown as the heavy continuous line $\Pi^A[t^A, t'']$. L^{XA} is chosen optimally in all cases. Note that (i) when $t^A = t''$ it is more profitable to free-ride ($\Pi^{A2}[t''] > \Pi^{A1}[t^A]$) as lobbying expenses of $wL^{S''}$ are saved (where $L^{S''}$ is the amount of lobbying needed to generate $t^A = t''$), and (ii) $\Pi^A[t^A, t'']$ itself is continuous in t^A.

Returning to our earlier notation, we also note for later use that:

$$\Pi^A[0, t^*] > \Pi^A[t^*, t^*] = \Pi^A[t^*, 0] > \Pi^A[0, 0].$$

The first inequality follows from the fact that, while the price faced by A's producers is the same in each case, in the first case it does no lobbying and, by revealed preference arguments, must be better off. The equality stems from our assumption regarding the relative magnitudes of demand and supplies—if B's producers free-ride on A's tariff it has no effect on A's producers. The second inequality follows from the optimality of t^* in a unilateral tariff setting context.

We consider the problem facing the industry in country A (by symmetry, that facing the industry in country B is identical). We wish to

construct a reaction function describing A's optimal tariff in response to
each t^B, taking the latter as given. Note that the industry's direct choice is
of lobbying efforts but this maps directly into the tariff that we are considering. Bearing in mind that if producers in B sell in country A this has
no effect on A's producers, for very "low" levels of t^B (described more
precisely below) the problem facing the industry in A is just that described in program (18.1) of Section 18.2 of the chapter, leading to $t^A = t^*$.

However, as t^B increases, the prospect of doing no lobbying and free-
riding on B becomes more attractive. Certainly if $t^B \geq t^*$ the industry in A
will do no lobbying. However, there is also a range of tariff levels less
than t^* for which this strategy is more profitable for the industry in A
than is lobbying for its own tariff. The reason is simply that it saves on
lobbying expenses. By continuity of the industry profit function in (18.1),
even though it is less profitable to sell at a price below $1 + t^*$, the loss in
profits when t^B is only slightly less than t^* is more than offset by the discrete gain in saved lobbying resources. This will be true for all levels of
the tariff in the partner above some critical minimum t' where $t' < t^*$. Formally, t' is defined by the following equality: $\Pi^A[0, t'] = \Pi^A[t^*, t']$ where
the latter also equals $\Pi^A[t^*, 0]$. We can illustrate this critical point in
Figure 18.2. If $t^B = t^*$ then $\Pi^{A2}[t^*] = \Pi^{A1}[t^*] + wL^{S*}$ (that is, free-riding is
more profitable than lobbying to the extent that lobbying expenditures
are saved.) The critical $t^B = t'$ occurs where the saved expenditures are
exactly offset by foregone profits from a lower price.

Thus Figure 18.3 illustrates the discontinuous reaction function for
country A as the two horizontal double lines labeled R^A and the symmetric function for B as the heavy vertical lines labeled R^B. Accordingly,
there are two pure strategy equilibria to this game at points E and E'
in the figure corresponding to $\{t^A, t^B\} = \{t^*, 0\}$ and $\{0, t^*\}$ respectively.
In the former, country B is a free-rider, $\Pi^A = \Pi^A[t^*, 0] = \Pi^A[t^*, t^*]$ and
$\Pi^B = \Pi^B[t^*, 0] > \Pi^B[t^*, t^*]$; in the latter the roles are reversed, country A
free-rides, $\Pi^A = \Pi^A[0, t^*] > \Pi^A[t^*, t^*]$ and $\Pi^B = \Pi^B[0, t^*] = \Pi^B[t^*, t^*]$.
These contrast to the unilateral tariff setting equilibrium (and FTA equilibrium of the analysis of section 18.2.3) at E^*.

However, there is also an equilibrium in mixed strategies in which
each industry lobbies for a tariff of t^* with probability α and does no
lobbying with probability $(1 - \alpha)$. In this equilibrium, expected profit to
each industry is $\Pi^i[t^*, t^*]$, $i = A, B$. To establish this as an equilibrium
we need to show both that the profitability of each element of the
strategy is the same in response to the strategy of the rival and that the
industry can do no better in response to the rival's strategy. Suppose

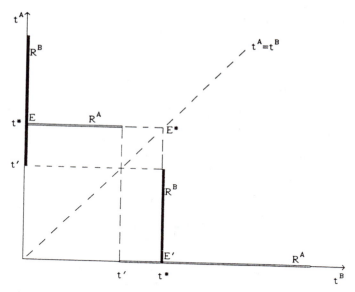

Figure 18.3

$t^A = 0$. Then, as B mixes over 0 and t^*, expected profits in A are $E\Pi^A = \alpha\Pi^A[0, t^*] + (1 - \alpha)\Pi^A[0, 0] \equiv \overline{\Pi}^A$. But if $t^A = t^*$ then $E\Pi^A = \alpha\Pi^A[t^*, t^*] + (1 - \alpha)\Pi^A[t^*, 0] = \Pi^A[t^*, t^*]$ by the equivalences listed earlier. But $\Pi^A[0, t^*] > \Pi^A[t^*, t^*] > \Pi^A[0, 0]$ so there exists some $\alpha \in (0, 1)$ such that $\overline{\Pi}^A = \Pi^A[t^*, t^*]$.[21] Overall expected profit from this strategy is $\Pi^A[t^*, t^*]$, as claimed. To see that the industry can do no better than this strategy, in response to the same strategy of the rival, note that L^{S*}, the optimal level of lobbying in the pure strategy equilibrium in which the industry in A lobbies, solves:

$$\frac{\partial E\left(\Pi^A[L^{SA}]\right)}{\partial L^{SA}} = \Pi_1^A[t^A, 0]\frac{dt^A}{dL^{SA}} - w = 0$$

In the mixed strategy equilibrium, the industry lobbies with only probability α. In these instances, the optimal level of lobbying solves:

$$\frac{\partial E(\Pi^A[L^{SA}])}{\partial L^{SA}} = \alpha\left\{\frac{dt^A}{dL^{SA}}[\alpha\Pi_1^A[t^A, t^B] + (1 - \alpha)\Pi_1^A[t^A, 0]] - w\right\}$$

$$= \alpha\left\{\frac{dt^A}{dL^{SA}}\Pi_1^A[t^A, 0] - w\right\} = 0$$

where the equality follows from the equivalence of $\Pi^A[t^A, 0]$ and $\Pi^A[t^A, t^B]$ for $t^A \geq t^B$. Thus the optimal degree of lobbying is L^{S*}, as claimed.

Notes

Alternatively, John Schorn has suggested [as a title], "A Farewell to Customs Unions." This chapter was written with financial support from a Georgetown University Summer Research Fellowship. I wish to thank, without incriminating, Costas Syropoulos and participants at the Southeast International Economics Meetings, Fall 1990, for comments on an earlier draft of this paper. I am also grateful to two anonymous referees for their helpful comments; the same disclaimer applies.

1. Dani Rodrik has noted that this argument is similar to one in the Federalist Papers concerning the benefits of a large republic. One such benefit is that, ceteris paribus, a faction is likely to have less power in a large than a small republic due to the increased likelihood of opposing cartels. So policies in a large republic are less likely to be hostage to the interests of any particular faction.

2. A referee has pointed out that the criteria of choice between a CU and a FTA are rather different in our setup and those of Dixit and Norman (1980) and Woodland (1982). They consider a country's welfare as traditionally defined in terms of a representative agent, whereas the choice in our model is implicitly determined by the profitability of firms. We argue that trade policy is effectively set by the lobbying activities of interested firms and demonstrate that a FTA may be more profitable to firms than a CU; accordingly firms will lobby for the former.

3. Wonnacott and Wonnacott (1981), however, provide an example in which a union of two small countries with "traditional" welfare-maximizing governments may be mutually beneficial in the presence of either transport costs or *non*-members tariffs.

4. Dixit and Norman (1980) show that any two tariff-ridden countries can form a CU and arrange internal taxies in such a fashion that neither is worse off (and each is strictly better off if there is any smooth transformation on the production possibility surface). That any FTA can be weakly dominated by an appropriately chosen CU is a direct consequence of this result; Richardson (1992) demonstrates that internal free trade in a FTA equalizes producer prices so that the result is weakened to equivalence between any FTA and some CU. However, the equivalent CU is unlikely to be optimal so, in general, the dominance result will still hold strictly.

5. We refer to "the tariff" henceforth but this is meant to include export subsidies.

6. In fact, we shall subsequently assume each country is identical in order to isolate the lobbying externality on which our argument focuses so even in a more general setting there would be no trade between member countries. The question then arises as to why these countries wish to form a FTA in the first place but this is a question that plagues any model of preferential trading arrangements between small countries, albeit for different reasons than in the present setting.

7. This activity is not bribery—we assume that resources devoted to lobbying represent a welfare loss to the economy as a whole and are not simply a transfer.

8. We take lobbying expenditures to be equal across these symmetric representatives but it does not matter if, instead, efforts are concentrated on only a few of them. With majority voting, lobbyists would be best to concentrate their efforts on only a fraction $((1/2) + 1)$ of the representatives but this does not affect our analysis.

9. This model of the political process can be formalized as the choice of prices p by policy-makers to maximize a payoff function $G[\mathscr{L}^S, V[p, I]]$ where $\mathscr{L}^S$ denotes per-representative industry lobbying, $V[.]$ is the typical voter's indirect utility function defined over prices and income, $\partial G/\partial \mathscr{L}^S > 0$ and $\partial G/\partial V > 0$. The number of representatives is assumed to be linear in L, the number of voters, so this problem determines a policy-maker's optimal tariff as a function of both L and L^S, total lobbying. We suppose that policy-makers care only about their own consumers, even when a CU is formed. Were they to care about the partner country's consumers too then resistance to a tariff in a CU would be greater, reinforcing our results.

10. This assumption is easily modified to include the n capital owners as voters also in which case the electorate is $L + n$. This change has no impact on our analysis.

11. Throughout this paper, square brackets contain function arguments.

12. While this is not critical to the argument that producer prices will be equalized, it does determine the *level* at which such equalization occurs.

13. It is this mixed strategy equilibrium that complicates the analysis if lobbying were plagued by a free-rider problem at the *national* level. If firms' lobbying were not coordinated then any mixed-strategy behavior by n firms between, say, $l^s = 0$ and l^{s*} would yield a total lobbying (and so tariff) distribution with $n + 1$ mass points $(L^S = 0, l^{s*}, 2l^{s*}, \ldots, L^{S*})$. Equilibrium would require that each firm's strategy be an individually optimal response to the others' given this profile in both the home and partner countries. As this wrinkle seems to add nothing to the analysis, we have concentrated here on a simpler case of coordinated domestic lobby groups.

14. I am grateful to an anonymous referee for suggesting the following approach instead of my earlier rather clumsy proof.

15. The fall in profitability for the industry that lobbies follows from the fact that lobbying was optimal in the FTA equilibrium, from the industry point of view.

16. Comparing (18.7) and (18.8) with (18.2) and (18.3), the latter two in the case where $p^{max} = p[L^{S*}, L]$, one can see the added free-rider effect here: the value of the marginal product of labor devoted to lobbying is equated to nw in the present case but w in our former specification. Clearly, per-firm lobbying is lower here.

17. In the manner of Section 18.2.2, (18.11) and (18.12) define upward-sloping locii of L^S and L^X and, by SOCs, (18.12) is steeper than (18.11). While (18.12) is satisfied at $L^S = L^{S**}$ and $L^X = L^{X***}$, the LHS of (18.11) is less than the RHS at this point. The value of the LHS of (18.11) is increasing in L^X, given L^S, thus the FTA point L^{S**}, L^{X**} must lie to the left of the locus satisfying (18.11): the values of L^S and L^X that jointly satisfy (18.11) and (18.12) must both be less than the FTA values.

18. Welfare analysis is rather more complex in the model of Section 18.2.1 for the following reasons. Consider the FTA equilibrium in which country A does no lobbying at all but country B does so A sells all its domestic production in B at a price $1 + t^B$. National income in A thus includes tariff revenue on total *consumption*. Formation of a CU now is definitely welfare-improving in the traditional manner in B: not only does the tariff fall but lobbying resources are saved *and* tariff revenue is earned on imports now sourced from outside the

union rather than tariff-free from A. In country A, however, things are not so rosy. The consumer price will rise (in the FTA there is no tariff, recall) and lobbying expenses increase.

19. In considering the transition from a FTA to a CU we wish to deal with large, discrete changes in L^S and L^X. Furthermore, as a CU is formed so the number of representatives to be lobbied increases; that is, the second argument of $p[.]$ also rises. Nevertheless, the expression above can be used directly in the case of two identical countries forming a CU. The reason we can ignore the increase in L is that in the symmetric equilibrium the effect of doubling the number of voters is exactly offset by the effect of doubling the number of firms, insofar as per-firm lobbying is unchanged, due to the homogeneity of $p[.]$. So the only net effect on the tariff is from changes in L^S and even though the magnitude of the tariff response for some dL^S is lessened in the CU, as $p_{12} < 0$, the qualitative effect is unchanged. The discrete changes in L^S and L^X leave the welfare conclusions unaltered because utility is monotonic in L^S and L^X where changes in L^S and L^X are related by FOCs (18.2) and (18.3).

20. I am grateful to a referee for suggesting this approach.

21. With risk-neutral firms this is all we need. With risk-aversion the equilibrium survives with the mixing proportions on the two elements of the strategy altered such that the certainty equivalent of profits when setting $t^A = 0$ equals $\Pi^A(t^*, t^*)$.

References

Dixit, A. and V. Norman, 1980, *Theory of International Trade* (Nisbet and CUP, Cambridge).

Hillman, A., 1982, Declining industries and political-support protectionist motives. *American Economic Review* 72 #5, 1180–1187.

Lloyd, P. J., 1982, 3 × 3 theory of customs unions. *Journal of International Economics* 12, 41–64.

Richardson, M., 1992, Some implications of internal trade in a free-trade area. *Working paper* #92-01, Department of Economics, Georgetown University.

————, 1993a, Endogenous protection and trade diversion. *Journal of International Economics* 34, 309–324.

————. 1993b, *Tariff revenue competition in a free trade area*. Mimeo, Department of Economics, Georgetown University.

Rodrik, D., 1986, Tariffs, subsidies and welfare with endogenous policy. *Journal of International Economics* 21, 285–299.

Wonnacott, P. and R. Wonnacott, 1981, Is unilateral tariff reduction preferable to a customs union? The curious case of the missing foreign tariffs. *American Economic Review* 71, 704–714.

Woodland, A. D., 1982, *International Trade and Resource Allocation* (North-Holland Publishing Co., Amsterdam).

III

"Dynamic" Time-Path Analysis: Issues of Sequential Expansion

Endogenously Determined
PTA Expansion

19

Regionalism versus Multilateralism: Analytical Notes

Paul Krugman

With the Uruguay Round still (at the time of writing) on the brink, with growing tensions between the United States and Japan, and with growing support in the United States for a more or less aggressive industrial policy, it is evident that the GATT-centred system of multilateral trade relations is in considerable trouble. At the same time, regional trading arrangements such as "EC 1992" and the North American Free-Trade Area (NAFTA) have appeared to be the cutting edge of whatever successful international negotiations have taken place. This apparent shift away from globalism to localism has created severe ambivalence among policy intellectuals. Should the rise of regional trading arrangements be welcomed, as a step on the road that will ultimately reinforce global free trade? Or should regional trading blocs be condemned, as institutions that undermine the multilateral system? Or, yet again, should they perhaps be accepted more or less grudgingly, as the best option we are likely to get in an age of diminished expectations?

This ambivalence, and the striking extent to which reasonable analysts find themselves in sharp disagreement, are not surprising. The issue of multilateralism versus regionalism is a difficult one to get one's arms around, on at least two levels. First, even in narrowly economic terms it is a tricky area: after all, it was precisely in the context of preferential trading arrangements that the byzantine complexities of the second best were first discovered.

Second, the real issues cannot be viewed as narrowly economic. International trading regimes are essentially devices of political economy; they are intended at least as much to protect nations from their own interest groups as they are to protect nations from each other. Any discussion of

Originally published, as chapter 3, in *New Dimensions in Regional Integration*, ed. Jaime de Melo and Arvind Panagariya (Cambridge, UK: Cambridge University Press, 1993), 58–79. Reprinted with permission.

the international trading system necessarily thus involves an attempt to discuss not what policy ought to be, but what it actually will be under various rule of the game. And the science of politics is, if possible, even less developed than that of economics.

In this realm of foggy discussion it is natural for economists to grab hold of any analytical tools they can find, even if they are ill-adapted to the work at hand. In an earlier paper (Krugman, 1991a), I offered a simple framework for thinking about the effects of the consolidation of a world of many nations into a smaller number of trading blocs. That framework (briefly reproduced in the Appendix to this chapter) had some merit as a concise way of thinking about the issues of trade creation and diversion, but was grossly unrealistic in its description of the trade-policy process. Nonetheless, it was one of the few games in town—at the very least, it offered a language for talking about the issue—and plunged me into the debate. In a follow-up paper (Krugman, 1991b) I used the original model as stiffening for a broader and looser analytical argument, which was in turn used to give some intellectual credibility to a largely model-free discussion of the political economy of trade. That paper proved startlingly controversial, to an extent that was bound to worry an economist who knew that he was speculating well beyond his analytical base.

The problem, of course, is that in spite of decades of intense research into the normative economics of trade policy, there are no widely accepted positive models of policy formation. And the multilateral–regional debate hinges crucially on how the institutions of the trading system will affect not just the consequences of given trade policies, but the choices by governments of what policies actually to adopt.

The purpose of this chapter is obviously not to propose a general theory of the political economy of trade policy—not only do I not have such a theory, I have no idea even where to start.[1] Instead, it offers a set of partial analyses that try to move the discussion of the trading bloc issue a little closer to giving a realistic account of trade policy, and thus a better account of the likely economic effects.

The chapter is in five sections. Section 19.1 reviews briefly the simple trading-bloc model originally developed in Krugman (1991a), then argues that its main *economic* conclusions are not too sensitive to the outrageously unrealistic trade-policy process that that paper assumed. Section 19.2 offers a stab at a more realistic description of unilateral trade-policy formation, based on the idea that governments maximise "weighted social welfare," and tries to relate this description to the issues raised earlier.

Section 19.3 turns to bargaining and international negotiations. Finally, section 19.4 combines the pieces to offer a loose second cut at the multilateralism–regionalism issue. Section 19.5 draws some summary conclusions.

19.1   The Narrow Economics of Trading Blocs

The pure economic theory of trading blocs is essentially part of the broader theory of preferential trading arrangements. This theory has been extensively studied. Unfortunately, it is a subject of inherent complexity and ambiguity; theory per se identifies the main forces at work, but offers few presumptions about what is likely to happen in practice. To make any headway, one must either get into detailed empirical work, or make strategic simplifications and stylisations that one hopes do not lead one too far astray. Obviously detailed empirical work is the right approach, but will not be followed in this chapter. Instead, I continue to use the stylised approach from Krugman (1991a).

19.1.1   A Political Economy Model (Krugman, 1991a)

In my initial trading-bloc model I tried to cut through the complexities of second-best analysis with a highly stylised model of a world economy. The structure of this world economy was as follows:

1. The world was assumed to consist of a large number of small geographical units ("provinces"), each specialised in the production of a distinct good.

2. The products of all provinces were assumed to enter symmetrically into world demand, with a constant elasticity of substitution σ between any two such products.

3. The world was assumed to be organised into B trading blocs of equal economic size, with free trade within each bloc and an ad valorem tariff rate t charged by each bloc on imports.

4. The blocs were assumed to set tariffs non-cooperatively, in order to maximise welfare.

The unrealism of this setup is obvious. Yet it had the virtue of offering a simple way to think about regionalism versus multilateralism. One could envision a move to regional trading blocs as involving a reduction in B. In the model, such a reduction in B leads to a mixture of trade creation and trade diversion. Trade creation occurs because a larger share of world trade takes place within blocs, and hence free from tariffs. Trade diversion occurs for two reasons. First, at any given tariff rate, enlarging blocs will lead to some diversion of trade that would otherwise take place between provinces in different blocs. Second, given the policy assumption (4), larger blocs, which have more market power, have an incentive to levy higher tariffs than small blocs; so as B falls, trade between blocs becomes less free.

Because of the mix of trade creation and diversion, consolidation into a smaller number of blocs has an ambiguous effect on welfare. Somewhat surprisingly, the best outcomes are with either very few or very many trading blocs. The intuition for the desirability of few blocs is obvious: when there is only one bloc, the world has achieved free trade. The converse case is perhaps less obvious: when there are many small players, each has limited market power and thus sets tariffs low—and imports are so large a share of consumption that a flat tariff has little distortive effect in any case. The worst case turns out to be for intermediate numbers of blocs, where potential inter-bloc trade is important yet tariffs distort it significantly.

The startling result is numerical: for a wide range of elasticities of substitution σ, the welfare-minimising number of blocs is three.

What is wrong with this model? The economic assumptions are grossly unrealistic, especially the absence of any structure of natural trading relations that defines natural blocs; we return to this point below. Even worse, however, is the description of trade politics embodied in assumption (4). Whatever it is that countries do when they set trade policy, they certainly do not choose the tariff level that satisfies the optimal tariff criterion. Even in Krugman (1991b), the problems with this assumption were acknowledged: "This setup is clearly both too cynical and not cynical enough about the political economy of trade. The internal politics of trade are not nearly this benign: governments do not simply (or ever) maximize the welfare of their citizens. At the same time, the external politics of trade show far more cooperation than this."

In fact, the numerical results themselves are a dead giveaway that the description of politics is very wrong. For any reasonable elasticity of substitution, the model predicts tariff rates that are far higher than what large industrial countries, which are presumably the ones with the most market power, impose in fact.

But do the conclusions about the shape of the relationship between the number of blocs and world welfare hinge crucially on the unrealism of the assumed trade-policy process? In fact, they do not.

19.1.2 Robustness of the Economics to Policy Description

The surprise of the basic trading-bloc model is its assertion that welfare is U-shaped in the number of trading blocs, and that welfare is minimised for a small number of blocs—which suggests that current trends could indeed be adverse.

The question is whether this result depends crucially on the political piece of the model. That is, does it depend crucially on (i) the very high tariff rates predicted by the model, and (ii) the tendency of larger blocs to impose high tariffs?

One might already have guessed that (ii) was not very important to the results from the charts presented in Krugman (1991a). It turned out that predicted tariff rates did not, in fact, rise very much with reductions in B. The reason was basically that sufficient trade diversion takes place as B falls that the share of a typical bloc in foreign markets does not rise much—for example, when we move from a four-bloc to a three-bloc world, interbloc trade falls so much that each of the three blocs has only a slightly higher share in the external market, and hence faces only a slightly lower elasticity of demand, than each of the previous four blocs. This suggests that trade diversion at a *constant* tariff rate is doing most of the work.

The easy way to confirm this hunch is to examine how welfare varies with B when one holds tariffs constant at much lower, more realistic levels. That is, we abandon assumption (4) and replace it with the simple assumption that all blocs maintain a common external tariff at the rate *t*, whatever the number of blocs. It is possible to show (see Krugman, 1991a) that if we normalise so that world welfare is 1 under global free trade, welfare with B blocs charging a tariff rate *t* is

$$U = \left[\frac{B}{(1+t)^{\sigma} + B - 1}\right][(1 - B^{-1}) + B^{-1}(1+t)^{\sigma-1}]^{\sigma/(\sigma-1)}. \qquad (19.1)$$

Figure 19.1 shows calculations of (19.1) for an elasticity of substitution of 4 (which implies optimal tariff rates of more than 35 percent), varying B while holding *t* at 0.1, 0.2 and 0.3. The U-shape appears in spite of the lack of an endogenous tariff rate. Indeed, for the higher tariff rates world

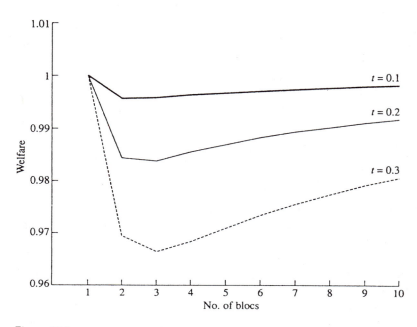

Figure 19.1
Number of blocs and welfare.

welfare continues to be minimised at $B = 3$, although at a 10 percent tariff the pessimum moves to two blocs.

The moral of this exercise is that the basic story about potential losses from consolidation into a limited number of trade blocs is not dependent on the specific model of tariff determination laid out in earlier papers. We may note also that this means that focusing on policy changes as a result of bloc formation may be missing the point. For example, suppose we ask whether NAFTA will hurt world trade. The participants may pledge solemnly not to raise external barriers, and may even honour that pledge. Nonetheless, this model suggests that the net effect is still one of trade diversion that could easily outweigh trade creation.

What could invalidate the story? The question is how the tariff rate depends on B. If the tariff rate rises as B falls, as in the case where t is set non-cooperatively to miximise bloc welfare, then the story is simply reinforced. In order to change the story sharply, one must offer a reason why a reduction in the number of blocs might actually lead each bloc to adopt lower rather than higher external tariffs.

We will turn to (crude) models of policy below. First, however, it is necessary to repeat a caveat that plays a key role in any attempt at realistic discussion: the importance of natural trading relations.

19.1.3   The "Natural" Trading-Bloc Issue

If transportation and communication costs lead to a strong tendency of countries to trade with their neighbours, and if free-trade areas (FTAs) are to be formed among such good neighbours, then the likelihood that consolidation into a few large trading blocs will reduce world welfare is much less than suggested by Figure 19.1. The reason is straightforward: the gains from freeing intra-regional trade will be larger, and the costs of reducing interregional trade smaller, than the geography-free story suggests.

Imagine, for example, a world of four countries, which may potentially consolidate into two trading blocs. Suppose that these countries are all symmetric, and that external tariffs are fixed at 10 percent. Then two blocs is the number that minimises world welfare, and hence this consolidation will be harmful. Suppose, however, that each pair of countries is on a different continent, and that intercontinental transport costs are sufficiently high that the bulk of trade would be between continental neighbours even in the absence of tariffs. Then the right way to think about the formation of continental FTAs is not as a movement from four to two, but as a movement of each continent from two to one—which is beneficial, not harmful.

In practice the sets of countries that are now engaging in FTAs are indeed "natural" trading partners, who would have done much of their trade with one another even in the absence of special arrangements. A crude but indicative measure of the extent to which countries are especially significant trading partners is to compare their current trade patterns (in a world of fairly low trade barriers) with "geographically neutral" trade, in which country B's share of A's exports is equal to B's share of gross world product outside of A.

Lawrence Summers (1991) has calculated the ratio of actual trade shares to those that geographically neutral trade would predict for major industrial countries; I reproduce his results in Table 19.1. They show that within North America, and especially within Europe, trade is much more intense than geographic neutrality would predict. The Western Pacific is less clearly a natural bloc than either of these, perhaps fitting its dubious status as a political reality as well.

Table 19.1
Regional Trading Patterns (Ratio of export share to share of gross product, 1989)

			Importer			
Exporter	US	Canada	Other Americas	Japan	Developing Asia	EC
United States	—	5.2	1.3	1.1	1.7	0.6
Canada	2.9	—	0.4	0.6	0.6	0.4
Other Americas	1.5	0.6	2.0	0.6	0.5	0.5
Japan	1.1	0.9	0.5	—	3.1	0.5
Developing Asia	0.8	0.5	0.2	1.5	3.3	0.5
EC	0.3	0.3	0.3	0.3	0.5	2.5

Source: Summers (1991).

In my policy discussion (Krugman, 1991b), I argued that this correlation between the lines of emerging FTAs and those of natural trading blocs implied that the move to free-trade zones is unlikely to reduce world welfare—that the main concern ought to be not global efficiency, but the problems of small economies that find themselves caught out in the cold. This issue will not be pursued in this chapter, however, which focuses more on the analytical issues than the practical ones.

The point of this section has been that the economic analysis of trade creation versus trade diversion in a simple trading-bloc model is not dependent on taking the assumption of optimal tariff warfare literally. But this still leaves open the question of how to think about what does determine policy.

19.2   Modelling Trade Policy

It is one of the well-known ironies of international trade theory that the only intellectually sound basis for a tariff, the terms of trade argument, plays virtually no role in actual policy discussion—even though most empirical estimates suggest that for large countries the unilaterally optimal tariff rates are startlingly high.[2]

Nor do modern, "strategic trade" arguments play much role. Even in the midst of widespread concern about technology and new calls for a sophisticated industrial policy, when George Bush went to Japan to demand market access he declared the purpose of his trip to be "jobs,

jobs, jobs"—and focused the political weight of his demands not on likely candidates for external economies but simply on politically visible sectors.

I have tried to summarise the apparent preferences of governments by a set of rules which can be described as "Gatt-think" (Krugman, 1991b). The essence of these rules is a desire for exports, an abhorrence of imports, but a willingness to trade off increased imports in some sectors for increased exports in others. This summary may or may not be helpful as a way to organise discussion; but in any case it does not lead on to any modelling. In this section I offer a crude further step that may prove usefully suggestive, particularly when (in section 19.3) we try to apply it to the issue of bargaining in trade.

19.2.1   An Approach to Trade Policy

It is obvious that governments act as if they care more about the interests of producers—import-competing or exporting—than they do about consumers. This concern may in turn be rationalised as the result of the superior organisation of producers, which enables them to influence government behaviour through, say, campaign contributions. And the superior organisation of producers itself may be modelled as resulting from the role of political activity as a public good, which is more easily provided by small concentrated groups of producers than by large diffuse groups of consumers.

Modelling all these levels explicitly is, however, a difficult task.[3] We do not have clear models either of how organised groups influence policy or of how groups get organised. Eventually we will have to devise such models. Meanwhile, however, we need a shortcut.

One such shortcut is simply to take the preference of the government for producer interests as a given. This is the "weighted social welfare" approach.[4] It has the disadvantage of telling us nothing about where the weights come from, but it can still give us some insights about trade-policy setting.

Consider, then, a country that is setting policy in a single market (an extension to a crude version of general equilibrium is considered below). In this market, there is an upward-sloping domestic supply curve $S(p)$, where p is the internal price of the good. There is also a downward-sloping domestic demand curve $D(p)$. Imports are available at a price p^*, which we take for the moment as given (i.e., we assume away any domestic market power). The internal price is related to the external price by the relationship

$$p = p^*(1 + t) \tag{19.2}$$

where t is the ad valorem tariff rate.

There are three key quantities here: producer surplus, consumer surplus, and tariff revenue. The two surpluses can most easily be defined in differential form, since the constants of integration are arbitrary:

$$d(PS) = S\,dp. \tag{19.3}$$

$$d(CS) = -D\,dp. \tag{19.4}$$

And revenue is simply

$$R = p^*t(D - S) = p^*tM. \tag{19.5}$$

Suppose the government were to choose t so as to maximise the sum of producer surplus, consumer surplus, and revenue. It is straightforward to show that the optimal value of t would be zero: in the absence of market power the government would choose free trade.

What we will assume instead is that the government has a preference for producer interests. Specifically, the government's objective function is

$$V = (1 + \pi)PS + CS + R. \tag{19.6}$$

In this function, π represents the premium placed on producer interests. The function may equivalently, and usefully, be written

$$V = [PS + CS + R] + \pi PS \tag{19.7}$$

where the term on the left-hand side represents "welfare," and the term on the right-hand side represents the extra preference the government gives to producers.

19.2.2 Implications of Preference for Producers

The conditions for maximising government behaviour may be seen by considering Figure 19.2. In Figure 19.2, we show a position in which there is some initial positive tariff t, and the effects of a small increase dt in that tariff.

First, ignore the preference for producers and consider the effect of a tariff increase on welfare. A tariff increase worsens both the production distortion and the consumption distortion. The increase in the production distortion is shown in Figure 19.2 as the area b; it is equal to

$$tp^* dS = tp^*S' dp. \tag{19.8}$$

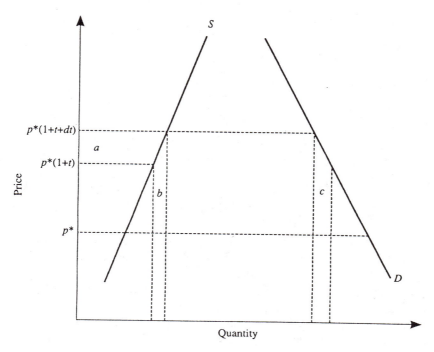

Figure 19.2
Tariff equilibrium when government favours producer interests.

The increase in the consumption distortion is shown in the figure as the area c; it is equal to

$$-tp^* \, dD = -tp^* D' \, dp. \tag{19.9}$$

These two areas measure the decline in social welfare $PS + CS + R$. The government is not, however, maximising social welfare; against these losses it sets the premium it places on benefits to producers. These benefits are equal to π times the area shown in Figure 19.2 as a; they are equal to

$$\pi S \, dp. \tag{19.10}$$

Suppose that t is a V-maximising tariff. Then it must be the case that a small increase in t has a zero impact on the government's objective function, i.e., the weighted extra payoff to producers must just offset the increase in distortions. So for an equilibrium tariff we must have

$$\pi S \, dp = -tp^* (D' - S') \, dp. \tag{19.11}$$

Define the following:

$$\mu = M/S \tag{19.12}$$

as the ratio of imports to domestic production, and

$$\varepsilon = -\frac{\partial M}{\partial p}\frac{p}{M} \tag{19.13}$$

as the elasticity of import demand. Then after some rearranging we find that the tariff rate that maximises the government's objective function must satisfy

$$\frac{t}{(1+t)} = \frac{\pi}{\varepsilon\mu}. \tag{19.14}$$

This equation contains endogenous variables on the right- as well as the left-hand side. Nonetheless, it offers a rather neat summary of the forces that should determine how much protection a given industry receives. It says that tariffs will be high in industries whose producers command an especially large premium in the government's welfare function (surprise), in industries which have a low elasticity of import demand (so that the distortionary costs of protection are less), or industries in which imports are low relative to domestic production (so a tariff is effective at transferring income to producers).

19.2.3   Relationship to Previous Analysis

Suppose that a relationship like (19.14), rather than optimal tariff-setting in the public interest, actually determines protection. How does the trading-bloc model of section 19.1 above hold up?

The key question is how tariffs will vary with the number of trading blocs. Recall that the basic story of trade creation versus trade diversion went through even with fixed tariffs—the rising tariffs that resulted from a reduction in the number of blocs in the original version of the model turned out not to be necessary. So what we need to ask is whether external tariffs will either rise, or at any rate not fall, as blocs become fewer in number.

We can take the preference for producers π as fixed, less out of conviction than as an application of what one of my colleagues calls the "principle of insignificant reason." The elasticity of import demand represents a more problematic variable. But there is a clear presumption that a larger bloc will, on average, have a smaller import share, other things being equal—that the ratio of imports to domestic production, both overall and industry by industry, will normally be lower in a large country or trading area than in a small one. And this will tend to imply that *if countries set tariffs unilaterally*, large economic units will be more protectionist than small.

This proposition cannot be tested by looking at modern industrial nations, which have operated under a regime of negotiated tariffs since the 1940s. In the pre-1939 era, however, a crude comparison does suggest that rates of protection were positively correlated with economic size. In particular, as Bairoch (forthcoming) points out, the United States, the largest economy even in the early 20th century, was notably more protectionist than any other major nation. Arguably it has also been the case that large developing countries such as Brazil and India have generally had higher rates of protection than smaller nations.

Thinking of tariff rates as set more with a view toward political pressure than as maximising national welfare does not thus, at first blush, invalidate the proposition that a move toward fewer, larger trading areas may well produce large trade diversion. This conclusion depends, however, on the assumption that tariff rates are set non-cooperatively—an assumption that was true before 1914 but has not (we hope!) been true under the GATT. So we need to turn next to the effects of negotiation on tariff-setting.

19.3   Negotiation and Protection

US protectionism actually peaked with the Smoot–Hawley tariff, and began a 45-year decline during the 1930s. The basic pattern was already visible during the Roosevelt years: the United States would offer nations increased access to the US market in sectors in which we had a comparative disadvantage, in return for reciprocal access in sectors in which we had the advantage. The political economy of this method was apparent: it set the interests of US exporters as a counterweight to import-competing industries.

Trade negotiations have been highly successful in reducing trade barriers. So to make sense of actual trade policy it is necessary to think in terms of a bargaining process in which there is linkage both across industries and between the trade policies of different nations.

19.3.1   Justifying Partial Equilibrium

As soon as we introduce multiple-industry complications, we must deal with general equilibrium. Yet full general equilibrium concerns do not seem to be of the essence in understanding trade negotiations, and are certainly not uppermost in the mind of, say, Carla Hills. So in this subsection I introduce a somewhat artificial framework that is formally general equilibrium in nature but can continue to be discussed using partial equilibrium techniques.[5]

This setup is as follows: in each of two countries, we suppose that $n + 1$ goods are produced. One of these goods, call it K, is a "residual" good: it plays a special role in both consumption and production. Utility is separable among the goods and linear in K:

$$U = K + \Sigma_i f_i(C_i) \tag{19.15}$$

where C_i is consumption of good i, and $f_i' > 0$, $f_i'' < 0$.

Production has a similar structure. There is an intersectorally mobile factor of production, labour, which can be used in all sectors. Labour is the only factor of production in K, so that there are constant returns in that sector:

$$Q_K = L_K. \tag{19.16}$$

In each of the n other sectors, however, there is a specific factor as well. This gives rise to diminishing returns with respect to labour:

$$Q_i = g_i(L_i) \qquad g_i' > 0, g_i'' < 0 \tag{19.17}$$

for all i.

The behaviour of this model is obvious. Demand for each of the n non-residual goods depends only on the price of that good relative to the residual good. Supply of each of the non-residual goods similarly depends on the price of the good relative to labour, or equivalently relative to the residual good.

Suppose that there are two countries that share this production and demand structure, and that all goods are tradeable. Under free trade, market equilibrium for the n non-residual goods can be determined in partial equilibrium fashion. In effect, we can draw back-to-back supply–demand diagrams, and set one country's excess supply equal to the other country's excess demand industry by industry. The residual sector's market must then clear because of Walras's Law.

A system of tariffs is also easy to introduce, as long as we maintain free trade in the residual good. Again, we simply do partial equilibrium good by good.[6]

What we have done with this setup, then, is rationalise (justify is too strong a word) the partial equilibrium approach used to discuss trade policy above. The main qualification is that even in the partial setting there will now necessarily be some market power on the part of the protecting nation in each industry, so that there is a terms of trade motive as well as a weighted social welfare motive for protection. Basically, however, we have now given ourselves licence to use the partial analysis in the context of multiple industry trade negotiations.

19.3.2   Trade Bargaining

Imagine that there are two countries and two non-residual industries. We suppose that under free trade each country would be an importer in one of these industries, and that each has a politically optimal tariff that it would choose in that industry if acting independently.[7]

Let t_1 be the tariff charged by the first country, and t_2 the tariff charged by the second. We can then illustrate the situation with Figure 19.3. The tariff rates t_1^* and t_2^* are the individual optima; a few contour lines are sketched in. These contour lines reflect the fact that an increase in either country's tariff hurts the other government's objective function, both by reducing welfare and additionally by hurting exporting producers.

If the two countries set tariffs non-cooperatively, the outcome will be at point N. But as is evident from Figure 19.3, both governments prefer

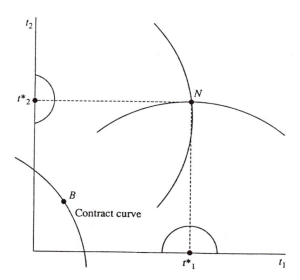

Figure 19.3
Tariff bargaining.

points to the southwest—again, this is both because they care to some extent about national welfare, and because they want to provide benefits to domestic producers.

An efficient bargain B will lie somewhere on the contract curve between the two governments, and will involve a reduction in both tariff rates from the non-cooperative outcome.

The interesting thing about this result is that it does not depend at all on the assumption that governments are maximising national welfare. If π were zero—if governments were not subject to interest group pressures—the contract curve would pass through the origin. In that case, free trade would be an efficient bargain from the governments' point of view (although not necessarily the bargain at which they would arrive). But international negotiation will lead toward free trade, even if not necessarily all the way, even if governments are strongly affected by interest group politics.

Trade bargaining in this description is characterised by a Prisoners' Dilemma. This dilemma arises in part from the terms of trade effect of conventional optimal tariff analysis, but also (and presumably in practice mostly) from the effect of each country's tariffs on the other country's producer interests.

Because of the Prisoners' Dilemma characteristic of trade negotiations, we can now invoke all the usual folk theorems of repeated games to help us think about the possibilities and difficulties of reaching cooperative solutions. Trade liberalisation must be supported by the belief of countries that if they cheat they will lose from the subsequent collapse of the cooperative outcome. And to make this sanction effective, countries must be able to observe each others' trade policies, and must find each others' promises credible.

To make any sense of the issue of regionalism versus multilateralism, we need to think in terms of how the range of countries included in negotiations affects the likelihood that the conditions for successfully achieving cooperation will be met.

19.4 Regionalism, Multilateralism, and Bargaining

At this point we turn to the weakest part of the discussion. To talk seriously about trade negotiations, we need to take an already loose analysis of trade bargaining between a pair of countries and try to apply it to multicountry issues. Obviously this discussion cannot be more than speculative. Indeed, for the most part I will simply state issues and a few hypotheses.

There are, I would argue, two basic issues. First, other things being equal, will the formation of regional trading blocs within a multilateral system tend to lead to lower or higher barriers to trade between blocs? Second, is the rise of regional trading blocs a second-best solution to the breakdown of a multilateral system?

19.4.1 Consequences of Regional Blocs

In section 19.1, I showed that consolidation of the world into a small number of trading blocs was likely, with unchanged external tariffs, to produce more trade diversion than creation—with the important practical caveat that to the extent that the blocs followed the lines of natural trading areas, the effect was likely to be more favourable. If blocs set trade policies non-cooperatively, consolidation will normally lead to higher external trade barriers, reinforcing the likelihood of adverse effects. But what if trade policies are set through negotiation?

Once upon a time, European nations came to multilateral negotiations as individual negotiators; now they come as a bloc. Does this make them more or less able and/or willing to compromise?

The answer seems to be that it can cut either way. On one side, consolidation into regional blocs could make it more likely that negotiated agreements would be reached simply because there were fewer players. A world trading system effectively run by a G-3 of NAFTA, the European Community, and Japan poses many fewer problems of free-riding than one in which France or Italy are free to make independent demands and cheat on their own.

On the other side, as argued in section 19.2 of this chapter, large blocs would in the absence of cooperation tend to impose higher tariffs than small players, i.e., their temptation to protect is higher. At the same time, in the realistic case where blocs follow natural geographic lines, a collapse of free trade to non-cooperative tariff-setting will probably do less harm if nations are organised into a few blocs—and therefore the prospect of such a collapse is less of a deterrent to cheating. So a consolidation into large trading blocs could undermine the sustainability of a cooperative international system.

All of this needs some careful modelling. But, overall, the answer seems to be definitely ambiguous. Regional trading arrangements could work either for or against global free trade.

19.4.2 Forces for Regionalism

In some sense, the question of whether regional trading arrangements are good or bad is a moot point. There is nobody who is in a position to decree regional blocs either into or out of existence. So we need to ask why such blocs are in fact emerging.

This come down to asking why nations may feel that they are able to negotiate more at a regional than at a global level. Or to put it more pessimistically, what are the problems of the GATT that lead countries to turn to their neighbourhood instead?

I would list four reasons, all of them tied to the Prisoners' Dilemma sketched out above.

First, there is the sheer number of participants in the multilateral negotiations. As a practical matter, this changes the character of negotiations. In the early, highly productive GATT rounds, the relatively small number of players were able essentially to carry on parallel bilateral negotiations, something like playing a game of Risk. By the time of the Kennedy Round, the numbers were too great, and it was necessary to resort to formulaic tariff reductions, which inevitably find it harder to strike the right political balance. Also, once there are many players the threat that cheating will bring down the system becomes less credible—will the GATT really collapse because, say, Thailand fails to honour its rules?

Second, the changing character of trade restrictions makes monitoring increasingly difficult. The rise of the New Protectionism of voluntary export restraints (VERs), orderly marketing agreements (OMAs), etc. has been massively documented; it represents both exogenous bureaucratic creativity and an end run around negotiated tariff reductions. What it does is to make the negotiation space vastly more complicated than indicated in Figure 19.3, and to make monitoring of adherence extremely difficult.

Third, the decline in the relative dominance of the United States has probably made the system more difficult to run. The political theory of 'hegemonic stability'—essentially, the view that some dominant power must be there to enforce the rules of a cooperative game—is not as well founded in theory as one might suppose. Nor is it universally accepted even among political scientists. But it is certainly reasonable to argue that a dominant America, preoccupied with trade as a binding agent in a political and military struggle, may have helped the GATT to work better a generation ago than it does now.

Finally, institutional differences among major countries pose problems for the system. (This means Japan.) The reason is not that there are no gains from trade between countries with different institutions. It is that at least a shared understanding is necessary to overcome the Prisoners' Dilemma. Suppose that a tariff reduction in country A, with its free-wheeling markets, really does open access to those markets; while a tariff reduction in Country J, whose markets are governed by informal under-standings and cartels, does little to open the gates. Then unless J can find something else to offer, the trade-bargaining game between the countries will break down. It may well be the case that A's welfare would be higher if it ignored this problem and simply pursued unilateral free trade. But as the GATT process itself recognises, governments do not maximise national welfare, and a successful trade regime must build on the motives governments actually have, not the ones we wish they did have.

Regional trading arrangements offer an opportunity to reconstitute the bargaining process at a level where all of these problems can be dimin-ished. They involve smaller groups of nations; they can (as in "EC 92") involve what Robert Lawrence has called "deep integration," which essen-tially removes borders and thus the possibility of creative protectionism. Because the numbers are small, the problem of finding a hegemon is pretty much eliminated. And regional trading blocs, at least so far, avoid including nations with institutional differences large enough to undermine faith in the process.

19.5 Summary Conclusions

We can pose two questions about the role of regional trading blocs. The normative question is, will the formation of such blocs lead to trade cre-ation or to trade diversion? The answer is clear; more research is needed. Small numbers tend to make cooperative solutions more likely; ability of players to fare well if bargaining fails make such solutions less likely; both effects are at work.

The positive question is whether there are deep-seated reasons for a move toward regional trading blocs. Although the discussion here is loose and speculative, I would argue that the answer is yes: for a mix of reasons, the ability to support a cooperative solution at the multilateral level is declining, while at the regional level it remains fairly strong.

Appendix: A Basic Trading-Bloc Model

This Appendix briefly restates the simple trading-bloc model of Krugman (1991a).

We imagine a world whose basic units are geographic units that we will refer to as "provinces." There are a large number N of such provinces in the world. A country in general consists of a large number of provinces. For the analysis here, however, we ignore the country level, focusing instead on "trading blocs" that contain a number of countries and hence a larger number of provinces. There will be assumed to be $B < N$ trading blocs in the world. They are symmetric, each containing N/B provinces (with the problem of whole numbers ignored). In this simplified world, the issues of free-trade zones reduces to the following: how does world welfare depend on B?

Each province produces a single good that is an imperfect substitute for the products of all other provinces. We choose units so that each province produces one unit of its own good, and assume that all provincial goods enter symmetrically into demand, with a constant elasticity of substitution between any pair of goods. Thus everyone in the world has tastes represented by the CES utility function

$$U = [\textstyle\sum_{i=1}^{N} c_i^{\theta}]^{1/\theta} \tag{19.A1}$$

where c_i is consumption of the good of province i, and the elasticity of substitution between any pair of products is

$$\sigma = \frac{1}{1 - \theta}. \tag{19.A2}$$

A trading bloc is a group of provinces with internal free trade and a common external ad valorem tariff. We ignore the realistic politics of trade policy, and simply assume that each bloc sets a tariff that maximises welfare, taking the policies of other trading blocs as given. This is a standard problem in international economics: the optimal tariff for a bloc is

$$t^* = \frac{1}{\varepsilon - 1} \tag{19.A3}$$

where ε is the elasticity of demand for the bloc's exports.

In a symmetric equilibrium in which all blocs charge the same tariff rate, it is possible to show that (see Krugman, 1991a)

$$\varepsilon = s + (1 - s)\sigma \tag{19.A4}$$

where s is the share of each bloc in the rest of the world's income measured at world prices. The optimal tariff is therefore

$$t^* = \frac{1}{(1-s)(\sigma-1)} \qquad (19.A5)$$

It is apparent from (19.A5) that the larger the share of each bloc's exports in the income of the world outside the bloc, the higher will be the level of tariffs on intra-bloc trade. This immediately suggests that a consolidation of the world into fewer, larger blocs will lead to higher barriers on interbloc trade.

One cannot quite stop here, however, because the share of each bloc in the rest of the world's spending depends both on the number of blocs and on the world-wide level of tariffs. Again after some algebra it is possible to show that this share equals

$$s = \frac{1}{(1+t)^\sigma + B + 1} \qquad (19.A6)$$

so that the share of each bloc's exports in the rest of the world's income is decreasing in both the tariff rate and the number of blocs.

Equations (19.A5) and (19.A6) simultaneously determine the tariff rate and the export share for a given number of blocs B.

It is straightforward to show that a reduction in the number of blocs will lead to a rise in both s and t.

Clearly this change will reduce the volume of trade between any two provinces that are in different blocs. Even at an unchanged tariff, the removal of trade barriers between members of the expanded bloc would divert some trade that would otherwise have taken place between blocs. This trade diversion would be reinforced by the rise in the tariff rate.

We now turn to welfare. Given the utility function (19.A1), it is possible to calculate the welfare of a representative province as a function of the total number of provinces N, the number of blocs B, and the tariff rate t on interbloc trade. Since N plays no role in the analysis, we can simplify matters somewhat by normalising N to equal 1. Again after considerable algebra, given in Krugman (1991a), we find that the utility of a representative province is

$$U = \left[\frac{B}{(1+t)^\sigma + B - 1}\right][(1-B^{-1}) + B^{-1}(1+t)^{\sigma\theta}]^{1/\theta} \qquad (19.A7)$$

If trade were free, this would imply a utility of 1. Since the tariff rate t is also a function of B, we can use (19.A5), (19.A6) and (19.A7) together to determine how world welfare varies with the number of trading blocs.

The easiest way to proceed at this point is to solve the model numerically. This grossly oversimplified model has only two parameters, the number of trading blocs and the elasticity of substitution between any pair of provinces; it is therefore straightforward to solve first for tariffs as a function of B given several possible values of the elasticity, and then to calculate the implied effect on world welfare. In Krugman (1991a) the values of ε considered are 2, 4, and 10.

Several points about the results are worth noting. First, the relationship between tariff rates and the number of blocs is fairly flat. The reason is that when there are fewer blocs, trade diversion tends to reduce interbloc trade, and thus leads to less of a rise in each bloc's share of external markets than one might have expected. Second, except in the case of an implausibly high elasticity of demand, predicted tariff rates are much higher than one actually observes among advanced nations. This is not an artifact of the economic model: virtually all calculations suggest that unilateral optimum tariff rates are very high. What it tells us, therefore, is that actual trade relationships among advanced countries are far more cooperative than envisaged here.

Finally, welfare calculations yield a striking result. World welfare is of course maximised when there is only one bloc, in other words, global free trade. As suggested informally in the text, however, the relationship between welfare and the number of trading blocs is not monotonic but U-shaped: world welfare reaches a minimum when there are a few large blocs, and would be higher if there were more blocs, each with less market power.

But where is the minimum? For the full range of elasticities considered, world welfare is minimised when there are three blocs.

Notes

1. Grossman and Helpman (1992) are currently engaged in a line of research that seems extremely promising; some of the discussion in this chapter was inspired by initial presentations of their work—although little of the flavour of their elegant analysis will seep through, and I of course bear all responsibility for any foolishness.

2. For example, Whalley (1985) estimates that in an "optimal tariff" war among major world trading areas, the tariff rate levied by the United States would be approximately 150 percent.

3. As mentioned above, Grossman and Helpman have made some important progress toward modelling the process by which organised groups exert influence.

4. Richard Baldwin has proposed using this approach for normative analysis of trade policy, and has proposed a catchy name: "politically realistic objective functions," or PROFs.

5. This framework was originally introduced by Samuelson (1964) in an attempt to psycho-analyse conventional views about the transfer problem. In his version the residual good, described below, was assumed to be non-traded. The version with a traded residual good has been part of the oral tradition in trade for some time, but as far as I know the recent work of Grossman and Helpman represents its first systematic application.

6. This partial approach can be badly misleading in one respect: it misses general equilibrium terms of trade effects. For example, suppose that a country imposes a tariff in an industry in which it has very little monopsony power. Does this tariff improve the terms of trade? One is tempted to say no; yet the tariff will pull resources out of other industries, which will include export sectors in which the country may have substantial market power. The assumption of a linear residual sector sterilises all such effects, but in reality they may be quite important.

7. This politically optimal tariff now combines the terms of trade and weighted social welfare motives.

References

Bairoch, P. (forthcoming) *Myths and Realities of Economic History*, London: Harvester Wheatsheaf.

Grossman, G. and E. Helpman (1992) 'Protection for Sale', Princeton University (mimeo).

Krugman, P. (1991a) 'Is Bilateralism Bad?', in E. Helpman and A. Razin (eds), *International Trade and Trade Policy*, Cambridge, Mass.: MIT Press.

————. (1991b) 'The Move to Free Trade Zones', Federal Reserve Bank of Kansas City, *Review* (December).

Samuelson, P. (1964) 'Theoretical Notes on Trade Problems', *Review of Economics and Statistics*, **46**, pp. 145–54.

Summers, L. (1991) 'The Move to Free Trade Zones: Comment', Federal Reserve Bank of Kansas City, *Review* (December).

Whalley, J. (1985) *Trade Liberalization among Major World Trading Areas*, Cambridge, Mass.: MIT Press.

20

Multilateral Trade Negotiations and Preferential Trading Arrangements

Alan Deardorff and
Robert Stern

The Welfare Effects of the Expansion of Trading Blocs

Having set out the advantages and limitations of both multilateralism and preferential arrangements, suppose now that the proliferation of preferential trading arrangements, in the form of FTAs or something similar, is inevitable. Is there anything that we can say theoretically about what this may portend for the welfare of the world?

There are many issues to be considered here, but we will confine our attention to only one: Is a world of a small number of trading blocs significantly inferior to a world of free trade? We say "significantly inferior" because it seems safe to assume that a world of perfectly free trade will never be reached by any mechanism. Experience suggests that multilateral negotiations can at best reduce trade barriers to low levels, but they cannot eliminate them. Since FTAs by definition reduce external barriers to zero within the included countries and do not presumably maintain or introduce intra-bloc barriers, it is potentially the case that a world of trading blocs, with each bloc forming an FTA, could raise would welfare closer to its free trade level than multilateral negotiations. In that case the world of blocs would not look altogether bad.

To illustrate this possibility in simple terms, imagine that we could measure welfare of a country or the world as a function of the size of trading blocs. Suppose, as we will discuss below, that world welfare rises rapidly as bloc size rises at first, then levels off and approaches the free trade level, W^F, as bloc size approaches the world as a whole, as drawn in figure 20.1. Then if multilateral negotiations can only achieve a level of welfare somewhere short of the free trade level, as at W^M in figure 20.1,

Originally published, as part of chapter 2, in *Analytical and Negotiating Issues in the Global Trading System*, ed. Alan Deardorff and Robert Stern (Ann Arbor: University of Michigan Press, 1994), 53–85. Reprinted with permission.

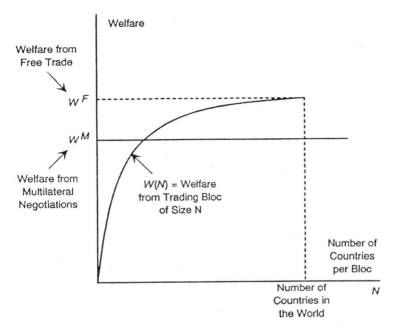

Figure 20.1
World welfare with trading blocks and multilateral negotiations.

there is a point beyond which blocs are large enough to yield a higher welfare than multilateral negotiations. Of course, it remains to be seen whether the effect of bloc size on welfare shown in Figure 20.1 can be correct.[1]

The Krugman Argument

Krugman 1991a,b, 1992b has addressed this question directly.[2] He examines a model of a large number of countries, each of which produces a distinctive good and each of which initially levies its optimal tariff on all imports. He then computes world welfare as these countries are combined into various numbers of equal sized trading blocs, each with zero tariffs internally, and each revising their external tariffs to remain optimal against goods from outside the bloc. While no general result can be obtained from this model, Krugman finds computationally that world welfare declines as the number of blocs decreases (and countries are therefore combined into ever larger FTAs) until the number of blocs reaches three.

World welfare then increases as the number of blocs is reduced still further to two, and it increases even more with the move to worldwide free trade in a single bloc. That is, world welfare is at a minimum when the number of blocs is three. Krugman therefore concludes in the context of his model that bilateralism is generally undesirable, since the formation of FTAs would reduce world welfare at almost every stage.

This is an ingenious argument. It is based, however, on a model that stacks the cards against bilateralism. In an alternative framework one might easily conclude that the formation of FTA trading blocs would be beneficial and that a world of a small number of blocs, even three, might be about as good as one could ask for.

A distinctive feature of Krugman's model is that the firms in each country are assumed to produce goods that are distinct from those produced by all other firms. This product differentiation allows him the simplicity of a single-sector monopolistic-competition model, and thus the kind of clean and simple theorizing that one has learned to expect from Krugman. However, the assumption also means that the countries of Krugman's model are subject to something very like the Armington assumption, which is that each country's products are imperfect substitutes for those of all other countries. This, we believe, is largely responsible for Krugman's results.

The Armington assumption has a long history in the construction of computable general equilibrium models of international trade.[3] However for some purposes, and especially for modeling the welfare effects of trade barriers, it has become increasingly recognized that the Armington assumption places an idiosyncratic stamp upon results.[4] In the context of FTAs and trading blocs, the Armington assumption seems especially likely to yield peculiar implications.

First, the Armington assumption makes it important for any country to import from every other country, since each has something unique to provide. This means that an extreme form of trading blocs in which blocs do not trade at all with each other would be welfare disasters. That is, depending on the functional form of the utility function, welfare would be either very low or infinitely low. This is not necessarily wrong, of course, but we find it rather implausible that each country's welfare should depend so sensitively on access to the products of each and every other country in the world.

Second, the Armington assumption increases the importance of trade diversion, as compared to trade creation, and therefore increases the likelihood that a preferential arrangement will be welfare reducing. Since this may be counter intuitive, the point requires some explanation.

As usually explained, trade diversion might seem to be impossible in a world of differentiated products. The classic description of trade diversion is the switch away from a low-cost external supplier of a good to a higher-cost supplier of the same good within an FTA. Since with differentiated products the same good is not available from different countries, this simple form of trade diversion is not possible. In addition, Krugman's model does not have differences in costs, and this too would seem to rule out trade diversion as usually described.

However, a more general definition of trade diversion would not involve identical products, and it would not require any particular differences in costs. Any time there is substitution away from one good in favor of another as a result of distorted price signals that incorrectly reflect costs, there will tend to be a welfare reduction.[5] If the two goods are both imported, then this substitution may usefully be labeled as trade diversion, for the welfare loss is from the same source as in the simpler, more familiar example.

Product differentiation in Krugman's model assures that any expansion of an FTA, short of subsuming the entire world, will involve such trade diversion. As long as any countries remain outside the union, there will be substitution away from their products when the FTA lowers the consumer prices of the products produced by new members of the FTA. Since the products of these two groups of countries previously faced the same tariffs, their relative prices within the FTA had been undistorted, and they become distorted by the FTA. Thus trade diversion necessarily occurs in Krugman's model, no matter how large the FTA becomes.

There is trade creation too, of course, as substitution also occurs away from previously protected domestic goods and towards imports from new members of the FTA. However it is easy in Krugman's model for trade diversion to dominate trade creation.

To see why, suppose that the welfare effects depend only on the number of goods for which there is trade creation and trade diversion. In a world of many countries, when only two of these form an FTA, there is creation of trade for the goods produced by the partners, but diversion of trade away from all of the goods produced by all other countries. Since the number of the latter countries, and therefore goods, is much larger than the number of countries and goods in the FTA, it is not surprising that diversion outweighs, creation. Then, as the FTA is made larger and larger, the number of countries inside the FTA—and hence the amount of trade creation—grows, while the number of countries still outside the FTA shrinks. But even when one enlarges the FTA to include one third of the world (the three-bloc case), there are still two thirds of the world's products from which trade is being diverted, and only one third for which trade is being created. Again, then, it is not surprising that each enlargement of the FTA up to this point lowers welfare and that the three-bloc case is the worst possible. Only when the goods and countries included in a bloc become as numerous as the goods and countries outside does trade creation finally have a reasonable chance of dominating trade diversion, and only then does the FTA raise welfare.

As this explanation is intended to suggest, then, the assumptions of complete product differentiation and the consequent exaggerated importance of each country and each country's goods for every other country's consumers may introduce a bias against the possibility that an FTA will be beneficial.

One other feature of the Krugman model should also be mentioned, since it may well contribute to his results even if it does not drive them. In his first paper on this subject, Krugman 1991a assumes that trading blocs maintain optimal tariffs against the rest of the would at all times. In part because of the high degree of product differentiation just discussed, these optimal tariffs tend to rise as bloc size increases, contributing to the welfare loss for the world as a whole. In a more recent analysis however, he questions the usefulness of this assumption and replaces it with a constant external tariff in his calculations. The conclusion that world welfare is minimized with either three or two blocs survives. Therefore, while the assumption of an optimal tariff may have exacerbated the welfare losses in the earlier analysis, it seems not to have caused them. The assumption of product differentiation instead seems to play the more important role.[6]

A Comparative Advantage Approach

As an alternative, suppose that trade among countries conforms more to the traditional model of comparative advantage. That is, all countries are capable of producing the same list of goods, but they differ in their abilities to do so either because of differences in technology or differences in factor endowments.[7] The effect of an FTA on world welfare then depends, we will argue first, on the differences among countries that join to form the FTA. Furthermore, as long as countries choose as partners others with whom enough differences in comparative advantage exist, they will tend to capture for themselves a significant portion of the gains from trade that would be available from a move to complete free trade by the world. In such cases it may well be that the majority of the gains from trade that would be possible with worldwide free trade can be captured by a group of trading blocs. The blocs would only need to be large enough and to include countries with a sufficiently divergent variety of comparative advantages.[8]

Unfortunately, we are not able to make these points with any great generality. However, we can illustrate them by means of simple examples, and that will be our approach.

A Four-Country Example

Consider first a four country version of the simple two-good Ricardian trade model that has been used for two centuries to illustrate the concept of comparative advantage.[9] Let the countries have identical preferences and labor endowments, and let unit labor requirements for producing the two goods, X and Y, be also the same in countries 1 and 2 and in countries 3 and 4, but differ between the two pairs of countries. That is, let countries 1 and 2 have a comparative advantage in good X relative to countries 3 and 4.

We will consider only the extremes of free trade and autarky to make our point. Suppose that prohibitive tariffs initially exist in all four countries, and that we now consider opening pairs of the four countries to free trade, thus forming trading blocs. It makes a great difference which pairs of countries we choose to form a bloc. If countries 1 and 2 were to form an FTA, they would not in fact trade with each other since their autarky prices are the same. They would gain nothing from trade. If countries 1 and 3 were to form an FTA, however, they would indeed trade and gain from trade exactly as in the traditional 2-country model. Thus it is only if countries with different comparative advantages join in an FTA that there can be trade creation, and only then are there gains from formation of the FTA.[10]

This example also illustrates our other point that worldwide free trade may not be necessary. In this example, with identical preferences and labor endowments and only two different sets of technologies, the worldwide free trade equilibrium is identical to the equilibrium that will be attained if any pair of countries with different technologies form an FTA, save only for size. That is, the equilibrium world price with free trade is also the equilibrium price within an FTA formed by, say, countries 1 and 3, and the quantities produced and consumed within each country are also the same. Only the total outputs are different, being twice for four countries what they are for two.

Thus, in this very special case, all of the gains from trade that can be achieved with worldwide free trade can also be achieved in two completely separate trading blocs, so long as each bloc includes countries with different technologies. This illustrates the point that trading blocs can in principle approximate (and in this case equal) the welfare levels of complete free trade.

In a more general model, one would not expect to find blocs equalling the welfare of free trade, but a tendency in this direction does seem likely. It seems plausible that blocs would in general achieve levels of welfare that are between autarky and free trade, being closer to the latter the larger are the blocs and the more diverse in terms of technologies represented. With only four countries we cannot capture much of this, but we can capture a part of it—and also foreshadow our next examples—by looking at blocs in terms of expected values.

Suppose in the four-country model that we are to form two blocs of two countries each, but that the composition of the blocs is to be decided randomly. What are the levels of welfare associated with two blocs in this sense, and how do they compare to autarky and complete free trade? The answer depends on what random mechanism is used for selecting blocs.

Let each possible pattern of blocs be equally likely. There are three such patterns: $(1, 2)(3, 4)$, $(1, 3)(2, 4)$, and $(1, 4)(2, 3)$. Of these only the first has the countries staying at autarky levels of welfare, while the other two have the countries attaining free trade levels. Thus the formation of two random blocs yields an expected gain in welfare that is two-thirds that of free trade.

To be a bit more formal in preparation for the next example, assume there are two types of countries in this four-country case. Let countries 1 and 2 be type A and countries 3 and 4 by type B. Let the welfare attained by a country of type i when it trades in an FTA including countries of types $j, k, l, \ldots$ be denoted $w^i_{jkl\ldots}$. Thus w^A_A is the autarky welfare of a country of type A, w^A_{AB} is the welfare of a country of type A in an FTA with a country of type B, and so on.

Now let $W(I)$ be the level of expected world welfare associated with an equal number of blocs of size I. In the four-country example, the only possibilities are $I = 1$ (autarky), 2 (two blocs) and 4 (free trade). Adding up over the four countries one can obtain world autarky welfare as

$$W(1) = 2w^A_A + 2w^B_B$$

and free trade welfare as

$$W^F = W(4) = 2w_{AB}^A + 2w_{BA}^B.$$

The world gains from free trade are then

$$G^F = G(4) = W(4) - W(1) = 2(w_{AB}^A - w_A^A) + 2(w_{BA}^B - w_B^B)$$

The expected welfare for a country of type A from two randomly chosen blocs is $(1/3)w_A^A + (2/3)w_{AB}^A$, and there is a similar expression for a country of type B. Therefore expected world welfare with two blocs is

$$W(2) = 2[(1/3)w_A^A + (2/3)w_{AB}^A] + 2[(1/3)w_B^B + (2/3)w_{BA}^B]$$

Comparing to $W(1)$, the expected gain in world welfare from two blocs is then

$$G(2) = W(2) - W(1)$$

$$= 2[(1/3)w_A^A + (2/3)w_{AB}^A] + 2[(1/3)w_B^B + (2/3)w_{BA}^B] - 2w_A^A - 2w_B^B$$

$$= (2/3)\ G^F$$

What this says is that the expected gain from forming two trading blocs, with the composition of the blocs randomly selected, is two-thirds of the gain that would arise from a single bloc, or free trade. That is, trading blocs do, on average, generate more than half of the gains from free trade.

A Six-Country Example

To allow for a slightly richer array of possibilities than the four-country model, now consider six. Again let there be just two goods and two technologies, so that the countries are of only two types, A and B, now with three of each. In addition to the extremes of autarky and free trade, there are now the possibilities of three blocs with two countries each, and of two blocs with three countries each. The two-country blocs have the same possibilities for welfare as before, but the three-country blocs do not: a country can join with zero, one, or two other countries of the same type as itself.

Levels of world welfare under autarky and free trade are the same as before, except that there are now six countries instead of three:

$$W(1) = 3w_A^A + 3w_B^B$$

$$W^F = W(6) = 3w_{AB}^A + 3w_{AB}^B$$

This gives a world gain from free trade of

$$G^F = G(6) = 3[w_{AB}^A + w_{AB}^B - w_A^A - w_B^B]$$

With blocs of two countries, there are fifteen ways that the six countries can be distributed across three blocs. In only six of these do all three blocs have one country of each type, so that they all attain the same welfare as under free trade. In the remaining nine, one bloc has two type-A countries, one has two type-B, and one has one of each. This leads to an expected world welfare of

$$W(2) = (2/5)[3w_{AB}^A + 3w_{AB}^B] + (3/5)[2w_A^A + 2w_B^B + w_{AB}^A + w_{AB}^B]$$

and an expected gain from trade of

$$G(2) = (3/5)G^F$$

Thus with more countries, blocs of two countries still produce more than half the benefit of free trade, but the expected gain is somewhat smaller than in the four-country case.

With two blocs of three countries there are ten ways that the six countries can be distributed across the blocs. One of those ways has all three type-A countries in one bloc and all three type-B in the other, leading to autarky levels of welfare in both. In the nine other ways that the two blocs can appear, each bloc has two countries from one type and one from the other. Expected welfare is therefore

$$W(3) = (1/10)[3w_A^A + 3w_B^B] + (9/10)[2w_{AAB}^A + w_{AAB}^B + w_{ABB}^A + w_{ABB}^B]$$

Interpretation of this expression does not lead to anything as simple as the other cases, and we will not try to carry it further here. It seems likely, though we have not been able to prove it, that it involves higher expected welfare than $W(2)$.

This example has one additional feature that would appear in a more general case but did not appear in the four-country case. It is quite possible for a country to achieve a level of welfare higher than world-wide free trade by joining an FTA. Consider a country of type A in an FTA with two other countries of type B, an "ABB" FTA in the notation used above. In a competitive model without increasing returns to scale, the free-trade equilibrium price in any group of countries is a weighted average of the autarky prices of the separate countries, the weights depending on the sizes of the countries. Thus the equilibrium price in an ABB FTA will be closer to the autarky price of the type B countries than will the equilibrium price under free trade where there are equal numbers of countries of the two types. Since the welfare of any country increases with the difference between the equilibrium price and its own autarky price, it follows that the type-A country is better off in the ABB FTA than it would be under free trade:

$$w^A_{ABB} > w^A_{AB}$$

A Many-Country Case

As our final example we consider a many-country case where comparative advantage is more generally defined in terms of relative autarky prices and may therefore reflect differences in technologies and/or factor endowments.

Suppose the world consists of $M + 1$ countries, numbered $i = 0, 1, \ldots, M$. Let these countries have, in general, different autarky prices but be otherwise identical in the following sense: each produces and consumes two goods, and their excess supplies of good one are

$$ES^i(p) = p - q^i$$

where p is the price of good one in terms of the numeraire good two, and q^i is the only parameter of this excess supply function that we allow to differ across countries. Since in autarky $ES^i = 0$, q^i is the autarky price of good one in country i.[11]

In addition to the autarky prices, one can also derive the world free-trade equilibrium price, p^F, from

$$\sum_{i=0}^{M} ES^i(p^F) = 0$$

as

$$p^F = \frac{1}{M+1} \sum_{i=0}^{M} q^i$$

which is simply the average of the autarky prices.[12]

Suppose that country O were to contemplate joining a trading bloc of some N other countries in addition to itself. If those N countries were $i = 1, \ldots, N$, then the resulting equilibrium bloc price, $P^{O,N}$, would be

$$p^{O,N} = \frac{1}{N+1} \sum_{i=0}^{N} q^i = \frac{1}{N+1} q^O + \frac{N}{N+1} p^N \tag{20.1}$$

where p^N is the equilibrium bloc price for countries $1, \ldots, N$ (without country zero). That is, if country O joins the bloc it will face an equilibrium price that is a weighted average of its own autarky price and that of the bloc excluding itself, the weight on the latter being larger the more countries are in the bloc. But suppose that, instead of the participants in the bloc being known, country O will join a bloc with N other randomly selected countries. In that case its equilibrium bloc price will still be given by equation (20.1), but the equilibrium price of the N-bloc, p^N, will be random. Since (20.1) is linear, the expected equilibrium price for the bloc of $N+1$ countries will be given in terms of the expected equilibrium price for the N-bloc:

$$Ep^{O,N} = \frac{1}{N+1} q^O + \frac{N}{N+1} Ep^N \tag{20.2}$$

To calculate Ep^N, let $c(N)$ be the number of possible N country blocs that can be formed out of the M countries $1, \ldots, M$. If each is equally likely, then

$$Ep^N = \frac{1}{c(N)} \sum_{j=1}^{c(N)} p^{N^j}$$

$$= \frac{1}{c(N)} \sum_{j=1}^{c(N)} \frac{1}{N} \sum_{i=1}^{n} q^{h^{ji}}$$

where p^{N^j} is the equilibrium bloc price for the jth possible bloc of size N, and h^{ji} is the index of the ith country in that j^{th} bloc. This is a simple average of all the autarky prices $q^1, \ldots, q^M$, with each one repeated by the number of blocs in which it appears. Since each bloc is equally likely and all possible blocs are represented in this summation, each autarky price q^i for $i = 1, \ldots, M$ must appear the same number of times in this summation, and thus have equal weight. Thus

$$Ep^N = \frac{1}{M} \sum_{i=1}^{M} q^i = p^M$$

which is just the equilibrium bloc price for the bloc of all M countries other than country zero. That is, the expected equilibrium price for a bloc of N countries chosen randomly from a larger group of M countries is just the equilibrium price for the M countries themselves as a bloc.[13] Substituting this into equation (20.2), the result for a randomly selected bloc of size $N + 1$ including country zero is therefore

$$Ep^{O,N} = \frac{1}{N+1}q^O + \frac{N}{N+1}p^M \qquad (20.3)$$

This result is illustrated in the top panel of figure 20.2. The horizontal axis measures the number of countries in a bloc in addition to country zero, while the vertical axis measures various prices. The autarky price in country zero, q^O, is shown as lower than the equilibrium bloc price for all countries excluding zero, p^M. As the above equation indicates, the expected equilibrium bloc price for a bloc of country zero plus N other randomly selected countries rises to half way between q^O and p^M for $N = 1$ and continues thereafter to approach p^M. The graph stops at $N = M$, where the free trade price p^F is reached just short of P^M.

The bottom panel of Figure 20.2 gives information about the welfare of country zero in these various circumstances. The welfare of a country is given by its indirect utility function, which in this case takes the simple form[14]

$$V^i(p) = (p - q^i)^2$$

Letting $G^O(N)$ be the expected gain in welfare of country zero from entering into a bloc with N other randomly selected countries,

$$G^O(N) = EV^O(p^{O,N}) \geq V^O(Ep^{O,N}) = (Ep^{O,N} - q^O)^2 \equiv \bar{G}^O(N) \qquad (20.4)$$

using the convexity of $V(\cdot)$. Thus the bottom panel of Figure 20.2 graphs $\bar{G}^O(n) = V^O(Ep^{O,N})$ as a function of N, taking $Ep^{O,N}$ as given by (20.3) from the top panel. From the inequality in (20.4), this graph provides a lower bound on the gain to country zero from entering into blocs of various sizes. This graph illustrates the conclusion discussed throughout this section of the chapter: that much of the gains from free trade can be achieved, in this case for an individual country, by entering into FTA trading blocs of larger and larger size.

The curve $\bar{G}^O(N)$ in Figure 20.2 provides only a lower bound for the expected gains from entering into blocs of various sizes for a particular country. We are not able to place an upper bound on this gain, which could extend well above the curve and even above the level of welfare in free trade. Indeed, one can easily find cases where the expected welfare

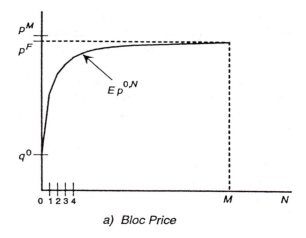

a) Bloc Price

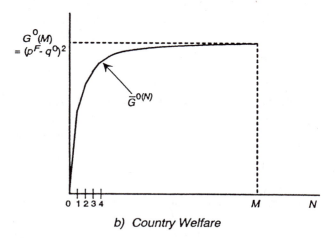

b) Country Welfare

Figure 20.2
Expected block price and country welfare with trading blocs.

for a country from entering into a bloc that includes only part of the world will be higher than its welfare from free trade. Suppose in a world of many countries that one of them has an autarky price equal to the free-trade price. Then it has nothing to gain from free trade at all. But by entering into trading blocs with only part of the world, it is quite likely to meet a bloc price that differs from its autarky price, and therefore enjoy greater welfare. Thus for a particular country it is quite possible that trading blocs are better than free trade.

This cannot be the case for the world as a whole, however. We know from the literature on the gains from trade that world welfare cannot be larger with trade barriers than without, and will usually be smaller. Therefore the upper bound on world welfare is given by free trade. Since the lower bound can be obtained by adding together vertically curves like $\bar{G}^0(N)$ in Figure 20.2, the world expected gains from trading blocs of various sizes are indeed constrained to lie between a curve like $W(N)$ in Figure 20.1 and the horizontal line shown for free trade, just as we surmised earlier.

Tariffs

Our discussion in this section has assumed that tariffs were always either prohibitive or zero. This may seem to be an important limitation in a world where actual tariffs are mostly neither of these. Furthermore, by excluding non-zero, non-prohibitive tariffs we have ruled out any possibility of trade diversion: with previously prohibitive tariffs there was no trade to be diverted by the formation of an FTA. Finally, this assumption has also made it unnecessary for us to consider the distinction between an FTA and a customs union: our FTAs continue to charge prohibitive tariffs against the rest of the world, and it therefore does not matter whether those tariffs are the same or not.

All of this seems to suggest that our analysis cannot be of much relevance. However, we would argue that our main result of the potential desirability of trading blocs can only be enhanced by now allowing for trade to occur over nonzero tariffs. As long as FTAs continue to involve zero tariffs internally, the presence of some trade externally can only raise welfare as compared to what it would have been in the prohibitive tariff case that we examined. Since we argued that expected welfare rises with the size of trading blocs and approaches the free-trade level as the blocs become large, the even higher welfare of blocs that do trade externally must have at least the second of these properties as well.[15]

Extensions and Caveats

The analysis here has included only three very simple examples. There are many directions in which it would be desirable to go with this, and it is premature to suggest that we know what such extensions would yield. However, these results do seem sufficient to at least raise the possibility that trading blocs may be welfare improving, and even that they may approach the level of welfare that could have been attained by free trade.

However, the examples here are at the opposite extreme from the model of Krugman, in the sense that they stack the cards in favor of trading blocs just as his model stacks them against. This suggests that an important consideration is whether in fact most trade is driven by differences in comparative advantage, as in the examples here, or by other considerations such as the product differentiation that drives Krugman's model. In a world where comparative advantage dominates and countries act cooperatively rather than noncooperatively in their trade policies, trading blocs of diverse countries may not be so bad.

Similarly, the examples here have assumed constant returns to scale and perfect competition. If instead there are increasing returns to scale and/or imperfect competition of various sorts, the argument here would have to be modified and possibly weakened. As long as trading blocs are too small to permit minimum efficient scale in many industries, or too small to permit a reasonable amount of competition, enlarging the blocs will increase welfare more than in the case considered here for these additional reasons. If this process can be completed while the blocs still encompass only a fraction of the world, then these effects strengthen our argument, since welfare will rise with bloc size even more rapidly when blocs are still small. On the other hand, if the entire world market is needed to surpass minimum efficient scale in many industries, or to permit a satisfactory level of competition, then these effects could conceivably turn our concave function into a convex one. In that case, any division of the world into trading blocs could fall well short of free trade in terms of welfare.

Note, finally, that the conclusion of our theoretical discussion is that a group of trading blocs, if they are large enough, can approximate the level of welfare that may be feasibly attainable from a multilateral system. However, it is also clear that if such blocs are too small and if the trade between them is too limited, then the gains we have described will not be achieved. In terms of our Figure 20.1, blocs must be sufficiently large to bring us up the curve to the free trade level, or else barriers to trade will be detrimental to world welfare. Therefore, our analysis argues in favor of trading blocs only if they are sufficiently large and only if they collectively encompass the entire world.

It is quite possible that a multilateral system of controls would be needed to assure that blocs do achieve this size and comprehensiveness, as well as to prevent the blocs from increasing levels of protection among themselves. Thus, as we will elaborate further in the concluding section, we do not view this simple theoretical analysis as undermining the case for GATT or for multilateral oversight of trade policy. We would only suggest on the basis of this analysis that trading blocs might have a legitimate place in a multilateral system, and that their presence should not be taken as necessary evidence that the gains from multilateral trade are being foregone.

Implications for the Design of Trading Blocs to Enhance World Welfare

From our institutional and historical discussion, it appears that preferential arrangements are an inevitable part of the world trading system. From our theoretical discussion, it appears that such arrangements are not necessarily the economic disasters that they have sometimes been supposed to be. It remains therefore to examine how the multilateral trading system should accommodate preferential arrangements, since it evidently must, in order to assure that their presence does not undermine other desirable features of the multilateral system and in order, if possible, to assure that they yield the greatest benefits and the fewest costs for the world as a whole. In this concluding section, therefore, we make several suggestions for how the multilateral trading system should be structured to this end.[16]

1. The GATT should recognize bilateral arrangements as an intrinsic part of any multilateral system, and not treat them as exceptions to the rule only to be tolerated. At present, in spite of Article XXIV, there is a tendency to regard new preferential arrangements as undermining the legitimacy of the GATT, and as long as they are treated that way they will indeed have that effect. Instead, much as the IMF came to accommodate the existence of flexible exchange rates in the 1970s, the GATT must accommodate preferential arrangements so that their presence will be seen as contributing to the system rather than tearing it apart.

2. The requirement, already embodied in Article XXIV, that new preferential arrangements should not lead to an increase in the level of protection, must be strengthened and enforced. In fact, the evidence does not suggest that such arrangements have historically added significantly to

the level of protection, so it should not be too difficult to enforce such a requirement. But, where cases can be brought to the GATT of violations of Article XXIV, they should be encouraged. That will not only serve in a minor way to restrain protectionism, but it will serve in a more major way to enhance the role of the GATT vis-a-vis such preferential arrangements and make it clear that the two can and should coexist.[17]

3. Language should be added to the GATT encouraging the formation of preferential arrangements where they are most likely to be beneficial to the countries involved and to the world. On the basis of comparative advantage, the GATT should favor arrangements that combine countries with large, rather than small, differences in their factor endowments and technologies. In particular, the GATT should encourage the inclusion of less developed countries within preferential arrangements, not involving only other developing countries like themselves, but involving also developed countries with whom they can benefit the most from trade.

4. Finally, and perhaps most importantly, the GATT should insist that preferential arrangements should have ways of accommodating new members, and that all countries (or at least all GATT members) should have access to joining some trading bloc, somewhere in the world. It will indeed be a disaster, politically as well as economically, if the formation of preferential trading arrangements leads not to an entire world of trading blocs, but rather to a world of blocs that include only the rich countries and a handful of their favored neighbors. Developments so far in Europe and America suggest a surprising and encouraging willingness to extend preferential treatment beyond the borders of the developed world. It remains to be seen whether this willingness will cease once the developed countries have acquired a comfortable buffer between themselves and the rest of the third world. The GATT could and should play an important role in preventing this from happening.

Notes

1. The assumption in Figure 20.1 is that the time path of welfare is monotonic as trading blocs increase in size. Krugman 1991a and Bhagwati 1992a suggest that there could be other paths in which world welfare would not consistently rise.

2. There is of course a large and venerable literature on the welfare effects of customs unions and free trade areas, including what determines whether particular combinations of countries forming trading blocs will raise or lower welfare. In addition to extensive discussions of trade creation and trade diversion, perhaps the most notable contribution is Kemp and Wan's 1976 demonstration that any grouping of countries into a customs union can be welfare improving, both for them and for the world as a whole, given a suitable selection of their

common external tariff. None of this literature, however, seems to bear directly on the issue here of the welfare effects of the size of trading blocs. For a recent analytical survey of pertinent theory relating to the welfare effects of trading blocs, see especially de Melo, Panagariya, and Rodrik 1992. See also Kennan and Riezman 1990 and Kowalczyk 1989, 1990, 1992.

3. See, for example, Whalley 1985 and subsequent work based on Whalley's model by Harrison and Rustrom 1991 and Nguyen, Perroni, and Wigle 1991.

4. Brown 1987 in particular has analyzed critically the implications of relying on the Armington assumption.

5. Although this is not certain, just as trade diversion by the narrower definition is not necessarily welfare worsening. See Kowalczyk 1990 for a recapitulation of this argument.

6. It is also noteworthy that Krugman 1991a,b, 1992b qualifies his analysis by noting that trade diversion may be lessened if the trading blocs consist of countries that are "natural" trading partners who would trade to a very large extent with each other in the absence of the formation of a trading bloc. While there may be some merit to this point, we have noted above that geographic proximity may not necessarily be a controlling factor. Bhagwati 1992a makes a similar point and also notes that relatively high substitution elasticities between nonmember and member country goods could prove detrimental to welfare.

7. We abstract from considerations of imperfect competition and increasing returns to scale. More will be said on this below.

8. The welfare gains would thus come mainly from an expansion of interindustry trade, and there would be presumably (transitional) costs of adjustment.

9. The example works just as well with Heckscher–Ohlin assumptions.

10. We assume here and in what follows that there are zero domestic barriers within any given country that would inhibit intra-bloc trade.

11. Note the assumption that price, p, appears in this function with a coefficient of one. What is important here is that each country have the same coefficient, indicating that behavior of both producers and consumers at the margin is identical across countries, and also that countries are in some sense equal in size (else a large country would have a much larger quantity response to a change in price than a small country). It is not important that the common coefficient happens to be one, which could always be assured by appropriate choice of units. A somewhat more general formulation would permit a different coefficient on p for each country. This would add complexity, and would also invalidate the result to be derived, without some additional assumption. Such an additional assumption will be suggested in a footnote below.

12. If countries have different coefficients on price in their excess supply functions, then this becomes a weighted average with those coefficients serving as weights.

13. This is the result we need, and it was in order to get it that we assumed the countries to be identical in such a strong way. If countries instead have different coefficients on price in their excess supply functions, it will not in general be true. (To see this, simply consider $N = 1$ and $M = 2$, with one country having a much larger coefficient and hence a large influence on the equilibrium price. The expected price in a one-country randomly chosen bloc is half way between their two autarky prices, while the equilibrium price for the two together is much closer to the autarky price of the high-coefficient country.) The result can nonetheless be salvaged if the coefficients are uncorrelated with the autarky prices.

14. This is obtained by integrating the excess supply function above, and normalizing on a level of welfare of zero in autarky.

15. Haveman 1992 has developed a model of trading blocs that encompasses comparative advantage and positive (optimal) tariffs that apparently negates this conclusion and reinforces Krugman's conclusion that the formation of trading blocs will be detrimental to world welfare as the number of blocs increases to two rather than three as in Krugman's model. In Haveman's model, however, this result does depend on the assumption that external tariffs are levied optimally at each stage.

16. See also Bhagwati 1992a,b and Whalley 1991 for related suggestions concerning the role and treatment of preferential arrangements within the multilateral system.

17. It is essential here, as Bhagwati 1992a,b and others have stressed, that measures be taken to constrain the use of antidumping measures and voluntary export restraints. The limitation of these measures is of course desirable in its own right and is ostensibly being dealt with in the Uruguay Round negotiations. The improvements here would then presumably carry over to the enforcement of Article XXIV.

References

Baldwin, Robert E. 1987. "Multilateral Liberalization," in J. Michael Finger and Andrzej Olechowski (eds.), *A Handbook on the Multilateral Trade Negotiations*. Washington, D.C.: The World Bank.

Bergsten, C. F. 1991. "Commentary" on Paul Krugman, "The Move Toward Free Trade Zones," in Federal Reserve Bank of Kansas City, *Policy Implications of Trade and Currency Zones*. Kansas City: Federal Reserve Bank of Kansas City.

Bhagwati, Jagdish N. 1990a. "Departures from Multilateralism: Regionalism and Aggressive Unilateralism," in David Greenaway (ed.), "Policy Forum: Multilateralism and Bilateralism in Trade Policy: Editorial Note," *Economic Journal* 100:1304–1317.

Bhagwati, Jagdish N. 1990b. "Multilateralism at Risk: The GATT is Dead. Long Live the GATT," *The World Economy* 13:149–169.

Bhagwati, Jagdish. 1992a. "Regionalism and Multilateralism: An Overview," in Jaime de Melo and Arvind Panagariya (eds.), *New Dimensions in Regional Integration*. New York: Cambridge University Press, forthcoming.

Bhagwati, Jagdish N. 1992b. "The Threats to the World Trading System," in Robert M. Stern (ed.), "Symposium on Issues for the Global Economy in the 1990s," *The World Economy* 15:443–456.

Brown, Drusilla K. 1987. "Tariffs, the Terms of Trade and National Product Differentiation," *Journal of Policy Modeling* 9:503–526.

Brown, Drusilla K., Alan V. Deardorff, and Robert M. Stern. 1992. "A North American Free Trade Agreement: Analytical Issues and a Computational Assessment," *The World Economy* 15:11–29.

Deardorff, Alan V. and Robert M. Stern. 1986. *The Michigan Model of World Production and Trade: Theory and Applications*. Cambridge: MIT Press.

de la Torre, Augusto and Margaret R. Kelly. 1992. *Regional Trade Arrangements*, Occasional Paper 93. Washington, D.C.: International Monetary Fund.

de Melo, Jaime, Arvind Panagariya, and Dani Rodrik. 1992. "Regional Integration: An Analytical and Empirical Overview," In Jaime de Melo and Arvind Panagariya (eds.), *New Dimensions in Regional Integration*. New York: Cambridge University Press, forthcoming.

Fieleke, Norman S. 1992. "One Trading World, or Many: The Issue of Regional Trading Blocs," *New England Economic Review*, May/June: 3–20.

Finger, C. Michael. 1992. "GATT's Influence on Regional Arrangements," in Jaime de Melo and Arvind Panagariya (eds.), *New Dimensions in Regional Integration*. New York: Cambridge University Press, forthcoming.

Finger, J. M. 1979. "Trade Liberalization: A Public Choice Perspective," in Ryan C. Amacher, Gottfried Haberler, and Thomas D. Willett (eds.), *Challenges to a Liberal Economic Order*. Washington, D.C.: American Enterprise Institute.

Harrison, Glenn W. and E. E. Rustrom. 1991. "Trade Wars, Trade Negotiations and Applied Game Theory," *Economic Journal* 101:420–435.

Haveman, Jon D. 1992. "Some Welfare Effects of Dynamic Customs Union Formation," in process.

Hoekman, Bernard M. 1991. "Multilateral Trade Negotiations and the Coordination of Commercial Policies," in Robert M. Stern (ed.), *The Multilateral Trading System: Analysis and Prospects for Negotiating Change*. Ann Arbor: University of Michigan Press, forthcoming.

Irwin, Douglas A. 1992. "Multilateral and Bilateral Trade Policies in the World Trading System: An Historical Perspective," in Jaime de Melo and Arvind Panagariya (eds.), *New Dimensions in Regional Integration*. New York: Cambridge University Press, forthcoming.

Jackson, John H. 1989. *The World Trading System: Law and Policy of International Economic Relations*. Cambridge: MIT Press.

Jackson, John H. and William J. Davey. 1986. *International Economic Relations*. Second Edition. St. Paul: West Publishing Co.

Kemp, Murray C. and Henry Wan, Jr. 1976. "An Elementary Proposition Concerning the Formation of Customs Unions," *Journal of International Economics* 6:95–97.

Kennan, John and Raymond Riezman. 1990. "Optimal Tariff Equilibria with Customs Unions," *Canadian Journal of Economics* 23:70–83.

Kowalczyk, Carsten. 1989. "Trade Negotiations and World Welfare," *American Economic Review* 79:552–559.

Kowalczyk, Carsten. 1992. "Paradoxes in Integration Theory," *Open Economies Review* 3:51–59.

Kowalczyk, Carsten. 1990. "Welfare and Customs Unions," National Bureau of Economic Research, Paper No. 3476. Cambridge: NBER.

Krugman, Paul R. 1991a. "Is Bilateralism Bad?" in Elhanan Helpman and Assaf Razin (eds.), *International Trade and Trade Policy*. Cambridge: MIT Press.

Krugman, Paul. 1991b. "The Movement Toward Free Trade Zones," in Federal Reserve Bank of Kansas City, *Policy Implications of Trade and Currency Zones*. Kansas City: Federal Reserve Bank of Kansas City.

Krugman, Paul. 1992a. "Does the New Trade Theory Require a New Trade Policy," in Robert M. Stern (ed.), "Symposium on Issues for the Global Economy in the 1990s," *The World Economy* 15:423–441.

Krugman, Paul. 1992b. "Regionalism vs. Multilateralism: Analytical Notes," in Jaime de Melo and Arvind Panagariya (eds.), *New Dimensions in Regional Integration*. New York: Cambridge University Press, forthcoming.

Ludema, Rodney D. 1991. "On the Value of Free-Trade Areas in Multilateral Negotiations," in process.

Nguyen, Trien T., Carlo Perroni, and Randall M. Wigle. 1991. "The Value of a Uruguay Round Success," *The World Economy* 14:359–374.

Nogués, Julio. 1990. "The Choice Between Unilateral and Multilateral Trade Liberalization Strategy," *The World Economy* 13:15–26.

Nogués, Julio and Rosalinda Quintanilla. 1992. "Latin America's Integration and the Multilateral Trading System," in Jaime de Melo and Arvind Panagariya (eds.), *New Dimensions in Regional Integration*. New York: Cambridge University Press, forthcoming.

Patterson, Gardner. 1989. "Implications for the GATT and the World Trading System," and "Comments" by John Whalley, in Jeffrey J. Schott (ed.), *Free Trade Areas and U.S. Trade Policy*. Washington, D.C.: Institute for International Economics.

Richardson, J. David. 1991. "U.S. Trade Policy in the 1980s: Turns—and Roads Not Taken," National Bureau of Economic Research, NBER Working Paper No. 3725 (June). Cambridge: NBER.

Saxonhouse, Gary. 1992. "Trading Blocs, Pacific Trade and the Pricing Strategies of East Asian Firms," in Jaime de Melo and Arvind Panagariya (eds.), *New Dimensions in Regional Integration*. New York: Cambridge University Press, forthcoming.

Schott, Jeffrey J. 1989. "More Free Trade Areas?" in Jeffrey J. Schott (ed.), *Free Trade Areas and U.S. Trade Policy*. Washington, D.C.: Institute for International Economics.

Schott, Jeffrey J. 1991. "Trading Blocs and the World Trading System," *The World Economy* 14:1–18.

Whalley, John. 1985. *Trade Liberalization Among World Trading Areas*. Cambridge: MIT Press.

Whalley, John. 1991. "Harnessing the New Regionalism," in process.

Whalley, John. 1992. "Regional Trade Arrangements in North America: CUSTA and NAFTA," in process.

Winters, L. Alan. 1990. "The Road to Uruguay," in David Greenaway (ed.), "Policy Forum Multilateralism and Bilateralism in Trade Policy: Editorial Note," *Economic Journal* 100:1288–1303.

Winters, Alan. 1992. "The European Community: A Case of Successful Integration," In Jaime de Melo and Arvind Panagariya (eds.), *New Dimensions in Regional Integration*. New York: Cambridge University Press, forthcoming.

Wolf, Martin. 1987. "Why Trade Liberalization is a Good Idea," in J. Michael Finger and Andrzej Olechowski (eds.), *A Handbook on the Multilateral Trade Negotiations*. Washington, D.C.: The World Bank.

Wonnacott, Paul and Mark Lutz. 1989. "Is There a Case for Free Trade Areas?" and "Comments" by Isaiah Frank and Martin Wolf, in Jeffrey J. Schott (ed.), *Free Trade Areas and U.S. Trade Policy*. Washington, D.C.: Institute for International Economics.

Yarbrough, Beth V. and Robert M. Yarbrough. 1986. "Reciprocity, Bilateralism, and Economic 'Hostages': Self-enforcing Agreements in International Trade," *International Studies Quarterly* 30:7–21.

Exogenously Determined
PTA Expansion

21

A Political-Economic Analysis of Free-Trade Agreements

Philip I. Levy

The recent pursuit of bilateral and regional trade agreements, marked most notably by the conclusion of the North American Free Trade Agreement (NAFTA) and the further lowering of trade barriers in Europe, raises questions about the wisdom of this approach to trade liberalization. Governments have asserted that bilateral free-trade negotiations are compatible with the goal of multilateral trade liberalization,[1] but others (e.g., Jagdish Bhagwati, 1992) have questioned whether bilateral arrangements will eventually lead to broader liberalization.[2]

If trade liberalization is to proceed in stages, a formal approach to the process should consider the decision to liberalize at each stage and explore how the decision to liberalize multilaterally is affected by bilateral liberalization. This chapter uses a median-voter setting to show a mechanism by which bilateral arrangements may undermine political support for a multilateral arrangement but can never enhance political support for broader free trade.

In the burgeoning literature on preferential trading arrangements and their effects, a number of studies address the impact of bilateral or regional free-trade agreements on trade relations with nonmembers. Unlike this chapter, most use the tariff on nonbloc members' goods as a measure of the agreement's effects.

Paul Krugman (1991) constructs a model in which the trading world divides symmetrically into blocs. Each bloc—a customs union rather than a free-trade agreement—sets tariffs non-cooperatively to take advantage of its market power and move terms of trade in its favor. The larger the individual blocs, the greater is their market power and the higher their tariffs.

Originally published in *American Economic Review* 87, no. 4 (September 1997): 506–519. Reprinted with permission.

Several works address the issues of free-trade agreements (FTAs). Kyle Bagwell and Robert Staiger (1993) focus on the transition period during which an FTA is being formed and posit that the effect of an FTA will be to reduce the volume of trade between the home country and non-participants once it is fully implemented. They find that the anticipation of a future drop in multilateral trade volumes interferes with the enforcement of low multilateral tariffs early in the FTA formation process, leading to temporarily higher multilateral tariffs. However, they find that, once an FTA is completed, tariff levels between the home country and non-participants will be no higher.

Martin Richardson (1993) considers the effect of an FTA in a different setting, in which governments maximize a political-support function which gives added weight to export- and import-competing producers' interests. In his model, the small home country has two trading partners supplying a good: the non-FTA partner, with perfectly elastic supply at a low price, and the FTA partner, with perfectly elastic supply at a high price. If an FTA were to make the FTA partners's price less than the tariff-ridden price of the nonpartner, Richardson argues that the home country would lower the tariff against the nonpartner. If it lowered the tariff to the point where the nonpartners's tariff-ridden price was equal to (or just below) the tariff-free price of the partner, the home country would gain tariff revenue on the good and would not harm consumers or import-competing producers (since the domestic post-FTA price would not change).

Panagariya and Ronald Findlay (1994) demonstrate one mechanism by which an FTA could lead to greater protection between blocs. In their model, an exogenously imposed function translates lobbying inputs (labor) into protection. When an FTA is enacted, the labor that was formerly employed lobbying for protection against the FTA partner countries will be released into the labor pool. The wage will be driven down, and thus more labor will be employed lobbying for protection against the rest of the world. Tariffs between blocs should rise.

In Levy (1996), I describe a different mechanism whereby exogenous introduction of a free-trade agreement could induce higher or lower tariffs between trading blocs. It is shown that, in a lobbying framework of the sort originated by Gene Grossman and Elhanan Helpman (1994), FTAs alter pressures for and against trade liberalization by shifting the payoffs to export industries and import-competing industries associated with any given level of protection. The net effect can be to raise or lower barriers between blocs, depending on the characteristics of FTA partners.

This chapter takes a very different approach by portraying national decisions on trade relations as binary choices; countries choose whether to join a free-trade agreement and then choose whether to participate in a broader multilateral agreement.[3] In such a setting, there are two readily apparent ways in which bilateral trade agreements could undermine multilateral liberalization: countries could abandon multilateralism in anticipation of future bilateral agreements; or countries could sign bilateral agreements before a multilateral accord is concluded and then lose the desire to pursue multilateralism further. The latter possibility is the topic of this chapter.

This possibility is addressed using a political-economy approach similar to that of Wolfgang Mayer (1984), in which a simple majority of voters is required to pass a proposal. Agents are presented first with a potential bilateral free-trade agreement and then with a multilateral free-trade agreement. Each potential agreement offers agents new equilibrium prices and product varieties in a trade model of the sort discussed by Helpman and Krugman (1985). A majority of voters must support a trade agreement for passage.

The sequence of votes is important, in that voters have perfect foresight. They will approve a bilateral agreement only if it is preferable to a multilateral arrangement or if the bilateral agreement will not prevent the adoption of a preferred multilateral agreement.

Agents have different holdings of capital and labor and thus react differently to any given proposal. In the rich version of the model, every trade agreement offers agents an increased number of product varieties, which uniformly enhances the welfare of agents. The shifts in goods and factor prices may be beneficial or detrimental depending on an agent's capital–labor ratio. In this approach the voter with the median capital–labor ratio is of primary importance, since that voter will always be in the majority on any vote.

The primacy of the median voter ensures that no proposal that diminishes the median voter's utility can ever pass. This means, for instance, that if a multilateral free-trade proposal is not politically feasible under autarky—because the median voter and thus at least half the populace oppose it—then that same multilateral proposal cannot be rendered feasible by any bilateral free-trade agreement. If a bilateral free-trade agreement is politically feasible, it will only raise the reservation utility level of the median voter to which the multilateral proposal will be compared.

For this reason, the chapter focuses on cases in which multilateral free trade is politically feasible in autarky. The most interesting cases are those in which the median agent is roughly indifferent between multilateral free trade and the status quo. For the median agent to be indifferent, multilateral free trade must offer a balance of additional product variety (a gain) and adverse price shifts (a loss).

A bilateral free-trade agreement can undermine support for multilateral free trade by offering the median agent disproportionately large gains with relatively small losses. If such a combination raises the utility of the median voter above the level offered by a multilateral free-trade agreement, then the multilateral agreement will no longer be politically viable. This undermining is more likely to occur in bilateral agreements, involving countries with similar capital–labor ratios and roughly indifferent median voters. In the extreme case, a bilateral agreement with an identical partner country would bring variety gains without any price shifts. The remaining variety gains offered by a move from the bilateral agreement to multilateral free trade could be insufficient to compensate the median agent for the factor-price losses, in which case the multilateral accord would be blocked.

The kinds of bilateral agreements that would do the least damage to the political feasibility of multilateral free trade would be those that leave the median voter's utility unchanged by combining price shifts with variety gains. This combination could be found in partner countries with capital–labor ratios different from that of the home country. Such agreements would also necessarily engender the most political opposition of any feasible bilateral agreement, since they do the least to enhance the welfare of swing voters.

To develop the point about undermining, this chapter begins with a two-good Heckscher-Ohlin model. In this model there are no variety gains to trade, and it is shown that in this setting voters will never forsake multilateral free trade in favor of a bilateral free-trade agreement. If a majority of voters in one country prefers a bilateral trade agreement with a given partner to multilateral free trade, the majority of voters in the partner country will prefer multilateral free trade to the bilateral accord. This result follows from the strict quasiconvexity of indirect utility as a function of the relative price; if a shift in relative prices increases an agent's utility, a further shift in the same direction will increase utility even more. Bilateral free trade can preclude multilateral free trade only in the trivial case when multilateral free trade would result in the same relative price as bilateral free trade, in which case there would be no incentive to trade on a multilateral basis once the bilateral agreement had been struck.

This result is reversed in the second half of the chapter with a specific trade model incorporating increasing returns to scale and product varieties. The introduction of product varieties allows agreements that would not be politically feasible in their absence. Specifically, these are agreements in which the median voter in one partner country would suffer from adverse price shifts but is compensated by increased variety gain. The introduction of product varieties into the welfare analysis also allows agreements between identical countries to raise the reservation utility levels in each. Thus, undermining is possible in the latter model, whereas in the former it was not.

An unusual feature of the analysis is the assumption that tariffs are either zero or prohibitive. While this has the virtue of simplicity, the chapter's reasoning would carry through with some different fixed level of tariff protection as the alternative to complete liberalization. The lack of tariffs allows a focus on the choice of trading regime and avoids the difficult question of how external tariffs might be determined simultaneously.

Although specific models are used, the lesson of the chapter is more general. When agents are roughly indifferent between an initial situation and multilateral free trade and that indifference results from a balance of gains (increased variety) and losses (adverse price shifts), then any intermediate agreement offering disproportionately large gains will undermine support for multilateral free trade. To the extent that the opinion of the broader public (or a subset thereof) plays an important role in determining trade policy, this chapter illustrates a potentially harmful effect of pursuing regional trade agreements.[4]

The next section will present the Heckscher-Ohlin model along with the voting procedure. The assertion that bilateral agreements cannot preclude multilateral agreements in such a setting will then be proved. In Section 21.2, a specific example of a model with differentiated products and intraindustry trade will be presented, along with a proof that in this setting, bilateral agreements can undermine multilateral agreements. Conclusions and implications will be presented in Section 21.3.

21.1   Bilateral Agreements in a Heckscher-Ohlin Model

This section will consider bilateral agreements in a standard two-good, two-factor[5] Heckscher-Ohlin trade model. Let there be many countries, distinguishable only by their fixed endowments of the two factors of production, capital (K) and labor (L). These factors are used in the constant-returns-to-scale production of goods X and Y. The internationally identical technologies will be assumed to be such that K is used relatively intensively in X (and L in Y) with no factor-intensity reversals. Perfect competition will ensure that profits are zero.

Agents in these economies own shares of their country's capital and labor stocks. If the return to a unit of labor is denoted as w and the return to a unit of capital as r, the income of an agent i is:

$$I_i = wL_i + rK_i, \tag{21.1}$$

where K_i and L_i are the number of units owned by agent i. Agents are assumed to have identical and homothetic preferences. Income is fully spent on goods X and Y. Arbitrarily, let Y be the numeraire good and p the relative price of X in terms of Y.

It will be assumed throughout this chapter that countries' relative endowments are sufficiently similar that when they join together in a free-trade area, bilateral or multilateral, there is factor-price equalization.[6] Within the trading area, the integrated economy that would result from factor mobility will be achieved instead through trade flows. It is also assumed that tariffs are either zero or prohibitive, so a country only trades with its free-trade partners.[7]

In this setting, when two countries with different capital–labor ratios form a free-trade area, the resulting relative price will lie between the autarky prices in the two countries and the capital-abundant country will export X and import Y (the Heckscher-Ohlin theorem).

When two or more countries join to form free-trade areas, the resulting capital–labor ratio of the integrated economy is likely to differ from any of the countries' autarky ratios (unless they originally had identical capital–labor ratios). The effects of these shifts on agents' utility can be characterized as follows:

Proposition 1   The utility of an agent i, with an endowment (L_i, K_i), can be depicted as a function of K/L, the integrated economy's capital–labor ratio. This function is strictly quasi-convex in K/L and has a unique minimum when the agent's capital–labor ratio is equal to that of the economy.

Proof   Let $H(p, K_j, L_j)$ represent the indirect utility of a country j where it will initially be assumed that there is a single agent. A. D. Woodland (1980) proves that

$$\frac{\partial H}{\partial p} = V_I(p, K_j, L_j)e_X^i(p, K_j, L_j).$$

where V_I is the marginal utility of income, which will always be positive, and $e_X(p, K_j, L_j)$ is defined as the excess supply of good X (production minus consumption). In autarky equilibrium, $e_X(p^A, K_j, L_j) = 0$ by definition. The law of comparative advantage requires that when $p > p^A$ country j exports good X and imports Y, so $e_X > 0$. Similarly, when $p < p^A$ it follows that $e_X < 0$. Thus,

$$\frac{\partial H}{\partial p} < 0 \quad \text{for } p < p^A$$

$$\frac{\partial H}{\partial p} > 0 \quad \text{for } p > p^A$$

$$\frac{\partial H}{\partial p} = 0 \quad \text{for } p = p^A.$$

In a Heckscher-Ohlin model without factor-intensity reversals, $p = p(K/L)$ and $p' < 0$, since p is the price of the capital-intensive good, X. Thus one can replace p in H with K/L, the capital–labor ratio of the broader integrated economy. It follows that H is strictly quasi-convex in K/L with a unique minimum at $K/L = K_j/L_j$, the autarky capital–labor ratio.

Finally, it can be seen that the parallel between a country in an integrated economy and an individual in a broader economy is exact. In both cases, an economic entity with some fraction of the total capital and labor stock uses those endowments to maximize utility, either through international or interpersonal trade. Therefore, there is an indirect utility function $U(K/L, L_i, K_i)$ for any agent i which is strictly quasi-convex in K/L with a minimum at $K/L = K_i/L_i$.

To illustrate the proposition given above, suppose an agent has a capital–labor ratio slightly higher than that of her country. For purposes of the agent's welfare, one can index all possible free-trade agreements by the continuum of possible capital–labor ratios that would result.[8] As depicted in Figure 21.1 any trade agreements with countries less capital-abundant than the agent's country will increase this agent's welfare by increasing the return to capital and raising the price of good X, which would then be the export good. Such agreements would lie to the left of the point labeled "Autarky" in Figure 21.1. Trade agreements that increase the integrated economy's capital–labor ratio will first hurt the agent. Then, as the capital–labor ratio rises above the agent's own, the agent's utility will

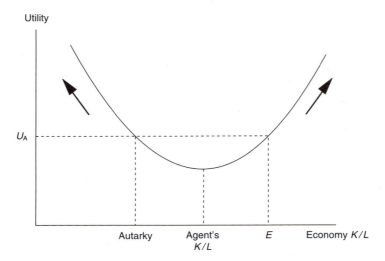

Figure 21.1
The strictly quasi-convex utility of an agent with a given capital—labor ratio as a function of the economy's capital-labor ratio (i.e., the capital-labor ratio of the entire trading region). *Notes*: If this represented the median voter in a country, she would reject trade agreements which resulted in economy capital—labor ratios in the range (Autarky, E). Outside of that range, utility increases as the distance from Autarky increases.

increase. To the right of point E in Figure 21.1, this agent's utility rises above its autarky level.

Next, I use this result to consider whether voters might ever opt for a bilateral trade agreement instead of multilateral free trade. The following voting structure will be assumed. Voters will be asked in a first period whether they would prefer a bilateral trade pact to autarky. Then, in a second period, voters are offered the choice between the existing trade regime (either autarky or bilateral free trade) and multilateral free trade.[9]

It is assumed that voters are fully informed about all aspects of endowments, economies, and voting. It is also assumed that the periods are close enough together in time or discount rates are sufficiently low that discounting may be ignored. Thus, agents all vote to maximize their expected utility under the final integrated trading economy.[10] Any proposal that garners the support of a majority of voters will be enacted.

Once a free-trade agreement has been approved, the participating countries retain their rights to veto an extension of the agreement to include a new country or countries. Thus free-trade agreements are distinct from political unions.[11]

While each voter has a single vote and the majority will prevail, one can predict the outcome of any vote by considering the behavior of the voter with the median capital–labor ratio. Suppose, for example, that a trade agreement under consideration would lead to a capital–labor ratio in the resulting integrated economy that was lower than the alternative economywide capital–labor ratio (either under autarky or a bilateral agreement). If this increases the utility of the voter with the median capital–labor ratio, one can deduce from Proposition 1 that all voters with higher capital–labor ratios than this median voter would also gain. Together, these agents must constitute a majority, by the definition of median. The same reasoning applies if an agreement would reduce the median voter's utility. Therefore, agreements will be approved if, and only if, they enhance the welfare of all participating countries' median voters. I will call such agreements politically feasible.

Now the major result of this section can be stated:

Proposition 2 In a Heckscher-Ohlin setting, there can be no politically feasible bilateral agreements that would supplant a politically feasible multilateral trade agreement.

Proof It is useful at this stage to enhance the notation. I will use k as generic notation for a capital–labor ratio. Next, let k_0^c represent the capital–labor ratio of the median agent in country c. Finally, I will distinguish between countries and integrated economies; the latter can consist of a single country (autarky) or two or more countries (free-trade areas). The ratio of all the capital to all the labor in an integrated economy e will be written as k^e. Now let the function

$$U_c(k_0^c, k^e)$$

denote the maximum attainable utility of the median agent in country c, given the capital–labor ratio in economy e, as in Proposition 1. Although the levels of capital and labor endowments determine utility, the ratios are sufficient to explore the welfare effects of policy changes, and thus the levels are omitted.

Consider two countries, A and B, which might pair to create a free-trade area. In the first stage of voting, voters in both countries decide whether to continue functioning in autarky or whether to join to form a free-trade area (AB). In the second stage, voters will determine whether to maintain the outcome of the first stage or join in a multilateral free-trade area (M) including the other countries. Since the proposition is only concerned with politically feasible multilateral free-trade agreements, assume

$$U_j(k_0^j, k^M) > U_j(k_0^j, k^j)$$

for each country j (i.e., all median agents prefer multilateral free trade to autarky).

Returning to the potential free-trade agreement, AB, one can see that if $k^A = k^B$ then there is no basis for trade between the two countries. Therefore, I will arbitrarily say that $k^A > k^{AB} > k^B$. For agreement AB to pass, both countries must approve it. This requires that

$$U_A(k_0^A, k^{AB}) > U_A(k_0^A, k^A)$$
$$U_B(k_0^B, k^{AB}) > U_B(k_0^B, k^B). \qquad (21.2)$$

Because of the strict quasi-convexity of utility functions, if condition (21.2) holds, this implies that the median voter in A must gain from decreases in the economy's capital–labor ratio at k^{AB}, while the median voter in B must gain from increases (see Figure 21.1).

Next consider the second stage of voting. The aim here is to show that there are no sets of capital–labor ratios (for the two countries A and B and the rest of the world) such that both A and B prefer the bilateral free-trade agreement to multilateral free trade. In relation to free-trade area AB, multilateral free trade can have one of three effects:

(i) Multilateral free trade could leave the integrated economy's capital–labor ratio unchanged ($k^M = k^{AB}$). In this case, there is no basis for trade, so both A and B would be indifferent.

(ii) Multilateral free trade could increase the integrated economy's capital–labor ratio ($k^M > k^{AB}$). In this case,

$$U_B(k_0^B, k^M) > U_B(k_0^B, k^{AB}) > U_B(k_0^B, k^B)$$

so B would approve of the change. It is possible that

$$U_A(k_0^A, k^M) > U_A(k_0^A, k^{AB})$$

only if k^M is sufficiently greater than k^A, in which case both countries would approve the change. If

$$U_A(k_0^A, k^M) < U_A(k_0^A, k^{AB}),$$

which will occur if A is capital-abundant relative to the world, then A would want to block multilateral free trade. However, country B would foresee the result and vote against the bilateral free-trade agreement in period 1.

(iii) Multilateral free trade could decrease the integrated economy's capital–labor ratio ($k^M < k^{AB}$). This case is simply the reverse of case 2. Country A would approve of the change. If B would want to block multilateral free trade, A would foresee the result and vote against the bilateral free-trade agreement in period 1.

Thus, the strict quasi-convexity of utility functions guarantees that no two countries that originally wanted multilateral free trade can establish a bilateral free-trade area that both prefer.

While the proof given above was tailored for a two-country free-trade agreement, the reasoning can be readily extended to regional trade agreement with two or more countries.

Corollary 1 In a Heckscher-Ohlin setting, there can be no politically feasible regional agreement that would supplant a politically feasible multilateral trade agreement.

Proof Define a regional agreement (R) as a free-trade agreement among any proper subset of the countries in a multilateral agreement. Denote the capital–labor ratio of the combined countries in the regional agreement as k^R. Let country A be any country that is capital-abundant relative to the combined countries in R. Let country B be any country that is relatively labor-abundant. Thus, $k^A > k^R > k^B$. For agreement R to pass, all member countries must approve it. One can now repeat the proof of Proposition 2 with k^R in place of k^{AB}.

The bilateral argument is demonstrated in Figure 21.2. A special case is depicted in which the median voters in countries A and B have the same capital–labor ratios as their countries. These capital–labor ratios are the minima of the two utility curves. The capital–labor ratio of a bilateral free-trade area between A and B must lie between these two points. The three cases in the proof given above correspond to situations when multilateral free trade would result in a capital–labor ratio the same as, to the right of, or to the left of the bilateral FTA point. In either of the latter two cases, at least one country would strictly prefer multilateral free trade to the bilateral agreement.

Of course, if the discount rate were sufficiently high or the periods sufficiently far apart, then it would be possible for a bilateral agreement to undermine multilateral free trade. This is a caveat applicable to almost any sequential result. The point remains that, in a Heckscher-Ohlin setting in which voters are asked to consider both a bilateral and a multilateral trade

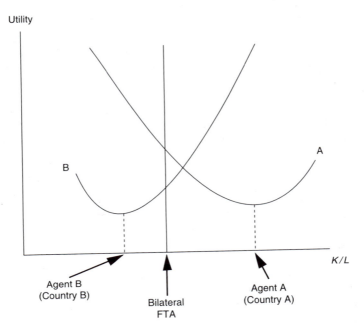

Figure 21.2
The impossibility of undermining in the Heckscher-Ohlin setting. For the special case depicted, utility curves are shown for two agents, A and B, each of whom is assumed, for simplicity, to have the same capital–labor ratio as his country. Also shown is the capital–labor ratio that would result in a free trade area involving the two countries.

agreement, there cannot be coalitions of countries that would prefer the bilateral agreement to multilateral free trade.[12]

It is worth noting that bilateral agreements are feasible in this model if, and only if, the capital–labor ratios of both participating countries lie on the same side of the multilateral integrated economy's capital–labor ratio. To see how this might happen, return to the example in which $k^A > k^B$. If both ratios were greater than that of the integrated economy under multilateral free trade, it is possible that country B would gain by both an initial increase in the broader economy's capital–labor ratio and a subsequent decrease sufficiently large that B became relatively capital-abundant. In Figure 21.2, this situation would involve a multilateral free-trade capital–labor ratio well to the left of country B's. The same argument could be made if both countries were labor-abundant relative to the multilateral economy. As shown in Proposition 2, though, these politically feasible bilateral agreements could not preclude multilateral free trade.

One can also readily see that a politically feasible bilateral agreement can never increase the political feasibility of multilateral free trade. If multilateral free trade is not politically feasible initially in a country j, $U_j(k_0^j, k^M) < U_j(k_0^j, k^j)$. If a bilateral free-trade agreement (ij) is politically feasible, then $U_j(k_0^j, k^{ij}) > U_j(k_0^j, k^j)$. By transitivity, then, $U_j(k_0^j, k^{ij}) > U_j(k_0^j, k^M)$, so there would not be political support for an expansion from a bilateral trade agreement to a multilateral trade agreement.

Finally, note that the logic of this section would also apply to political unions. A political union between two countries would imply that majority support from the *pooled* populations would be necessary for expanding the union. Under such an arrangement, there would likely be a new median voter. However, if the voters in the two partner countries are fully informed, they would block the bilateral political union unless they concurred with the predictable ensuing choice on multilateral union.

21.2 A Differentiated-Product Model

In this section it will be shown that, in a richer model, the result of the previous section can be overturned; there may be bilateral trade coalitions that can supplant multilateral free trade. To demonstrate this, a standard differentiated-product model will be introduced. This model will retain the important features of the Heckscher-Ohlin model but will add another dimension to agents' utility: the number of varieties of the differentiated product that are available. It is this new dimension that allows bilateral agreements to undermine multilateral agreements.

This section will begin by extending the model of the previous section and deriving the effect of trade agreements on agents' welfare. It will be shown that the median voter is still the agent with the median capital–labor ratio. Finally, it will be shown that trade agreements between similar countries can win voter approval and undermine support for multilateral free trade.

The only differences between countries will be their endowments of the two factors of production—capital (K) and labor (L)—and the distribution of factor ownership. I now add the simplifying assumption that each agent i will be assumed to own one unit of labor and some amount of capital, k_i, where

$$\sum_{i=1}^{L} k_i = K. \tag{21.3}$$

Since labor ownership is assumed not to vary, k_i also measures an agent's relative wealth.

The two factors receive returns per unit of w for labor and per unit of r for capital. Thus, agent i enjoys an income of

$$I_i = rk_i + w. \tag{21.4}$$

I turn now to the two sectors of production and adopt a specific functional form. Y will denote the economy's output of the homogeneous product. The constant-returns production process uses factors in the following way:

$$Y = \gamma_Y K_Y^\mu L_Y^{1-\mu}, \tag{21.5}$$

where all parameters are assumed to be positive and $\mu \in (0, 1)$. Y will be assumed to be the numeraire good.

The goods in the X sector are now differentiated products produced under increasing returns to scale. For an individual variety x, the production function is

$$x = \gamma_x K_x^{\xi\eta} L_x^{\xi(1-\eta)}, \tag{21.6}$$

where parameters again are positive, $\eta \in (0, 1)$, and the returns to scale are reflected by $\xi > 1$. In equilibrium, n will denote the number of varieties in production, and X will denote the sum of output over all n varieties in an economy.[13]

Agents are assumed to have identical utility functions of the following form:

$$U = U_X^\alpha Y^{1-\alpha}, \tag{21.7}$$

$$U_X = \left(\sum_{i=1}^n D_i^\beta \right)^{1/\beta}$$

$$\beta = \left(1 - \frac{1}{\sigma} \right) \quad \sigma > 1, \tag{21.8}$$

where D represents the consumption of an individual variety x and i indexes the varieties. The homotheticity of (21.7) ensures that expenditure patterns will not vary as income is redistributed or augmented. The parameter α lies in the range $(0, 1)$. The Spence-Dixit-Stiglitz (SDS) sub-utility function implies that individuals prefer variety and have a constant cross-price elasticity of substitution (σ) between varieties.[14]

In this framework, each firm in sector X produces at an identical optimal level of output, denoted by x, where

$$x = \frac{\sigma}{\xi(\sigma - 1)}$$

and sells at an identical equilibrium price, p. For a large number of firms, σ approximates the elasticity of demand facing each firm.[15] The number of firms, n, is thus determined by

$$X = nx. \tag{21.9}$$

Returning to the utility of agents, by substituting equilibrium values into the utility function described by (21.7) and (21.8), I derive an indirect utility function for an agent i:

$$U_i = I_i(1 - \alpha)^{1-\alpha}\alpha^\alpha n^{\alpha/\sigma-1}p^{-\alpha}. \tag{21.10}$$

Next, I use this result to explore the effect of any free-trade agreement on agents' utility. From equation (21.10) the change in agent i's utility due to a trade agreement can be described as

$$\frac{U_i^{FT}}{U_i^{AUT}} = \left(\frac{I_i^{FT}}{I_i^{AUT}}\right)\left(\frac{p^{FT}}{p^{AUT}}\right)^{-\alpha}\left(\frac{n^{FT}}{n^{AUT}}\right)^{\alpha/(\sigma-1)}, \tag{21.11}$$

where FT denotes values after a free-trade agreement and AUT denotes values in autarky. Define λ_K as the percentage increase from an economy's capital stock to the capital stock of the integrated economy resulting from a free-trade agreement (and λ_L as the percentage increase in the labor stock). The final term of (21.11) can be shown to equal

$$\left(\frac{n^{FT}}{n^{AUT}}\right)^{\alpha/(\sigma-1)} = [(1 + \lambda_K)^\eta(1 + \lambda_L)^{1-\eta}]^{\alpha/(\sigma-1)}. \tag{21.12}$$

Since λ_K and λ_L are always greater than zero, this "variety" effect always exceeds one (i.e., it has a positive effect on utility). Note that, if an agreement offered only this variety effect, it would raise the welfare of all agents and win unanimous support.

I call the remaining effect on utility the "comparative advantage" effect.[16] This is the effect that would remain if σ went to ∞ and the differentiated product became homogeneous. It is a specific example of the utility arguments underlying Section 21.1. To sign to this effect, first parameterize the shift in the economy's capital–labor ratio by the variable φ, where φ is implicitly defined by

$$\frac{K^{FT}}{L^{FT}} = \frac{(1+\lambda_K)K^{AUT}}{(1+\lambda_L)L^{AUT}} = \varphi\frac{K^{AUT}}{L^{AUT}}. \tag{21.13}$$

Note that the free-trade capital–labor ratio is that obtained by pooling the endowments of the partner countries. I assume, as before, that endowments are such that the integrated equilibrium can be replicated through trade. Therefore, φ will be greater than 1 if a country's counterpart is relatively capital-abundant and less than 1 if the counterpart is relatively labor-abundant.

One can also parameterize agent i's capital holdings by ρ_i, where ρ_i is implicitly defined by

$$\left(\frac{K}{L}\right)_i = k_i = \rho_i\left(\frac{K^{AUT}}{L^{AUT}}\right). \tag{21.14}$$

Therefore, $\rho_i > 1$ if agent i is relatively capital-abundant, $\rho_i < 1$ if agent i is relatively labor-abundant, and $\rho_i = 1$ if agent i has the same capital–labor ratio as the country.

With these parameterizations, the comparative-advantage effect is

$$\left(\frac{I_i^{FT}}{I_i^{AUT}}\right)\left(\frac{p^{FT}}{p^{AUT}}\right)^{-\alpha} = \varphi^{1/1+\theta}\left(\frac{\dfrac{\rho^i}{\varphi}+\theta}{\rho_i+\theta}\right) \tag{21.15}$$

where[17]

$$\theta \equiv \frac{1}{\mu(1-\alpha)+\eta\alpha} - 1.$$

Thus, the comparative-advantage effect of an agent's utility change can be seen to depend on the capital abundance of the agent and the capital–labor ratio of the partner country. It will prove useful to work with the natural logarithm of equation (21.15). Define

$$f(\varphi, \rho, \theta) = \frac{1}{1+\theta}\ln \varphi + \ln\left(\frac{\rho}{\varphi}+\theta\right) - \ln(\rho+\theta) \tag{21.16}$$

so that $f > 0$ implies an increase in utility and $f < 0$ implies a decrease in utility due to a free-trade agreement. Then,

$$\frac{\partial f}{\partial\varphi} = \frac{\theta(\varphi-\rho)}{\varphi^2(1+\theta)\left(\dfrac{\rho}{\varphi}+\theta\right)}, \tag{21.17}$$

which describes the change in desirability of an agreement as the factor abundance of a partner country changes.

It is now possible to establish the identity of the median voter in this new framework.

Proposition 3 The median voter for a country will be the agent with the median capital–labor ratio in that country.

Proof Consider a given free-trade agreement characterized by φ. Consider the agent with the median capital–labor ratio, whom we can identify as ρ_{median}. From the log of the utility ratio, $f(\varphi, \rho_{median}, \theta)$, one can derive

$$\frac{\partial f}{\partial \rho} = \frac{\theta(1 - \varphi)}{(\rho + \varphi\theta)(\rho + \theta)}. \tag{21.18}$$

The sign of this expression depends only on whether the partner country is relatively capital-abundant ($\varphi > 1$) or labor-abundant ($\varphi < 1$). One can thus say, in terms of the comparative-advantage effect, that, if the partner country is relatively capital-abundant, then all agents with $\rho > \rho_{median}$ are worse off than the median agent and all agents with $\rho < \rho_{median}$ are strictly better off. Since variety gains affect all voters equally, this demonstrates that the agent with the median capital–labor ratio is the median voter.

If a median voter gains from both the comparative-advantage effect and the variety effect, the arguments from Section 21.1 against a bilateral agreement undermining a multilateral agreement will still apply. The interesting counterexample will occur when the median voter is abundant in the same factor as the partner country. Equation (21.17) indicates that as φ moves from 1 toward ρ_{median}, the corresponding comparative-advantage effect on the median voter's utility will be negative and declining.

Balanced against this comparative-advantage loss is a gain from the variety effect. In terms of Figure 21.1, it is now possible for trade agreements to occur in the region between Autarky and E if, and only if, variety gains compensate for the adverse shifts in goods and factor prices.

I now return to the sequential consideration of a free-trade agreement among a subset of countries and a multilateral free-trade agreement involving the entire set and state the following results:

Proposition 4 No agreement involving a proper subset of countries can render politically feasible an otherwise infeasible agreement involving the full set of countries.

Proof Return to the notation of Proposition 2, in which k_0^c represents the capital–labor ratio of the median agent in country c and the ratio of all the capital to all the labor in an integrated economy e will be written as k^e. Let the possible values of e be: MFT for multilateral free trade, c for autarky in country c, and FTA for a free-trade agreement involving a subset of the countries. The utility notation must now also include n^e to represent the number of varieties in economy e. Now the utility function for an agent in country c can be written as

$$U_c(k_0^c, k^e, n^e).$$

Suppose that

$$U_c(k_0^c, k^{\mathrm{MFT}}, n^{\mathrm{MFT}}) < U_c(k_0^c, k^c, n^c).$$

This implies that multilateral free trade is politically infeasible. An agreement involving a proper subset of countries is politically feasible if, and only if,

$$U_c(k_0^c, k^{\mathrm{FTA}}, n^{\mathrm{FTA}}) \geq U_c(k_0^c, k^c, n^c).$$

But that implies

$$U_c(k_0^c, k^{\mathrm{FTA}}, n^{\mathrm{FTA}}) > U_c(k_0^c, k^{\mathrm{MFT}}, n^{\mathrm{MFT}}).$$

Therefore multilateral free trade must remain infeasible.

Proposition 5 An agreement involving a proper subset of countries can render politically infeasible an otherwise feasible agreement involving the full set of countries.

Proof Using the same notation, suppose that

$$U_c(k_0^c, k^{\mathrm{MFT}}, n^{\mathrm{MFT}}) > U_c(k_0^c, k^c, n^c)$$

so that multilateral free trade is initially politically feasible. If

$$U_c(k_0^c, k^{\mathrm{FTA}}, n^{\mathrm{FTA}}) > U_c(k_0^c, k^{\mathrm{MFT}}, n^{\mathrm{MFT}})$$

then the subset agreement will have rendered an otherwise politically feasible multilateral agreement infeasible. For an agreement that does this, consider an FTA between country c and a country that is identical to country c in every respect. Such an agreement would leave goods and factor prices unchanged.[18] Thus, the income of any agent i, with capital k_i, remains unchanged by the opening of trade. By equation (21.10), utility increases with n. All agents in each economy benefit from the liberalization, so under any distribution of capital, agents would choose the free-trade agreement over autarky.[19] If k_0^c is such that

$$U_c(k_0^c, k^{\mathrm{MFT}}, n^{\mathrm{MFT}}) - U_c(k_0^c, k^c, n^c)$$

is sufficiently small (i.e., the variety gain just outweighs the comparative-advantage loss for the median voter), then the variety gains offered by the FTA would render the move to multilateral free trade undesirable (since the comparative-advantage loss would be unaffected). This would necessarily hold for the identical partner country as well.

This result can be generalized beyond the case of countries with equal capital–labor ratios. For any pair of countries, the closer their capital–labor ratios are, the more variety gains they offer in proportion to comparative-advantage effects, the more popular the agreements are likely to be, and the more potentially damaging they are to multilateral free trade.

It is of some interest to explore how a country could avoid undermining support for multilateral liberalization in this setting. One answer, of course, is to pursue only a policy of multilateral liberalization from the start. If bilateral free-trade agreements are to be sought, though, the answer would be to pursue agreements with countries or groups of countries with different factor endowments. A capital-abundant country needs partner countries with less capital and more labor. A free-trade agreement will preserve the feasibility of multilateral free trade so long as it balances variety gains and comparative-advantage effects in such a way as to leave the median voter in each country preferring multilateral free trade to the subset free-trade agreement.

21.3 Conclusion

This chapter has shown that in a Heckscher-Ohlin setting it is politically impossible for a bilateral trade agreement to supplant multilateral free trade. In contrast, it was shown that, in a model with differentiated products and variety gains, bilateral free trade can undermine support for multilateral free trade. Conditions were described under which this could happen. To explain the difference, it is important to understand that the differentiated-product setting permits trade agreements that would have been politically impossible in the setting of Section 21.1 by allowing gains through variety gains as well as price shifts. In the Heckscher-Ohlin setting, a voter's utility depended solely on the capital–labor ratio. For undermining to occur in the differentiated-product setting, the median voter would have to experience lower utility under free trade in the absence of variety gains and higher or equal utility once variety gains are taken into account.

Throughout, the distribution of factors was shown to be crucial. The task of maintaining political support for multilateral free trade when countries negotiate side agreements in a differentiated-product setting was shown to require a clear understanding of the political situation (i.e., factor distribution) in all participating countries as well as a careful selection of those participating countries. The general principle emerged that the more politically popular a bilateral agreement is, the more likely it is to undermine political support for further multilateral liberalization.

The applicability of these results to more intricate models merits further research. Still, the general lesson should remain: intermediate accords can upset the balance of gains and losses offered by multilateralism and can therefore undermine political support. Only when such balances are impossible (as in the Heckscher-Ohlin setting) do these concerns subside.

As stated above, all such difficulties are readily avoidable if countries are restricted to pursuing multilateral liberalization. This is not necessarily an argument against more lenient World Trade Organization rules of the sort endorsed by Alan Deardorff and Robert Stern (1991). The World Trade Organization must accommodate the strong desires of its most powerful members if it is to survive as an institution. Were it to veto major policy initiatives put forward by the United States or the European Community countries, it would be more likely to come apart at the seams than to prevail. Instead, this paper suggests that those powerful member countries might wish to return their attentions to the task of multilateral liberalization.

Notes

I would like to acknowledge the financial support of the Center for Economic Policy Research at Stanford. I also thank the participants in the Stanford Workshop on International Trade, Anne Krueger, Alice Enders, and anonymous referees for their comments. I am especially grateful to Bob Staiger for his guidance. All remaining errors are my own.

1. A recent report of the Council of Economic Advisors (1995 pp. 217–19) considers several arguments for free-trade agreements as "building blocks" or "stumbling blocks" and concludes that they will further multilateral liberalization.

2. Bhagwati (1992) does not formally answer that question but does conclude that many of the arguments in favor of preferential arrangements are of dubious merit. For further general work on regionalism and multilateralism, see the collections edited by Jaime De Melo and Arvind Panagariya (1993) and Kym Anderson and Richard Blackhurst (1993).

3. An example would be the United States's choice to participate in NAFTA and then its choice of whether to pursue free trade with the fuller membership of the World Trade Organization. In each case, liberalization proceeds through agreements which are adopted or rejected.

4. Public opinion is likely to be one important mechanism among several in the actual formation of trade policy. Intuitions about other mechanisms, such as interest-group lobbying, are addressed elsewhere in the literature, as described above. For a general standard reference on public choice, see Dennis C. Mueller (1989). For a recent survey of the political economy of trade, see Dani Rodrik (1994).

5. The assumption that there are only two factors of production is important for the median-voter analysis that follows, in that it permits identification of a median voter (the holder of the median capital–labor ratio). With n factors of production ($n > 2$), it might be impossible to array voters along a single dimension, which would preclude the identification of a median voter. However, even in a more general case, if one were able to identify a key voter (who determined whether or not an agreement would be adopted) the rest of the chapter's analysis would pertain.

6. A sufficient condition for this to hold is that the endowments of all countries lie in the intersection of the cones of diversification of the country with the highest, and the country with the lowest, capital–labor ratio.

7. This assumption is restrictive; participants in free-trade agreements do trade with non-participants. If there were some fixed tariff level that applied against all nonparticipants, then the magnitudes of effects would be altered, but the basic arguments of the present chapter would not. If, however, trade barriers against nonparticipants were endogenous, this might or might not affect the basic arguments of the chapter, depending on the nature of the endogeneity. Such a case is beyond the scope of this chapter, but models of endogenous tariff determination and free-trade agreements can be found in Richardson (1993), Panagariya and Findlay (1994), and Levy (1996).

8. It should be noted that, as in the proof of Proposition 1, the relative price p decreases monotonically with increases in the capital–labor ratio. I omit descriptions of most price changes in the chapter because of this immediate correspondence.

9. This is not the only possible vote ordering, of course. There are permutations in which a multilateral pact could be voted on before a bilateral offer or in which voting sequences are repeated. These permutations can affect some of the results of this chpater, and I hope to explore them in later work. For this chapter, though, the voting structure is assumed to be the one described above.

10. I assume that agents vote their utility whether or not they believe their vote will decide the election, perhaps as a civic duty. This avoids the issue of agents' expectations about other agents' voting behavior. While that issue may be of theoretical interest, empirically one observes elections in which the winner wins by a substantial margin.

11. As an empirical basis for this assumption, it should be noted that the EC has moved the furthest toward political union of any existing regional trade group, yet for admission of new members even the EC has relied upon the unanimous approval of its members.

12. If countries were able to dissolve a bilateral agreement, then one could see bilateral agreements formed in cases in which one country preferred the multilateral outcome to the bilateral outcome. There would be no incentive to form such an agreement unless sufficient time passed between voting stages. Of course, in such a setting, it would still be the case that a bilateral agreement could not undermine a multilateral agreement.

13. The results do not depend on the Cobb-Douglas form of the production functions. They do depend, however, on the assumption of homotheticity in production.

14. An alternative assumption described by Helpman and Krugman (1985) is that subutility preferences are of the Lancaster variety. In this case, consumers have an ideal variety and prefer products which are closer to the ideal. Lancaster preferences would not fundamentally alter the results of this paper but would make the analysis more complicated.

Avinash Dixit and Joseph Stiglitz (1977) interpret the SDS subutility function as a Samuelsonian social utility function rather than that of an individual, and caution is necessary in extending its use to describe the preferences of individuals. While the functional form is used here mostly for its convenience, it is quite appropriate for a large number of commodities, although certainly not all. It is reasonable to assume that, at least within a certain range, individuals benefit from the availability of greater product variety. As real-world examples of commodities for which increased product variety typically raises an individual's utility, one may think of apparel products, toys, food, and beverages.

15. For a fuller discussion of the demand structure, see Helpman and Krugman (1985 Ch. 6). Note also that the fixed level of firm production is a by-product of the Spence-Dixit-Stiglitz approach. Under Lancaster's approach, x would vary.

16. Alternatively, one could refer to this as the Stolper-Samuelson effect, since this effect of liberalization on real returns to factors is that identified by W. Stolper and Paul Samuelson (1941).

17. To interpret θ, note that the denominator of the fraction term can be seen as a weighted average of the capital-intensity parameters in the two sectors. Recall also that α denotes the utility weight on the capital-intensive differentiated product sector.

18. The result that prices remain unchanged requires homotheticity in production. The fixed-optimal-output result, as stated above, is particular to the Spence-Dixit-Stiglitz subutility assumption. With increasing returns, if the optimal output level increased, it is possible that the relative price of the differentiated product would fall while factor returns remained constant. This could further enhance welfare.

19. This proposition readily extends to an agreement involving n identical countries, where $n > 2$, since a larger group simply implies a larger number of varieties. Thus, the results apply to regional agreements as well as to bilateral agreements.

References

Anderson, Kym and Blackhurst, Richard, eds. *Regional integration and the global trading system.* New York: St. Martin's Press, 1993.

Bagwell, Kyle and Staiger, Robert. "Multilateral Tariff Cooperation During the Formation of Regional Free Trade Areas." National Bureau of Economic Research (Cambridge, MA) Working Paper No. 4364, May 1993.

Bhagwati, Jagdish. "Regionalism and Multilateralism: An Overview." Columbia University Discussion Paper Series No. 603, April 1992.

Council of Economic Advisers. *Economic report of the President.* Washington, DC: U.S. Government Printing Office, 1995.

De Melo, Jaime and Panagariya, Arvind, eds. *New dimensions in regional integration.* Cambridge: Cambridge University Press, 1993.

Deardorff, Alan and Stern, Robert. "Multilateral Trade Negotiations and Preferential Trading Arrangements." Unpublished manuscript presented at the Conference on Analytical and Negotiating Issues in the Global Trading System, Ann Arbor, Michigan, October 31–November 1, 1991.

Dixit, Avinash and Stiglitz, Joseph. "Monopolistic Competition and Optimum Product Diversity." *American Economic Review*, June 1977, 67(2), pp. 297–308.

Grossman, Gene and Helpman, Elhanan. "Protection for Sale." *American Economic Review*, September 1994, 84(4), pp. 833–50.

Helpman, Elhanan and Krugman, Paul. *Market structure and foreign trade*. Cambridge, MA: MIT Press, 1985.

Krugman, Paul. "Is Bilateralism Bad?" in Elhanan Helpman and Assaf Razin, eds., *International trade and trade policy*. Cambridge, MA: MIT Press, 1991, pp. 9–23.

Levy, Philip I. "Free Trade Agreements and Inter-Bloc Tariffs." Mimeo, Yale University, 1996.

Mayer, Wolfgang. "Endogenous Tariff Formation." *American Economic Review*, December 1984, 74(5), pp. 970–85.

Mueller, Dennis C. *Public choice II*. Cambridge: Cambridge University Press, 1989.

Panagariya, Arvind and Findlay, Ronald. "A Political-Economy Analysis of Free Trade Areas and Customs Unions." World Bank Policy Research Working Paper No. 1261, March 1994.

Richardson, Martin. "Endogenous Protection and Trade Diversion." *Journal of International Economics*, May 1993. 34(3–4), pp. 309–24.

Rodrik, Dani. "What Does the Political Economy Literature on Trade Policy (Not) Tell Us That We Ought to Know?" National Bureau of Economic Research (Cambridge, MA) Working Paper No. 4870, 1994.

Stolper, W. and Samuelson, Paul. "Protection and Real Wages." *Review of Economic Studies*, November 1941, 9(1), pp. 58–73.

Woodland, A. D. "Direct and Indirect Trade Utility Functions." *Review of Economic Studies*, October 1980, 47(5), pp. 907–26.

It is then straightforward to analyze the impact of such bilateral arrangements upon the incentives faced by member countries for multilateral liberalization. Trade-diverting preferential arrangements generate rents for producers within the agreement that are tied to preferences granted by the agreement, and these rents are lost if these preferences are eliminated. If governments care sufficiently about producers and if the increased access to external markets that would come with multilateral liberalization does not generate sufficient rents to make up for the elimination of preferences, then preferential agreements may be preferred over multilateral free trade.[5] Multilateral liberalization that would have been politically feasible in the absence of the preferential arrangement is rendered infeasible. This is the paper's second conclusion.[6]

22.2 The Model

The model presented here is a simple extension of the Brander-Krugman [1983] model. In Vinerian fashion and without loss of generality, the world is split into country X, country Y (where X and Y are the potential partners in a bilateral arrangement) and the rest of the world, denoted by Z. There is a single good that is produced by firms from each of the countries. The market structure is one of imperfect competition, with oligopolistic firms producing goods that are perfect substitutes for each other. The markets in the different countries are assumed to be segmented. The equilibrium concept is that of Cournot-Nash. We follow Dixit [1984] in assuming that firms do not incur any transportation costs in supplying the good abroad, but that such costs are prohibitive for any third party arbitrageurs. As in Brander and Krugman, it is also assumed that a competitively produced numeraire good also exists and that it is freely traded. This numeraire good is transferred across countries to settle the balance of trade.

To facilitate the analysis, the notation is set up as follows: Let

$i = X, Y, Z$ and $j = X, Y, Z$ be country indices. Then, let

$q_j^i =$ the quantity supplied by a single firm from country i in country j's markets

$P_j =$ the equilibrium price of the good in country j's markets

$\pi_j^i =$ the profits made by any firm from country i in country j's markets

$t_j^i =$ the specific tariff imposed by country j on imports from i

$n_i =$ number of firms in i

$n = n_x + n_y + n_z$ is the total number of firms.

There are assumed to be no fixed costs of production and marginal costs are assumed to be constant at c in terms of the numeraire good. Aggregate utility in country j is assumed to take the form,

$$U_j(K, Q_j) = K + (A_j Q_j - Q_j^2/2),$$

where K denotes the consumption of the competitively produced numeraire good and where $Q_j = \Sigma_i n_i q_j^i$ denotes the total sales of the oligopolistically produced good in country j's markets by firms from X, Y, and Z.

The price of this good in country j is therefore a linear function of the total output,

$$P_j = A_j - Q_j. \tag{22.1}$$

Uniform nondiscriminatory tariffs are initially assumed to be applied by all countries on imports from other countries. Therefore, to start with,

$$t_j^i = \begin{cases} t & \text{if } i \neq j \\ 0 & \text{if } i = j. \end{cases}$$

In the usual manner, these tariffs simply add on to marginal costs of firms, whose effective marginal costs of exports then become $c + t$. Each firm regards each country as a separate market and therefore chooses its optimal quantity for each country separately. Under the Cournot assumption, firms are assumed to be maximizing profits taking other firms' outputs as given with all firms choosing their quantities simultaneously. Firms from country i, choosing the quantity to supply in country j, therefore solve the following problem:

$$\max_{q_j^i} \pi_j^i = q_j^i[A_j - Q_j - (c + t_j^i)].$$

This yields

$$q_j^i = \left[\Theta_j + \left(\frac{\Sigma_k n_k t_j^k}{n+1} \right) - t_j^i \right], \tag{22.2}$$

where $\Theta_j = (A_j - c)/(n+1)$ and $k = X, Y, Z$, as the Nash equilibrium output level.

From (22.2) we can derive the following comparative statics results that help establish the basic intuition of the model. First,

$$\frac{dq_x^y}{dt_x^y} = \left(\frac{n_y}{n+1} \right) - 1 < 0. \tag{22.3}$$

This implies that as tariffs are reduced by X on the partner country Y, the quantity supplied by the firms from Y in X's markets increases. Second, we have

$$\frac{dq_x^z}{dt_x^y} = \left(\frac{n_y}{n+1}\right) > 0. \tag{22.4}$$

That is, the opposite is true for Z's firms: as tariffs are reduced by X on imports from Y, the quantity supplied by firms from Z in X's market decreases. Finally,

$$\frac{dq_x^x}{dt_x^y} = \left(\frac{n_y}{n+1}\right) > 0. \tag{22.5}$$

Thus, just as for Z's firms, a reduction in tariffs by X against Y will decrease the quantity supplied by X's firms in their own domestic markets.

From (22.1) and (22.2) it can also easily be seen that

$$\pi_j^i = [q_j^i]^2. \tag{22.6}$$

It follows that with a change in tariffs, firm profits would change in the same direction as changes in equilibrium quantities sold by them (as given by equations (22.3), (22.4), and (22.5)).

The political economy framework is one where producers play a decisive role in shaping trade policy.[7] We have in mind an agenda-setting government that considers both bilateral and multilateral reciprocal tariff reductions. Firms lobby[8] either for or against these proposed trade regime changes depending upon whether or not they would see an increase in their profits following a given change in regime. For instance, a proposed bilateral arrangement between countries X and Y will be supported by firms from X if they see a *net* increase in their profits following this bilateral arrangement. With a reciprocal reduction in tariffs, firms from either country would see a reduction in profits in their home market and an increase in profits made abroad (from (22.3) and (22.5)). In our segmented markets and constant costs framework, firm profits in any single market are independent of profits in other markets. Therefore, we can separately compute the losses on the import-competing side and the gains on the exporting side. Overall, since in this framework the same firms constitute both the exporting sector and the import-competing sector, firms from each country would either all gain or all lose following any trade policy change. If the gains are greater than the losses, it is assumed that the proposed trade policy change is implemented. Alternatively, if exporting firms and import-competing firms were to be modeled separately, this assumption regarding the determination of trade policy would be equivalent to assuming that the winners would be willing to lobby the government to the full extent of their expected gains, while the losers would be willing to lobby the government to the full extent of their losses. Thus, if the winners gain more than the losers lose, the proposed change will be implemented. Our analysis of the conditions under which the three countries would reduce tariffs against each other (preferentially or otherwise) is therefore carried out by looking exclusively at the impact of various trade arrangements on relevant producer profits.[9]

The remainder of this chapter is structured as follows. We first examine the conditions under which a bilateral arrangement will be entered into by X and Y. We then examine the impact on the incentives for multilateral liberalization vis-à-vis the rest of the world, Z, by comparing the incentives for such a liberalization both before and after the bilateral arrangement is in place.

22.3   Bilateral Tariff Reductions

Article XXIV of the GATT Articles of Agreement permits Customs Unions and Free Trade Areas. However, these preferential arrangements are sanctioned only as long as "duties and other regulations of commerce" on "substantially all trade" are eliminated. Here, the GATT rules are interpreted as requiring that goods be freely traded between the parties to the agreement. Accordingly, a bilateral arrangement between X and Y implies that t_y^x and t_x^y have to be set equal to zero.

Let $_Bq_j^i$ denote the equilibrium quantities that would be sold once the bilateral arrangement is in place, and let $_B\pi_j^i$ denote the corresponding profits. Since producer profits are decisive, for a bilateral arrangement to be supported in country X and country Y, we need[10]

$$\sum_j (_B\pi_j^x) > \sum_j \pi_j^x \quad \text{and} \quad \sum_j (_B\pi_j^y) > \sum_j \pi_j^y;$$

i.e., we need

$$\sum_j (_Bq_j^x)^2 > \sum_j (q_j^x)^2 \quad \text{and} \quad \sum_j (_Bq_j^y)^2 > \sum_j (q_j^y)^2. \tag{22.7}$$

Simplifying the above expressions gives us Proposition 1.

Proposition 1   A bilateral arrangement will only be supported by X and Y if

$$[q_x^x + {}_Bq_x^x]n_y < [q_y^x + {}_Bq_y^x](1 + n_z + n_y) \qquad (22.8)$$

and

$$[q_y^y + {}_Bq_y^y]n_x < [q_x^y + {}_Bq_x^y](1 + n_z + n_x). \qquad (22.9)$$

These conditions can be derived directly using (22.2), (22.7), and our assumptions regarding the symmetry of initial tariffs (see Appendix 22A.2). They can be interpreted, roughly, as requiring the sales in the partner country to be sufficiently large relative to home country sales for the agreement to be supported by the home country. The intuition here is clear: with a bilateral arrangement you gain better access to the partner's market; the larger the partners market, the greater the gains. What you lose, however, is market share in your own market. The gains have to be greater than the losses for the arrangement to be supported. This gives us conditions that require the size of the partner's market to be sufficiently large relative to the size of the domestic market for the arrangement to be supported.

Condition (22.8) has to hold for X to support the arrangement. Note that in addition to the terms denoting the sales in Y's market, the term $(1 + n_z + n_y)$ enters on the right-hand side of this condition and the term n_y enters on the left-hand side of this equation. These can be interpreted as follows. The gains in Y's market come from two sources.

1. The reduction in the tariffs imposed by Y against X, which reduces their effective marginal costs in Y from $c + t$ to c. This is the direct effect. This accounts for the "1" in the $1 + n_y + n_z$ term.

2. The reduction in marginal costs of X's firms relative to firms from Y and Z shifts the equilibrium quantities in X's favor. Firms from X gain a competitive advantage over the n_y firms from Y and the n_z firms from Z. This is the "strategic" effect. This accounts for the $n_y + n_z$ in the $1 + n_y + n_z$ term. The larger the number of firms $(n_y + n_z)$ over which firms from X gain a strategic advantage, the greater the strategic effect.

In their own domestic market there is no direct effect on X's firms, since their effective marginal costs remain the same. There is a strategic loss relative to firms from Y (whose marginal costs in X similarly fall from $c + t$ to c), and this accounts for the n_y term on the left-hand side of the equation. Condition (22.9) which may be interpreted, mutatis mutandis, in exactly the same manner as (22.8), needs to hold for Y to support the bilateral arrangement.

One question that naturally arises is whether conditions (22.8) and (22.9) could hold simultaneously. In other words, could X's market be sufficiently large relative to Y, and could Y's market be sufficiently large relative to X's market at the same time? To answer this question, we first specify (22.8) and (22.9) in terms of the primitives: the parameters of the demand and cost functions. Using (22.2), these conditions can be re-written as

$$\alpha_x < \frac{1}{2n_y}\alpha_y(2 + 2n_y + 2n_z) - 2tn_y n_z + t(n_z)^2 - t(n_y)^2 - t(1 + n_y)^2$$

$$(22.10)$$

and

$$\alpha_y < \frac{1}{2n_x}\alpha_x(2 + 2n_x + 2n_z) - 2tn_x n_z + t(n_z)^2 - t(n_x)^2 - t(1 + n_x)^2,$$

$$(22.11)$$

where $\alpha_j = A_j - c$.[11] Equations (22.10) and (22.11) give us our second proposition.

Proposition 2   If conditions (22.10) and (22.11) are both satisfied by $(\alpha_x, \alpha_y, \alpha_z, n_x, n_y, n_z)$, they are necessarily satisfied by $(\alpha_x, \alpha_y, \alpha_z, n_x, n_y, n_z')$ $\forall n_z' > n_z$.

This is easily verified by examining the right-hand side of conditions (22.10) and (22.11). Note that from (22.2), with initial trade being nonzero,

$$\alpha_x - tn_x = (n + 1)q_x^y + t > 0$$

and

$$\alpha_y - tn_y = (n + 1)q_y^x + t > 0,$$

implying that the right-hand sides of conditions (22.10) and (22.11) are increasing in n_z. With a larger number of firms from Z, both conditions are more likely to hold. The intuition for this result is as follows. With larger n_z, the number of firms over which firms from X (in Y) and from Y (in X) gain a strategic advantage, is larger. The strategic effect (causing a larger diversion of sales away from the rest of the world's firms to partner country firms), is therefore larger for both firms from X selling in Y and for firms from Y selling in X.[12] This gives us a strong result: the larger the trade diversion[13] that would result from the preferential arrangement, the more likely it is that the arrangement will be supported by the partner countries.[14]

To interpret conditions (22.8) and (22.9) better, it is useful to think of the case with $n_z = 0$. In this case we (trivially) have no trade diversion. In X, firms from Y take market share away only from the domestic firms. Similarly in Y, X's firms take market share away only from Y's firms. There is increased competition in both markets implying that the strategic effect on net is negative in the absence of trade diversion. However, due to the direct effect (reduction in effective marginal costs), it may still be possible, for both X and Y to gain with the bilateral arrangement. To the extent that direct effects are large enough, they dominate the losses due to the increased competition, and (22.10) and (22.11) are both satisfied. On the other hand, if strategic losses on net dominate the direct effects, firms from both countries see reduced profits, and the bilateral arrangement is not entered into.

From the above discussion, and comparing the left- and right-hand sides of (22.8) and (22.9) when $n_z = 0$, it would also appear that, absent any trade diversion gains for partner country firms, it would be the case that countries of roughly the same size would enter into bilateral arrangements. However, as discussed above, to the extent that direct effects (gains) are dominated by strategic losses, (22.8) and (22.9) may, of course, not be satisfied even if the two countries are completely symmetric. Most importantly, and this serves to highlight the role of trade diversion in this model, the diversion of trade away from the rest of the world relaxes both these conditions (as illustrated in Figure 22.1), thus permitting higher profits for firms from both countries even with asymmetry in partner country sizes and the number of firms.[15]

Figure 22.1 illustrates this point. XX represents (22.10), and YY represents (22.11) for any given number of firms from Z, n_z. $X'X'$ and $Y'Y'$ are the loci if the number of firms from Z is $n'_z > n_z$. With n_z firms, the bilateral arrangement will be supported by X at all points above XX. The arrangement will be supported by Y at all points below YY. The area XOY is where both countries would support the bilateral arrangement. With n'_z firms, $X'O'Y'$ is the area within which both X and Y would support the bilateral arrangement. Note that XOY is contained entirely within $X'O'Y'$. It can easily be verified that the loci shift in the manner indicated in Figure 22.1. The proof is contained in Appendix 22.A.4.

The welfare effects of the bilateral arrangement can be analyzed using the standard surplus measures. From Appendix 22.A.1, we know that overall world welfare increases with the bilateral arrangement. Importantly, however, due to trade diversion, welfare unambiguously decreases in the rest of the world (consumer surplus and tariff revenues stay the same while producer profits decrease—from (22.4) and (22.6)). Thus, the

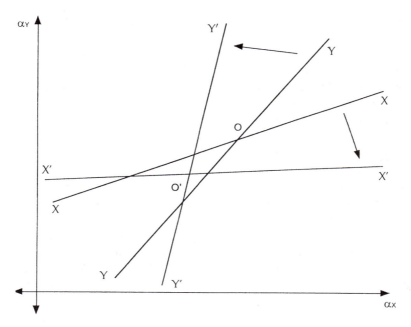

Figure 22.1
Trade diversion and preferential liberalization.

partner countries gain in sum. Producer profits increase (by (22.7)), and consumer surplus increases as well (since a larger quantity is sold in each market with any tariff reductions; see Appendix 22A.1) for both partner countries. However, tariff revenues fall (since tariffs on imports from the partner reduce to zero and imports from the rest of the world are reduced). Since the partner countries gain in sum, in the symmetric case, clearly, producer and consumer gains dominate these tariff revenue losses. With some asymmetry, however, tariff revenue losses may outweigh consumer and producer gains for one of the partner countries whose welfare will consequently fall.[16]

22.4   Multilateral Tariff Liberalization

For the rest of this analysis, we assume that (22.10) and (22.11) are satisfied, that a bilateral arrangement is in place between X and Y, and examine the incentives that X and Y face for multilateral tariff liberalization vis-à-vis Z. As stated above, by multilateral liberalization we mean an elimination of tariffs by all countries on imports from other countries.[17] Prior to the bilateral arrangement, this implies an equal reduction in tariffs by X, Y, and Z. After the bilateral arrangement between X and Y, multilateral liberalization implies that X and Y eliminate their tariffs against a reciprocating Z and that the tariffs imposed by X on imports from Y and vice versa continue to be zero.

Let

$$\prod_x = \sum_j \pi_j^x,$$

$$_B\prod_x = \sum_j (_B\pi_j^x)$$

and

$$_M\prod_x = \sum_j (_M\pi_j^x)$$

denote the total profits of a firm from X prior to the bilateral arrangement, after the bilateral arrangement and after total multilateral liberalization, respectively.

As a simplification, we now assume that the partner countries are identical; i.e., that $A_x = A_y$ and $n_x = n_y$. This allows us to examine the effects of the bilateral arrangement on any one partner country (instead of having to carry out the analysis for both of the partner countries separately). Without any further loss of generality, we now only look at these effects on firms from X.

Consider first the increase in profits with multilateral liberalization before the bilateral arrangement:

$$_M\prod_x - \prod_x = (_M\pi_x^x - \pi_x^x) + (_M\pi_y^x - \pi_y^x) + (_M\pi_z^x - \pi_z^x), \qquad (22.12)$$

where

$(_M\pi_x^x - \pi_x^x) =$ gain in the domestic market < 0,

$(_M\pi_y^x - \pi_y^x) =$ gain in Y's market > 0, and

$(_M\pi_z^x - \pi_z^x) =$ gain in Z's market > 0.

Next we consider the increase in profits with multilateral liberalization after a bilateral arrangement is in place between X and Y:

$$_M\prod_x - _B\prod_x = (_M\pi_x^x - _B\pi_x^x) + (_M\pi_y^x - _B\pi_y^x) + (_M\pi_z^x - _B\pi_z^x), \qquad (22.13)$$

where

$(_M\pi_x^x - {}_B\pi_x^x) =$ gain in the domestic market < 0,

$(_M\pi_y^x - {}_B\pi_y^x) =$ gain in Y's market < 0, and

$(_M\pi_z^x - {}_B\pi_z^x) =$ gain in Z's market > 0.

We are finally interested in comparing $(_M\Pi_x - \Pi_x)$ with $(_M\Pi_x - {}_B\Pi_x)$. Clearly, the change in profits in Z, the third term in (22.12) and (22.13)), is the same, before and after the bilateral arrangement. The second term, the change in profits in Y, is positive in (22.12) and negative in (22.13). The first term is negative in both cases, but it is less negative in (22.13), due to the fact that with the bilateral arrangement, some market share is already lost by X's firms to Y's firms and with the multilateral reduction in tariffs, X's firms have less to lose in their own domestic markets than they would have with direct multilateral liberalization. It may therefore appear that the sign of the difference between the right-hand sides of (22.12) and (22.13) may have to be determined parametrically, depending upon the relative magnitude of these two opposing factors. However, introducing (22.7) into (22.12) and (22.13) immediately resolves this and allows us to state that "politically supported" preferential arrangements necessarily reduce domestic incentives to seek multilateral tariff liberalization; i.e., $(_M\Pi_x - \Pi_x) - (_M\Pi_x - {}_B\Pi_x)$ is always > 0. This can be seen by noting, first, that

$$\left(_M\prod_x - \prod_x\right) - \left(_M\prod_x - {}_B\prod_x\right) = -\left(\prod_x - {}_B\prod_x\right),$$

and, second, that from (22.7), for the bilateral arrangement to be supported in the first place,

$$_B\prod_x > \prod_x,$$

which readily gives us

$$\left(_M\prod_x - \prod_x\right) - \left(_M\prod_x - {}_B\prod_x\right) > 0.$$

The point here is simply that the fact that the bilateral arrangement was supported by X and Y in the first place gives us information about the impact of the bilateral arrangement on multilateral liberalization incentives and helps us determine unambiguously that preferential arrangements reduce the incentives for multilateral liberalization.[18]

While it is now clear that these incentives will be reduced, we need to ask whether these incentives would ever be reversed; i.e., could multilateral liberalization that was initially feasible be rendered infeasible by the bilateral arrangement? This consideration gives us Proposition 3.

Proposition 3 Politically supported bilateral arrangements could critically reduce internal incentives for multilateral liberalization. That is, multilateral liberalization that was otherwise feasible could lose support due to a bilateral arrangement. This is more likely the larger the trade diversion associated with the bilateral arrangement.

For this, we need to see whether the following conditions could hold together.

$$_M\prod_x - \prod_x > 0 \quad \text{and} \quad _M\prod_x - _B\prod_x < 0. \tag{22.14}$$

With substantial algebraic manipulation,[19] (22.14) can be rewritten as

$$h(n_z) < \alpha_z < g(n_z)$$

where

$$h(n_z) = \left(\frac{t}{2(1+n_z)}\right)[(n_y + n_z)^2 + (1+n_y)^2 + (1+n_z)^2] + \frac{\alpha_x(n_z - 1)}{1 + n_z}$$

and

$$g(n_z) = \left(\frac{t}{2(1+n_z)}\right)[(2(n_z)^2 + (1+n_z)^2] + \frac{2\alpha_x n_z}{1 + n_z},$$

as the condition under which the bilateral arrangement can render infeasible multilateral liberalization.

It is easily verified that

$$h(n_z) < g(n_z) \tag{22.15}$$

and that

$$[d(g(n_z) - h(n_z))]/dn_z > 0. \tag{22.16}$$

If α_z lies between $h(n_z)$ and $g(n_z)$, the bilateral arrangement would impede multilateral liberalization.[20]

Figure 22.2 illustrates this point by appropriately partitioning the (α_z, n_z) space. HH is the locus of points that satisfies $h(n_z) = \alpha_z$, and GG is the locus of points that satisfies $g(n_z) = \alpha_z$. HH and GG therefore correspond

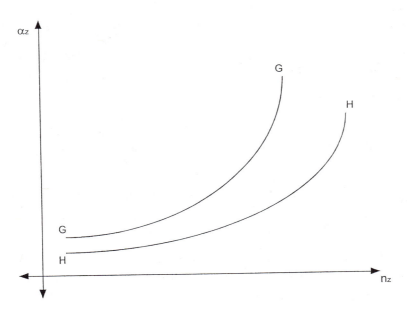

Figure 22.2
Bilateral arrangements and reduced incentives for multilateral liberalization.

to points at which multilateral liberalization is just feasible, initially and after the bilateral arrangement is in place, respectively. Initially, multilateral liberalization is feasible above HH and infeasible below. After the bilateral arrangement is in place, multilateral liberalization is feasible above GG and infeasible below. Therefore, between GG and HH, the bilateral arrangement would render infeasible multilateral liberalization. The intuition is as follows. For a given value of n_z, a larger α_z (a direct measure of the size of Z's market) implies larger gains for both X and Y, following a reciprocal reduction in tariffs against Z. After the bilateral arrangement is in place, for multilateral liberalization to be feasible, an even larger α_z is required. With multilateral liberalization, Z's firms gain equal access to the markets in X and Y. This eliminates the gains that X and Y had enjoyed due to the preferential access to each other's markets. A larger α_z is therefore required to offset this. This is why the GG locus is above the HH locus. As inspired by (22.16), note also that with larger n_z, there is a wider range of values of α_z for which the bilateral arrangement would render multilateral liberalization infeasible. This follows directly from the fact that with larger n_z, the bilateral arrangement results in larger trade diversion gains for X and Y (Proposition 2) which would now be eliminated, requiring even higher values of α_z for multilateral liberalization to still be supported by X and Y. Therefore, the larger the trade diversion resulting from the preferential arrangement, the more likely it is that multilateral liberalization loses support.[21]

22.5   Summary and Conclusions

This chapter examines the impact of Free Trade Areas (FTAs) on the internal incentives for multilateral liberalization and challenges the contention that Free Trade Areas are superior to GATT style (multilateral) trade liberalization as a way of getting to multilateral free trade for all. Using a model of imperfect competition in segmented markets, preferential trading arrangements are analyzed from the viewpoint of the "new political economy" which views trade policy as being determined by lobbying by concentrated interest groups (producers in this case). Within this framework this chapter reaches two conclusions: first, that preferential arrangements that divert trade away from the rest of the world are more likely to be supported politically; and second, that such preferential arrangements will reduce the incentives for multilateral liberalization. It is also shown that in some cases this reduction in incentives could be critical: multilateral liberalization that is initially feasible could be rendered infeasible by preferential arrangements.[22] The larger the trade diversion resulting from the preferential arrangement, the more likely this will be the case.

In considering producer interests exclusively, this chapter makes a rather extreme assumption that has the benefit that it yields an analytically convenient and tractable way to express the idea that the trade diversion resulting from bilateral arrangements could critically impede multilateral liberalization efforts. While this incentive effect on countries, driven here by producer interests, is a rather general point that we expect will survive other settings,[23] it should also be mentioned that one may expect these effects to be overwhelmed if government preferences are substantially different from those assumed in this chapter.

While it is tempting to conclude that countries should be restricted to pursuing GATT style multilateral liberalization in order to avoid these difficulties, it must be recognized that the question of preferential trade arrangements is a difficult one. This chapter does not take into account several complex features of the real world. Specifically, no account has been taken of asymmetries in government preferences across countries, capital mobility in response to trade policy changes, path dependencies that may be caused due to the presence of adjustment or sunk costs or other factors. The inclusion of these factors in the analysis is important and constitutes topics for future research.

Appendix

Appendix 22A.1:   Welfare Analysis

Given the quasi-linear form of the aggregate utility function, welfare analysis can be conducted using the standard surplus measures:

World welfare $= W$

$$= \sum_j (A_j Q_j - Q_j^2/2) - c \sum_j Q_j$$
$$= \sum_j ((A_j - c)Q_j - Q_j^2/2).$$

Therefore,

$$\frac{dW}{dQ_j} = ((A_j - c) - Q_j) > 0, \quad \text{using } (A_j - c) > Q_j.$$

From (22.3), (22.4), and (22.5) it is easy to see that Q_j is decreasing in tariffs; therefore welfare increases with an increase in each Q_j. We therefore have welfare being maximized at global free trade.

Appendix 22A.2:   Derivation of (22.8) and (22.9)

Consider the incentives for country X. Expanding the terms in (22.7) gives us

$$(Bq_x^x)^2 + (Bq_y^x)^2 > (q_x^x)^2 + (q_y^x)^2.$$

This reduces to

$$(Bq_x^x + q_x^x)(q_x^x - Bq_x^x) < (Bq_y^x + q_x^x)(Bq_y^x - q_y^x).$$

From (22.2) we have

$$q_x^x - Bq_x^x = \frac{n_y}{n+1} t \quad \text{and} \quad Bq_y^x - q_y^x = \frac{1 + n_y + n_z}{n+1} t.$$

Substituting these into the previous expression, we get condition (22.8). Condition (22.9) can be entirely analogously derived.

Appendix 22A.3:   Numerical Example

Example: Let $n_x = n_y = n_z = 1$. Expressions (22.10) and (22.11) can be rewritten as

$$2\alpha_x < 6\alpha_y - 6t$$

and

$$2\alpha_y < 6\alpha_x - 6t.$$

Let $\alpha_x = \alpha_y/2$. The conditions translate into $\alpha_y > 6t/5$ and $\alpha_y > 6t$, both of which clearly hold if $\alpha_y > 6t$.

Appendix 22A.4: Loci in Figure 22.1

To verify that the loci YY and XX shift in the manner indicated in Figure 22.1, note that (22.10), with equality, could be rewritten as

$$\alpha_y > \alpha_x f(n_z) + s(n_z),$$

where $f'(n_z) < 0$. This proves that the slope of XX shifts in the manner indicated. Also, (22.10) implies that with a larger n_z, the right-hand side increases. Therefore, ceteris paribus for (22.10) to hold with equality, α_x has to increase. Therefore, XX shifts lower as shown.

Appendix 22A.5: Trade Diversion

To see that a larger number of firms from Z, n_z, implies greater trade diversion, note that from (22.2), X's initial volume of imports from Z equals $(n_z/(n+1))(\alpha_x - (1 + n_x)t)$. The volume of imports with a bilateral arrangement $= (n_z/(n+1))(\alpha_x - (1 + n_x + n_y)t)$. Thus, volume of trade diverted $= (n_y n_z/(n+1))t$, which is increasing in n_z.

Appendix 22A.6: Derivation of $h(n_z)$ and $g(n_z)$

Consider first the expression, $_M\Pi_x - \Pi_x > 0$. Using (22.6) and (22.12) and proceeding in steps analogous to the ones in Appendix 22A.2 above, this can be expressed as

$$(_Mq_x^x + q_x^x)(_Mq_x^x - q_x^x) + (_Mq_y^x + q_y^x)(_Mq_y^x - q_y^x)$$
$$+ (_Mq_z^x + q_z^x)(_Mq_z^x - q_z^x) > 0.$$

Using (22.2), the fact that $\alpha_x = \alpha_y$, and noting that all tariffs reduce to zero with the multilateral arrangement, the above expressions can be reduced to $h(n_z) < \alpha_z$, where

$$h(n_z) = \left(\frac{t}{2(1 + n_z)}\right)[(n_y + n_z)^2 + (1 + n_y)^2 + (1 + n_z)^2] + \frac{\alpha_x(n_z - 1)}{1 + n_z}.$$

The expression for $g(n_z)$ can be analogously derived using (22.2), (22.6), and (22.13). Finally, using (22.7), (22.10), (22.11), and expressions derived for $h(n_z)$ and $g(n_z)$, and some simple algebra yields (22.15) and (22.16), respectively.

Appendix 22A.7: Numerical Example

Let $A_x = A_y = 10$ and $A_z = 10$. Let $c = 5$ and $n_x = n_y = n_z = 1$. Instead of using the assumption made in the chapter that producer profits exclusively determine government decisions, let us assume that governments maximize a weighted welfare function of the form,

$$W = 0.45(CS + TR) + 0.55(PS),$$

where CS, TR, and PS denote consumer surplus, tariff revenues, and producer surplus, respectively. Initial (nondiscriminatory) tariffs can be derived by assuming that governments maximize the welfare function while taking the other countries' tariffs as given. Numerically simulating the model for the parameter values mentioned above, we get initial tariff $t_x = t_y = 1.8$ and $t_z = 1.8$. Also, initial (weighted) welfare levels are $W_x = W_y = 5.07$ for X and Y, respectively. With bilateral tariff reductions between X and Y, the welfare levels are $_BW_x = {_B}W_y = 6.13$. With global free trade, $_MW_x = {_M}W_y = {_M}W_z = 5.74$. While all three countries would have reduced tariffs multilaterally (since $_MW_x > W_x$, $_MW_y > W_y$, and $_MW_z > W_z$), once the bilateral arrangement is in place, X and Y would clearly not want to reduce tariffs multilaterally against Z (since $_MW_x < {_B}W_x$ and $_MW_y < {_B}W_y$).

Appendix 22A.8: Estimates Using Data from the U.S. Automobile Market

The data used for this analysis were obtained from Dixit [1987]. While Dixit's analysis of trade policy interventions in the U.S. automobile market were carried out under the assumption that U.S. cars and Japanese cars are imperfect substitutes for each other, the model presented in this chapter assumes that the goods produced by firms in any country are perfect substitutes for each other in every market. The present calculations make suitable modifications to Dixit's numbers to adjust for this. The overall point made below regarding the possibility of bilateral arrangements raising profit levels above that of multilateral free trade and the rough magnitude of this effect are unaffected by variations in these numbers.

In particular, for 1979, the following are assumed:

a. Total sales in the U.S. auto market = 10 million cars;

b. Initial U.S. tariffs are 2.9 percent, the MFN tariffs for the United States reported in Dixit [1987];

c. The cost of automobile production = $5000;

d. The inverse demand function is assumed to be given by

$$P = 12{,}000 - 6 * 10^{-4}Q, \tag{22.17}$$

where Q denotes the total quantity sold in the U.S. market;

e. The market price for cars = $5600.

Assumptions (a), (b), (c), (d), and (e) imply a Cournot equivalent total firm number of twelve. With demand given by (22.17), sales in each country, analogous to (22.2), are given by

$$q_j^i = \frac{1}{6 * 10^{-4}}\left[\Theta_j + \left(\frac{\Sigma_k n_k t_j^k}{n+1}\right) - t_j^i\right], \tag{22.18}$$

where $\Theta_j = 12{,}000 - 5000 = 7000 \;\forall j$.
    Profits are given by

$$\pi_j^i = 6 * 10^{-4}[q_j^i]^2. \tag{22.19}$$

For the purposes of this analytical exercise, it is assumed that the home country X, the partner country Y, and the rest of the world Z are of equal size; i.e., that the demand curve in each is identical to (22.17) and that these markets are each supplied by four firms from each country.

Using (22.18) and (22.19) and under the assumptions, regarding supply and demand in the world market made above, we can easily compute profits for each firm in each of the partner countries, initially, with a bilateral arrangement between two countries and with multilateral free trade. These gives us

22A.8.1. Initial total (from sales in all markets) home firm profits equal 1.43 billion dollars;

22A.8.2. With multilateral free trade, they stand at 1.45 billion dollars (1.4 percent increase over the initial level); and

22A.8.3. With a bilateral arrangement they rise to 1.53 billion dollars (a 7 percent increase over the initial level and 5.5 percent over the multilateral level);

22A.8.4. Due to trade diversion, rest of the world profits fall from 1.43 billion dollars to 1.28 billion dollars (a reduction of 10.5 percent).

From 22A.8.1 and 22A.8.3, a bilateral arrangement would be supported by home firms. From 22A.8.1, 22A.8.2, and 22A.8.3, the bilateral arrangement, once in place, would render initially feasible (from 22A.8.1 and 22A.8.2) multilateral free trade unfeasible. Under assumptions (a), (b), (c), and (d), but assuming a smaller number of firms in the third country (three firms instead of four), the corresponding figures are 1.65 billion dollars initially, 1.74 billion dollars with a bilateral arrangement, and 1.70 billion dollars with multilateral free trade. Home firms profits with a bilateral arrangement are 5.3 percent above the initial level (thus lower in terms of absolute difference and in proportion than when the number of firms in the third country was four). This illustrates the point regarding greater trade diversion made in Proposition 2.

Notes

I am extremely grateful to Jagdish Bhagwati for numerous conversations on this topic and for his advice and suggestions. I am also grateful to Alessandra Casella, Donald Davis, Vivek Dehejia, Ronald Findlay, Carsten Kowalczk, Kala Krishna, Thomas Krebs, John McLaren, Devashish Mitra, Arvind Panagariya, J. David Richardson, Dani Rodrik, T. N. Srinivasan, Sang Seung Yi, Olivier Blanchard, and two anonymous referees as well as seminar participants at Brown University, the Universities of California at Santa Barbara and Riverside, the University of Chicago, Columbia University, Dartmouth College, Georgetown University, New York University, and the NBER's Universities Research Conference on International Trade Rules and Regulations for discussions and comments.

1. Bhagwati [1993] has characterized the current revival of interest in such preferential trading arrangements, which are largely regional as well, as the Second Regionalism, contrasting it with the First Regionalism that broke out in the latter half of the 1950s and in the 1960s. He has argued that the former is likely to endure while the latter did not. For additional arguments in support of that thesis, also see Bhagwati [1994].

2. Bhagwati [1993] offers a number of arguments on this question distinguishing among different incentives facing outsiders and insiders, and Baldwin [1993], in an approach that complements the one taken in this chapter, provides theoretical analysis of a "domino" effect that investigates the incentive of outsiders to join an FTA.

3. As Staiger [1994] notes, there have been several attempts to evaluate the basis for this concern: one approach, taken by Ludema [1994], asks how regional integration may affect multilateral bargaining outcomes. A second approach, taken by Bagwell and Staiger [1993a,

1993b], analyzes the impact of FTAs and CUs on enforcement issues at the multilateral level. A third approach, adopted by Levy [1994] and this chapter, is to consider how internal support for multilateral liberalization would be affected by regional integration opportunities. While a complete answer might attempt to address all of these questions together, useful insights can be obtained by examining each of these questions in isolation, which is what the literature to date has done. Adopting a slightly different approach, Yi [1995] examines how PTA membership rules may be modified to achieve global free trade advocating finally "open membership" rules to achieve this goal.

4. Grossman and Helpman [1994a] develop a theory of the political economy of trade policy that takes specific account of the influence exerted by organized groups. Grossman and Helpman [1994b] analyze the politics of the formation of preferential arrangements using this framework. Another contribution that takes into account political economy factors in a preferential arrangements context is the recent paper by Findlay and Panagariya [1994], who conclude that entering into a PTA would increase member country incentives to raise tariffs against the rest of the world.

5. I am grateful to an anonymous referee for suggesting this statement to describe a central result of the chapter.

6. In a different approach to the same question, Levy [1994], using a median-voter model in a differentiated products-monopolistic competition setting and quite different economic reasoning, arrives at similar conclusions: that bilateral arrangements can undermine political support for multilateral trade liberalization.

7. This may easily be understood to result from the public good nature of political activity which is more easily provided by a concentrated group of producers rather than by large diffuse groups of consumers. The theoretical and empirical literature on the effectiveness of such interest groups in bending policy in a direction that is to their benefit is, of course, quite well developed by now. For the classic theoretical arguments, see Olson [1965], Stigler [1971], Peltzman [1976], and Becker [1983]. O'Halloran [1994] provides a comprehensive survey. An alternative framework in which producer profits would be decisive is if any proposed trade policy changes had to meet the approval of both consumers and producers and where tariff revenues were consumed directly by the government. Ignoring tariff revenue, consumers would always support any tariff reductions, since consumer surplus always increases with any reduction in tariff levels. Producers may or may not support tariff reductions, and so they become critical.

8. Similar to the well-known Findlay and Wellisz [1982] model of trade policy determination, the actual lobbying process is not explicitly modeled here and is left as somewhat of a black box.

9. While this assumption has the benefit of yielding tractable closed-form solutions, the results of this chapter can be generated under more general specifications of the political economy process inter alia. Appendix 22A.7 works out a numerical example in which consumer interests play a role in the political process as well and in which the initial tariffs are endogenously determined.

10. Clearly, profits made in Z's markets by firms from either X or Y do not change following the bilateral arrangement.

11. It can easily be verified that equations (22.10) and (22.11) hold together for a range of parameter values (a numerical example is presented in Appendix 22A.3).

12. The signs of the direct and strategic effects discussed here can be shown to hold for more general demand functions than the linear form considered here. See Dixit [1986] for a general discussion.

13. That a larger number of firms in Z indeed translates into greater volume of trade diverted is shown in Appendix 22A.5.

14. Since this chapter was written, independent work by Grossman and Helpman [1994b] arrives at a conclusion that is similar in spirit: that a preferential arrangement would be politically viable if it resulted in "enhanced protection" for partner country firms.

15. A literal interpretation of these results would imply that observed PTAs between substantially asymmetric countries must have involved large trade diversion. However, an important caveat that would limit the applicability of this interpretation in understanding actually implemented preferential arrangements such as NAFTA relates to the fact that the underlying model of trade employed here is one of intraindustry trade. When comparative advantage and specialization dominate, as may be the case between the United States and Mexico, for instance, the strategic losses for import-competing home firms in the home market are likely to be smaller in comparison with gains in the partner's market that accrue to exporting firms. Indeed in the extreme case, if the partner countries are completely specialized, bilateral tariff reductions will involve no strategic losses in the home market for home country firms and only the usual gains in the partners market due to direct effects and any trade diversion. While a greater degree of trade diversion, as argued above, will still provide greater incentives to enter into a bilateral agreement, trade diversion may not be as necessary for gains, in aggregate, to accrue to firms in both countries, as in the case where the underlying pattern of trade is that of intraindustry trade.

16. This result that politically supported, trade-diverting PTAs may result in welfare improvement for member countries, in contrast to the popular intuition regarding trade-diverting PTAs being welfare decreasing, is similar, though not entirely identical, of course, to the perfectly competitive cases as analyzed by Lipsey [1957, 1960], Bhagwati [1971], and Michaely [1976]. These authors variously showed, in elaboration and partial contradiction of the classic analysis by Viner [1950], that Vinerian intuition regarding trade diversion being welfare decreasing resulted from the exclusion (as in Viner's original analysis) of producer and consumer gains from the calculus. Thus, they showed that more general analysis of PTAs that permitted producer and consumer gains could easily result in welfare improvement even with trade diversion, just as in the present analysis. Additionally, in an important contribution that is closer in its workings to the present analysis due to its consideration of PTAs which involve *reciprocal* tariff reductions (in contrast to the analysis of Viner and most subsequent researchers who analyzed PTAs with *unilateral* preferential reductions instead), Wonnacott and Wonnacott [1981] have argued that, with reciprocity, the scope for terms of trade losses itself is reduced and we have an even greater possibility of welfare improvement even when the PTA is trade diverting. The possibility of welfare reduction, particularly when countries are asymmetric, remains, again just as in the present analysis.

17. For analytical convenience, this chapter only considers this dichotomous choice—a feature that we share with Levy [1994] and Fischer and Serra [1996] among others. For an elegant analysis of optimal multilateral tariff choices made by governments in a dynamic context and in the presence of bilateral arrangements (CUs and FTAs), see Bagwell and Staiger [1993a, 1993b].

18. Note that, given our political economy setup, the statement regarding politically supported preferential arrangements necessarily reducing the incentives to seek multilateral tariff liberalization, is quite general and holds independently of the other specific assumptions of this model like market segmentation or constant marginal costs.

19. Details are in Appendix 22A.6.

20. While the focus of this paper is on internal incentives for multilateral liberalization, it could be that a bilateral arrangement between X and Y makes an initially uninterested Z seek multilateral trade liberalization if the bilateral arrangement diverts a large amount of trade away from it; i.e., if $\Pi_z > {}_M\Pi_z > {}_B\Pi_z$.

21. It is easy to show that if we started with four countries, X, Y, R, and Z, and considered bilateral arrangements in sequence (between X and Y first and then between X and Y and R), the GG curve would be pushed even higher following the second bilateral arrangement, resulting in a larger range of values of α_z and n_z for which total multilateral liberalization would become infeasible.

Using 1979 data from Dixit's [1987] well-known calibration study of the U.S. automobile market, Appendix 22A.8 presents some rough calculations that are suggestive of the magnitudes of the effects at work here. To summarize: in a symmetric three-country world in which demand in each of the countries is represented by parameters taken from Dixit estimates of demand for the United States, and where total the number of firms, twelve, is the Cournot equivalent number of firms such that, given our assumptions regarding demand and cost functions (also taken from Dixit [1987]), the price level implied by this exercise matches the actual price data reported by Dixit for the United States, and starting from an initial MFN tariff level of 2.9 percent (U.S. auto tariffs in 1979), firm profits are calculated to be 1.43 billion dollars, 1.56 billion dollars, and 1.45 billion dollars at the initial level, with a bilateral arrangement and with multilateral free trade, respectively. Clearly, bilateral profits are greater than both the initial level of profits and the final multilateral level. (Indeed, the bilateral level of profits is equal to what the profit level would be if the home firm raised its non-discriminatory initial tariffs *unilaterally* from 2.9 percent to 4.2 percent, thus giving a sense of the effective increased "protection" received by the home firm due to the bilateral arrangement.) Also, multilateral profits are greater than the initial profit level. Thus while multilateral free trade is initially feasible, it could be rendered infeasible by a bilateral arrangement. Also, due to trade diversion, there is a 10.5 percent reduction in profits of firms from the rest of the world. Appendix 22A.8 also shows that this increase in profits with a bilateral arrangement is lower if less trade is diverted from the third country.

22. As an important caveat, it should be pointed out that the scope of the three-country analysis presented here is limited in that it does not include such possibilities as, for instance, the formation of pairs of trading blocs where, then, multilateral free trade implies a symmetric elimination of preferential access in both bilateral arrangements, thereby maintaining its attractiveness to countries in both bilateral arrangements. Thus, it is "unbalanced preferentialism" rather than preferential arrangements per se that creates problems for multilateralism here.

23. See Appendix 22A.7.

References

Bagwell, K., and R. Staiger, "Multilateral Cooperation during the Formation of Free Trade Areas," NBER Working Paper No. 4364, 1993a.

Bagwell, K., and R. Staiger, "Multilateral Cooperation during the Formation of Customs Unions," NBER Working Paper No. 4543, 1993b.

Baldwin, R., "A Domino Theory of Regionalism," NBER Working Paper No. 4465, 1993.

Becker, G., "A Theory of Competition among Pressure Groups for Political Influence," *Quarterly Journal of Economics*, XCVII (1983), 371–400.

Bhagwati, J., "Trade-Diverting Customs Unions and Welfare Improvement: A Clarification," *Economic Journal*, LXXXI (1971), 580–587.

————, "Regionalism and Multilateralism: An Overview," in A. Panagariya and J. De Melo, eds., *New Dimensions in Regional Integration* (Washington, DC: World Bank, 1993).

————, "Threats to the World Trading System: Income Distribution and the Selfish Hegemon," Columbia University Working Paper No. 696, 1994.

Brander, J., and P. Krugman, "A Reciprocal Dumping Model of International Trade," *Journal of International Economics*, XV (1983), 313–321.

Deardorff, A., and R. Stern, "Multilateral Trade Negotiations and Preferential Trading Arrangements," *Analytical and Negotiating Issues in the Global Trading System* (Ann Arbor, MI: University of Michigan Press, 1994).

Dixit, A., "International Trade Policy for Oligopolistic Industries," *Economic Journal*, XCIV (1984), 1–16.

————, "Comparative Statics for Oligopoly," *International Economic Review*, XXVII (1986), 107–122.

————, "Tariffs and Subsidies under Oligopoly: The Case of the U.S. Automobile Industry," in H. Kierzkowski, ed., *Protection and Competition in International Trade* (Oxford: Basil Blackwell, 1987).

Findlay, R., and A. Panagariya, "Political Economy Analysis of Free Trade Areas and Customs Unions," unpublished manuscript, 1994.

Findlay, R., and S. Wellisz, "Endogenous Tariffs, the Political Economy of Trade Restrictions, and Welfare," in J. Bhagwati, ed., *Import Competition and Response*, National Bureau of Economic Research (Chicago, IL: University of Chicago Press, 1982).

Fischer, R., and P. Serra, "Income Inequality and Choice of Free Trade in a Model of Intra-industry Trade," *Quarterly Journal of Economics*, CXI (1996), 41–64.

Grossman, G., and E. Helpman, "Protection for Sale," *American Economic Review*, LXXXIV (1994a), 833–50.

Grossman, G., and E. Helpman, "The Politics of Free Trade Arrangements," *American Economic Review*, LXXXIV (1994b), 667–690.

Krugman, P., "Is Bilateralism Bad?" in E. Helpman and A. Razin, eds., *International Trade and Trade Policy* (Cambridge, MA: MIT Press, 1992).

Levy, P., "A Political Economic Analysis of Free Trade Arrangements," mimeograph, Stanford University, 1994.

Lipsey, R. G., "The Theory of Customs Unions: Trade Diversion and Welfare," *Economica*, XXIV (1957), 40–46.

————, "The Theory of Customs Unions: A General Survey," *Economic Journal*, LXX (1960), 498–513.

Ludema, R., "On the Value of Preferential Trade Agreements in Multilateral Negotiations," Mimeo, University of Western Ontario, 1994.

Michaely, M., "The Assumptions of Jacob Viner's Theory of Customs Unions," *Journal of International Economics*, VI (1976), 75–93.

O'Halloran, S., *Politics, Process, and American Trade Policy* (Ann Arbor, MI: The University of Michigan Press, 1994).

Olson, M., *The Logic of Collective Action: Public Goods and the Theory of Groups* (Cambridge, MA: Harvard University Press, 1965).

Peltzman, S., "Toward a More General Theory of Regulation," *Journal of Law and Economics*, XVIIII (1976), 211–248.

Staiger, R., "International Rules and Institutions for Trade Policy," mimeograph, University of Wisconsin at Madison, 1994.

Stigler, G., "The Theory of Economic Regulation," *Bell Journal of Economic and Management Science*, II (1971), 3–21.

Srinivasan, T. N., "Discussion on Regionalism vs. Multilateralism: Analytical Notes," in A. Panagariya and J. De Melo, eds., *New Dimensions in Regional Integration* (Washington, DC: World Bank, 1993).

Viner, J., *The Customs Union Issue* (New York: Carnegie Endowment for International Peace, 1950).

Wonnacott, P., and R. Wonnacott, "Is Unilateral Tariff Reduction Preferable to a Customs Union? The Curious Case of the Missing Foreign Tariffs," *American Economic Review*, LXXI (1981), 704–714.

Yi, S. S., "Endogenous Formation of Customs Unions under Imperfect Competition: Open Regionalism Is Good," Working Paper, Dartmouth College, 1995.

23

A Domino Theory of Regionalism

Richard E. Baldwin

23.1 Introduction

In the past 10 years, regional trade liberalisation has swept the world trading system like wildfire while the multilateral GATT talks proceeded at a glacial pace. This conspicuous contrast raises the question: "Why are countries eager to open markets regionally, but reluctant to do so multi-laterally?" Perhaps the most widely heard answer to this question focuses on two assertions.[1] The first is that regional integration has prospered as an alternative to multilateralism since multilateral trade negotiations have become too cumbersome to deal with today's complex trade issues. The second assertion is that the "conversion" of the US from a strong backer of multilateralism to an avid participant in regional schemes has been a driving force.

This chapter discusses the shortcomings of these assertions, and pro-poses an alternative answer. The chapter has four sections after the Introduction. Section 23.2 presents a few facts about recent regionalism, criticises the standard explanation for the recent rise in regionalism and proposes an alternative answer. Section 23.3 presents the basic economic and political economic model. Section 23.4 discusses how the domino effect operates in the model, and Section 23.5 contains a summary and some concluding remarks.

23.2 Facts, the Standard Explanation and an Alternative

Before discussing the shortcomings of the standard assertions and pro-posing an alternative answer, it is necessary to get a few facts straight.

Originally published, as chapter 2, in *Expanding Membership of the EU*, ed. Richard Baldwin, P. Haaparanta, and J. Kiander (Cambridge, UK: Cambridge University Press, 1996), 25–48. Reprinted with permission.

First, it is important to be more precise about the nature of the recent wave of regionalism. The initiatives that constitute the recent revival of regionalism should be thought of as falling into two categories: deep initiatives and shallow initiatives. Second, it is necessary to understand the relative size (as measured by the amount of trade covered) of these various initiatives. Lastly, one must get the facts straight on the timing and motives of the two major regional initiatives—those in Europe and in North America.

23.2.1 *Deep and Shallow Regional Integration Arrangements*

Deep regional integration schemes go far beyond the liberalisation of statutory border measures such as tariff and quantitative restrictions. These schemes involve the further opening of product and service markets to international competition by removing regulatory and fiscal barriers to competition from foreign firms. Typically, this involves modification of laws, regulation, practices and policies that many nations view as purely domestic matters. Most of these deeper integration schemes are in West Europe. Examples are the completion of the Single Market, the Treaty on European Union signed in Maastricht, the European Economic Area (EEA) agreement and the accession of Spain, Portugal, Austria, Finland and Sweden to the EU. These involved a substantial deepening of preexisting arrangements, or promises thereof. For instance, the Single Market programme instituted free movement of capital in the EU, and alleviated many non-border barriers to trade in goods and services.[2] It harmonised VAT rates, required mutual recognition of product standards (with minimum harmonisation), strengthened rights of establishment and further opened public procurement. The EEA basically extended the Single Market to EFTA countries (except Switzerland), and prohibited all anti-dumping and countervailing duties on intra-EEA trade.

These initiatives did not expand regional integration. They merely deepened existing schemes. Before the Single Market programme (also known as EU "92"), West European regional integration was marked by two concentric circles. The outer circle, which encompassed all EU and EFTA members, was a "virtual" free-trade area for industrial goods. That is, the confluence of the Treaty of Rome, the Stockholm Convention (EFTA's founding document) and the bilateral EU–EFTA free-trade agreements ensured duty-free treatment for industrial trade between each pair of these countries. The inner circle consisted of the EU's common market, which went beyond duty-free industrial trade. The EU "92" programme and the EEA deepened the extent of integration in both the inner and outer circles. The 1986 EU enlargement brought one new country (Spain) into the system and moved another (Portugal) from the outer to the inner circle. The 1995 EU enlargement merely switched three countries from the outer to the inner circle.

The Australia–New Zealand Closer Economic Relations Trade Agreement, ANZCERTA, is also a deep integration scheme. It applies to most food trade in addition to duty-free trade in industrial goods. Moreover, it goes far beyond border measures in that it includes explicit commitments to harmonise standards and other regulations that may impede trade, and to make business laws and regulatory practices compatible. Labour mobility in the area is also relatively free.

Most of the other recent regional schemes—such as the US–Canada free-trade area (FTA), the US–Israel FTA, NAFTA, MECOSUR—and the revivals of old regional schemes in Latin America and Africa have involved fairly shallow integration. These are principally limited to liberalisation of tariffs and quantitative restrictions over longer transition periods. For example, the NAFTA tariff and quota liberalisations will not be completed until the year 2009.

23.2.2 The Size of Regional Integration Arrangements

The second point of fact that needs to be mentioned is the size of the various regional schemes. In terms of the volume of trade affected, Western European schemes dominate all others. Table 23.1 shows that the EEA now covers about a third of world exports. This figure is more than $4\frac{1}{2}$ times larger than the amount of trade covered by the next largest regional scheme, NAFTA.[3] All of the other successful regional initiatives are tiny. de Melo and Panagariya (1993) considered all regional integration arrangements in the world (well over 100 in number) and defined as "successful" only those for which intra-arrangement trade was at least 4 percent of the members' total exports on a sustained basis. As they point out, this is a very permissive definition of "successful." As table 23.1 shows, none of the other arrangements covers even as much as 1 percent of world trade. Several of them cover less than one hundredth of 1 percent of world trade. The main point is that in terms of the volume of world trade covered, the European and North American regional integration schemes are really the only important ones.

Table 23.1
West European Regional Arrangements

1990 data	Intra-regional exports ($ billion)	Intra-regional exports as share world exports (%)
West Europe free trade zone (EU + EFTA)	1128.5	33.9
of which:		
EU-12	821.8	24.7
NAFTA	237.9	7.1
ANZCERTA	3.8	0.1
ASEAN	26	0.8
Andean Pact	1.4	0.0
CACM	0.5	0.0
LAFTA	12.0	0.4
ECOWAS	1.2	0.0
PTA	0.6	0.0

Source: IMF, *Direction of Trade Yearbook 1992*, EFTA, *Trade 1991*, and de Melo and Panagariya (1993) for smaller arrangements.
Note: 0.0 per cent indicates less than one-hundredth of 1 per cent. ANZCERTA is the Australia–New Zealand arrangement, ASEAN is the South-east Asian arrangement, the Andean Pact is an FTA among South American nations, CACM is the Caribbean common market, LAFTA is the Latin America FTA, ECOWAS is the West African arrangement and PTA is the Eastern and Southern African preferential trading area. Many of the last six arrangements cover substantially less than all intra-group trade, so the figures in table 23.1 are overestimates of the trade actually influenced directly.

23.2.3   The Timing and Motivation of Regional Arrangements

Given the dominance of Europe and North America in the recent revival in regionalism, it is therefore worth reviewing the timing and motives of regional integration on these two continents.

American Regionalism   In the Western hemisphere, the recent wave of regionalism may be traced back to the US–Canada FTA. According to Schott (1988), the germ of this initiative was a March 1985 summit meeting between President Reagan and Prime Minister Mulroney. Reagan formally announced his intention to negotiate this FTA in December 1985. It is important to note that this was almost a year *before* the Uruguay Round was launched. The US–Canada talks in fact proved difficult, and the agreement did not come into force until 1989.

The following year, the US and Mexico announced their intention to form an FTA. This bilateral FTA was initiated by President Salinas of Mexico as a means of fostering stability in Mexico by boosting growth and locking-in unilateral pro-market reforms. The motives for this initiative had little to do with the US's desire to liberalise trade. In 1990, US exports to Mexico accounted for only 7.2 percent of its total exports, so it seems highly unlikely that the US viewed this politically exacting, yet commercially unimportant, initiative as substituting in any way for global trade liberalisation. Since the Mexican economy is smaller than that of the Los Angeles basin, Mexico is not likely to become an important trading partner of the US in the coming decades.

Canadian concerns that the US–Mexico FTA might erode their preference margins, especially in automotive parts, led to NAFTA. Canada requested that the bilateral US–Mexico talks be broadened into a trilateral negotiation. The US and Mexico agreed and the North American Free-Trade Agreement (NAFTA) was born.

Following the resurgence of regional integration in North America, many smaller regional initiatives were launched, re-launched or seriously discussed in Latin America. For instance, Chile, Brazil, Argentina, Uruguay and Paraguay, formally or informally, approached the US to begin bilateral FTA talks. Moreover, interest in President Bush's Enterprise for the Americas Initiative boomed in 1991, with 26 countries signing so-called Framework Agreements. These require the countries to make unilateral concessions on trade and investment to the US in exchange for the promise of closer US relations, leading eventually to an FTA.

Few of these came to fruition, and it seems likely that even fewer will be ever carried out. De la Torre and Kelly (1992) analyse the reasons why South–South preferential trade arrangements are typically plagued by a low rate of implementation. The recent discussion of regional integration in the Asia–Pacific area is certainly a development to watch. However, it seems quite likely that nothing substantial will come of this. Trade frictions among the major trading nations, China, Japan and the US have been rising rather than diminishing: for instance, one may rightly question the likelihood of the US Congress agreeing to abolish all tariffs on Japanese and Chinese imports.

European Regionalism   Recent European regionalism was sparked by the Single Market programme. In 1985 Jacques Delors took office with the intention of rekindling European integration. His strategy was to embark on a massive liberalisation that would turn the common market into a single market. The first formal step towards the Single Market programme was Lord Cockfield's June 1985 *White Paper*. This listed 282 measures necessary to complete the single market. The treaty that implemented these measures (along with many other changes) was the Single European Act. This was signed in February 1986 by the EU heads of government. In the same year, Spain and Portugal acceded to the EU after 6 years of membership negotiations.

The Single Market programme harmed the competitiveness of EFTA-based firms by lowering the costs of their EU-based rivals, as Krugman (1988) points out. In the mid-1980s, EFTA governments had decided that they must react. The idea of countering the threat with a new plurilateral agreement was first suggested at a meeting of EFTA and EU ministers in Luxembourg in 1984, even before the *White Paper* was published. This produced the so-called "Luxembourg Declaration." However, the difficulties of such an initiative, and the EU's preoccupation with the Single European Act and the Maastricht Treaty, led to long delays. Indeed very little was done until January 1989 when Jacques Delors proposed the European Economic Area (EEA) agreement (initially called the European Economic Space agreement). Talks on the EEA began informally in 1989, continuing more formally in 1990 and 1991.

The first version of the EEA, signed in 1991, was rejected by the European Court of Justice as inconsistent with EU law. Negotiations were reconvened and the second version of the EEA was signed on 2 May 1992 in Oporto. This was acceptable to the European Court; however, Swiss voters rejected it in a December 1992 referendum. Since the EEA formally included all EFTAns, this required a technical rewriting of the agreement. More important, since the EEA obliged the EFTAns to make financial transfers to poor EU regions, the withdrawal of Switzerland also forced a renegotiation of the size of these transfers. The final version of the EEA was signed in 1993, with implementation starting in January 1994.

Since the Single Market involves such a deep degree of integration it proved difficult for the EU to extend the Single Market to non-members. In particular, EU "92" constrains many economic policies that are not traditionally viewed as trade policy. It requires supranational surveillance and enforcement of competition policy (known as anti-trust policy in the US), state aids to industry, national public procurement policies, and regulation of the behaviour of state-owned monopolies. The member states of the EU can accept this sort of supranational control by the European Commission since the Commission itself is controlled by national political leaders via the Council of Ministers. Since non-member governments cannot vote or attend the Council of Minister meetings, the EEA agreement involved "regulation without representation" for the EFTA side.

This so-called "influence deficit" made the EEA a relatively unpalatable means of offsetting potential discrimination from EU "92." As it turned out, virtually none of the EFTA governments were willing to live with the EEA. Even before the final version was adopted, all the EFTAns (except Iceland and Liechtenstein, which have a combined population of 0.29 million) had applied for full EU membership. Obviously, the end of the East–West conflict in Europe was also critical to this membership drive in that it removed traditional resistance to the EU. Applications were received from Austria (July 1989), Sweden (July 1991), Finland (March 1992), Switzerland (May 1992) and Norway (November 1992). For these countries, the EEA was viewed as a transitional arrangement, not a long-term solution (note that the EU froze the Swiss application in response to the negative outcome of their EEA referendum). Accession talks for the four EFTAns were concluded in 1994, with entry to occur in 1995 subject to national referendums. Austrian, Finnish and Swedish voters responded positively in 1994. Norwegian voters said no.

The collapse of Communism also opened the Central and Eastern European countries (CEECs). The EU and EFTA (separately) signed bilateral free-trade agreements with several of these countries in the early 1990s. Since nearly all industrial trade in West Europe is duty-free and West Europe is the dominant market for the exports of Central and Eastern European nations, these bilateral free-trade agreements were essential to levelling the playing field for CEEC exporters. Most CEECs have applied, or plan to apply, to become full EU members, and the EU heads of state have agreed that they will eventually be admitted.

23.2.4 Critique of the Standard Explanation of Recent Regionalism

There is certainly some truth in the first pillar of the standard account of resurgent regionalism. Many contemporary trade issues are much more complicated than those (e.g. tariff liberalisation) dealt with in earlier GATT rounds. However, this assertion does not directly answer the question of why "regional" instead of "global." We will first consider how relevant this explanation is to elucidate the recent deep integration schemes in Europe.

The primary forces behind European economic integration in the post-Second World War period have always been strategic and geopolitical motives. It seems quite far-fetched to propose that European frustrations with the GATT are what triggered EU governments to endorse Jacques Delors' proposal for completing the internal market. Two historical facts reinforce this assertion. Even when the GATT multilateral process was widely perceived as functioning well (in the 1950s and 1960s), West Europe continued to proceed with regional integration. Also, the Single Market programme, which is the first cause of most of the deeper integration schemes, was proposed and adopted long before frustration with the GATT talks emerged.

Given that the first part of the standard explanation is irrelevant to understanding European regionalism, we will turn to the second part. According to Bhagwati (1993), the single most important reason why regionalism is making a comeback is the conversion of the US from devoted multilateralist to ardent regionalist. Recall, however, that the US conversion dates back only to late 1985. The resurgence of regionalism in Europe and the US thus occurred at approximately the same time. This timing suggests that the second part of the standard explanation also has little explicatory power when it comes to deep integration initiatives in Europe.

This line of argument, if accepted, should be enough to reject the standard explanation. If the standard explanation does not account for recent regionalism in Europe, then it does not account for the bulk of regionalism. At the very best, it accounts for the relatively small regional arrangement in North America and the tiny arrangements in Africa, Latin American and Asia. Taken together, all the non-European schemes deemed successful by de Melo and Panagariya (1993) cover only 8.5 percent of world trade. As we shall see, however, the standard explanation has many shortcomings when applied to even these small arrangements.

Again we start with the first pillar of the standard explanation. Is it reasonable to assert that the shallow regional arrangements in Africa, Asia and the Western hemisphere are prompted by a disappointment with the lack of progress in the Uruguay Round and the functioning of the multilateral trading system? Consider the Canada–US FTA (CUSTA). The political decision to start negotiations was taken in the year before the Uruguay Round was launched. One would have to tell a very complicated story about American and Canadian motives to assert that sluggish progress on the GATT talks prompted the Canada–US FTA. The US–Mexico FTA talks and NAFTA were started after the Uruguay Round talks became bogged down. However, the motives for the triggering event, the US–Mexico FTA, had virtually nothing to do with global trade. It was pursued on both sides as a means of locking-in pro-market reforms in Mexico. It thus seems that the "frustration-with-GATT" part of the argument is not applicable to the other major regional initiatives in the world, namely those in North America.

Next consider the second pillar of the traditional argument. When it comes to North American initiatives, all of which involve the US, the second pillar is a tautology. Indisputably the US acceptance of regionalism was a key to explaining NAFTA, but this sort of logic has no explanatory power.

Where does this leave the traditional explanation of regionalism? If it does not account for European or North American regionalism, then it is irrelevant. According to the figures in Table 23.1, all the other schemes cover less than 2 percent of world trade.

The traditional explanation is appealing at first glance, and it has won over many adherents. Unfortunately, it is not consistent with the facts. West European and North American regionalism arrangements are the only ones that cover a significant fraction of global trade. Resurgent regionalism in both regions started well before the GATT talks became sluggish and cumbersome. Moreover, European regionalism was revitalised for purely European reasons. The US attitude was irrelevant.

23.2.5   The Domino Theory of Regionalism

This chapter proposes a very different explanation of the question: "Why are countries eager to open markets regionally, but reluctant to do so multilaterally?" The stark contrast between the ease of regional liberalisation and the glacial GATT talks does not reflect a GATT failure: GATT Rounds have always been protracted, have always been slow, and have always been difficult. Indeed it does not even reflect a systemic phenomenon. I propose that the current wave of regionalism stems from two idiosyncratic events—one in the New World and one in the Old—that have been multiplied many times over by a "domino effect."

The idiosyncratic event in the Western hemisphere was the US–Mexico FTA, which was itself motivated by the unilateral reforms undertaken by Mexico in the 1980s. Announcement of the US-Mexico FTA destroyed the status quo of trade relations in the Americas. Other countries in the region, which are heavily dependent on the US market, were faced with a fait accompli. Mexico-based producers would gain preferential access to the US market, thereby increasing the competition facing third-country exporters and diverting foreign investment to Mexico. Despite continuing domestic opposition to its first regional liberalisation—the Canada–US FTA—Canada decided that it has to be at the negotiating table. Other countries in the hemisphere, such as Chile, Brazil, Argentina, Uruguay and Paraguay enquired about the possibility of a bilateral FTA with the US. Faced with a flood of requests for bilateral FTAs, the Office of the US Trade Representative encouraged South American countries to form regional groups among themselves before applying en groupe for an FTA with the US. Similar pressures explain the booming interest in President Bush's Enterprise for the Americas Initiative.

The idiosyncratic event in Europe was the completion of the Single Market. Again the timing and motives for this suggest that this regional initiative was in no way a substitute for multilateral liberalisation, nor did it have anything to do with the US attitude towards the GATT system. This event triggered a domino effect. Austria, which had been previously restrained from joining the EU by pressure from the Soviet bloc, applied for EU membership in 1989. The deepening of the EU and pending enlargement of the EU to include several large EFTA countries made the potential loss of competitiveness even more threatening to EFTA nations that chose to remain outside the EU. That is, each EFTA nation individually faced the prospect of losing out in the EU-12 markets *and* in the markets of those EFTAns acceding to the EU. Since the combined EU and EFTA markets on average account for three-quarters of EFTA exports, the pressure on the holdouts mounted. Sweden put in its application in 1991 and Finland, Norway and Switzerland requested EU membership in 1992. The Icelandic government, which gave much thought to joining in the early 1990s, was deterred by the EU's common fishery policy. By the time Iceland changed its mind in 1994, it was told by the EU that it was too late to participate in the 1995 EU enlargement, so Iceland did not put in an application.

The first draft of this chapter was completed before the accession negotiations were finished. However, additional evidence of the importance of the domino effect can be found in the ordering of the four referendums. Leaders of Austria, Finland, Sweden and Norway agreed to sequence the national votes in order of descending EU popularity. The heavily populated eastern part of Austria was occupied by Soviet forces until 1955, so intrinsic resistance to joining the West via EU membership was quite weak in Austria. Also, Austria is the EFTA country most heavily dependent on the EU market for its manufactured exports. Owing to this, it was decided that Austria should go first. Finland held its vote next. Parts of Finland were lost to the USSR in the Second World War, and the country was "Finlandised" during the Cold War so, as with Austria, EU member-ship promised significant non-economic gains. Sweden came after Finland and before Norway. It was hoped that the widely anticipated positive results in Austria and Finland would tilt the fine balance in Sweden towards the "Yes" side. Norway was last. Norway's current exports are dominated by oil and so are not threatened by the Single Market pro-gramme. Norwegian exports of manufactured goods (SITC 5–8) to the EU account for only 19 percent of its total exports, the figure rises to 27 percent when manufactured exports to other EFTA nations (mainly Sweden and Finland) are included.

As figure 23.1 shows, there is strongly positive correlation between the fraction of the population voting for EU membership and the impor-tance of manufactured exports to the EU + EFTA area as a share of total exports. The exception, of course, is Switzerland whose voters rejected even the EEA despite the fact that about 60 percent of its exports face discrimination from EU92.

The political economy forces driving this domino effect are strength-ened by a peculiar tendency of special interest groups; they usually fight harder to avoid losses than they do to secure gains. In this light, it is im-portant that joining the regional integration in Europe and North America would allow countries to avoid damage as well as to gain new commercial

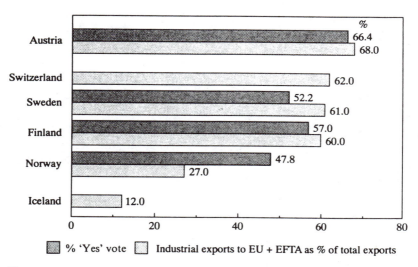

Figure 23.1
Importance of manufactures trade with EU and EFTA and referendum results.

opportunities. While there may be many explanations for this asymmetric phenomenon, Baldwin (1993) proposes a simple economic interpretation based on sunk costs.

Entry into most industries and markets involves large unrecoverable investments in product development, training, brand name advertisement and production capacity. In such situations, established firms can earn positive profits without attracting new firms only in as far as these profits constitute a fair return on the entry investments. Another way to say this is that sunk costs create quasi-rents. In such industries, consider the incentive to lobby. If a country's exporters obtain additional access to foreign markets, their sales and profits will typically rise. The increase in pure profit, however, will attract new competition, so the size of the gains must be limited. In the extreme, entry continues until all pure profit disappears. Correspondingly, the incentive to lobby for new export opportunities will be limited, and in the extreme will disappear altogether. Next consider the reaction of an established firm to an unanticipated policy change (such as the "1992" programme, or the US–Mexico FTA) that would reduce its relative competitiveness and profitability. To be concrete, suppose that the change would wipe out half its quasi-rents. Since it would not actually be losing money, the firm would not shut down. More to the point, the firm should be willing to spend up to half its quasi-rents on lobbying for membership, if doing so would reverse the loss of relative competitiveness.

23.3   The Basic Model

Formalisation of the domino effect presented in the Introduction requires a model that first shows how closer regional integration affects the fortunes of industries based in non-member countries, and then connects these changing fortunes to the political decision making process. The economic framework adopted is closely related to the setup used by Krugman (1991) in examining economic geography issues. The political economy model employed is related to Grossman and Helpman (1993).

23.3.1   The Economic Framework

Consider a world of g countries, h of which are members of the regional trade bloc. Without loss of generality, we refer to the trade bloc as the EC. Each country has two sectors: a differentiated-products sector (referred to as manufacturing) which is marked by increasing returns and imperfect competition, and a perfectly competitive, constant-returns sector (referred to as the A sector). Technology and preferences over goods are identical in all countries. There are two classes of workers, labourers and firm owners. The preferences of the firm owners are:

$$U^F = C_A^{1-\phi} C_M^\phi; \quad C_M = [\sum_i c_i^{(\sigma-1/\sigma)}]^{\sigma/(\sigma-1)},$$
$$\sigma > 1, \quad 0 \le \phi \le 1 \tag{23.1}$$

where the summation is over goods that are actually available, σ is the elasticity of substitution between any two varieties and c_i is the consumption of food i. The income of firm owners derives solely from profits. The preferences of labourers are given by:

$$U^L = C_A^{1-\lambda} C_M^\lambda; \quad C_M = [\sum_i c_i^{(\sigma-1)/\sigma}]^{\sigma/(\sigma-1)}, \tag{23.2}$$

where σ is less than unity and λ is between zero and unity.

Utility maximisation by the representative consumers, subject to budget constraints, yields a typical country's demand function for a typical variety of manufactured good. This is:

$$c_j = \left(\frac{p_j}{P}\right)^{-\sigma} E, \quad P = [\sum_i (p_i)^{-(\sigma-1)}]^{-1/\sigma} \tag{23.3}$$

where E is the total expenditure of consumers on manufactured products. Labourers and firm owners spend a fraction $1 - \lambda$ and $1 - \phi$ on A respectively, so the demand for the A good is:

$$A = [(1 - \lambda)E^L + (1 - \phi)E^F]/p_A \tag{23.4}$$

where p_A is the price of A, and E^L and E^F are the total expenditures of labourers and firm owners.

The labour input requirement for a typical manufactured variety is:

$$l_i = \alpha + \beta x_i, \quad \alpha, \beta > 0 \tag{23.5}$$

where x_i is the output of variety i. α is a fixed cost. The cost of introducing a new variety is zero so, as usual, there will be only one firm producing each variety. Entry is ruled out, so the number of active firms is exogenous and equal to k per country. Each firm is owned entirely by the residents of the country in which it produces.

Two very strong assumptions on trade costs are made for tractability. Trade in the A good is costless while trade in manufactures is costly, with the costs being of the "iceberg" type.[4] That is, shipping of manufactured

goods between any two countries melts a fraction of the shipment. These
trade costs are lower for intra-EC trade than for all other international
trade. An EC-based firm that wants to sell a unit of manufactured goods in
another EC country must ship $\mu > 1$ units. All other trade, that is all non-
intra-EC trade, requires that $\tau > 1$ units be shipped for every unit sold.
The essence of EC membership in this chapter is that $\mu < \tau$. There are no
trade costs for domestic sales.

The production function of good A is linear homogeneous. Units of A
are chosen such that A's unit labour input coefficient is unity. With perfect
competition and costless trade prevailing, this choice of units implies that
the price of A is equal to the wage rate. As long as all countries produce
in both sectors, competition in the A good equalises the equilibrium wage
in all countries. We take labour to be the numeraire.

Given the demand function, the typical manufacturer faces an isoelastic
demand curve.[5] For producers based in a non-EC country, the first order
conditions are:

$$p\left(1 - \frac{1}{\sigma}\right) = \beta, \quad p\left(1 - \frac{1}{\sigma}\right) = \beta\tau, \tag{23.6}$$

for home and foreign sales respectively. Here the ps are consumer prices,
that is, c.i.f. prices. For a firm based in the EC, the first order conditions for
sales to the home market and non-EC markets are the same as those for a
non-EC firm; however they are:

$$p\left(1 - \frac{1}{\sigma}\right) = \beta\mu \tag{23.7}$$

for sales to other EC markets.

Manufactured goods are measured in units that are chosen so that the
unit input coefficient β just equals $(1 - 1/\sigma)$. This implies that optimising
firms charge the same f.o.b. price (namely unity) for all sales regardless of
destination. The c.i.f. prices for home sales are unity in all countries, for
intra-EC sales price equals μ and all other exports are priced at τ.

To simplify calculations of the general equilibrium demand patterns, we
assume ϕ to be unity and λ to be strictly between unity and zero. By
carefully choosing the units with which to measure national workforces,
we can take E^L to be unity. Given that manufactured-goods prices are determined by profit maximisation, it is easy to calculate sales in the various
markets using the demand curve. With a constant demand elasticity of σ,
operating profits (i.e. profits gross of fixed costs) in manufacturing equal
$(1/\sigma)$ times sales. In what follows, a crucial quantity will be the differ-

ence between equilibrium operating profit earned by the typical firm when it is based in a member nation and when it is not. This difference equals:

$$\Pi^{in} - \Pi^{out} = \lambda \frac{h(\mu^{1-\sigma} - \tau^{1-\sigma})}{\sigma} P_{ec}^{\sigma} + \frac{\lambda}{\sigma}(P_{ec}^{\sigma} - P_{non}^{\sigma}), \tag{23.8}$$

where

$$P_{ec} = (k[l - \mu^{1-\sigma} + h(\mu^{1-\sigma} - \tau^{1-\sigma}) + g\tau^{1-\sigma}])^{-1/\sigma} \tag{23.9}$$

and

$$P_{non} = (k[1 + (g - 1)\tau^{1-\sigma}])^{-1/\sigma}. \tag{23.10}$$

The first term in (23.8) is positive and represents the increase in profits the firm would experience in all incumbents' markets. The second term, which shows the change in profits earned on home market sales, is negative. The profit earned on sales to third nations is unaltered by EC membership and therefore cancels out.

23.3.2 *General Political Economy Modelling Considerations*

The median-voter model (see Mayer, 1984) is a popular and elegant framework much used in the political equilibrium literature. However, it does not seem to capture the principal aspects of the policy formation process affecting EC membership. Indeed, one of the most remarkable facts about the trend towards regionalism is the gap between the positions of governments and the positions of their electorates (as portrayed by public opinion polls). Both in Europe and North America, governments tend to espouse the views of pro-integrationist business leaders (and labour leaders as well in most of Europe), while the populace tends to be more wary. It would thus appear unreasonable to adopt a model of the political process in which the government was simply a mouthpiece for the people. In fact, direct democracy is not the usual way in which a country's government decides whether it wants to join a regional trade bloc.[6] Even if a referendum is held on the final negotiated accession treaty, the decision to engage in the negotiations is usually taken in the setting of representative democracy. The decision is thus influenced by pressure groups.

Both Hillman (1989) and Baldwin (1985) point out that under realistic assumptions elected officials may not be fully aware of the economic interests of their constituents. And their constituents may not be familiar with all the policies (and their economic consequences) championed by their elected representatives. Consequently, as Baldwin (1985) notes, groups of voters "may have to engage in time-consuming and costly lobbying activities to bring its viewpoint to the attention of legislators. Similarly office-seekers need funds to inform the voters of how they have served them or will do so in the future." The so-called pressure group model, or lobbying model, developed by Olson (1965) and others, focuses on the costs and benefits of lobbying and its impact on policy. Grossman and Helpman (1993) provide a modern, rigorous treatment of the lobbying model.

The basic political influence technology adopted in this chapter is similar to the Grossman and Helpman (1993) approach to the pressure group model. Two assumptions in the Grossman-Helpman approach are crucial to tractability: the policy maker's objective function is linear in campaign donations and social welfare, and interest groups can make donations contingent on the actions of the policy maker. Grossman and Helpman (1993) provide several justifications of the fixed-weight linear objective function. First, it can be taken as a reduced form for a political process where politicians' true objective is re-election and the odds of survival increase linearly in aggregate campaign donations and utilities of individual voters. Alternatively, they conjecture that it can be interpreted as a reduced form of a broad class of political process models in which

politicians may value donations not only for the marginal effect that advertising and other campaign expenditures have on voter behaviour, but also because the funds can be used to retire campaign debts from previous elections (which many times are owed to the politician's personal estate), to deter competition from quality challengers, and to show the candidate's abilities as a fund raiser and thereby establish his or her credibility as a potential candidate for higher political or party office.

Regardless of the justification, this fixed-weight linear objective function allows us to think of campaign donations as direct payments to risk-neutral policy makers.

Grossman and Helpman (1993) also assume that organised special interest groups can specify donation contracts, or "contribution schedules" that stipulate how large a donation will be made for each possible policy stance chosen. In the first of the two stages in the Grossman–Helpman model, contracts are announced by private groups and in the second, the government sets policy and collects donations. It is useful to think of these schedules as enforceable employment contracts where special interest groups "employ" policy makers to do their bidding in exchange for performance-related compensation. Note that the donations are ex post in the sense that they are paid *after* the policy has been chosen by officials that have already been elected. Each group chooses the donation contract that maximises its own welfare, taking the contracts of other special interest groups as given.

Plainly one does not observe formal, enforceable contacts between policy makers and special interest groups (except when they are entered as evidence by the prosecution). It is, therefore, worth justifying the assumption in more depth. Even if not all real-world donations are made on this "contractual" basis, one can think of the donation contracts as a simple way of capturing the potentially very complicated real-world compacts struck between special interest donors and policy makers. After all, regardless of the actual details of the informal agreements between policy makers and interest groups, the practical intent of these agreements is to reward the policy makers if and only if they choose policies that benefit the donating special interest group.

It would seem that the enforceability assumption could be dropped in a more complex model. For instance, using a repeated game set-up and the Folk theorem, I conjecture that ex ante donations would have the same effect as enforceable donation contracts. The equilibrium would involve politicians faithfully sticking to the bargain in order to avoid an off-equilibrium punishment consisting of the donators backing the politicians' opponents. It would be very interesting to model such a situation explicitly.

The fixed-weight linear objective function, together with performance-contingent donation contracts, makes it easy to frame the political process as a principal–agent problem where the government is the 'agent' and competing interest groups are the "principals." This, in turn, allows direct access to the well developed literature on principal–agent problems. Grossman and Helpman (1993) draw on the very general analysis of Bernheim and Whinston (1986a, 1986b), which enables them to consider an extremely broad class of "contracts" between special interest groups and policy makers. This high level of generality makes it difficult to say very much about the nature of the resulting political equilibrium, apart from the fact that it exists. To characterise further the political equilibrium, Grossman and Helpman (1993) impose more structure on the problem in two steps. First they consider all donation contracts that are differentiable around the equilibrium. Second they focus on the Bernheim–Whinston notion of a "truthful Nash Equilibrium," which restricts the contracts to a very specific form:[7] the donation of any special interest group equals the group's gross welfare minus a fixed amount that is chosen optimally. Bernheim and Whinston defend this concept by showing that such contracts would never be suboptimal and that equilibria supported by truthful contracts, and only these equilibria, are stable to non-binding communications among the players.

23.3.3 Specific Political Influence Technology

The government of the typical country chooses whether to join the EC or not. We capture this choice with the variable u, which equals unity if they decide to join, and zero otherwise. The choice is taken to maximise political support, which in turn depends positively upon the level of donations by industry, the level of social welfare net of donations, and on a third term R which reflects the support of groups that oppose EC membership on non-economic grounds. The government's problem is thus to choose u in order to maximise:

$$u[(1-a)D^{in} + aW^{in}] + (1-u)[(1-a)D^{out} + aW^{out} + R] \qquad (23.11)$$

where a is a parameter that lies between zero and one, the D and Ws are the levels of donations and social welfare when the country is "in" or "out" of the EC respectively, and R is the support from anti-EC groups that the government receives if it decides not to join the EC. R, which measures the country's general resistance to membership, varies across countries. The parameter a measures the extent of the political distortion. If a equals unity, the government acts as a social welfare maximiser. The further is a from unity, the greater is the political distortion. In this model, greater political distortion leads to the interest of exporters receiving greater weight in the policy making process. We take social welfare to be the sum of utilities, that is $W = U^L + U^F$, so:

$$W^{in} = (1-\lambda)^{1-\lambda}(\lambda)^{\lambda}P_{ec}^{\lambda\sigma/(1-\sigma)} + k\Pi^{in}$$
$$W^{out} = (1-\lambda)^{1-\lambda}(\lambda)^{\lambda}P_{non}^{\lambda\sigma/(1-\sigma)} + k\Pi^{out}. \qquad (23.12)$$

Following Grossman and Helpman (1993), the donation contracts in this chapter are restricted to be "truthful" in the Bernheim–Whinston jargon and actual donations to be non-negative. All manufacturing firms in a country are organised into a lobbying group. The group's truthful donation contract is:

$$D^{in} = k\Pi^{in} + B, \quad D^{out} = k\Pi^{out} + B \tag{23.13}$$

where B is a scalar and k is the number of manufacturing firms per country.

Given the donation contract, a typical government decides to join the EC if and only if:

$$R \leq (1 - a)\, k[\Pi^{in} - \Pi^{out}] + a[W^{in} - W^{out}]. \tag{23.14}$$

Which can be rewritten as:

$$R \leq k[\Pi^{in} = \Pi^{out}] + a(1 - \lambda)^{1-\lambda}(\lambda)^{\lambda}[P_{ec}^{-\lambda\sigma/(\sigma-1)} = P_{non}^{-\lambda\sigma/(\sigma-1)}]. \tag{23.15}$$

23.3.4 The Supply Side of Membership

The model so far describes only the demand for membership. We now turn to the "supply" of memberships. As was mentioned in the Introduction, the truly remarkable fact is that the demand for membership in regional trading blocs has spread rapidly. The actual enlargement of the blocs has proved much slower.

To focus on why so many countries wish to join trading blocs, as opposed to focusing on how many actually get in, we assume that the supply of membership is perfectly elastic. That is to say, that the EU is an open club: any one who requests membership is admitted. Of course, this assumption does quite a bit of violence to the reality of EU politics. In future research, it would be quite interesting to specify a more realistic supply of membership schedule.

Having restricted special interests to "truthful" donation contracts, the political choice of manufacturers is limited to the size of the constant term in the donation contract. Since there is only one organised donor, the level of B has no influence on the shape of policy, as long as the government is willing to accept the donation contracts. The way to tie down B in this simple principal–agent problem is to use the voluntary participation constraint.[8] That is if the agent (in this case, the government) is to accept the contract offered, the level of its equilibrium "utility" must be at least as great as its reservation level. In our case, the government could refuse all contingent donation contracts. Thus if the lobbying groups are to have any influence over the government, they must choose a B such that the government is at least indifferent to refusing their donation contract.

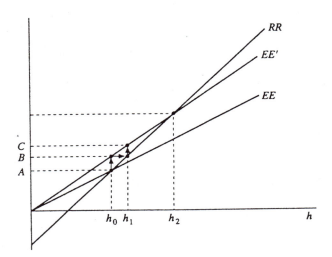

Figure 23.2
Non-economic resistance to EU membership.

Although all countries are symmetric economically, we assume that they differ in terms of the degree of non-economic resistance to EU membership. Arranging the countries in order of increasing resistance, we can plot the degree of resistance against the number of EU members. In figure 23.2, this is shown as RR. Clearly, we can think of there being a continuum of countries, so that h is a continuous variable, or we can view RR as the line that connects the points representing individual countries. In figure 23.2 we have assumed that there is negative resistance to membership in some countries. That is to say, the government loses political support for non-economic reasons if it does not choose membership.

23.4   The "1992" Programme and the Domino Effect

The political equilibrium, for a given τ and μ, can be found with the help of figure 23.2. The locus EE plots the right-hand side of (23.14). Since P_{ec} is decreasing in h, and $\Pi^{in} - \Pi^{out}$ is increasing in h, it is straightforward to show that right-hand side of (23.12) is upward-sloping, as shown in figure 23.2. The equilibrium number of members will be below the maximum of g, if there are countries in which there is sufficient resistance to EU membership to ensure that the locus RR will eventually rise above the EE schedule. The equilibrium number of members, h_0 in figure 23.2, is given by the intersection of the EE and RR schedules. For all countries to the right of h_0, the non-economic resistance to membership exceeds the net economic benefit from switching from non-member to member status. For all those to the left, the political support gained from being "in" versus being "out" outweighs the political resistance to membership. More precisely, respecting the integer constraint, we can say that equilibrium h is the highest integer that is less than h_0.

Given the economic and political economic components of the model, it is quite simple to see how a domino effect could occur. Consider the impact of a policy change, such as the Single European Act, that makes intra-EC trade cheaper. In our model this is reflected by a lowering of μ. The impact of a reduction in μ shows up in figure 23.2 as a shift of EE to EE'. To show this, note that the derivative of the right-hand side of (23.14) with respect to μ is:

$$a(\lambda)^\lambda (1 - \lambda)^{1-\lambda} \left(\frac{-\lambda\sigma}{\sigma - 1} \right) P_{ec}^{(-\lambda\sigma/\sigma-1)-1} (dP_{ec}/d\mu) + d(\Pi^{in} - \Pi^{out})/d\mu.$$

Since the EU price index falls with μ and the operating profit difference increases with μ, the derivative is clearly positive. Of course at $h = 0$, the price and operating profit differences are zero. The new equilibrium number of members is h_2. The difference between h_1 and h_2 is caused by the "domino" effect: falling trade barriers in one set of countries triggers a fall in the barriers of other countries. Although there are no formal dynamics in this model, it is useful to illustrate the domino effect by telling the story of the increase from h_0 to h_2 as if the increase in EU applications took place over time.

The initial shock of closer EU integration (lower μ) raises the political economic gains from membership enough to overcome the intrinsic resistance to membership in some countries. In particular in the first round of effects, the political economy support for membership rises from A to B in Figure 23.2. Thus, in the first round, all countries whose resistance is between A and B would join, thus boosting membership from h_0 to h_1. The rise in h, however, affects the choices of the remaining non-members. In particular, governments would judge that the political economy support for membership was equal to C in figure 23.2. This would prompt applications from all non-members whose resistance was between B and C. Of course, this further rise in membership would provoke a fresh batch of membership applications, and the process would continue until the new equilibrium was reached. Thus although the fundamental cause of enlargement is the exogenous deepening of EU integration, this initial shock is amplified by the way in which enlargement makes non-membership even more costly.

23.5 Summary and Conclusions

This chapter presents a simple model of how an idiosyncratic shock, such as deeper integration of an existing regional bloc, can trigger membership requests from countries that were previously happy to be non-members. The basic logic is simple. The stance of a country's government concerning membership is the result of a political equilibrium that balances anti- and pro-membership forces. Among the pro-EU forces are firms that export to the regional bloc. Since closer integration within a bloc is detrimental to the profits of non-member firms, closer integration will stimulate the exporters to engage in greater pro-EU political activity. If the government was previously close to indifferent (politically) to membership, the extra activity may tilt the balance and cause the country to join the bloc. If the bloc enlarges, the cost to the non-members increases, since they now face a cost disadvantage in an even greater number of markets. This second-round effect will bring forth more pro-EU political activity in non-members, and thus may lead to further enlargement of the bloc. The new political equilibrium will involve an enlarged regional trading bloc. Meanwhile it would appear that regionalism is spreading like wildfire.

In future research, it should be possible to develop a set of hypotheses based on this simple model that could be tested against the experience of the EU. Stepping away from the strong symmetry in the model, it should be possible to show that those countries that partake in the enlargement depend rather heavily on exports to the EU (since their export profits would be greatly affected), and have a rather small home market (since the loss of profits on home sales due to the market opening would be small).

Notes

1. See for instance, discussions by Bhagwati and Krugman in de Melo and Panagariya (1993).

2. The European Economic Community (EEC) was one of the four communities. The Treaty of European Union changed its name to the European Union (EU). This chapter uses EU throughout.

3. Under NAFTA, tariffs and other border measures are to be phased out between 1994 and 2009, so it is hard to know how much trade it will cover. The figure in table 23.1 shows the sum of exports between Canada, Mexico and the US in 1990.

4. As will become clear below, these two assumptions facilitate calculation of the equilibrium, since costless trade in the constant returns goods pins down the prices of labour in terms of A in all countries and iceberg costs allow consideration of trade costs without altering the homogeneity of the manufacturers' first order conditions.

5. Actually the elasticity is only approximately constant, with the approximation improving as the number of varieties increases.

6. In the one country where direct democracy is the political norm, Switzerland, the government's demand for membership was effectively overturned by a referendum on the EEA agreement.

7. The adjective "truthful" comes from the fact that in the principal–agent set-up, these contracts imply that the principals pay the agent her full marginal product minus some fixed amount. This, of course, means that the incentives of the agent to change her behaviour on the margin truthfully reflects the worth of such changes to the principals.

8. Grossman and Helpman (1993) show how to find the equilibrium Bs when the problem is too complicated to use the participation constraint.

References

Anderson, K. and E. Blackhurst (eds.), 1993. *Regional Integration and the Global Trading System*, Brighton: Harvester-Wheatsheaf.

Baldwin, R. E., 1985. *The Political Economy of US Import Policy*, Cambridge, MA: MIT Press.

————. 1992. "The economic logic of EFTA membership in the EEA and the EC," EFTA, *Occasional Paper*.

————. 1993. "Asymmetric lobbying: why governments pick losers," GIIS, mimeo.

Bernheim, B. and M. Whinston, 1986a. "Common agency," *Econometrica*, **54**, 923–42.

————. 1986b. "Menu auctions, resource allocation and economic influence," *Quarterly Journal of Economics*, **101**, 1–31.

Bhagwati, J., 1993. "Regionalism and multilateralism: an overview," in K. Anderson and R. Blackhurst (eds.), *Regional Integration and the Global Trading System*, Brighton: Harvester-Wheatsheaf.

CEPR, 1992. "Is bigger better? The economics of EC enlargement," *Monitoring European Integration*, **3**, London: CEPR.

De la Torre, A. and M. Kelly, 1992. "Regional trade arrangements," IMF, *Occasional Paper*, **93**, Washington, DC: IMF.

de Melo, J. and A. Panagariya, 1993. "Introduction," in J. de Melo and A. Panagariya (eds.), *New Dimensions in Regional Integration*, Cambridge: Cambridge University Press.

de Melo, J. and A. Panagariya (eds.), 1993. *New Dimensions in Regional Integration*, Cambridge: Cambridge University Press.

Dixit, A. and J. Stiglitz, 1977. "Monopolistic competition and optimal product diversity," *American Economic Review*, **67**, 297–308.

Grossman, G. and E. Helpman, 1993. "Protection for sale," CEPR, *Discussion Paper*, **827**, London: CEPR.

Hillman, A., 1989. *The Political Economy of Protection*, New York: Harwood Academic.

Krugman, P., 1979. "Increasing returns, monopolistic competition and international trade," *Journal of International Economics*, **9**, 496–80.

————. 1988. "EFTA and 1992," EFTA, *Occasional Paper*, **23**, Geneva: EFTA Secretariat.

————. 1991. "Increasing returns and economic geography," *Journal of Political Economy*, **99(3)**, 483–99.

————. 1993. "Regionalism versus multilateralism: analytic notes," in K. Anderson and R. Blackhurst (eds.), *Regional Integration and the Global Trading System*, Brighton: Harvester-Wheatsheaf.

Mayer, W., 1984. "Endogenous tariff formation," *American Economic Review*, **74**, 970–85.

Olson, Mancur, 1965. *The Logic of Collective Action*, Cambridge MA: Harvard University Press.

Schott, J., 1988. "United States–Canada free trade: an evaluation of the argument," *Policy Analyses in International Economics*, **24**, Washington, DC: Institute for International Economics.

IV

Theoretical Analyses: Modeling Institutional Features

24

Will Preferential Agreements Undermine the Multilateral Trading System?

Kyle Bagwell and
Robert W. Staiger

Is bilateralism bad? This question was the title of Paul Krugman's provocative paper on regionalism (Krugman, 1991a), and the pursuit of an answer has spawned the *regionalism versus multilateralism* debate. The answer to this question turns largely on how one answers the related question posed by Jagdish Bhagwati (Bhagwati, 1991): will regional agreements— or more accurately, *preferential* agreements—undermine the multilateral trading system? On one side of the debate are those who argue that preferential agreements can complement existing multilateral efforts to foster greater economic integration among countries, and should therefore be encouraged. On the other side are those who see such agreements as a threat to the multilateral system.

But what is "the multilateral system" that may or may not be threatened by preferential agreements? Much of the literature treats it as a "black box" synonymous with the goal of "multilateral free trade," and proceeds to ask whether preferential agreements contribute to or interfere with the attainment of this goal. Introductory references are typically made to the GATT/WTO, but the analysis is often carried out with little or no reference to the structure of this multilateral institution. In this chapter we argue that understanding GATT's structure is vital to the debate over regionalism versus multilateralism.

There are three components that together comprise the cornerstones of the GATT system: the principles of *reciprocity* and *non-discrimination*, which are regularly identified as the "pillars" of the GATT architecture, and the *enforcement* mechanisms, which Dam (1970, p. 81) calls the "heart" of the GATT system. Below we describe how preferential agreements may be expected to interact with the multilateral system in light of each of its three principle components.

Originally published in *Economic Journal* 108 (July 1998): 1–21. Reprinted with permission.

We approach the question posed at the outset in two parts. We first ask, will preferential agreements undermine a multilateral trading system that is built on the pillars of reciprocity and non-discrimination? A remaining question is then, how do preferential agreements affect the enforcement provisions of the GATT? To lay the foundation for an answer to the first question, we describe a framework within which the pillars of reciprocity and non-discrimination can themselves be interpreted and understood. From this perspective, we then offer support for the view that preferential agreements pose a threat to the multilateral system. An answer to the second question requires an understanding of how GATT agreements are enforced. Observing that these agreements must be *self-enforcing*, we describe circumstances under which preferential agreements can either enhance or detract from the performance of the GATT system through their impacts on enforcement at the multilateral level.

In order to establish these answers, we must first articulate a theory of the multilateral trading system within which the workings of reciprocity, non-discrimination and enforcement mechanisms can be understood. Any attempt to construct such a theory immediately confronts a most-basic question: Why have governments found reciprocal trade agreements to be appealing? One view is that these agreements provide governments with an escape from a terms-of-trade driven Prisoners' Dilemma. This view has a long history, originating with Torrens (1844), Mill (1844), Scitovsky (1942) and Johnson (1953–4), who posed their arguments in the context of national-income maximising governments that set "optimal tariffs" to exploit monopoly power in world markets.

While the terms-of-trade view is logically correct, many economists are skeptical of its practical relevance: a common position is that these arguments become secondary in explaining the appeal of reciprocal trade agreements once more realistic government objectives that include political concerns are introduced. A popular view is then that governments are attracted to such agreements as a means to achieve political objectives.

To evaluate these two views, we therefore begin in the next section by constructing a general model in which governments are motivated by both political and terms-of-trade considerations. Our framework is sufficiently general to include all the major political economy models of trade policy formulation as special cases. Within this framework, we show that more general government objectives do not change the view that trade agreements provide an escape from a terms-of-trade driven Prisoners' Dilemma, and that this is *all* that trade agreements do. Political forces shape the trade objectives that governments seek to achieve, but political considerations play no role in explaining why governments seek reciprocal trade agreements. Rather, it is the terms-of-trade externality that creates an inefficiency when policies are set unilaterally and that therefore explains why governments need a reciprocal trade agreement in order to accomplish their objectives.[1]

As it turns out, this observation both clarifies the purpose of trade agreements in the leading models of trade policy and, as we will demonstrate, reveals a simple logic to GATT's principles of reciprocity and nondiscrimination. Furthermore, with this theory of the multilateral trading system at hand, we are then able to offer our answers concerning the consequences of preferential trading agreements for the functioning of the multilateral trading system.

24.1   The Purpose of Reciprocal Trade Agreements

We develop here a general model of the trade policy choices of politically motivated governments. Our initial goal is to understand the appeal of reciprocal trade agreements for such governments. We present a full treatment of the issues contained in this and the next section in Bagwell and Staiger (1997a).

24.1.1   The Economic Environment

We first describe the economic environment, which is a standard two-good two-country general equilibrium trade model. A home (no *) and foreign (*) country trade two goods, x and y, which are normal goods in consumption and produced in competitive markets under conditions of increasing opportunity costs. With x (y) the natural import good of the home (foreign) country, define $p = p_x/p_y$ to be the local relative price facing home producers and consumers, and similarly define $p^* = p_x^*/p_y^*$ to be the local relative price facing foreign producers and consumers. Letting τ denote one plus the (non-prohibitive) ad valorem import tariff imposed by the home country, and defining τ^* analogously for the foreign country, it then follows that $p = \tau p^W \equiv p(\tau, p^W)$ and $p^* = p^W/\tau^* \equiv p^*(\tau^*, p^W)$, where $p^W \equiv p_x^*/p_y$ is the "world" (i.e., untaxed) relative price. The home country (foreign country) terms of trade is then given by $1/p^W(p^W)$.

Within each country, local relative prices determine competitive production decisions, which we represent by the domestic and foreign production functions $Q_i = Q_i(p)$ and $Q_i^* = Q_i^*(p^*)$ for $i = \{x, y\}$, respectively. National consumption is determined by the local relative price, which defines the tradeoff faced by consumers and implies the level and distribution of factor income in the economy, and by tariff revenue, which is distributed to consumers lump-sum. In the usual way, tariff revenue can be expressed as a function of local and world prices, so that we may represent national consumption in each country as $C_i(p, p^W)$ and $C_i^*(p^*, p^W)$. Finally, home country imports of x, denoted by $M_x(p(\tau, p^W), p^W)$ are given by the difference between home country consumption and production of x, while home country exports of y, denoted by $E_y(p(\tau, p^W), p^W)$, amount to the difference between home country production and consumption of y. Foreign country imports of y, $M_y^*(p^*(\tau^*, p^W), p^W)$, and exports of x, $E_x^*(p^*(\tau^*, p^W), p^W)$, are similarly defined.

We may now express the trade balance and equilibrium conditions. For any world price, home and foreign budget constraints imply that

$$p^W M_x(p(\tau, p^W), p^W) = E_y(p(\tau, p^W), p^W) \quad \text{and} \qquad (24.1a)$$

$$M_y^*(p^*(\tau^*, p^W), p^W) = p^W E_x^*(p^*(\tau^*, p^W), p^W). \qquad (24.1b)$$

The equilibrium world price, $\tilde{p}^W(\tau, \tau^*)$, is then required to clear the market for good y:

$$E_y(p(\tau, \tilde{p}^W), \tilde{p}^W) = M_y^*(p^*(\tau^*, \tilde{p}^W), \tilde{p}^W), \qquad (24.2)$$

with market clearing for good x then implied by (24.1) and (24.2). Hence, given any pair of non-prohibitive tariffs, the equilibrium world price will be determined through (24.2), and the equilibrium world price and the given tariffs then determine in turn the local prices and thereby production, consumption, import, export and tariff revenue levels. Throughout we assume that the Metzler and Lerner paradoxes are ruled out, so that $dp/d\tau > 0 > dp^*/d\tau^*$ and $\partial \tilde{p}^W/\partial \tau < 0 < \partial \tilde{p}^W/\partial \tau^*$.

24.1.2 Government Objectives

We adopt a representation of government objectives which is general enough to include as special cases national income maximisation as well as each of the major modelling approaches to the political economy of trade policy. The key observation is that politically motivated governments are sensitive to the distributional as well as the efficiency properties of the local price implications of their trade policy choices. We thus represent the objectives of home and foreign governments by the general functions $W(p(\tau, \tilde{p}^W), \tilde{p}^W)$ and $W^*(p^*(\tau^*, \tilde{p}^W), \tilde{p}^W)$, respectively. The only structure we place on these functions is that, holding local prices fixed, each government is assumed to achieve higher welfare when its terms-of-trade improve:

$$\partial W(p,\tilde{p}^W)/\partial\tilde{p}^W < 0 \quad \text{and} \quad \partial W^*(p^*,\tilde{p}^W)/\partial\tilde{p}^W > 0. \tag{24.3}$$

For fixed local prices, an improvement in a country's terms of trade amounts to an income transfer from its trading partner (brought about by an increase in the country's tariff and a corresponding decrease in the tariff of its trading partner). Throughout, we also assume that the second-order conditions associated with the maximisation problems developed below are globally satisfied.

24.1.3 Unilateral Trade Policies

Consider first the unilateral trade policies that governments would choose in the absence of a trade agreement. Supposing that each government would set its trade policy to maximise its objective function taking as given the tariff choices of its trading partner, the associated home and foreign reaction functions are defined implicitly by:

Home: $\quad W_p + \lambda W_{p^W} = 0,$ (24.4a)

Foreign: $\quad W_{p^*}^* + \lambda^* W_{p^W}^* = 0,$ (24.4b)

where subscripts denote partial derivatives, and where $\lambda \equiv (\partial\tilde{p}^W/\partial\tau)/(dp/d\tau) < 0$ and $\lambda^* \equiv (\partial\tilde{p}^W/\partial\tau^*)/(dp^*/d\tau^*) < 0$. As (24.4) illustrates, the best-response tariff of each government is determined by the combined impact on welfare of the induced local and world price movements.

The best-response conditions can be further interpreted with the aid of Fig. 24.1. An initial tariff pair is given by point $A \equiv (\tau,\tau^*)$. Associated with the point A is an iso-local-price locus, denoted as $p(A) \to p(A)$, and an iso-world-price locus, labelled $p^W(A) \to p^W(A)$.[2] If the home government were to raise its tariff unilaterally to τ^1, then a new tariff pair would be induced, represented by the point $C \equiv (\tau^1,\tau^*)$ in Fig. 24.1, and this tariff pair rests on a new iso-local-price locus $(p(C) \to p(C))$ and also a new iso-world-price locus $(p^W(C) \to p^W(C))$. Hence, with a unilateral increase in its tariff, the home government induces a local price that is higher and a world price that is lower as compared to the prices associated with the original point A.

In analogy with (24.4a), Fig. 24.1 can be used to disentangle the overall movement from A to C induced by a unilateral tariff increase by the

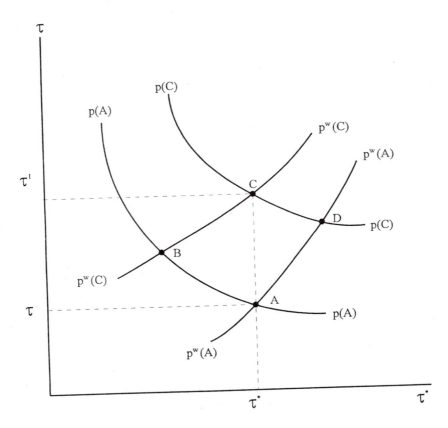

Figure 24.1

domestic government into separate movements in the local and world prices, respectively. The movement from A to B isolates the induced reduction in the world price, and its welfare significance for the domestic government is captured in (24.4a) by the term W_{p^w}. Similarly, the movement from B to C isolates the local price change, and its welfare significance for the domestic government is captured in (24.4a) by the term W_p. The welfare implications of the local-price change implied by the movement from B to C reflect a weighing of the costs of the associated domestic distortions in production and consumption against any domestic distributional benefits. The welfare implications of the change in the world-price implied by the movement from A to B, in contrast, reflect the benefits accruing to the domestic government as it shifts the costs of its policy onto the foreign government through a terms-of-trade improvement. It follows that, if the home government seeks to implement a local price corresponding with the iso-local-price locus $p(C) \to p(C)$, then a unilateral increase in the domestic import tariff will shift a portion of the costs of achieving this policy goal onto the foreign government. A similar interpretation holds for (24.4b).

A tariff pair that simultaneously satisfies (24.4a) and (24.4b) constitutes a Nash equilibrium of the game that arises when both governments set tariffs unilaterally. We will assume that such a tariff pair, which we take to be unique, corresponds to the tariff choices that governments would make in the absence of a trade agreement, and we will denote this tariff pair by (τ^N, τ^{*N}). The next task is to determine whether these tariff choices are inefficient for the governments making them and, if they are, to identify the source of the inefficiency that a trade agreement can correct.

24.1.4   Why Unilateral Trade Policy Choices Are Inefficient

To determine whether the tariff choices made by governments in the absence of a trade agreement are efficient for the governments given their objectives, we need to characterise the set of tariff pairs that lie on the efficiency frontier and ask whether (τ^N, τ^{*N}) is an element of this set. The efficiency frontier can be given the general representation $(d\tau/d\tau^*)|_{dW=0} = (d\tau/d\tau^*)|_{dW^*=0}$, but it can also be represented more concretely as the set of tariffs that satisfy:

$$(1 - AW_p)(1 - A^* W_{p^*}^*) = 1, \tag{24.5}$$

where $A \equiv (1 - \tau\lambda)/(W_p + \lambda W_{pW})$ and $A^* \equiv (1 - \lambda^*/\tau^*)/(W_{p^*}^* + \lambda W_{pW}^*)$, with $A \neq 0$ and $A^* \neq 0$ under the further assumption that the partial derivatives of the welfare functions are always finite.[3]

It is now immediate from a comparison of (24.4) and (24.5) that Nash tariffs are inefficient. This is not surprising since, as we have described above, when governments set their trade policies unilaterally they are motivated to shift costs onto one another through the world-price changes that their tariffs imply. It is perhaps also not surprising that these cost-shifting motives will lead governments to adopt trade policies that are unambiguously too restrictive relative to efficient choices given their objectives: it can be shown that both governments can achieve welfare gains relative to the Nash equilibrium only if each agrees to lower its tariff below the Nash level.[4]

What is perhaps more surprising is that this terms-of-trade externality is the *only* inefficiency that a trade agreement can remedy, despite the fact that we have allowed governments to have political motivations of a quite general nature. To establish this, we consider a hypothetical world in which governments are not motivated by the terms-of-trade consequences of their trade policies. To this end, we define *politically optimal tariffs* as any tariff pair (τ^{PO}, τ^{*PO}) satisfying the following two conditions:

Home: $W_p = 0$ (24.6a)

Foreign: $W_{p^*}^* = 0.$ (24.6b)

We assume that a unique set of politically optimal tariffs exists and that the associated second-order conditions are globally satisfied.

When governments set politically optimal tariffs, it is as if they ignore any welfare gains attributable to changes in the world price that would be induced by their tariff choices. If both governments sought to maximise national income, politically optimal tariffs would correspond to reciprocal free trade. More generally, however, government objectives may reflect political considerations as well, and in this case there is no presumption that politically optimal tariffs will correspond to free trade.

It can now be seen that politically optimal tariffs are efficient, as tariffs that satisfy (24.6) will lie along the efficiency locus defined by (24.5). As a consequence, once the terms-of-trade motivations are eliminated from the trade-policy choices of governments, there is no further scope for Pareto improving changes in trade policy. To gain intuition for this finding, suppose that tariffs have been set at their politically optimal levels, so that the terms-of-trade motivations have been removed from trade-policy choices and each government has set its trade policy so as to achieve its preferred local prices. Consider now a small increase in the tariff of the domestic country. This change has three effects. First, it induces a small increase in the local price in the domestic economy, but this has no first-order effect on domestic government welfare as domestic local prices were already at their preferred level. Second, the domestic tariff increase induces a small reduction in the local price of the foreign country, but this has no first-order effect on the welfare of the foreign government since it too has already achieved its preferred local prices. Finally, the domestic tariff increase causes the world price to fall, but this cannot generate an efficiency gain as it represents a pure international transfer of tariff revenue. Hence, once the terms-of-trade motivations have been removed from trade-policy choices, there are no further Pareto gains for governments to achieve.

Fig. 24.1 illustrates the essential inefficiency that prevents governments from reaching the efficiency frontier with unilateral trade policy decisions. We suppose again that, beginning at point A, the home government considers a unilateral tariff increase to achieve the local price associated with point C. If the government allows the terms-of-trade consequences (i.e., the movement from D to C) of its tariff selection to influence its decision concerning whether to proceed with this tariff increase, then it will recognise that some of the costs of achieving the higher local price at C can be shifted onto its trading partner as a result of the reduced world price, and the tariff increase will look especially attractive. As a consequence, Nash tariffs are always inefficient, leading to tariffs (trade volumes) that are too high (low). Alternatively, if the government were not permitted to let the terms-of-trade consequences of its tariff selection influence its decision of whether or not to proceed with the tariff increase, then it would prefer choosing the higher tariff to induce point C if and only if it also prefers point D to point A. In this case, the potential appeal of point C to the home government is independent of any cost-shifting benefits that may arise with the consequent change in the world price, and so it has the "right" incentives when deciding whether to proceed with a tariff increase.[5] If each government were to choose tariffs in this way, then a resulting set of consistent tariffs is politically optimal and efficient.

The findings described here can be summarised with the aid of Fig. 24.2, which depicts the locus of efficient tariff pairs by the curve $E \rightarrow E$, the politically optimal tariffs by the point on the efficiency locus labeled PO, and the Nash tariffs by the point labelled N positioned to the northeast of the efficiency locus.[6] Notice that the iso-welfare curves of the two governments are tangent at every point along the efficiency locus, including the political optimum. The novel feature of the politically optimal tariffs is that the iso-welfare curves at these tariffs are also tangent to the iso-world-price locus (the locus labelled p_{PO}^W). The bold portion of the efficiency locus corresponds to the contract curve.

Fig. 24.2 clarifies the central task that governments face when they design a trade agreement. Without cooperation, governments would set trade policy unilaterally, leading to the Nash outcome N. A trade agreement can then offer governments a means to cooperate and move from the inefficient Nash point to some alternative tariff pair that rests on the contract curve. Among the points on the contract curve, the politically optimal tariffs are focal, as they remedy in a direct fashion the terms-of-trade inefficiency that keeps governments from reaching the contract

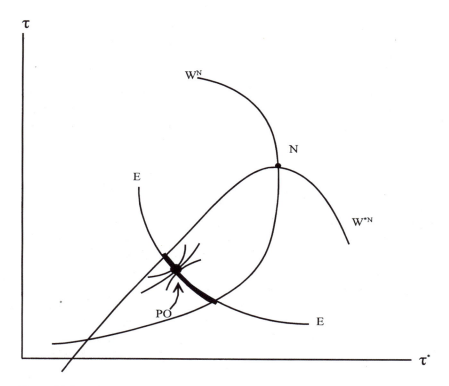

Figure 24.2

curve with their unilateral choices. As Fig. 24.2 makes clear, when governments have political objectives the efficiency locus need not pass through
the point of reciprocal free trade. But while political concerns will effect
government preferences over tariffs (e.g., the location of the efficiency
locus), it is the terms-of-trade externality that creates a "problem" with
unilateral tariff choices which an appropriately designed trade agreement
can "solve."[7]

24.2 Reciprocity, Non-discrimination and Preferential Agreements

With the basic framework now described, we are prepared to consider the
principles of reciprocity and non-discrimination, and how preferential
agreements will affect a multilateral trading system built on these two
pillars.

24.2.1 The Meaning of Reciprocity

Within GATT, the term "reciprocity" refers broadly to the ideal of mutual changes in trade policy that bring about equal changes in import volumes across trading partners.[8] Using the model presented above, we may define reciprocity more formally as follows: a set of tariff changes $\Delta\tau \equiv (\tau^1 - \tau^0)$ and $\Delta\tau^* \equiv (\tau^{*1} - \tau^{*0})$ conforms to *the principle of reciprocity* provided that

$$\tilde{p}^{W0}[M_x(p(\tau^1, \tilde{p}^{W1}), \tilde{p}^{W1}) - M_x(p(\tau^0, \tilde{p}^{W0}), \tilde{p}^{W0})]$$
$$= [M_y^*(p^*(\tau^{*1}, \tilde{p}^{W1}), \tilde{p}^{W1}) - M_y^*(p^*(\tau^{*0}, \tilde{p}^{W0}), \tilde{p}^{W0})]$$

where $\tilde{p}^{W0} \equiv \tilde{p}^W(\tau^0, \tau^{*0})$, $\tilde{p}^{W1} \equiv \tilde{p}^{W1}(\tau^1, \tau^{*1})$, and where we have measured changes in import volumes at existing world prices. Using the trade balance condition (24.1) and the equilibrium condition (24.2), this expression may be rewritten as

$$[\tilde{p}^{W1} - \tilde{p}^{W0}]M_x(p(\tau^1, \tilde{p}^{W1}), \tilde{p}^{W1}) = 0. \tag{24.7}$$

Hence, as (24.7) makes clear, mutual tariff changes that conform to reciprocity leave world prices unchanged. The potential significance of this property can be appreciated when viewed from the perspective of the finding, reported above, that a government's tariff choice will be inefficient if and only if it is motivated by the *change* in the world price that its tariff choice implies.

24.2.2 The Practice of Reciprocity in GATT

Having now defined the general meaning of the principle of reciprocity, we turn to the application of this principle within GATT practice. To understand the importance of the principle of reciprocity in GATT, it is useful to distinguish between two broad circumstances in which reciprocity applies. A first circumstance is when governments seek greater access to the markets of their trading partners, and engage in a "round" of negotiations under GATT's Article XXVIII bis. In the context of these negotiations, opening one's own market is deemed a "concession." In this circumstance, the principle of reciprocity reflects the "balance of concessions" that governments seek through a negotiated agreement. This practice is described by Dam (1970, p. 59), who explains that, under the language of Article XXVIII bis, negotiations are voluntary and are to be conducted in a "reciprocal and mutually advantageous basis." Dam (1970, p. 59) explains further that:

This permissive approach to the content of tariff agreements is often referred to under the heading of *reciprocity*. From the legal principle that a country need make concessions only when other contracting parties offer reciprocal concessions considered to be "mutually advantageous" has been derived the informal principle that exchanges of concessions must entail reciprocity.

The emphasis that governments place on reciprocity in this sense stands in contrast to standard economic logic, which holds that optimal unilateral policy for a country is free trade. From this perspective, it is perplexing that a government would require a "concession" from its trading partner in order to do what is in any event best for its country. Appealing to this apparent violation of economic logic, it is tempting to interpret the observation that governments seek reciprocity in negotiated agreements as direct evidence that government negotiators adopt a mercantilist perspective that is incompatible with basic economic reasoning and that therefore derives from underlying political forces.[9]

Here we simply note that the mercantilist logic that drives actual trade negotiations admits a simple economic interpretation within the framework developed in the preceding section. In particular, the nature of the terms-of-trade externality described above ensures that, in the absence of a trade agreement (i.e., at the Nash point), each government would prefer to reduce its tariff and induce lower import-competing prices and greater imports *if the increased trade volume could be obtained without a deterioration in the terms of trade* (see (24.4)).[10] Acting unilaterally, a government cannot achieve this. But by balancing one country's "concessions" against another's, this is precisely what liberalisation conforming to the principle of reciprocity will deliver.

While reciprocity in this circumstance reflects the broad manner in which governments appear to approach rounds of trade negotiations under Article XXVIII bis, there is in fact no requirement in GATT that negotiations proceed in this manner. There is, however, a second broad circumstance in which the principle of reciprocity applies in GATT practice, and in this case GATT rules do require reciprocity. Here we refer to the circumstance in which a government wishes to reduce foreign access to its markets below a previously negotiated level. An important mechanism through which GATT provides for this possibility is contained in Article XXVIII.[11] Under this article, a country may at any time propose to modify or withdraw a concession agreed upon in a previous round of negotiation. In this circumstance, if the country and its trading partner cannot agree on a renegotiated tariff structure, then the country is free to carry out the proposed changes to its tariffs, and the notion of reciprocity is then invoked to moderate the allowable response of the country's trading partner, who is permitted to withdraw *substantially equivalent concessions* of its own.

This suggests that GATT negotiations may be understood as a multistage game, in which governments first agree to an initial set of tariffs, and then each government considers whether to propose a more restrictive tariff knowing that, under GATT's reciprocity rules, its trading partner can do no more than respond with reciprocal withdrawals of concessions which preserve the world price implied by the original agreement. Viewed from this perspective, it is clear that when governments evaluate the desirability of a proposed initial agreement, they must take account of any future incentives to renegotiate the agreement under GATT's reciprocity rules. But it should now also be clear that an initial agreement will be renegotiated if either government decides that the protection from imports provided under the agreement is inadequate at the existing world price. The implications of this observation can be illustrated with the help of a figure.

Consider then Fig. 24.3, which depicts three possible tariff pairs that might represent an initial agreement. We represent these tariff pairs by the points A, B, and PO. Each tariff pair is efficient (all three points lie on the efficiency locus), but the political optimum point PO is distinguished from the others by the fact that the iso-world-price locus running through PO is tangent to the iso-welfare contours of each government at this point.

Consider first an initial agreement that corresponds to point A. Observe that in this case the foreign government would request a renegotiation to raise its tariff and further restrict imports knowing that, under GATT's reciprocity rules, the domestic government would then withdraw a substantially equivalent concession that would preserve the world price and therefore deliver the tariff pair at point A'. Thus, while the tariff pair at point A is efficient, it is not robust to the type of renegotiation that GATT allows through Article XXVIII. A similar argument applies to the efficient tariff pair at point B, except that the roles of the foreign and domestic government are now switched. In fact, there is only one efficient tariff pair which, if agreed to originally, would not be lost in the renegotiation process. This tariff pair is the politically optimal tariff pair, since this is the only point on the efficiency locus at which each government achieves its preferred local prices given the associated world price.

This suggests that the principle of reciprocity can be viewed as a mechanism by which governments are guided in GATT negotiations to

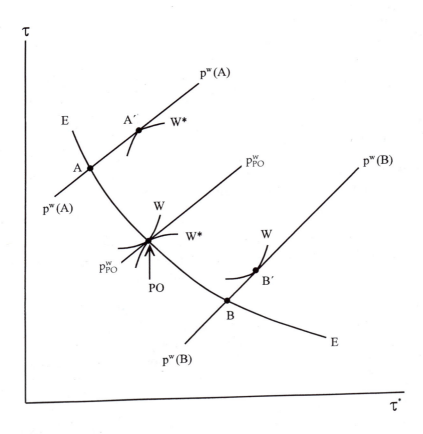

Figure 24.3

efficient politically optimal outcomes.[12] There is a certain appeal to this finding, since the politically optimal tariffs are also those tariffs which arise when the source of the inefficiency—government's motivations to influence the terms of trade—is eliminated.

24.2.3 The Importance of MFN

If the principle of reciprocity reveals a basic economic logic, can the importance of the principle of non-discrimination in GATT practice be similarly understood? Is there a *reason* for these two principles to coexist in the same multilateral institution? This is a crucial question for the debate over regionalism versus multilateralism, since preferential agreements amount to blatant violations of the principle of non-discrimination. Hence we would like to know whether the ability of reciprocity to implement an efficient trade agreement depends in any fundamental way on the restriction that tariffs conform to MFN. We now confront this question and ask, Can reciprocity implement an efficient multilateral trade agreement that allows for discriminatory tariffs? To address this question, we must extend our two-country model to a many-country framework. This is done in Bagwell and Staiger (1997a), and here we simply provide an intuitive account of the results.

It is perhaps easiest to begin by imagining a multi-country world in which all tariffs conform to MFN, and consider whether reciprocity can still deliver an efficient agreement in this environment. The key observation is that, by requiring that a government levy the same tariff on imports of a good regardless of the identity of the source (i.e., exporting) country, the principle of non-discrimination preserves the simple pattern of externalities found in the two-country setting depicted above. That is, with all tariffs conforming to MFN, a common world price will prevail, and externalities continue to pass through this world price. As a consequence, reciprocity, by neutralising the world price implications of a government's tariff decisions, can guide governments to efficient politically optimal outcomes when their tariffs are non-discriminatory.

Now consider a world in which tariffs are discriminatory. If a country imports the same good from several sources and its government applies different tariff rates to imports from each source, then all else equal it would prefer to import relatively more of the good from the country to which it applies a higher tariff owing to the lower associated world (i.e., export) price and the greater associated tariff revenue. But this implies that the pattern of externalities is now more complicated, as the government's interest in the pattern of bilateral imports from its trading partners provides a reason for concern over both world prices *and* the local prices in the markets of its trading partners (since these determine the relative shares of the import good coming from each supplying country). As a consequence, reciprocity, which serves well to neutralise externalities which travel through the world price but which is ill-equipped to handle the local-price externalities that are created when tariffs are discriminatory, fails to deliver an efficient trade agreement in this environment.

These arguments suggest a fundamental efficiency link between the principles of reciprocity and non-discrimination. Reciprocity serves to neutralize the world-price effects of a country's trade policy decisions. Provided that the externalities associated with trade intervention travel through the world price, reciprocity therefore works well as a principle with which to undo the terms-of-trade driven restrictions in trade and achieve efficient trade volumes. The principle of non-discrimination thus complements reciprocity, since it ensures that all externalities indeed are channelled through the world price.

24.2.4 Why Preferential Agreements May Undermine GATT

Having identified a basic economic logic to GATT's principle of reciprocity and an efficiency link between reciprocity and the principle of non-discrimination, we turn next to consider how preferential agreements will affect a multilateral trading system built on these two pillars. GATT's Article XXIV permits preferential agreements, provided that member countries eliminate tariffs on substantially all trade between them in a reasonable period of time. This exception to the principle of non-discrimination was controversial in its inception and has met with renewed controversy recently as many GATT members—but most especially the United States —have increasingly exercised their rights under this article to negotiate preferential trading agreements. These agreements may take either of two forms. When countries form a *free trade area*, they eliminate barriers to internal trade but maintain independent external trade policies. Under a *customs union*, member-countries also agree to harmonise their external trade policies and create a common external-tariff-setting authority.

We start with free trade areas. An immediate implication of the preceding discussion is that an efficient set of tariffs cannot be implemented under reciprocity when a free trade agreement is present. Intuitively, a free trade agreement violates MFN, and as a consequence externalities travel through both local and world prices in its presence. In this environment, as we have seen, reciprocity cannot serve to implement an efficient trade agreement. The broader implication is that the efficiency properties of a multilateral trading system founded on the principles of reciprocity and non-discrimination will be undermined when exceptions from MFN are granted for the formation of free trade areas.

Consider next the implications of customs unions for the multilateral trading system. We cannot immediately conclude from the above discussion that the introduction of a customs union is incompatible with the pursuit of an efficient set of multilateral tariffs through reciprocity. This is because the formation of a customs union creates a new environment in which, while there is now tariff discrimination, there are also fewer external-tariff-setting authorities operating, and thus it does not immediately follow from our earlier discussion that the presence of tariff discrimination will again undermine the efficiency properties of reciprocity. Nevertheless, the arguments above provide the essential intuition, once it is noted that a customs union will be analogous to a single country so long as the countries that form the union are similar in an appropriate sense. This would imply that the principle of reciprocity can then deliver an efficient agreement in the presence of a customs union between such countries so long as all *external* tariffs continue to conform to the principle of non-discrimination.

The required similarity among customs-union members that permits this result is that member-countries must share similar political goals so that the elimination of tariffs between them is internally efficient. When this relationship fails, customs unions will be like free trade areas, and it will be impossible to implement efficient tariffs under reciprocity when either type of preferential agreement is present.

More generally, we have identified a basic tension between a multilateral system built on the principle of reciprocity and the formation of preferential trading arrangements. We have shown that there is a logic to the principle of reciprocity when it is combined with the principle of non-discrimination, in the sense that the former principle serves well to deliver efficient tariffs provided that tariffs also satisfy MFN. When preferential agreements are introduced, tariffs no longer satisfy MFN, and the presumption that a multilateral system based on reciprocity will deliver an efficient outcome is severely undermined.

24.3   Preferential Agreements and Enforcing Multilateral Commitments

Up to this point we have compared non-cooperative outcomes with efficient trading arrangements, finding that the difference is entirely attributable to terms-of-trade externalities and that the principles of reciprocity and non-discrimination can serve to implement an efficient arrangement. We have abstracted, however, from the way in which such arrangements might be enforced. We now turn to issues of enforcement, and consider how preferential agreements can affect the ability to enforce trade commitments at the multilateral level.

24.3.1   The Problem of Enforcement

As there is no "world jail," an international agreement must be self-enforcing if it is to be credible (see, for example, Dam, 1970), and an agreement to open markets is in turn self-enforcing only if it also specifies credible retaliatory measures against any country that places additional restraints on trade in a way that violates the agreement. In this light, GATT can be seen as an agreement that specifies cooperative trade policies and acceptable retaliatory measures, with the maintenance of the former resting on the strength of the latter. Starting from this vantage point, the task of enforcing a reciprocal trade agreement amounts to maintaining a balance between (i). the short-term temptation to deviate unilaterally from an agreed-upon trade policy and enjoy the corresponding terms-of-trade benefits, and (ii). the long-term penalty of a consequent future loss of cooperation (i.e., the cost of a future retaliatory "trade war").[13] Viewed in this way, it is evident that any event that alters the current temptation to cheat or the value of maintaining cooperation into the future can upset this balance, and thus that the enforceable level of cooperation may fluctuate with underlying market conditions.

A preferential agreement introduces one possible source of "imbalance," and raises the question of whether such agreements might affect the level of multilateral cooperation that can be enforced. Various implications of preferential agreements for the ability to enforce multilateral commitments have been explored in a number of papers, including Bagwell and Staiger (1997*b*, *c* and 1998), Bond and Syropoulos (1996), and Bond et al. (1996). Here we review a number of the themes from this literature.

24.3.2   Transition Effects

Preferential agreements are typically formed over a lengthy *transition period* during which the trade policy changes associated with the agreement are being phased in, and so we begin by asking how emerging preferential agreements may affect the ability to enforce multilateral cooperation during this period of transition.[14] Our interest in this question is due in part to historical and current experiences with regard to preferential agreements and multilateral tariff cooperation. Beginning in 1957, the EC customs union was formed over a twelve year phase-in period, and it underwent a period of major expansion to include Great Britain, Denmark and Ireland beginning in 1972. These episodes of customs union formation and enlargement corresponded with periods of enhanced multilateral tariff cooperation and, as a recent WTO report concludes (WTO, 1995b, pp. 53–4), were factors behind the launching of the GATT Dillon Round (1960–2), Kennedy Round (1964–7) and Tokyo Round (1973–9) of multilateral negotiations. More recently, important preferential agreements include the 1988 U.S.-Canada free trade agreement and its expansion to include Mexico in the NAFTA. The implementation of these agreements, by contrast, appears to have taken place against a backdrop of strained multilateral relations in which preferential initiatives are viewed as a potential threat to the GATT system.[15]

In Bagwell and Staiger (1997b, c), we present formal models broadly consistent with these observations. To interpret the findings of these papers, we note that there are two principal effects of preferential agreements that are crucial in determining how they will affect enforcement at the multilateral level: a *trade diversion effect*, under which trade volumes among member countries increase at the expense of trade between member and non-member countries; and a *market power effect*, which occurs if the member countries form a customs union and adopt a common external tariff policy that enables them to impose higher tariffs on their multilateral trading partners should such punitive tariff action be desired.

Consider first the transition to a free trade area. The main ideas can be understood in terms of a three-country setting. Once countries A and B become firmly engaged in the lengthy transition process that will culminate in a free trade area, country C faces the prospect that it is currently trading more extensively with country A than it is likely to in the future, since more of country A's future trade will be diverted to its free trade partner once the free trade agreement is fully implemented. Thus, while country C's current temptation to exploit its power over the terms of trade with country A is largely unaffected, owing to its as yet undiminished current trade volume with country A, country C is no longer as fearful of a future trade war with country A, since it expects that it will in any case trade less with country A in the future. Incentives are thus temporarily thrown out of balance as the transition to a free trade area between countries A and B begins, and as a result the trade policies that countries A and C can enforce will be less cooperative during the associated transition phase. It follows that the transition to a free trade area will bring about a period of temporarily heightened multilateral trade tensions in which trade disputes proliferate and further efforts to reduce multilateral tariffs become temporarily stalled. These predictions seem broadly compatible with recent experiences.

On the other hand, when countries A and B are in the lengthy transition process that will culminate in a customs union, country C is faced with the emergence of a new 'market power' effect. Intuitively, when a customs union is formed, its common external tariffs enable it to exert greater power over the terms of trade. As a consequence the union will find high import tariffs more tempting than do its individual member countries prior to uniting. This suggests that a trade war initiated in the transition phase might have heightened negative consequences for country C once the union is formed, as countries A and B will retaliate even more aggressively once they select a common tariff. Accordingly, country C's current temptation to cheat in the transition phase is now more than outweighed by its fear of the retaliation that a customs union could later mete out. Country C's incentives are again temporarily out of balance, but in this case it will tolerate even more liberal multilateral tariffs before the difficulty of enforcement again begins to bind. In this way, the transition to a customs union involves a period of improved multilateral tariff cooperation, much as historical experience suggests.

24.3.3   Steady State Effects

Finally, in a more recent paper (Bagwell and Staiger, 1998), we ignore the transitional effects of preferential agreements and consider instead a three-country world in which two countries are better at cooperating than is the third. In particular, we assume that countries A and B are more patient, and are thus better able to enforce liberal trading policies, than is country C. Within this setting, we compare two trading regimes.

Consider first the case in which countries are constrained to adopt MFN tariffs. Countries A and B then cooperate best by acting as "hegemons," extending tariff cuts to country C that exceed the cuts that country C offers in return. The impatient country is therefore "pooled in" with the patient countries under MFN, and it gets to free ride on their liberalisation efforts.

Consider next a second regime, in which countries A and B form a preferential agreement, enabling them to offer a tariff to country C that differs from the zero tariff that they extend to one another. With the ability to discriminate, the patient countries need no longer cooperate multilaterally to cooperate bilaterally, and so the impatient country loses its free rider benefits.

The discriminatory tariff that is offered to country C in this second trading regime will often exceed the tariff it would face were the preferential agreement not allowed, and this leads to an overall deterioration in multilateral tariff cooperation once the preferential agreement is formed. However, the opposite can also occur, as it is possible that the discriminatory tariff offered to country C falls with the introduction of the preferential agreement between countries A and B. Which outcome occurs, and hence whether preferential agreements act as "stumbling blocs" or "building blocs" for multilateral tariff cooperation, depends in this setting on how close the multilateral system can get to an efficient trade agreement in the absence of tariff discrimination, which depends in turn on how patient the two "hegemons" are. Weighing these factors, we find that preferential agreements can facilitate multilateral liberalisation, and that they have their most desirable effects on the multilateral system precisely when multilateral enforcement mechanisms are ineffective and the multilateral system is working poorly.

24.4   Is Bilateralism Bad?

We have argued that the multilateral trading system can be understood as a cooperative arrangement among governments that is designed to eliminate the inefficient trade restrictions that are associated with governments' ability to manipulate the terms of trade. In the absence of enforcement difficulties, we find that GATT's principles of reciprocity and non-discrimination can work in tandem to implement an efficient outcome. As a corollary, we find that reciprocity cannot serve to implement an efficient agreement in the presence of free trade areas. An efficient agreement can be implemented under reciprocity in the presence of a customs union, but only if the union members have similar political preferences. These conditions are quite stringent, and so we offer little support for the hypothesis that reciprocity can deliver an efficient multilateral trade agreement in the presence of preferential trade agreements. Instead our results offer support for the view that preferential agreements pose a threat to the existing multilateral system.

Enforcement concerns, however, should not be ignored, as the threat of future retaliation may not be sufficient to deliver a fully efficient multilateral agreement. Consequently, significant changes in the trading environment, such as occur when major preferential integration initiatives are undertaken, can have an impact on the level of multilateral cooperation that can be enforced. This impact will depend critically on the period of analysis, i.e., transition or steady state, on the form that the preferential agreement takes, i.e., free trade agreement or customs union, and on the strength of the multilateral enforcement mechanism. Nevertheless, these results serve to qualify the more negative view of preferential agreements that obtains in the absence of serious limitations to the multilateral enforcement mechanisms, and the implied qualifications achieve their greatest force when multilateral enforcement mechanisms are at their weakest.

Finally, as to the question we posed at the outset, our results suggest that the efficiency of the multilateral trading system will be compromised by the creation of preferential agreements unless multilateral enforcement mechanisms are sufficiently weak. In this light, further strengthening of the enforcement mechanisms of the GATT/WTO will undercut the case for preferential agreements.

Notes

This chapter was completed while Staiger was a Fellow at the Center for Advanced Study in the Behavioral Sciences. Staiger is also grateful for financial support provided by The National Science Foundation Grant # SBR-9022192.

1. Political considerations might provide a separate motivation for reciprocal trade agreements if governments seek such agreements to gain commitment relative to their private sectors, a possibility explored by Maggi and Rodriguez-Clave (forthcoming) and Staiger (1995). It has not yet been demonstrated, however, whether this hypothesis could account for the principles of reciprocity and non-discrimination that form the pillars of GATT.

2. Absent the Metzler and Lerner paradoxes, the iso-local-price locus is negatively sloped while the iso-world-price locus has positive slope.

3. If governments maximise national income, the efficiency locus reduces to the form $\tau = 1/\tau^*$, as Mayer (1981) demonstrates. In this case, tariffs are adjusted along the efficiency locus so as to maintain equality in relative local prices between the domestic and foreign countries, with different tariff pairs along the efficiency locus reflecting different world prices and therefore different distributions of income across trading partners. In the more general representation of government preferences considered here, the efficiency locus still determines a relationship between domestic and foreign tariffs, but it need no longer be the case that this relationship equates relative local prices across trading partners.

4. A reduction in tarrifs from the Nash level, however, is not sufficient to guarantee mutual welfare gains. For example, as Johnson (1953–4) and Kennan and Riezman (1988) demonstrate, a large country may be worse off under reciprocal free trade than in the Nash equilibrium if countries are asymmetric.

5. The movement from point A to point D in Fig. 24.1 induces no externality through the terms-of trade but it does alter the foreign local price. If the foreign government also selects tariffs that are politically optimal, however, then a small change in the foreign local price will have no first-order effect on foreign government welfare.

6. We draw this picture under the assumptions that a unique Nash equilibrium exists, a unique political optimum exists, and that the political optimum lies on the contract curve (i.e., it is on the efficiency locus and yields greater-than-Nash welfare for each government). The last assumption is new to our discussion, and it will be satisfied if countries are sufficiently symmetric.

7. The degree to which countries are able to affect their terms of trade significantly is an issue of some debate. We note the following points of support. First, at the level of theory,

even ostensibly small countries have some power over their terms of trade, if the industry is monopolistically competitive (Gros, 1987). Second, our theory does not require that all countries have the ability to alter world prices, but it does imply that only those countries that can alter world prices will be actively involved in reciprocal tariff negotiations, an implication that is consistent with the 'principle supplier' rules of GATT negotiations (see Bagwell and Staiger, 1996). Third, with regard to empirical evidence, a large literature documents imperfect 'pass-through' in the face of exchange rate shocks. If symmetric empirical patterns arise when the cost increase is associated with a tariff increase, then the finding of imperfect pass-through would offer evidence of a reduction in the world price, i.e., a terms-of-trade externality. Feenstra (1989) provides empirical support for the symmetric pass-through hypothesis. Finally, we note that empirical studies of trade policy confirm that the potential world-price implications of alternative trade policy choices can have important effects on the national desirability of intervention (see, for example, the discussion in Feenstra, 1995, p. 1579).

8. The meaning of reciprocity in GATT, and the various ways in which reciprocity has been implemented in practice, is discussed in Dam (1970, pp. 58–61 and pp. 87–91), and WTO (1995a, p. 949).

9. Many have expressed this view. Krugman (1991b, 1997) provides an especially clear articulation of this position.

10. This follows from (24.3) and (24.4a) which indicate that $W_p < 0$ along the domestic government's reaction curve. A similar observation holds for the foreign government.

11. For further discussion of Article XXVIII and its importance in GATT practice, see Dam (1970, pp. 79–99), Jackson (1989, p. 119) and Enders (1997). Provisions for temporary suspension of GATT obligations are provided in Article XIX, where similar reciprocity rules apply.

12. Actually, we establish in Bagwell and Staiger (1997a) that governments will indeed negotiate to politically optimal outcomes in this setting unless sufficient asymmetries are present.

13. We draw a distinction between *unilateral deviations* from an agreed-upon trade policy and the lawful *withdrawal or modification of a previously negotiated concession* under Article XXVIII. The former may go undetected for some time but, once observed by trading partners, would trigger a retaliatory "trade war." The latter must be pre-announced to trading partners who are then free to simultaneously withdraw substantially equivalent concessions under the procedures of Article XXVIII described in Section 24.2.2 above.

14. GATT's Article XXIV acknowledges the practical need for "interim agreements" to facilitate the process of preferential integration, and only requires that the transition to a completed free trade area or customs union be accomplished "within a reasonable length of time."

15. According to the WTO report, existing preferential agreements were a less significant factor in the 1986 launching of the Uruguay Round of GATT negotiations, because "... at the time, regional integration was still confined mainly to Western Europe, with the United States maintaining its traditional multilateralism" (WTO, 1995b, p. 54). Nevertheless, while the failure of these negotiations to conclude at the Brussels Ministerial in December 1990 reflected the strained multilateral relations of the time, this failure together with the subsequent increase in new preferential initiatives after 1990 were "... major factors in eliciting the concessions needed to conclude the Uruguay Round" in 1994 (WTO, 1995b, p. 54), as they raised the specter that a failed Uruguay Round would lead to a world in which future trade and economic relations would be based primarily upon preferential agreements.

References

Bagwell, Kyle, and Staiger, Robert W. (1996). "Reciprocal trade liberalization," NBER Working Paper no. 5488, March.

Bagwell, Kyle, and Staiger, Robert W. (1997a). "An economic theory of GATT," NBER Working Paper no. 6049, May.

Bagwell, Kyle, and Staiger, Robert W. (1997b). "Multilateral tariff cooperation during the formation of customs unions," *Journal of International Economics*, February.

Bagwell, Kyle, and Staiger, Robert W. (1997c). "Multilateral tariff cooperation during the formation of free trade areas," *International Economic Review*, May.

Bagwell, Kyle, and Staiger, Robert W. (1998). "Regionalism and multilateral tariff cooperation," in (John Piggott and Alan Woodland, eds.), *International Trade Policy and the Pacific Rim*, London: Macmillan.

Baldwin, Richard, (1987). "Politically realistic objective functions and trade policy," *Economic Letters*, vol. 24.

Bhagwati, Jagdish, (1991). *The World Trading System at Risk*. Princeton, New Jersey: Princeton University Press.

Bond, Eric W., and Syropoulos, Costas (1996). "Trading blocs and the sustainability of interregional cooperation." in M. Canzoneri, W. Ethier, and V. Grilli, (eds.) *The New Transatlantic Economy*, Cambridge: Cambridge University Press.

Bond, Eric W., Syropoulos, Costas and Winters, Alan A., (1996). "Deepening of regional integration and external trade relations," CEPR Discussion Paper No. 1317.

Dam, Kenneth W., (1970). *The GATT: Law and International Economic Organization*, Chicago: University of Chicago Press.

Enders, Alice, (1997). 'The origin, nature and limitations of reciprocity in GATT 1947,' mimeo. (WTO, Geneva: October 1997).

Feenstra, Robert C., (1989). "Symmetric pass-through of tariffs and exchange rates under imperfect competition: an empirical test," *Journal of International Economics*, vol. 27, pp. 25–45.

Feenstra, Robert C., (1995). "Estimating the effects of trade policy," in (Gene M. Grossman and Kenneth Rogoff, eds.) *The Handbook of International Economics*, vol. 3, North Holland.

Gros, D., (1987). "A note on the optimal tariff, retaliation and the welfare loss from tariff wars in a framework with intra-industry trade," *Journal of International Economics*, vol. 23, pp. 357–367.

Jackson, John H., (1989). *The World Trading System*. Cambridge: The MIT Press.

Johnson, Harry G., (1953–4). "Optimum tariffs and retaliation," *Review of Economic Studies*, vol. 21, no. 2.

Kennan, John and Riezman, Raymond (1988). Do big countries win tariff wars? *International Economic Review*, vol. 29, pp. 81–5.

Krugman, Paul R., (1991a). "Is bilateralism bad?" in (Elhanan Helpman and Assaf Razin, eds.) *International Trade and Trade Policy*, Cambridge, MA and London, England. The MIT Press, pp. 9–23.

Krugman, Paul R., (1991*b*). "The move toward free trade zones," in *Policy Implications of Trade and Currency Zones*, A Symposium Sponsored by the Federal Reserve Bank of Kansas City, Jackson Hole, Wyoming, August 22–24.

Krugman, Paul R., (1997). "What should trade negotiators negotiate about?," *Journal of Economic Literature*, vol. 35, March 1997, pp. 113–20.

Maggi, Giovanni, and Rodriguez-Clare, Andres, (1998). "The value of trade agreements in the presence of political pressures." *Journal of Political Economy*, forthcoming.

Mayer, Wolfgang, (1981). "Theoretical considerations on negotiated tariff adjustments," *Oxford Economic Papers*, vol. 33, pp. 135–53.

Mill, John Stewart, (1844). *Essays on Some Unsettled Questions of Political Economy*, London: Parker.

Scitovszky, Tibor, (1942). "A reconsideration of the theory of tariffs," *Review of Economic Studies*, vol. 9.

Staiger, Robert W., (1995). "International rules and institutions for trade policy," in Gene M. Grossman and Kenneth Rogof, eds.) *The Handbook of International Economics*, vol. 3, North Holland.

Torrens, Robert, (1844). *The Budget: On Commercial and Colonial Policy*. London: Smith, Elder, 1844.

WTO (1995a). *Analytical Index: Guide to GATT Law and Practice*, vol. 2. (WTO, Geneva: 1995).

WTO, (1995b). *Regionalism and the World Trading System*. (WTO, Geneva: April 1995).

25

Regionalism and the (Dis)advantage of Dispute-Settlement Access

Philip I. Levy and
T. N. Srinivasan

The Uruguay Round (UR) of multilateral trade negotiations (MTN), the most ambitious of all such rounds initiated by the General Agreement on Tariffs and Trade (GATT), was successfully concluded after nearly eight long and frustrating years with the signing of its Final Act in April, 1994. As of the end of October 1995, 110 countries had formally become members of the World Trade Organization (WTO), and several others, including China and Russia, are negotiating entry.

The UR negotiations came to a virtual breakdown several times during the eight years. At its midterm review in December 1988, the prospects for the round even to conclude successfully, let alone on schedule in 1990, did not appear bright. The fear that the negotiations might fail and the world collapse into warring trade blocs was a significant reason for the revived enthusiasm in the late 1980's for regional trading arrangements (RTA's), particularly among small nations who were afraid of being marginalized and squeezed out of their traditional export markets.

Surprisingly, after the successful conclusion of the negotiations the enthusiasm for RTA's did not wane, but rather waxed. New free-trade areas (FTA's) have been proposed, such as one encompassing the European Union and NAFTA (the North American Free Trade Agreement), one for the Western Hemisphere, and one for the Asia-Pacific region.

The recent RTA's are qualitatively different from earlier ones that failed (with the exception of the European Community and European FTA). They envisage "deep integration" that involves coordination at a minimum, and complete harmonization at a maximum, of domestic institutions and policies that influence international competition.

Where the proliferation of RTA's will lead is a contentious analytical, empirical, and policy issue. Some economists, notably Lawrence Summers

Originally published in *American Economic Review*, Papers and Proceedings 86, no. 2 (May 1996): 93–98. Reprinted with permission.

(1991), view any and all liberalization of trade, whether unilateral, bilateral, plurilateral, or multilateral, as worthy of support. This school of thought considers such "trade agreements stepping stones to global free trade ... [embodying] principles of openness and inclusion consistent with the GATT" (Council of Economic Advisers, 1995 p. 215). Many other economists, with Jagdish Bhagwati (1993) notable among them, see the proliferation of RTA's as a threat to a liberal world trading system. These critics argue that RTA's "are a particularly damaging institutional arrangement to legitimate in the world trading system when the WTO has been jumpstarted and can be used to proceed with nondiscriminatory, multilateral trade liberalization through fresh rounds of MTN" (Bhagwati and Arvind Panagariya, 1995 p. 41). There is a substantial and growing literature on RTA's that addresses these issues (Kym Anderson and Richard Blackhurst, 1993; Jaime de Melo and Panagariya, 1993; Philip Levy, 1994; Bhagwati and Anne O. Krueger, 1995).

In this chapter we focus on one particular feature that distinguishes regional trading arrangements from the multilateral trading system: the difference in private parties' access to the arrangements' dispute-settlement mechanisms. Unions, business groups, and activists do not have standing to force actions by the WTO, whereas they do have some ability to press complaints under the rules of the European Union and NAFTA. A closer tie between interest groups and the machinery of the regime governing their economic environment has been cited as a major attraction of the regional format. Miles Kahler (1995 p. 86) cites as a source of strength of European institutions "their linkages to the domestic political institutions and interests within member states, connections that are far more substantial and intricate than those of any other international institution."

We explore whether or not such ties offered by regional agreements are advantageous relative to the more remote structure of global trade agreements. Since a world of liberalized trade on a most-favored-nation basis, ceteris paribus, is superior to a world of RTA's, it is of great interest to uncover the motivations for pursuing RTA's. If the benefit of offering private parties greater access to the dispute-resolution mechanisms is a rationale for RTA's, then changing the institutional structure of the WTO to provide such access would be superior to pursuing RTA's.

25.1   The Role of Dispute Settlement

A natural way of looking at an agreement (multilateral or regional) is that it sets the "rules of the game," in this case the game of international exchange that participants play. It is the analogue of a contract, implicit or explicit, between private agents, which stipulates what the two parties are to do (and not do) under the various future contingencies envisaged in the contract. Clearly, contracts are needed whenever the quid and quo of exchange between parties are not contemporaneous.[1]

Contracts could be incomplete, in that some contingencies may not be covered in the contract, either because they were not foreseen when the contract was written or because it was too costly to specify actions contingent on them even if foreseen. Complete and enforceable long-term contracts encourage mutually beneficial relationship-specific investments, reduce risk, and generate efficient (i.e., Pareto optimal) outcomes. In contracts between two parties subject to the same legal jurisdiction, enforcement is usually not an issue except that enforcement through courts may be costly, in which case parties might choose to enter into contracts that are "self-enforcing" (e.g., through appeals to custom, good faith, or reputation). If contracts are incomplete, as they more often are, it is possible that they are not first-best (i.e., Pareto optimal) even in situations where there are no information asymmetries and there is also no risk aversion among the parties.

International agreements also reduce uncertainty and allow beneficial relationship-specific investment by agents in different countries. For example, if countries A and B enter into a bilateral agreement or become parties to a multilateral agreement that lays out the contingencies and terms under which trade-restricting actions could be taken, the countries' exporters and importers are less uncertain of their trading environment and can undertake investments that are specific in trading with each other. However, there is no third party to enforce an international contract, so such agreements must be self-enforcing. Besides, unless the agreement itself provides for it, private disputants in different countries have to rely on their governments to act on their behalf in getting their grievances with respect to any violation of contracts redressed. International agreements are also incomplete contracts. Thus, while the desirability of entering into a self-enforcing and complete agreement is clear, an agreement that does not attain this ideal could be superior to no agreement at all.

Contracts usually specify a dispute-settlement system. This is crucial, since most contracts are incomplete, and a dispute between parties can arise both with respect to whether an actual situation corresponds to one of the contingencies specified in the contract and with respect to whether one of the parties violated the provisions stipulated in the contract. Article 3 of the Understanding on Rules and Procedures Governing the Settlement of Disputes in the WTO explains the role of such a system nicely. "The Dispute Settlement System of the WTO is a central element in providing security and predictability to the multilateral trading system. The Members recognize that it serves to preserve the rights and obligations of Members under the covered agreements, and to clarify the existing provisions of those agreements in accordance with customary rules of interpretation of public international law" (GATT Secretariat, 1994 p. 405).

As noted earlier, in the WTO's system and that of most other international agreements only national governments have standing to bring a case to the dispute-resolution system, even though the ultimate incidence of the costs and benefits of the terms of the settlement of a dispute often fall largely on private agents. The sustainability of an agreement could depend on how satisfied the private agents are with its dispute-settlement system. It is this concern that motivates this paper and its model.

The most prominent RTA's, the European Union and NAFTA, allow private agents some measure of access to the agreements' dispute-settlement mechanism. Under NAFTA, this access is limited to the side agreements on labor and environmental issues. Any organization or individual can trigger the process by complaining of a failure to enforce national laws governing these issues. The ultimate remedy offered by the process is trade sanctions (Gary Clyde Hufbauer and Jeffrey J. Schott, 1993 pp. 160–62).

The European Union offers the best example of "deep integration" and private access to the dispute-resolution mechanism. The dispute-settlement mechanism is embodied in the European Court of Justice. While private parties do not have direct access to the European Court, they may take their case to a domestic court and make the claim that they have been denied a benefit of European law. The domestic court may either apply European law as it sees fit or ask the European Court for a ruling (Geoffrey Garrett and Barry R. Weingast, 1993 pp. 193–94). Thus, private parties have indirect access to the system.

25.2   A Simple Model

Consider a model in which two governments sign a trade agreement in either a regional or a multilateral setting. In either setting, the agreement will specify the states in which a government may take a particular action and the states in which it may not. A regional or multilateral body will verify the state and authorize the action. We assume that the governments find such a contractual arrangement to be valuable.[2]

Aside from the two governments, called "home" and "foreign," the other actors are private groups or individuals within the two countries. There could be many of them within each country, but since their heterogeneity plays no role in our model, we assume that there is a representative private individual in each country.

We contrast two cases. First, we assume that only the governments decide whether an action that is allowable is taken—for example, filing a complaint to a dispute-resolution mechanism. The assumption of access being limited to governments corresponds with the rules of the WTO, so we label this the "multilateral" case. In contrast, in the "regional case," both governments and the private agents may have the right to induce settlement action.

There are two state variables, P and E, assumed to be stochastic. Each is meant to represent a different aspect of relations between the two countries. P represents the state of political relations (e.g., military incidents, domestic political tensions, etc.) while E represents the state of economic relations (e.g., trade flows, corporate earnings, etc.). These can encompass both interactions between the two countries and variables within a country. We treat them as scalars, since this will be sufficient to demonstrate our argument.

To simplify further, we assume each variable is binary, assuming the value "high" or "low." The variables are independent and

$$\Pr(P = \text{high}) = p = 1 - \Pr(P = \text{low})$$
$$\Pr(E = \text{high}) = m = 1 - \Pr(E = \text{low})$$

(25.1)

where $0 < p$ and $m < 1$.

Both P and E will be observable, in that both governments and both sets of private individuals will know their values. Only E will be contractable, however; while governments may both know whether the state of political relations is high or low, this will not be verifiable by an independent body in a dispute-settlement proceeding. Thus, any agreement that the governments reach on whether actions are allowable will depend only on E, and not P.

We assume that the welfare function, W, of each government (G) depends on the political and economic state variables, which are exogenous, and on whatever actions it might take, represented by the binary variable A, with values "file" or "no action." Thus, for the Home government:

$$W_G = W_G(P, E, A).$$

(25.2)

Private agents are only concerned with the economic state variable and with whatever action their government takes in response to that variable. Thus, for individuals (I) in the home country

$$W_I = W_I(E, A). \tag{25.3}$$

It is this difference in welfare functions that will account for the effects of allowing private access to the dispute-resolution process. If private individuals' welfare depended on political relations the same way the governments' welfare does, allowing them access would make no difference. This would also be true if the government did not care about the value of P.

In state $E =$ high, viewed as positive, neither the governments nor private individuals will wish to take any action. Thus, any interesting role for dispute resolution will come only in the negative state, $E =$ low, and from now on, we ignore $E =$ high. We assume that government preferences take the following shape:[3]

$$W_G(P = \text{high}, E = \text{low}, A = \text{file}) > W_G(P = \text{high}, E = \text{low}, A = \text{no action})$$

$$W_G(P = \text{low}, E = \text{low}, A = \text{no action}) > W_G(P = \text{low}, E = \text{low}, A = \text{file}).$$

$$\tag{25.4}$$

Thus, the home government prefers to act if and only if the state P of political relations is positive.

Private individuals, who place no weight on political relations, have the following preferences:

$$W_I(E = \text{low}, A = \text{file}) > W_I(E = \text{low}, A = \text{no action}). \tag{25.5}$$

Thus, regardless of P, the private individuals will always prefer to take action.

We now consider a game with four stages:

i. the two governments negotiate a contract that specifies when action may be taken conditional on E;

ii. the values of P and E are realized;

iii. the government decides whether or not to take action;

iv. if allowed to do so, private individuals decide whether or not to take action.

At each stage, actors choose their actions with full information and perfect foresight.

We first solve, by working backwards, the simplest case in which private individuals have no decision to make (i.e., there is no stage (iv)). In stage (iii), if the government is allowed to by contract, it will take action "file" if and only if the economic state is "low" and the political state is "high." In stage (i), the government will wish to sign the contract, since it is assumed to have value and never compels the government to take any suboptimal action.

This is our multilateral case. Two governments negotiate an accord facilitating trade liberalization. Each has the option (but not the responsibility) to press a complaint should it encounter a negative economic state.

In our regional case, there is a stage (iv). Private individuals will compel the government to take the action "file." Stage (iii) now becomes meaningless. If the political state is high, the government will prefer to take the action file; if the political state is low, the government will prefer no action. The stage-(i) decision on adopting the contract is now more difficult for the government. Not all contracts that are gainful in a multilateral setting will be adopted in a regional setting, since adopting the contract compels the government to file when it would have preferred not to (i.e., if P is low). If the government is risk-neutral, it will wish to adopt a contract if and only if the probability-weighted gain of filing (optimal action) when P = high is greater than the gain it forgoes by adoption (i.e., the probability-weighted gain from not filing when P = low). That is, the government adopts the contract if

$$p[W_G(P = \text{high}, E = \text{low}, A = \text{file})$$

$$- W_G(P = \text{high}, E = \text{low}, A = \text{no action})]$$

$$> (1 - p)[W_G(P = \text{low}, E = \text{low}, A = \text{no action})$$

$$- W_G(P = \text{low}, E = \text{low}, A = \text{file})]. \tag{25.6}$$

Three remarks are in order. First, since there is no interesting role for dispute settlement if E = high, probability m has to be strictly less than 1, but its precise value does not affect the government's decision to adopt. Second, given welfare levels, the higher the probability p of P = high the greater is the likelihood of adoption. Finally, given p, the likelihood of adoption is greater, the greater the welfare gain from filing in P = high relative to that from no action in P = low.

To sum up, since private individuals compel the government to file when it would prefer not to, their access to dispute-resolution mechanisms will limit the scope of agreements signed. This effect will be more pronounced if the government perceives a large penalty from pressing a complaint in a time of low political relations or if the government is risk-averse.

25.3   Conclusion

Our model clearly invites generalization. For example, the foreign country could be allowed a more active role in determining the economic and political states, or foreign private agents could be allowed to act in a similar fashion to home private agents. Also, heterogeneity among private agents could be allowed to play a role. Any one of these generalizations will complicate the game. However, the principal point—that altering the structure of the dispute-settlement procedure is not necessarily beneficial, and that it is likely to alter the type of agreements that governments are willing to sign—will hold despite such complications.

Notes

1. For a broad discussion of contracts, see Oliver Hart and Bengt Holmstrom (1987).

2. Specifically, since agreements are voluntary, each government's welfare has to be higher with a long-term arrangement than without one if the governments are to sign.

3. We describe the preferences only of the home government and the home private individual. One can imagine a separate state variable E^* over which the home actors have no preferences and take no actions, but over which the foreign government and foreign private individual act symmetrically.

References

Anderson, Kym and Blackhurst, Richard, eds. *Regional integration and the global trading system*. New York: Harvester Wheatshaft, 1993.

Bhagwati, Jagdish. "Regionalism and Multilateralism: An Overview," in Jaime De Melo and Arvind Panagariya, eds., *New dimensions in regional integration*. Cambridge: Cambridge University Press, 1993, pp. 22–57.

Bhagwati, Jagdish and Krueger, Anne O. *The dangerous drift to preferential trading arrangements*, Washington, DC: American Enterprise Institute Press, 1995.

Bhagwati, Jagdish and Panagariya, Arvind. "Preferential Trading Arrangements and Multilateralism: Strangers, Friends and Foes." Unpublished manuscript presented at the Conference on Capital Flows and Regionalism, 12–13 June 1995, University of Maryland at College Park, 1995.

Council of Economic Advisers. *Economic report of the President*. Washington, DC: U.S. Government Printing Office, 1995.

de Melo, Jaime and Panagariya, Arvind, eds. *New dimensions in regional integration*. Cambridge: Cambridge University Press, 1993.

Garrett, Geoffrey and Weingast, Barry R. "Ideas, Interests, and Institutions: Constructing the European Community's Internal Market," in Judith Goldstein and Robert O. Keohane, eds., *Ideas and foreign policy*. Ithaca, NY: Cornell University Press, 1993, pp. 173–206.

General Agreement on Tariffs and Trade. *The results of the Uruguay Round of Multilateral Trade Negotiations*. Switzerland: Geneva, GATT Secretariat, 1994.

Hart, Oliver and Holmstrom, Bengt. "The Theory of Contracts," in T. Bewley, ed., *Advances in economic theory: Fifth World Congress*. New York: Cambridge University Press, 1987, pp. 71–155.

Hufbauer, Gary Clyde and Schott, Jeffrey J. *NAFTA: An assessment*, Rev. Ed. Washington, DC: Institute for International Economics, 1993.

Kahler, Miles. *International institutions and the political economy of integration*. Washington, DC: Brookings Institution, 1995.

Levy, Philip. "A Political-Economic Analysis of Free Trade Agreements." Economic Growth Center Discussion Paper No. 718, Yale University, 1994.

Summers, Lawrence. "Regionalism and the World Trading System," in Federal Reserve Bank of Kansas City, *Policy implications of trade and currency zones*. Kansas City, MO: Federal Reserve Bank of Kansas City, 1991, pp. 295–301.

26

Implementing Free Trade Areas: Rules of Origin and Hidden Protection

Kala Krishna and
Anne O. Krueger

26.1 Introduction

In recent years, considerable progress has been made in understanding the effects of trade policy, especially when markets are imperfectly competitive. It is now well understood that the same instrument may have different effects under alternative market structures. However, little attention has been focused on the role of implementation. The precise manner of implementing trade restrictions may also alter incentives, resource allocations and results, both when markets are competitive and when they are not. The relative lack of attention paid to the details of implementation has resulted in the neglect of a number of interesting real world phenomena. When these are studied, conventional wisdom on a number of issues is challenged and needs to be rethought.

In this chapter we focus on one such area, where market structure and particulars of implementation turn out to be highly important. That is, we focus on the contrasting incentive and resource-allocation effects of different rules of origin (ROO)[1] within free trade agreements (FTAs). There are, of course, many other areas where the details of implementation are critical. These include issues like the effects of different forms of implementing other direct controls such as quotas on imports[2] or limits on emissions of pollutants or market access requirements, to mention a few.

The North American Free Trade Agreement (NAFTA) has focused attention on regional trading arrangements. Many analysts have tended to view NAFTA and other FTA arrangements as being preferential trading arrangements similar to customs unions (CU). And indeed, in some respects they are.

Originally published, as part of chapter 6, in *New Directions in Trade Theory*, ed. Alan Deardorff, James Levinsohn, and Robert Stern (Ann Arbor: University of Michigan Press, 1995), 149–179. Reprinted with permission.

However, ROO, which are part of both FTAs and customs union agreements, can have significantly different effects under these two arrangements. In a customs union, members have a common external tariff. Therefore, when a ROO is agreed upon, its purpose is simply to determine when members will provide preferential treatment for fellow members. For example, the European Community (EC) has rules governing treatment of imports of semiconductors: if diffusion is undertaken within the Community, then importation to another EC country is duty free. If, however, diffusion is undertaken abroad, then the import is treated as having been produced outside the EC, and the (common) external tariff applies.[3]

In an FTA, members maintain their own external tariffs. As such, tariffs may differ between member countries. ROO, therefore, assume a function additional to that under customs unions: ROO are established because, in their absence, imports of any particular commodity would enter through the country with the lowest duty on the item in question and be reexported to other countries in the FTA. Without ROO, an FTA could be highly liberalizing, as the lowest tariff would apply to each category of imports.[4]

However, unlike ROO in customs unions or domestic content requirements in developing countries, ROO in an FTA can also serve to export protection! Suppose one FTA producer, say A, is a high-cost (relative to nonmember countries) producer of intermediate goods used in producing a final product that is subject to protection by A and is exported or exportable by the other partner, B. Then A can impose a ROO on B's assembly of the final product and make it profitable for B's producers to shift their purchases of intermediates from the rest of the world (even if there is a zero tariff on these) to A, in order to satisfy the ROO and realize A's internal (tariff driven) price for the final product. In other words, it can pay producers to buy from a higher cost FTA source than from the rest of the world, in order for them to qualify for preferential treatment on their sales to their FTA partner.[5] Thus, trade patterns and investment flows needed to sustain them can be profoundly affected by a FTA.

In what follows, we first provide some background on ROO, and relate our work to previous work on domestic-content requirements and customs unions. Thereafter, we deal with the implications of alternative ROO in the long and short run. A final section contains some ideas on future research.

That ROO may be protectionist does not, of course, prove that they are. Indeed, many may not be.[6] However, in the NAFTA agreement, ROO turned out to be a significant source of contention. ROO for automobiles and apparel were the last items on which agreement was reached. The intensity of U.S. industry pressures for ROO certainly gave the appearance that the affected industries, especially automobile producers, viewed higher ROO as in their self-interest. That ROO are regarded as important was reflected not only in industry pressure for them, but in the fact that ROO occupy 200 pages of the NAFTA agreement.

26.2 Background

ROO can be defined in a variety of different ways. From a legal point of view, there appear to be four alternative criteria: (a) requirements in terms of domestic content; (b) requirements in terms of a change in tariff heading (CTH); (c) requirements in terms of specified processes that must be performed within the FTA or CU; and (d) requirements that the product has been "substantially transformed."

However, for our purposes, these criteria are both too broad and too narrow. They are too narrow, we argue below, as some of these categories are analytically similar. They are too broad for two reasons. First, some of the four methods may differ in the details that could be specified in a number of alternative ways that alter their economic effects. For example, domestic content can be defined in terms of value added or in physical terms.[7] Moreover, the required share of value added can be defined in terms of cost or price.[8] For example, NAFTA provides that value added can be calculated in terms of a transaction value (price) method or a net-cost method.[9] These differences matter in terms of their incentive effects and therefore their effects on resource allocation. Second, more than one test may need to be met. For example, the Australia-New Zealand Closer Economic Relationship (CER) relies on a 50% value-added standard in conjunction with the requirement that the last process performed in manufacture be in the territory of the exporting member state.[10]

ROO set in terms of a change in tariff heading are specified in terms of tariff categories. To satisfy origin requirements, a product must change its tariff heading in a specified way. However, by making the necessary changes more or less extensive, the origin requirement can be made more or less restrictive. For example, in the U.S.-Canada FTA, the production of aged cheese from fresh milk does not confer origin.[11]

Exceptions to rules on changes in tariff headings can also be used for the same purpose, namely to make the origin requirement more restrictive. For example, under NAFTA, transformation from any other chapter (2 digit classification level) of the harmonized system, to tomato catsup, chapter 21, confers origin, *except* transformation from tomato paste that falls in chapter 20![12]

When origin is instead conferred by performing particular steps in the production process, restrictiveness depends entirely on the steps prescribed and the nature of the production technology. In the case of American imports of apparel under NAFTA, the rule is one of "triple transformation." Only if each step of the transformation from raw material to finished garment has been undertaken within the FTA will preferential treatment be given. American textile producers, of course, benefit from this rule. The difference in this and the CTH criterion is only that the CTH criterion is based on some commonly used descriptions such as the tariff code, while the specified process definition is defined in terms of production processes specific to each industry.

Substantial transformation on the other hand is more loosely defined. In the United States, the term "substantial transformation" has come to mean the determination of origin based on common law, reasoning from case to case. It then results in a commodity-specific ROO that falls into one of the earlier three categories. We therefore do not discuss this criterion further.

From an analytical viewpoint, the legal classification makes little sense. We choose to categorize ROO in terms of: (a) content requirement, sub-categorizing them by the particular form of the requirement; or (b) in terms of transformation steps needed to confer origin. We focus on (a) since we have little to say about (b) other than that it must raise costs.[13]

If ROO specify minimum requirements for domestic value added, they can be defined in different ways. For example, a ROO can be defined as requiring a minimum proportion *relative to unit cost* of domestic value added. Alternatively, value added domestically can be defined as the price obtained less the value of imported unit intermediate input requirements, with value-added share defined *relative to price*.[14] A further variation is to put a minimum value share of FTA unit input requirements relative to price. Since cost information is harder to get than price information, the price-based definition is favored on grounds of implementation. Yet the effects of these three variations differ; little work has been done on this issue. Especially with the price definition of value added, since the price of the product is itself endogenous, the assumptions made in terms of timing and technology turn out to be vital.

From the above description, it is evident that ROO under FTAs bear a resemblance to the domestic content requirements often imposed by developing countries' governments. Content protection schemes specify requirements on the share of domestic content in production. Failure to meet these requirements results in a penalty tariff on inputs for domestic producers or a penalty tariff on the import of the final good if the final good is imported.

Content protection policies have been previously analyzed in the literature at both a theoretical and empirical level; we focus on the former. Johnson 1971 and Corden 1971 contain some of the early work on the subject. McCulloch and Johnson 1973 pointed out that a content protection scheme is basically a proportionally distributed quota, as the ability to import foreign inputs depends on the use of domestic inputs. Content protection has been favorably compared to a tariff on inputs in Mussa 1984. The argument given there is that while content protection distorts the input mix, thereby raising costs, costs rise less than under a tariff that leads to the same input mix. The reason is that foreign input prices do not rise in the former case. Mussa 1984 also analyzes the implications for technological progress of such schemes.

Grossman 1981 analyzes physical and value added restrictions on domestic content. He examines the case where not meeting the content requirement results in a penalty tariff on the imported intermediate good, with a focus on the case where the domestic and foreign inputs are perfect substitutes. He points out that while content protection causes substitution towards domestic inputs, it also raises the cost, and hence the price, of the final good. The former effect raises the use of domestic inputs while the latter reduces it, since demand for inputs is a derived demand. He demonstrates that a value-added content requirement could reduce value added in some cases if domestic and imported intermediates are complementary. He also looks at the effects of having domestic monopoly in the intermediate input and argues that content protection, like a quota, would augment this monopoly power by restricting the ability of competitive foreign suppliers to compete.

Content preference policies, studied by Grossman 1981, allow preferential tariff treatment for imports from less developed countries (LDCs), provided that a minimum content requirement is satisfied by the exporting country. Content preference then, with the preferential tariff set at zero, is similar to the effects of rules of origin specified by a FTA. However, with content preference policies, the content requirement is on the amount of intermediates from the *developing country* given preference. In implementing FTAs, the requirement is on the use of intermediates from *the FTA*. With ROO in a FTA, not only does the tariff on the final good fall if the requirement is met (as occurs with content preference), but the price of inputs from the FTA also falls. Input use is thus distorted towards *all* FTA inputs, and not just towards the inputs of the exporting country as under content preference policies.

Grossman points out that content preference leads to foreign final-goods producers distorting their use of inputs towards those made internally.[15] This could serve to protect the LDC intermediate good industry from foreign competition, a point similar to that made in Krueger 1992.

More recently, Krishna and Itoh 1986 analyzed the effects of content protection when input suppliers are oligopolistic. They showed that, counter to the case of monopoly, domestic input suppliers could lose from such protection even when content requirements are set at free-trade levels. Hollander 1987 looks at the effect of content protection when the final-good market is monopolized by a foreign multinational. De Silanes, Markusen and Rutherford 1993 look at the effect of ROO in oligopolistic industries. They show that if foreign multinationals rely on imported inputs to a greater degree than do domestic producers, ROO can reduce output and shift profits to domestic firms. In addition, if output falls, the demand for domestic inputs could also fall.

In the following sections we look at the effects of some different ways of specifying ROO. We look for some simple ideas that might be helpful in guiding policy. The simplest setups that can do so are used throughout. We think of our work not as the last word on the subject, but rather as a beginning that could stimulate further work.

26.3   Perfect Competition

In this section we look at the effects of specifying ROO in terms of price or of cost.[16] We ask what the effects of this choice might be on the outcome under the FTA. To do so, we must first analyze the effects of these rules.

Assume that in order to qualify for the FTA treatment, the firm (exporting to the United States from Mexico) must show that the cost of all intermediate inputs imported from outside the FTA divided by the total cost of production does not exceed a given proportion $(1 - \alpha)$. Let there be three kinds of inputs. For simplicity we will assume there is only one input of each kind. First we have nontraded inputs, whose price is given by W^N. In addition there are traded inputs produced in the FTA whose price is given by W^T. Finally, there are traded inputs produced outside the FTA whose price is given by W^{T*}.

Assume that the United States is a small country so that it does not affect world prices. Also assume that there are constant returns to scale

(CRS) in making the final good. Further, assume that Mexican tariffs on this final good, as well as on all imported input goods are zero,[17] and that there is some Mexican production of the final good so that the world price equals the Mexican cost of production.

A Cost-Based Definition

Let $C(.)$ be the unrestricted cost function and equal the world price. Let $R(W^N, W^T, W^{T*}, \alpha)$ be the restricted average and marginal cost function for the firm.[18] It is the value function for the cost minimization problem faced by the Mexican firm confronted by the restriction that the value of inputs used from within the FTA be at least a minimum share, α, of costs. Two results are worth pointing out. First, that the value added constraint acts like a tax on the use of T^* and a subsidy at the same rate on N and T; in this way the FTA acts to export protection. Second, that the value added constraint does not affect the *ratio* of the marginal products of N and T.

The firm has the choice of accepting the restriction and obtaining $P^{US} - R(., \alpha)$, or ignoring it and getting $P^{US} - C(.)(1+t)$.[19] It chooses the option with the higher payoff. Hence, if $R(., \alpha) < C(.)(1+t)$, it chooses to accept the restriction. If the converse is true, it does not. Since $R(., \alpha)$ is increasing in α, and for low enough levels of α, $R(., \alpha) < C(.)(1+t)$, the relationship between $R(.)$ and $C(.)(1+t)$ is as shown in figure 26.1, Therefore, if α is below α_1 in figure 26.1, then the value-added constraint is not binding and $R(., \alpha) = C(.)$. In this case the creation of an FTA will result in the effective lowering of U.S. tariffs on the final good to zero, and the U.S. price of the final good will equal the world price which equals the Mexican price. All imports will be *produced* in Mexico. U.S. welfare must increase in this region, as the consumer surplus gain exceeds the tariff revenue loss.

If the constraint on value added binds, that is, $\alpha > \alpha_1$, and it is worthwhile accepting the value-added constraint, then the U.S. price equals the restricted cost function $R(., \alpha)$, which exceeds the price in Mexico and the world price. Again, all imports come from Mexico. In this region, U.S. welfare could fall, as the gain in consumer surplus can fall short of the loss in tariff revenues. If α is so high that it is not worth accepting the value-added restriction, that is, $\alpha > \alpha_2$, the FTA has no effect on the U.S. price which equals $C(.)(1+t)$. Welfare is also unaffected, relative to the absence of an FTA.

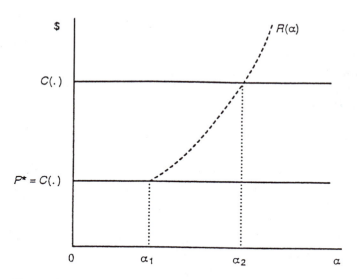

Figure 26.1
A cost-based ROO.

To summarize, the FTA need not equalize the price of the good within the FTA, and an FTA can have drastic effects on trade patterns as outlined above. Mexico can shift the source of inputs away from the low cost supplier even though there is no Mexican tariff. In addition, the investment flows into Mexico needed to enable it to serve the entire U.S. market are likely to be substantial. Also, U.S. welfare is not monotonic in the restrictiveness of the ROO. ROO could raise U.S. welfare compared to the absence of an FTA, as long as they are not too restrictive.

However, the effect on the U.S. price depends on factors such as the time period in question: in the short run, constant returns to scale are unlikely to prevail and investment flows do not materialize. Thus in the short run, as opposed to the long run where costs are constant, all imports are not going to come from Mexico. In the short run, output in Mexico will expand, but as it does, Mexican marginal costs rise choking off supply. Assuming there is no change in the world price and given that Mexico cannot meet all of U.S. demand, the U.S. price will be unchanged. All that will happen is a reallocation of imports from the rest of the world and production in the United States to Mexico, causing a reduction in U.S. welfare arising from the loss in tariff revenues. In the longer run, investment will flow into Mexico, leading to the long-run effects outlined above, assuming no effect on world prices and the price of inputs in Mexico.

These results are in sharp contrast to those which would prevail in the absence of any ROO's. In the absence of transport costs and under the same assumptions as made above, welfare would have to rise in the U.S. due to the FTA, as the gain in consumer surplus would outweigh the loss in tariff revenue. However, *production* in Mexico need not be affected.

A Price-Based Definition

Assume that in order to qualify for the FTA treatment, the firm (exporting to the United States from Mexico) must show that the U.S. price less the cost of all intermediate inputs imported from outside the FTA divided by the U.S. price exceeds a given proportion, α. We will be assuming that before the FTA, the U.S. price exceeds the world price because of a tariff on the final good. If the good is also produced in the United States under CRS, there must be tariffs on imported inputs or differences in other input costs which make the domestic cost equal to the tariff-ridden price. We keep the same notation as in the previous subsection.

Let $R(W^N, W^T, W^{T*}, \alpha, P^{US})$ be the restricted unit-cost function for the firm. It is the value function for the cost minimization problem for the Mexican firm, which faces a given U.S. price and is confronted by this value-added restriction.

Let subscripts denote partial derivatives from here on. Note also that by the envelope theorem,

$$R_{pus}(.) = -\lambda(1 - \alpha) < 0 \quad \text{for all } \alpha \in [0, 1].$$

Thus, the restricted cost function *shifts downward for all α* as the U.S. price rises. This makes intuitive sense, as raising the U.S. price makes the constraint on value added easier to meet. In addition,

$$R_\alpha(.) = \lambda \quad P^{US} > 0.$$

Thus, an increase in the required value-added share raises costs of production as expected, as long as the constraint is binding.

The Mexican firm can choose to accept the constraint and get $P^{US} - R(.)$, or not to accept it and pay the tariff to get $P^{US} - C(.)(1 + t)$. If

$$R(.) < C(.)(1 + t),$$

it is preferable to accept the restriction and avoid the tariff. If

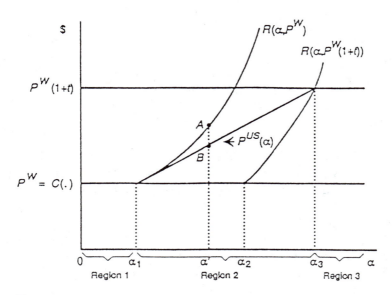

Figure 26.2
A price-based ROO.

$$R(.) > C(.)(1 + t),$$

it is preferable to accept the tariff. In other words, the restriction is accepted if the restricted cost function lies below the tariff-inclusive import price.

If α is low enough, the restriction on value added will not be binding, and the restricted cost function, $R(.)$, will be identical with the unrestricted one, $C(.)$. As α rises, the restriction becomes binding and $R(.)$ exceeds $C(.)$. Finally, as α rises further, $R(.)$ exceeds $C(.)(1 + t)$. This progression is depicted in figure 26.2. For a *given* P^{US}, since $R(.)$ is increasing in α, the firm will choose to accept the value-added restriction if α is low and not accept it if α is high. Where the switchover points occur depends on the level of P^{US}.

However, P^{US} is itself *endogenous*. As the U.S. price rises, $R(.)$ falls as shown in figure 26.2. This makes the point at which the value-added constraint becomes binding rise as well. Note α_2 exceeds α_1 since an increase in the U.S. price reduces the $R(.)$ function for all levels of α. Thus, we need to specify the effect of α on the U.S. price to proceed further. We will denote this function by $P^{US}(\alpha)$. Many different treatments are possible here, corresponding to different assumptions on the technological and timing side. One set of assumptions consistent with the approach so far is elucidated below.

Assume, as before, that the United States is a small country that does not affect world prices. Also assume that there are CRS everywhere and that factor prices are fixed, as this is a partial equilibrium framework. Assume that Mexican tariffs on this final good as well as on the imported input good are zero, and that there is some Mexican production of the final good so that the world price equals the Mexican cost of production. Our assumptions so far ensure that Mexico has the ability to serve all U.S. demand should it wish to do so.

Due to the FTA, the U.S. price always equals the lower of the world price plus U.S tariffs and restricted unit costs from Mexico. Thus, even though the United States has protection, its domestic price can equal the world price if Mexico can produce at a cost equal to the world price. Given our assumptions, Mexico can do so if the value-added constraint is not binding. Therefore, let us begin by assuming that the U.S price is the world price and seeing when this assumption is met. If α is very low, below α_1 in figure 26.2, then the value-added constraint is not binding, assuming the U.S. price equals the world price, and so the U.S. price will in fact equal the world price in this region. In this case, the creation of an FTA will result in the effective lowering of U.S. tariffs on the final good to zero, and the U.S. price of the final good will equal the world price. All imports to the U.S. of the final good will come from Mexico, and by assumption this level of production is possible using a CRS technology.

What if the constraint on value added binds? Again, the U.S. price equals the lower of the world price plus U.S. tariffs and the restricted unit cost from Mexico. Start from where the constraint just becomes binding, at α_1, and increase α. This raises the restricted cost and hence the U.S. price, as the U.S. price equals the restricted cost function $R(., \alpha, P^{US})$. Since we assume that the United States is a small country, and since we have CRS, *all trade* will still go through Mexico. Then if P^{US} remained unchanged at the world price, the constraint would bind, so P^{US} would rise. How far would it have to rise? Until $P^{US} = R(., \alpha, P^{US})$, assuming that Mexico has the resources to satisfy the entire U.S. market. Differentiating the above equality gives $dP^{US} = R_{pus}(.)dP^{US} + R_\alpha(.)d\alpha$, implying that

$$\frac{dP^{US}(\alpha)}{d\alpha} = \frac{R_\alpha(.)}{1 - R_{pus}(.)} > 0.$$

Thus, increasing α would raise P^{US}.

Since in this region $R(.,\alpha,P^{US}) = P^{US}$, it is clear that the total derivative of $R(.)$, accounting for the fact that P^{US} is endogenous, equals that of $P^{US}(\alpha)$ with respect to α:

$$\frac{dR(.,\alpha,P^{US}(\alpha))}{d\alpha} = R_{pus}(.)\frac{dP^{US}}{d\alpha} + R_{\alpha}(.)$$

$$= R_{pus}(.)\left(\frac{R_{\alpha}(.)}{1 - R_{pus}(.)}\right) + R_{\alpha}(.)$$

$$= R_{\alpha}(.)\left[\frac{R_{pus}(.) + 1 - R_{pus}(.)}{1 - R_{pus}(.)}\right]$$

$$= R_{\alpha}(.)\left[\frac{1}{1 - R_{pus}(.)}\right].$$

Note that the slope of $P^{US}(\alpha)$ is less than that of $R(.,\alpha,P^{US})$ for a fixed U.S. price, but remains upward sloping as depicted in figure 26.2. Hence for α between α_1 and α_3, P^{US} rises as α rises. When α has risen so much that $R(.,\alpha,P^{W}(1+t)) = P^{W}(1+t)$, the firms will stop accepting the value-added restriction, and the FTA will *not* affect the domestic price in the United States at all! Thus, the price in the United States is $C(.)$ is Region 1 in figure 26.2 and equals $P^{US}(\alpha)$ defined above in Region 2. It equals $C(.)(1+t)$ in Region 3 since the U.S. price cannot exceed the world price inclusive of the tariff on the final good.

Again, the same points made earlier where cost-based restrictions were discussed are worth noting. The FTA need not equalize prices in Mexico and the United States and can have dramatic implications for trade patterns and investment flows in Regions 1 and 2. It has no impact in Region 3.

What can we say about the price-based versus cost-based definitions? From derivations, the two appear to have different effects, as the programs look quite different. However, we argue that they do not differ in the long run under certain conditions. But they do differ in the short run in the presence of capacity constraints. Consider the two programs below:

Program 1 Minimize $W^N a^N + W^T a^T + W^{T*} a^{T*}$ subject to

$$\frac{P^{US} - W^{T*} a^{T*}}{P^{US}} \geq \alpha$$

$$F(a^N, a^T, a^{T*}) \geq 1.$$

Let the value function for the problem be denoted by $R(\alpha, P^{US})$.

Program 2 Minimize $W^N a^N + W^T a^T + W^{T*} a^{T*}$ subject to

$$\frac{W^N a^N + W^T a^T}{W^N a^N + W^T a^T + W^{T*} a^{T*}} \geq \alpha$$

$$F(a^N, a^T, a^{T*}) \geq 1.$$

Let the value function for this problem be denoted by $C(\alpha)$.

We ask what the relationship is between $R(\alpha, C(\alpha))$ and $C(\alpha)$. That is, what can we say about the value function for Program 1 when $P^{US} = C(\alpha)$ and that of Program 2 when the domestic content requirement is common at share α?

Let the solution values of a^N, a^T, a^{T*} for Program 1 be denoted by the Vector

$$A^1(\alpha) = \begin{bmatrix} a^{N1}(\alpha) \\ a^{T1}(\alpha) \\ a^{T*1}(\alpha) \end{bmatrix}$$

Let $R(\alpha, C(\alpha))$ be the corresponding value function.

Similarly, let the Vector

$$A^2(\alpha) = \begin{bmatrix} a^{n2}(\alpha) \\ a^{T2}(\alpha) \\ a^{T*2}(\alpha) \end{bmatrix}$$

denote the solution values of a^N, a^T, a^{T*} for Program 2. Let $C(\alpha)$ be the corresponding value function. We can show that the following relationships hold.

Lemma 1 $R(\alpha, C(\alpha)) \leq C(\alpha)$.

Proof Since $\dfrac{C(\alpha) - W^{T*} a^{T*2}(\alpha)}{C(\alpha)} \geq \alpha$, the Vector $A^2(\alpha)$ is feasible for Program 1. Thus, $R(\alpha, C(\alpha)) \leq C(\alpha)$ for all α.

Lemma 2 $R(\alpha, C(\alpha)) \geq C(\alpha)$.

Proof Again, since $\dfrac{C(\alpha) - W^{T*} a^{T*1}(\alpha)}{C(\alpha)} \geq \alpha$, and as $C(\alpha) = W^N a^{N1}(\alpha) + W^T a^{T1}(\alpha) + W^{T*} a^{T*1}(\alpha)$,

$$\frac{W^N a^{N1}(\alpha) + W^T a^{T1}(\alpha)}{W^N a^{N1}(\alpha) + W^T a^{T1}(\alpha) + W^{T*} a^{T*1}(\alpha)} \geq \alpha.$$

Hence $A^1(\alpha)$ is feasible for Program 2. Thus, $R(\alpha, C(\alpha)) \geq C(\alpha)$ for all α. This shows that $R(\alpha, C(\alpha)) = C(\alpha)$.

Now recall that when the price definition of content requirement was used, the price itself was endogenous. With CRS, this endogenous price was defined by $P^{US}(\alpha)$, where

$$R(\alpha, P^{US}(\alpha)) = P^{US}(\alpha)$$

for $\alpha \in [\alpha_1, \alpha_3]$. Thus is this region, $P^{US}(\alpha) = C(\alpha)$.

For $\alpha < \alpha_1$, the constraint on content is not binding and the U.S. price equals the world price. For $\alpha > \alpha_3$, the FTA is ignored and P^{US} equals the tariff inclusive world price under both definitions.

Thus, Lemmas 1 and 2 show that when the *endogeneity* of price is taken into account, and all factors are variable with CRS, as would be expected in the long run, both price and cost definitions of content are *equivalent*! This gives us Proposition 1.

Proposition 1   In the long run, with CRS, specifying ROO on a price or cost basis is equivalent.

How then can specifying the definition of origin on a price or cost basis matter? We show next that even if price is endogenous, if capacity constraints exist, it can matter which definitions of origin is used.

Assume that Mexican capacity is *fixed* at $\overline{T}$. Output levels up to $\overline{T}$ can be produced at unit cost $C(\alpha)$ or $R(\alpha, P^{US})$ depending on the restriction. Output levels in excess of $\overline{T}$ cannot be produced at costs below $P^W(1 + t)$. In this case, assuming $\overline{T}$ is insufficient to meet U.S. demand, the U.S. price is unaffected by the FTA and remains at $P^W(1 + t)$. The cost in Mexico under a cost based rule is $C(\alpha)$, while the Mexican price, assuming no Mexican tariffs, is P^W. All Mexican consumption is met by imports, and Mexican producers earn quasi-rents of $P^W(1 + t) - C(\alpha)$ per unit in the short run in the event of a cost based rule.

However, if the rule is price based, they will earn more. The logic is obvious. Recall that Mexican costs are $R(\alpha, P^W(1 + t))$ for output up to $\overline{T}$. Also recall that $R(\alpha, C(\alpha)) = C(\alpha)$. Since $P^W(1 + t) > C(\alpha)$, and $R(\alpha, P^{US})$ decreases as P^{US} increases, $R(\alpha, P^W(1 + t)) < R(\alpha, C(\alpha)) = C(\alpha)$. Thus, in the short run, the quasi-rents earned are $P^W(1 + t) - R(\alpha, P^{US})$, which are in excess of $P^W(1 + t) - C(\alpha)$. Hence, Mexican producers will lobby for a price-based definition over a cost-based one in the interests of short-run profits. This gives us Proposition 2.

Proposition 2   In the presence of capacity constraints, Mexican producers will prefer a price-based definition of origin to a cost-based one.

26.4   Concluding Remarks

In this chapter we have just begun to look at how ROO and different definitions of them can have very different effects; much remains to be done. An area we did not touch upon deals with the effects of FTAs and the accompanying ROO on intermediate goods markets when there is market power in these markets. Here Krishna and Itoh 1986 might provide a starting point. In addition, we had little to say about non content-based-definitions of origin and the effects of multiple layers of requirements as often occur in the real world. Perhaps the most important issue we treat in a very simple manner is the effects of FTAs on foreign direct investment (FDI). In contrast to content requirements on imports, which tend to lead to FDI in the importing country in order to evade the content requirement on imports, ROO tend to lead to FDI in the lower cost country in the FTA, as this provides access to the FTA market at a lower cost to the investor. Such concerns are common in discussions dealing with NAFTA and need further study. Nor have the implications of different ways of defining origin been explored in this context. The work begun here suggests that such issues might be well worth addressing.

Notes

This is an abbreviated version of the original article that includes a section on ROOs under imperfect competition and a mathematical appendix. We are indebted to Donald Davis, Robert Feenstra and Will Martin for helpful comments, and to Jan Herin and Bernard Hoekman who provided useful insights in correspondence on an earlier draft of this paper.

1. These rules of origin are used to determine whether a good is eligible for preferential treatment or not.

2. See Krishna and Tan 1993 for one illustration. They analyze the effects of transferable permits versus nontransferable ones. They show that, contrary to conventional wisdom, transferable permits need not raise more revenue than nontransferable ones and that, depending on the weight given to revenues in welfare, transferable permits need not dominate nontransferable ones.

3. ROO in customs unions bear a strong resemblance to domestic content requirements, often used by developing countries. See below, where these content requirements and their effects are discussed.

4. This statement assumes that transport costs among members of the FTA are not so high as to offset tariff differentials. When transport costs are significant, an FTA could have adverse welfare consequences that a ROO might prevent or reduce. An example, due to Will Martin, illustrates why. Assume that two countries in an FTA have the same transport costs from the rest of the world. Both import the good in question before the FTA. The high tariff country has a 10% tariff while the partner has a zero tariff. Transport costs are just under

10% for intra-FTA trade. In this situation, without a ROO, all imports will enter through the zero-tariff country and be shipped to the partner country. Consumer prices would be essentially unchanged but the high-tariff country would get no tariff revenues (which would be dissipated in paying real transport costs). Thus, welfare would be lowered, relative to the status quo, by an FTA with no ROO present. ROO that prevented this could result in a welfare improvement relative to the FTA without ROO.

5. See Krueger 1992 for an example with a fixed coefficients technology.

6. Will Martin has pointed out in correspondence that a high ROO might reduce trade-diversion costs of a preferential trading arrangement and thus be welfare enhancing.

7. One example of physical-content requirements occurs in the cigarette industry in Australia. Cigarette manufacturers must meet a domestic-content requirement on tobacco leaf use, defined by weight. See Beghin and Lovell 1992 for an empirical analysis of the effects of this requirement.

8. There are many variations possible. Are capital costs included or not? Are intermediate imports from the partner country counted in domestic content or not? How is the origin of inputs determined?

9. See Palmeter 1993, fn. 10, p. 12, for more on this.

10. See Steele and Moulis 1993 for details.

11. See Palmeter 1993, fn. 4, for details.

12. See Palmeter 1993, p. 4, for details.

13. However, note that input decisions in this case are affected only by the absence of tariffs on imports from the partner country and not by a content requirement on their use.

14. This is equivalent to specifying a maximum value share of unit imported inputs relative to price.

15. The careful reader of Grossman's paper will notice that there is a problem in the derivation of his Figure 1. The segment EB is not part of the net demand for domestic components.

16. We ignore the fact that providing appropriate documentation to demonstrate origin can be costly. Herin 1986, p. 7, reports that costs to Finnish firms of satisfying EC ROO for entry of Finnish exports range from 1.4 to 5.7 percent of the value of shipments.

17. By assuming that there are no tariffs on all inputs even before the FTA, we are abstracting from the effects of changes in tariffs on inputs from the partner country due to the FTA.

18. Our notation in the future suppresses the price of inputs, including them in the "." or suppressing them totally.

19. We assume throughout that tariffs are levied on cost, which here equals the fob price.

References

Beghin, John C., and C. A. Knox Lovell. 1992. "Trade and Efficiency Effects of Domestic Content Protection: The Australian Tobacco and Cigarette Industries," *Review of Economics and Statistics*.

Corden, W. M. 1971. *The Theory of Protection*. London: Allen and Unwin.

De-Silanes, Florencio Lopez, James R. Markusen and Thomas F. Rutherford. 1993. "Anti-Competitive and Rent Seeking Aspects of Domestic-Content Provisions in Regional Trading Blocs," mimeo.

Grossman, Gene M. 1981. "The Theory of Domestic Content Protection and Preference," *Quarterly Journal of Economics*, 96:583–603.

Herin, Jan. 1986. "Rules of Origin and Differences between Tariff Levels in EFTA and in the EC," EFTA Occasional Paper No. 13, February, Geneva.

Hollander, Abraham. 1987. "Content Protection and Transnational Monopoly," *Journal of International Economics*, 23:283–97.

Johnson, H. G. 1971. *Aspects of the Theory of Tariffs*. London: Allen and Unwin.

Krishna, Kala and M. Itoh. 1988. "Content Protection and Oligopolistic Interactions," *Review of Economic Studies*, 55:107–125.

Krishna, Kala and L. H. Tan. 1993. "Transferability Versus Non Transferability: What is the Difference?" mimeo.

Krueger, Anne O. 1992. "Free Trade Agreements as Protectionist Devices: Rules of Origin." Forthcoming in Festschrift in honor of John Chipman's 65th Birthday.

McCulloch, R. and H. G. Johnson. 1973. "A Note on Proportionally Distributed Quotas," *American Economic Review*, 63:726–32.

Mussa, M. 1984. "The Economics of Content Protection," National Bureau of Economic Research, Working Paper No. 1457.

Palmeter, N. David. 1993. "Rules of Origin in a Western Hemisphere Free Trade Agreement," mimeo.

Steele, Keith and Daniel Moulis. 1994. "Country of Origin: The Australian Experience," in Edwin Vermulst, Paul Waer, and Jacques Bourgeois (eds.), *Rules of Origin in International Trade: A Comparative Study*. Ann Arbor: University of Michigan Press.

V

Policy Papers

27

Regionalism and the World Trading System

Lawrence H. Summers

Increasing economic integration has been one of the major forces driving the world economy's impressive growth over the last forty-five years. Today, however, more than at any time since World War II, the future of the world trading system is in doubt. Ironically, just as the Soviet Union, Eastern Europe, and many developing countries rush to join the General Agreement on Tariffs and Trade (GATT), many in the developed world have become disillusioned with the GATT process. The nearing completion of Europe's 1991 process, the North American Free Trade Agreement (NAFTA) apparently on the way, and even the dissolution of Comecon has forced the question of regional trading blocs increasingly to the fore. It is useful at the outset to consider how the world trading system is now faring. World trade grew 3 percent a year faster than GNP in the 1960s, 2 percent a year faster in the 1970s, and 1 percent a year faster in the 1980s. The good news is that integration has continued; the bad news is that it has increased ever more slowly.

Why did integration increase less rapidly in the 1980s? I think there are two important reasons. First, the technological push toward integration has slowed. Transportation and communication costs fell less quickly in the 1980s than in previous decades. Air transport, for example, is usually thought of as a dynamic industry. Yet the last major innovation was the jumbo jet, introduced nearly a generation ago. Moreover, as the total share of transportation and communication costs declines, incremental reductions have ever smaller effects; a reduction from $5 a minute to $2.50 a minute will have a greater impact on communication than a fall from 50 cents a minute to 25 cents a minute. Progress in this sense reduces the potential for future progress.

Originally published in *Policy Implications of Trade and Currency Zones* (Kansas City: Federal Reserve Bank, 1991), 295–301. Reprinted with permission.

Second, the momentum of trade liberalization has slowed as well. While sixty developing nations significantly reduced barriers to imports over the last decade, twenty of twenty-four Organization for Economic Cooperation and Development (OECD) countries, including the United States, raised such barriers. The United States, which on some measures has trebled the protectionist impact of its policies, has a particularly ignominious record.

In the long run, however, it is those sixty liberalizing developing countries and those that emulate them that are ultimately of greatest importance for the future development of the world trading system. Ninety-five percent of the growth in the world's labor force over the next twenty-five years will occur in what are now developing nations. Even assuming only modest productivity performance, these demographic trends imply that these nations will be the most rapidly growing markets in the world over the next two decades. And this is a moment of historic opportunity in the developing world. There is abundant evidence—most obviously in Eastern Europe, but also in large parts of Latin America, in China, where industrial production has grown at a 30 percent annual rate over the last six years, in India, where a new finance minister has pledged radical change, and even in Africa, where twenty nations are undertaking adjustment programs—that the desirability of market systems has become apparent. Our top priority must be to reinforce these trends.

Trade policy not only needs to proceed on all fronts to lock in the gains that have occurred but also to provide examples that will lead to new trade gains, and even to insure viable investment opportunities for OECD companies—GATT yes, but regional arrangements as well. I therefore assert and will defend the following principle: economists should maintain a strong, but rebuttable, presumption in favor of all lateral reductions in trade barriers, whether they be multi, uni, bi, tri, plurilateral. Global liberalization may be best, but regional liberalization is very likely to be good.

This position is based on four propositions: (1) given the existing structure of trade, plausible regional arrangements are likely to have trade creating effects that exceed their trade diverting effects; (2) there is a very good chance that even trade diverting regional arrangements will increase welfare; (3) apart from their impact on trade, regional trading arrangements are likely to have other beneficial effects; (4) reasonable regional arrangements are as likely to accelerate the general liberalization process as to slow it down.

Are trading blocs likely to divert large amounts of trade? In answering this question, the issue of natural trading blocs is crucial because to the

Table 27.1
Trading Neighbors: Ratio of Share of Trade to Partner's Share of World Output, 1989

(Trader with)	U.S.	Canada	Other Americas	Japan	Developing Asia	EC
United States	—	6.06	2.38	0.87	2.34	0.61
Canada	2.63	—	0.66	0.47	0.97	0.39
Other Americas	1.13	0.63	3.16	0.31	0.57	0.67
Japan	0.95	1.15	0.75	—	4.33	0.53
Developing Asia	0.73	0.62	0.43	1.26	4.83	0.54
EC	0.22	0.30	0.42	0.17	0.63	1.75

extent that blocs are created between countries that already trade disproportionately, the risk of large amounts of trade diversion is reduced. Table 27.1 sheds some light on the importance of natural trading blocs. It compares the ratio of observed trade for various entities to the trade one would expect if it were equiproportional to GNP. For example, the number in the upper lefthand corner indicates that the United States and Canada engaged in six times as much trade as they would if U.S. trade with Canada were proportional to Canada's share of world, non-U.S., GDP. Looking at the table, I draw three conclusions:

1. Existing, and many contemplated, regional arrangements link nations that are already natural trading partners. Note the disproportionate share of U.S. trade with Canada, of trade within the developing Asian countries, and of trade within industrialized Europe. If I included Mexico in the table it would have a ratio of about 7 with the United States, Korea would have a ratio of nearly 4, and even Israel would have a ratio well in excess of unity.

2. There is very little sense in which the United States and Canada have a natural affinity with the rest of the Western Hemisphere. American, and to an even greater extent Canadian, trade is disproportionately low, with Europe about equivalent between developing Asia and Latin America. This suggests that America should not be content with an Americas-based approach to trade reduction.

3. What is striking about the numbers in Table 27.1 is the isolation of industrial Europe, which trades disproportionately with itself. This is not an artifact of the fact that Europe is broken up into many countries; this rationalization would fail to explain why it occupies so small a fraction of both Asian and Western Hemisphere trade.

Table 27.2
Trading Neighbors: Ratio of Share of Trade to Partner's Share of World Output, 1975

(Trader with)	U.S.	Canada	Other Americas	Japan	Developing Asia	EC
United States	—	6.42	2.68	0.60	1.56	0.51
Canada	2.32	—	0.90	0.37	0.58	0.36
Other Americas	1.19	0.74	2.81	0.55	0.23	0.72
Japan	0.65	1.17	1.12	—	4.70	0.26
Developing Asia	0.71	0.65	0.19	1.53	3.68	0.56
EC	0.18	0.37	0.46	0.09	0.44	1.25

I conclude from this exercise that most seriously contemplated efforts at regional integration involving industrialized countries cement what are already large and disproportionately strong trading relationships. To this extent they are likely to be trade creating rather than trade diverting. The one idea that looks bad from this perspective is that of a North Atlantic trading bloc which would be building on a weak trading relationship. Amongst regional groups of smaller developing countries, even trade disproportionate to GDP may constitute a small fraction of total trade and hence the argument carries less force.

It is sometimes suggested that whatever may have been true in the past, today's market is worldwide and regional arrangements are therefore more likely to be damaging than would once have been the case. Table 27.2 provides a fragment of evidence on this issue by redoing the exercise reported in Table 27.1 for 1975. It is striking how similar the pattern of trade is. Perhaps this should not be too surprising; it is well known that intra-European trade has risen much faster than Europe's external trade.

Let me come now to my second point: trade diverting regional arrangements may be desirable despite their trade diverting effects. I find it surprising that this issue is taken so seriously—in most other situations, economists laugh off second best considerations and focus on direct impacts. Further, it is a consequential error to think that just because a regional trading agreement's trade diverting effects exceed trade creating effects it is undesirable. Suppose that Korea and Taiwan were identical —a free trade area between the United States and Korea would divert Taiwanese trade to Korea but would have no welfare costs. Only where trade diversion involves replacing efficient producers with inefficient producers is it a problem.

I think this point had considerable force. We too often forget that more than half of U.S. imports are either from U.S. firms operating abroad or to foreign firms operating within the United States. And the fraction is rising rapidly. Under these circumstances, trade and investment decisions are inseparable. With many similar sites for investment by U.S. firms producing for the U.S. market, it is far from clear that trade diversion would have important welfare impacts.

While trade diversion is unlikely to involve large efficiency costs, trade creation is much more likely to involve real efficiency gains. First, it will help realize economies of scale which can be gained through creation, but are unlikely to be lost due to trade diversion. Second, especially where agreements link developed and developing countries, or developing countries that are heavily specialized, the trade they create is likely to be substantially welfare enhancing.

My third reason for eclectically favoring integration schemes is a reading of where the real benefits are. To the chagrin of economists, the real gains from trade policies of any kind cannot, with the possible exception of agriculture, lie in the triangles and welfare measures we are so good at calculating. Instead, they can be found in the salutary effects of competition and openness on domestic policy more generally. Pedro Aspe in his speech yesterday clearly thought more of NAFTA as a device for locking in good domestic policies and attracting investment than as a mechanism for gaining market access. To the extent that the benefits of trade integration lie in these areas, it may not be important how geographically general it is, or whether it is trade diverting. Take the case of Enterprise for the Americas. If the rest of Latin America desires to follow in Mexico's footsteps, a standstill on future U.S. protection for reassurance, and the political and symbolic benefit that it can bring in promoting domestic reform, it seems almost absurd to resist them on the grounds that some trade might be diverted from some part of Asia that would produce a little more efficiently.

It is instructive to consider the breadth of the European Community (EC) 1992 and GATT agendas. No small part of what is good about 1992 is the downward pressure on regulation created by mutual recognition policies. Similarly, competition for investment within the EC will have salutary effects on tax and regulatory policies. But there are diminishing returns to increasing numbers of policy competitors. A significant part of the benefits of trade liberalization in improving domestic policy may be realizable within small groups of countries.

The fourth and final part of the case for supporting regional arrangements is their impact on the multilateral system. I do not share the view held by some that GATT is to trade policy what the League of Nations became to security policy. I believe that a successful completion of the Uruguay Round and its successors would be highly beneficial to the world economy and that the developed nations especially must work to bring one about.

But I am far from persuaded that over time regional arrangements make multilateral trade reduction impossible. The essential reason for concern is that large blocs will have more monopoly power than small ones—and will then use it. The argument is that the resulting reduced cross bloc trade would do more harm than increased within bloc trade would do good. This is a legitimate concern. But it is also true that three parties with a lot to gain from a successful negotiation are more likely to complete it than are seventy-one parties, each with only a small amount to gain. It may be well that a smaller number of trade blocs are more likely to be able to reach agreement than a larger number of separate countries.

This is not just a theoretical proposition. I doubt that the existence of the EC has complicated the process of reaching multilateral trade agreements. Instead, I suspect that the ability of Europe to speak with a more common voice would have helped, not hurt, over time.

Furthermore, there is the beneficial effect of successful arrangements in attracting imitation and in providing a vehicle for keeping up the momentum of liberalization. Those concerned that the U.S.-Mexico or possible follow-on agreements will divert attention from the Uruguay Round ought to consider whether they will also divert Congress' attention from the Super 301 process, or that of the business community from negotiating further import restrictions.

Even strong presumptions remain rebuttable. Obviously some past and current proposals for regional integration would fail to satisfy the conditions. Agreements within groups of small, highly distorted, and protectionist countries that diminish momentum for greater overall liberality are clear candidates for welfare worsening regional agreements.

But the crux of the argument is this: regional arrangements will necessarily speed up the GATT, and moving the GATT along is important if it is possible. But, holding the degree of multilateral progress constant, the world will be better off with more regional liberalization. And the case that regional integration will slow multilateral progress is highly speculative at best. The Uruguay Round may well be the best hope for the world trading system, but it is surely not the last best hope.

28

Beyond NAFTA: Clinton's
Trading Choices

Jagdish Bhagwati

Although the debate over the North American Free Trade Agreement (NAFTA) will be loud and distracting, its passage seems assured, albeit with some tougher environmental and labor standards. It is time, then, for President Bill Clinton to plan his next, critical step on trade. He must now decide whether to continue with a free trade area (FTA) approach, be it global or confined to the Americas, or to throw his weight exclusively behind a multilateral approach based on the General Agreement on Tariffs and Trade (GATT). Unfortunately, the president seems to be headed down the least attractive of those paths: the embrace of more regional FTAs in the Americas alone.

The president and U.S. Trade Representative (USTR) Mickey Kantor have occasionally remarked, without making a formal policy statement, that they would carry the NAFTA process southward. In a policy statement on March 30, 1993, Larry Summers, the Treasury Department's assistant secretary for international affairs, supported the trade component of the broader Enterprise for the Americas Initiative, which was launched in 1990. After Mexico, then, the Clinton administration is likely to embrace Chile and thus, wittingly or unwittingly, the regional FTA approach—without seriously examining the other options.

Inertia, however, is not a sound basis for policy. Analysis of the choices at hand and an appreciation of the history of such choices are essential if the administration is to make such a momentous decision with vision and wisdom. Indeed, history is most enlightening on this question. When GATT was crafted at the end of World War II, the United States was wedded to the cause of open, multilateral trade. It resolutely fought the British, who favored discrimination in defense of Imperial Preference. Because of U.S. efforts, non-discrimination became a central principle of

Originally published in *Foreign Policy* 91 (Summer 1993): 155–162. Reprinted with permission.

GATT: If trade barriers were lowered for one trading partner, they had to be lowered for all trading partners. Virtually the only exception to that rule is found under Article 24 of GATT, which allows a group of countries to dismantle all trade barriers only among themselves.

That was the door through which the European Community (EC) passed in 1957, with U.S. approval. Though Americans were not at the time interested in Article 24 for themselves, the EC effort led to an outpouring of short-lived FTAs in the developing countries, with the 1960 Latin American Free Trade Association being the most prominent. But the time was not yet ripe for their success. Few developing countries were willing to adopt a regime under which free trade, not planning, would regulate economic activity.

In the 1960s, the use of Article 24 by the United States emerged as a real possibility in a manner that has immediate relevance today. Several influential economists, politicians, and intellectuals in Great Britain and North America came up with the proposal for a NAFTA. But NAFTA then stood for the North *Atlantic* Free Trade Area, which was nonregional at its inception and meant to push outward to the Pacific for new members—with the United States right in the middle of it all. The economist Harry Johnson and Senator Jacob Javits (R—New York) were among the first NAFTA proponents.

The 1960s NAFTA initiative, much like the early 1980s turn to FTAS by the United States, was essentially prompted by the fear that the GATT-based multilateral-negotiations route to lowering trade barriers worldwide had run its course. FTAs, open to new members on a nonregional basis, seemed to offer an alternative, indeed the only, route to free trade everywhere. Thus, at the time, there was a widespread feeling that the Kennedy Round would turn out to be the last opportunity under GATT to lower trade barriers. NAFTA proponents also viewed the EC as an inward-looking customs union that would resist efforts to liberalize world trade under GATT. At the same time, Atlanticists in Britain and the United States preferred to see Britain link its destiny with the United States rather than with the EC. As British efforts to join the EC met with French president Charles de Gaulle's continuing *non*, others felt that Britain might well have no option but to turn to other initiatives.

De Gaulle's opposition to British entry was, of course, driven wholly by the fear that Britain would act as the Americans' Trojan horse within the EC, bringing in the interests and influence of the United States and undermining the French policy of independence from U.S. hegemony. British prime minister Harold Wilson recalled a 1965 cartoon from the

Observer where a diminutive Wilson says, in short, "I even wake up tired!," to which a towering de Gaulle, a stethoscope in his ear, responds: "Hm. It's all those late night telephone calls to Washington. What you need is an independent policy on Vietnam." Indeed, de Gaulle made no secret of his suspicions about the British. Thus, immediately before his resounding November 1967 rejection of British membership in the EC, de Gaulle had queried Wilson on precisely that issue. As Wilson put it: "The whole situation would be very different if France were genuinely convinced that Britain really was disengaging from the U.S. in all major matters such as defense policy and in areas such as Asia, the Middle East, Africa and Europe."

As it happened, it was precisely the flip side of de Gaulle's concerns that made the American government eager, for political reasons, that Britain join the EC and hence unenthusiastic about the NAFTA proposal. Britain would help moderate, it argued, Gaullist anti-Americanism. In fact, American leaders were also wary of a NAFTA on economic grounds because they were in no mood to give up on multilateralism and GATT. Both Secretary of State John Foster Dulles and Secretary of the Treasury Douglas Dillon had supported the European Community on political grounds. In 1950, the U.S. House of Representatives had amended the Economic Cooperation Act to include among its objectives the "economic unification of Europe" as part of the effort needed to restore Western Europe to prosperity, strengthening it against the Soviet menace. Both Dulles and Dillon opposed a Europe-wide free trade area, as distinct from the then six-member EC. Thus, any FTA that focused on free trade alone, as the first NAFTA was designed to do, the American government found unacceptable. It saw America's interests in multilateralism and non-discrimination, as typified by GATT: A trading regime embodying those principles would provide a predictable and orderly framework for trade among all countries and hence benefit the United States in turn. By contrast, the North Atlantic initiative, despite its ultimate objective of free trade worldwide, would have entailed preferences and discrimination at the outset.

The 1960s NAFTA initiative then came to naught: The U.S. government refuse to play. But the conjunction of factors encouraging a U.S. policy shift to FTAs had returned in the early 1980s and, this time, the United States changed its mind and its course. Faced with European refusal to start multilateral trade negotiations in 1982, and with growing protectionism at home that required countervailing moves to expand trade, the Reagan administration initiated the talks culminating in the Canada-U.S.

Free Trade Agreement now turning a decade later into NAFTA, the North *American* Free Trade Agreement, with Mexico.

The new NAFTA is clearly a regional FTA, and extending it to South America would undoubtedly stamp it as regionalism par excellence. Yet, it is noteworthy that, as with the aborted 1960s NAFTA initiative, the policy shift to Article 24-blessed FTAs by the United States in the 1980s was not conceived as being narrowly regional in scope. When the U.S.-Canadian agreement was first negotiated, its supporters could be roughly divided into two camps, both of them anti-regionalist.

The first group, the GATT optimists, thought that the U.S.-Canadian agreement would push the EC and the developing countries into a new GATT round. Without the United States, all would realize, GATT would have little future and world trade would revert to the law of the jungle, which would be most painful to the weak. The strategy worked, and the American embrace of Article 24 through the Canada-U.S. FTA did indeed prompt countries to come to the table with the GATT Uruguay Round of multilateral trade negotiations. When completed, the Uruguay Round will radically transform GATT, implementing many of the reforms for which the United States has been fighting over the last decade. According to that school of thought, the turn to FTAs was a tactical move designed to jumpstart the GATT multilateral negotiations. Having succeeded in doing so, it is now time for America to return to its original commitment to GATT as the best means to liberalize world trade.

A second group, the GATT pessimists, also favored the Canada-U.S. FTA. But much like the earlier proponents of the North Atlantic initiative, they saw FTAs as part of a global strategy that sought to build FTAs that were open-ended, not regionally exclusive. Ambassador William Brock, the USTR in the early years of the Reagan administration, offered FTAs even to members of the Association of Southeast Asian Nations. He would have no doubt offered them to the moon if only he could have found life there and a government with whom to negotiate.

The GATT pessimists thought of the GATT process of trade negotiations as less effective and rapid than the FTA approach to worldwide trade liberalization. But that is a hasty and ill-considered view. A comparison of the two processes of trade liberalization is surprising. It turns out that the problems that plague the one also afflict the other. As the economists Bernard Hoekman and Michael Leidy have pointed out, the holes (areas left out) and the loopholes (areas where the disciplines of free trade are avoided) are practically identical in either case. As for slowness, consider the European Community: The process began in 1957, with the Treaty of Rome pledge to eliminate trade barriers as required by GATT Article 24. As of 1993, it still has not succeeded—not exactly a record of alacrity. The NAFTA talks, which aim to bring together only three countries, have taken nearly a decade, while the Uruguay Round, with 112 countries participating, has so far taken only seven years.

Nonetheless, the nonregional FTA approach embraced by Brock became the U.S. trade policy in the early 1980s, downgrading the option of sticking to multilateralism despite its revival at the Uruguay Round. Yet, down the road, that policy turned into the narrow regional FTA option that is the least attractive of those available. Some of the blame lies with the U.S. Treasury Department, which was able to capture the FTA idea for its own purposes, offering preferential trade to South America in lieu of debt relief. When the South Americans responded positively, the State Department muscled in, turning the trade initiative into a foreign policy initiative and making it an integral part of the Enterprise for the Americas Initiative. That program harked back to President John Kennedy's Alliance for Progress, except that the latter did not include an offer of regional FTAs because the United States was correctly devoted to multilateralism at the time.

The effect of that narrower vision has been to encourage the notion that the United States is interested in trade regionalism no matter how strong its professed commitment to multilateralism. Since the United States also recognizes its vital trade interests in the rapidly expanding markets of the Far East, it has found itself in an awkward position. George Bush's secretary of state, James Baker, was trying to convince the Asian countries not to form their own Japan-centered FTA even as he worked on the NAFTA and its exclusive extension to the south—an incoherent position that argues that what is good for me is not good for you.

Many have even tried to convince themselves that an Asian trade bloc is unlikely because the Asian countries will not soon forget Japan's wartime cruelties—conveniently forgetting that other countries have learned to live with and profit from Germany despite the unparalleled crimes of the Holocaust. The profit motive can help numb the grey cells of memory.

Indeed, few would have thought that anti-Yanqui sentiments would so quickly evaporate from the Mexican scene, allowing President Carlos Salinas de Gortari's splendid team to hitch Mexico's economic destiny to America's. Salinas turned on its head Porfirio Diaz's famous dictum: "Poor Mexico, so far from God and so near the United States."

But if the United States pushes FTAs only southward, it will certainly invite a defensive, if not retaliatory, bloc in Asia. Divisions will be sharpened and the world economy fragmented into four blocs: an expanded EC, a NAFTA extended to the Americas, a Japan-centered Asian bloc, and a marginalized group of developing countries, many with low incomes and only just turning to export-oriented strategies. We should not favor that scenario.

If the United States continues to pursue FTAs, the least it can do is to return to the Brock agenda, to the vision of the 1960s North Atlantic initiative. That would mean developing a new strategy of openness before adding any new members, especially from South America.

Such a policy would have to be unambiguously stated and diplomatically credible. Negotiations to add one or more non-hemispheric countries before adding hemispheric ones would help. Then again, if U.S. domestic politics drives America farther south, well beyond the Rio Grande, Canada could be explicitly encouraged to seek out new NAFTA members from the British Commonwealth, countries to which Canada surely has stronger economic and historical links. Indeed, instead of playing the complaisant junior partner in NAFTA, Canada could itself play a leadership role; prime ministers like Lester Pearson and Pierre Trudeau did not shy away from the world stage.

But all that is more readily urged than undertaken. Clayton Yeutter, the former USTR who negotiated the U.S.-Canadian agreement, has candidly described the enormous difficulties of such talks. Then again, the politics of pushing the next agreement through Congress could be quite a challenge. Imagine what would happen if the Congress were considering an FTA with India—or with Japan.

Yet many analysts seem drawn to FTA blocs, to a power-political conception of trade that sees the world as a jigsaw puzzle. Some call for a U.S.-Japanese Pacific free trade area, with the two economic superpowers bringing along their respective regions to provide a counterweight to the enlarging EC. In turn, taking a cue from Margaret Thatcher—the irrepressible Atlanticist—and from the Japanophobes, columnist Charles Krauthammer recently argued that the three NAFTA countries should free up trade with the EC instead. "A transatlantic free-trade zone would signal Japan that if it had thoughts of creating a rival Asian bloc or did not modify its predatory drive for market dominance, it might find itself shut out of the new world economic order," he wrote in *Time*. And thus each of us will act out our own fantasies, seeking allies against imagined adversaries, lining up our preferred blocs against the others, and vying for political attention and action.

The more deeply one thinks about the issue, and about the basic choice between multilateralism and FTAs as ways of bringing down trade barriers worldwide, the more disenchanted one is likely to be about the latter. Even the popular notion that the two processes and policies can coexist—the "GATT-plus" proposition—and even be benignly symbiotic, is too simplistic. Lobbying support and political energies can readily be diverted to preferential trading arrangements such as FTAs, where privileged access to markets is obtained at the expense of outside competitors (such as the EC and Japan in NAFTA). That deprives the multilateral system of the support it needs to survive, let alone be conducive to further trade liberalization.

The wisest option for the Clinton administration, therefore, is to move NAFTA with Mexico through Congress, conclude the Uruguay Round, and then focus exclusively on the multilateral trading regime of GATT. Will the administration rise to that challenge or, in choosing the least attractive option of regional FTAs, continue the sorry spectacle of thoughtless trading choices?

Index